MW00845933

Security
Essentials

by
Linda K. Lavender

Publisher
The Goodheart-Willcox Company, Inc.
Tinley Park, IL
www.g-w.com

The Goodheart-Willcox Company, Inc. Brand Disclaimer: Brand names, company names, and illustrations for products and services included in this text are provided for educational purposes only and do not represent or imply endorsement or recommendation by the author or the publisher.

The Goodheart-Willcox Company, Inc. Safety Notice: The reader is expressly advised to carefully read, understand, and apply all safety precautions and warnings described in this book or that might also be indicated in undertaking the activities and exercises described herein to minimize risk of personal injury or injury to others. Common sense and good judgment should also be exercised and applied to help avoid all potential hazards. The reader should always refer to the appropriate manufacturer's technical information, directions, and recommendations; then proceed with care to follow specific equipment operating instructions. The reader should understand these notices and cautions are not exhaustive.

The publisher makes no warranty or representation whatsoever, either expressed or implied, including but not limited to equipment, procedures, and applications described or referred to herein, their quality, performance, merchantability, or fitness for a particular purpose. The publisher assumes no responsibility for any changes, errors, or omissions in this book. The publisher specifically disclaims any liability whatsoever, including any direct, indirect, incidental, consequential, special, or exemplary damages resulting, in whole or in part, from the reader's use or reliance upon the information, instructions, procedures, warnings, cautions, applications, or other matter contained in this book. The publisher assumes no responsibility for the activities of the reader.

The Goodheart-Willcox Company, Inc. Internet Disclaimer: The Internet resources and listings in this Goodheart-Willcox Publisher product are provided solely as a convenience to you. These resources and listings were reviewed at the time of publication to provide you with accurate, safe, and appropriate information. Goodheart-Willcox Publisher has no control over the referenced websites and, due to the dynamic nature of the Internet, is not responsible or liable for the content, products, or performance of links to other websites or resources. Goodheart-Willcox Publisher makes no representation, either expressed or implied, regarding the content of these websites, and such references do not constitute an endorsement or recommendation of the information or content presented. It is your responsibility to take all protective measures to guard against inappropriate content, viruses, or other destructive elements.

References to CompTIA and CompTIA Security+ Certification Exam details in this textbook and its ancillary products do not imply partnership with or endorsement by the CompTIA association.

Cover image: hywards/Shutterstock.com; photos cropped: https://creativecommons.org/licenses/by/Willh26

Preface

Information security is among the top concerns of IT professionals. The prevalence of Internet-ready devices, combined with the ease of connectivity, has made digital attacks far more prevalent than traditional threats to businesses. Consider how many times you have heard of a data breach or compromised user data in the last few years. It is estimated that cybercrime will cost businesses over $6 trillion by 2021. As such, it is imperative for IT professionals to understand how to prevent network breaches and loss of data. Equally important is the knowledge, skills, and ability to assess the security posture of an enterprise environment; implement identity and access controls; adhere to applicable laws and policies; and use appropriate tools or utilities to identify, analyze, and respond to incidents by implementing or recommending solutions.

Security Essentials prepares learners with the skills and information needed to work as a security professional. More than just a test-prep book, *Security Essentials* presents technical topics in an easy-to-read, relatable format. Each chapter's learning outcomes align directly to the top-level headings, chapter summary points, and review questions. This alignment ensures valuable information is learned, relearned, and reinforced as users progress through the text. Coverage of topics includes the following:

- overview of data security
- threats, attacks and vulnerabilities
- implementation of security controls and protocols
- governance, risk, and compliance
- operations and incident response
- digital forensics
- secure network architecture and design
- secure network protocols and administration
- wireless device security
- cloud security
- secure mobile solutions
- secure application development
- secure systems policy enforcement
- device hardening
- cryptography
- public key infrastructure
- incident response
- business continuity
- data sanitization
- management through a command-line interface
- employment and soft skills

In addition to the textbook, hands-on learning opportunities are available by using the supplemental Study Guide and Lab Manual. These valuable ancillary products improve the user's level of preparation for earning an industry-recognized certification as well as serve as a reference when studying for the exam.

Intended Audience

Security Essentials is designed for students, as well as professionals, preparing for the CompTIA Security+ SY0-601 Certification, one of the most sought-after entry-level certifications in digital and information security. Earning CompTIA Security+ certification validates baseline skills needed to become an IT security professional.

The concepts discussed in this textbook build off an assumed understanding of computer systems, including operation, installation, troubleshooting, maintenance, and repair. Additionally, the reader should have foundational networking knowledge, such as topologies, installation, devices and media, IPv4 and IPv6 addressing, troubleshooting, administration, and management. An ideal user of this textbook is an information technology student or professional who has already obtained CompTIA A+ and Network+ Certifications, or the equivalent study or professional experience.

Securing computing devices is an advanced topic, and it relies on a foundational knowledge of basic computer hardware, processing, and networking. As such, CompTIA recommends a minimum of two years in IT administration as well as a CompTIA Network+ Certification before sitting for the Security+ Certification Exam.

About the Author

Linda K. Lavender is an adjunct instructor of information technology for Tidewater Community College in Virginia Beach. She holds a Master of Science in cybersecurity and a Bachelor of Science in computer information systems from Saint Leo University.

She has been named teacher of the year by several organizations, including ACTE, and received the Virginia Affiliate Educator Award of the NCWIT Award for Aspirations in Computing. She is certified in CompTIA Security+, Network+, A+, CySA+, and CTT+; Microsoft MCTS, MCTIP, MCP, MOS, and MTA; and CIW Foundations.

Reviewers

Goodheart-Willcox Publisher would like to thank the following individuals for their honest and valuable input in the development of *Security Essentials*.

Shane Archibald, M.S., Cybersecurity Instructor, Gwinnet Technical College, Lawrenceville, Georgia

Mark Bayley, Adjunct Professor and Penetration Tester, Metropolitan Community College of Kansas City, Kansas City, Missouri

Dr. Adam Beatty, Associate Professor of Information Technology, Washington State Community College (WSCC), WSCC/Marietta, Ohio

Dr. Scott Bell, Assistant Professor of Computer Science, Northwest Missouri State University, Maryville, Missouri

Bryan Bennett, Assistant Professor of Network and Systems Administration, Kirkwood Community College, Cedar Rapids, Iowa

Constance Boahn, Engineering and Computer Information Technologies Department Chair, Central Carolina Community College, Sanford, North Carolina

Donald D. Casper, Computer Networking Instructor, College of Eastern Idaho, Idaho Falls, Idaho

Dr. Tingting Chen, Associate Professor of Computer Science, California State Polytechnic University at Pomona, Pomona, California

Jenny Dawkins, Professor, Department of Computer & Information Technology, West Virginia University at Parkersburg, Parkersburg, West Virginia

Kim Doane, Technology Professor, Mott Community College, Flint, Michigan

Gayle E. Francis, MBA, Instructor, Computer Science and Technology, Tarrant County College District, Northeast Campus, Hurst, Texas

Dr. Bill Hammerschlag, Computer Information Technology Faculty, Dallas College, Dallas, Texas

Amy Hertel, Professor, Texas State Technical College, Marshall, Texas

Ryan Hill, Professor, Computer Science Department, Houston Community College, Houston, Texas

Dr. Shweta Jain, Associate Professor, Mathematics & Computer Science Department, CUNY John Jay College of Criminal Justice, New York, New York

Timothy Jansen, Adjunct Professor for NET Courses, Information Technology Department, Harper College, Palatine, Illinois

Junhua (Jason) Jia, PhD, Professor (Tenured), Computer Science and Information Technology Department, Sinclair Community College, Dayton, Ohio

Kyle Jones, Chair and Associate Professor of Computer Science and Information Technology, Sinclair College, Dayton, Ohio

Jon Juarez, Regents Professor/Department Chair for Computer and Information Technology, Dona Ana Community College, Las Cruces, New Mexico

Kees Leune, PhD, CISO and Assistant Professor, Mathematics and Computer Science, Adelphi University, Garden City, New York

Andrew Lutz, MS, Associate Professor and Information Technology Chair, Johnson County Community College, Overland Park, Kansas

Dr. Rick L. Massengale Sr., Associate VP Sponsored Programs and University Initiatives, Computer Science Professor, North Arkansas College, Harrison, Arkansas

Arden Meyer, Adjunct Instructor, Cyber Security, Des Moines Area Community College, Ankeny, Iowa

Robert C. Nelson II, Information Technology Program Coordinator, Blinn College, Bryan, Texas

Thalya Nero, Education Manager/Adjunct Faculty, AZStRUT/South Mountain Community College, Phoenix, Arizona

Alicia Pearlman, Adjunct Faculty, Computer Science Department, Schoolcraft College, Livonia, Michigan

Zhengrui Qin, Assistant Professor, Computer Science Department, Northwest Missouri State University, Maryville, Missouri

Dennis Roebuck, Computer Science and Information Technology Faculty, Delta College, University Center, Michigan

Kenneth Schaffer, IT Security Instructor, Southeast Technical College, Sioux Falls, South Dakota

Michael Sletten, Adjunct Professor for NET Courses, Information Technology Department, Harper College, Palatine, Illinois

Michael Vest, Networking Technology Instructor, Ozarks Technical Community College, Springfield, Missouri

Minhua Wang, Cybersecurity B.S. Program Coordinator, SUNY Canton, Canton, New York

Student Resources

Student Text

Security Essentials is a comprehensive text detailing introductory topics in information security and securing computer systems. It provides the foundational skills and knowledge for managing and mitigating security risks, detecting and preventing network intrusion, and managing and responding to threats. The text is aligned to CompTIA Security+ Certification SY0-601 Objectives. The CompTIA Security+ Certification Exam is an industry-recognized certification and starting point for a career in IT. It is the first security certification IT professionals should earn, as it provides groundwork for future career growth. Obtaining the Security+ Certification opens doors to career pathways such as auditing, penetration testing, and security or network administration.

Study Guide

The supplemental study guide provides users with a valuable means of review and practice essential for important knowledge and skills. The first half of the study guide provides practice exercises that reinforce concepts and skills learned in the corresponding textbook chapters. The completion of these activities greatly enhances the comprehension of the topics covered in the corresponding textbook chapter. The second half of the study guide includes a CompTIA Security+ Reference Guide to help learners study and prepare for the CompTIA Security+ Exam. The reference guide includes a detailed review of each CompTIA objective, including examples and related concepts.

Lab Manual

The supplemental lab manual encourages the application of concepts learned in the text. It provides an opportunity to perform many of the tasks required in a typical workplace setting and incorporates review questions at the end of each lab to reinforce understanding of the practicality and purpose of the activities. For ease of reference, the table of contents shows both the topic covered and the corresponding textbook chapter.

Instructor Resources

LMS Integration

Integrate Goodheart-Willcox content within your Learning Management System for a seamless user experience for both instructors and learners. LMS-ready content in Common Cartridge® format facilitates single sign-on integration and enables control of enrollment and data. With a Common Cartridge integration, you can access the LMS features and tools you are accustomed to using and G-W course resources in one convenient location—your LMS.

G-W Common Cartridge provides a complete learning package. The included digital resources help users remain engaged and learn effectively:

- **eBook content.** G-W Common Cartridge includes the textbook content in an online, reflowable format. The eBook is interactive, with highlighting, magnification, note-taking, and text-to-speech features.
- **Lab Manual and Study Guide content.** Learners can have access to digital versions of the corresponding Lab Manual and Study Guide.
- **Drill and Practice.** Learning new vocabulary is critical to success. These vocabulary activities, which are provided for all key terms in each chapter, provide an active, engaging, and effective way to learn required terminology.

When you incorporate G-W content into your courses via Common Cartridge, you have the flexibility to customize and structure content to meet the educational needs of learners. You may also choose to add your own content to the course.

For instructors, the Common Cartridge includes the Online Instructor Resources. QTI® question banks are available within the Online Instructor Resources for import into your LMS. These prebuilt assessments help measure student knowledge and track results in your LMS gradebook. Questions and tests can be customized to meet your assessment needs.

Online Instructor Resources (OIR)

Online Instructor Resources provide all the support needed to make preparation and classroom instruction easier than ever. Available in one accessible location, the OIR includes Instructor Resources, Instructor's Presentations for PowerPoint®, and Assessment Software with Question Banks. The OIR is available as a subscription and can be accessed at school, at home, or on the go.

Instructor Resources

One resource provides instructors with time-saving preparation tools such as answer keys, editable lesson plans, and other teaching aids.

Instructor's Presentations for PowerPoint®

These fully customizable, richly illustrated slides help you teach and visually reinforce the key concepts from each chapter.

Assessment Software with Question Banks

Administer and manage assessments to meet your classroom needs. The question banks that accompany this textbook include hundreds of matching, completion, multiple choice, and short answer questions to assess understanding of the content in each chapter. Using the assessment software simplifies the process of creating, managing, administering, and grading tests. You can have the software generate a test for you with randomly selected questions. You may also choose specific questions from the question banks and, if you wish, add your own questions to create customized tests to meet your classroom needs.

Focus on Certification

Security Essentials is designed with certification in mind. This text reflects current programs, systems, and practices in the information technology industry. It adheres to the CompTIA Security+ SY0-601 Exam Objectives, ensuring users are up to date with the most recent testing domains.

Learning Outcomes

At the beginning of each chapter, a list of outcomes guides learning as users read the material presented. Each outcome is aligned with a content heading, as well as with a summary bullet point and review question at the end of the chapter. This alignment provides a logical flow through each page of the material so learners may build on individual knowledge as they progress through the chapters.

Security+ Objectives

CompTIA Security+ Exam Objectives are listed in the opening of each chapter to engage readers and highlight important testing points presented in the content. The list of objectives serves as a checklist to verify understanding of the Security+ standards as presented in the material. In addition, objectives are noted by an icon in the margin where material is covered and provides a visual clue as to where each objective is met.

Security+ Note

The Security+ Note feature provides tips and facts regarding the CompTIA Security+ Certification Exam. These tips will help users study for the certification exam.

Tech Tip

The Tech Tip feature highlights supplemental information about practical application of security concepts. These tips vary in scope, ranging from simple definitions of discussed material to real-world insight.

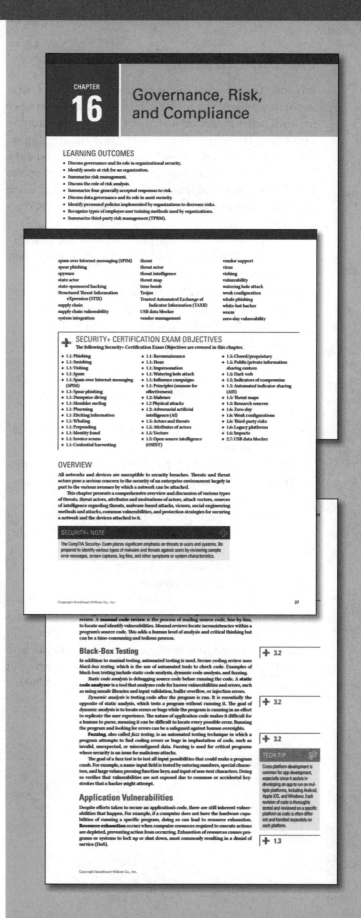

End-of-Chapter Content

End-of-chapter material provides an opportunity for review and application of concepts.

- A concise **Summary** reiterates the Learning Outcomes and provides a brief review of the content for reference. The summary helps students review important concepts presented in the text.
- **Review Questions** highlight basic concepts presented in the chapter to evaluate understanding of the material.
- **Sample Security+ Exam Questions** provide an opportunity to answer questions similar to those on the CompTIA Security+ Certification Exam, providing a sample of what to expect on the exam.
- **Lab Exercises** offer hands-on opportunities to apply the concepts presented in the chapter in real, meaningful ways. These labs can be utilized as formative assessment after the chapter has been completed or at point of presentation as topics are encountered during study.
- A **Case Study** provides a real-world scenario of a security concept related to the chapter content. Users can read the example and answer questions to reflect on the content.

Appendices

Appendices containing valuable material that complements the chapter content are included at the end of the text. These appendices contain the following information:

- Correlation chart that identifies where each Security+ objective is fulfilled within the textbook
- Table of commonly used ASCII characters
- List of acronyms encountered on the CompTIA Security+ Certification Exam
- Conversion table for decimal, binary, octal, and hexadecimal numbers

---

SUMMARY

Evaluating Security

- A security assessment is a periodic exercise that evaluates a company's security preparedness. Its purpose is to keep networks, devices, and data safe by discovering vulnerabilities and threats and offering recommendations to lessen the risk for future attacks.
- A comprehensive IT security strategy incorporates technological solutions, policies, procedures, and a detailed security assessment of an organization. It is necessary to assess the security posture of an enterprise environment so that security solutions can be recommended and implemented. This evaluation is a structured and detailed approach to locate IT vulnerabilities.
- The types of assessments conducted in an organization varies based on the organization's mission and technology and can cover a wide spectrum. Regardless of the type of assessment used, it is necessary for an organization

REVIEW QUESTIONS

1. Summarize *hardening*.
2. State the difference between a host, a client, and an endpoint.
3. Identify and explain three endpoint-protection tools used to protect host devices.
4. Which type of firewall can run at all levels of the OSI model?
5. Discuss securing a network through network hardening.
6. Summarize techniques used for hardening a server.
7. Identify and explain hardening techniques for operating systems.
8. Which type of port does not have a process actively listening to it?
9. What is the difference between manual patch management and centralized patch management?
10. List three critical areas that must be continuously patched and monitored for updates.
11. How do you update Linux?
12. Identify hardware system hardening techniques.
13. Which keys can be used to access the UEFI during the boot process?
14. Briefly explain the three common elements to boot integrity.
15. Define a *full-device encryption (FDE)* and its importance on mobile devices.
16. Identify procedures used to harden applications.
17. What is a database?
18. Explain three methods used for hardening a database.
19. Explain the importance of hardening external storage devices.
20. Define a USB data blocker.

➕ SAMPLE SECURITY+ EXAM QUESTIONS

1. Which statement *best* describes operating system hardening?
   A. Uninstalling older programs
   B. Patching systems to potential vulnerabilities in the operating system
   C. Installing a packet filtering firewall
   D. Creating a system baseline
2. Which of the following should be ensured before shutting down a service?
   A. The service startup-type is set to manual.
   B. Other services depend on this service running.
   C. Components are needed for this service to run.

Lab Activity 1-2: Locating and Evaluating Security Guides

Security guides are often published by non-profit organizations, security firms, and even IT bloggers and researchers. In this lab, we will compare guidelines for the Linux operating system. Since Linux is open-source code, the distributor of the operating system you are using may not have any published guides, but many individuals and companies have created detailed documents.

1. Launch a web browser, and search for hardening Linux operating systems.
2. Choose a link and review the suggestions. Did this link address the two major Linux distribution platforms (Debian and RedHat)?
3. Who provided the link you chose; was it a blogger, security company, non-profit etc.?
4. Return to your search results and choose another response. Compare this list to the first one you reviewed. Did they provide similar suggestions and recommendations?
5. Return to your browser, repeat the same search, but add +password in the search request. (The + ensures the term password must be in the results.)
6. Review one or more of the results. Notice that adding a password allows you to focus on a specific task to assist in confidentiality goals.
7. Discuss your observations and favorite sites with classmates.

CASE STUDY

HIPAA-Compliant Security

In March 2020, the Office for Civil Rights (OCR) at the US Department of Health and Human Services (HHS) issued temporary waivers and guidance regarding HIPAA and telehealth services rendered during the COVID-19 health emergency. These measures were intended to encourage the use of telehealth services and enable social distancing. In their directive, the OCR announced they would use enforcement discretion not to impose penalties for HIPAA violations against healthcare providers with their good-faith provision of using telehealth communication methods. *Telehealth* is described as the use of electronic information and telecommunication technologies to support and promote long-distance clinical health care using technologies such as video conferencing, the Internet, store and forward imaging, streaming media, and landline and wireless communications.

1. Summarize what you believe constitutes an organization's *good-faith effort* in protecting the confidentiality and integrity of data. Provide relevant examples.
2. Telehealth relies on the use of video conferencing tools. Therefore, providers should be aware of the differences between nonpublic-facing services, such as Apple Face Time and Zoom, and public-facing services, such as TikTok or Facebook Live. Prepare a statement to a medical practice differentiating these technologies and how some of them may violate the basic principles of confidentiality and integrity.
3. Consider the security domains identified in this chapter. Which areas will be most affected by the incorporation of telehealth practices? Support your answer with detailed analysis.

CompTIA Security+ Certification

How to Become CompTIA Certified

The *Security Essentials* textbook can help learners prepare for the CompTIA Security+ Certification SY0-601 Exams. The Computing Technology Industry Association (CompTIA) is a nonprofit information technology (IT) trade association. Its certifications are designed by subject-matter experts. Each certification is vendor-neutral, covers multiple technologies, and requires demonstration of skills and knowledge widely sought after by employers in the IT industry. There are four general steps to achieving CompTIA certification:

1. Choose the desired IT certification from CompTIA
2. Gain familiarity with the exam, its objectives, and the types of questions used
3. Begin studying, learning, and preparing for the exam
4. Register for the exam, read and sign the Candidate Agreement, and take and pass the exam

For more information about CompTIA certifications, such as industry acceptance, benefits, or updates, visit www.comptia.org/certifications.

Preparing for Your CompTIA Security+ Exam

Preparing for an exam is a highly individualized activity, meaning each person prepares differently. However, the CompTIA organization recommends a simple strategy that you can follow to get, and stay, organized and prepared for a Security+ Certification Exam:

- Understand what the exam will assess by reviewing the objectives.
- Complete practice exams to determine what you already know and what you need to study.
- Obtain additional resources and continue practicing in problematic areas to help close the knowledge gap between what you already understand and what needs to be practiced.

How Long Does It Take to Obtain Security+ Certification?

The amount of time needed to obtain a Security+ Certification varies by person. It depends heavily on what a person already knows, how much has to be learned, and how quickly a person learns information. It can also be affected by how much confidence a person has in their ability to demonstrate their knowledge. It is recommended that you give yourself enough time to prepare for the exam thoroughly.

CompTIA Security+ Correlation Charts

A complete mapping (correlation chart) of the CompTIA Security+ Exam Objectives to the content of the *Security Essentials* textbook is located on the G-W website at www.g-w.com. The correlation chart lists the exam objectives and corresponding page numbers where the related content can be found. This correlation chart is also included as an Appendix; however, the printed chart contains the correspond chapter number and heading, not an exact page reference.

How to Use this Text

The *Security Essentials* text and accompanying resources will help you prepare for the CompTIA Security+ Certification Exam. You will learn the skills and knowledge for managing and mitigating security risks, detecting and preventing network intrusion, and managing and responding to threats. In addition to learning about security, the last chapter of the text helps identify qualities employers seek in job candidates. These are concepts you will need to understand for not only the certification exam but also your career as an IT security professional.

Each chapter in *Security Essentials* begins with a set of Learning Outcomes. These are the goals you should focus on accomplishing by the time you complete each chapter. For each outcome, there is a corresponding top-level heading in the content, chapter summary bullet point, and end-of-chapter review questions to help ensure you comprehend material covered in the chapter. There is also a list of CompTIA Security+ Certification Exam Objectives at the beginning of each chapter that identify CompTIA concepts that will be discussed.

In addition to Learning Outcomes, the chapter-opening material lists a set of key terms discussed throughout the material. These terms are in boldface when they appear in the content, which makes them easily distinguishable. There are also important words or phrases printed in italic text to which you should pay special attention and consideration. Studying these key terms and italicized words will help you understand the material and better prepare you for taking the certification exam.

Each chapter concludes with a summary of important points to remember, organized by level-one headings. This summary will help you review important topics from each section of the chapter.

Following the suggested guidelines will help you make the most of your introduction to security.

- Read the Learning Outcomes listed in the chapter opener. Each outcome is tied directly to a heading within the content. In addition, these objectives are repeated in the chapter summary and applied in end-of-chapter review questions. The connection of Learning Outcomes throughout the content helps you focus and apply important information as you read each chapter.

- Read the list of CompTIA Security+ Objectives in the chapter-opening material. These objectives are also noted in the margin with an icon where the material is covered. Use the list of objectives in the chapter opener as a checklist to take inventory of CompTIA standards you understand as well as information you need to review. The icons in the margins are there to direct you to the coverage of each objective for review.

- Pay attention to the illustrations. Each illustration is strategically created to highlight important information. By studying these, you will extend your learning and improve retention and application of the content.

- Read all Security+ Note and Tech Tip features as you progress through the material. This information supplements your learning by highlighting study tips and providing useful industry information.

- Review the summary at the end of each chapter. This will help you retain important information from the chapter.

- Answer the review questions and sample Security+ questions in the end-of-chapter material. These questions provide exposure to the types of questions likely to be on the CompTIA Security+ Certification Exam. By practicing these questions, you increase your chances of successfully earning CompTIA Security+ certification.

- Complete the lab exercises provided at the end of each chapter. These exercises provide an opportunity to apply the chapter content through hands-on activities in real, meaningful ways.

- Read the case study at the end of each chapter and answer the questions that accompany each case. Each case provides a real-world scenario related to the chapter in which it appears.

Brief Contents

Contents

CHAPTER 1

Introduction to Information Security

LEARNING OUTCOMES

- Define *information security*.
- Summarize information assurance.
- Identify the top frameworks adopted by organizations.
- List and discuss commonly referenced security domains.
- Explain regulatory compliance.

KEY TERMS

ARP poisoning
attack surface
authentication
availability
CIA triad
compliance
confidentiality
defense in depth
framework

industry standard
information assurance (IA)
information security
information security plan
integrity
Internet of Things (IoT)
nonrepudiation
nonrepudiation process
pen register

pretexting
risk
risk management
secure-configuration guide
security domain
security posture
vendor-specific guide
Wi-Fi

SECURITY+ CERTIFICATION EXAM OBJECTIVES

The following Security+ Certification Exam Objectives are covered in this chapter.

+ 1.4: Address resolution protocol (ARP) poisoning
+ 2.5: Technologies
+ 2.5: Vendors
+ 2.5: Controls
+ 5.2: Regulations, standards, and legislation

+ 5.2: Center for Internet Security (CIS)
+ 5.2: National Institute of Standards and Technology (NIST) RMF/CSF
+ 5.2: International Organization for Standardization (ISO) 27001/27002/27701/32000

+ 5.2: SSAE SOC 2 Type II/III
+ 5.2: Benchmarks/secure configuration guides

2

OVERVIEW

Computer systems are more complex than ever before, and they often interconnect with other organizations to share information and resources. These complexities have not just changed business operations; they have also increased the need for a robust security plan to protect all forms of data. Businesses have a responsibility to protect data and often must comply with national, local, or international regulations.

The protection of data begins with an understanding of how data is used in a business, classifications of data, and the importance of data privacy. In this chapter, coverage of basic security concepts, compartmentalizing a business into security domains, and the importance of data management will be discussed in detail.

SECURITY+ NOTE

For the CompTIA Security+ Exam, you will be expected to identify various security acronyms. Many answers provide only the acronym. It is up to you to know not only what the letters of an acronym mean, but also the definition of the acronym itself. For example, you should know that PHI stands for Protected Health Information, which includes all "individually identifiable health information."

Defining Information Security

Protecting data, whether it is electronic or printed, is the ultimate responsibility of an organization. The process of protecting and securing data is accomplished through policies, tools, design, and technology. Collectively, these measures are known as information security. **Information security**, sometimes referred to as *infosec*, refers to the processes and procedures designed to prevent the loss of data integrity, detect ongoing vulnerabilities and threats, and mitigate and respond to threats. It is a broad term that includes many aspects of an organization's security-management functions, which include identifying the organization's assets and developing, documenting, and implementing policies and procedures to protect those assets. Above all else, information needs to be protected from unauthorized use and modification and available when needed.

Businesses are increasingly interconnected with external environments. Interconnectivity increases the likelihood of potential vulnerabilities being exploited within computer systems as well as exposing users to a large variety of risks. The complexity of systems and the growing use of technology—including the Internet of Things (IoT), artificial intelligence (AI), autonomous systems, and the many choices among software applications and technology—intensifies the need for strong, detailed information security plans. The **Internet of Things (IoT)** describes the connection of nontraditional computing devices to the Internet. Internet connectivity is added to nontraditional devices such as home appliances, wearable devices, trash cans, and light bulbs.

Companies often seek, hire, and rely on industry experts who possess the necessary knowledge, skills, and experience in IT security measures. The most sought-after industry experts are generally those who hold industry-approved certifications. One such certification that is widely respected and desired by organizations is the CompTIA Security+ Certification.

The CompTIA Security+ Certification Exam addresses the essential and key concepts of IT security. It covers a wide range of topics, including physical security, network design and infrastructure, cryptography, authentication, and access control. In addition to technical measures, this certification addresses core business principles,

TECH TIP

If you are considering a degree in information or data security, you can choose from information assurance or cybersecurity. While both require knowledge of similar areas, including threats and technology, they differ in the respect that information assurance focuses on how a company uses data and its value, while a security professional specializes in the technical aspects of protecting the data.

including risk management, incident response, and administrative and technical policies. This text covers all the objectives required for a student to master the CompTIA Security+ Exam.

Information Assurance

Information assurance (IA) is the process of protecting an information system, including identifying vulnerabilities and risks for using, storing, and transmitting data. IA also includes planning and creating security policies, as well as budgeting for the cost of operation. One key component of information assurance includes risk management. **Risk** is a situation that could cause harm, create a hazard, or otherwise cause problems for an organization. **Risk management** is the process of identifying and evaluating assets and their vulnerabilities while taking steps to avoid or minimize loss, should it occur.

One of the most important assets for an organization is data, and when it comes to protecting data, there is much to consider. This includes the physical access to—as well as the storing, transmitting, and processing of—information. A security professional needs to understand a business's processes and the progression of data through the organization's systems. This understanding enables those professionals to assist in the design and implementation of systems and technology, which includes network and database design, software applications, and related systems.

Information assurance is a term often used interchangeably with *information security*. While there are elements associated with both processes, there are also some differences. Information assurance deals with a comprehensive understanding of IT in general along with how the variety of IT systems are interconnected, while information security is the practice in which the data is secured.

Key Areas of Information Assurance

Information assurance involves five key areas, as shown in Figure 1-1. Each area represents tasks, policies, and procedures needed to protect an organization's data. These processes are not sequential; rather, they are interconnected systems that illustrate core principles followed by an organization's information technology department.

Consider the application of both information assurance and information security in practice, using the following example. A graphic design firm partners with a production firm to send their digital content to be printed on a variety of platforms. An information assurance specialist will review the flow of data and systems that connects the two companies together, evaluate the potential vulnerabilities and risks, and propose security measures such as system design, authorization, and

Figure 1-1 The five areas of information assurance include confidentiality, integrity, authentication, availability, and nonrepudiation.

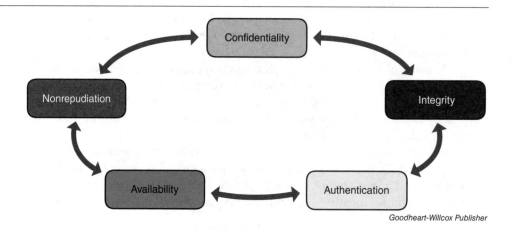

Goodheart-Willcox Publisher

cryptography to protect the assets and the systems. An information security professional will also perform the technical steps such as assigning the permissions, configuring firewalls, and implementing cryptography where required.

Confidentiality

Confidentiality is the condition of being private or secret. Providing confidentiality is the practice of ensuring users have access only to the data they need, which protects the data against unauthorized or unintentional access. Often, the phrase "need to know" is used to determine the level of access a user has to data, if at all. If a worker does not "need to know" the information to perform a job, then access is not granted to the data.

Confidentiality is implemented by the rights and privileges granted to individual computer users. For example, an employee who edits a company's social media accounts probably does not need access to corporate payroll information. It is not so much a matter of not trusting an employee; rather, the employee simply does not "need to know" information about other employees. Consider what could happen if a hacker or another employer were to steal that user's password. The thief could log in as the user and access whatever data the employee has rights to view or manage. Another way to incorporate confidentiality is through encryption. *Encryption* converts data into a format that can only be read by the holder of the decryption key.

Integrity

Integrity refers to an unchanged, unimpaired, or unaltered state. In context of data, integrity means ensuring data is not changed or altered when it is stored or is transmitted to another destination. For example, an employee in the payroll department should not be able to change a personal wage. Nor should such an employee be able to delete a bad performance review for a friend. In both cases, doing so would severely compromise the integrity of the data. Integrity applies to all data uses, such as ensuring that files downloaded or transmitted remain unchanged from their original state.

A practical example of ensuring integrity is using folder and file permissions. Figure 1-2 shows the permissions settings for a user. A user was given Windows file permissions to the payroll folder to view *and* read data. However, the person cannot make changes to files in this folder. In this way, the integrity of the data in the folder cannot be affected. You will learn how to view and grant permissions in Chapter 3.

Availability

Availability means data can be accessed when needed. A problem such as a hardware failure or a hacking attack might prevent access to data. Security managers must have solutions to ensure data can be accessed when a problem occurs. For example, if a server that provides user authentication fails, another server should be able to provide these services quickly so users do not lose access to the systems. Some hacking attacks against organizations are attacks against the availability of the data, including attacks such as denial of service attacks and ransomware. Both types of these attacks will be covered in detail in a future chapter.

Authentication

Authentication is the process of validating or verifying a user's identity. It is a critical function that must be performed before a user is given access to data. Common methods include the combination of a username and password, fingerprints, and access cards. Hackers often target the authentication process, so strong measures should be taken to incorporate and protect this process.

Figure 1-2 This user was given permission to read the files in the Payroll folder. However, the user cannot write (save) to the folder. This means that this person cannot make changes to the data in the folder.

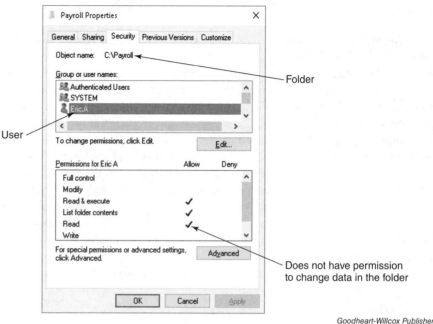

Goodheart-Willcox Publisher

Nonrepudiation

Nonrepudiation is the assurance that an individual or group of people cannot deny the validity of something. Essentially, nonrepudiation proves that a person performed a given action. Nonrepudiation plays an important role in information assurance because it ensures the integrity of a given file, data set, or action. Ensuring nonrepudiation is often achieved through a nonrepudiation process. A **nonrepudiation process** is a systematic process in which the origins and alterations to a data set are tracked according to the user account that made them.

CIA Triad

A fundamental guiding principal among security professionals is to maintain data confidentiality, integrity, and availability. This principle is known as the CIA triad, shown in Figure 1-3. The **CIA triad** consists of the three underlying core security principles of data protection: confidentiality, integrity, and availability. IT security decisions, such as evaluating new software or implementing technology in the workplace, should always apply the principles outlined in the CIA triad. For example, suppose your organization is going to move to a new payroll software application. What impact could this new software have on the availability of employee data? Are there any risks that could allow unauthorized people to view the data they should not see? A business will also want to ensure that user payroll information is not changed without proper authorization. This security model allows a company to view decisions using these strategic goals.

Information Security Plan

 5.2

An **information security plan**, also referred to as a *security plan*, is a set of procedures that describes an organization's computer network and details how company data will be protected and kept confidential. It also documents how threats to the

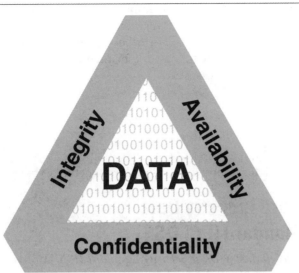

Goodheart-Willcox Publisher

Figure 1-3 The CIA triad provides three basic principles guiding information security professionals.

organization can be eliminated. Information security plans are designed to incorporate preventive measures and oversee various areas of protection, such as access to data stored on local systems or in the cloud, web and mobile applications, cryptographic measures and implementations, infrastructure design, and much more.

Organizations depend on many sources for guidance, such as frameworks, secure-configuration guides, and vendor-specific guides when creating a security plan.

 5.2

- **Frameworks** are documents that define policies and processes that outline the way in which information is managed in an organization.
- **Secure-configuration guides** are guides that provide assistance to security personnel for the secure configuration of hardware devices in an effort to prevent unauthorized access or attacks.
- **Vendor-specific guides** are guides written by a vendor for specific models of hardware. These guides are particularly helpful for web servers, operating systems, application servers, and network infrastructure devices.

The usage and purpose of these documents and publications is to provide guidance for organizations to help plan defenses.

Frameworks

Frameworks help break down the aspects of a business and security domains into manageable task areas and responsibilities. In turn, this helps create procedures and actions to defend against security threats. Companies face a daunting task of complying with regulations from states, industry, and federal and international governments, as well as company-specific edicts. Creating a security plan improves an organization's **security posture**, which is the actions, philosophies, and strategies for ensuring the security of an organization's software, hardware, network, and data.

Frameworks are often developed collaboratively by multiple organizations and individuals and are generally available at no charge for organizations to use to create their own security plans. Frameworks are often regulatory, meaning a company *must* abide by its requirements. In most cases, these are laws that businesses must follow. The frameworks discussed in this section are non-regulatory. *Non-regulatory frameworks* are those that are not overseen or controlled by a law or rule and may be optional. Frameworks can also be categorized as *industry-standard frameworks*, or *reference architecture*, which means the framework applies within a specific industry and outlines best practices for a given topic. According to the *Trends in Security Framework Adoption Survey* produced by cybersecurity firm Tenable, 84 percent of US organizations use a security framework for their organization. Some of the top frameworks adopted by businesses are

- PCI DSS;
- ISO Standards;
- CIS Critical Security Controls;
- SSAE SOC 2; and
- NIST Framework for Improving Critical Infrastructure Cybersecurity.

✚ 5.2

Payment Card Industry Data Security Standard (PCI DSS)

The *Payment Card Industry Data Security Standard (PCI DSS)* is a non-regulatory industry framework used for all merchants who process credit card transactions. It is a *set of standards* and requirements that apply to businesses using services from a credit card vendor, such as a bank. This framework provides guidance to businesses on their responsibilities in protecting credit card and related personal data of customers. It includes elements of protection such as firewall configuration, antivirus software, encryption of information, physical access restriction, and additional elements.

The PCI council was founded in 2006 by American Express, Discover, JCB International, MasterCard, and Visa. The council developed 12 different requirements that businesses that process credit card payments must follow to protect credit card and user information. The 12 standards are based on six goals shown in Figure 1-4.

According to a 2019 Nilson report, the United States leads the world in credit card fraud. Credit card data has long been sought by criminals, and most stolen credit card numbers are sold to other criminals who use them to create fake credit cards. They then sell the fake cards because theft of credit card numbers is a very lucrative market.

Figure 1-4 The PCI DSS contains 12 standards based on six goals.

Goals	PCI DSS Standard
Build and Maintain a Secure Network	1. Install and maintain a firewall to protect cardholder data.
	2. Do not use vendor-supplied defaults for system passwords and other security parameters.
Protect Cardholder Data	3. Protect stored cardholder data.
	4. Encrypt transmission of cardholder data across open, public networks.
Maintain a Vulnerability Management Program	5. Use and regularly update antivirus software or programs.
	6. Develop and maintain secure systems and applications.
Implement Strong Access Control Measures	7. Restrict access to cardholder data by business need-to-know.
	8. Assign a unique ID to each person with computer access.
	9. Restrict physical access to cardholder data.
Regularly Monitor and Test Networks	10. Track and monitor all access to network resources and cardholder data.
	11. Regularly test security systems and processes.
Maintain an Information Security Policy	12. Maintain a policy that addresses information security for employees and contractors.

Goodheart-Willcox Publisher

There are many examples of stolen credit card data. Companies such as J.C. Penney, The Home Depot, Target, Dairy Queen, and Jimmy Johns have seen breaches, and the list goes on. Any organization that processes credit cards must do its part in protecting the data. The PCI DSS provides the tools to understand what must be done for compliance and provides the framework to implement data protection.

The key aspect of the PCI DSS is that it applies to *all* organizations, regardless of the size or number of transactions conducted. If an organization accepts, transmits, or stores cardholder data, PCI DSS applies to the transaction. For example, suppose you sell crafts and use a tool such as Square on your iPhone or Android device to process the credit card transaction. You must comply with the mandates in the PCI DSS.

The PCI DSS has four levels of compliance based on a merchant level, which is determined by the number of transactions a business conducts per year. The four levels of PCI compliance are:

- Level 1: Merchants processing over 6 million card transactions per year
- Level 2: Merchants processing 1 to 6 million card transactions per year
- Level 3: Merchants handling 20,000 to 1 million card transactions per year
- Level 4: Merchants handling fewer than 20,000 transactions per year

In the previous example, your small business selling crafts would likely be level 4. However, a company that processes over 6 million transactions per year would be at level 1. Some of the compliance requirements differ depending on the merchant-level assignment, as outlined in Figure 1-5. In addition to the PCI merchant-level requirements shown, each credit company may have its own security programs requiring merchant-based safeguards for processing credit data. There are potential penalties for noncompliance of the standards. Fines could run as high as $5,000 to $100,000 per month. The credit card bank may choose to pass the cost of the fines to the merchant or terminate the payment relationship with the merchant. This would be in addition to any possible civil litigation from cardholders.

ISO Standards

 5.2

The International Organization for Standardization (ISO) creates "standards that support innovation and provide solutions to global challenges." The ISO is an independent, nongovernmental international organization. The following are examples of standards from ISO that are useful to organizations of any size.

- *ISO 27001* focuses on information security management systems (ISMS). This standard guides an organization to manage risks and the security of their assets.
- *ISO 27002* is a security standard that defines establishing and continuing improvement of an information security management system. Also included is information on assessing information security risks.

TECH TIP

Credit card data is often exposed due to the many areas where it can be stored. This can include browser history, bookmarks, and data located in Internet temporary files and cache. There are also scanning tools that can be used to locate stored card numbers in systems. Therefore, it is a necessary measure to ensure credit data is wiped from a device as often as it is used.

Figure 1-5 There are four levels of PCI compliance, each with their own set of compliance regulations.

Merchant Level	PCI Requirements
1	Merchants are required to produce an Annual Report on Compliance (ROC) by a Qualified Security Assessor (QSA) or internal auditor, and they are also required to participate in a quarterly network scan conducted by an approved scanning vendor (ASV).
2	Merchants must complete a PCI DSS self-assessment. They must also complete
3	and obtain evidence of a passed vulnerability scan with an approved scanning
4	vendor (ASV).

"CUNY PCI-DSS Guideline" bcc.cuny.edu

- *ISO 27701* provides guidance on establishing and continuously improving a Privacy Information Management System (PMIS) of a business. It provides guidance for those who are responsible for managing personally identifiable information (PII).
- *ISO 31000* contains standards that relate to risk management. These standards provide guidelines on risk management for organizations.

CIS Critical Security Controls

5.2

The Center for Internet Security (CIS) Top 20 Critical Security Controls is a simplified approach to protecting data written in an easily understandable format. CIS is a nonprofit organization that maintains best practices developed by experts around the world. Content included in the controls includes how to manage hardware and software assets, recommendations for securing mobile devices such as laptops, controls regarding the use of administrative privileges, and wireless control.

SSAE SOC 2

5.2

The *Statement on Standards for Attestation Engagements (SSAE)* is an auditing standard that governs ways in which companies report on compliance with laws and regulations rather than financial information. *Attestation* means proof or evidence, and through the audit process of an accounting firm, business must provide proof of compliance. These standards serve as frameworks and are written by the Institute of Certified Public Accountants (AICPA) Auditing Standards Board. At the conclusion of the audit, a *Service Organization Control (SOC) report* is created of a company's nonfinancial reporting controls that relate to items of security, availability, processing integrity, confidentiality, and privacy of a system. These five items are called *Trust Principles* that are applied during the audit.

There are two types of SOC reports generally used: Type I and Type II. An *SOC Type II report* is designed to be used by organizations that store customer data in the cloud and is for the organization's use only. It reports on the trust principles and requires strict polices relating to customer security. A third report type, *SOC Type III*, contains the same information as Type II; however, this report removes privacy information so that it can be distributed to the general public.

NIST Framework for Improving Critical Infrastructure Cybersecurity

5.2

The framework for improving critical infrastructure cybersecurity is a voluntary, risk-based framework for critical infrastructure in the United States. Critical infrastructure includes networks that manage water systems, electrical grids, banking institutions, energy companies and other crucial systems. This framework is the result of an executive order by President Barack Obama in 2013. The framework was initially developed to offer guidance to US businesses that operate and manage critical infrastructure systems. However, the framework was expanded and made available to any organization that wishes to provide risk management and security strategies to protect its computer network. It is used to help a company assess its security, and improve its ability to prevent, detect, and respond to any cyber threats.

The *NIST Cybersecurity Framework (CSF)* is a framework that helps an organization manage its cybersecurity risks. This framework consists of three parts: a framework core, which is a set of cybersecurity activities; framework implementation tiers, which include context on how a company views cyber risk and the processes for managing risk; and framework profiles, which represent outcomes based on business needs. NIST also includes the *NIST Risk Management Framework (RMF)*, which outlines and employs a mandatory six-step process for managing risk and loss to a business.

Security Domains

A **security domain** refers to a list of people, devices, and systems that must comply with a security policy. Attacks can occur from many sources, so it is important to design layered solutions that assist with prevention and protection. A security domain allows you to define various aspects of your organization logically into manageable and related functions for security planning and implementation. Security domains help to manage the task of protecting data by dividing and distributing an organization's information into job-specific divisions.

When considering security domains, you must identify the attack surface. The **attack surface** is all the locations where an attacker can enter and cause a security risk. It is a point or area in a system that could be used or compromised to allow hackers entry into the system. These are areas you need to recognize in order to develop prevention and detection strategies. As part of the planning, it is helpful to create multiple levels of protection. Having multiple, redundant levels of protection in the event that one level fails is known as **defense in depth**. Examples of defense in depth include control diversity, vendor diversity, and user training. Defense in depth is also known as *layered security*.

Consider a comparison from medieval times: the defense of castles, as shown in Figure 1-6. Castles were often placed on hills so defenders could scan below them for attacking forces. Trees were cleared to provide clear lines of sight around the castles. Moats were added for additional protection. Turrets provided cover for defenders who could attack incoming forces. Access to the castle was limited to entrances protected with iron gates. Each of these defensive measures is unique and separate from each other. Having different security control types is an example of *control diversity*.

To liken this to a business, defense in depth might include security guards to access the building. Then, employees might have to use a code to access a door lock. To log in to the computer network, a fingerprint might be required. Therefore, for an intruder to gain access to the network, the person would need to

1. slip past the security guards;

2. know or hack the door-lock code; and

3. hack the fingerprint lock on the network.

Another best practice of defense in depth is *vendor diversity*, which means using equipment from multiple vendors. For example, if you were using only Cisco routers and there is a network weakness that is exploited by hackers, it would affect all your routers. If you had a diversity of routers from different manufacturers, you would still have the ability to continue limited operations and not suffer a complete failure. This is known as *systems resilience*.

 2.5

Similar to vendor diversity is *diversity of technologies*, which refers to the use of many types of technology in an effort to lessen impact of a cyberattack or outage. For example, if an organization relies only on antimalware solutions, malware could still infiltrate the network. If telephone contact is the only technology to relay critical information to employees in a crisis, a business could have major problems if cellular traffic is impacted.

Policies are another aspect of security management, as they provide direction for the security plan. *Control diversity* refers to establishing multiple policies, procedures, or methods for enforcement. *Administrative controls*, also called *procedural controls*, are processes and policies put in place for security. These include topics

Figure 1-6 Medieval castles practiced the concept of defense in depth. Multiple layers of security must be overcome to breach the castle.

Moat

Towers and turrets

Drawbridge

Gate

Goodheart-Willcox Publisher; (castle) Aerovista Luchtfotografie/Shutterstock.com

such as security awareness training and cyber insurance, which protects the company against losses caused by cybersecurity incidents. A procedural control outlines the other types of security controls that should be in place. It is also referred to as an administrative control since it establishes other controls, methods, or policies.

Diversity in cryptographic systems should also be explored. *Cryptography* protects data by encrypting the data and provides confidentiality. There are different methods of cryptography available, depending on use and security needs. Diversifying cryptographic methods will further protect data in the event one method is compromised. Cryptography will be discussed in detail later in this text.

Technical controls consist of technology used to automate security functions. This automation may include scheduled actions taken due to events in the system logs. It can also include the implementation of firewalls. Firewalls restrict unwanted traffic to or from the network. A firewall is a security tool that acts as a barrier or protection against an unwanted data transfer.

Another important technical control that should be part of the security plan is auditing. *Auditing* is the process of tracking the actions of an individual using a resource. It is an essential security measure. Auditing may be done internally, though many companies hire an outside firm to perform audits. Audits should be performed on a regular basis.

When evaluating the security of a business or organization, it can be overwhelming to consider the many areas that must be secured. To make the goal of protecting data and assets a more manageable process, security teams often break down the areas of a business or organization into sections called *information technology security domains*. Commonly referenced IT domains include the following:

- user
- workstation
- LAN
- WAN
- remote access
- system

These sections are based primarily on network infrastructure with the exception of the user domain.

User

A *user domain* is about people. This domain includes all employees of a business. However, it could also include vendors or contractors who use the network as well as guests who are provided Wi-Fi access. **Wi-Fi** is a wireless networking technology that uses radio waves instead of copper-core or fiber-optic cable.

Users often represent the weakest link in the security chain. They often provide the potential for data breaches. For example, users might reveal confidential data, have weak passwords, leave confidential papers on desks, or lose flash drives containing important data. It is critical to create a domain to deal with these issues. Simple measures such as proper trash disposal, not using sticky-notes on monitors, and locking computers when not near them can go far in securing systems. Another security strategy is a screen saver that locks the computer and requires a password to unlock so that unauthorized users cannot access the system.

A security plan for the users in an organization would not be complete without providing user training. The impact of untrained users to a computer system or individual device can be widespread. Without proper training, users can unknowingly download malware, reveal classified information, or even provide access to unauthorized users. It is the responsibility of an organization to ensure users have the knowledge they need to protect the data and resources within an organization. User training can be conducted in many formats, including online training, a traditional classroom model, or small group training. An efficient security plan should include awareness of threats and vulnerabilities most encountered by users; compliance with laws, regulations, and company policies; and best practices such as some of those listed previously. In addition to training, frequent security awareness measures should be provided. These could include posters, e-mails, newsletters, and videos. Using these awareness tools will keep security a prominent reminder to employees.

Workstation

The *workstation domain* deals with the issues surrounding workstations or other devices used by people. Workstations are computers such as desktop or laptop units. These items may be system-owned or personal devices, including tablets, smartphones, and IoT devices.

The actions or system settings for these devices often produce an avenue of attack from many threats. Protecting these devices against potential intrusion or threats is an essential security management responsibility. Security administrations should use appropriate preventive software, such as antivirus, local firewalls, and even global positioning system (GPS) tracking tools for mobile devices.

A number of policies should be examined and implemented for these devices. Suggested policies include technical policies, such as preventing users from installing software or changing system settings; alerting policies, such as those that notify administrators of potential threats or misuse; and other security measures, such as directing data storage to central locations instead of local access. Additional policies to consider are lock-down policies that reduce threats from network services, filter Internet browsing, and prevent unauthorized scripts from running.

LAN

A *local area network (LAN)* is a network infrastructure within a small area. This area is usually a single building. Issues related to the LAN may be related to servers, switches, routers, and media. The *LAN domain* covers these items.

The devices in this domain are critical elements of an organization's network. The ability for data to move successfully within a network relies on properly configured routers, switches, and other networking devices. Since these devices are often managed through remote access and use of configuration files, strong security settings must be in place for all devices on a LAN domain. Attackers often try to access these devices through open connections, such as Telnet, or easily cracked passwords. Switches are particularly vulnerable to **ARP poisoning**, also called *ARP spoofing*, which is an attack in which a spoofed Address Resolution Protocol (ARP) message is sent onto a LAN and causes network traffic to be sent to the attacker.

Servers are among the most critical devices in this domain. They hold files and data vital not only to an organization's operation, but also to its infrastructure. Poorly configured permissions or a lack of authentication or strong preventive policies increase the likelihood of data exposure and unauthorized access. Network security is usually employed through *security protocols*, which define processes and actions to secure a network from unauthorized attempts to access or modify data. There are many security protocols, most of which will be discussed throughout this text.

WAN

A *wide area network (WAN)* is a network infrastructure for more than one geographic location. The Internet is an example of a WAN. There are distinct threats and vulnerabilities that could occur in this part of the network infrastructure. The *WAN domain* covers these issues.

Important considerations in this security domain include ensuring firewalls are correctly configured and routers properly secured, patched, and updated. In many WAN configurations, sites are connected through public networks, and data and access must be protected, especially at the endpoints where the local business network connects to the public infrastructure.

Another important element includes potential threats to supervisory control and data acquisition (SCADA) systems. SCADA systems are used to monitor and control processors in many manufacturing, oil and gas facilities, nuclear power plants, electrical grids, and other critical systems. These systems allow for collection of real-time information from the manufacturing plant, and/or production environments, which are then processed and distributed to networked devices. This information can then be accessed remotely. Due to the critical nature of this information, threats against these systems could have a serious or catastrophic effect.

Remote Access

In today's workplace, businesses are increasingly allowing employees, or other users, to connect remotely to the computer network. The *remote access domain* addresses challenges presented by remote access. These challenges include securing data in transit over the Internet, verification of the authorized users and their locations, and the security of the remote system.

Remote access presents a weak point in the system, primarily due to the fact that devices connecting remotely are not managed by the organization whose network is being used for access. In addition, the organization has no physical controls over the location where access connection originates, or the networks traversed in order to establish connections. There are many strategies that can be implemented for remote users to secure this type of access, including strong authentication methods, incorporation of encryption method, incorporation of the virtual private network, updated antimalware programs, and use of network firewalls at the remote client and enterprise network.

TECH TIP

The ARP protocol was replaced in IPv6 with Neighbor Discovery Protocol (NDP) and Internet Control Message Protocol v6 (ICMPv6). As with ARP, NDP messages are not authenticated and can be used to spoof legitimate network hosts on a network. Simply eliminating IPv4 from a network will *not* prevent these type of attacks.

System

A system domain includes the services and software used to provide access to data and other resources. *System domain* is a generic term. This domain covers web servers, database servers, and any server operating system or feature used to support data access.

Some of the top threats to an organization come from access through web services, which provide a portal to the company through its web pages. Websites are designed with many features, including scripts and access to stored data, which leave data and services vulnerable to many different types of attacks. Security administrators need to be aware of threats to web services and system resources as well as the proper configurations to lock down undesired access.

Web servers are not the only element in this domain that pose a security risk. Any service that runs on servers contains its own vulnerabilities, including e-mail systems, domain name services, authentication services, and the operating system powering the servers. Each network service must be evaluated for specific threats, such as outdated systems and open ports. A rigorous plan to evaluate each network service is important, as is the implementation of features and configurations required to reduce the risk of attacks.

In the various domains, it is necessary to configure and secure a myriad of software applications, network servers, and related services, such as web servers, directory servers, IoT devices, computer hardware, operating systems, and network infrastructure. Configuration can be an overwhelming project; each manufacturer has different procedures, and all systems come with default settings that do not necessarily provide security measures. The responsibility of configuring these systems in a secure fashion is known as hardening the system. *Hardening* is the practice of configuring a system securely, including technical measures, procedures, and processes. This means closing or locking down unnecessary paths on an operating system that can be used for unapproved access.

To assist in system hardening, IT security technicians look to technical guides to provide details and recommendations to configure these systems securely. These guides can come from vendors to provide information on configuring devices and software such as web servers, operating systems, application servers, and other network infrastructure guides. Examples include Cisco guides to harden their Internetwork Operating System (IOS) devices and Microsoft's security configuration frameworks for their operating systems. Security guides may be published by independent organizations like The Open Web Application Security Project (OWASP), a nonprofit organization that provides details on application and website hardening techniques. Many independent organizations and security vendors publish guides for operating systems, browsers, and other software and hardware devices. Additionally, there are many general-purpose guides that provide excellent information on both device and system hardening. General-purpose guides offer best practices and suggest configuration settings across a wide variety of platforms and are not vendor specific.

Regulatory Compliance

As you plan security measures, it is important to understand that in a business, you can establish policies that the information technology department and management team enforce to help the organization comply to laws.

Some laws are generic in nature and apply to all systems. Other laws apply only to certain types of businesses or data. Failure to abide by laws could result in criminal or civil penalties. A business may also lose the ability of providing a service, such as processing credit cards, if laws are not followed.

When a requirement is a legal or regulatory directive, you are responsible for ensuring compliance with the terms. **Compliance** means adhering to laws, regulations, and standards as set forth by a governing body, such as a professional organization or governmental agency. Since technology is key to data storage and access, many laws are established to ensure that data and privacy are protected. While most laws are enacted at a federal level, states may also have their own laws. Companies that work with other businesses or customers located outside the United States may also have to comply with international legal regulations set by those countries. For example, the European Union (EU) adopted the General Data Protection Regulation (GDPR), a set of strong data privacy rules. All companies with business or customer interests in the EU must be compliant with this act.

In addition to federal law, international law, and compliance regulations, many individual states have their own computer security laws. These rules must be followed if a company conducts business within the state that enacted the law.

Standards are different from laws. An **industry standard** is a set of rules adopted by a particular industry. Businesses in that industry have agreed to follow the rules in the standard. However, laws are enacted by a governmental body and are *compulsory*, meaning they must be followed. In the United States, state laws are passed by individual state legislatures, and they apply only within their respective states. Federal laws are passed by Congress and apply everywhere throughout the country. Some of the major federal and international laws that apply to security measures include the following:

- Computer Fraud and Abuse Act (CFAA)
- Electronic Communication Privacy Act (ECPA)
- Gramm-Leach-Bliley Act (GLBA)
- Sarbanes-Oxley Act (SOX)
- Health Insurance Portability and Accountability Act (HIPAA)
- EU General Data Protection Regulation (GDPR)

Computer Fraud and Abuse Act

The *Computer Fraud and Abuse Act (CFAA)* defines and outlines unauthorized access of computers. It primarily covers *protected* computers located on US governmental systems, financial institutions, and interstate or foreign communication. The law was originally enacted in 1986 and has been updated several times since it first took effect. In theory, most computers and cell phones are likely included within the scope of this law. While there are many specific aspects to the law, some of its main points deal with individuals who knowingly access computers for which they do not have authorization. The four essential elements of the CFAA state that a defendant

- has accessed a protected computer;
- has done so without authorization or by exceeding such authorization as was granted;
- has done so knowingly and with intent to defraud; and
- as a result, has furthered the intended fraud and obtained something of value.

The law covers both criminal and civil litigation. Many computer hackers have found themselves prosecuted under this law. Criminal penalties include fines and imprisonment, including potential fines assessed for civil litigation.

The CFAA has been used to prosecute unauthorized computer access and cited in many civil cases as well. In July of 2019, the US Justice Department announced a series of indictments against 12 Russian nationals working on behalf of the Main Intelligence Directorate (the GRU). These hacks were directed against the Democratic National Committee, the Democratic Congressional Campaign Committee, and Hillary Clinton's presidential campaign. Each individual was charged with two separate violations of the CFAA along with other criminal charges. Another newsworthy attack was the indictment of Paige A. Thompson, who is charged with a single count of computer fraud and abuse pursuant to the CFAA. Paige Thompson was arrested for alleged hacking into servers rented by Capital One Financial Corporation in the summer of 2019. And in May of 2019, the founder of WikiLeaks, Julian Assange, was arrested and charged with violating one count of the CFAA. The case has raised a great deal of interest, as Julian himself did not access the systems to illegally obtain information, but helped crack a password which allowed access to the classified data.

There are many critics of CFAA. Much of the criticism is based in part due to the very broad nature of the law. This criticism has led to controversy surrounding prosecutions under the law. Two of the most debated indictments for computer fraud were against Aaron Swartz for downloads of information from the MIT network in July of 2011 and the previously attempted prosecution of Lori Drew for a fake social media profile.

Aaron Swartz was a popular programmer and helped co-found the website Reddit.com and create *RSS (Really Simple Syndication)*, a web format in which regularly changing web content can be delivered to subscribers. Beginning 2010 and continuing through 2011, Swartz connected a personal computer to the MIT network and downloaded 2.7 million academic papers that were freely available to anyone on campus, including visitors, by using the JSTOR service. Despite JSTOR not filing a criminal complaint, the Justice Department charged him with 13 felony counts with possible penalties including jail time of 50 years and up to one million dollars in fines.

Electronic Communication Privacy Act

The *Electronic Communication Privacy Act (ECPA)* protects wire and electronic transmissions of data. This law covers communication such as e-mail, telephone conversations, and data stored electronically. Essentially, the law protects electronic communication whether made orally (by voice) or by digital data transmissions. Protection of communication begins as soon as a transmission is started and remains in effect through the data transmission and even while the data is stored in its destination, as shown in Figure 1-7. The ECPA has three parts: the Wiretap Act, the Stored Communications Act (SCA), and the Pen Register Act.

The *Wiretap Act* prohibits the intentional interception, use, disclosure, or procurement of any communication. Data collected in these ways cannot be used as evidence in court. In addition, even the attempt to commit these actions is prohibited.

The *Stored Communications Act (SCA)* protects the privacy of the content of files stored by service providers. It also protects records including subscriber names, billing records, and IP addresses.

The *Pen Register Act* requires governmental entities to obtain a court order on these devices. A **pen register** is a device that captures *outgoing* phone numbers, e-mail data, or Internet addresses of communications between parties. Most of the information collected includes the contact information, such as phone number, e-mail address, IP address, and time and location data. The only data that can be provided through the pen register act is the content of SMS messages. This differs from a *trap and trace*, which captures *incoming* numbers, e-mail addresses, and IP addresses.

There are many issues with the ECPA, and amendments have been made for compliance with the USA PATRIOT Act. There are also issues of conflict with the Fourth Amendment rights to protect individuals from unreasonable search and seizure. Currently, stored data older than 180 days is considered to be abandoned, and thus, not subject to a warrant. This applies to e-mail and data stored in the cloud. Proposals have been made in Congress to address these conflicts and privacy issues.

Figure 1-7 ECPA protection begins at the start of the transmission and continues to the end, including the data stored on computers.

ECPA Protection

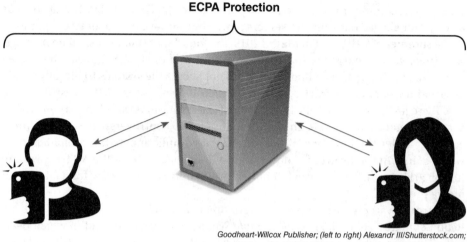

Gramm-Leach-Bliley Act

The *Gramm-Leach-Bliley Act (GLBA)* ensures that financial businesses are protecting a customer's private data. It was enacted in 1999 and is also known as the *Financial Services Modernization Act of 1999.* This act applies to companies of all sizes that provide financial services and products. *Financial services* can include loans, insurance, and financial and investment advice. Any business that provides these services is subject to the provisions outlined in the GLBA. The GLBA also covers other businesses, such as retail stores offering financing or credit cards, check-cashing companies, tax-preparation services, and even real-estate appraisers.

To implement the GLBA, the Federal Trade Commission (FTC) issued the Safeguards Rule. The *Safeguards Rule* mandates that all businesses must develop, implement, and maintain a comprehensive information-security program that contains administrative, technical, and physical safeguards appropriate to the size and complexity of an organization. Companies must anticipate likely threats and hazards that could affect the security and integrity of the data. This not only includes potential security threats to IT systems but also the employees who have access to customer information. Additionally, it includes potential system failures.

The other key provision of the GLBA is the Financial Privacy Rule. The *Financial Privacy Rule* regulates the collection and disclosure of a consumer's nonpublic personal information (NPI). Under this rule, businesses must provide customers with written notice describing their privacy policies and practices. Consumers should be given the opportunity to opt out of the sharing of some of their personal financial information.

Another protection under this act is for pretexting protection. **Pretexting** is using a lie or scam to obtain private information. Pretexting may include requests from fraudulent e-mails, telephone calls, or direct mail. Companies must train their employees and implement practices to reduce the success of a pretexting act.

There are some criticisms of the Gramm-Leach-Bliley Act. Some privacy advocates believe too great of a burden is placed on the individual consumer to protect personal data. These advocates believe consumers should have the right to opt in and decide for themselves what data, if any, can be shared. Also, there are no standards on notices required by the GLBA. This can create confusion to consumers, especially regarding confusing legal terminology.

Sarbanes-Oxley Act

The *Sarbanes-Oxley Act (SOX)* prevents company executives from hiding or destroying electronic records for a minimum of five years. In the early 2000s, there were a few large corporations, such as Enron and WorldCom, who engaged in deceptive and fraudulent financial and accounting practices. When these issues were discovered, some of the companies closed. This cost investors, stockholders, and employees millions of dollars, retirement pensions, and jobs.

Sarbanes-Oxley was named after its two sponsors in Congress: Senator Paul Sarbanes of Maryland and Representative Michael Oxley of Ohio. It became law in 2002. Enforcement of this law is made through the Securities and Exchange Commission (SEC).

SOX is designed to crack down on corporate fraud. Some of its provisions included creating a Public Company Accounting Oversight Board to oversee the accounting industry. Company loans to its executives were banned. Rules were instituted to protect whistleblowers who came forward to report fraudulent practices.

Some of the key provisions required executives to certify the accuracy of financial information and statements personally. A person who violates these provisions can be penalized with up to 20 years in prison. Internal control structure and procedures must be maintained. It is here that an IT department has a significant role in protecting and retaining data, including files and e-mail.

One of the contributing companies that prompted the legislation was the deeds of Arthur Andersen, a prominent accounting firm. In an effort to hide actions of fraudulent work for the company Enron, employees deleted relevant files and shredded paper copies of the files and e-mail.

Health Insurance Portability and Accountability Act

The *Health Insurance Portability and Accountability Act (HIPAA)* protects electronic medical records and personal health information, including patient demographics, medical history, tests and labs and the resulting diagnosis. Any company that handles medical records or insurance information must comply with the requirements of this legislation. It applies to medical practices and hospitals. In addition, it covers pharmacies and other businesses that handle personal health-care information. It even applies health-care–related employee information within a business.

Health-care information can reveal much about a person and can be exploited and used improperly. It can even be used as a form of identity theft in which a criminal can impersonate a victim to obtain medical care. Stolen medical records can result in fraudulent billing.

HIPAA is managed by the US Department of Health and Human Services (HHS). In addition to numerous rules and regulations, HIPAA provides two key rules that are important to consumers: the Privacy Rule and the Security Rule.

Privacy Rule

The Privacy Rule establishes a set of national standards for the protection of all "individually identifiable health information." This information is also known as *protected health information (PHI)*. PHI can be in the form of electronic data, paper records, or even spoken conversation. Not complying with the Privacy Rule can result in civil fines. For "willful actions," criminal charges could be filed.

Security Rule

Most medical practices use some form of digital or electronic platform for health records. A record in this form is called an *electronic health record (EHR)*. The Security Rule establishes a set of national standards to protect personal health information in electronic form. These standards help organizations understand the safeguards they must undertake to ensure the confidentiality, integrity, and security of information. Safeguards can be physical, administrative, or technical in nature.

EU General Data Protection Regulation

The *EU General Data Protection Regulation (GDPR)* is a set of privacy laws approved by the European Union Parliament in April 2016, and enforcement began on May 25, 2018. It provides regulations on data protection and privacy for all individuals in the European Union and European Economic area. While it does not directly cover citizens or businesses outside the European Union, many global organizations are affected by this regulation as they do business with companies and individuals that are covered by the law.

Some of the main elements of the GDPR outline the technical and organization safeguards that must be implemented to protect data. These include anonymization where it is appropriate, privacy settings configured at the highest level possible, and other aspects including consent of the individual. Data breaches must be reported within specific time frames, and the GDPR also lays out fines for noncompliance.

SUMMARY

Defining Information Security

- Information security is the act of securing data through processes, procedures, and technical measures.
- Part of information security is developing an information security plan that describes an organization's computer network and details how a company's data will be protected and kept confidential.
- Individuals can validate their skills in information security by earning certifications such as Security+ from CompTIA.

Information Assurance

- Information assurance (IA) deals with the big picture aspect of securing data in an organization including setting and maintaining policies and procedures, budgeting, and oversight.
- There are five core principles of information assurance: confidentiality, integrity, availability, authentication, and nonrepudiation.
- The CIA triad of confidentiality, integrity, and availability identifies the three core security principles of data protection.
- An information security plan provides guidelines that help organizations incorporate preventive measures, oversee various areas of protection, and plan defenses.

Frameworks

- Segmenting an organization into security domains allows an organization to categorize differing data protection needs.
- Frameworks are documents and checklists that enable an organization to create structured plans to identify, manage, and monitor security plans.
- Some of the top frameworks adopted by businesses are PCI DSS, ISO Standards, CIS Critical Security Controls, SSAE SOC 2, and NIST Framework for Improving Critical Infrastructure Cybersecurity.

Security Domains

- Security domain refers to a list of people, devices, and systems that must comply with a security policy. It allows an organization to define various aspects of the business logically into manageable and related functions for security planning and implementation.
- When considering security domains, an individual must identify the attack surface, which is all the locations where an attacker can enter and cause a security risk. These are areas an individual needs to recognize in order to develop prevention and detection strategies.
- The most commonly created domains include user, workstation, LAN, WAN, remote access, and system.
- Hardening is the process of locking down a system to make it more secure. Technical guidelines from vendors and industry assist security technicians by identifying vulnerable areas in the attack surface.

Regulatory Compliance

- Compliance means adhering to laws, regulations, and standards as set forth by a governing body, such as a professional organization or governmental agency.
- In addition to federal law, international law, and compliance regulations, many individual states have their own computer security laws.
- Standards are different from laws. An industry standard is a set of rules adopted by a particular industry. However, laws are enacted by a governmental body and must be followed.
- Some of the major federal and international laws that apply to security measures include the following: Computer Fraud and Abuse Act (CFAA), Electronic Communication Privacy Act (ECPA), Gramm-Leach-Bliley Act (GLBA), Sarbanes-Oxley Act (SOX), Health Insurance Portability and Accountability Act (HIPAA), and EU General Data Protection Regulation (GDPR).

REVIEW QUESTIONS

1. What is information security?
2. Summarize information assurance.
3. State the difference between *information assurance* and *information security*.
4. What is the term that describes the process of tracking changes to the user who made them?
5. What is an *information security plan*?
6. Identify and explain the top frameworks adopted by businesses.
7. What are the four levels of PCI compliance?

8. Which NIST framework consists of three parts that help an organization manage its cybersecurity risks?

9. List and discuss each of the security domains covered in this chapter.

10. What is defense in depth?

11. Provide an example of how control diversity demonstrates defense in depth.

12. What is the purpose of technical guides that govern system hardening?

13. Explain regulatory compliance.

14. What are possible outcomes if a business does not comply with laws?

15. List and summarize three examples of laws or standards related to information security.

16. Identify the four essential elements of the CFAA.

17. Summarize the three parts of the Electronic Communication Privacy Act (ECPA).

18. Summarize the two rules covered in the Gramm-Leach-Bliley Act (GLBA).

19. What are the two key HIPAA rules that are important to consumers?

20. How do international standards, such as the GDPR, apply to companies outside the European Union?

✚ SAMPLE SECURITY+ EXAM QUESTIONS

1. Which of the following compliance requirements would Christina, the security officer, follow to protect PHI?

   A. Sarbanes-Oxley

   B. PCI DSS

   C. HIPAA

   D. GDPR

2. Which of the following is used to *best* help Juan harden a web server?

   A. Platform-based technical guides

   B. Data classification

   C. Security Domains

   D. CIA triad

3. Which of the following is not a law that must be followed but a non-regulatory industry regulation for a clothing retailer?

   A. HIPAA

   B. GDPR

   C. PCI DSS

   D. GLBA

4. Which of these is *not* true regarding Carla, the data steward of an organization?

   A. Carla is responsible for the policies of data storage.

   B. Carla must be aware of how data is transferred and accessed.

   C. Carla is the legal owner of the stored data.

   D. Carla must be aware of the methods that collect the business's data.

5. A company wants to ensure that users are aware of how data should be categorized, such as Internal, Public, or Confidential. Which of the following will they use to ensure this process?

   A. Determine legal ownership of the data

   B. Use an industry framework

   C. Establish clear data classification methods

   D. Create security domains

6. Jenna is configuring settings to a network switch that connects multiple workstations to her organization's network. In which security domain is she working?

   A. User

   B. Workstation

   C. System

   D. LAN

7. What is a primary goal of using an industry framework?

   A. Reduce business costs

   B. To obtain technical instructions on hardening

   C. Identify vulnerabilities and establish protection measures

   D. Ensure legal and regulatory compliance

8. A company needs to ensure data is available after its initial usage. Which two measures should be used when making this decision? (Choose 2)

   A. The cost of storing data

   B. Regulatory compliance rules

   C. The size of the stored data

   D. Corporate retention policies

9. A company must demonstrate their compliance with security controls. Which of the following will they use?

   A. DPO

   B. SSAE SOC 2

   C. ISO 31000

   D. Reference architecture

10. Michael recommends classifying data to include labels such as Confidential, Private, Public, and Proprietary. Which is the *best* reason to follow this approach?

    A. Easier to create data retention policies

    B. Easier to establish data access policies

    C. Easier to back up the data

    D. Easier to encrypt data

LAB EXERCISES

Lab Activity 1-1: Exploring an Industry Framework

The Center for Internet Security (CIS) provides controls for a security framework. In this activity, we will explore an example of a security framework. As you view the framework, consider that it can be used as a baseline for an organization to develop its own specific documentation and security planning. In this exercise, you will take a brief look at an example of some frameworks.

1. Launch a web browser, and navigate to the Center for Internet Security website (www.cisecurity.org).

2. Locate the **About us** link, which is likely at the bottom of the page, and click it. Review the information about this group, including its goals and mission. What do you think the benefits of using a volunteer method to create these controls offers over a for-profit organization?

3. Click on the **CIS Controls** link at the top of the page, as shown

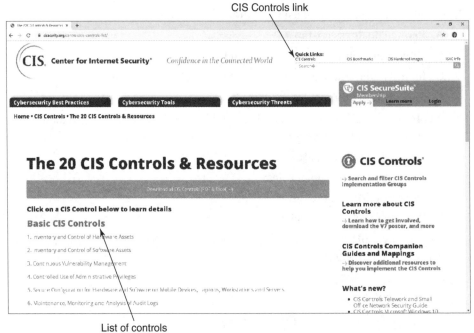

CIS Controls link

List of controls

4. From the right side of the screen, select **Learn about the 20 individual CIS Controls and other resources**.

5. How many controls are offered?

6. Review the first five controls. Click the name of each control to display detailed information about the control.

7. Discuss with your classmates why control 5 is an important control to implement.

8. Review the complete list of the 20 controls. Discuss with your class how these controls can help plan your security defenses.

Lab Activity 1-2: Locating and Evaluating Security Guides

Security guides are often published by non-profit organizations, security firms, and even IT bloggers and researchers. In this lab, we will compare guidelines for the Linux operating system. Since Linux is open-source code, the distributor of the operating system you are using may not have any published guides, but many individuals and companies have created detailed documents.

1. Launch a web browser, and search for hardening Linux operating systems.
2. Choose a link and review the suggestions. Did this link address the two major Linux distribution platforms (Debian and RedHat)?
3. Who provided the link you chose; was it a blogger, security company, non-profit etc.?
4. Return to your search results and choose another response. Compare this list to the first one you reviewed. Did they provide similar suggestions and recommendations?
5. Return to your browser, repeat the same search, but add +password in the search request. (The + ensures the term password must be in the results.)
6. Review one or more of the results. Notice that adding a password allows you to focus on a specific task to assist in confidentiality goals.
7. Discuss your observations and favorite sites with classmates.

CASE STUDY

HIPAA-Compliant Security

In March 2020, the Office for Civil Rights (OCR) at the US Department of Health and Human Services (HHS) issued temporary waivers and guidance regarding HIPAA and telehealth services rendered during the COVID-19 health emergency. These measures were intended to encourage the use of telehealth services and enable social distancing. In their directive, the OCR announced they would use enforcement discretion not to impose penalties for HIPAA violations against healthcare providers with their good-faith provision of using telehealth communication methods. *Telehealth* is described as the use of electronic information and telecommunication technologies to support and promote long-distance clinical health care using technologies such as video conferencing, the Internet, store and forward imaging, streaming media, and landline and wireless communications.

1. Summarize what you believe constitutes an organization's *good-faith effort* in protecting the confidentiality and integrity of data. Provide relevant examples.
2. Telehealth relies on the use of video conferencing tools. Therefore, providers should be aware of the differences between nonpublic-facing services, such as Apple Face Time and Zoom, and public-facing services, such as TikTok or Facebook Live. Prepare a statement to a medical practice differentiating these technologies and how some of them may violate the basic principles of confidentiality and integrity.
3. Consider the security domains identified in this chapter. Which areas will be most affected by the incorporation of telehealth practices? Support your answer with detailed analysis.

Threats, Attacks, and Vulnerabilities

LEARNING OUTCOMES

- Define *threats*.
- Discuss threat actors, types, and attributes of actors.
- Differentiate types of hackers.
- List examples of vectors used to exploit system vulnerabilities.
- Summarize threat intelligence sources and resources.
- Identify and explain various malware attacks.
- Discuss viruses.
- Explain an adversarial artificial intelligence (AI) attack.
- Summarize social engineering and reconnaissance.
- Identify types of social engineering attacks.
- Discuss vulnerabilities.
- Identify examples of protection strategies against threats to networks and data.

KEY TERMS

advanced persistent threat (APT)
adversarial AI attack
adware
armored virus
artificial intelligence (AI)
attribute
backdoor
black-hat hacker
bug-bounty program
card cloning
closed threat intelligence source
command and control (C&C) attack
credential harvesting
criminal syndicate
cryptomalware
cyberattack
cybercrime
cybersecurity
dark web
denial of service (DoS) attack
distributed denial of service (DDoS) attack
doxing

drive-by download
dumpster diving
encryption
enterprise environment
fileless virus
gray-hat hacker
hacking attack
hacktivist
heuristic methodology
hoax
hybrid warfare
identity fraud
impersonation
indicators of compromise (IoC)
influence campaign
information sharing center (ISC)
invoice scam
insider
keylogger
legacy platform
logic bomb
machine learning (ML)
macro virus

malicious USB cable
malware
malware attack
nondisclosure agreement (NDA)
open port
open service
open-source intelligence (OSINT)
payload
pharming
phishing
polymorphic virus
potentially unwanted program (PUP)
prepending
ransomware
reconnaissance
remote access Trojan (RAT)
rootkit
script kiddie
shadow IT
shoulder surfing
skimmer
smishing
spam

spam over Internet messaging (SPIM)
spear phishing
spyware
state actor
state-sponsored hacking
Structured Threat Information eXpression (STIX)
supply chain
supply chain vulnerability
system integration

threat
threat actor
threat intelligence
threat map
time bomb
Trojan
Trusted Automated Exchange of Indicator Information (TAXII)
USB data blocker
vendor management

vendor support
virus
vishing
vulnerability
watering hole attack
weak configuration
whale phishing
white-hat hacker
worm
zero-day vulnerability

SECURITY+ CERTIFICATION EXAM OBJECTIVES

The following Security+ Certification Exam Objectives are covered in this chapter.

+ 1.1: Phishing
+ 1.1: Smishing
+ 1.1: Vishing
+ 1.1: Spam
+ 1.1: Spam over Internet messaging (SPIM)
+ 1.1: Spear phishing
+ 1.1: Dumpster diving
+ 1.1: Shoulder surfing
+ 1.1: Pharming
+ 1.1: Eliciting information
+ 1.1: Whaling
+ 1.1: Prepending
+ 1.1: Identity fraud
+ 1.1: Invoice scams
+ 1.1: Credential harvesting

+ 1.1: Reconnaissance
+ 1.1: Hoax
+ 1.1: Impersonation
+ 1.1: Watering hole attack
+ 1.1: Influence campaigns
+ 1.1: Principles (reasons for effectiveness)
+ 1.2: Malware
+ 1.2 Physical attacks
+ 1.2: Adversarial artificial intelligence (AI)
+ 1.5: Actors and threats
+ 1.5: Attributes of actors
+ 1.5: Vectors
+ 1.5: Open source intelligence (OSINT)

+ 1.5: Closed/proprietary
+ 1.5: Public/private information sharing centers
+ 1.5: Dark web
+ 1.5: Indicators of compromise
+ 1.5: Automated indicator sharing (AIS)
+ 1.5: Threat maps
+ 1.5: Research sources
+ 1.6: Zero-day
+ 1.6: Weak configurations
+ 1.6: Third-party risks
+ 1.6: Legacy platforms
+ 1.6: Impacts
+ 2.7: USB data blocker

OVERVIEW

All networks and devices are susceptible to security breaches. Threats and threat actors pose a serious concern to the security of an enterprise environment largely in part to the various avenues by which a network can be attacked.

This chapter presents a comprehensive overview and discussion of various types of threats, threat actors, attributes and motivations of actors, attack vectors, sources of intelligence regarding threats, malware-based attacks, viruses, social engineering methods and attacks, common vulnerabilities, and protection strategies for securing a network and the devices attached to it.

SECURITY+ NOTE

The CompTIA Security+ Exam places significant emphasis on threats to users and systems. Be prepared to identify various types of malware and threats against users by reviewing sample error messages, screen captures, log files, and other symptoms or system characteristics.

Threats

The terms *vulnerability* and *threat* are used interchangeably, but they actually have different meanings. A **vulnerability** is a flaw or potential for harm, while a **threat** is an event or action in which a vulnerability is exploited, endangering an enterprise environment. An **enterprise environment** is the devices, architecture, and design of a professional organization's computer network system.

A security threat can be physical or nonphysical. A *physical threat* is one that endangers devices and the systems. A *nonphysical threat*, also called a *logical threat*, is one that endangers data and operations.

Cybersecurity is the process of protecting an enterprise environment against unintended or malicious changes or use that involves access from individuals and systems on the Internet. However, to many, the term *cyberattack* has come to mean any attack against a business, its systems or users. In actuality, a **cyberattack** is an attempt to steal, damage, or destroy data or a computer system. Cyberattacks are one example of cybercrime. **Cybercrime** is an umbrella term that describes any criminal activity committed using a computer or the Internet. There are many costs associated with cybercrime. Costs include actual damage to a system, theft of confidential and intellectual property, lost productivity, and harm to an organization's reputation.

Threat Actors

✛ 1.5

Cybercrime is committed by threat actors. A **threat actor**, also called a *threat agent* or *malicious actor*, is an individual, nation state, or organization responsible for a security incident, attack, or other type of event that affects an organization's security. *Threat actor* is a broad term that covers those who instigate threats, regardless of type of incident including errors, accidents, and network breaks. Conversely, those who primarily aim to break into computer systems to steal data are referred to as *hackers*.

Types of Actors

There are many types of threat actors, including the following:

- script kiddies
- hacktivists
- criminal syndicates
- state actors
- insiders
- competitors

Script Kiddie

✛ 1.5

Script kiddie is a slang term used to describe an individual who uses premade tools to perform an attack. Script kiddies often attack systems to challenge their skills or for the thrill of breaking into a system.

Hacktivist

✛ 1.5

Hacktivists are hackers who are motivated to hack based on ideals or personal beliefs. *Hacktivism* is the aim to target and harm companies or individuals with whom the person has a fundamental disagreement. This term is a play on the word's *hacker* and *activism*. One of the most familiar hacktivist groups is *Anonymous*, which is a leaderless group in which individuals associate with other like-minded individuals.

Its members often target organizations or businesses that they view as hindering free speech and Internet use.

Hacktivist attacks may include defacement of web pages, denial of service attacks, and doxing. A **denial of service (DoS) attack** is a cyberattack that prevents rightful users from accessing systems. **Doxing** is the theft and release of personal, private, or identifying information.

Criminal Syndicate

A **criminal syndicate** is a group of criminals in local, national, or international enterprises who engage in illegal activity for profit. These groups are often behind credit card breaches, such as the Capital One Financial Corporation attack that revealed information from 100 million applications and customers. Money is often the driving factor for criminal syndicates.

State Actor

A **state actor** is a hacker who is financially supported by a sovereign political entity. **State-sponsored hacking** is the work of a governmental body to disrupt or impair an organization, individual, or other governments. The purpose of this type of hacking is to obtain data, disrupt actions, or create internationally significant incidents. Governments are vulnerable to these attacks when you consider a nation's economy, infrastructure, and transportation systems are based on IT systems and services.

Cyberwarfare is attacks against a government's critical IT systems. The goal of cyberwar programs is often to weaken, disrupt, or destroy the targeted country. During the 2016 US presidential election, Russian operatives committed large-scale attacks designed to disrupt the free-election process. These hacks targeted the servers at the Democratic National Committee. In the attack, Hillary Clinton's campaign chairperson received and fell victim to a phishing e-mail, resulting in unauthorized access to his e-mails. The FBI has since warned that the security of the US elections from nation-state actors remains an *advanced persistent threat*. In response, the US Director of National Intelligence appointed an election threats executive to deal with persistent threats posed by this type of cyberwarfare. An **advanced persistent threat (APT)** is a stealth network attack, typically state-sponsored, that gains unauthorized access to a computer system or network and intentionally remains undetected for extended periods of time.

Insiders

An **insider** is a threat actor who has infiltrated an organization with the intent of committing cybercrime against the employer. Insider threats can be difficult to prevent but are often easy to troubleshoot through monitoring activity, reviewing logs, and maintaining appropriate security controls. These threat actors are often motivated by financial gain or revenge hacking. *Revenge hacking* is an attack against a person or company by which a hacker believes to have been wronged.

Shadow IT is the use of information systems, devices, hardware, applications, or services without explicit approval of a central IT staff. Users installing their own personal devices or software can threaten the security posture of an enterprise environment in a number of ways. For example, suppose an employee uses a personal external storage device to take files home. If the external drive is infected with malware, the entire network is rendered vulnerable to infection. Shadow IT can be prevented through user education, availability of company-owned devices, and strict usage policies that are enforced throughout the organization.

Competitors

Competitors are organizations that compete with a business. Competitors sometimes engage in cybercrime to gain an advantage against another business in terms of revenue or market share. Some businesses engage in the unethical activity of stealing information from their competitors to damage the competing business or use proprietary information for its own gain. Such an attack was committed by David W. Kent, a founder of a professional networking site. Kent was convicted of hacking into a competitor's site to steal information and use it to boost the value of his own company. He then tried to sell his company to the competitor. Kent was ultimately sentenced to one year in jail for his actions.

Attributes of Threat Actors

Threat actors have specific **attributes**, which are characteristics a person possesses. Threat actors are a diverse group of individuals, each having a specific degree of skills and interests. Common attributes of threat actors are as follows.

- Some actors are *internal* and work with or for the organization, such as employees or trusted vendors. Internal actors have access to the enterprise environment and can elevate access to systems and data. *External* actors are people outside the organization who do not have physical access to systems and data. For them to execute an attack, they must discover methods and vulnerabilities to access the systems.
- Actors can be *sophisticated*, which means they have experience and knowledge about hacking. A sophisticated actor has reliable tools to launch an attack. Conversely, an unsophisticated actor lacks experience and hacks primarily on instinct and desire rather than experience.
- Executing a security attack requires resources and funding. Some threat actors are associated with hacking groups, such as criminal syndicates or nation states, which have funds for equipment and tools. Other actors have no backing and are on their own to finance an attack.
- Threat actors have different intent and motivations to launch attacks. They may have a political agenda, desire for financial gain, crave attention, or be out for revenge.

Hackers

The term *hacker* has traditionally referred to an individual who attacks computers and systems for malicious purposes. A **hacking attack** is an attempt to break into a computer system to steal data. Hackers focus on computers and systems and *are not* usually associated with other security threats contributed to actions of a threat actor. Hackers are classified by intent as follows.

- **White-hat hackers** are generally ethical and law-abiding individuals who often break into networks with permission to study or reveal vulnerabilities, such as in penetration tests. These individuals are examples of why the word *hacker* does not always mean something bad.
- A **black-hat hacker** usually operates outside the law. They commit hacks for malicious purposes or personal gain.
- A **gray-hat hacker** does not necessarily harm others but does not ask permission before conducting attacks or accessing systems. These hackers fall somewhere between the other two. Many participants in bug-bounty programs are gray-hat hackers.

Vectors

A *vector* is the means by which a threat actor attempts to access or compromise a system. A vector is not necessarily the hacker's end goal, but rather the pathway an actor uses to access systems and launch attacks.

To protect against vectors, apply the least privilege principle, layer defenses, and monitor user credentials. Examples of vectors used to exploit a system vulnerabilities are as follows.

- *Direct access.* A direct access vector is one in which a threat actor has physical connection to the system or resource targeted in the attack. With direct access, an actor has the ability to download files, upload or install malware, eavesdrop on communications, and log in to systems to steal data.
- *Wireless.* A wireless attack vector is one in which wireless security and settings are the path used to attempt to gain access to networks in a wireless environment. Actors attempt to break encryption keys to exploit vulnerabilities or poison systems so traffic routes through unauthorized equipment.
- *E-mail.* E-mail is a vector often used with social engineering attacks. It provides an easy path to entice users to click on malicious links or download files.
- *Supply chain.* Rather than attack an organization directly, a threat actor may opt to use the organization's supply chain to gain access to an organization. By infiltrating a supplier, a backdoor is provided to an organization that buys from the supplier.
- *Social media.* Social media is a common path used to launch an attack. Actors can attempt to obtain personal and other useful information to build a record of information about a victim and create a fraudulent scheme.
- *Removable media.* Removable media provides a portable path for attacking an organization. Flash drives, SIM cards, and CD/DVDs can be used for data exfiltration or as the source for malicious uploads. Removable media can be small and easy to hide, and it is ubiquitous in an organization.
- *Cloud.* The cloud environment is a significant platform for many companies, from storage to data availability and resiliency. Since direct access is not likely, actors can use Internet connections to access data and systems stored at these partner sites.

Threat Intelligence Sources

Threat intelligence is information regarding threats, threat actors, and other potentially harmful actions that could occur in an enterprise environment. It includes critical information such as the nature of an attack, file names, IP addresses, domain names, hackers (if known), and other essential details. Threat intelligence helps IT personnel understand past security events so current events can be remedied and remedies for future defenses be put in place.

Threat intelligence sources reveal information for security teams as they work to find indicators of compromise. **Indicators of compromise (IoC)** are evidence that identify a cyberattack. IoC examples include data stored in system logs that signify malicious activity has occurred on a network. After malicious activity is identified, remaining forensic artifacts provide clues to the activity identified. Analyzing these artifacts in context with additional correlated information may provide detailed intelligence about the type of attack and its mission, as well as enable analysts to discover patterns and link similar security incidents. Identifying and monitoring IoCs provides critical intelligence that can help further evaluate attempted cyberattacks.

TECH TIP

In Microsoft Windows, logs can be reviewed for IoCs using Windows Event Viewer or PowerShell. In Linux, logs are plaintext files and found in the directory structure of **/var/log**. Both operating systems maintain a variety of logs, including applications, operating system, and security issues.

Indicators of attack (IoA) try to pinpoint the goal an attacker wants to accomplish. The focus is the intent and techniques of the attack rather than the tools used for the attack.

There are four main type of threat intelligence.

- *Strategic intelligence* is data for organizational strategy that helps achieve goals of a company. Rather than provide technical detail, this information is for management to make high-level decisions for the organization.
- *Tactical intelligence* is detail about cyberattacks that is needed to help meet the strategic plan. This information is for IT personnel to help identify threat actors and understand how to approach attacks.
- *Technical intelligence* identifies indicators of threats, such as malware and social engineering. Technical intelligence changes quickly because threat actors execute many types of attacks every day.
- *Operational intelligence* defines day-by-day tasks to identify detail of cyberattacks. This type of data is gathered by breaking into hacker chat rooms and other secret activity resources.

Open-Source Intelligence (OSINT)

Threat intelligence comes from many sources. **Open-source intelligence (OSINT)** is data collected from public sources as well as government sites. The information is available to anyone who seeks it and is free of charge. OSINT is a research source used to find critical cybersecurity data.

Security teams must remain vigilant and monitor resources that can inform them to potential advisories, new vulnerabilities, and technology that could provide additional protection for their businesses. There are many OSINT resources available to obtain credible and accurate information.

- *Threat feeds* are real-time data streams that provide detailed information about known threats, including IP addresses, malware signatures, and domain names. These streams enable security professionals to obtain real-time information about pending threats and vulnerabilities.
- *Vulnerability feeds* are subscriber-based information threads that provide real-time information about new vulnerabilities. These can be generalized or specific to a product or business type.
- *Local industry groups* are organizations founded by businesses that operate in a given industry. These groups often provide relevant information to communities and similar organizations. This is often the quickest way to push information to professionals and provide timely information about threats and links for further engagement.
- The Internet provides several sources of information, such as social media and search engines. *Vendor websites* are the definitive source for information regarding products used specifically within an organization. Each vendor likely provides alerts, patches, and cyber threat information specific to its unique products.
- *Academic journals* are high-quality formal documents drafted by committees or teams that provide detailed information and/or request feedback. Additionally, other professional and academic publications can be used as an open-source resource.
- *Requests for comments (RFC)* are formal documents drafted by the Internet Society (ISOC) and the Internet Engineering Task Force (IETF) that describe methods, activities, research, and developments regarding the Internet and its connected systems. Security personnel can use these documents to learn about

innovations or discover preferred methodologies recommended by the ISOC and IETF.

- Databases from corporations and industry are valuable sources of intelligence. *Adversary tactic, techniques, and procedures (TTP)* are knowledge bases that provide publicly available information about tactics and techniques used by hackers to conduct their attacks. These articles enable security professionals to get insight into *how* hackers behave and initiate attacks so they can learn to lock down potential avenues of attack.

- *Conferences* are formal meetings attended by cybersecurity professionals. These gatherings enable security professionals to network with other professionals to exchange information, receive training, or hear the latest in technology innovations.

Closed/Proprietary Sources

 1.5

Closed threat intelligence sources, also known as *proprietary intelligence sources*, are commercial products that require an account and payment to access their resources to extract information. These intelligence sources are often highly reliable and employ specialized tools and security analysts to gather and convey detailed information regarding threats. Closed sources often have a higher sense of trustworthiness than open-source data since they often have contracts with the organizations that use them. Vendors providing this intelligence often have access to specific resources not available to the public at large, making them valuable tools in the collection of data regarding threats and potential hacking attacks.

These sources offer threat maps for a subscription charge. **Threat maps**, also known as *cyberattack maps*, are visual representations of cyber threats occurring at any given time across the world. Typically laid out on the background of a world or country map, these maps identify known threats, locations of threats and their targets, and the type of attacks discovered. Threat maps convert data into useful intelligence such as attack frequency, type, and impact. Security teams can make connections and predictions based on the data generated by the threat maps to determine how vulnerable their organizations may be to any given threat. Vendors display maps differently according to their data collection and analysis techniques. Popular examples of threat maps include Kaspersky Cyberthreat Real-Time Map, FireEye Cyber Threat Map, and Digital Attack Map from Arbor Networks.

 1.5

Information Sharing Centers

 1.5

An **information sharing center (ISC)** is an industry-specific consortium of business owners and IT personnel working together to collect, analyze, and distribute timely information to its members about cyber threats. A vulnerability or threat can have an instant impact on the security of a network. When security data is discovered, timely notification to appropriate organizations can help prevent widespread attacks. The ability for federal, state, local, and private sector partners to share accurate information is essential for improving cyber resilience. One of the best-known ISCs is the Cyber Information Sharing and Collaboration Program (CISCP) sponsored by the US Department of Homeland Security. CISCP enables trusted partnerships to exchange relevant, timely, and unclassified information. This shared data results in a benefit to all organizations through published alerts, advisories, reports, and bulletins.

Automated Indicator Sharing

 1.5

The Department of Homeland Security's (DHS) Automated Indicator Sharing (AIS) program is a free resource that enables the exchange of cyber threat indicators between the federal government and the private-sector participants. The goal of this program is to receive timely indicators from nonfederal entities, remove all personally identifiable information (PII), and disseminate the information between stakeholders.

AIS functions through the development of two standards: Structured Threat Information eXpression (STIX) and Trusted Automated Exchange of Indicator Information (TAXII). These standards are necessary for the automated exchange of relevant data from security indicators.

Structured Threat Information eXpression (STIX)

Structured Threat Information eXpression (STIX) is a standardized language developed by the MITRE Corporation and the OASIS Cyber Threat Intelligence (CTI) technical committee to discuss cyber threat information. Information included in the STIX language standard includes the scope and structure of information to provide consistency in sharing information between partners. This standard focuses on the format and inclusion of data to be shared trough AIS.

Trusted Automated Exchange of Indicator Information (TAXII)

Trusted Automated Exchange of Indicator Information (TAXII) is an AIS standard that defines the method of information exchanges, including data formatted with STIX standards between partners. The three principal models for TAXII include the following:

- *Hub and Spoke* is a sharing model in which one organization assumes the role of the central facilitator of information, called the hub. The organization's partners serve as the spokes. The spokes can produce and send information to the hub or receive information from the hub.
- *Source/Subscriber* is a sharing model in which a single generator of information, called a source, collects and disseminates threat indicators to organizations that have subscribed to that particular source.
- *Peer-to-peer* is a sharing model in which organizations can share information directly with other partners. TAXII empowers organizations to share threats and security awareness intelligence with the partners they choose.

Dark Web

The **dark web**, or *darknet*, is a part of the Internet that is not easily accessible to the average user. The dark web provides threat intelligence through forums and markets selling stolen credentials and credit card information, hacking tools, malware, and other cyber products. Monitoring the dark web can provide valuable information, from hacking methods to determining if an organization is targeted for an attack.

Often, cybercriminals attempt to recruit inside personnel from a specific company through dark web posts in an effort to coordinate an attack against the company that employs the recruits. Security professionals can also search the dark web for leaked credentials from their organizations to determine if their networks are vulnerable. The dark web can be accessed using special software such as the *Tor browser*, which consists of open-source software that enables anonymous communication. However, for untrained individuals, locating information within the unstructured nature of the dark web can be difficult. Instead, obtaining threat information from the dark web can be accomplished through specialized monitoring tools, such as AlienVault's Alien App, or Digital Shadows Dark Web Monitoring Services.

Malware Attacks

Malware, also known as *malicious software*, is computer code intentionally written to cause some form of harm. It can range from stealing or destroying data to collecting information or allowing remote access to a system. A **malware attack** is the action of a hacker installing malicious software on another person's device with the intent of accessing data for personal gain. The purpose, or intent, of malware is in its payload. The **payload** is the actions of malicious code. Malware succeeds in its goal by exploiting vulnerabilities in the targeted systems.

There are many reasons why malware is developed, such as for criminal intent, data disruption, or even as an act of cyberwarfare. Malware represents an ongoing threat to an organization because of vulnerable user actions, poorly written application software, flaws in operating system services, and the numerous variations of malware that exist.

Malware can be designed to infect a single system or to spread on its own to infect as many devices as possible. In some cases, malware is installed on a device and controlled remotely. This type of malware is activated through a command and control attack. **Command and control (C&C) attack** is a malware attack that programs the infected machine to signal the attacker's server for instruction. The attacker's server then sends commands to the infected machine, giving the attacker full control of the remote computer. With command and control, malware lies dormant until it receives instructions from a remote location. Additionally, multiple computers can be infected in this method, creating a network of remote hacking devices for the attacker.

Malware can also direct an infected device to perform actions automatically. In these cases, the infected device is called a *zombie* or a *bot*, which is short for *robot*. A series of interconnected infected bots are called *botnets*. This type of infection can spread to millions of devices, including IoT hosts. Often, botnets are created through multiple C&C attacks on one network. Botnets can collectively perform large operations of deploying a malware payload that will have a greater impact than a single device.

An example of a powerful botnet is one composed of approximately 402,000 IoT devices that attacked an undisclosed streaming service in the spring of 2019. This attack appeared to originate from Brazil and caused a massive distributed denial of service attack over a 13-day period. A **distributed denial of service (DDoS) attack** is a DoS attack in which many hosts are contributing in attacking the victim, as illustrated in Figure 2-1. In both DoS and DDoS attacks, a target is flooded with network traffic to the extent that its servers are unable to keep up with the requests being sent, meaning the requests from authorized users go largely unfulfilled. In this particular attack, the devices attempt to exhaust the resources of the server that handled authentication requests by issuing hypertext transfer protocol (http) requests at an average of over 100,000 requests per second. A DoS attack is intended to prevent access or disrupt service rather than destroy information.

Malware remains a significant problem to all Internet-ready devices, including computers, web servers, and IoT devices. Compared to the original malware threats prevalent in the 1980s, the threat of malware has increased exponentially. Cyber criminals have become more skilled in the complexity of the malware as well as the targeting of their victims. According to a report by the cyber technology firm SonicWall, over 7.2 billion malware attacks were launched in the first three quarters of 2019 alone. While these numbers show a decline in the number of overall attacks, there is significant concern regarding attacks on IoT devices and encryption threats and attacks on web apps. Moreover, the complexity and danger posed by today's malware contribute to serious challenges in protecting data.

Figure 2-1 A distributed denial of service (DDoS) attack involves many hosts, usually infected with malware, attacking a single server.

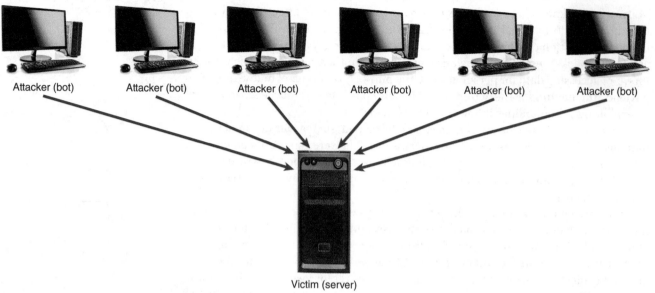

Victim (server)

✦ 1.2

Keylogger

A **keylogger** is software or a hardware device that tracks a user's keystrokes on a keyboard. In some cases, a computer screen is recorded as well as the individual's keystrokes. It is a form of **spyware**, which is a type of software that unobtrusively spies on a user's activities. Keyloggers run in stealth mode, meaning they do not appear as a running application or process on the system, which makes detecting the intrusion a challenge.

A software keylogger is most common and easily installed on a user's device. A hardware keylogger can be embedded in a device or plugged into a computer, as shown in Figure 2-2. A keyboard is then plugged into the back of the device.

Adware

Adware is not malware, but it can behave as such. **Adware** is software installed on a computer that collects data about the user, such as websites the person visits, and then redirects advertising sites to the web browser based on browsing habits. Adware is not always considered malware. For example, advertisements installed alongside a program or the result of visiting a specific website is not malware. Adware becomes malware when it is installed without a user's permission or knowledge and causes problems for users, such as multiple pop-up windows on web browsers. More importantly, it also raises security and privacy concerns about an individual's web surfing.

Cookies

Unfortunately, cookies are sometimes used in a malicious manner and are malware in disguise. *Cookies* are small text files saved on a computer for use with web browsers and websites. If a website uses a cookie, the cookie contains information about the user's visit to the site. A cookie stores personal preferences so when the user returns to the site, user information does not need to be provided again. The idea behind cookies is simple: they make your web surfing personalized to your browsing.

Most reputable companies publish a cookie policy. A *cookie policy* states if the site uses cookies. If cookies are used, the policy should explain how they are used. In

Figure 2-2 Hardware-based keyloggers are widely available and can be used to record every keystroke on a keyboard.

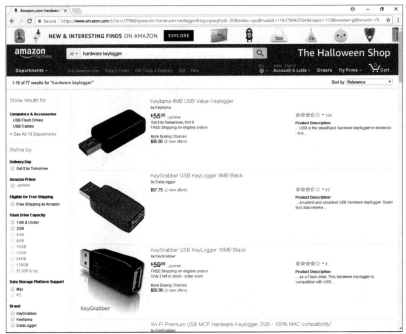

some cases, the user may be able to opt out. Most web browsers also have a setting to prevent cookies from being saved.

There are different types of cookies of which to be aware:

- session cookies
- persistent cookies
- secure cookies
- third-party cookies

Session Cookies

A *session cookie* exists only as long as the web browser is open. This type of cookie is intended to exist only while you are visiting the website in that browser visit. Session cookies will remain active while this browser session is open, enabling you to open other tabs and retain the settings of a website session. Closing an individual browser tab does not delete the session cookie by default, but when a browser is closed, session cookies are deleted.

Persistent Cookies

A *persistent cookie* stays on a computer until an expiration date, as shown in Figure 2-3. Because these cookies remain after a browser is closed, they are sometimes referred to as *tracking cookies*. They are called tracking cookies because adware or other programs will read the cookies on a computer to record information about your browsing history and your habits.

Secure Cookies

A *secure cookie* can only be sent in an encrypted session. The data in the cookie is sent using the Secure Hypertext Transfer Protocol (HTTPS).

Figure 2-3 A persistent cookie will remain on a computer until a predetermined date has passed.

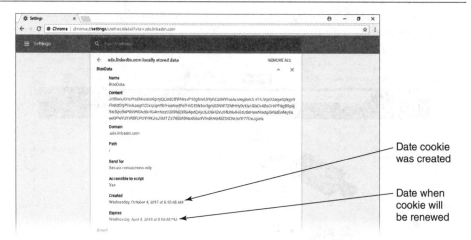

Date cookie was created

Date when cookie will be renewed

Third-Party Cookies

A *third-party cookie* originates from a visit to a website but references a different website. For example, suppose you visit the news.com website. This site may create a session or persistent cookie. The page you visited on news.com displayed an ad from the computers.com website. The computers.com website may create a cookie on your computer despite the fact you never visited that site. In this example, the cookie from computers.com is a third-party cookie.

Trojan

A **Trojan** is malware hidden inside software that appears to be harmless. This type of malware takes its name from the ancient story of Greek soldiers hiding inside a wooden horse so they could invade the city of Troy. In computing, a Trojan represents the same type of threat: malicious or dangerous code hidden inside something that appears innocent. It may be inside a screen saver, game, or other type of file. Like the residents of Troy, a user is unaware of this threat lurking in the file. As soon as someone downloads, executes, or installs the program, the person has put the computer system at risk.

A **remote access Trojan (RAT)** is a form of malware that allows a hacker to use an embedded backdoor to gain administrative control of a victim's computer. The victim is infected by downloading a seemingly normal file that contains the malware. The RAT is installed on a system, and it piggybacks on legitimate files and programs. This allows the RAT to hide behind the legitimate program when it runs. RATs can carry a variety of payloads, including allowing remote administrative access. Some RAT programs may also monitor a system to obtain keystrokes, activate microphones on the remote systems to eavesdrop electronically, and turn on webcams discreetly.

Potentially Unwanted Program (PUP)

A **potentially unwanted program (PUP)** is a program that has been approved for download, but may not be wanted, by a user. For example, a user may download and install audio software, which also installs a web browser. In this scenario, the web browser is an unwanted program that was authorized to be downloaded by the user. These programs can contain spyware or adware. They also are capable of slowing or locking up a computer, collecting private information, and adding unwanted features to installed programs or browsers.

Worm

1.2

A **worm** is a form of malware that infects a system with its payload, but the method of infection differs from other malware. Unlike many other forms of malware, a worm moves or spreads from one infected computer to another through open network connections. Worms normally move from machine to machine through computer networks. A worm exploits a security vulnerability in software, such as e-mail systems or vulnerabilities in an operating system. Because they use common everyday software, they often can bypass protections in firewalls. Worms can be very destructive and difficult to remove.

Time Bomb

A **time bomb** is malicious software that does not launch immediately when a system is infected. Instead, it relies on some type of trigger, which can be a date, time, or condition. The malware remains dormant while waiting for the trigger. When the trigger occurs, the payload is unleashed.

A time bomb deploys its payload when a date or time occurs. An early example of a time bomb is a virus called *Michelangelo*. This virus delivered its payload only on the month and day of Michelangelo's birthday, which is March 6. When the payload delivered, it reformatted the infected system's hard disk by overwriting data with random characters.

Logic Bomb

1.2

Similar to a time bomb, a **logic bomb** is malicious software that deploys when conditions exist that the malware is seeking; the time and date are irrelevant. The *Stuxnet virus* illustrates this concept. The Stuxnet virus was very sophisticated and only targeted computers running Windows 7 and Siemens Step7 software. Stuxnet did nothing to systems that did not have the Siemens software installed. In that example, Siemens created software specifically for programmable logic boards used only by Iran for nuclear enrichment. It only activated its payload when this software was present.

Ransomware

1.2

Ransomware is malware that does not steal or destroy data; rather, it encrypts data so the user cannot access it unless a fee, or ransom, is paid to the hacker. **Encryption** is the process of converting data into unreadable characters by applying a security key. To read the data, the correct key, or algorithm, is used to convert data back to readable data, as shown in Figure 2-4. With ransomware, hackers hold data hostage until a ransom is paid for a decryption key.

Figure 2-4 Encryption makes data unreadable without the proper key to unlock the encryption.

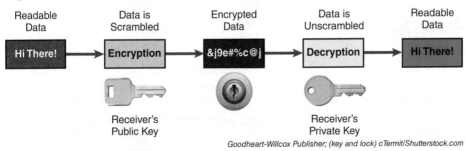

Goodheart-Willcox Publisher; (key and lock) cTermit/Shutterstock.com

Usually, money is demanded to be paid via bitcoins or other forms of cryptocurrency, which makes the source of the ransomware difficult to trace. *Cryptocurrency* is a digital form of payment exchanged online for goods and services. It does not include a central bank, and transactions occur on a peer-to-peer basis. Bitcoin is probably the most familiar and largest traded of the cryptocurrencies currently in use. Ransomware, or any other malware, that requires the use of cryptocurrency for return of access to data is **cryptomalware**.

A computer system is usually infected with ransomware when a user opens an infected e-mail attachment. However, ransomware is also spread by a drive-by download. A **drive-by download** attack occurs when a user visits an infected web page from which ransomware is automatically downloaded to a computer without a user's knowledge.

Rootkit

A **rootkit** is a type of malware that infects a computer before the operating system loads, making it difficult to remove. The term rootkit comes from combining the words *root* and *kit*. *Root* is the term for administrator in Linux/UNIX systems. *Kit* refers to the malicious programs within the virus.

Rootkits often deliver serious payloads. A payload may include the ability to access a computer remotely without needing or knowing user credentials for the system. An infected computer must be booted with a repair disc, recovery disc, or flash drive in order to remove the rootkit.

Backdoor

A **backdoor** is a type of malware that creates a secret or unknown access point into a system. It can take the form of a hidden program embedded in the firmware of a computer, or it can be an account that is hardcoded in an operating system or program. Backdoors are often created using RAT malware. However, a backdoor does not always imply the presence of software or a virus; it could be a user with administrative privileges of whom you are not aware.

Virus

A **virus** is malicious software code that is unleashed and attempts to perform destructive content on computer systems or data. To be classified as a virus, malware must have the ability to self-replicate and spread copies of itself to other devices.

Most people hear the term *malware* and think "computer virus." This is misleading. *Computer viruses* are programs written specifically to infect a device and are one form of malware. While all viruses are malware, not all malware are viruses.

The Internet plays an important role in the spread of viruses. Because online devices are interconnected, malware, such as viruses, can spread farther and faster than they can through simple sharing of disks or other storage media.

Armored Virus

An **armored virus** is a computer virus designed to prevent security analysts from reading source code by attempting to disassemble or prevent access to the code. Armored viruses use specifically coded mechanisms to attempt to ward off antivirus software, technicians, and, ultimately, detection. Armored viruses use extra code that masks the actual virus code, making it appear either unimportant or to be running elsewhere on the system.

Polymorphic Virus

A **polymorphic virus** is a virus that changes its characteristics in an attempt to avoid detection from antivirus programs. Polymorphic viruses use a *mutation engine*, which randomizes the decryption process of the virus codes. In most traditional virus infections, a virus uses an encryption key that changes each time the virus infects another file or host, ensuring the virus appears differently on each infected system. However, antivirus companies target specific decryption processes to locate these malware infections. When creating a polymorphic virus, programmers add a mutation engine to ensure the virus-decryption process varies from one infection to the next. This allows it to avoid detection by antivirus programs searching for specific byte sequences associated to a decryption routine.

Fileless Virus

➕ 1.2

A **fileless virus** is a virus that uses a computer system's software, files, and applications to launch malware, often through PowerShell scripts. Fileless viruses are difficult to find since they do not attach to specific files and therefore do not leave digital footprints.

Macro Virus

A **macro virus** is a macro written in the same language as software applications and programmed to carry out a malicious intent. A macro virus infects the software application in which it is embedded, and the sequence of actions inside the code execute automatically when the application is opened.

Macros are small scripts often created to perform repetitive tasks and enable developers to automate tasks. In Microsoft Office programs, macros are created using the programming language Visual Basic for Applications (VBA). These mini programs can be inserted into files created with Word, PowerPoint, Excel, and Access.

Adversarial Artificial Intelligence (AI) Attack

➕ 1.2

Artificial intelligence (AI) is a branch of computer science aimed at simulating intelligence in machines. Using algorithms and computer-based training, AI machines are able to evaluate and perceive their environments to respond to stimuli and achieve desired goals. An **adversarial AI attack** is malicious development and use of sophisticated AI systems to behave in a manner that benefits an attacker. These attacks impact enterprise environments by showing the ability of AI devices to exploit machine-learning algorithms to automate e-mail responses and reveal sensitive information. Adversarial AI often attacks through two methods: tainting training data for machine learning and compromising the security of machine-learning algorithms.

➕ 1.2

An important element of developing artificial intelligence is to allow the machines to train themselves through persistent practice using data called *training data*. Systems repeatedly use this data to learn and fine-tune its response. Training data often includes voice recordings, photos, and text. If training data were sabotaged or tainted, machine learning would be compromised, resulting in unexpected or undesired outcomes. For this reason, the security of machine-learning algorithms must be maintained at all times. **Machine learning (ML)** is the ability for computer algorithms to improve automatically through experience. *Machine-learning algorithms* enable a computer to "learn" through experience. Adversarial AI attacks manipulate the process of data training by writing an algorithm to function in unintended ways. Even minor changes to machine-learning algorithms result in irrational output, malfunction, data loss, or machine lockup.

Because AI is considered a comparatively new technology, it is not as easy to detect threats and indicators of compromise with existing tools and technology. However, some traditional methods can help identify *potential* threats and protect the data and networks. For example, if network traffic or disk activity differs greatly from established baselines, this could be an indicator of a potential threat. Additionally, AI systems can be used to police themselves through training by monitoring systems and analyzing application usage data. With enough time, these systems can adapt enough to be able to detect and respond to AI-generated threats.

Social Engineering

+ 1.1

Social engineering is the use of manipulation techniques to lure individuals to reveal personal and confidential information to a cybercriminal. It is a *vector*, or means, by which a threat actor attempts to access or compromise a system. It involves the use of social tools to obtain information, which often includes deceptive practices that result in the acquisition of personal information about individuals or business practices. Social engineering attacks are believable and effective for some of the following reasons.

- *Authority.* In a social engineering attack, a hacker portrays authority to take information from a victim. Many times, hackers pretend to be from a help desk or human resources in an effort to make their authority clear.
- *Intimidation.* Social engineering tactics employ intimidation and instill fear or concern in the victim to provide information. The victim is fearful that not providing information can result in harm to the person.
- *Consensus.* Attackers sometimes try to convince the victim that there is a consensus of other people already participating or providing information to make that person feel okay doing the same. This provides a level of comfort and makes the victim feel safe to provide sensitive information due to the perception that everyone else is already doing so.
- *Scarcity.* Scarcity is the feeling or idea that something is limited or in short supply and therefore valuable. Many times, a threat actor will create a sense that a document, service, or system-related necessity is of limited supply, manipulating a user into taking action. People tend to fall victim to these types of attacks because of lack of knowledge.
- *Familiarity.* Familiarity is a situation in which a scammer injects friendliness in an attempt to make a victim feel a familiar connection to the attacker. Often, an attacker will talk or reference items the victim enjoys to establish familiarity. This familiarity encourages the victim to be friendly and supply information to the attacker.
- *Trust.* Exhibiting trust is a way in which an attacker incorporates a level of confidence with the victim. This type of social engineering forces the victim to believe the attacker can be trusted with personal information.
- *Urgency.* Urgency conveys a sense of immediate action or attention to pressure an individual into providing information. The attacker tries to convince a victim that time is running out and manipulates the victim to make a quick decision.

+ 1.1

The first phase of a social engineering attack is reconnaissance. **Reconnaissance** is the act of eliciting information from or about a target. One approach is *pretexting,* which occurs when a scammer creates a fake story to lure a victim into providing information. Other techniques to gather information about a person include

- asking people to reveal information;
- looking through social media sites for information;
- using public records stored online or available via public-library searches;
- using advanced web searches;
- dumpster diving; and
- shoulder surfing.

Eliciting Information

✚ 1.1

One of the easiest ways to get information is simply ask for it! Of course, going to an employee and asking for an account number is not likely to work. However, if the hacker has credible information to support the request, the hacker will appear entitled to the information.

In his book *The Art of Deception*, hacker Kevin Mitnick explains how easy it was for him to get individuals to tell him things. He uses inquiries such as: "I am writing a book and want to make sure I am using the correct terminology. Can you tell me if BankCU is the correct name of the ATM software company?"

Most people want to be helpful and provide information when requested. Mitnick would then take that information, and call another department, asking questions such as: "This is Chris from BankCU. I am doing a quality assurance check. Can I confirm you are using our correct new support number of 1-800-555-1111?"

This user will likely say, "No, we are using a different number," since the hacker is providing an invalid number. Over time, the hacker will have enough credible information to call a company and pretend to be an employee from the bank. Then, the person can obtain specific information being targeted.

Another convincing scheme to gain information is simple friendliness. A hacker can strike up a conversation with a target. The scheme could work like this: after chatting with a person, the hacker might say, "Didn't you go to elementary school with my mom? Your name seems so familiar!" The victim might say, "Where did your mom go to school? My mom went to Kennedy Primary in Houston." This may seem like innocent information, but many websites often ask security questions that in theory only the authorized person should know. The schools a user attended or the streets the person lived on as a child are often on those preconfigured lists.

Social Media

✚ 1.5

Social media sites, such as Facebook, Twitter, Instagram, and LinkedIn, are treasure troves of information for hackers. Many users do not realize some of their information is not fully private. Other users simply are not concerned about the information they post on the Internet. In addition to posting too much confidential information, users also make the mistake of accepting friend or follow requests from people they do not know. If a user has access to your social media site, information posted on your profile can be read by anyone. Because of this, maintaining organizational security often includes not allowing employees to use social media while signed in to the organization's network.

Many organizations often have an employee who manages the company's social media profiles. In this instance, that person should be the only one who is able to access social media websites. However, this person must be cautious about the information posted to the company profiles. Social media platforms are like breadcrumbs that hackers can follow. For example, suppose a company held a luncheon to celebrate the retirement of a long-term employee. The social media manager took photos, posted them to the company's Facebook page, and tagged the employees shown in the photos. Now suppose a hacker wants to obtain access to that company's network. The hacker may look at the company's publicly accessible Facebook page and collect the names of those shown in the photos. Next, the hacker could access the Facebook pages of those employees and learn a great deal about them. Using this information, the hacker could attempt social engineering practices to circumvent network security and gain access. In this scenario, a company policy that defines the type of information that can be posted or tagged on the organization's social media accounts could prevent the network intrusion.

Public Records

City and state governments post an abundance of taxpayer information online, such as data about property ownership. Hackers can use this information in public records to learn about an individual's personal business.

For example, assume a home in Boston is listed on a real estate website. A hacker can record the home's address, navigate to the official website for the city Boston, and use a property-information search tool to obtain a great deal of personal information, such as the property tax assessment, property value, homeowner's name, and other private information. One successful example of this is shown in Figure 2-5.

Some cities and counties create free public records directories. There are also websites that collect public records and provide a centralized search engine. Collecting data from various sources is called *aggregating* data. In some cases, the

Figure 2-5 Public records, including real estate records, can provide much information about a person.

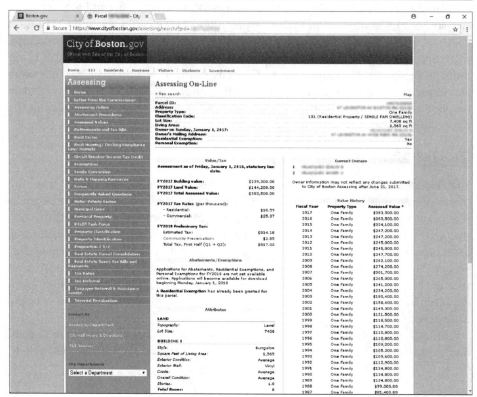

information provided includes obituaries that reference families and places of birth. This can be valuable information to a hacker.

Court records are also in public databases. Most states offer access to databases at no charge. In some states, such as California, a small fee may be required to access the records. Figure 2-6 shows an example of a court record from Alexandria, Virginia, that is available online. On this site, you can search for a hearing by date, name, type of hearing, or other criteria.

Advanced Internet Searches

Internet searches are often used to find personal information and other data on a target's digital footprint. Most Internet search engines have advanced options to help find data. Figure 2-7 shows five tips for conducting advanced searches. Most average users are not aware of these practices. For purposes of this discussion, the search engine Google is used. However, the tools often work in any search engine.

Enclosing specific keywords within quotation marks tells the search engine all of those words must be present in the results. For example, entering "John Smith New York NY" into Google will only return results that contain *all* of those words. By contrast, entering the same words without the quotation marks will return results that contain *any* of those words.

Goodheart-Willcox Publisher

Figure 2-6 Often, court records can be located online. This is an example from Alexandria, Virginia.

Tip #1	Enclose specific keywords in quotation marks.
Tip #2	Use a hyphen (-) to exclude words or a plus sign (+) to ensure words are included.
Tip #3	Conduct the search on a specific website.
Tip #4	Limit searches to specific dates or a range of dates.
Tip #5	Search for only specific file types.

Goodheart-Willcox Publisher

Figure 2-7 Most Internet search engines have advanced options such as those listed here to help find specific data.

A hyphen (-) can be used to exclude words from the search. For example, entering eagles -football -Philadelphia into Google will search for anything that contains the word *eagles*. However, of those found, those that include the word *football* or *Philadelphia* will not be included in the list of results. In effect, this search is focused away from the popular NFL team. Similarly, a plus sign (+) can be used to ensure certain words are included in the results.

A search can be conducted to retrieve information from a specific site. For example, entering site:Microsoft.com Bill Gates into Google will only return results from sites within Microsoft.com. This search can be further refined by enclosing Bill Gates in quotation marks. That would limit the results to only items within Microsoft.com that include both Bill and Gates.

Searches can be limited to a specific numeric value, such as a date or range of dates. For example, to find information about PlayStation in only the current year, enter Playstation..20XX into Google (substituting the last two digits of the current year for XX). The two periods (dots) tell Google not to display any results before this year. To specify a range of dates, separate the dates with two periods. Figure 2-8 shows an example of searching for information on car hacking, but only from 2018 through 2019. This can also be used to limit searches to a specific year. For example, cybersecurity 2019..2019 will display results only from the year 2019.

A search can be limited to a specific file type. For example, the file type for a Microsoft Excel spreadsheet is XLS or XLSx. To limit a search to only the XLS file type, enter filetype:xls and a keyword into Google. To search for an Excel file that contains the word *password*, enter filetype:xls password into Google. Since there are two native file formats for Excel, you may want to do this search twice, once for each file type.

+ 1.1

Dumpster Diving

Dumpster diving is digging through trash for useful or valuable information. Stealing information from trash is not a new technique, and information gained from dumpster diving can be employed maliciously. Often, important documents, such as utility bills, credit card statements, and bank statements, are thrown in the trash

Figure 2-8 Entering the search phrase **car hacking 2018..2019** will display results only from those years.

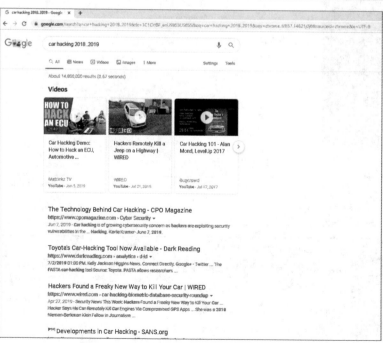

Goodheart-Willcox Publisher

instead of destroyed. Those who steal these discarded documents from the trash can then use the information in social engineering attacks.

To help protect against dumpster diving, documents should be shredded when no longer needed. Private or confidential papers and other documents that contain sensitive information should always be shredded to prevent someone from using it.

Shoulder Surfing

➕ 1.1

A common technique to obtain information such as passwords is shoulder surfing. **Shoulder surfing** is observing a person keying their information, such as passwords, on a keyboard. This technique is used by many hackers who use phones to record actions of a victim while pretending to look in another direction.

Shoulder surfing can be avoided by being aware of your surroundings when keying sensitive information. To discourage shoulder surfing, you can install screen filters that can block sensitive information on a screen so others cannot see it. When keying information, sit with your back to a wall so no one behind you can view your screen and keyboard. You can also use a type of guard or shield when keying information, such as the PIN guards or PIN shields commonly installed at most point-of-sale terminals and ATMs.

Social Engineering Attacks

The second phase of social engineering is the attack phase, in which information gathered in reconnaissance is used to launch an attack. The hacker uses the information to appear believable and effective while encouraging a response from the victim.

Part of the success of social engineering attacks is that they are difficult to troubleshoot. It can often be difficult to determine how an attacker gained access to a network or secure area of an organization, especially if personnel are fooled into granting access. The best defense against social engineering is diligence and enforcement of policies that not only state what employees can and cannot do while online, but also outline types of information that can and cannot be disclosed to unauthorized parties.

An interesting note about social engineering attacks is they are sometimes indirectly used against an individual who is not the intended victim. For example, a hacker could target an employee in order to obtain information about that employee's boss. The boss is the victim, but the scammer targets the employee as another method of reconnaissance.

Phishing

➕ 1.1

Phishing is a social engineering attack in which an attacker attempts to obtain a user's personal information, such as bank account numbers, through fake e-mails that appear to be real. Phishing can be quite successful and is one of the most critical attack vectors. An *attack vector* is the means in which a hacker can gain access to a target. Phishing attacks generally contain a link to a falsified website that also appears real. The website may contain malware or may ask the user to enter a name, password, account number, and other information, which is stolen by the hacker as it is entered.

Phishing attacks play on a user's willingness to believe that the message is a personal e-mail directed to the user. Often, the e-mail details a serious situation or security incident. It may describe a situation that would be of concern to most people. This may be something like a problem with a bank account or a problem with the Internal Revenue Service (IRS). Phishing e-mails commonly appear to be from a bank or organization like PayPal, as shown in Figure 2-9.

Figure 2-9 A phishing attack often appears as a legitimate e-mail asking the user to click a link to log in to the account.

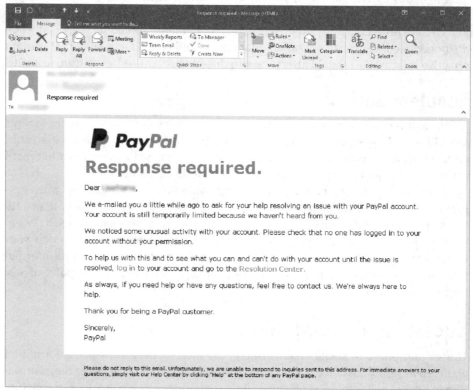

Goodheart-Willcox Publisher

In early phishing attacks, hackers often sent e-mails directly asking users to respond with their credentials. Once the hacker possessed the credentials, user accounts could be accessed with no issue. As security personnel tightened policies surrounding external e-mails, threat actors had to learn how to obtain information more covertly through variations of phishing attacks. Two common variations of general phishing scams are whale phishing and spear phishing. Other variations include vishing and smishing.

Whale Phishing

1.1

Whale phishing, also known as *whaling*, is a phishing attack targeting individuals who have a high net worth or a high business status. Often, company executives are the recipients of such attacks. The popular social media platform Snapchat is an example of the seriousness of whale phishing. In this example, a Snapchat employee released employee payroll information to someone impersonating the CEO. Similarly, the data-storage manufacturer Seagate was a victim of a whale phishing attack in which an executive revealed tax forms for current and former employees. This attack resulted in income tax information being exposed for nearly 10,000 individuals.

Spear Phishing

1.1

Spear phishing is a variation of a phishing attack in which a recipient is deliberately chosen as a target of an attack. What differentiates this type of phishing from whaling is that the target may not be wealthy or prominent. By hypertargeting just a few users, these e-mails tend to stay off the radar longer. This also allows the e-mails to be highly personalized, which increases the chances the victim will follow the instructions in the e-mail.

Vishing

Vishing is an attack like phishing, but it involves an attack conducted by phone. The term comes from a combination of the words *voice* and phishing. A common feature of vishing attacks is the use of a spoofed caller ID, which appears to be a legitimate phone number to the victim. Vishing attacks are unexpected, and often, the victim does not have a great deal of time to consider legitimacy of the phone call. Vishing attacks are generally successful against the elderly or individuals who are not technologically aware. Attackers are always improving their abilities to appear realistic or legitimate to their victims in order to gain a broader attack surface.

The best defense against a potential vishing attack is to distrust the authenticity of the phone call and confirm any anomalies by direct contact with the real bank or company.

Smishing

1.1

Smishing is an attack in which a user is tricked into downloading malware or providing confidential information via text message. For example, imagine a scenario in which a user registers an account on a social media site. That user may receive a text message containing a link to verify a device or unsubscribe to notifications. In reality, the link connects the user to malicious code. Smishing, often styled as *SMiShing*, is a combination of *SMS* (short messaging service) and *phishing*.

Prepending

1.1

Prepending is a technique in which characters are added to the beginning of a text, phrase, word, etc. with the goal of influencing how a user receives or interprets the message. For example, a common prepending technique in social engineering is to add a reference for a specific user in a Tweet (@user) to entice the person to click on link. Adding a legitimate company name to the beginning of a fake URL draws users' attention to a valid name and may trick a user into believing the URL is legitimate.

Credential Harvesting

1.1

Credential harvesting is a technique designed to obtain a user's login name and password for systems. Credentials are often harvested using a phishing e-mail to trick a user into accessing a link to enter personal credentials. Once credentials have been obtained, a hacker can access an enterprise environment at will.

Watering Hole

1.1

A **watering hole attack** occurs when an attacker targets an individual in a specific group, organization, or IP address range. This attack is designed to get specific information from a victim. For example, threat actors may hack a specific brand or version of a software application used by many financial institutions. As these organizations run the software, hackers are able to collect transaction and banking information regarding the organizations' customers.

Pharming

1.1

Pharming is the process of setting up a website that looks legitimate and credible but used to steal personal information entered by users. It is another attack used to entice users into revealing information or clicking on malware links or attachments. Because it is difficult to expect users to find the pharmed site on their own, hackers use pharming and phishing to get malware on the victim's computer. The malware redirects the user's browser to the fake site without the victim's knowledge by using DNS poisoning.

Hoax

1.1

Another technique to bait users into clicking on suspicious links or downloading malicious software is tricking them into an action by using a hoax. A **hoax** is a falsehood that a person believes is genuine. Some examples of hoaxes include pop-up ads on browsers. A common trick is a pop-up alert that states your computer is infected with viruses and click on the link to scan your system. This technique is often referred to as *scareware*, as it is an attempt to frighten a user into clicking on malicious code.

E-mail is another delivery mechanism of hoaxes and urban legends. Even if the hoax does not contain malware, or links to malware, it can increase bandwidth in networks and reduce productivity of workers. Users should be educated on how to determine the legitimacy of information by using credible websites recommended by the US Cybersecurity and Infrastructure Security Agency (CISA). Additionally, users can use fact-checking websites to determine if a questionable e-mail is genuine or a hoax. One such example of an online fact-checking website is snopes.com.

Spam

1.1

Spam is unsolicited bulk messages. Typically, spam consists of nuisance e-mails, but it may also contain phishing messages, which makes it a form of social engineering.

Spam over Internet Messaging (SPIM)

1.1

Spam over Internet messaging (SPIM) is a specific form of unwanted messages that arrive as Internet messages, instant messages, or notifications. SPIM usually contains embedded web links that are malicious in nature.

Identity Fraud

1.1

Identity fraud is a social engineering attack in which a hacker uses stolen information to obtain additional data or access to a secure account of a victim. Hackers often steal and use information such as Social Security numbers or credit card information to access secured information.

Impersonation

1.1

Impersonation is a social engineering technique in which hackers pretend to be another person to obtain information. Impersonation often goes hand-in-hand with identity fraud, as hackers typically steal personal information of a victim and pretend to be that person.

Invoice Scams

1.1

An **invoice scam** is a social engineering attack in which fraudulent invoices are submitted to targeted organizations in an effort to obtain money. The invoices are typically labeled as past due so the organization sends payment without investigating.

Influence Campaigns

1.1

Social engineering relies heavily on the psychological manipulation of human behavior that entices users to disclose information or act in a specific manner. In this regard, influence campaigns are effective tools for validating social engineering schemes. An **influence campaign** is a wide-scale operation that focuses on the spread of false or misleading information in an effort to make a group of people think or behave a certain way. Influence campaigns are effective in part due to a concept called *social proof*, which is a phenomenon in which users view behaviors and information as correct if they see others performing or agreeing with an idea.

Users are especially vulnerable to manipulation if the information's source appears to be knowledgeable, familiar, or widely accepted. Influence campaigns are typically conducted through hybrid warfare or social media.

Hybrid Warfare

 1.1

Hybrid warfare is a military strategy that combines political, conventional, and cyberwarfare to disseminate false information. This term also refers to the ever-changing landscape of *battlespaces*, which are military operations conducted to achieve desired goals. By blending typical warfare tactics with contemporary methods, an aggressor can retain anonymity and avoid retribution or blame. Elections are also highly targeted by warfare campaigns, particularly using social media platforms, such as the highly documented Russian influence in the US 2016 presidential campaign.

Social Media

1.1

Social media platforms such as Facebook, LinkedIn, Twitter, Snapchat, and Instagram have an extensive reach. Often, social media sites are used to influence perceptions, distort reality, or shape content otherwise. The use of social tools provides anonymity, ease of access, lack of geographical borders, and the ability to reach multitudes of people. Combining misinformation campaigns with traditional attacks increases the believability of social engineering attacks.

In a successful influence campaign, social media is weaponized to launch disruptive information and psychological campaigns. Social media provides a great deal of intelligence about targets, but it can also be used to launch attacks, such as taking over a trusted Twitter account to send erroneous information.

Vulnerabilities

A *vulnerability* is a flaw or potential for harm and represents a weakness that can be exploited by threat actors or inadvertent user actions to cause harm to a business and its data or operations. A vulnerability represents a flaw that can result in a security breach and must be identified before a threat actor causes harm.

Vulnerable systems present a high risk for exploitation through attacks and errors. When a system is exploited, impacts can range from a minor inconvenience to catastrophic loss. Examples of impacts felt from exploited vulnerabilities include the following:

- *Data loss.* Data loss can occur due from hardware failures, theft, attacks, exploits, and mistakes made by internal personnel. Data loss is a significant security concern that has wide-ranging implications, such as potential loss of proprietary information and legal ramifications if the lost data was private in nature or otherwise protected by data laws.

1.6

- *Data breach.* A data breach occurs when private, confidential, or protected data is released to an unprotected environment. This allows data to be discovered and accessed by people outside the trusted organization. This could produce significant security concerns, including loss of financial data, theft of intellectual property, and identity theft. Data breaches can be the result of an attack, insiders, or unintentional exposure of data.

- *Data exfiltration.* Data exfiltration occurs when there is any unauthorized movement of data. This includes external actors who copy or transmit data from an organization as well as internal personnel who transmit protected data via e-mail or portable storage. Just as with a data breach, data sent from an organization is a security concern as the data can be used maliciously. For example, employees can sell confidential information to competitors or publish private information in an attempt to destroy a person or company's reputation.
- *Identity theft.* Identity theft is the result of stolen personal private information used to assume the identity of an individual. Identity theft can have serious security concerns, including altered personal credit history and stolen tax refunds. Additionally, victims of identity theft may be left with a criminal record or damaged reputation as a result of actions committed by the perpetrator.
- *Financial impact.* Financial impacts are security concerns because they affect an organization's financial stability. Financial impacts can also turn into security implications, including financial losses from theft of corporate information; theft of financial information such as credit cards, bank account information, costs incurred to reimburse others for losses, or replacement of credit cards and technology; and disruption of services and revenue resulting from an attack.
- *Damage to reputation.* Reputational damage can occur with cyber incidents. There is a level of trust that customers and others have in your organization that can be damaged by a cyber incident. The chief security concern with reputation damage is the erosion of customer trust, which could lead to a loss of customers, sales, and profits.
- *Loss of availability.* Availability loss is the result of production, services and system usage that stop a business from using their resources and equipment in normal operations. Availability loss can be the result of hardware failures, configuration mistakes, or cyberattacks. Security concerns with availability loss include lost revenue due to downtime and loss of customers' trust in the company's ability to deliver products and services.

Zero-Day Vulnerability

1.6

An example of a vulnerability is a zero-day attack. A **zero-day vulnerability** is a serious flaw that exists in software and remains unknown until exploited by hackers. Because it is unknown to the developer, there is usually no immediate fix or patch available. It is difficult to protect against an unknown vulnerability. The best defense is to keep a system and software patched. Also monitoring forums and support logs for announcements about zero-day attacks is necessary so immediate action can be taken to remedy or possibly avoid an issue. Many software developers have bug-bounty programs in place to try to identify zero-day vulnerabilities. A **bug-bounty program** is an initiative that offers rewards to those who identify flaws and vulnerabilities found in their program. When a bug is reported, it can be patched before discovered and exploited by hackers.

Weak Configurations

1.6

Weak configuration of security properties in devices or systems can create vulnerabilities due to a lack of appropriate controls. A **weak configuration** is inadequate security controls in a device or system. Weak configurations cover a great deal of settings from unprotected privileged user accounts, overly permissive permissions, use of unsecure protocols or solutions, and failing to recognize and protect inherent system settings. Poor configuration settings and solutions greatly increase the vulnerability of a system and make it easier to breach defensives. The following are common vulnerabilities that often exist in enterprise environments and should be evaluated and strengthened.

Open Permissions

✛ 1.6

User permissions control access to data and technology. *Open permissions* are file permissions that provide unlimited access to open and modify files or execute commands. Since accounts with open permissions are given more access than needed to perform job duties, these accounts provide attackers the ability to penetrate entire areas of a network they normally would not be able to reach. Users with more permissions than they need may also make mistakes that can compromise data security. For example, they may accidentally change data instead of just viewing it, or accidentally delete content in a shared folder. Administrators should evaluate which permissions employees need and only provide what is necessary. Audits on secure resources can determine who has access and the type of permissions granted.

Unsecured Root Accounts

✛ 1.6

A common weak configuration is an *unsecured root account*, which is an administrative account for which a known default password has not been changed. *Root accounts*, sometimes called *administrator accounts*, provide complete system access to a device.

Limits on root access should be tightly controlled as they are the most powerful accounts and their security is essential. When unsecured, attackers are able to exploit these vulnerabilities and guess passwords or use unchanged default credentials. Once accessed, threat actors can use root accounts to gain entry into programs or files or create additional root accounts. If a root account cannot be disabled, passwords should be changed.

Errors

✛ 1.6

Mistakes or errors in design, operations, or configurations make a system vulnerable to threats or loss of availability. Hardware and software systems often come pre-configured with default configurations, or out-of-the box settings. Left unchanged, systems are vulnerable to attacks. However, errors often occur when proper preliminary steps are not taken or users are rushed or unskilled when configuring a system.

Errors in the secure configuration of a device or network are misconfigurations. A *misconfiguration* is a mistake or error in design, operation, or configuration that makes a system vulnerable to threats or loss of availability. Examples of misconfigurations include a typo in a command, which could shut down servers or services; e-mailing confidential information to the wrong individual, which could result in lawsuits; or configuring DNS incorrectly, which could disrupt traffic navigation.

Ensuring there are appropriate recovery methods to counter errors is important, along with testing major changes and commands in a protected environment before executing them in a live production network.

Weak Encryption

✛ 1.6

Weak encryption is a vulnerability that can enable an attacker to crack encryption keys and subsequently read encrypted information thought to be secure. A weak encryption implementation is particularly vulnerable to brute-force attacks designed to crack encrypted keys. One reason for weak encryption is the use of outdated hardware or software that is unable to support newer standards. Systems should be upgraded, if possible, to ensure only secure encryption methods are used.

Unsecure Protocols

Unsecure protocols are those that contain weaknesses, specifically by not providing confidentiality, integrity, or authentication mechanisms. One of the most common vulnerabilities is not using encryption to protect the confidentiality of the data. Unsecure protocols expose data such as remote system credentials or data in transfer, to packet sniffers, which can intercept and read information stored within packets. Protocols that do not require authentication will respond to any request without validating the source. Companies should establish policies preventing their use, and restrict communications conducted on these protocols through firewalls and other security appliances.

Default Settings

Most systems come preconfigured with default settings that enable initial access and login. Default settings, such as usernames, passwords, and configurations for hardware and software are typically found online. Failure to change these settings leaves your system vulnerable for attackers to use default credentials for high-level access. The need to change default settings permeates to all networks, not just enterprise environments. Often, consumers do not properly remove default configurations, leaving their residential networks vulnerable to unauthorized access. Additionally, Internet-enabled devices left in a default state are vulnerable to infection with malware that can turn the devices into bots in a larger botnet. Systems should be audited to verify that default settings have been removed. Some IoT devices are not able to be changed, so those devices should run on a separate network away from enterprise systems.

Open Ports and Services

Open ports and services can communicate with other devices through these communication channels. *Ports* are virtual connections used by an operating system to allow IP protocol communication and traffic exchange. An **open port** is a communication port that actively accepts TCP or UDP connections. Any open port not being used presents a possible attack vector that could allow access into a device for malicious activity. Ports can be closed network-wide using network firewalls or on individual machines using host-based firewalls.

A *service* is any program running in the background of an operating system that provides specific features and functionality. An **open service** is a service permitted to run on a computer. Services advertise their functionality through ports, making them susceptible to remote exploitation. However, not all services are essential for computer operation, and unneeded services should be stopped, or blocked, to prevent them from serving as attack vectors.

Legacy Platforms

A common vulnerability on enterprise networks are legacy platforms. A **legacy platform**, also called a *legacy operating system*, is an operating system or embedded system that is no longer in widespread use. Often, legacy equipment is unable to support strong encryption, meaning weak encryption methods secure data on the devices. This vulnerability can result in successful attacks on cryptographic systems exposing encrypted data, such as passwords, or an encryption key, which could be used to gain access to all the data protected with that key.

As operating systems are replaced by newer, secure platforms, outdated systems are no longer supported by the vendor that created the system. This includes patches and updates for security monitoring, virus protection, and system vulnerabilities. By including legacy platforms on a network, an organization risks a potential attack due to the lack of continuous updates on legacy devices.

Third-Party Risks

 1.6

A *third-party risk* is a vulnerability an organization assumes when it hires an outside vendor to provide products or services for the business. IT personnel typically use the services of a third party for tasks such as software development, systems issues, and other tasks internal personnel are unavailable to perform. Using outside sources is an efficient way to expedite tasks that need attention.

When a third party develops IT products or services, that party has access to privileged information and systems of an organization. Allowing outsiders access to an enterprise environment is a risk in itself as it creates a security concern. Some of these risks can be managed by instituting a secure vendor management strategy.

Vendor Management

 1.6

Vendor management is the process of procuring and managing the services of a third party. *Vendors*, also known as *suppliers*, are businesses that provide product or services. Most organizations use a bidding process when purchasing third-party services. A *bidding process* is a series of steps the buyer takes to obtain the best price and schedule for a purchase. Most organizations require a bidder to sign a nondisclosure agreement before submitting a bid. A **nondisclosure agreement (NDA)** is a legal contract between two parties that restricts the signing party from distributing or sharing confidential information to anyone outside of the agreement. This helps eliminate security concerns. The *bid* is a formal written proposal that lists all details of the project. The bidding process enables a manager to control the risks of a third party. After bids are evaluated and the job is awarded, a written contract is put into place.

System integration is a security issue when using a third party. **System integration** is the process of linking various IT systems, services, and software to enable a unified functional system between companies. Vendors typically need access to systems of an organization when providing IT services. It is a risk to manage as integrated systems can allow attacks to spread between systems or be used as an attack vector to provide the means to target a business network.

Vendor management includes facilitating the relationship with the third party. Because you do not control the security of vendors, you must rely on their security expertise or lack thereof. Having a vendor management plan enables development of best practices to reduce vulnerabilities and threats from partners while still enabling a strong working relationship. Some of these practices include clear, consistent communication including expectations of services; security measures; and notification of changes. Monitoring interactions with vendors is important to ensure compliance with established procedures. Monitoring is accomplished with site visits, reports, and audits.

Lack of Vendor Support

 1.6

Vendor support is the act of a vendor providing training, help desk responses, and other follow-up services for a contract. Some contracts call for these services to end at the conclusion of the project. Other contracts extend the support for a specified time. Using third party contracts should not be taken lightly. A detailed vendor management plan that includes specifications for vendor support can eliminate future issues, such as the following:

- If issues arise at the end of the contract and vendor support is required, the hiring organization could be in a bind and need to contract for additional services if these services were not included in the original third-party agreement.
- If a vendor creates software or other IT products and future upgrades are needed, the vendor may no longer support the product to fix vulnerabilities.
- If systems are old, end-of-life systems, vendors generally will not support or if they do, charge high prices for services.
- A vendor could potentially go out of business, leaving the hiring organization with unpatched systems and potential downtime for lack of parts or assistance.

1.6

Supply Chain

A **supply chain** is the businesses, people, and activities involved in turning raw materials into products and delivering them to end-users. **Supply chain vulnerabilities** are potential malicious events that can occur in the supply chain.

Vulnerabilities can originate at points along the supply chain, often at less-secure elements or vendors in the process. Supply chain risks include the installation of rootkits in hard drives, phishing schemes designed to inject malware into systems, or embedding malicious scripts into websites and systems. Preventing supply chain attacks involves creating a detailed risk analysis of the potential threats as part of a vendor management plan. A robust security defense is required, including the use of intrusion-detection systems, firewalls, antimalware, and compliance agreements.

1.6

Outsourced Code Development

Outside code development can expedite application development for an organization. However, when a company chooses to have a third party develop code, the contracting organization loses some degree of control, and potential problems may arise, including the following:

- When code is outsourced, it should be clear in the contract as to who owns the code. Otherwise, the third-party developers may have a legal claim to it.
- Although vendors are screened in order to be deemed reputable, security concerns can arise. Rogue programmers working for the vendor could intentionally put in software vulnerabilities.
- The outside vendor may subcontract the job to another party that was not screened for security purposes. Therefore, the contract should either explicitly disallow subcontracting or set forth parameters for screening subcontractors.

A vendor-management plan should include strategies to control code development. An independent security audit can ensure data privacy and security is addressed. In addition, code ownership must be defined to avoid lockout of an owner from accessing and modifying the code to address security problems and future upgrades.

1.6

Data Storage

Vendor management includes plans for secure data storage. A company must protect the confidentiality and integrity of data. Cloud storage is a common option for an organization. *Cloud storage* is using remote serves hosted on the Internet to store data rather than process data. The service may be free or pay-per-use. For many businesses, the cloud provides vital services, from redundancy to deployment of resources.

Customers use cloud service so they can store data at a location other than their server or personal computers. By storing data in the cloud, the information is away from the user's primary location, which means there are inherent security risks. Because information is shared elsewhere, there have to be assurances that data is secure and not subject to hacking.

Protection Strategies

There is no perfect defense against security attacks to networks and data. In fact, network and system defense is a multifaceted approach involving software developers, skilled security professionals, specialized software, established policies and procedures, and educated users. All elements must work together to provide protection. A great deal of media coverage and oversight are given to attacks in which data was lost or compromised by intentional actions of a criminal. However, a company must consider *all* possibilities of data loss, including unforeseen natural events and human error.

Antimalware Software

The best defense against attacks is prevention. However, sometimes attacks slip past all precautions and defenses. Using an antimalware software program is critical to catching threats that may be installed without your knowledge. *Antimalware software* with multiple layers should be in place. Often, antimalware software also uses heuristic methodology. **Heuristic methodology** is an approach to finding previously undetected, unwanted programs or variants of known viruses. Antivirus companies have designed heuristic approaches to search for potentially malicious software. Some of the approaches include deep inspection of files, such as determining intent or looking for key words or phrases in the file. Others include running the code in an isolated environment to test it before determining if it is safe. Looking at file signatures is another technique for malware defense that entails looking for files that are variations of known virus files. Heuristic scanning can be successful but can also result in false positives. A *false positive* occurs when the software incorrectly flags a valid file as a threat.

Caution should be shown when downloading programs from the Internet. Ensure the URL displayed in the browser matches the site. For example, www.microsoft.com is the correct URL. However, a hacker may set up a website to *look* like the official site, but the URL may be micr0s0ft.com. Notice the zeros where there should be the letter *O*. Pay extra attention to website URLs that have been shortened using URL-shortening services such as bitly.com, as it masks the complete URL name. Likewise, a system should be in place to scan e-mail messages and attachments as received by a company's e-mail system as many malware infections are transmitted via e-mail.

Physical Attacks

Organizations should implement an equipment policy that prohibits the use of removable media, such as flash drives. Users could pick up malware or viruses from their home computers and unknowingly transfer it to their work computers when they insert flash drives or other removable storage devices. Therefore, removable media not vetted or assigned by the company should be prohibited.

Malicious USB Cables

A **malicious USB cable** is a USB cable that, when plugged into a USB device, injects keystrokes onto a computer enabling an attacker to download malware. Often, users are unaware of problems until unusual activity or communication is noticed or they become a victim of identity theft. There is no fix for this type of attack vector; however, IT personnel can minimize the risk by

- purchasing USB cables only from reputable vendors;
- establishing and enforcing policies to prohibit employee sharing of cables; and
- locking down use of external cabling.

Malicious Flash Drives

Hackers have long targeted flash drives with malware as a method to deliver malicious code to devices used by the drives. Malware-infected drives typically contain backdoors, ransomware, Trojans, and browser hijacking tools that redirect a user's browser to other sites that typically contain additional malware. Systems with up-to-date antimalware programs detect most threats when a drive is inserted or files accessed. Not *all* malware may be detected, but unusual activity including logins, data or identity theft, and atypical browsing requests may all be symptoms of a malware attack. Prevention consists of prohibiting flash drives through group policy configuration, user awareness, and maintaining up-to-date antimalware programs.

USB Data Blocker

A **USB data blocker** is a device that prevents unauthorized transfer of information as well as the installation of malware to a device. USB data blockers serve as a filter between public USB ports for Internet connection or device charging and users' devices. In organizations that allow employees to use USB devices, the use of a data blocker cannot be undervalued. Given the size of most USB devices, employees can easily and covertly withdraw information from or install malware onto a network. Therefore, locking down USB data transfers through the installation of data blockers is a vital step in securing a network from a physical attack.

Card Cloning and Skimming

Card cloning, also called *skimming*, is the act of stealing a credit card by copying card numbers and data and attaching them to a bogus card. A **skimmer** is a hardware device that attaches to a Point of Sale (PoS) device, reads credit card data simultaneously with the PoS device, and then copies the information from the card's magnetic strip into memory. The skimmed data is sent to a hacker who copies it to a bogus card.

To avoid cloning, businesses using PoS devices should conduct regular inspections on terminals to ensure skimmers have not been placed on the device.

System Updates

One of the most important protection strategies is ensuring systems are updated with the latest security patches, hotfixes, or other system updates. It is important to keep an operating system fully patched. A *patch* is an update provided by the vendor to correct errors or bugs. A *hotfix* is a small piece of code intended to correct or patch a specific vulnerability as quickly as possible. Many viruses exploit vulnerabilities left in place due to uninstalled patches.

TECH TIP

Businesses that use Windows 10 often manage their updates through special servers and policies that push the updates to computers. Similarly, Windows 10 Home users can manually check for updates through system settings. However, Linux uses commands to retrieve updates. For Debian-based Linux distributions, the command to check for updates is **sudo apt-get upgrade**, and Red Hat versions use the **yum** command.

Most home users are familiar with Microsoft's update policies and procedures for personal Windows computers. In an organization, it is the responsibility of IT personnel to ensure system updates are in place. Update managers and policies are commonly used to push updates to networked systems, but stand-alone devices, including laptops, must be protected. Updates are not limited to operating system software, either. Browsers, applications, and customized programs and scripts should be updated frequently.

SUMMARY

Threats

- A vulnerability is a flaw or potential for harm. A threat, however, is an event or action in which a vulnerability is exploited, and a computer system is endangered. A threat may or may not lead to an attack.
- A threat can be physical or nonphysical. A physical threat is one that endangers devices and the systems. A nonphysical threat is one that endangers data and operations.
- It is IT's responsibility to monitor threats and protect the enterprise environment. This process of protecting the enterprise environment is known as cybersecurity.

Threat Actors

- A threat actor is an individual, nation state, or organization responsible for a security incident, attack, or other type of event that affects an organization's security. Conversely, those who primarily aim to attack a network to steal data are referred to as hackers.
- There are many types of threat actors. Common types include script kiddie, hacktivist, criminal syndicate, state actor, insiders, and competitors.
- Threat actors have specific attributes, which are characteristics a person possesses. Common attributes include internal or external actors, sophisticated or unsophisticated, part of a hacking group or are individuals, and different intentions or motivations behind the attacks.

Hackers

- The term *hacker* has traditionally referred to an individual who attacks computers and systems for malicious purposes. Hackers focus on computers and systems and are not usually associated with other security threats contributed to a threat actor.
- A hacking attack is an attempt to break into a computer system to steal data.
- Hackers are classified by intent. White-hat hackers are generally ethical and law-abiding individuals who often break into networks with permission to study or reveal vulnerabilities, while black-hat hackers operate outside the law for personal gain. Gray-hat hackers fall in the middle. They do not necessarily harm others but do not ask permission before conducting attacks or accessing systems.

Vectors

- A vector is the means by which a threat actor attempts to access or compromise a system. It is the pathway a threat actor uses to access systems and launch attacks.
- To protect against vectors, apply the least privilege principle, layer defenses, and monitor user credentials.
- Examples of vectors used to exploit system vulnerabilities include direct access, wireless, e-mail, supply chain, social media, removable media, and the cloud.

Threat Intelligence Sources

- Threat intelligence is information regarding threats, threat actors, and other potentially harmful actions that could occur in an enterprise environment. Intelligence helps IT personnel understand past security events so current events can be remedied and remedies for future defenses be put in place.
- Threat intelligence sources reveal information for security teams as they work to find indicators of compromise. After the malicious activity is identified, remaining forensic artifacts provide clues to the activity identified.
- Identifying and monitoring IoCs provides critical intelligence that can help further evaluate attempted cyberattacks.
- Sources and resources of threat intelligence include OSINT, closed/proprietary sources, information sharing centers, automated indicator sharing, and the dark web.

Malware Attacks

- Malware is computer code intentionally written to cause some form of harm. A malware attack is the action of a hacker installing malicious software on another person's device with the intent of accessing date for personal gain.
- Malware represents an ongoing threat to an organization. It can be designed to infect a single system or many devices as possible. Malware can also direct an infected device to perform actions automatically.
- Types of malware attacks include keyloggers, adware, cookies, Trojan, potentially unwanted program, worm, time bomb, logic bomb, ransomware, rootkit, and backdoor.

Virus

- A virus is malicious software code that is unleashed and attempts to perform destructive content on computer systems or data. It has the ability to self-replicate and spread copies of itself to other devices. While all viruses are malware, not all malware are viruses.
- An armored virus is a computer virus designed to prevent security analysts from reading source code by attempting to disassemble or prevent access to the code. It uses extra code to mask the actual virus code, making it hidden from users.
- A polymorphic virus changes its characteristics in an attempt to avoid detection from antivirus programs. It uses a mutation engine, which randomizes the decryption process of the virus codes.
- Fileless viruses use a computer system's software, files, and applications to launch malware. It is difficult to find since they do not attach to specific files and do not leave digital footprints.

- A macro virus is a macro written in the same language as software applications and programmed to carry out a malicious intent. It infects the software application in which it is embedded and starts running as soon as the application is opened.

Adversarial Artificial Intelligence (AI) Attack

- Artificial intelligence (AI) is a branch of computer science aimed at simulating intelligence in machines. It is able to evaluate and perceive their environments to respond to stimuli and achieve desired goals.
- An adversarial AI attack is malicious development and use of sophisticated AI systems to behave in a manner that benefits an attacker. These attacks impact enterprise environments by showing the ability of AI devices to exploit machine-learning algorithms to automate e-mail responses and reveal sensitive information.
- Adversarial AI often attacks through two methods: tainting training data for machine learning and compromising the security of machine-learning algorithms.

Social Engineering

- Social engineering is the use of manipulation techniques to lure individuals to reveal personal and confidential information to a cybercriminal. It involves the use of social tools to obtain information, such as personal information or business practices.
- Social engineering tasks are believable and effective for the following reasons: authority, intimidation, consensus, scarcity, familiarity, trust, and urgency.
- Reconnaissance is the first phase of a social engineering attack. Reconnaissance is the act of eliciting information from or about a target.
- One common approach of reconnaissance is pretexting, which occurs when a scammer creates a fake story to lure a victim into providing information.
- Additional reconnaissance techniques include asking people to reveal information, looking through social media sites for information, using public records stored online or in public-library searches, using advanced web searches, dumpster diving, and shoulder surfing.

Social Engineering Attacks

- The attack phase is the second phase of social engineering. In this phase, the hacker uses the information gathered in reconnaissance to launch an attack.
- Social engineering attacks are successful due to the difficulty in troubleshooting them and determining how an attacker gained access. The best defense against attacks is diligence and enforcement of online access and information disclosure policies.
- Phishing is a social engineering attack in which an attacker attempts to obtain a user's personal information. Phishing attacks include whale phishing, spear phishing, vishing, and smishing.
- Additional types of social engineering attacks include prepending, credential harvesting, watering hole, pharming, hoax, spam, spam over Internet messaging, identity fraud, impersonation, and invoice scams.
- Influence campaigns are another type of attack. It is a wide-scale operation that focuses on the spread of false or misleading information in an effort to make a group of people think or behave a certain way. This attack includes hybrid warfare and social media.

Vulnerabilities

- A vulnerability is a flaw or potential for harm and represents a weakness that can be exploited by threat actors or inadvertent user actions to impact a business and its data or operations. When a system is exploited, impacts can range from a minor inconvenience to catastrophic loss.
- A zero-day vulnerability is a serious flaw that exists in software and remains unknown until exploited by hackers. It is difficult to protect against an unknown vulnerability. The best defense is to keep a system and software patched.
- A weak configuration is inadequate security controls in a device or system. This greatly increases the vulnerability of a system and makes it easier to breach defensives. Examples include open permissions, unsecured root accounts, errors, weak encryption, unsecure protocols, default setting, and open ports and services.
- A legacy platform is an operating system or embedded system that is no longer in widespread use. This vulnerability can result in successful attacks on cryptographic systems exposing encrypted data, which could be used to gain access to all the data protected with that key.
- A third-party risk is a vulnerability an organization assumes when it hires an outside vendor to provide products or services for the business and can occur for various reasons. Examples include lack of vendor support, supply chain vulnerabilities, outsourcing code development, and unsecure data storage.

Protection Strategies

- Network and system defense is a multifaceted approach involving software developers, skilled security professionals, specialized software, established policies and procedures, and educated users. All elements must work together to provide protection.
- The best defense against attacks is prevention. However, sometimes attacks slip through systems. Companies can utilize various protection strategies to protect against threats.
- Examples of protection strategies include installing antimalware software, implementing an equipment policy that prohibits the use of removable media, and ensuring systems are up to date with the latest security patches, hotfixes, or other updates.

REVIEW QUESTIONS

1. Define *threats*.
2. Identify and explain three types of threat actors.
3. Briefly explain common attributes of threat actors.
4. State the difference between types of hackers.
5. List examples of vectors used to exploit system vulnerabilities.
6. Summarize threat intelligence sources and resources.
7. Define each of the four main types of threat intelligence.
8. What two standards does AIS function through?
9. Identify and explain five types of malware attacks.

10. Which type of cookie stays on a computer until an expiration date?

11. Discuss four types of viruses.

12. Explain an adversarial artificial intelligence (AI) attack.

13. Define *machine learning (ML)* and its algorithm.

14. Summarize social engineering and reconnaissance.

15. Identify types of social engineering attacks.

16. Explain the two forms of influence campaigns.

17. Discuss vulnerabilities.

18. List common types of weak configurations.

19. Identify examples of protection strategies against threats to networks and data.

20. How can IT personnel minimize the risk from malicious USB cables?

✚ SAMPLE SECURITY+ EXAM QUESTIONS

1. Deborah's computer was found to be infected with malware that compromised the host device prior to the operating system loading. What type of malware has infected this system?

    A. Worm

    B. Rootkit

    C. Cryptomalware

    D. Trojan

2. Adrian is investigating a slow computer and observes unusual traffic from the computer to an unknown Internet address. What is the *most likely* type of malware he has discovered?

    A. Keylogger

    B. RAT

    C. Worm

    D. Polymorphic virus

3. E-mail spam filters have intercepted an e-mail targeting the sales team. This e-mail contained a malicious link. What type of attack was prevented?

    A. Hoax

    B. Spear phishing

    C. Whaling

    D. Vishing

4. In an e-mail to several employees, the sender indicated they were the only employees who had not yet signed up for a new employee benefit. The attack was using which principle to convince the individuals to click the embedded link?

    A. Authority

    B. Consensus

    C. Impersonation

    D. Hoax

5. Jeremy was browsing the Internet on his lunch break and downloaded a game. The next day when he tried to access his data, he received a message informing him his data was encrypted and he had to pay a fee to gain access to an unlock code. Which of the following has caused this attack?

   A. Hoax

   B. Ransomware

   C. Trojan

   D. Adware

6. Which type of attack *most likely* occurred when the victim is the chairman of a company's board of directors?

   A. Whaling

   B. RAT

   C. Smishing

   D. Keylogger

7. Malware was inserted on a web page that is frequented by utility companies. The attacker is conducting what type of attack?

   A. Spyware

   B. Backdoor

   C. Watering hole

   D. BOT

8. Xavier wants to stay on top of current threat situations so he can make adjustments on security settings. Which threat intelligence will provide this information in a timely fashion?

   A. Threat feeds

   B. Academic journals

   C. Vendor websites

   D. Strategic intelligence

9. A company has a poor environmental record. It is hit with a cyberattack that reveals its poor practices along with employee names and their salaries. Which is *most likely* the motivation of the hacker?

   A. Hacktivism

   B. Thrill of the attack

   C. Revenge

   D. Cyberwarfare

10. A cyberattack against a country's water system infrastructure would *most likely* be the actions of which type of hacker motivation?

    A. Cyberwarfare

    B. Money (criminal)

    C. Thrill of hacking

    D. Hacktivism

LAB EXERCISES

Lab Activity 2-1: Viewing Cookies with Google Chrome

Many, if not most, websites use some type of cookie. Most web browsers have settings for managing cookies. In Google Chrome, you can search for cookies by a particular website.

1. Launch the Google Chrome web browser, and navigate to the AOL web page (www.aol.com).

2. Click the **Customize and Control Google Chrome** button, and click **Settings** in the drop-down menu. A new tab is opened that contains the Chrome settings.

3. Click the **Advanced** or **Advanced Settings** link at the bottom of the page.

4. In the Privacy area, click the **Content settings** link, and then click the **Cookies** link (this link may be labeled **All cookies and site data**).

5. Review the settings for cookies. Notice there are options to keep cookies and block third-party cookies.

6. Scroll down until the Search cookies text box is displayed, and enter aol in the text box, as shown. All of the cookies stored by Chrome are filtered to show only those set by AOL.

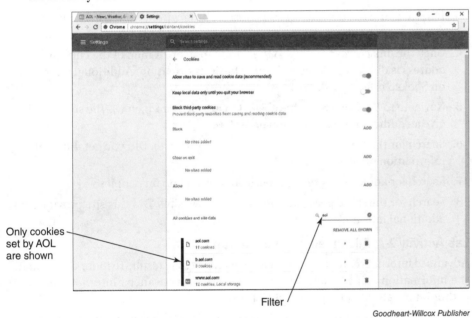

Only cookies set by AOL are shown

Filter

Goodheart-Willcox Publisher

7. Click on a set of cookies to see the individual cookies. Click an individual cookie to see data about it, including when it will expire. For some cookies, you will not be able to read the content as some content is written in JavaScript.

8. Close Chrome, and then relaunch it.

9. Display the cookies, and filter for AOL cookies. Are there any cookies still present from AOL? Explain why or why not.

Lab Activity 2-2: Recognizing Phishing

Phishing has become very prevalent. Many phishing e-mails appear very convincing. The challenge for users is determining if an e-mail is fake or real.

1. Launch a web browser, and navigate to the Sonic Wall website. (If this site is unavailable, search for another phishing quiz online.)
2. Using the site's search function, enter the search phrase phishing IQ.
3. In the results, click the link for **Phishing IQ Start**.
4. Read the information on the page, and then start the test.
5. Compare your results with those of your classmates.

Lab Activity 2-3: Personal Data Online

There are many websites that aggregate personal data from various sources. Many of the sites charge a fee to obtain information, but there are some that will provide information for free.

1. Launch a web browser, and navigate to the Spokeo website (www.spokeo.com).
2. In the search box, enter your name or a parent's name, and click the **Search** button. All matches will be returned. Depending on how common the name is, there could be quite a few selections.
3. If needed, use the tools to filter the results by location. Notice that relatives are connected to each result. This may help in identifying the correct person.
4. Click the link corresponding to the correct person. A map of the current address is displayed along with some basic information. Additional information on Spokeo is fee-based.
5. Navigate to the Zaba Search website (www.zabasearch.com). The search will give an address for a person you enter.
6. Search for the same person as on the Spokeo website. Did you get different information or was it identical?
7. Search for additional sites that perform free lookup on people.
8. Search for the same person as on the other two sites. Did this site provide any additional information?

Lab Activity 2-4: Advanced Internet Search

Advanced Internet searches can be useful in refining the results to more closely match the information being sought. Hackers may also use advanced Internet searches to gather information about potential victims.

1. Launch a web browser, and navigate to the Google website (www.google.com).
2. In the search box, enter cyberhacks 2019..2020, and press the [Enter] key to conduct the search. Google looks for information on hacks that occurred in the years 2019 and 2020.

3. Conduct a new search by entering filetype:pdf "computer hackers". This search looks for any PDF file that contains the phrase *computer hackers*.

4. Conduct a new search by entering allintitle:computer hackers. This command ensures the words *computer* and *hackers* appears in the title of the search results. Notice, however, that the words can appear in any order and do not even need to be next to each other in the title.

5. Conduct a new search by entering cache:http://lifehacker.com. The result is not a search, but rather a cached version of the website is displayed. A cached version is a saved version, which may not be the most current version.

Lab Activity 2-5: California Online Privacy Protection Act

One of the most definitive sources for defining PII (Personally Identifiable Information) is the California Online Privacy Protection Act (CalOPPA). A look at some of the specifics of this law can be informative to see how it applies to consumers.

1. Launch a web browser, and navigate to the Consumer Federation of California website (www.consumercal.org). This is a nonprofit advocacy organization for consumer rights.

2. Click the **About CFC** link in the menu at the top of the page, and then click the **CFC Education Foundation** link in the menu on the left, as shown.

Goodheart-Willcox Publisher

3. On the CFC Education Foundation Privacy Protection Consumer Guide page that is displayed, scroll down to the Online Privacy Protection section, and click **The California Online Privacy Protection Act (CalOPPA)** link. A new page is displayed that provides an overview of the act, as shown.

Goodheart-Willcox Publisher

4. When does this law apply to businesses located in other states?
5. What happens if a website does not display the information required?
6. The recent amendment added tablets and other mobile device apps. If an app is not in compliance, what fine would the business pay?
7. What is AB 370? Are you in favor of this? Defend your answer.
8. Locate a website that you believe tracks PII. Does it abide by the CalOPPA? Explain your answer.

CASE STUDY

Android Phones and Updates

Unlike Apple iPhones and iPads, smartphones using the Google Android operating system have to rely on Google to release security patches to individual phone manufacturers, which then incorporate updates to their individual operating systems. After the manufacturer OS is updated, users can download and install the updates. In May of 2020, a popular Android support website ranked models of smartphones to determine the delay in updates from Google to the end-user. Of the three devices that scored a top score of 10, two of them were Google-manufactured phones, the Pixel 3 and Pixel 4, and the Samsung-manufactured Galaxy 10. The remaining scores ranged from 8 to under 1 with delays ranging from 10 days to over 60 days until manufacturers produced the updates in their product.

Security vulnerabilities are common in smartphones, and Google releases security patches on a monthly basis. The delay in availability from the manufacturer increases the vulnerability of the device to malware and other attacks.

1. Based on this data, do you think Google should mandate a minimum time frame by which other manufacturers of Android-enabled phones should have their operating systems patched and available for downloads? What would that time frame be? Explain your reasoning.

2. Beginning with Android 10, Google is attempting to provide system patches through an initiative called Project Mainline, which will provide select updates through the Play Store. Even so, this will have no impact on older phones running legacy Android operating systems that predate Android 10. In your opinion, is it the responsibility of Google, the manufacturer, or the end-user to ensure devices are consistently patched? Explain your reasoning.

3. Should businesses allow nonvendor phones on their networks due to the delays described above? This means networks would be exclusive to either Apple or Google productions. Provide support for your argument.

Security Evaluation

LEARNING OUTCOMES

- Summarize reasons to perform a security evaluation.
- Discuss threat hunting.
- Explain the use of a vulnerability scan as a component of a security assessment.
- Summarize penetration testing.
- Differentiate between passive and active reconnaissance.
- Recognize types of penetration techniques.
- Summarize penetration testing cleanup.
- Discuss the importance of system baselines and performance monitoring.
- Identify and explain types of log files.
- Summarize syslog.
- Identify the features of a security information and event management system (SIEM).
- Summarize SOAR.
- Discuss log management.
- Explain viewing of event logs.

KEY TERMS

active reconnaissance
application scanning
automated alert and trigger
banner grabbing
baseline
black box test
Common Vulnerabilities and
    Exposure (CVE)
Common Vulnerability Scoring
    System (CVSS)
configuration-compliance scanner
configuration review
credentialed scan
data input
escalation of privilege
ethical hacking
event deduplication
false negative
false positive
footprinting
gray box test

initial exploitation
intelligence fusion
intrusive test
lateral movement
log aggregation
log analysis
log collector
log file
log management
log review
network vulnerability scanner
noncredentialed scan
non-intrusive test
NXlog
orchestration
packet capture
passive reconnaissance
penetration exercise
penetration testing
penetration testing authorization
persistence

pivot
port scanner
port scanning
PowerShell
predictive analysis
rules of engagement (RoE)
rsyslog
security assessment
security automation
security information and event
    management (SIEM) system
sentiment analysis
SIEM correlation
SIEM dashboard
SIEM log
SMTP querying
SOAR
system logging protocol (syslog)
time synchronization
threat hunting
threat intelligence feed

user behavior analysis (UBA)	war driving	WORM device
vulnerability scan	war flying	white box test
vulnerability scanner	web application scanner	

SECURITY+ CERTIFICATION EXAM OBJECTIVES

The following Security+ Certification Exam Objectives are covered in this chapter.

+ 1.1: Reconnaissance
+ 1.7: Threat hunting
+ 1.7: Vulnerability scans
+ 1.7: Syslog/Security information and event management (SIEM)
+ 1.7: Security orchestration,

automation, response (SOAR)
+ 1.8: Penetration testing
+ 1.8: Passive and active reconnaissance
+ 1.8: Exercise types
+ 2.1: Baseline configuration

+ 4.3: Vulnerability scan output
+ 4.3: SIEM dashboards
+ 4.3: Log files
+ 4.3: syslog/rsyslog/syslog-ng
+ 4.3: journalctl
+ 4.3: nxlog

OVERVIEW

An organization's network can be vulnerable to an attack in a number of ways that may not be obvious or clear to security personnel. To prevent unsecure network operation, security evaluations should be performed to discover vulnerabilities present, including those on individual devices and the software installed on them.

This chapter discusses methods of evaluating the security of an organization's network. Topics include threat hunting; vulnerability scanning; common vulnerabilities and exposures; penetration testing, types, and techniques; reconnaissance; baselining; and assessing and managing log files.

SECURITY+ NOTE

The topics of attacks, threats, and vulnerabilities comprise nearly one-fourth of the CompTIA Security+ Exam. To complete this portion of the exam successfully, you must not only be able to identify an attack type but also assess and evaluate the security of a network prior to attack attempts. Be prepared to answer questions regarding vulnerability assessments and scans and the proper identification of assessment techniques, threat hunting, log management, and penetration testing.

Evaluating Security

The former director of the FBI, Robert Mueller once said, "There are two companies, those that have been hacked, and those that will be." This provocative statement is nearly a decade old but still rings true today, maybe even more so. Technology integration in business is pervasive, and its widespread use has made it a clear target for hackers. Organizations that fail to perform security assessments are leaving their networks and their companies at a high risk of compromise.

Awareness is the first stage in developing a culture of security within the organization. A **security assessment** is a periodic exercise that evaluates a company's security preparedness. The assessment looks at business practices, physical security measures, and associated technology incorporated throughout an enterprise network. The purpose of a security assessment is to keep networks, devices, and data safe by discovering vulnerabilities, threats, and offering recommendations to lessen the risk of future attacks.

A comprehensive IT security strategy incorporates technological solutions, policies, procedures, and a detailed security assessment of an organization. It is necessary to assess the security posture of an enterprise environment so that security solutions can be recommended and implemented. This evaluation is a structured and detailed approach to locate IT vulnerabilities. It looks at business practices, physical security measures, and associated technology incorporated throughout an enterprise network. Companies often consider this function a type of security audit, as its intent is to review security measures in place, locate possible threats against a business, and identify vulnerabilities and the potential for attacks and threats. The results from this analysis provide guidance and data for an organization to incorporate measures to protect against vulnerabilities and remediation strategies for recovering from attacks.

The types of assessments conducted by an organization vary based on the organization's mission and technology. Included are activities such as vulnerability scanning, which are tools that run on systems such as servers to identify known or suspected vulnerabilities. In addition, proactive measures can also be used to assess the security posture of an organization. It is necessary to locate and monitor current threat intelligence to identify current threats, actively search for threats on a network through threat-hunting measures, and conduct penetration tests, which are simulated attacks originating from trained individuals to actively test the company's cyber defenses.

Threat Hunting

1.7

Proactive techniques for security assessments must be applied in an enterprise environment, making threat hunting an essential element of an organization's cyber security program. **Threat hunting** is the practice of proactively searching for cyber threats and vulnerabilities not already detected or identified in a network.

1.7

Effective threat hunting requires *threat intelligence*, which is knowledge about threats, threat actors, and other potentially harmful actions to an enterprise environment that helps prevent cyberattacks. It is analyzed information used by a company to understand the threats that have, will, or are currently targeting an organization. **Intelligence fusion** is the combination of intelligence information from many sources to create a comprehensive threat profile. The profile provides security teams with comprehensive analysis and correlation of information to respond to potential imminent threats effectively. This heightened awareness enables teams to focus on known attack vectors and methods of attack to harden and monitor those systems. This improves efficiency and security by focusing on likely areas of vulnerabilities and threats.

Threat Intelligence Feeds

1.7

Threat intelligence feeds are real-time streams of data that provide information on potential cyber threats and risks. Time is of the essence when protecting the security of an organization. It is important to have security information and event management (SIEM) tools that can take the information and analyze in real time.

Feeds come from sources outside of the organization that provide information used to protect the network, such as blocking IP addresses associated with malicious activity or searching the network to see if those IP addresses were used within your network.

There are many threat intelligence feeds and some are open source. Examples include the FBI's InfraGard Portal, which provides information relevant to the 16 sectors of critical infrastructure, including organizations that protect critical assets such as power plants, financial institutions, and transportation systems. Another free feed is the Automated Indicator Sharing feed from the US Department of Homeland Security (DHS). This service facilitates exchange of cyber threat indicators from many organizations as a threat feed.

Advisories and Bulletins

✚ 1.7

Another source for obtaining cyber threat intelligence comes from *advisories and bulletins*. Governmental agencies, cyber companies, and vendors are examples of sources that provide current information about cyber threats and incidents.

One of the most informative advisory and bulletin systems is the National Cyber Awareness System from the Cybersecurity and Infrastructure Security Agency (CISA). From the web page, you can view current activity, such as critical security updates or weekly bulletins that provide a summary of current vulnerabilities. In addition, vendors often publish advisories and bulletins that identify threats to their products.

Maneuvers

✚ 1.7

Another method for obtaining cyber threat intelligence is to perform *cyber maneuvers*. This is a proactive approach to searching and navigating a network for potential anomalies or threats to the system. Instead of waiting for an alert from a security product, a security team can search for a specific threat and then maneuver through the network searching for evidence of the potential threat. In this method, the security team becomes cyber hunters by actively searching for threats.

Vulnerability Scan

A **vulnerability scan** is a security assessment that searches a computer or network for potential vulnerabilities or weak security configurations. A *weak security configuration* is a poorly designed or inadequate security structure. For a comprehensive security assessment, vulnerability scanning is completed in conjunction with penetration testing (pen testing). An *external scan* is one conducted outside an organization's firewall, and an *internal scan* is a scan conducted within the system.

There are two general categories of vulnerability scans.

✚ 1.7

- A **noncredentialed scan**, also called *nonauthenticated*, is a scan that does not require credentials to access the system. The scan is similar to an outsider's view.
- A **credentialed scan**, also called *authenticated*, requires credentials of an account registered to a device being scanned. By using a username and password registered to a computer, users have access to files and folders that a scan run outside the network would not have.

Vulnerability Scanners

A **vulnerability scanner** is software that automates the process of scanning computer systems for potential security weaknesses in software, configurations, and other settings. Vulnerability scanners are tools used to assess an organization's security posture and identify potential attack vectors.

- A *passive scanner* examines systems and monitors network activity. Since the scanner only monitors activities, it does not interfere with any client or network operations. Passively testing security controls can provide a great deal of information about vulnerabilities, including vulnerable software programs, unusual activities, or open ports.

- An *active scanner* simulates attacks and threats, and if the scanner's configuration options allow, it can respond to a potential threat in real time.

Most commercial vulnerability scanners provide options to select the level of *intrusiveness* desired in a scan. A scanner performs a non-intrusive or intrusive test.

- A **non-intrusive test** is one in which a system is scanned without causing harm to its target. This could involve searching for keys in the registry, open ports, missing software patches, and similar vulnerabilities. During this type of scan, the scanner reads and records the requested information.
- An **intrusive test** is one in which the scanner tries to exploit vulnerabilities. A script automates the attack to prove the target is vulnerable. Intrusive scanning could have a major impact on a system or network being scanned. For example, the scan may cause business functions to be disabled. Even worse, a target could be left vulnerable if the attack is successful.

Vulnerability Scanning Techniques

Vulnerability scanners are not limited to identifying vulnerabilities in operating systems; they also enable users to scan applications, web applications, and networks to identify potential problems.

- **Application scanning** is scanning software applications to identify weak configurations, out-of-date software patches, and other vulnerabilities. Some application scanners can also scan mobile applications running on iOS or Android platforms to identify vulnerabilities related to malware, personal e-mail and data leakage, weak encryption implementations, and other vulnerabilities specific to mobile platforms.
- **Web application scanners** are tools that scan web applications for web-based vulnerabilities, such as scripting attacks, dangerous files, out-of-date versions, and unsecure configurations.
- **Network vulnerability scanners** are vulnerability scanners that focus on potentially vulnerable network activities. Network vulnerability scanners identify preventive measures in an organization. Often, these scanners monitor firewalls, ports, and servers and conduct packet analysis. This type of scanning can identify unusual traffic by comparing current traffic with historical data and identifying open ports.
- A **configuration-compliance scanner** is a security configuration assessment that determines if a target's configuration settings comply with an organization's configuration guidelines. This type of scan is different from simply locating vulnerabilities on a system, such as outdated patches. Similar to a vulnerability scanner, configuration-compliance scanners help assess or affirm a company's security posture by identifying potential flaws with system hardening policies.

Scanner Output

A vulnerability scanner identifies weaknesses in a system. However, there can be false positives and false negatives that occur. **False positives** occur when a scanner registers a vulnerability when none is present. **False negatives** occur when a scanner is unable to find vulnerabilities when there really are vulnerabilities present.

Scan output identifies missing *internal* security controls, which could include a lack of up-to-date security patches and no installed firewall or antivirus software. *Security controls* are tools or processes used to reduce risk to assets by slowing, minimizing, or stopping a threat. Scanning a system with these tools can also identify

1.7

TECH TIP

When choosing a vulnerability scanner, consider the fact that for-purchase commercial products often provide deeper scans and better reporting systems than free or open-source scanners.

1.7

1.7, 4.3

common misconfigurations on computers that leave the systems vulnerable to hackers. *Misconfigurations* include settings such as open ports, default credentials and passwords, default directories, and even sensitive data, such as looking for patterns of Social Security numbers or keywords that could indicate confidential information.

Scanning systems for vulnerabilities and compliance not only allows for identification and remediation of vulnerabilities and potential threats, but also enables the ability to conduct a **configuration review**, which is the act of monitoring and assessing settings and policies set forth for a system. For example, if a network scan reveals suspect traffic coming from a website that does not have a business purpose, the site can be blocked using firewalls or other tools. If a high number of anomalies are present on a non-credentialed scan, the local policies may need review and adjustment to provide higher protections.

 1.7

As part of the vulnerability scanning process, scanners generate logs that record events, vulnerabilities, and other security incidents. Logs play an integral part of a comprehensive security assessment. A **log review** is an assessment and analysis of vulnerability scan logs. Through log review, administrators can obtain a list of vulnerable devices, dates and times of incidents, and data regarding baseline deviation and trends. The logs may also be necessary as part of a forensic analysis of security incidents. Effective log management and analysis can help identify long-term problems and potentially detect threats before they become major incidents.

1.7

Common Vulnerabilities and Exposure Resource

1.7

The **Common Vulnerabilities and Exposure (CVE)** is a list of known security threats identified by the US Department of Homeland Security. The CVE divides threats into two categories: vulnerabilities and exposures. This list was established when vendors used their own databases and naming conventions to identify security vulnerabilities. The CVE list provides a standardized format to identify known vulnerabilities. CVE is maintained by the MITRE Corporation. This corporation oversees the vendors, researchers, bug-bounty programs, and more that provide information about vulnerabilities. That information is collected and distributed through a free searchable list. The list is available through the MITRE website.

An entry in the CVE uses this type of format: CVE-2020-10001. The first four digits after *CVE* represent the year of identification, and the next set of numbers is a unique identification number. Within the entry will be a brief description of the security vulnerability and any references to provide additional resources and information.

Another tool called the Common Vulnerability Scoring System (CVSS) provides characteristics and severity of software vulnerability. The **Common Vulnerability Scoring System (CVSS)** is an open industry standard used to assess system vulnerabilities and their severity. Each vulnerability is assigned a numerical severity score, which enables security teams to prioritize their responses to these vulnerabilities.

1.7

Penetration Testing

1.8

Penetration testing, commonly called *pen testing*, is a process in which white-hat hackers are given permission to access a system in an attempt to penetrate defenses to locate vulnerabilities. Pen testing is a form of **ethical hacking**, which is an umbrella term that refers to all hacking methods performed and sanctioned by an organization to identify potential vulnerabilities or attack vectors within a system.

Penetration tests are recommended as they perform different tasks than a vulnerability scan. *Pen tests* exploit weaknesses in a system of an organization whereas a *vulnerability scan* assesses for potential vulnerabilities in a computer system. A penetration test uses skilled ethical hackers to test the security of a system and only for a specified time. A skilled *ethical hacker*, also referred to as a *certified tester*, uses skill and knowledge in an attempt to bypass a company's security features, break into a network, and obtain information to return to the organization conducting the test.

In Chapter 2, you learned about bug-bounty programs that organizations use to prevent zero-day attacks. A *bug-bounty program* is an initiative that offers rewards to those who identify flaws and vulnerabilities found in their program. Bug-bounty programs are not penetration tests; rather, they are continuous monitoring programs that ethical hackers use to find vulnerabilities. Many people could be searching for the bugs at the same time. When a bug is reported, it can be patched before being discovered and exploited by hackers.

 1.8

Rules of Engagement

Rules of engagement (RoE) is a document that specifies in detail the manner in which penetration testing will be conducted. The RoE consists of testing details including scope of testing and type of testing.

Scope

The *scope* of a project is the description of the pen test, its complexity, size, and other details needed to perform a complete and accurate job. Without a defined scope, it is difficult to determine specific tasks to be performed as well as price for the services provided by the pen tester. In addition, without a scope, the testers may do too much or too little and the outcome not be as planned.

Types of Pen Tests

After scope is defined, it is necessary to identify the type of test to be performed, which determines specific information that the company will provide to the tester. There are three general types of penetration tests.

- *Black box:* A **black box test** is a penetration test in which the tester has no knowledge of the system. The organization does not provide any information.
- *Gray box:* A **gray box test** is a penetration test in which the tester has some knowledge of the system. The organization provides specific and limited amounts of information.
- *White box:* A **white box test** is a penetration test for which the tester is given complete information and full knowledge of the system.

All three types of tests have merit. Having advanced knowledge of a system allows a tester to focus on the system and its configurations. On the other hand, if a tester has no knowledge of a system, the tester can approach the system just as a potential hacker may. This approach can reveal information that may lead to an actual hack.

Exercise Types

Penetration exercises are tests that examine the security defenses of an organization. Penetration exercise types are specific tests that simulate hacking attempts in targeted areas such as wireless, network intrusion, social engineering attacks, or on applications. These exercises locate weaknesses and vulnerabilities in an organization's security configurations and evaluate the effectiveness of responses. However, some penetration exercises do more than conduct offensive security testing and may test the security responses or defenders.

1.8

1.8

Rather than work alone, penetration testers often work in teams. The four main types of teams include red, blue, white, and purple teams.

- *Red teams* are *offensive* security professionals. They are the individuals who attempt to break into the systems. Red team members will simulate attacks against the network.
- *Blue teams* are the *defensive* security professionals. The blue teams respond to network threats and are responsible for the security and defenses of the network.
- *White teams* set the rules of engagement since they oversee the exercises designed to test the strength and defense of the business. They do not conduct any testing or provide defensive measures.
- *Purple teams* represent the blending of red and blue teams and enhance information sharing between the teams to maximize each team's respective and combined effectiveness. However, purple teams are not needed if effective communication happens organically between red and blue teams.

Testing Authorization

Pen tests are usually conducted by an outside firm rather than internal personnel. Since outside resources are used, an organization should sign a penetration testing authorization with the contractor. In addition, the contractor should sign a nondisclosure agreement.

Penetration Testing Authorization

Penetration testing authorization is permission given by a company or organization to another party to access or hack a system in an effort to determine how susceptible the system is to unauthorized access or penetration. There are a number of reasons for seeking authorization before conducting an assessment including the following:

- Authorization provides legal permission to conduct the assessment.
- Authorization gives approval to conduct an assessment and limits the legal responsibilities of the tester should an outage or disruption in connectivity occur.

In addition to pen testing and vulnerability testing authorization, written permission may be required for third-party vendors, such as Microsoft. The tester is responsible for obtaining and following the policies of each third-party vendor involved. For example, if assets are stored on a cloud, the tester must obtain permission from the cloud vendor, such as Microsoft, Amazon, or Rackspace.

Nondisclosure Agreement (NDA)

An organization may also consider asking a pen tester to sign a nondisclosure agreement. A *nondisclosure agreement (NDA)* is a legal contract between two parties that restricts the signing party from distributing or sharing confidential information to anyone outside of the agreement. By requesting an NDA, an organization is assured that information uncovered during the test will not be distributed to anyone outside of the company.

1.1, 1.8

Reconnaissance

Gathering information about an organization or network can provide clues to a tester for gaining entry into a building or system. In black box and gray box testing, a penetration tester collects as much information as possible about an organization and its network. Intelligence gathering is *reconnaissance* that can be either passive or active. *Reconnaissance* is discovering and gathering information.

1.8

Passive Reconnaissance

Passive reconnaissance is the discovery and gathering of data without the target being aware it is happening. This type of reconnaissance is accomplished by a tester conducting research or using tools to gather information. Passive reconnaissance includes the following:

- **War driving** is the act of moving around, usually in a vehicle, and searching for wireless networks. This includes mapping the location and security settings of an organization.
- **War flying** is the act of detecting wireless networks using airplanes or drones/unmanned aerial vehicles to search for open access points. Due to the expense of airplanes, drones are more probable. Drones can also carry devices that can detect wireless networks.
- *Social engineering* is the use of social tools and techniques to obtain information. Job-posting websites, such as CareerBuilder or Indeed, are good examples as they often reveal information about the organization posting an advertisement.
- *Open-source intelligence (OSINT)* is publicly available information freely obtained from multiple sources.
- **Footprinting**, or *pre-attack technique*, is gathering information about a system. This is typically the first step a hacker generally takes in an attack.

1.8

Active Reconnaissance

Active reconnaissance is the active discovery and gathering of data by using tools to interact with a system. This type of activity may be as simple as trying a door to see if it is unlocked or using tools to look for information.

Active reconnaissance includes port scanning, banner grabbing, and SMTP querying, all of which are likely noticed by a company's defenses.

- **Port scanning** is a method that determines the status of communication ports on a system. Ports are either open, which indicates a port is able to listen and receive information, or closed, meaning the port cannot accept any communication through that channel. A **port scanner** is an application designed to probe a server or host for open ports. Scanning the system will identify all communication entry points on a system. Testers can identify unnecessary ports and running services and use this information to allow for potential access and exploitation.
- **Banner grabbing** is the act of requesting information about computer systems or services on a remote system. The banner is a message transmitted from a system to the requesting device. The banner could contain system information about services and version. This information can be used to identify server functionality and known vulnerabilities that may exist in those software programs.

- **SMTP querying** is the act of using the Simple Mail Transfer Protocol (SMTP) system to obtain e-mail account information. This operation will directly query an e-mail server to locate valid e-mail addresses. E-mail servers run the SMTP protocol and can be located using DNS lookup functionality. These servers maintain a database of every e-mail address in its organization. Using the SMTP command or other utilities can provide these addresses if not blocked by security configurations.

Penetration Techniques

There are multiple techniques used to conduct a penetration test. These techniques test the controls that are supposed to prevent access to the network, as well as movement and gaining higher privileges within the network.

Initial Exploitation

After research is complete, a pen tester moves on to the initial exploitation stage of the test. An **initial exploitation** is the act of a pen tester using the information gathered during reconnaissance in an attempt to gain entry to a network. At this stage, the tester will also attempt to exploit any vulnerabilities found.

Pivot

 1.8

When a network is breached, the tester will conduct a pivot. A **pivot** is a point of a penetration test in which the tester refocuses attention from the initial point of entry to begin looking for targets and other resources on a network. Pivoting allows a tester, and potentially a hacker, to use a system, collect more information, and access other areas of a computer or network.

Lateral Movement

1.8

Another pen testing technique used is lateral movement. **Lateral movement** is moving from one compromised host to another host within the network. When the initial access of the network has been gained, the tester maintains ongoing access to the network by moving through compromised areas using tools to gain higher-level privileges.

Persistence

1.8

Persistence is the act of a pen tester attempting to maintain a connection after a successful exploit. One way to do this is to place tools on key devices in the network so data can still be obtained. Examples include installing *keyloggers*, which are devices or software that track a user's keystrokes, and *rootkits*, which are viruses that infect computers before their operating systems load. They may also create fake user accounts to establish backdoors and change passwords.

Escalation of Privilege

 1.8

An **escalation of privilege** is a test that attempts to move from a normal user to achieve root or admin privileges while accessing a system. If successful, the tester takes control of the system. In addition to creating higher-level administrative backdoors, areas can be accessed where the tester can remove log files, change metadata, and make other changes to hide hacking actions.

1.8

Penetration Testing Cleanup

At the conclusion of the penetration testing, it is important to perform a cleanup of the environment. During the test, the team may have made changes, installed software and tools, and created accounts. The cleanup includes removing executable scripts, temporary files, backdoors, or rootkits used during the test. If user accounts were created during the test, they should also be removed. Reconfigured devices or software must be reset to their original state.

Baselines and Performance

Conducting security evaluations requires a point of reference for which to compare findings. A **baseline** is a starting point from which data comparisons are made. Establishing and reviewing baselines related to how a system is used is referred to as *usage auditing*.

For example, when evaluating security of a computer system or network, baselines are set that show the network's data rate, traffic statistics, or CPU speed under normal usage. The information is the baseline to compare the same type of data recorded during sluggish performance or an outage to help determine which operations are essential to the system. If a system seems sluggish and slow in responding to requests, the current amount of network traffic or CPU speed is compared with the baseline. A *baseline deviation* is a change or difference in data when compared to an original baseline. A large deviation may indicate a problem, such as a user streaming media or downloading large volumes of information.

Companies victimized by advanced persistent threats often do not recognize symptoms of an attack. Symptoms of persistent threats typically include large, unexpected flows of data and collection of large amounts of data before it is moved off-site. If a company establishes a baseline and sees unusual patterns that deviate from the normal patterns, it may help identify and ward off a larger security attack.

 2.1

Establishing Baselines

Establishing baselines provides insight into varying levels of network usage under normal circumstances. Microsoft Windows has built-in tools that can assist with creating baselines and monitoring systems, such as Resource Monitor and Performance Monitor, as shown in Figure 3-1. A Resource Monitor is a comprehensive utility that displays real-time data on various hardware elements. A Performance Monitor tracks specific data over a wide range of components, such as

- network traffic;
- memory usage;
- CPU usage; and
- disk space.

To establish a baseline, the Performance Monitor is used when a system is known to be in normal operating condition. Then, data can be recorded for elements you wish to track. Be sure to save the file in a secure location for future reference.

By knowing the baseline data, you could view, for example, if there is an unexpected spike in disk usage. This may indicate a large number of downloads or a high number of files being saved or deleted. Someone downloading a large quantity of files could point to a hacked system or an insider threat. High network traffic can also indicate malware or the presence of a remote user accessing the system.

Performance data is used to monitor the operating condition of hardware. Spikes in disk usage can indicate a failing hard drive, which would result in the loss of critical business data. If the CPU or memory usage is increasing over time or is

TECH TIP ⚙️

Consider establishing baselines that could indicate other potential vulnerabilities such as physical disk activity. If a drive containing sensitive or confidential information shows an unusual spike in activity, it could be indicative of an excessive number of files being copied or accessed. Additionally, in Windows, the Performance Monitor can be configured to monitor read, write, and idle time on a disk, which can further indicate unusual activity.

Figure 3-1 In Microsoft Windows, the Resource Monitor and Performance Monitor can be used to establish baselines and check usage of system resources. The Resource Monitor (A) is more detailed overall. The Performance Monitor (B) allows for more specificity regarding which counters to track.

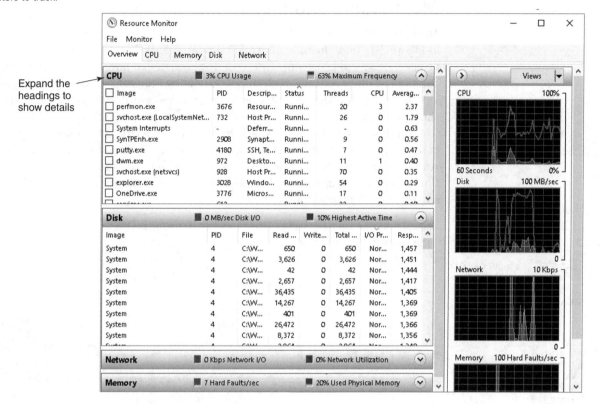

A

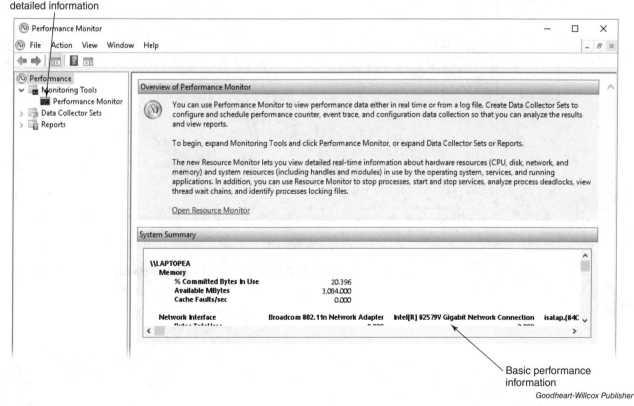

B

consistently high, the system may not be meeting performance goals and an upgrade in processor or RAM may be needed.

Monitoring Performance

The default view of the Performance Monitor displays a few key counters, as shown in Figure 3-1. These include information related to the memory, network interface, physical disk, and processor (CPU). To display detailed information and to change counters or other settings, click the **Performance Monitor** branch in the tree in the left-side pane. The view changes to display processor utilization in a line graph, as shown in Figure 3-2.

Another way to monitor data is to use data collector sets. A *data collector set* gathers information and saves it as a report so the information can then be further studied. Data collectors are created as if you were viewing data in real time. In addition, alerts can be created with a data collector set to inform instantly if there is a spike in a performance indicator.

Figure 3-2 The Performance Monitor can be used to display usage data over time.

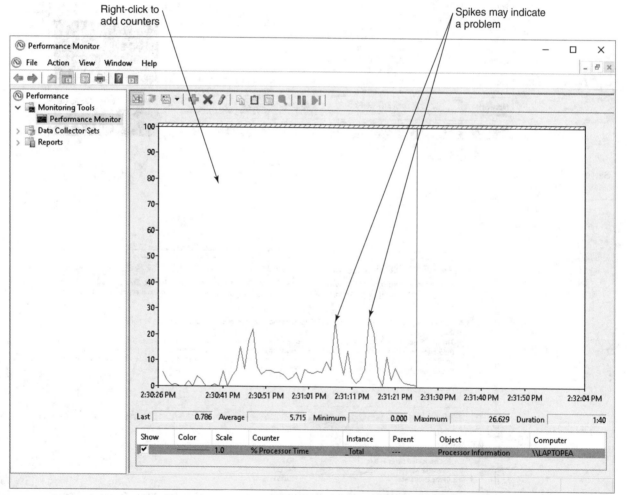

Log Files

4.3

A **log file**, also called *event log*, is a record of events that occur during a server or computer operation. A *log* is accumulated data about a system and its services, time and dates of user actions, and other activities that affect the security of an organization.

An event can indicate informational announcements and help troubleshoot serious or critical errors and event anomalies. Event logs are instrumental in troubleshooting and investigating possible security incidents. They are also a key aspect of forensic investigations and used for documentation or evidence.

There are multiple types of logs used for security purposes, including the following:

- *System logs* record events generated from the operating system components. For example, if a server is restarted, the event would be recorded in the system log.
- *Network logs* are generated by specific network services or devices, such as NAT, routers, firewalls, VPNs.
- *Application logs* record events are triggered by applications, such as an update to Windows Defender.
- *Security logs* are used to track events related to auditing established configurations. For example, this log can audit failed attempts of logging in as a specific user.
- *Web logs* are generated by web servers and contain information regarding each website visited by a user.
- *PowerShell logs* allow administrators to view which PowerShell providers are accessed. **PowerShell** is a powerful command-line interface shell integrated in Windows.NET technologies. In some cases, the PowerShell programs used are also logged.
- *DNS logs* are created and stored on servers that provide DNS services. These logs record information sent and received by a DNS server.
- *Authentication logs* allow administrators to view successful and failed logins and authentication methods.
- *Dump files* are not traditional logs in that they record data about a service or application, but are usually generated when a system crashes, and the contents of memory are compiled, or dumped, into files.
- *Voice over IP (VoIP) logs* are used to store data related to VoIP sessions, such as logs of each call, whether it was answered or sent to voice mail, date, and duration of the call. *Call manager logs* provide detailed call information such as diagnostics and the amount of data sent and received. *Call managers* are solutions for managing not only IP-based phones and calls, but also other applications including videos and messaging.
- *Session initiation protocol (SIP) logs* contain information about the SIP process, which manages voice-based data.

Security professionals use logs to monitor events that could indicate a potential security breach. Event logs are coded in Windows. Figure 3-3 shows event codes that may indicate a security incident.

Figure 3-3 In Windows, events are coded. Some codes may indicate a security issue.

Event Code	Description	Potential Security Concern
1102	Deletion of the security log	This could be a normal administrative task, but it could mean someone tried to cover his or her tracks by deleting the contents of this log.
4663	An attempt to access an object	If a large number of files are being deleted, this event will be recorded. This may indicate someone is trying to remove critical company information.
4724	Password reset (a privileged user changed this user's password)	While this is a normal function of networking, it could be tracked for administrative accounts or service accounts.
4704, 4717	Change to user's rights or permissions assignments	This could indicate a hacker has given an account more rights than it should have.
4740	User account locked out	This is normal; users do forget their passwords. However, frequent occurrences of this event, or it occurring on service, administrative, or manager accounts, should be investigated.

Goodheart-Willcox Publisher

1.7, 4.3

Syslog

System logging protocol (syslog) is the standard event logging protocol used to send system and event log information to a specific server, called the *syslog server*. Syslog enables the aggregation of multiple logs into one central log for monitoring and review.

Syslog process is supported natively by both Linux and Unix platforms, but third-party tools must be used to collect Windows Event Viewer log information. A variation of syslog called **rsyslog** is an open-source software utility used with Unix and Linux systems to forward messages. *Syslog-ng* is a portable version of rsyslog that is available on additional operating systems platforms.

Syslog solutions offer differing review reports options and functionality. A *review report* is a document containing findings from a review of logs or data. Generally, data in a review report is analyzed by auditing event logs by severity or specific action. Syslog systems provide event correlation that tracks attack patterns that occur across the network. It also serves as a source of data to support an investigation.

4.3

Similar to syslog and rsyslog, **NXlog** is a multiplatform log management tool that includes support for Android and Windows platforms. NXlog is capable of collecting event logs from multiple servers and can support or convert between formats. It is also capable of processing logs offline.

In many modern Linux distributions, the systemd init software suite is used to collect and manage system, boot, and kernel logs. This logging system includes a journal component that stores log data in binary format. Journals are retrieved using a tool called journalctl, which queries and displays system journal contents.

4.3

Syslog event collection is to ensure event logs around the network can be in one location. At that point, analysis of the correlated data must occur to identify potential threats, incidents, or possible vulnerabilities. Syslog servers may provide tools to query and filter information, but the syslog server does not analyze the information. Depending on the size of your network and the event logs that are collected, the amount of data can become overwhelming. Another solution is to use an SIEM system, which can provide the event analysis on correlated event data.

Security Information and Event Management (SIEM)

4.3

In a large network that includes multiple servers and systems, it can be extremely difficult to collect event log data, analyze it appropriately, and act on urgent matters quickly. Even with event forwarding, the amount of data collected could make it difficult to locate critical information. To help with these tasks, a security information and event management (SIEM) system can be used. A **security information and event management (SIEM) system** is a software product that supports organizational security by real-time collecting and compiling log data generated in a network and producing analyzed results and reports.

There are many SIEM software products available; some are open-source, and others may have limitations on gathering data based on the host operating system. Some of the implementations of SIEM software programs can become quite costly. For this reason, SIEM systems are not common on smaller networks. However, many security companies offset cost by managing the SIEM process remotely. Some popular SIEM programs include SolarWinds, AlienVault, Splunk Enterprise Security, and LogRhythm NetGen SIEM.

An SIEM system is a combination of two separate security components: Security Information Management (SIM) and Security Event Management (SEM). SIM systems handle the collection of log files stored centrally for later analysis of the data. SEM products identify, gather, and monitor systems in real-time. SIEM systems combine the functionality of each component to take real-time and historical data from network devices and apply analytical rules to identify patterns, threats, and suspicious activity. Together, the two components create the blended SIEM product:

- *Security Information Management (SIM)* is the practice of automating the collection of event-log data from computer logs and other security devices including firewalls, intrusion detection systems, proxy servers, and antivirus software. The data is then *normalized*, which is the process of breaking up the fields in raw data, placing them into a standardized format, and combining them into views that are relevant to security administrators.

- *Security Event Management (SEM)* automates log collection and performs real-time analysis on data including event correlation to establish relationships between events. By using SEM, threats can be identified and alerts provided in a timely manner.

An SIEM system typically provides the following features:

1.7

- *Log aggregation.* **Log aggregation** is the automated gathering of log and event data from hosts and network devices throughout the network. This is an important step, as it provides a complete picture of the overall health status of the network.

- *Log Collection.* A **log collector** is a service that assembles logs from various event sources through a network environment. Log collectors are often configured on endpoint devices, along with syslog services, to send resulting data to syslog servers.

- *Data input.* **Data input** is the methods used in syslog to collect and record data within logs. One method of data input is to identify each data source such as files, directories, or network inputs. In addition, data inputs can be used to forward TCP or UDP data to a syslog server.

- *Packet capture.* **Packet capture** is the act of intercepting a data packet as it crosses a specific network point. Packet capture provides another source of data collection.
- *SIEM correlation.* **SIEM correlation** is an SIEM feature that searches through aggregated data and reports common characteristics. This allows the software and system administrators to search for patterns, similarities, attempted or actual breaches, potential failures, or other incidents.
- *Automated alerts.* Administrators often create **automated alerts and triggers**, which are rules that generate and inform administrators about specific events or incidents to streamline the process of reviewing data. Alerts are triggered automatically if the conditions for the rule are met.
- *Event deduplication.* **Event deduplication** is a process that merges identical events into a single event. There can be a significant number of duplicate events in an event log, and processing duplicate information can result in extensive overhead and latency. Allowing an SIEM product to perform deduplication saves a significant amount of time and overhead.
- *Time synchronization.* **Time synchronization** is a process that ensures all devices agree on the correct time. This is a critical configuration element, especially when analyzing log data and potential incidents or data breaches. The data analyzed by SIEM systems relies on accurate time reporting throughout the network and devices. Therefore, it is important that the devices are coordinated through time synchronization.
- *User behavior analysis (UBA).* **User behavior analysis (UBA)** is a security assessment that monitors user behavior and compares it to established baseline information. For example, UBA software identifies patterns of unusual behavior, such as applications launched, Internet or network activity, and downloads, by comparing data to existing baselines and alerting administrators of anomalies. In addition to baselines, user activity can be compared with data sourced from packet collection and event logs.
- *Sentiment analysis.* **Sentiment analysis** is a security feature that assesses social attitudes and opinions to make predictions about likely outcomes. A major source of informing sentiment analysis comes from logged data of online social networks, e-mail, and instant messages. When used correctly, sentiment analysis can help identify intentions or motivations and provide warning of forthcoming cyberattacks.
- *SIEM logs.* **SIEM logs** are records of events that are reviewed or analyzed. In addition, the logs can be used as evidence to prove compliance to regulations. Logs create critical output and must be protected from changes whether intentional, accidental, or malicious. SIEM software can save the logs to a write-once-read-many (WORM) device. A **WORM device** is a storage device that allows data to be saved but not changed. These devices are either optical discs or ROM chips.

✦ 4.3

SIEM systems typically have a presentation tool that displays for easy analyzation. An **SIEM dashboard** is a tool that summarizes data and transforms it into useful information to provide simple security monitoring. SIEM products allow for flexibility in designing an effective dashboard. Often, SIEM dashboards display

- *alerts* or anomalies from critical hardware;
- notifications and data from *sensors* that have been deployed on a system; and
- options for focusing on data sensitivity activities.

Using a dashboard is helpful to highlight trends in activities, such as an uptick in web traffic, or unusual traffic patterns. Trends can be evaluated against current business practices or investigated as potential threats.

SIEM is a comprehensive solution that incorporates log management, analysis, alerts, and reporting, but a company may want to configure a log management system that is not as comprehensive or full-featured as SIEM. This option can be fulfilled by using a syslog mechanism for log management.

SOAR

 1.7

SOAR, which stands for *Security Orchestration, Automation, and Response*, is a security solution that uses an array of software tools and solutions that allows for a collection of data from multiple sources and generates an automatic response. Using SOAR solutions, security operations are executed automatically through collection of data from the broadest of resources without human intervention. SOAR is similar to SIEM as it collects information. However, SOAR takes information from multiple sources and centralizes the results.

SOAR is a technique that enables an organization to simplify security operations in three key areas: threat and vulnerability management, incident response, and security operations automation. In a business not using SOAR techniques, security analysts must make decisions based on information available and may not be able to respond as quickly as needed. In addition, companies often use a multitude of products to collect information and then must manually aggregate the data to get a comprehensive overview of the situation. The amount of data can be quite large, and it is possible that relevant information is overlooked.

Orchestration

Orchestration is the integration of different technologies, including security and non-security tools to work together. SOAR functionality makes efficient use of the integration of existing security tools and equipment to investigate and respond to vulnerabilities. For example, if a suspicious IP address is identified during a scan of a log, a response could include changes in a network firewall.

Automation

Security automation is the automatic handling and processing of security-related tasks to identify vulnerabilities without human intervention. Security teams initially define the steps and actions using SOAR tools. Automation performs these tasks, such as querying logs, scanning e-mails, or managing user privileges. Automation replaces the need for human intervention.

Incident Management

The final piece of SOAR is improved incident response functionality. The response is based on intelligent decision making and the automated process, which increases security of the hosts and network. This allows for immediate triage of a vulnerability before it becomes an actual threat. Consider a scenario in which a user logon account exceeds the maximum attempts of failed logons. SOAR can generate a response to the user and confirm if the user made the error. If it is true, a password reset can be initiated. However, if the user did not perform these attempts, SOAR can quickly disable the account and begin an investigative response such as identifying the IP and MAC addresses of the attempts.

Log Management

Log management is the process of generating, transmitting, analyzing, archiving, and disposing of log data. *Log management software (LMS)* enables aggregation of files from endpoint devices so the security posture of an organization can be monitored to support investigation of network events. Conversely, SIEM aggregates files across the infrastructure rather than just endpoint devices.

Every Windows desktop and server maintains various log files created by virtually every software application and system resource. Therefore, evaluating and managing logs can be challenging and include the following factors.

- The quantity of logs can be overwhelming since devices can have multiple logs, and by default, logs are located throughout the network.
- Resources to collect and analyze the logs can be time-consuming and can be costly to store vast amounts of data.
- To be effective, logs should be analyzed in real-time so immediate threats can be mitigated. Depending on the number of logs and data, the time needed for real-time analysis could be affected.
- Correlation of data from logs can provide a big picture overview of network security. Without this correlation of information, security administrators do not have a complete picture of the current security posture.

Log analysis is the process of setting policies regarding the collection, review, and analysis of log data. Log analysis can occur at different stages of a data life cycle. Real-time log reviews should focus on identification of vulnerabilities and threats to initiate immediate remediation. Based on regulatory and internal compliance requirements, logs are analyzed during a routine audit of operations or to satisfy compliance requirements. Logs may also provide forensic insights following a security incident.

Many organizations use predictive analysis as they fight cybersecurity. **Predictive analysis** is the examination of data, statistical modeling, and machine learning techniques to quantify the likelihood of a future cyber threat. Predictive analysis technology combines machine- and self-learning analytics with detection techniques to monitor network activity, report on real-time data, and use historical data to predict a breach before it happens. Predictive analysis monitors real-time network activity and sends an alarm before an attack begins.

As a comparatively new method of cyber defense, predictive analysis does not focus on defending an attack or establishing general preventative measures. Instead, it enables a company to focus on establishing cyber defenses before damage can be inflicted.

Viewing Event Logs

Event log data is reviewed in Windows operating systems using Event Viewer. *Event Viewer* is a versatile program that allows administrators to view, save, and back up logs. It also allows for the creation of alerts that can notify administrators of potential concerns as a problem occurs, such as a cleared log.

When Event Viewer is first opened, the main screen provides a dashboard for quick analysis. Multiple logs from different machines can be forwarded to one combined log. Windows event logs are categorized by type, as shown in Figure 3-4. They include the following:

- critical
- error
- warning
- information
- audit success
- audit failure

With Event Viewer, other hosts can be set up to forward entire logs or specific events to a single source log, and you can back up your log data. A forwarded event log can be set up on a single machine to allow the tracking of events of logs from other systems, as shown in Figure 3-5. To gather data, a subscription to events is created on a remote computer. Data from all events is gathered, or as an alternative, data can be customized and limited to specific events such as errors or warnings.

Logs in Linux distributions are stored in plaintext and found in the /var/log directory and subdirectories. Linux maintains logs on many features, including system, services, events, and applications. Logs can be read from the command line or in a text editor. Other log management tools can be used to collect, correlate, and view log data.

Type	Meaning
⊗ Critical	A serious error. It indicates something is broken. An example of when this entry may appear is if the system is powered off without a clean shutdown.
❗ Error	Indicates a significant problem that could include a loss of functionality or data. For example, if a service failed to start as instructed, this entry may be created.
⚠ Warning	Indicates a potential problem or possible future problem. For example, a warning can be logged if the system is low on disk space.
ⓘ Information	Describes a successful operation of an application, driver, or service. For example, an event will be recorded for downloading and installing a Windows update.
🔑 Audit Success	An audited security access that was successful. A common example is a user's successful attempt at logging in.
🔒 Audit Failure	An audited security event that fails. For example, an unsuccessful logon attempt is recorded as a failure.

Figure 3-4 Event codes in Windows are classified by type that indicates their potential severity.

Goodheart-Willcox Publisher

Figure 3-5 Logs can be forwarded from individual machines into a single location on an administrator's machine.

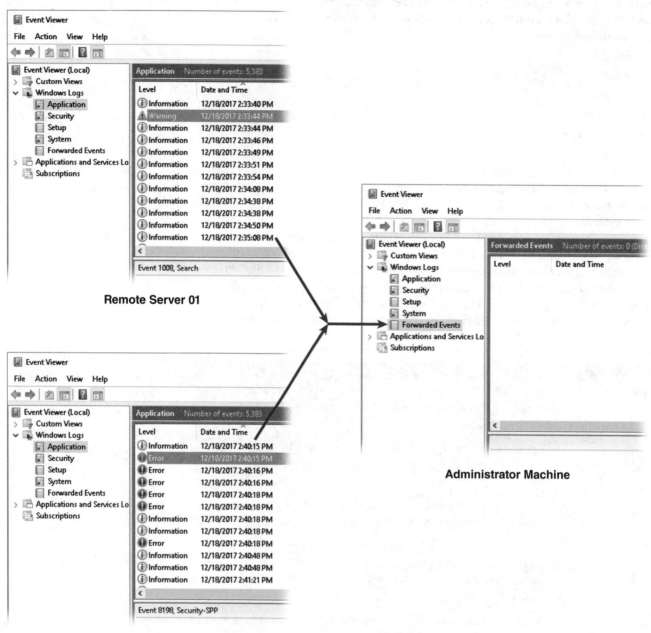

Remote Server 01

Remote Server 02

Administrator Machine

Goodheart-Willcox Publisher

SUMMARY

Evaluating Security

- A security assessment is a periodic exercise that evaluates a company's security preparedness. Its purpose is to keep networks, devices, and data safe by discovering vulnerabilities and threats and offering recommendations to lessen the risk for future attacks.

- A comprehensive IT security strategy incorporates technological solutions, policies, procedures, and a detailed security assessment of an organization. It is necessary to assess the security posture of an enterprise environment so that security solutions can be recommended and implemented. This evaluation is a structured and detailed approach to locate IT vulnerabilities.

- The types of assessments conducted in an organization vary based on the organization's mission and technology and can cover a wide spectrum. Regardless of the type of assessment used, it is necessary for an organization to locate and monitor current threat intelligence to identify any current and potential future attacks.

Threat Hunting

- Threat hunting is the practice of proactively searching for cyber threats and vulnerabilities not already detected or identified in a network.

- Effective threat hunting requires threat intelligence. The intelligence is analyzed information used by a company to understand the threats that have, will, or are currently targeting an organization.

- Intelligence infusion is the combination of intelligence information from many sources to create a comprehensive threat profile. The profile provides security teams with comprehensive analysis and correlation of information to effectively respond to potential imminent threats.

Vulnerability Scan

- A vulnerability scan is a security assessment that searches a computer or network for potential vulnerabilities or weak security configurations. For a comprehensive security assessment, vulnerability scanning is completed in conjunction with penetration testing.

- Two general categories of vulnerability scans include noncredentialed scan and credentialed scan.

- A vulnerability scanner is software that automates the process of scanning computer systems for potential security weaknesses in software, configurations, and other settings. A scanner can also enable users to scan applications, web applications, and networks to identify potential problems.

- Scan output identifies missing internal security controls, which could include a lack of up-to-date security patches and no installed firewall or antivirus software. Scanning a system can also identify common misconfigurations on computers that leave the systems vulnerable to hackers.

Penetration Testing

- Penetration testing is a process in which white-hat hackers are given permission to access a system in an attempt to penetrate defenses to locate vulnerabilities. It is a form of ethical hacking.
- Pen testing is recommended because a pen exploits weaknesses in a system of an organization. It uses skilled ethical hackers to test the security of a system for a specified time.
- Three key items that are important in penetration testing are establishing the rules of engagement (RoE), identifying the exercise types, and giving testing authorization an outside source.

Reconnaissance

- Reconnaissance is information gathered. It can be either passive or active.
- Passive reconnaissance is the gathering of data and information without the target being aware this is happening. This is accomplished by a tester conducting research or using tools to gather information. Methods include war driving, war flying, social engineering, OSINT, and footprinting.
- Active reconnaissance is the active discovery and gathering of data by using tools to interact with a system. Methods include port scanning, banner grabbing, and SMTP querying, all of which are likely noticed by a company's defenses.

Penetration Techniques

- Penetration techniques test the controls that are supposed to prevent access to the network, as well as movement and gaining higher privileges within the network.
- Penetration techniques include initial exploration, pivot, lateral movement, persistence, and escalation of privilege.

Penetration Testing Cleanup

- At the conclusion of the penetration testing, it is important to perform a cleanup of the environment.
- The cleanup includes removing executable scripts, temporary files, backdoors, or rootkits used during the test. If user accounts were created during the test, they should also be removed. Reconfigured devices or software must be reset to their original state.

Baselines and Performance

- A baseline is a starting point from which data comparisons are made. Establishing and reviewing baselines related to how a system is used is referred to as usage auditing.
- Establishing baselines are important because they provide insight into varying levels of network usage under normal circumstances. The Performance Monitor is used to establish and monitor a baseline.
- Another way to monitor data is to use data collector sets. A data collector set gathers information and saves it as a report so the information can then be further studied.

Log Files

- A log file is a record of events that occur during a server or computer operation. A log is accumulated data about a system and its services, time and dates of user actions, and other activities that affect the security of an organization.
- Event logs are instrumental in troubleshooting and investigating possible security incidents. They are also a key aspect of forensic investigations and used for documentation or evidence.
- Types of log files include system logs, network logs, application logs, security logs, web logs, PowerShell logs, DNS logs, authentication logs, dump files, VoIP logs, and SIP logs.

Syslog

- System logging protocol (syslog) is the standard event logging protocol used to send system and event log information to a specific server, called the syslog server. It enables the aggregation of multiple logs into one central log for monitoring and review.
- Syslog solutions offer differing review reports options and functionality. Syslog systems provide event correlation that tracks attack patterns that occur across the network. It also serves as a source of data to support an investigation.
- Two variations of syslog include rsyslog and syslog-ng. Another variation is Nxlog, which is a multiplatform log management tool that includes support for Android and Windows platforms.

Security Information and Event Management (SIEM)

- A security information and event management (SIEM) system is a software product that supports organizational security by real-time collecting and compiling log data generated in a network and producing analyzed results and reports.
- An SIEM system is a combination of two separate security components: Security Information Management (SIM) and Security Event Management (SEM).
- An SIEM system provides several features including log aggregation, log collection, data input, packet capture, SIEM correlation, automated alerts, event duplication, time synchronization, user behavior analysis, sentiment analysis, and SIEM logs.
- For easy analyzation of the information, an SIEM system uses the SIEM dashboard, which is a tool that summarizes data and transforms it into useful information to provide simple security monitoring.

SOAR

- SOAR, or Security Orchestration, Automation, and Response, is a security solution that uses an array of software tools and solutions that allows for a collection of data from multiple sources and generates an automatic response.
- Using SOAR solutions, security operations are executed automatically through collection of data from the broadest of resources without human intervention. It takes information from multiple sources and centralizes the results.
- SOAR enables an organization to simplify security operations in three key areas: threat and vulnerability management, incident response, and security operations automation.

Log Management

- Log management is the process of generating, transmitting, analyzing, archiving, and disposing of log data.
- Log management software (LMS) enables aggregation of files from endpoint devices so the security posture of an organization can be monitored to support investigation of network events.
- Log analysis is the process of setting policies regarding the collection, review, and analysis of log data. Log analysis can occur at different stages of a data life cycle. Reviewing logs in real-time should focus on identification of vulnerabilities and threats to initiate immediate remediation.

Viewing Event Logs

- Event log data can be reviewed in Window using Event Viewer, which is a versatile program that allows administrators to view, save, and back up log files.
- When Event Viewer is first opened, the main screen provides a dashboard for quick analysis. Multiple logs from different machines can be forwarded to one combined log.
- With Event Viewer, other hosts can be set up to forward entire logs or specific events to a single source log. Organization can also back up log data.

REVIEW QUESTIONS

1. Summarize the reasons to perform a security evaluation.
2. Discuss threat hunting.
3. List three sources for obtaining cyber threat intelligence.
4. Explain the use of a vulnerability scan as a component of a security assessment.
5. Identify and explain four types of vulnerability scanning techniques.
6. Summarize penetration testing.
7. State the difference between the three types of pen tests.
8. Which team for penetration testing is known as the defensive security professionals?
9. State the difference between passive and active reconnaissance.
10. Briefly explain three types of penetration techniques.
11. Summarize penetration testing cleanup.
12. Discuss the importance of system baselines and performance monitoring.
13. List four components a Performance Monitor tracks.
14. Identify and explain five types of log files.
15. Summarize syslog.
16. Identify and explain four of the features of a security information and event management (SIEM) system.
17. What two components create the blended SIEM product?
18. Summarize SOAR.
19. Discuss log management.
20. Explain viewing of event logs.

SAMPLE SECURITY+ EXAM QUESTIONS

1. Trevor is on a security team hired to conduct a pen test for a company. Which of the following will he need to understand the depth and type of testing required?

    A. White box testing

    B. Threat intelligence

    C. RoE

    D. NDA

2. Amy is on a red team conducting reconnaissance. Which of the following is most likely to be detected by a blue team?

    A. War driving

    B. Banner grabbing

    C. Footprinting

    D. Collecting personal information of managers from social media platforms

3. What security benefit does performance monitoring offer administrators?

    A. The CPU is fast enough to keep up with requests.

    B. The server's hard disk can be monitored before it runs out of space.

    C. It can show an unusual amount of traffic is being recorded on the network adapters.

    D. It maintains the status of antivirus and vulnerability software.

4. An administrator notices a high amount of disk activity. What would the administrator use to determine if this is an unusual occurrence?

    A. Baseline

    B. System event log

    C. Stateful firewall

    D. Vulnerability scanner

5. A security administrator needs to review auditing results. Where will this information be found?

    A. Security log

    B. Properties of the object being audited

    C. Group policy

    D. In a firewall

6. In reviewing a system log, which of the following events should have the *highest* priority in a security investigation?

    A. A warning message indicates that the DHCP server failed to start on first attempt.

    B. The date and time the payroll report was printed

    C. The Google updater service terminated with an error.

    D. The computer entered sleep mode.

7. In order for log data to be aggregated to a single server, what is needed to provide this functionality?

   A. Syslog

   B. SOAR

   C. Event Viewer

   D. SIEM dashboard

8. Which type of vulnerability scan can provide the most accurate and detailed feedback regarding the state of vulnerabilities on a system?

   A. Credentialed scan

   B. Configuration compliance scan

   C. Non-credentialed scan

   D. Intrusive scan

9. Which security feature provides real-time analysis of centralized log data?

   A. Syslog

   B. SIM

   C. UBA

   D. SEM

10. Which of the following would indicate the *best* use of using SOAR techniques in an enterprise network?

    A. The creation of standard baselines

    B. An immediate response to a potential threat can be launched.

    C. Provides the capabilities to correlate events from multiple servers

    D. It can normalize event data, making it more efficient for analysis.

LAB EXERCISES

Lab Activity 3-1: Startup Programs and Scheduled Tasks

In Windows, an easy way to locate startup programs is to run a Microsoft utility called msconfig. The Task Scheduler should also be examined for commands set to execute at a specific time.

1. Click the Windows **Start** button, and then enter msconfig in the search bar. Select msconfig.exe or System Configuration in the search results to launch the System Configuration utility.

2. In the System Configuration utility, click the **Startup** tab. In Windows 10, click the **Open Task Manager** link. In older versions of Windows, the startup information is accessed directly in the System Configuration utility.

3. From the **Startup** tab, select a program in the list, and right-click and choose the **Disable** button to prevent the program from loading, as shown. In older versions of Windows, uncheck the check box for a service to disable it.

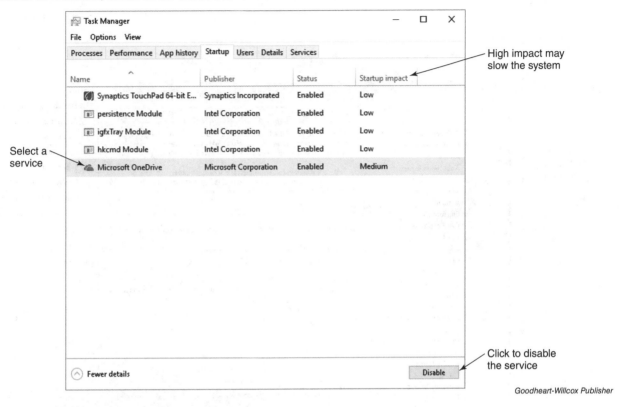

High impact may slow the system

Select a service

Click to disable the service

4. Close the Task Manager and the System Configuration utility.

5. Enter task scheduler in the Windows search bar. Select the Task Scheduler application in the search results.

6. The initial view is a dashboard that allows you to view information on tasks, including recently run tasks. How many tasks ran in the last 24 hours? The last hour?

7. Click **Action>Display All Running Tasks** in the pull-down menu. A new window is displayed that shows all tasks currently running. Click the **Close** button after viewing the tasks.

8. In the left-side pane, expand the Task Scheduler Library tree, as shown. You can view scheduled tasks for various components, those scheduled through the Event Viewer, or other programs.

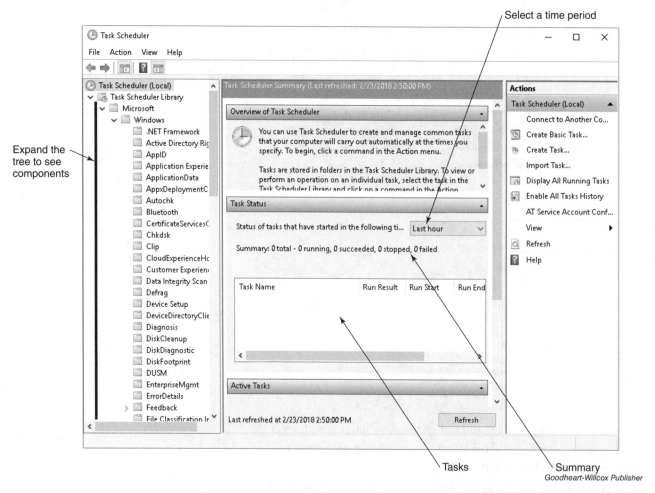

Goodheart-Willcox Publisher

9. Expand the Microsoft branch, and then expand the Windows branch. Scroll down to find the DiskCleanup branch, and select it. Information for this specific component is displayed. When was the last time this program ran?

10. With the DiskCleanup branch selected, click the **Actions** tab in the middle view. The path to the actual executable program is displayed.

11. Click the **General** tab. Can the program run if the user is not logged on? Will it run hidden (not visible to the logged in user)?

12. Close the Task Scheduler.

Lab Activity 3-2: Parameters in Performance Monitor

The Performance Monitor is a versatile tool in Microsoft Windows. It can be used to monitor and collect various information about the system.

1. Click the Windows **Start** menu, and then enter performance monitor in the search box. Select the Performance Monitor application in the search results.

2. In the Performance Monitor, expand the Monitoring Tools branch, and then select the Performance Monitor branch in the left-hand pane. A graph is displayed in the right-hand pane.

3. Click the arrow next to the **Change graph type** button on the toolbar above the chart. Notice the options in the drop-down menu. The view can be changed from the default line graph to bar graphs (histogram) or see the raw data value (report). Change to each type to see the views.

4. Click the **Add** button on the toolbar. This is used to add more counters to monitor. The **Add Counters** dialog box is displayed, which contains a list of available counters.

5. Scroll through the list, and select the down arrow next to **Network Adapter**. In the expanded list, click Bytes Total/Sec, as shown. Select your network adapter in the **Instances of selected object**: box, and click the **Add** button to add it to the list on the right-hand side. Then, click the **OK** button to add the counter.

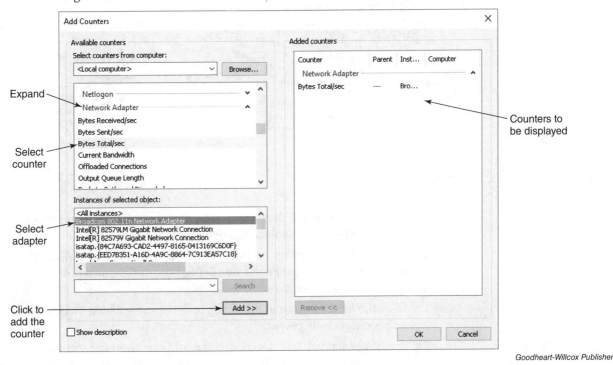

Goodheart-Willcox Publisher

6. Applying what you have learned, display the data as a line graph.

7. Click the **Properties** button on the toolbar. The **Performance Monitor Properties** dialog box is displayed.

8. Click the network adapter counter in the list on the **Data** tab, and then click the **Color:** drop-down arrow. Change the color to blue. Also, use the **Width:** drop-down arrow to change the width to the thickest option.

9. Click the **Graph** tab, and then check the **Horizontal Grid** check box. This places horizontal markers on the graph. Click the **OK** button to update the display.

10. Leave the Performance Monitor open, and launch the command prompt.

11. Using the command prompt, use the **ipconfig** command to obtain the default gateway, and then ping your default gateway. Notice how the graph in the Performance Monitor changes.

12. Expand the Data Collection Sets branch in the left-hand pane of the Performance Monitor, and then click the User Defined branch. The right-hand pane is empty as no data collector sets have been defined.

13. Right-click in the right-hand pane, and click **New>Data Collector Set** in the shortcut menu. A wizard appears to guide you through creating a data collector set.

14. On the first page of the wizard, name the data collector set Practice Set, and click the **Create from a template** radio button. Then, click the **Next** button.

15. On the next page of the wizard, select the Basic template, and click the **Next** button.

16. On the next page of the wizard, click the **Finish** button to accept the default location for saving the file. The Practice Set data collector set appears in the right-hand pane, as shown. Notice that by default it is not running.

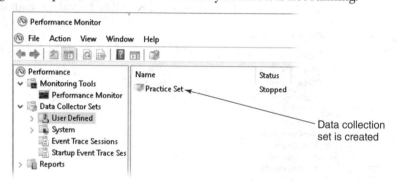

17. Double-click Practice Set in the right-hand pane to expand this branch. Notice the options now available in the right-hand pane.

18. Double-click Performance Counter in the right-hand pane to display the **Performance Counter Properties** dialog box. By default, a processor counter is included. Other counters can be added.

19. Click the **Add...** button in the dialog box. The same dialog box used earlier to add counters is displayed.

20. Applying what you have learned, add a bytes received per second counter for the network adapter. Then click the **OK** button to close the **Performance Counter Properties** dialog box.

21. Right-click on Practice Set in the left-hand pane, and click **Start** in the shortcut menu. Notice the icon for Practice Set changes to indicate it is running.

22. Leave the Performance Monitor open, launch a web browser, and navigate to a few web pages.

23. Return to the Performance Monitor. Right-click on Practice Set in the left-hand pane, and click **Stop** in the shortcut menu.

24. Expand the Reports branch in the left-hand pane, and then the User Defined branch. Select the Practice Set branch to see the report that was generated, as shown.

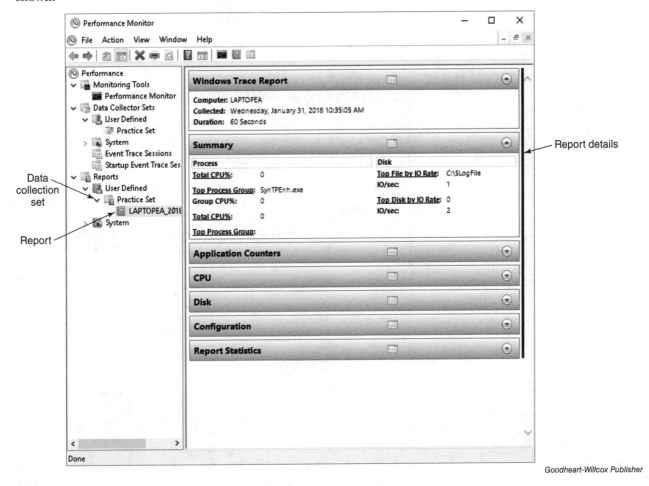

Goodheart-Willcox Publisher

25. Double-click the report in either the left- or right-hand pane. The details are displayed in the right-hand pane.

26. Investigate the data that was saved to the data collection set.

27. Close the Performance Monitor and any other open windows.

Lab Activity 3-3: Event Logs

Event logs can provide much information on the operation of a system. In Windows, the Event Viewer is used to not only view logs, but also manage or export them.

1. Click the Windows **Start** button, and enter event viewer in the search bar. Select the Event Viewer application in the search results.

2. The left-hand pane of the Event Viewer contains items organized in a tree format. Click the Windows Logs branch. The middle pane displays the different logs for the machine. The logs listed will depend on the machine and its installed services. How many logs are listed (in the Name column)?

3. Expand the Windows Logs branch. Notice the branches listed below it match the logs listed in the middle pane. Select the System branch, as shown. The system log is displayed in the middle pane.

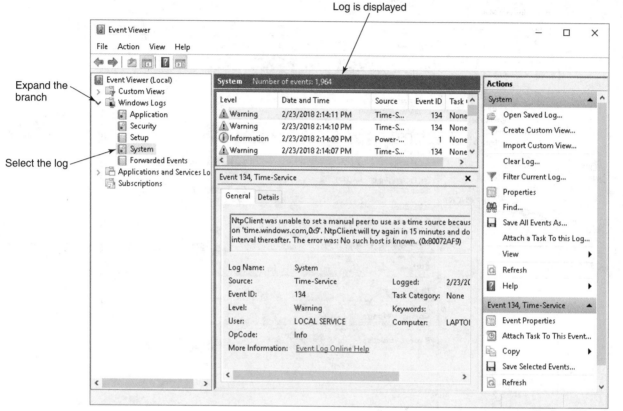

Goodheart-Willcox Publisher

4. Click the Source column heading. The events are sorted in order by the name of the source. By clicking any of the column headings, the view can be sorted in ascending or descending order by column. The default order of events is by date and time with the most recent event at the top.

5. Double-click any event in the list. Additional information about that event is displayed in a dialog box. Click the **Close** button to exit the information.

6. The right-hand pane is the **Actions** pane. This is where you can perform additional tasks, such as searching, filtering, and saving. Click **Find...** to display a search box, and enter DHCP. The first event that references DHCP is selected in the list (it may take a few seconds to find). Click the **Find Next** button to jump to the next related event, and then click the **Cancel** button to end the search function.

7. Click **Filter Current Log…** in the **Actions** pane. The **Filter Current Log** dialog box is displayed, as shown. This dialog box allows you to define multiple parameters to filter the search, such as looking for any warnings and DHCP or disk.

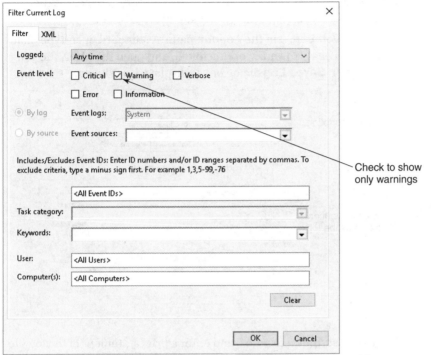

Check to show only warnings

8. Check the **Warning** check box, and then click the **OK** button. The logs are filtered to show only those categorized as warnings.

9. Click **Save filtered log as…** in the **Actions** pane. A standard save-type dialog box is displayed. The log can be saved in comma separated value (CSV), extensible markup language (XML), text (TXT), or event log (EVTx) format. Navigate to your working folder for this class, and save the file as LogTest.csv.

10. Click **Clear Filter** in the **Actions** pane. This removes the filter you just applied, and the full list of events is again displayed in the middle pane. Note, do *not* click **Clear Log…** in the **Actions** pane!

11. Click **Attach Task To This Event…** in the **Actions** pane. A wizard is launched to guide you through setting an alert for the specific event that was selected in the middle pane. Click the **Cancel** button to close the wizard without adding an alert.

Lab Activity 3-4: Event Log Backup

The ability to manage logs is a skill important to IT professionals. Part of log management is creating backups of logs.

1. Applying what you have learned, launch the Windows Event Viewer.

2. Expand the tree in the left-hand pane, and select the branch for the log you wish to back up.

3. Click **Save All Events As…** in the **Actions** pane. A standard save-type dialog box is displayed.

4. Navigate to your working folder for this class, name the file *LogName_Year_Month* (such as System_2019_June), and select **Event Files (.evtx)** in the **Save as type:** drop-down list. Click the **Save** button to save the file. The **Display Information** dialog box is displayed. Click the **OK** button to accept the default setting and close the dialog box. The backup file is created.

5. Click **Open Saved Log…** in the **Actions** pane. A standard open-type dialog box is displayed. Navigate to your working folder, and open the EVTX file you just saved. The **Open Saved Log** dialog box is displayed, as shown.

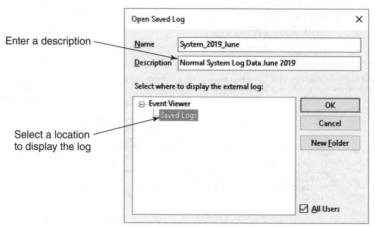

Goodheart-Willcox Publisher

6. Click in the **Description** text box, and enter a brief statement of the log file. For example, you may enter Normal System Log Data June 2019. Also, notice you can choose where the log will be displayed. By default, opened logs are displayed in the Saved Logs branch.

7. Click the **OK** button to finish opening the log. The log is automatically selected in the tree, and the events it contains are displayed in the middle pane. Notice the log name appears above the events, and it also is the name of the branch in the left-hand pane.

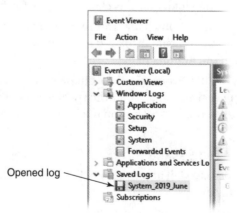

Goodheart-Willcox Publisher

8. Close the Event Viewer.

Lab Activity 3-5: Audit Policy

Suppose your sales manager is working on a bid proposal and wants to track everyone who opens the file or changes its content. These events can be audited to help protect the integrity of the data in the bid proposal. Note: this exercise is based on Windows 10, and you will need administrative access to the system.

1. Create a new document in Microsoft Word, and add your name to the file.
2. Save the file as SalesBid in your working folder for this class, and exit Word. You will audit for users who are able to view and make changes to the file.
3. Click the Windows **Start** button, and enter group policy in the search box. Select **Edit group policy** in the results to open the Group Policy Editor application.
4. In the left-hand pane, expand the tree **Computer Configuration**>**Windows Settings**>**Security Settings**>**Local Policies** and select the Audit Policy branch.
5. In the right-hand pane, double-click Audit object access. The **Audit object access Properties** dialog box is displayed, as shown.

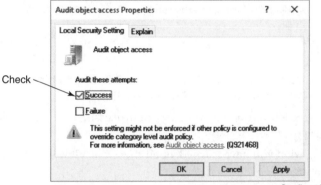

Goodheart-Willcox Publisher

6. Check the **Success** check box, and then click the **OK** button. Editing and saving the word-processing file is a "success event."
7. Close the Group Policy Editor.
8. Launch File Explorer, navigate to your working folder, right-click on the SalesBid document, and click **Properties** in the shortcut menu.
9. In the **Properties** dialog box, click the **Security** tab, and then click the **Advanced** button.
10. In the **Advanced Security Settings** dialog box, click the **Auditing** tab. Click the **Continue** button in the middle of the tab to acknowledge the warning.
11. Click the **Add** button at the bottom of the tab. A new dialog box is displayed for adding an auditing entry. You first need to select the principal, which is the user to audit.
12. Click the **Select a principal** link. In the new dialog box that is displayed, click in the **Enter the object name to select:** text box, enter everyone, and click the **OK** button.

13. Click the **Type:** drop-down arrow, and click **Success** in the list. Also, check **Modify, Read & execute,** and **Write** check boxes, as shown. Then, click the **OK** button. If you get any errors regarding enumeration, just click through them.

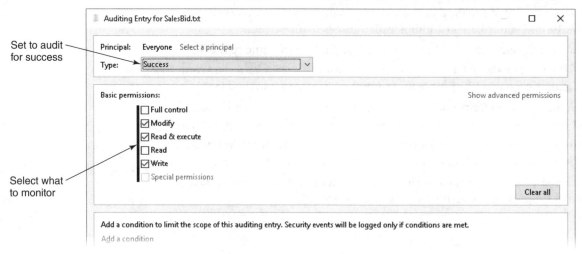

Goodheart-Willcox Publisher

14. Click the **OK** button to exit the **Advanced Security Settings** dialog box, and then the **OK** button to exit the **Properties** dialog box.

15. Open the SalesBid document in a word processor. Add today's date, and save and close the file.

16. Applying what you have learned, open the Event Viewer, and display the security log.

17. Applying what you have learned, open the **Filter Current Log** dialog box.

18. Enter the event ID 4660, as shown. Then, click the **OK** button to show only those events with this code.

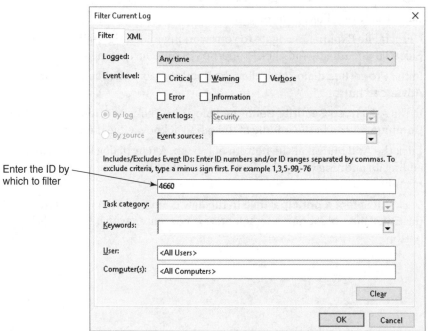

Goodheart-Willcox Publisher

19. Select the event in the middle pane of the Event Viewer. Look at the details for the event in the **General** tab at the bottom of the middle pane. The **Security ID:** entry is the user who changed the file. The program used to access the file is also listed. For example, if Microsoft Word was used to modify the file, the path to winword.exe will be given.

20. Close the Event Viewer.

CASE STUDY

Alternative Worksites

One of the outcomes of the COVID-19 pandemic in early 2020 was the transition to alternative worksites for many employees. Many of these worksites consisted of employees' homes using personal equipment. As employees shifted to this working environment, the *Harvard Business Review* published an advisory over the potential increase in cyberattacks. The security consulting company Artic Security subsequently revealed a global increase of compromised systems since March 2020 due to COVID-related phishing e-mails, a push to issue company equipment quickly, use of personal equipment, lack of technical oversight by employees, and equipment located outside of organization offices.

1. Since many employees were directed to work from home unexpectedly, organizations that issued company-owned equipment may not have fully secured and patched each device. What are some suggestions an IT staff could provide to ensure the business devices are secured, even though they are not onsite? Keep in mind the need for physical distancing measures.

2. List strategies you would recommend to employees to reduce the vulnerabilities of using their personal equipment.

3. Nationwide conducted a small business owner survey in 2019 and found that only four percent of business owners implemented the cybersecurity practices and recommendations outlined by the Small Business Administration. How could an IT department convince management of the importance of strong cybersecurity practices in this unprecedented working environment?

4. Moving forward, it is possible that businesses will be forced to return to this work-from-home model if a similar situation arises. How can companies prepare to protect remote hosts and its own environment should another pandemic occur?

Managing User Security

LEARNING OUTCOMES

- Discuss authentication and access control.
- Summarize potential problems associated with password authentication.
- Identify factors and attributes of multifactor authentication.
- Compare and contrast types of access management controls.
- Explain three processes for system login.
- Differentiate among examples of single sign-on deployments.
- Summarize account management practices.
- Identify best practices for ensuring accounts are configured in a uniform, secured fashion.
- Evaluate two types of file system permissions.
- Explain three types of permissions assigned to a user.

KEY TERMS

account audit
account expiration
account maintenance
Active Directory (AD)
attribute-based access control (ABAC)
behavioral biometrics
biometric authentication
CAC reader
common access card (CAC)
credential management
crossover error rate (CER)
directory
disablement
discretionary access control (DAC)
efficacy rate
explicit permission
facial recognition
false acceptance rate (FAR)
false rejection rate (FRR)
federated identity management (FIM)
fingerprint scanner
gait analysis
geofencing

geolocation
GPS tagging
group-based access control
implicit permission
inherited permission
iris scanner
Kerberos
LDAPS
Lightweight Directory Access Protocol (LDAP)
location-based policy
mandatory access control (MAC)
multifactor authentication
New Technology File System (NTFS) permission
offboarding
onboarding
password complexity
password lockout
password recovery
permission
permission audit and review
policy

recertification
Remote Authentication Dial-In User Service (RADIUS)
retinal scanner
right
role-based access control (RBAC)
rule-based access control
secondary logon
Security Assertion Markup Language (SAML)
share permission
Shibboleth
single sign-on (SSO)
standard biometrics
standard naming convention
Terminal Access Controller Access-Control System (TACACS)
time-of-day restriction
token
usage audit and review
user account control (UAC)
vein scanner
voice recognition

SECURITY+ CERTIFICATION EXAM OBJECTIVES

The following Security+ Certification Exam Objectives are covered in this chapter.

+ 2.1: Standard naming conventions
+ 2.4: Directory services
+ 2.4: Federation
+ 2.4: Biometrics
+ 2.4: Attestation
+ 2.4: Short message service (SMS)
+ 2.4: Token key
+ 2.4: Authentication applications
+ 2.4: Biometrics
+ 2.4: Multifactor authentication (MFA) factors and attributes
+ 2.4: Authentication, Authorization, and Accounting (AAA)
+ 3.1: Directory services
+ 3.4: Remote Authentication Dial-In User Server (RADIUS)
+ 3.7: Identity provider (IdP)
+ 3.7: Attributes
+ 3.7: Tokens

+ 3.7: Account types
+ 3.7: Password complexity
+ 3.7: Password history
+ 3.7: Password reuse
+ 3.7: Time of day
+ 3.7: Network location
+ 3.7: Geofencing
+ 3.7: Geotagging
+ 3.7: Geolocation
+ 3.7: Access policies
+ 3.7: Account permission
+ 3.7: Account audits
+ 3.7: Lockout
+ 3.7: Disablement
+ 3.8: Knowledge-based authentication
+ 3.8: RADIUS
+ 3.8: Single sign-on (SSO)
+ 3.8: Security Assertions Markup

Language (SAML)
+ 3.8: Terminal Access Controller Access Control System Plus (TACACS+)
+ 3.8: OAuth
+ 3.8: OpenID
+ 3.8: Kerberos
+ 3.8: Attribute-based access control (ABAC)
+ 3.8: Role-based access control
+ 3.8: Rule-based access control
+ 3.8: MAC
+ 3.8: Discretionary access control (DAC)
+ 3.8: Privilege access management
+ 3.8: File system permissions
+ 5.3: Least privilege
+ 5.3: Onboarding
+ 5.3: Offboarding

OVERVIEW

The security of a company relies on strong digital protections, including policies, technical solutions, and the ability of the IT team to recognize and respond to threats. However, despite all protections established, one aspect of data protection that leads to many vulnerabilities is the end-user. Users in an organization often do not understand the ramifications of their decisions, such as password choice, opening e-mail attachments, and the risks involved to the data they use to perform their duties. It is up to IT security personnel to implement restrictions to reduce user-generated vulnerabilities and protect both data and systems.

This chapter will discuss restrictions such as password protections, requirement of multiple factors to prove user identity, and limiting the permissions and rights users have to data. Additionally, single sign-on options to manage user access across diverse systems will be explored.

SECURITY+ NOTE

On the CompTIA Security+ Exam, a great deal of attention is focused on the various methods of authentication. Be sure you can summarize uses, features, and implementation of all authentication methods introduced in this chapter.

Authentication and Access Control

Authentication is the process of validating a user or verifying the person's identity. It is one of the most important tasks in a security plan. Authentication helps ensure that only authorized users are accessing the network and its resources. An *authorized user* is a person approved to access a system. After a user is authenticated, controlling the user's access to network locations, alter data, and perform actions becomes a critical management aspect. *Access control* is restricting user access to specific locations and resources. Access control is often bolstered or hindered by access management. *Access management* is the measures taken and policies enforced to grant authorized users access to services while ensuring unauthorized users are prohibited from accessing the network.

Network users are often the weakest link in a security chain, and insufficient policies or poor decisions often lead to vulnerabilities in system security. When an individual logs in to a network, that person is given a key to access various resources of that network, including hardware, software, and data. Poor decision making by users, such as having a weak password or leaving a workstation unattended without first securing its access, can have serious effects on network security. Since humans cannot be automated, security administrators must put policies and configurations in place to reduce risks associated with users.

2.4

A critical area that must be protected is the login process. One framework that defines policies for granting access to users is *AAA*, which is a suite of protocols used to facilitate network access. AAA stands for authentication, authorization, and accounting. However, AAA also includes identification. The AAA process is as follows:

- *Identification* is the first step of the AAA process, in which a user makes a claim of identity. Identification is generally accomplished by entering a username. The user does not provide evidence of identity at this stage.

- *Authentication* is the process of validating a user. During this step of the AAA process, the user provides evidence of identity. Authentication is generally accomplished by entering a password, though additional authentication practices can be employed.

- *Authorization* confirms a user is permitted to access a system and its resources. At this step, permission sets are assigned that define actions an authenticated user can or cannot perform when accessing the network. Authorization is often determined through access control lists and the assignment of rights and permissions.

- *Accounting* provides a measurement of resources used by an employee during access of the system. It also allows administrators to track user activity throughout the system.

While creating strong authentication policies is essential, it is equally important to control access to data and system functionality after a user is granted access to a system.

It is important to try to predict and troubleshoot issues that could result in authentication vulnerabilities. For example, since passwords have inherent weaknesses, establishing policies that promote strong password choices and frequent changes can help eliminate vulnerabilities before they occur. Examples of additional options will be discussed later in this chapter.

Many companies also like to utilize an in-house recovery service for password resets and employ nontraditional questions to improve security. Additionally, they often attempt to add security measures so authentication requires multiple actions, such as sending a text message to a user's personal mobile device to confirm identity. Organizations should develop policies that can immediately suspend a user's access if credentials are lost or stolen while considering the storage and security of private data, such as passwords and phone numbers.

Passwords

The most common type of user authentication is a password. Access to operating systems and related applications is often granted using a login account secured with a password. Before a user is granted access, the person must enter the correct password for the user account. However, password authentication is one of the *least* secure methods of authentication. Some of the problems associated with password authentication include

- weak passwords;
- reuse of passwords on multiple sites;
- weak password policies; and
- password cracking tools.

Weak Passwords

Weak passwords are those that can be guessed, as demonstrated in Figure 4-1. Most users choose a password and security-reset question based on personal information. Caution should be applied when using personal information as it can lead to unauthorized access.

An example of a person exploiting a personal-information vulnerability is Chris Chaney, the so-called *Hollywood Hacker*, who successfully guessed Gmail account names of celebrities. Using the Gmail account names along with personal information retrieved from the Internet Movie Database website, the hacker gained access to their accounts and then revealed private and sensitive information about the celebrities.

Repetition of Passwords

Often, people create a password and use it repeatedly for many sites. For example, a user may use the same password for network access, bank accounts, and social media. If a user's password is stolen or cracked, the hacker has access to all these other sites. Always insist that employees use a different password for each system they access.

TECH TIP

 3.8

To mitigate the possibility of weak passwords, password keys can be employed for user access. Password keys are token devices roughly the size of a USB flash drive that stores authentication credentials. These keys can be used to authenticate users and enforce account policies and permissions once a user logs in to a system.

Figure 4-1 A good or strong password is key to effective password protection. Here, the password **123ABC** is identified as a poor password.

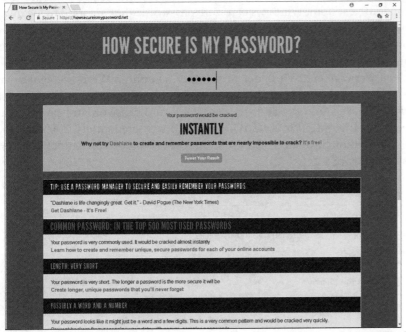

Goodheart-Willcox Publisher

In fall of 2019, users of the then-recently launched Disney Plus streaming service complained of compromised accounts and hacking. The resulting investigation into the service revealed that Disney's streaming service was secure. The accounts that were taken over belonged to users who had recycled old usernames and passwords from other accounts that had been previously hacked. Data taken from those previously compromised accounts, such as e-mail addresses, usernames, and passwords, were sold on the dark web. By reusing compromised passwords, users were essentially inviting anyone who had purchased that stolen data into their new Disney Plus accounts.

Weak Password Policies

If not forced to change passwords, many users will continue to use the same password indefinitely. Weak password policies allow this to happen. A technical setting can be made to force users to change passwords at a specific interval, such as once a month or annually. There is some debate about how often passwords should change. The Better Business Bureau suggests a monthly change. Most security professionals suggest passwords be changed every 30, 60, or 90 days. The decision on the number of days to change a password is often made based on the type of data a user accesses. The more secure or confidential the data, the more common it is to have a shorter time requirement for password use. Even though users dislike changing passwords, it can prevent someone who obtained the current password from accessing the account.

Password-Cracking Tools

There are many password-cracking tools that individuals can obtain in an effort to uncover passwords. These tools can often be found on the Internet for free. Hackers can use these tools to breach the password level of defense. The only real defense against a hacker using a free password-cracking tool is to make a password as complex as possible and employ more than one form of authentication.

Stored Passwords

Security administrators should be aware of the use of stored passwords in the Windows operating system. Windows can store passwords that are used to log in, access network shares, or access other shared devices. While these passwords are capable of being shared securely using encryption, some passwords may be stored insecurely and thus subject to potential exploits.

When you connect to a folder on another computer, Windows allows you the ability to save your password in a credentialed file. The credentialed file is stored in a "digital locker," and the address, username, and password are saved. Windows also provides the option to save Windows and web credentials. You can view the stored information by opening **Control Panel**>**User Accounts**>**Credential Manager** as shown in Figure 4-2.

TECH TIP

Password-cracking tools should *not* be run on your own network without consulting company policies. Even though you may locate insecure passwords, there may be an ethical or legal liability in discovering a user's password.

Figure 4-2 Users can view stored credentialed files containing information such as passwords, usernames, and web addresses through **Credential Manager**.

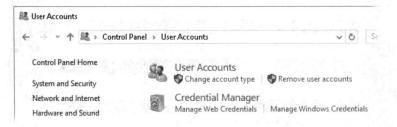

One of the concerns regarding stored web credentials lies in the risk of a user walking away from an unattended and unlocked computer. Anyone who knows the user's domain or local password would be able to retrieve the stored password. Accessing the web credentials option provides the stored list of credentials. The logon information is visible in plain text, and while the password is hidden, you can click **Show** to view the password in plain text. See Figure 4-3.

In Windows 10, the option for password-protected sharing is enabled by default. This option ensures that only those users who have a password-protected user account on the local machine will be able to access the shared files, folders, and printers that are locally attached. If you want to allow other people the ability to access a shared folder, this feature must be disabled, which potentially allows anyone on the network to access the folder. This option can be set in **Control Panel>Network and Sharing>Change advanced sharing settings**. In the **Advanced sharing settings** dialog box expand the **All Networks** section at the bottom of the screen and select either **Turn on password protected sharing** or **Turn off password protected sharing**.

Multifactor Authentication

✚ 2.4

Passwords alone are not a sufficient defense for systems, and there are other methods that can be used to authenticate users. Using only one type of identification is called *single-factor authentication*. Using multiple independent credentials, rather than just one, to verify user identification is called **multifactor authentication**. Multifactor authentication is a form of security that requires multiple independent factors and attributes to verify user identification.

Factors

A *factor* is evidence or proof of identity. Multiple factors may be used to confirm an individual's identity, including

- what you know;
- what you have; and
- what you are.

What You Know

✚ 3.8

A password is an example of "what you know." Some programs and websites might ask a user to provide the answer to a security question. This is *not* an example of multifactor authentication. It is one-factor, or single-factor, authentication; the only factor in this situation is knowledge of an answer. Asking a security question provides for stronger authentication than a password alone, but it does not provide a second factor.

Figure 4-3 Credentialed files are a potential vulnerability for computer systems due to their ability of displaying sensitive information in plain text.

Goodheart-Willcox Publisher

What You Have

To fulfill the "what you have" factor, the user must possess a device that contains security information. This authentication factor is comparable to someone possessing a key to a lock. In this case, the key is the device a user has to enable authentication. The most common types of devices are common access cards (CACs) and tokens.

Common Access Card (CAC)

A **common access card (CAC)** is a smart card that contains security information about the user stored on a microchip similar to microchipped credit cards. CACs work in conjunction with a **CAC reader**, which is a device that senses the microchip in the CAC and determines if it contains the correct information to allow access. A CAC reader can be installed on computers or computerized devices, embedded into keyboards, or attached to a computer via a USB device. USB devices are not used to replace a password. Rather, the user must insert the card into a reader and then enter a username and password. This is an example of using two factors for authentication: 1) password, and 2) CAC.

CACs are generally the size of most credit cards. These cards are common in military facilities, as shown in Figure 4-4. Smart cards generally work with digital certificates for authentication.

⊹ 3.7

Tokens

A **token** is a device that acts as a key to gain access to a resource. It may be a hardware token, or *hard token*, which is a physical device that often resembles a USB device in size and appearance and has ROM storage that can store a certificate or unique identifier. Most hardware tokens have a small LCD screen display to reveal an alphanumeric value at fixed intervals, usually every 60 seconds. The number is generated by an algorithm that uses a predetermined or shared secret called a *seed value* in its computation. When the user enters the value displayed on the token screen, the

Figure 4-4 The US military uses common access cards as its standard identification for service personnel.

token's value must be verified by the authenticating device. The authenticating server confirms the user's login credentials and associated serial number of the token they have been assigned. Each hardware token is assigned a unique seed value associated with its serial number.

A software token, commonly called a *soft token*, is software that contains the authentication token. These types of tokens are not physically tangible and are often accessed from an app running on a smartphone or software configured on a desktop or laptop computer.

What You Are

The third factor is "what you are," which involves biometrics. *Biometrics* refers to measurements and calculations based on characteristics of a person. **Biometric authentication** is an identity and access management concept and physical security control in which a user must provide a physical characteristic in addition to a username and password. Biometric systems rely on the inherent difficulty of spoofing biological credentials of the targeted user.

Two types of biometrics typically used in information security include standard biometrics and cognitive biometrics.

Standard Biometrics

Standard biometrics are the unique physical characteristics of a person used for authentication. Standard biometrics include the following:

- A **fingerprint scanner** is a device that reads the unique skin layers of a person's fingerprint to confirm that person's identity.
- A **retinal scanner** is a device that scans a person's retina to confirm their identity.
- An **iris scanner** confirms a person's identity by reading the characteristics of a person's iris.
- A **vein scanner** is a device that identifies characteristics of a person's blood vessels using infrared light.
- **Facial recognition** uses software that scans a person's facial features to confirm identity.
- **Voice recognition** uses software that authenticates a person's unique vocal characteristics.
- **Gait analysis** is identity confirmation based on analysis of the way a person walks.

Since standard biometrics rely on unique biological features, they tend to offer a great deal of security. However, this system is not perfect, and there are some potential risks associated with a standard biometric system's efficacy rate. An **efficacy rate** is the frequency in which an intended result is achieved. In this context, the intended result is the acceptance of authorized personnel and the rejection of unauthorized individuals. When measuring a system's efficacy rate, three important measurements are considered: false acceptance rate, false rejection rate, and crossover error rate.

- **False acceptance rate (FAR)** is a measurement of how likely a biometric feature incorrectly grants access to an unauthorized person. A *false acceptance* occurs when biometric credentials are authorized on invalid characteristics. FAR is calculated by dividing the number of false acceptances by the number of identification attempts.
- **False rejection rate (FRR)** is a measurement of how likely a biometric feature will incorrectly deny an authorized person access to the system. A *false rejection*

occurs when a person authorized to access the system employs biometric credentials and is denied access. FRR is calculated by dividing the number of false rejections by the number of identification attempts.

- The **crossover error rate (CER)** is the point where the false acceptance rates and false rejection rates are equal, as illustrated in Figure 4-5. This measurement is often the best method for determining a biometric system's efficacy rate, as settings are often made to achieve a balance between providing security and easy user access.

Cognitive Biometrics

Cognitive biometrics incorporates a person's understanding and perceptions. For example, a person might be required to identify a familiar object as a means of authentication. It relies on a person responding to the method rather than being personally scanned or measured.

Attributes

Multifactor authentication also considers personal attributes. An *attribute* is a quality, feature, or characteristic of a person. Attributes provide evidence of an individual's identity including

- somewhere you are;
- something you can do;
- something you exhibit; and
- someone you know.

Somewhere You Are

This attribute refers to physical location. Identifying the location of an individual can help identify unusual patterns, such as if a person is logging in using a different computer, or from a different geographic location. Wi-Fi triangulation and GPS can be

Figure 4-5 The crossover error rate (CER) is the point where the FAR and FRR are equal.

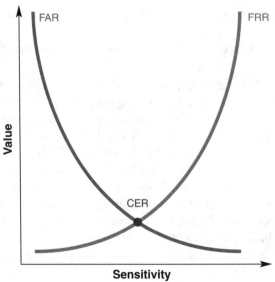

Goodheart-Willcox Publisher

used to determine where a person is located and can be cross-referenced to a list of accepted locations. Authentication is granted if the locations match. This practice often includes the following GPS-based activities:

- **Geofencing** is the process of using GPS or RFID to create a virtual boundary, allowing management to establish a geographic area and disable or allow devices or features based on the user's proximity to that area.
- **GPS tagging**, also known as *geotagging*, is the act of including GPS information to media, such as photos taken from a mobile device. Through geotagging, a person's location is identified from the information tagged to documents, photographs, or videos.
- **Geolocation** is the act of identifying the geographical coordinates of a device. GPS must be enabled on the device and tracking software must be loaded in order for geolocation to function.

Something You Can Do

Behavioral biometrics is a study that identifies measurable patterns in human activities. This factor is better described as "something you can do." One aspect of this type of authentication is called *keystroke dynamics*, which measures the patterns of rhythm and timing generated when a person is using the keyboard on a system. Examples of keystroke measurements include the following:

- speed of keystrokes
- variations as the user moves between different keys
- common errors (typos)
- how long a key is pressed

Something You Exhibit

Something you exhibit is who you are and an evaluation of personal biometrics. It is a measurement of physical and psychological characteristic exhibited by an individual. This includes fingerprints as well as the retina or iris of the eyes. It could also be a person's face or the way a person walks. These are physical and psychological characteristics that can only be exhibited by the person who possess them.

Someone You Know

This type of authentication attribute is a form of human authentication in which one user helps authenticate another. Consider the following example. A user needs to provide a CAC for login, but does not have the CAC on hand. In this scenario, a trusted person can authenticate the user and provide temporary access to the resources the user is trying to access.

Access Management Controls

An important security decision deals with how to give users access to resources and data on a network. Imagine a company with several hundred employees. Assigning individual user access rights would be a tedious process, but more important, the probability for error is high. It would also be difficult to determine a user's access instantly. To make this process easier and potentially more secure, access control methods can be used, such as mandatory access control (MAC), discretionary access control (DAC), and attribute-based access control (ABAC).

3.8

Mandatory Access Control (MAC)

The first access management control used most often is mandatory access control (MAC). **Mandatory access control (MAC)** is a security strategy that sets a strict level of access to resources based on criteria set by a network administrator. MAC is often used by the military and supporting organizations. In a military setting, MAC is commonly implemented with classifications such as confidential, secret, and top secret. These levels form a hierarchy of access, as shown in Figure 4-6. When data or resources are identified and configured using a category, only users with the matching credential can have access. Because credentials are mandatory, exceptions are not permitted. Administrators are not permitted to make changes, such as allowing someone with a credential for *secret* to read data categorized as *top secret*.

 3.8

Discretionary Access Control (DAC)

The next access management control is discretionary access control (DAC). With **discretionary access control (DAC)**, a user can be granted additional rights to data beyond what is allowed by the individual's assigned access level. The user who owns the data can grant permissions to another user. For example, suppose an instructor wants to share a folder with students. If the instructor owns the data (folder), the instructor can decide who else has rights to access the folder.

A common access control implementation method is role-based access control (RBAC). With **role-based access control (RBAC)**, rights are assigned to a role instead of manually to each individual user. Users are associated as a member of a role or group, as shown in Figure 4-7. When permissions are set or changed to a role, each member of the role is automatically assigned new or updated permissions. A user's access to the role's resources are instantly revoked when the user is removed from the role. This helps eliminate mistakes and provides a higher level of security.

If a role is not used, as illustrated in the example in Figure 4-7, permissions are assigned to each user one at a time. However, by creating a role, or group, a user can be assigned to a group that already has the appropriate permission levels applied to it. For example, if a new engineer is hired, assigning the correct permissions is as simple as adding the individual to the Engineering group.

Rule-based access control is a control strategy in which user access is determined by a set of rules established by an administrator. A common example of a rule-based control is users may only log in to the network during specific hours or from specific workstations. Rule-based control applies to everyone for whom the rule applies, regardless of group or other identifying characteristics.

Attribute-Based Access Control (ABAC)

The next level of access control models that is popular is attribute-based access control (ABAC). **Attribute-based access control (ABAC)** is an access control system that uses attributes or characteristics assigned to a user and compares them to

Figure 4-6 The US government uses three levels of access. A user with confidential- or secret-level access can only use data at that level. A user with top secret-level access can use data at any level.

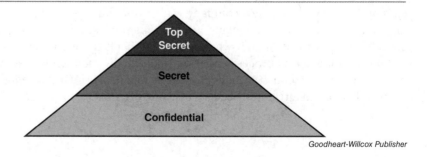

Goodheart-Willcox Publisher

Figure 4-7 By using roles, or groups, permissions can be assigned to many users in a single step.

Accountant   Sales Rep   Engineer   Engineer   Sales Rep   Accountant   Engineer   Sales Rep   Engineer

Engineering group   Accounting group   Sales group

Goodheart-Willcox Publisher; (vector art) Rawpixel.com/Shutterstock.com

attributes or characteristics that are assigned to the data. This type of control allows businesses to adopt a more dynamic and granular approach in assigning access than more generalized rule-based controls. For example, Ella is the project manager for Project A. In Ella's account, Ella has the property or attribute of project manager based on position title, and Project A will be the value of the project field. This data assigned to Ella is matched to the data and its attributes for determining the level of access. This means that if Ella were to attempt to gain access to files pertaining to Project A, permission would be granted based on the role as project manager.

System Login

When a user logs in to a computer in a Windows environment, the person is utilizing *access services*, which are preloaded services that provide users with network access. System login can be achieved in one of three ways:

- The computer is a workstation on a network located in an *organizational domain*, which is a database that stores all the resources on the network in a centralized server.
- The computer is a stand-alone computer that operates independently from the rest of the computers on the network.
- The user logs in through one account, then logs in to a secondary account to run specific programs or execute commands.

Domain-Based Login

When logging on to a workstation located on a network, the user provides a login name and password established on the network server. If multifactor authentication is used, other credentials must also be entered. The authentication information is

TECH TIP

Attribute-based access control is an effective tool for creating specialized and granular access, but it requires critical maintenance and upkeep of the users' attributes. Forgetting to remove this information when it is no longer required can lead to potential vulnerabilities or unauthorized access.

passed to the server's security database, where it is cross-referenced against what has been established for the user. If the information matches, the user is authenticated. If not, authentication fails, and access is denied. Figure 4-8 shows an example of a security database (domain) on a network.

Directory Services

➕ 2.4, 3.1

A **directory** is a location or hierarchical folder structure for storing files on a computer. *Directory services* are software systems that create, store, organize, and allow access to directory information and resources. One such directory services often used to create security domains in Microsoft is the Active Directory. The **Active Directory (AD)** is a directory service developed by Microsoft for Windows networks that authenticates users in a Windows network. Think of Active Directory as a database of network resources, such as objects, user and group accounts, computers, servers, and printers. The central database holding this information in the directory is a *domain*. Directories are based on the **Lightweight Directory Access Protocol (LDAP)**, which is a protocol that provides standards and ensures that directories or directory services are constructed and used in the same manner. This allows a user on a Microsoft directory to access resources on another platform's directory, such as Apple's directory. **LDAPS** is the secure form of LDAP, where LDAP is used with SSL to send directory communications encrypted. The default port for LDAPS is 636.

Directories are needed to help locate resources in a database. For example, when you print to a network printer, you do not have to identify its location in the directory. The LDAP will perform that function.

All directories are constructed in a hierarchical manner commonly referred to as the *tree approach*. Within the hierarchy, or tree, network administrators define the objects, resources, and users. Objects that represent resources, such as users or printers, are called *leaf objects*. A directory can be further organized using objects called *organizational units*, which can be customized to a company's needs. For example, a company can create organizational units based on geographic location,

---

Figure 4-8 When logging in to a network security domain, the user's credentials are checked against the security database.

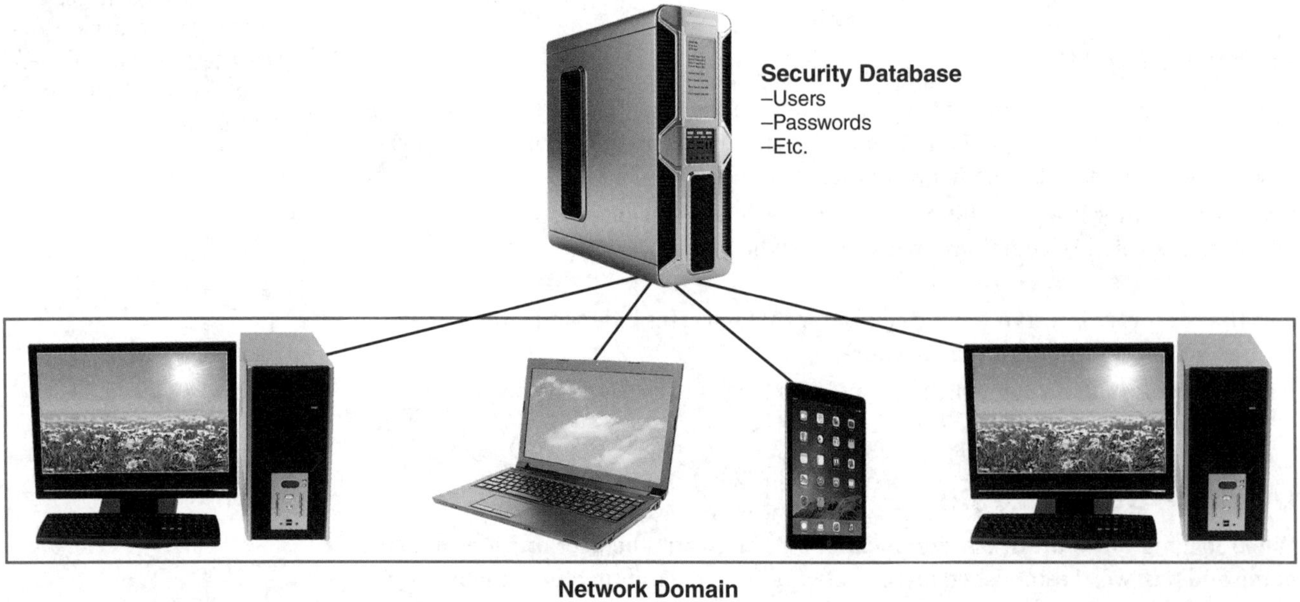

Security Database
—Users
—Passwords
—Etc.

Network Domain

such as individual states. Then, each organizational unit can be divided into multiple levels to describe regional areas within each state.

Consider the example shown in Figure 4-9. The network administrator has named the domain Wagner Accounting. In this example, Wagner Accounting chose to organize resources by department. There is an organizational unit for each of the IT, accounting, and support staffs. Within each of these organizational units are the leaf objects.

LDAP compliance ensures that all objects follow specific rules. For example, suppose that Kari Johnson is a customer service representative for Wagner Accounting. Kari's user object's complete name, which is called a *distinguished name*, includes all levels of the tree. Each level has a prefix that identifies the level. Therefore, Kari's distinguished name is:

cn=kJohnson.ou=supportstaff.dc=WagnerAccounting.dc=com

Notice the prefixes. They identify the following levels:

- cn = common name
- ou = organizational unit
- dc = domain controller (domain components)

Directory Authentication

 3.8

In Microsoft server operating systems, the authentication model used is called Kerberos (pronounced *ker-ber-os*). **Kerberos** is the standard authentication protocol on all versions of Microsoft Server when using the Active Directory. This is an advanced protocol and offers several key characteristics to provide security. In it, two key main functions comprise the role of the *Key Distribution Center (KDC)*:

- Authentication Service (AS) exchange
- Ticket Granting Service (TGS) exchange

Figure 4-9 The directory structure is created as a hierarchy.

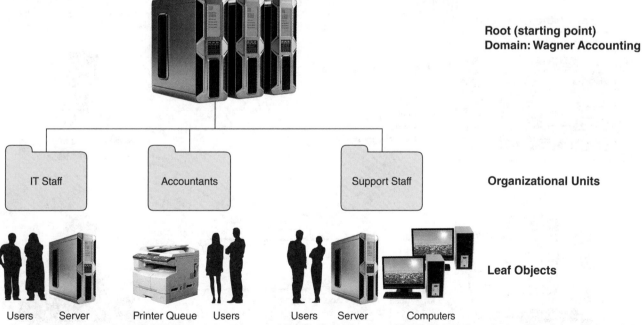

Root (starting point)
Domain: Wagner Accounting

IT Staff   Accountants   Support Staff   Organizational Units

Users   Server   Printer Queue   Users   Users   Server   Computers   Leaf Objects

Goodheart-Willcox Publisher; (printer) R-O-M-A/Shutterstock.com; (computers) Elnur/Shutterstock.com; (servers) Sashkin/Shutterstock.com; (vector art) Rawpixel.com/Shutterstock.com

The KDC is a service running on a server that has a copy of the Active Directory. Its job is to manage the main functions listed previously. Figure 4-10 illustrates the communication between the KDC and devices. This process occurs whenever a user requests *any* type of network resource. In this way, there are constant security checks during a user's session.

Trust Relationships

An important access level of which security professionals must be aware is called a trust relationship. A *trust relationship* is a logical link formed between two separate domains in LDAP-configured directories. One domain is known as the trusting domain, and the second domain is known as the trusted domain. Once the trust is established, the trusting domain will honor and accept the logon authentication of the trusted domain.

There are many ways a trust relationship can be configured between domains. One common configuration is a transitive trust, which occurs when the trust relationship is considered two-way. A *transitive trust* is an access management concept in which a user is authenticated in one security domain and is automatically authenticated into another security domain. It is important to be aware of trust relationships and their potential impact on authentication of users throughout the organizations.

Figure 4-10 The KDC processes the exchange of tickets to provide authorization whenever the user requests any type of network resource.

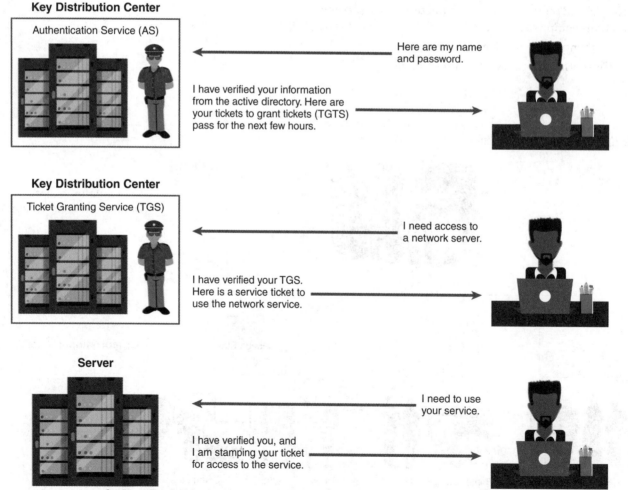

One example of the use of a transitive trust is Microsoft's Active Directory. Suppose you configure an Active Directory domain called ACME.com. ACME.com is considered the highest, or parent, domain. Another domain called NYC.ACME.com is created. NYC is a child domain located under the ACME.com domain. In this Microsoft relationship, child domains and their parent domains automatically establish transitive trust. It is important to note that having transitive trust does not automatically grant permissions to resources in the domain and security tasks must still be performed. Transitive trust simply allows authentication automatically into the other domain.

Local Machine Login

When a user is not connected to a network, it is called a *stand-alone machine* or *local machine*. In this type of connection, logon accounts must be stored directly on the stand-alone machine. Every Windows computer maintains a local database of user accounts that can be used in the event AD is not available. This local database is called the *Security Account Manager (SAM)*.

SAM is a nonhierarchical database, meaning the information contained within it is not organized or divided into levels of importance. SAM contains not only the local user account names but also passwords stored in a hashed format. A *hash* is a computed value that uniquely identifies data. Passwords stored in a hashed format are unreadable. The Security Account Manager database is stored in C:\%systemroot%\ system32\config\SAM. It is important to be aware of both SAM's location and the local accounts stored within it, as these accounts are often prime targets for hackers and since local accounts can be used to perform diagnostics or troubleshooting on a local machine.

In a scenario in which a Windows server is not part of a domain or AD, users logging in to it must first log in through a remote SAM database. In this case, the user's credentials are stored on the remote system, and the authentication used to verify the user is called the Windows Challenge/Response (NTLM) authentication protocol. NTLM uses a series of steps to verify the user's credentials. NTLM is demonstrated in Figure 4-11, where Zach is entering credentials on a local computer, but authentication is occurring on a remote system. During this process, the remote Windows computer attempts to authenticate Zach with a series of challenges and request information that only Zach and the remote computer possess.

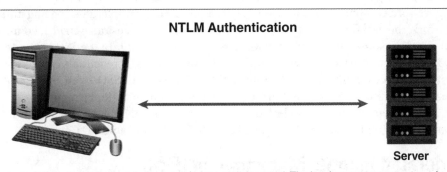

NTLM Authentication

Figure 4-11 The Windows Challenge/Response (NTLM) authentication protocol uses a series of steps to verify the user's credentials.

Server

1. Zach logs in locally by entering a username and password. The local computer computes a hash of the password and discards the password. It is never sent to the server.
2. The client sends only the user's name to the server.
3. The server creates a random number of 16 bytes. This is called a *nonce*. It is sent back to the client. This is the challenge.
4. The client computer will then encrypt the nonce using Zach's password. This encrypted text is the response to the challenge.
5. The server will use Zach's password it has stored locally and encrypt the nonce previously sent. If this encryption is the same as the response from Zach's computer, access is granted.

Goodheart-Willcox Publisher; (monitor icon) romvo/Shutterstock.com; (server) Sujith RS/Shutterstock.com

While most businesses use Windows operating systems on their desktop and mobile devices, many organizations use Linux-based servers and networking devices. Therefore, it is important to understand where and how login information, including usernames and passwords are stored on Linux-based operating systems. In Linux, usernames and passwords are stored in separate files. The logon or user information is located on the /etc/passwd file, which contains information such as the username, unique user ID information, default group ID, and other pertinent content such as the home directory. Passwords are stored in the encrypted file ~/etc/shadow, along with information such as when the password was last changed, the number of days until the password must be changed again, and the number of days to warn a user of an expiring password.

Secondary Logon

A **secondary logon** provides a way for entering a secondary set of credentials. This allows a person to be logged in as a standard user but run specific programs as an administrator. Users with administrative rights can access and configure all aspects of a computer. Therefore, they need to be especially careful with their logon information. A hacker who gains access through an administrator account can make any changes the administrator can make. Security and network administrators should consider using a secondary logon. The secondary login can be accessed two different ways:

- A secondary logon can be accessed from the graphical interface by right-clicking on a desired program and choosing **Run as Administrator**.
- A secondary logon can also be accessed from the command line using the **Runas** command. On Linux operating systems, this can be done with the **su** command, which means *switch user*.

For routine work, the administrator logs on to the system without administrative rights. Many tasks can be completed without the need for administrative rights. Then, when higher-level tasks must be completed, the administrator accesses the secondary logon that has administrative rights needed to perform those tasks. Limiting the initial login to a standard user reduces the potential exposure to hackers.

Single Sign-On (SSO)

3.8

Single sign-on (SSO) is an authentication service that allows a user to use one login and password combination to access a set of services. For example, after logging into a network, the user does not have to provide credentials to access an e-mail account. In many Microsoft-enabled services, Kerberos is used to facilitate the SSO requests. SSO is not without risks, however. A hacker obtaining the SSO credentials can access all other services configured with that SSO authentication. SSO is an important access management concept that presents itself in a number of deployments. Examples of SSO deployments include federated identity management (FIM), Security Assertion Markup Language (SAML), Shibboleth, OAuth, and OpenID Connect.

Federated Identity Management (FIM)

2.4

Federated identity management (FIM) is an agreement between a group of organizations to allow subscribers to use one set of credentials to access all networks belonging to the organizations in the group. *Federated* means a collection of smaller units or organizations. Using FIM provides a form of SSO and enables semi-independent systems to work together. The goal of a federated system is to allow users of one system to access resources from another system. Most social media and web users are familiar with options to "Log in with Facebook" or "Log in with Google." In these instances, the requesting app looks to Facebook or Google for user authentication. This eliminates the need to have its own way to create and manage user accounts.

Security Assertion Markup Language (SAML)

3.7, 3.8

Security Assertion Markup Language (SAML) is an open standard that allows the exchange of authentication and authorization information to provide SSO options over the Internet with federated systems. It is a set of specifications that use an XML format to exchange information during the SSO process. In SAML, an organization or entity hosts the user identification information in a database, known as an Identity Provider (IdP). An IdP is set up to allow assertions regarding identity to be made to partner organizations called Service Providers or SPs. The user makes a request to access the SP, which activates federated identity software, such as SAML, to facilitate the login process. The IdP then authenticates the user on its system and sends an assertion through a message to the SP. There are three types of assertions. The first type of assertion contains authentication assertions that prove identification of the user. The second assertion is called the *attribute assertion* and passes on attributes, or specific pieces of information about the user, to the SP. The third assertion deals with authorization; this assertion indicates if the user is authorized to use the service or if the IdP denied the request. This process is transparent to the user. Many products incorporate SAML standards. Some notable products include Active Directory Federated Systems from Microsoft.

Shibboleth

Shibboleth is an open-source project that provides single sign-on and allows websites to make authorization decisions on an individual level. It is another popular SSO option that began with a research organization dedicated to solving the problems of sharing information between organizations with incompatible systems. Shibboleth was developed during the same time period as SAML, and some of its features were well received and included in later versions of SAML. Shibboleth is used on web pages and implements its SSO capabilities through HTTP requests and assertions from SAML standards.

OAuth

3.8

OAuth is an open standard for single sign-on, but it does not provide authentication services; instead, it issues access to third-party clients through an authorization server. For example, if a user elects to login to a music app such as Spotify using their Facebook ID, the OAuth standard allows the third party (in this case Facebook) to use information, but not reveal the user's password. The OAuth standard implements a series of tokens to exchange information and is illustrated in Figure 4-12.

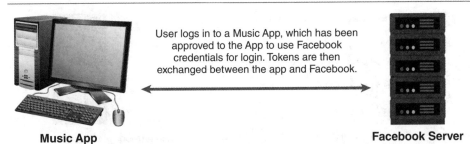

User logs in to a Music App, which has been approved to the App to use Facebook credentials for login. Tokens are then exchanged between the app and Facebook.

Music App   **Facebook Server**

Figure 4-12 The OAuth standard does not provide authentication services; instead, it issues access to third-party clients through an authorization server.

3.8

OpenID Connect

OpenID Connect, or simply *OpenID*, is another open-standard authentication protocol that supports single sign-on. It differs from OAuth, which is primarily concerned with authorization. OpenID focuses on allowing data access by providing authentication services. You can compare OpenID and OAuth in this manner. OAuth eliminates the need for a user to share a password with a third-party site. Using the previous example, Spotify does not need to know or store Jen's password. If Facebook trusts Jen, its severs will authorize Jen's account. OpenID requires users to be authenticated by an OpenID identity provider. Any site that accepts OpenID authentication will then be able to accept the user's access based on the provider's authentication process. This allows many webmasters to eliminate the need to maintain their own databases of user logins and passwords. OpenID Connect will allow the third-party site (replying party) to authenticate the user with the account the user already possesses (identity provider).

In Figure 4-13, Kira, a college student, is accessing the learning management website. However, Kira's college has chosen to use an identity provider to provide the authentication services instead of maintaining users and passwords on their own

Figure 4-13 OpenID focuses on allowing data access by providing authentication services. It requires users to be authenticated by an OpenID identity provider, and any site accepting OpenID authentication can accept the user's access based on the provider's authentication process.

Step 1

Kira goes to the school's Learning Portal's provider web page. Kira clicks on the **Login** button.

Step 2

During an exchange of information, the Service Provider will prompt the Identity Provider for information. If Kira has previously signed in, it will use previous info. If not, Kira will be prompted to provide authentication.

Step 3

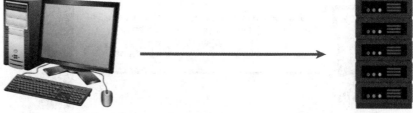

Once Kira's identity has been proven, the service provider will authorize Kira to use requested services.

Goodheart-Willcox Publisher; (monitor icon) romvo/Shutterstock.com; (server) Sujith RS/Shutterstock.com

servers. As soon as Kira has authenticated through the Identity Provider, authorization is granted to use the learning management system.

Remote Access Authentication

It is incredibly common for organizations to allow users to access files and technicians to manage systems and networking equipment remotely, meaning the connection is made over the Internet from a device not physically attached to an organization's network. Remote authentication protocols help provide the security required for authenticating users remotely. Two remote authentication protocols often used in networking are RADIUS and TACACS+. Both services provide the AAA framework by offering authentication of users, authorization of access to resources, and accounting of which users logged in and what those users did.

Remote Authentication Dial-In User Service (RADIUS) is a connectionless protocol that uses the User Datagram Protocol (UDP) as its transport protocol. RADIUS is an open-standard protocol, meaning it can work with any server or vendor. Despite containing the phrase *dial-in*, RADIUS is used for many purposes including VPNs; secure wireless connections; and logins to routers, switches and firewalls. RADIUS uses port UDP 1812 for authentication and authorization and UDP port 1813 for accounting since it is performed independently from the first two elements.

Terminal Access Controller Access-Control System (TACACS) is a Cisco proprietary protocol and authentication service that forwards user credentials to a central server. The most recent version of TACACS is known as *TACACS+*, which is an open standard but still used almost exclusively on Cisco products and UNIX software. TACACS+ is more reliable than RADIUS since it uses TCP as its transport protocol. Additionally, each concept of AAA is encrypted and separately managed in TACACS+, and RADIUS only encrypts a user's password.

Account Management Practices

Account management is actions taken by a network or security administrator to establish, configure, and set rights and permissions for individual user accounts. A **right**, or *privilege*, is the ability to perform a type of action on the computer. This includes the right to log in or the right to install or remove software. For example, a user may not be allowed to install software or change Windows settings. A **permission** is an authorization assigned to a user that allows the individual to access a given resource within a computer network. Permissions typically further define specific abilities within a right or with files and folders. Examples of permissions include the ability to delete or create a file and the ability to submit a job for printing.

An important aspect of account management is credential management. **Credential management** is actions taken to manage a user's login credentials, including a user's login name and password, and other factors associated with a user's account. Additional issues included in account management include distinguishing among account types and enforcing account policies.

Account Types

Various account types exist in a network. The most used account type is *a user account,* which is associated with an individual user. This is likely the type of account you use to log into your school or work network. However, there are several other types of accounts that exist on a network.

- A *shared account,* or *generic account,* is an account used by multiple individuals. Shared accounts are often deployed for general purpose, such as kiosks, but are not recommended for most situations because it can be difficult to audit individual actions. Shared accounts also make it difficult to manage passwords. If one user changes the password, the new credentials need to be shared with all other users.

- A *guest account* is an account that can be used for temporary purposes, such as visiting customers or temporary access to systems. Microsoft Windows has a built-in account called Guest, but it is disabled by default. For security reasons, guest accounts should remain disabled or prohibited.

- A *service account* is an account used primarily to view and provide security information for services run through a server. These accounts are not intended for user login and should be configured carefully to prevent granting more permission than is necessary. They are also used to allow operating services to load on local systems.

- A *privileged account* is one that has extensive access to a system, often root access. Privileged access should only be given to individuals who need this access to perform their jobs. A recommended best practice is to only log in with the privileged account when it is necessary for performing higher-level operations. This limits the access to the system in the event of malware or other security incidents. *Privileged access management (PAM)* is the strategies and technologies used to maintain control of privileged accounts in an enterprise environment.

Account Policy Enforcement

Most Windows settings are configured through policies. In computing, a **policy** is a set of rules that can automatically control access to resources. Policies are generally run when a computer boots and the operating system is loaded into memory, but they can also be configured to run when a user successfully authenticates to the system.

+ 3.7

When an account no longer meets the requirements established in policies, the account can and should be disabled. **Disablement** is the act of leaving an account intact but unable to be used for authentication. A user with a disabled account will not be able to access the network. Administrators may disable an account if a user leaves for an extended period or if the account is set to be removed from the system. Disabling the account without removing it enables an opportunity to review and audit the account. Similar to disablement, an expiration date can be established. **Account expiration** is a process that will automatically disable an account after the expiration date is met.

There are a number of important policies to consider implementing after creating a user account. Among those are local policies, group policies, and password policies.

Local Policy vs. Group Policy

Policies are often defined specifically on local computers. User rights established and managed on a local computer are referred to as *local policies*. However, policies can also be defined within the Active Directory. Policies configured through the Active Directory or on a server are called *group policies*. There are more options available with group policies because they potentially apply to a great deal of users and services. Local policies take precedent and are applied before group policies, but in the event of any conflicts, the last policy applied prevails.

+ 3.7

Password Policy

One of the most important policies is a password policy. A preferred *password policy* provides rules that must be followed when a password is created or changed. Figure 4-14 shows the available options for a password policy. A password policy

Figure 4-14 Password policies allow a system administrator to enforce rules for passwords.

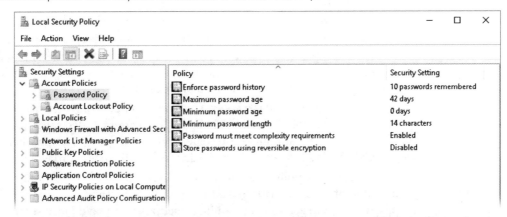

Policy	Description
Enforce password history	The user password cannot match a password used within this numerical range of previous passwords.
Maximum password age	Once a password has been used for the number of days set in this policy, the user will be forced to change the password.
Minimum password age	A password must be used for the number of days in this policy before it can be changed. This helps prevent the user from changing the password back to the previous one after being forced to change the password when it expires.
Minimum password length	The password must contain at least this number of characters. To help prevent password hacks, this number should be set no lower than eight.
Password must meet complexity requirements	Enabling this option forces the user to create a password at least six characters in length and containing at least three of these four criteria: an uppercase letter a lowercase letter a number a special character (such as #, %, @, etc.)
Store password using reversible encryption	Enabling this option stores passwords in plain text. Unless specifically needed by an authentication protocol, this setting should be disabled as enabling it makes the system much more vulnerable.

Goodheart-Willcox Publisher

helps ensure that users are providing strong passwords. This can help prevent someone from trying to hack into a user's account by trying to guess the user's password.

Most password policies dictate the complexity of passwords. **Password complexity** refers to the level of difficulty associated with a password. Often, password complexity rules determine what characters are required for a password. For example, a password policy may dictate that in order to satisfy complexity rules, a password must consist of uppercase letters, lowercase letters, numbers, and non-alphabetic characters, such as exclamation points, pound signs, and at symbols. The following consists of optional rules included in Windows Group Policy that can help enforce strict password guidelines:

- *Password history* is a control that determines how many days a new password must be used before a user can change it. This figure is measured in days and can be set anywhere between 0 and 999 days. It is recommended that administrators require users to keep a password for at least one day before being able to change it.

- *Password reuse* is a control that establishes how many unique passwords a user must create before an old password can be reused. The maximum number of unique passwords a user can create is 24, which is also the recommended setting. Forcing users to create unique passwords makes it more difficult for a hacker to guess a password.

- *Password length* is a control that determines the minimum number of characters required for a password. It is recommended that passwords should be at least 12 characters, but this control can require passwords of up to 28 characters. The minimum length of a password also affects complexity rules, as the longer a password is, the more complex it will be.
- *Password expiration* is a control that determines how long a user can use a password before it must be changed. The recommended setting for this control is 90 days, but administrators can require new passwords anywhere between 0 and 999 days. An expiration of 0 days means the password will never expire.

A password policy should also include information regarding how to handle attempted logins with invalid passwords. Sometimes, a user simply forgets the password for an account, but an incorrect password could also stem from a hacker attempting to guess a password. For users who forget their passwords, a recovery process must be in place. **Password recovery** is a process for providing an existing or new password to a user as a replacement for a lost password. A password recovery should consist of user authentication before a password is retrieved. Recovery can apply to an account's username as well as its password.

In the event an incorrect password is actually a hacker attempting to gain access through brute force, a lockout policy should be enforced. A **password lockout** is a policy that prevents access to an account after an established number of failed login attempts is met, as shown in Figure 4-15.

Figure 4-15 A password lockout is a policy that prevents access to an account after an established number of failed login attempts is met.

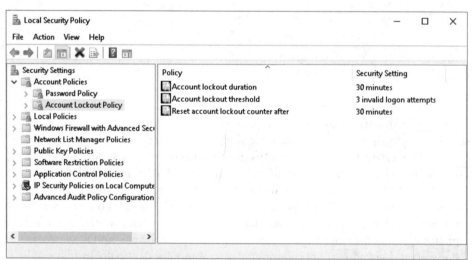

Policy	Description
Account lockout duration	This setting identifies how long an account will be disabled after the account lockout threshold is reached.
Account lockout threshold	This setting identifies the number of incorrect logon attempts before the account will be locked out.
Reset account lockout counter after	Incorrect logons will be only tracked for the time duration set here.

Password-Protected Screen Savers

A simple and effective way to limit access to a local computer is to set a password-protected screen saver. After a period of inactivity, the screen saver will turn on. To turn off the screen saver and gain access to the computer, a password must be entered. The option for requiring a password is part of the basic screen saver settings, as shown in Figure 4-16. Check the **On resume, display logon screen** check box. Also, enter the number of minutes of inactivity for the screen saver to turn on.

Similarly, a password can be required to start a computer from a power-saving "sleeping" state. This is part of the power settings. To require a password to wake a computer, navigate to the computer's power options, choose **Require a password on wakeup**, and then select the **Require a password (recommended)** radio button.

User Account Control (UAC)

Another way to limit a user's ability to make changes is with the user account control setting. The **user account control (UAC)** is a Microsoft technology used to govern security by limiting what a standard user is able to do on a system. Additional privileges require a higher UAC setting or administrative rights. For example, a user with a low UAC setting is prompted to provide appropriate credentials before changing settings or installing software. Setting an appropriate level of the UAC is important since changes to configurations can be made by software programs without the user's knowledge or interaction. The setting in the UAC helps prevent unknown or potentially dangerous settings from being made without knowledge of the user who is logged in.

Figure 4-16 Adding a password to a screen saver is an easy way to add simple protection to a computer system.

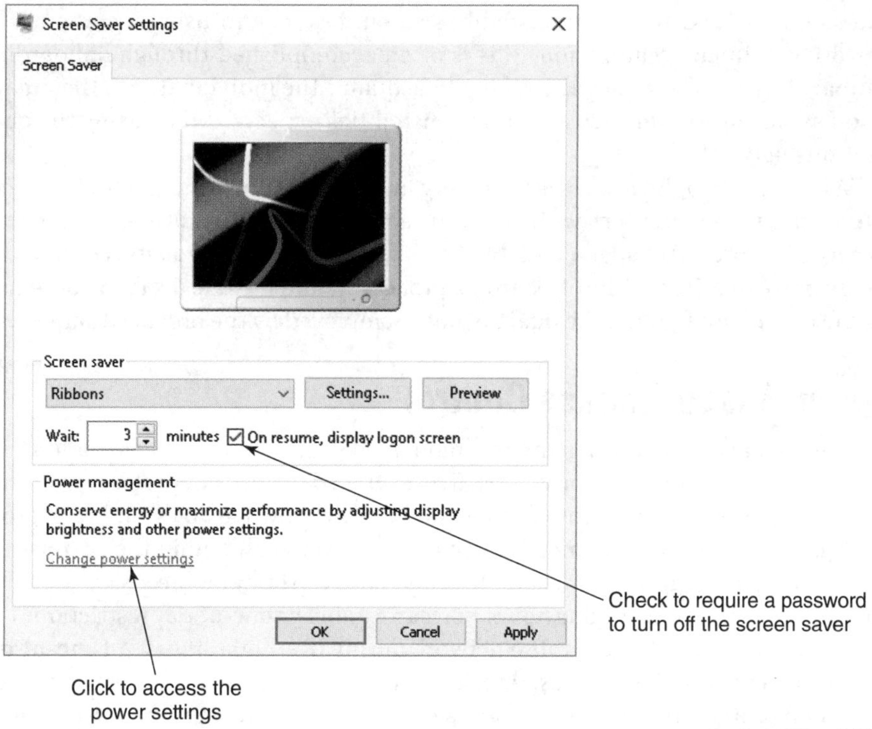

Check to require a password to turn off the screen saver

Click to access the power settings

Goodheart-Willcox Publisher

Best Practices

Account management includes best practices for ensuring each account is configured in a uniform, secure fashion. These concepts include incorporating a standard naming convention, establishing least privilege, conducting employee onboarding and offboarding, implementing group-based access, ensuring methods for account maintenance, and conducting account auditing on a regular basis.

Standard Naming Convention

2.1

A **standard naming convention** is a set of rules that dictates how account names are created or established. When accounts are established for users, an organization should create a standard naming convention. For example, a naming convention could consist of a user's first name and last name separated by a period, such as Tom.Smith, or a user's fist initial and last name, such as TSmith. Regardless of which naming convention is selected, all user accounts should follow this pattern.

Least Privilege

5.3

It is critical that employees have only the privileges needed to perform their job responsibilities. This concept is known as *least privilege*. It is always easier to grant additional privileges than it is to take them away. Removing privileges may cause resentment when a user discovers an action cannot be performed that was previously possible. It is important to consider all aspects of computer and software usage to maintain a balance between tools and resources users need to perform job duties and protecting data and systems from unnecessary access.

Employee Onboarding and Offboarding

5.3

Since permissions and privileges are granted to users, it is important that individuals understand their responsibilities when it comes to using a computer or network within an organization. This is often accomplished through onboarding. **Onboarding** is new-employee training to acquaint the individual with the organization as well as explain rights and responsibilities expected when using the organization's network.

When an employee leaves an organization, offboarding should occur. **Offboarding** is an interview with an exiting employee to gather all login credentials, such as CAC cards, ID badges, and tokens, as well as a debrief of digital content that person possesses. Part of the offboarding process should include disabling or removing a user account for an individual no longer employed by the organization.

Group-Based Access Control

3.7

Group-based access control is the recommended practice for managing and monitoring user permissions and privileges. **Group-based access control** is a procedure in which users are assigned into groups, sometimes known as *roles*, and each group is assigned permissions. All members of a given group will obtain the permissions set for that specific group. For example, if you have a group that needs access to the networking during nonworking hours, you can establish time-of-day restrictions that allow only that group to access the network during overnight hours. A **time-of-day restriction** is a control that is used to limit when a user or group of users can access an account. Alternatively, administrators can limit access to a group based on location. A **location-based policy** is a control used to grant or deny access based on a user's location. Location-based policies are known as *network location settings*.

Security changes can be made for all group members by editing the permissions or privileges of the group account as opposed to updating each user's permissions manually. However, if one user needs different or additional permissions, then those should be assigned manually, not as part of the group.

Account Maintenance

Account maintenance is the routine review of accounts, including permissions and usage patterns, compared against an organization's operational and security needs. Maintenance is often conducted on accounts to ensure that there are no vulnerabilities associated with a given account. For example, if a person's role changes within an organization, the associated account should be reviewed to ensure the appropriate permissions and restrictions are established.

Account Auditing

+ 3.7

In addition to account maintenance, it is important that account audits are performed regularly. An **account audit** is an examination, assessment, or evaluation of an account. Account audits help ensure that user actions are verified. There are three important audits that should be performed on accounts:

- A **permission audit and review** is the process of re-evaluating the permission set established for an account to determine if the same permission set can be renewed, or if more or fewer restrictions are necessary. Permission audits enable administrators to restructure group access controls or adjust permission sets.
- A **usage audit and review** is the process of evaluating the types, frequency, and purpose of applications used by a given account. This type of audit allows administrators to determine if a specific application is still needed by a user.
- **Recertification** is the process of renewing a user account, including permissions, access control, and group membership. Recertification allows administrators to ensure a given account is still valid and necessary. If an account is discovered that is no longer needed, such as an account for a former employee, it can be deleted during the recertification process.

File System Permissions

+ 3.8

Data is one of the largest and most important assets for a company or organization. Employees must be able to access the data they need to perform their jobs. However, they should not have more privileges than necessary. Protecting data access (confidentiality) and preventing unwanted changes (integrity) are high priorities for security officers.

Permissions should be assigned with careful consideration and thought. The importance of determining what each employee, or group of employees, is able to do with a given a file cannot be diminished. Furthermore, consideration must be given to the type of permissions applied to a user or group of users. In a Microsoft Windows environment, there are two types of access permissions that apply to the file system: share permissions and NFTS permissions.

Share Permissions

Sharing a file or folder is allowing another user access to it. **Share permissions** are permissions that determine the level of access to a given file or folder for other network users. As the name describes, share permissions allow you to share items stored on a network. Anyone connecting to the folder from a remote connection can have access to the files in a shared folder. Share permissions have no effect on user access when logging in directly at the machine. Following the concept of least privilege, only allow users to have the shares needed to perform their tasks.

Consider the example shown in Figure 4-17. Valeria needs to use the notes in the Marketing Campaign folder on Damien's computer. Since the folder and files are on Damien's computer, Damien has *discretionary access control*. This means the only one who can choose to share the folder is Damien, who can give Valeria permission to access the folder and files.

Sharing a Folder in Windows

Before a folder can be shared in Windows, sharing must be enabled. Sharing is configured in Control Panel under **Network and Internet>Network and Sharing Center**. Select **Change advanced sharing settings**, and then choose the **Turn on file and printer sharing** radio button.

The user who owns the folder has full-control permissions. This user is able to share the folder to selected individuals. When a folder is shared, the owner selects the individuals who are granted access. Then, the owner gives these users the appropriate permissions.

There are only three permissions available when sharing a folder: read, change, and full control, as described in Figure 4-18. The setting for a permission is either allow or deny. *Allow* explicitly grants the user the permission. *Deny* explicitly excludes the user from the permission. This is an important distinction. A user can receive permissions from multiple sources, such as a group of which the person is a member of or directly on the user's account. Unless a deny selection is present, the permissions *combine*.

Figure 4-17 Share permissions are permissions that determine the level of access to a given file or folder for other network users.

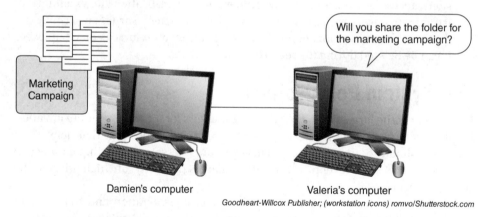

Damien's computer   Valeria's computer

Goodheart-Willcox Publisher; (workstation icons) romvo/Shutterstock.com

Figure 4-18 Permissions that can be assigned for sharing files and folders include Read, Change, and Full Control.

Share Permission	Description
Read	Allows a user to see the files and read their contents, but changes are not allowed.
Change	Allows a user to see and read files and to make changes to files as well as rename files, delete files, and create new files.
Full Control	Allows a user to see, read, and change files and give other users permissions.

Goodheart-Willcox Publisher

Consider the following example. Rashad is given the read permission to the Sales folder (allow). Rashad is in a group called SalesStaff. This group is given read and change permissions (allow) to the same folder. In this case, Rashad receives the combination of the allow permissions. The net result is Rashad's *effective* permission to Sales of read *and* change. Rashad is able to create files, delete them, and make modifications along with reading and viewing the files.

Now assume Rashad is given the read permission to the Sales folder (allow). The change permission to the sales folder is set to deny. Because the change permission includes the read permission, read permission is also applied to the folder. However, Rashad is in a group called SalesStaff. This group is given read and change permissions (allow) to the same folder. In this case, Rashad receives the combination of the allow permissions, but the deny permission is also considered. The net result is Rashad's *effective* permission to Sales will be deny for read and change. This is because whenever the deny and allow permissions conflict, deny *always* prevails.

TECH TIP

Microsoft Windows creates several hidden administrative shares by default. These include the folder where the operating system is installed and each drive is recognized by the system (C$, D$, etc.). These shares are protected by requiring administrative access but can be removed if necessary.

Sharing a Folder in Linux

File sharing in Linux/UNIX systems is most commonly accomplished by using the Network File System (NFS) protocol. The system in Linux must be configured to run the NFS server. Once configuration is completed, the file of /etc/exports is configured with the list of directories that are to be shared, and the **exportfs** command is executed. On the remote machine, the client must use the **mount** command to make the shared directories available. In the exports file, you can configure the directory, include the host(s) to which you want to share the folder, and the type of permissions you are granting.

Security Considerations of Sharing Folders

Folders can be shared by any user who has full control of a folder, and shares can be found by searching the network where they have been created. Additionally, users can view all shares created on a local machine. The ease of access to shared folders presents a possible access point for a hacker or employee to use to exploit other system vulnerabilities or access confidential data. Therefore, shared folders should be monitored for unnecessary access.

Shares can be created and hidden. Many default administrative shares are hidden. These include sharing of fixed and removable drives such as C: or D:, the folder containing the Windows operating system, and a special communication share called IPC. Administrators sometimes hide other shares for ease of use. However, hidden shares may also be used by a hacker in an attempt to hide that person's actions. A hidden share is only accessible if you know the correct name and path to the folder. Administrators create a hidden share in the advanced settings by putting a dollar sign ($) at the end of the share name. For example, if the folder Notes is shared as Notes$, only users who know this name and the path to the folder will be able to access it.

NTFS Permissions

 3.8

Sharing folders makes them available to users logged into another machine on the network. However, it has no impact on a user who logs in directly on the local machine. When a user logs into a local computer, the person has complete access to the files and folders within the individual's Users folder by default. To secure the folders for users with local access, NTFS permissions must be used. **New Technology File System (NTFS) permissions** are permissions that are used to manage access to folders, files, or resources stored on an NTFS-based system.

NTFS provides more options for permissions than share permissions. Additionally, share permissions are not very flexible when compared to NTFS permissions. For example, suppose a user needs to be able to add files. With sharing, this user must be given change permission, which also allows files to be deleted. NTFS allows an administrator to be more specific when assigning permissions. NTFS permissions also use allow and deny options when assigning permissions.

Figure 4-19 describes the different types of NTFS permissions. Notice that the full control permission allows the user to *take ownership* of the files. The owner of the file or folder is normally the person who created the object. As the owner, the user has discretionary control over the file or folder. In some cases, however, an administrator might need to take ownership of a file or folder. For example, if an employee has left the company and the individual's user account is deleted, an administrator can take ownership of the files, and thus obtain full control access to the files.

Permission Type

There are three types of permissions assigned to a user: explicit, implicit, and inherited.

- **Explicit permissions** are permissions given to a user to access a specific folder, file, or network drive. These permissions are often set by default when an object is created, but they can also be established by a user or administrator.

- **Inherited permissions** are permissions a user receives by default when a child of a parent object is created. For example, suppose a user is assigned explicit permissions of read, list, and write for Folder1. The user inherits the same permissions in all subfolders within Folder1 because each subfolder is a child of the Folder1 parent object.

- **Implicit permissions** are permissions a user receives through another object, such as a group. Suppose a user is a member of the Engineers group. All permissions the group has will be indirectly assigned to the user as well.

Implicit and explicit permissions factor into a user's effective permissions. However, there is a hierarchy of permission order:

1. Explicit deny
2. Explicit allow
3. Inherited deny
4. Inherited allow

Figure 4-19 New Technology File System (NTFS) permissions are permissions that are used to manage access to folders, files, or resources stored on an NTFS-based system.

NTFS Permission	Description
Full control	Gives the user the ability to take ownership; provides the ability to read, change, and give other people permissions.
Modify	The user can modify the properties of a file and create and delete files.
Read & execute	The user can read and run any executable files.
List folder contents	The user can see the files in the folder, but cannot view the contents of files; only applicable to folders, not files.
Read	The user can see files in the folder and read their contents.
Write	The user can edit contents of files.
Advanced	This button accesses more advanced options that are more granular, such as allowing files to be created, but denying the ability to delete files.

Goodheart-Willcox Publisher

Figure 4-20 illustrates three scenarios and details the effective permissions for each scenario.

Combining NTFS and Share Permissions

3.8

In many cases, when a folder is shared, the options for permissions are not flexible or specific enough to satisfy the owner or originator of the folder. In these situations, NTFS permissions are also given to the share. When the two permission sets are combined, the permissions are set according to their restrictions. The more restrictive permission takes precedence.

Consider the following example. The marketing department has created the folder structure shown in Figure 4-21. These folders will be used to save the data for online research. The marketing manager shares the Research Data folder with the Marketing group and grants the group the *share* permission of read. The manager then assigns the Marketing group the NTFS permissions of read & execute, list, and write. This allows all users to add more data to the databases. However, in this scenario, the Marketing group will only have read permissions assigned by the share since that is more restrictive than the NTFS permissions for the group. This applies to the Telephone Surveys and Online Surveys subfolders as well.

In many cases, it makes more sense to first share the folder with the target user or group with the full-control permission. Then, assign the specific NTFS permissions you actually want the user or group to have. In this case, the most restrictive permissions will be the NTFS permissions.

Security Considerations of NTFS Permissions

NTFS permissions offer the ability to assign very specific permissions to users or groups. A user can have permissions from many areas, including share permissions and memberships in other groups. This can present security risks. Administrators should confirm each user's actual abilities by verifying effective permissions.

Figure 4-20 Implicit and explicit permissions factor into a user's effective permissions.

Scenario	Effective Permissions
Marissa is explicitly allowed read, list, and write permissions for the **Marketing Campaign** folder. She has no other explicit or implicit permissions.	Marissa can list, read, and write for both the **Marketing Campaign** folder and the **Videos** subfolder.
Drew is explicitly allowed read, list, and explicitly denied write permissions for the **Marketing Campaign** folder. He is a member of the Marketing group, which is explicitly allowed read, list, and write permissions for the **Marketing Campaign** folder.	Drew's rights are read and list. The deny permission on write took away his allow write permission. These permissions are then inherited in the **Videos** subfolder.
Carlos is a member of the **SocialMedia** group. This group is allowed list, read & execute, and write permissions for the **Marketing Campaign** folder. Carlos also is explicitly allowed modify permission for the **Videos** subfolder.	Carlos can list, read & execute, and write for the **Marketing Campaign** folder through his implicit permissions from the **SocialMedia** group. For the **Videos** subfolder, he inherits all of the above permissions and he also is allowed to modify the folder.

Goodheart-Willcox Publisher

Figure 4-21 In many cases, when a folder is shared, the options for permissions are not flexible or specific enough to satisfy the owner or originator of the folder.

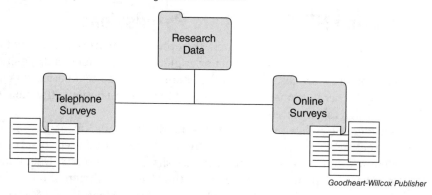

Goodheart-Willcox Publisher

3.8

Linux File Permissions

Permissions are handled in a different format for Linux than they are in Windows. Each file and folder handles permissions in the same way. There are three basic permission groups that are used to assign permissions.

- The first set of permissions lists the file's owner. These are permissions that only affect the owner of the file or directory and have no impact on any other user.
- The next set of permissions lists the assigned group. Any member of the group would have those permissions applied.
- The last set of permissions applies to all other users on the system.

Directories and files have three basic types of permissions that can be assigned to each permission group listed previously. The first is the Read (R) permission. This permission gives the user the ability to read the content of a file. The Write (W) permission allows the user to write or make changes to a file or a directory. The last permission is called Execute (X). This permission is used to allow a user to view contents of a directory and execute or run file, as indicated in Figure 4-22.

You can review a file and easily view the permissions of a file by issuing the **ls -l filename** command. The results of this command are displayed in a specific format. The file will show with permission information displayed after the file name or directory. The permissions apply not only to the user issuing the command, but also to the group to which the user belongs and then anyone else who may access the file. The order in which these permissions appear details for whom the permissions apply, as illustrated in Figure 4-23.

Figure 4-22 Directories and files have three basic types of permissions: Read (R), Write (W), and Execute (X).

Permission Type	Explanation
Read (R)	This permission allows a user to read a file.
Write (W)	This permission allows a user to write or make changes to a file or directory.
Execute (X)	This permission allows a user to view the contents of a directory and execute a file.

Goodheart-Willcox Publisher

In the previous example, the **ls -l** command produced the output shown in Figure 4-20 for **ls myfile -l**. The user lklavender in Figure 4-21 has read and write permissions to the file, the default group of lklavender has read and write permissions, and anyone else accessing this file would have just read permissions. Notice the – that appears before the first set of permissions in Figure 4-24. This means that the object in question is a file. If the item were a directory, the permission sequence would begin with a d, for example drw-rw-r--.

Figure 4-23 Permissions apply not only to the user issuing a command, but also to the group to which the user belongs and anyone else who may access the file.

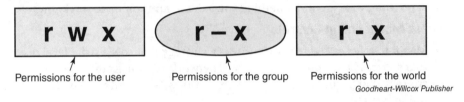

Permissions for the user   Permissions for the group   Permissions for the world

Goodheart-Willcox Publisher

Figure 4-24 In this example, the user and group both have read and write permissions, but anyone else accessing the file only has read permissions. The – preceding the first permission set means the object is a file, not a directory.

```
lklavender@ubuntu:~$ ls myfile -l
-rw-rw-r-- 1 lklavender lklavender 0 Oct  9 11:26 myfile
```

Goodheart-Willcox Publisher

SUMMARY

Authentication and Access Control

- Authentication is the process of validating a user and verifying the person's identity. It helps ensure that only authorized users are accessing the network and its resources.
- An authorized user is a person who is approved to access a system.
- Access control refers to the intentional restriction of user access to specific locations and resources.
- AAA is a key framework for granting and facilitating network access to users. AAA is defined as identification, authentication, authorization, and accounting.

Passwords

- Most accounts used a secret word and/or phrase called a password to prove a user's identity to a system.
- Password authentication is one of the least secure methods of authentication. Some of the problems include weak passwords; reuse of passwords on multiple sites; weak password policies, which allows users the ability to use the same password indefinitely; and password-cracking tools, which allow hackers to uncover passwords.

Multifactor Authentication

- Multifactor authentication involves using multiple independent credentials, rather than just one, to verify user identification. It includes using factors and attributes to verify an individual.

- A factor is evidence or proof of identity. Multiple factors to confirm an individual's identity include what you know, what you have, and what you are.

- An attribute is a quality, feature, or characteristic of a person. Attributes provide evidence of an individual's identity including somewhere you are, something you can do, something you exhibit, and someone you know.

Access Management Controls

- Mandatory access controls security is a strategy that sets a strict level of access to resources based on criteria set by a network administrator. An example is a strategy that permits access based on non-negotiable criteria, such as secret, top secret, etc.

- Discretionary access control (DAC) allows a user to be granted additional rights to data beyond what is allowed by the individual's assigned access level. The user who owns the data can grant permissions to another user. Two types of DAC controls are role-based access control and rule-based access control.

- Attribute-based access control (ABAC) uses attributes or characteristics assigned to a user and compares them to attributes or characteristics assigned to the data. This allows businesses to adopt a more dynamic approach in assigning access.

System Login

- There are three ways a user can log in to a computer on a network: through an organizational domain, on a stand-alone machine, or by a secondary logon.

- When logging on to a workstation located on a network, also known as an organizational domain, the user provides a login name and password. Authentication information is passed to the server's security database where it is cross-referenced against what has been established for the user. If it matches, the user is authenticated. If not, authentication fails, and access is denied.

- Security domains for servers are often implemented with the use of directory services. They are created and managed by the Lightweight Directory Access Protocol (LDAP) or its secure form LDAPS.

- Kerberos, a key ticketing service, is the standard authentication protocol used by Microsoft's Active Directory.

- When a computer is not connected to a network, it is called a stand-alone or local machine. In this type of connection, logon accounts must be stored directly on the stand-alone machine. Authentication is accomplished through data stored in the Security Account Manager (SAM) and an authentication process called NTLM.

- Secondary logon is the practice of logging in as a non-administrator account and using the secondary login to access programs on an administrative level for that application only.

Single Sign-On (SSO)

- Single sign-on (SSO) is an authentication service that allows a user one login and password combination to access a set of services. Examples of SSO deployments include federated identity management (FIM), Security Assertion Markup Language (SAML), Shibboleth, OAuth, and OpenID Connect.

- Federated identity management allows users of one system to access resources in another system. It enables semi-independent systems to work together.
- Security Assertion Markup Language (SAML) is an open standard that allows the exchange of authentication and authorization information to provide SSO options over the Internet with federated systems. It is a set of specifications that uses an XML format to exchange information during the SSO process.
- Shibboleth is an open-source project that provides single sign-on and allows websites to make authorization decisions on an individual level.
- OAuth open standard for single sign-on that issues access to third-party clients through an authorization server. It implements a series of tokens to exchange information.
- OpenID Connect is an open SSO protocol that allows an Identity Provider to provide the authentication services between participating businesses and the authorization access to local resources.

Account Management Practices

- Account management refers to actions taken by a network or security administrator to establish, configure, and set rights and permissions for individual user accounts.
- Credential management is an important aspect of account management. It refers to actions taken to manage a user's login credentials, including a login name and password as well as other factors associated with an account.
- Account management practices include identifying account types within an organization, establishing an account policy and enforcing it, setting a password-protected screen saver, and using a user account control to limit what a standard user is able to do on a system.

Best Practices

- Organizations can implement best practices to help ensure accounts are configured in a uniform, secure fashion.
- A standard naming convention is a set of rules that dictates the manner in which account names are created or established. An organization often establishes rules to follow for all user accounts.
- The concept of least privileges involves employees having only the privileges needed to perform their job responsibilities.
- When an employee starts, the individual will go through onboarding, which is new-employee training to acquaint the individual with the organization as well as explain rights and responsibilities expected when using the organization's network. When an employee leaves an organization, offboarding occurs. Offboarding is an interview with an exiting employee to gather all login credentials.
- Group-based access control is a procedure in which users are assigned into groups, and each group is assigned permissions. All members of a given group obtain permissions set for that specific group, which helps an organization monitor user permissions and privileges.
- Account maintenance is the routine review of accounts compared against an organization's operational and security needs. It is often conducted to ensure that there are no vulnerabilities associated with a given account.

- An account audit is an examination, assessment, or evaluation of an account. Account audits help ensure that user actions are verified. Three important audits conducted include permission audit and review, usage audit and review, and recertification.

File System Permissions

- Microsoft uses two levels of permissions to grant local and remote folder/file access: share permissions and NTFS permissions.
- Share permissions are permissions that determine the level of access to a given file or folder for other network users. It allows a user to share items stored on a network. Anyone connecting to the folder from a remote connection can have access to the files in a shared folder.
- NTFS permissions provide more granular control over permissions to files and folders and apply to local and/or remote files and folders. NTFS basic permissions include List, Read, Read & Execute, Modify, Write, and Full Control. Advanced permissions include the ability to create specific permission threats.

Permission Type

- Explicit permissions are permissions given to a user to access a specific folder, file, or network drive. Inherited permissions are permissions a user receives by default when a child of a parent object is created. Implicit permissions are permissions a user receives through another object, such as a group.
- Combining share and NTFS permissions relies on the principle that the most restrictive of the two permissions prevails.
- Linux permissions are granted to the owner, the default group, and all other users (known as the world). Linux permissions on files or directories can be viewed with the ls -l filename command syntax.

REVIEW QUESTIONS

1. Explain authentication and access control.
2. Summarize the AAA framework.
3. Explain common problems associated with password authentication.
4. Identify factors and attributes of multifactor authentication.
5. Compare a hard token to a soft token.
6. What three GPS-based activities are used to identity a user through location?
7. Compare and contrast types of access management controls.
8. State the difference between a role-based access control and rule-based access control.
9. Explain three processes for system login.
10. Explain how SAM authentication protects the confidentiality of the password while providing authentication.
11. How does a secondary logon reduce the attack surface?
12. List and discuss examples of single sign-on deployments.
13. A company decides to implement access to software using an Identity Provider. Which single sign-on option will be used in this scenario?

14. Summarize account management practices.

15. What is the difference between a right and a permission?

16. List three common account polices that can be implemented after a user account is created.

17. Identify and explain three different best practices an organization can use to ensure accounts are configured in a uniformed, secured fashion.

18. Summarize three key account audits that organizations should perform on accounts.

19. Evaluate two types of file system permissions.

20. What are the three permission options for shared folders in Windows?

21. How can a shared folder be set to hidden?

22. Which NTFS permission allows a user to take ownership of files?

23. Explain three types of permissions assigned to a user.

24. What occurs when shared permissions and NTFS permissions are combined?

25. What are the three types of permissions in a Linux operating system?

✚ SAMPLE SECURITY+ EXAM QUESTIONS

1. A user logs in and provides a password and a token ID value. This is an example of _____.
   A. biometric login
   B. hash value
   C. one-time password
   D. multifactor authentication

2. Which of these is *not* considered multifactor authentication?
   A. Use of a password and a retinal scan
   B. Use of a fingerprint and an iris scan
   C. Using a token and a palm print
   D. Using a password and CAC device

3. Which two technologies are single sign-on options? (Choose 2)
   A. SAML
   B. LDAPS
   C. Federation
   D. Kerberos
   E. NTLM

4. Royse is an authorized employee of his firm and when providing biometric credentials, access was denied. Which describes what happened?
   A. FAR
   B. OTP
   C. FRR
   D. CER

5. Which of the following *best* describes eliminating potential threats?

    A. Attack surfacing

    B. Policy implementation

    C. Hardening a system

    D. Hashing

6. How does the **Enforce Password History** setting help create a strong password strategy?

    A. It prevents users from ever reusing a previous password.

    B. It prevents users from adding numbers to the end of a previous password.

    C. It prevents users from using a previous password for a specified number of changes.

    D. It prevents passwords that are already being used by others.

7. Which security strategy is *most* effective in preventing a normal user from automatically installing software on a computer?

    A. Grant the user only read and execute permissions to the computer.

    B. Set an appropriate UAC level.

    C. Join the computer to the network domain.

    D. Do not allow share permissions.

8. Luis is a forensic investigator for a firm. Which access control policy will allow easy configuration of his rights and permissions based on his job function?

    A. ABAC

    B. SAML

    C. MAC

    D. Rule-based access

9. Restricting a user to allowed logins between the hours of 7 am to 6 pm is configured in which option?

    A. OAUTH

    B. Rule-based access

    C. Secure token

    D. HOTP

10. Which setting will ensure Cameron will not change his password to a previously used password?

    A. Password complexity

    B. Credential management

    C. Password reuse

    D. CAC implementation

LAB EXERCISES

Lab Activity 4-1: Local User Accounts

A computer that is not connected to a network does not have access to the network's Active Directory. However, it still has a local database of user accounts.

1. On a Windows computer, click **Start**>**All Apps**>**Windows System**>**Command Prompt** in Windows 10 or enter command prompt into the search bar to open the local command prompt window.

2. At the command prompt, enter net users. When the [Enter] key is pressed to execute the command, all local users in the SAM file are displayed, as shown.

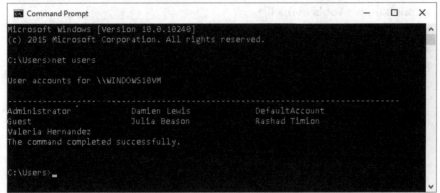

3. Enter the **set** command. This shows the local variables. Look through all the variables stored on the machine. Which variable do you believe represents the logged-in user?

4. Enter the **net localgroup** command. The local security groups on the system are displayed, as shown.

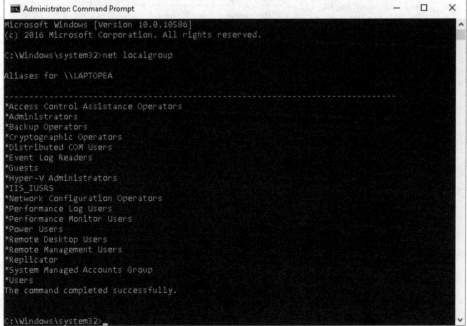

5. Type net accounts to identify local settings including password settings and lockout settings. Evaluate each of the settings if the logged-in user was an administrative assistant to the Chief Information Officer. List the settings and indicate on each whether you would change it and the new recommended value, or keep it the same. Justify your reasoning.

Lab Activity 4-2: Local Password Policies

Password policies are an important part of securing not only the local computer, but also the network. These policies can be viewed on the local machine.

1. Log in to Microsoft Windows as a local user with administrator rights.

2. Click the **Start** button, enter administrative tools in the search box, and click **Administrative Tools** in the list.

3. In the window that is displayed, double-click the **Local Security Policy** shortcut. The **Local Security Policy** window is displayed.

4. Click the arrow next to Account Policies to expand the tree, and then select the Password Policy branch.

5. Double-click the Enforce Password History setting to display details, as shown. Click the **Explain** tab in the dialog box to view information about the policy. What is the maximum number of new unique passwords that can be remembered?

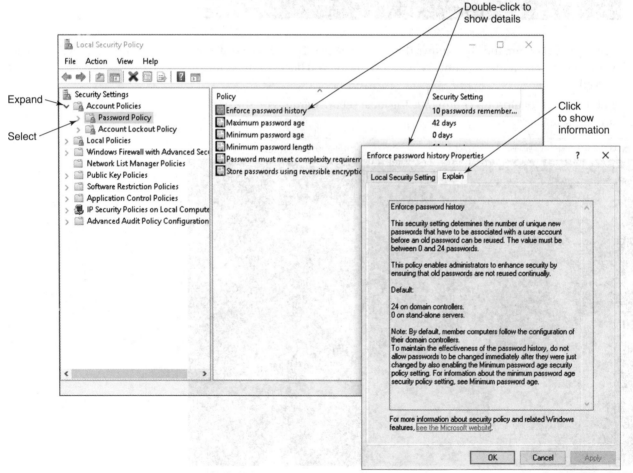

Goodheart-Willcox Publisher

6. Which setting would you choose to have the maximum password option never expire?

7. Click the **Cancel** button to close the details window.

8. In the **Local Security Policy** window, expand the Local Policies branch, and select the User Rights Assignment branch.

9. By default, which accounts can change the system time?

10. Close the **Local Security Policy** window. Be sure you have not made changes to any of the local policies.

Lab Activity 4-3: Share Permissions

It is easy to share folders. When doing so, it is important to consider which permissions are allowed and which are denied.

1. Launch Windows File Explorer and navigate to your Users folder. This is the folder under Users named with your login name.

2. Right-click on your folder and click **New>Folder** in the shortcut menu. Name the new folder Classnotes.

3. Right-click on the Classnotes folder and click **Properties** in the shortcut menu.

4. In the **Properties** dialog box, click the **Sharing** tab. There are two ways to share the folder, using the **Share...** button or the **Advanced Sharing...** button.

5. Click the **Share...** button. A new window is displayed in which users are selected, as shown.

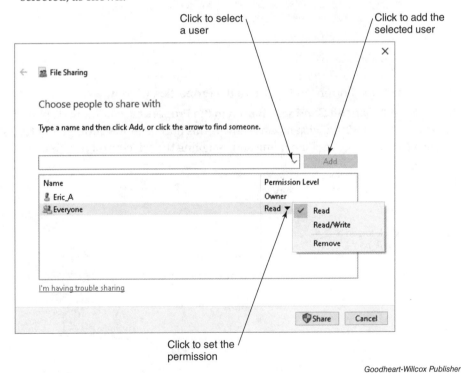

Click to select a user

Click to add the selected user

Click to set the permission

Goodheart-Willcox Publisher

6. Click the drop-down list and select **Everyone**. Then, click the **Add** button. Note: this is for practice only; selecting **Everyone** allows *every* user on the network access to this folder!

7. Click the permission setting for the Everyone user, which is currently Read. Notice the three options available in the shortcut menu.

8. Leave the settings as the default Read. Then, click the **Share** button at the bottom of the window. When the system finishes sharing the folder, a link for user access is provided, as shown.

Link to shared folder

Goodheart-Willcox Publisher

9. Click the **Done** button, and return to the **Properties** window.

10. Click the **Advanced Sharing...** button in the **Properties** window to display the **Advanced Sharing** dialog box, as shown. This option allows additional settings, such as changing the share name and assigning the full control permission.

Uncheck to stop sharing folder

Click to add a share name

Add a comment

Click to change sharing permissions

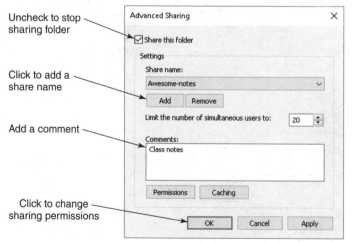

Goodheart-Willcox Publisher

11. Click the **Add** button below the **Share name:** drop-down list, and enter the name Awesome-notes in the **New Share** dialog box that appears. Click the **OK** button to return to the **Advanced Sharing** dialog box.

12. Click in the **Comments:** text box, and enter Class notes.

13. Click the **Permissions** button. The **Permissions** dialog box is displayed, as shown. Notice how there are settings for each of the permissions.

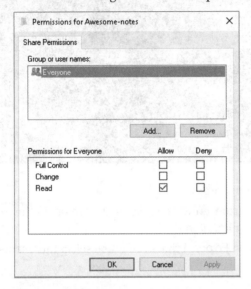

Goodheart-Willcox Publisher

14. Check the check box in the **Deny** column for the change permission. What happens to the read permission? Why did that happen?

15. Click the **Cancel** button so as not to change the permissions.

16. Click the **OK** button in the **Advanced Sharing** dialog box to save the new share.

17. Click the **Close** button in the **Properties** dialog box.

Lab Activity 4-4: Shared Folders on a System

Shared folders on a system can be viewed using the command prompt. This will show all shared folders, including hidden folders.

1. On a Windows computer, click **Start>All Apps>Windows System>Command Prompt** in Windows 10 or enter command prompt into the search bar to open the local command prompt window.

2. Enter net share on the command line. All shared folders are listed, as shown. How many *hidden* shares do you see?

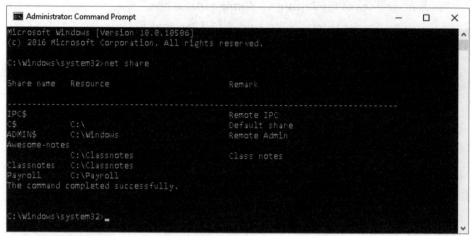

3. Close the command prompt.

4. Click the **Start** button, enter computer management in the search box, and click **Computer Management** in the list.

5. Expand the Shared Folders branch, and then select the Shares branch, as shown.

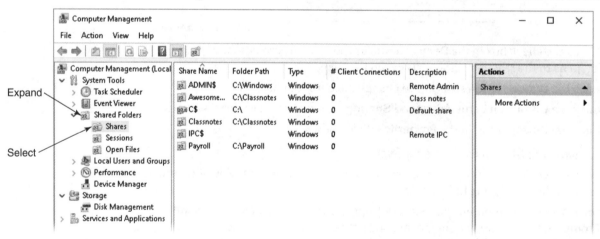

6. Based on what you see, are the shares for C$, IPC$, and ADMIN$ security concerns?

7. Notice the share you created named Awesome-notes. Click *once* on Awesome-notes to select it. Then, in the right-hand panel, click **More Actions** under the **Awesome-notes** heading (*not* the **Shares** heading). A shortcut menu is displayed.

8. Click **Stop Sharing** in the shortcut menu. When prompted, click the **Yes** button. This folder is no longer shared. Notice it is no longer listed as a shared folder.

CASE STUDY

Biometric-Authentication Technology

Election officials are often concerned with voter fraud. To combat this, the idea of using biometric voting systems is being considered as an alternative to existing election systems. Many African and Latin American countries have already embraced this technology. In the United States, a handful of states including Utah, Colorado, and West Virginia deployed mobile biometric voting in the 2018 and 2019 elections for overseas users, particularly members of the US military. According to the West Virginia secretary of state, while there was an initial hacking attempt during the 2018 pilot, the hackers were unable to gain access. Similarly, a mobile app was used in April of 2020 in Utah for the Republican convention due to COVID-19 restrictions.

1. What are some of the ethical and privacy concerns related to these types of systems?

2. In what way(s) do these concerns specified in the previous question outweigh the security benefits these devices provide?

3. Describe your feelings toward the use of biometric technology.

4. Explain which biometric technologies make you comfortable. Which technologies make you uncomfortable?

5. Describe how comfortable you would feel casting a ballot using a biometrically secured device.

Physical Security

LEARNING OUTCOMES

- Summarize security controls.
- Discuss physical security controls used by an organization.
- Explain physical controls used within an IT system.
- Summarize examples of threats posed by insiders of an organization.
- Compare and contrast methods of data destruction.

KEY TERMS

administrative control
air gap
air-gap network
bollard
compensating control
corrective control
closed-circuit television (CCTV)
data center
data purging
degaussing
detective control
deterrent control
disk sanitization

electromagnetic radiation (EMR)
EMI shielding
Faraday cage
hot and cold aisle
IEEE 802.1X
industrial camouflage
Jersey wall
mantrap
object detection
personal identity verification (PIV)
physical control
physical network segregation
preventive control

protective distribution system (PDS)
pulping
screen filter
secure token
security control
smart card
smart card authentication
SNMPv3
tailgating
technical control
TEMPEST
turnstile

SECURITY+ CERTIFICATION EXAM OBJECTIVES

The following Security+ Certification Exam Objectives are covered in this chapter.

+ 1.1: Tailgating
+ 2.4: Time-based one-time password (TOTP)
+ 2.4: HMAC-based one-time password (HOTP)
+ 2.4: Smart card authentication
+ 2.7: Bollards/barricades
+ 2.7: Mantraps
+ 2.7: Badges
+ 2.7: Alarms
+ 2.7: Signage
+ 2.7: Cameras

+ 2.7: Closed-circuit television (CCTV)
+ 2.7: Industrial camouflage
+ 2.7: Personnel
+ 2.7: Locks
+ 2.7: Lighting
+ 2.7: Fencing
+ 2.7: Fire suppression
+ 2.7: Sensors
+ 2.7: Visitor logs
+ 2.7: Faraday cages
+ 2.7: Air gap

+ 2.7: Protected cable distribution
+ 2.7: Secure areas
+ 2.7: Secure data destruction
+ 3.1: Simple Network Management Protocol, Version 3 (SNMPv3)
+ 3.4: 802.1X
+ 3.7: Tokens
+ 3.7: Smart cards
+ 3.8: 802.1X
+ 4.1: Data sanitization
+ 5.1: Control type

OVERVIEW

Physical security controls are of utmost importance to an organization so assets are protected from harm. Not all threats to data and systems come from hackers through the Internet. There are many risks from local threats, including employees and unauthorized persons posing as employees. It is also important to consider the problems faced by environmental threats, including the threat of overheated systems or accidental water damage.

This chapter will explore physical controls for an organization and its computer network; insider threats; and methods of secure data destruction and sanitization.

SECURITY+ NOTE

The Security+ Exam emphasizes a candidate's ability to assess an organization's security plan. Be prepared to evaluate technology usage and physical building layouts in scenarios and recommend appropriate physical security measures.

Security Controls

Security controls are tools or processes used to reduce risk to assets by slowing, minimizing, or stopping a threat. When planning security measures, design or implement physical controls that will help with three key goals in mind:

- preventing a problem
- detecting a problem
- recovering from a problem through corrective action

It is preferable to prevent a problem from occurring rather than to deal with the aftermath of an incident. By using security controls, you can organize various methods and policies needed to protect a business.

There are different types of controls, including the following:

- An **administrative control** is a type of control that develops and enforces policies, procedures, and processes in an effort to regulate human interaction with a device or network.
- A **compensating control** is a type of control that provides an alternative action in the event a typical control cannot be used.
- A **corrective control** is a type of control that isolates and limits damage caused by an incident.
- A **detective control** is a type of control that identifies incidents that are in progress or have recently occurred and categorizes them according to specific characteristics.
- A **deterrent control** is a type of control that attempts to dissuade attacks or violations from occurring.
- A **physical control** is a tangible control used to protect the physical assets of an organization.
- A **preventive control** is a type of control that prevents an incident from occurring.
- A **technical control** is a type of control that uses technology that automates device management for access and application of confidential data.

A good security plan will incorporate all the aforementioned types of controls. These controls are explained further in Figure 5-1.

 5.1

Figure 5-1 Security controls can help organize the various methods and policies needed to protect a business.

Goal	Control Type	Description
Preventing	Physical Controls/ Deterrent Controls	These controls are used to prevent or deter an incident from occurring. An example is a gated parking lot.
Preventing	Technical Controls	These controls are usually software programs or policies that are implemented to protect systems. An example of a technical control is requiring a password of a specific length.
Preventing	Procedural Controls/ Administrative Controls	These controls are specified by policies or management to ensure something is done or not done. An example is to conduct annual training for all employees by a specific date.
Detecting	Detective Controls	These controls send notification to appropriate individuals when an incident is discovered so the threat can be addressed. An example is an alert that appears if malware is detected on a removable storage drive.
Preventing, detecting, or recovering (depends on specific control)	Legal/Regulatory Controls	Some controls are not optional. Legal or industry regulations may determine the level of control allowed. An example is a vendor that processes credit cards must conduct a vulnerability scan every 90 days.
Preventing, detecting, or recovering (depends on specific control)	Compensating Controls	Sometimes a control is not possible to implement. A compensating control, or an alternate control, is one in which a similar control can be conducted that meets the same criteria. An example is an administrative control that requires several employees to sign off on a task, which can be provided by a similar safeguard if there are not enough employees to perform that control.

Goodheart-Willcox Publisher

Physical security controls are tangible controls used to protect the physical assets of an organization, including its computer systems. Physical controls are a form of *access-management control*, which is a system of approving or denying individuals access to a facility or network.

Facility Physical Controls

A number of physical controls can be used to help prevent physical user access to a facility or sensitive area, including the following:

- industrial camouflage
- gated entrance
- fencing
- lighting
- alarms
- barricades
- personnel
- screen filters
- identification badges
- smart cards
- tokens
- safes and vaults
- protected distribution and cabling
- lock access and cable locks
- CCTV
- mantraps
- turnstiles
- signage
- logs

Keep in mind, not every approach can stop all intrusions. A good strategy is to create a plan based on defense in depth that calls for multiple layers of defensive strategies. *Defense in depth* means having multiple levels of protection. If one plan fails to stop an intruder, subsequent layers may still stop the attack. Physical barriers should be only one layer of defense in depth.

Industrial Camouflage

Industrial camouflage is a concept in which a company designs a facility in a way that makes it unappealing or uninteresting to a potential attacker. Examples of industrial camouflage on a building's exterior include limited or misleading identification and markings to mask what is inside, establish underground operations, or choose a location in a remote or mountainous area to help prevent electronic eavesdropping.

Gated Entrance

The first layer of defense is to control physical access to the business site. A common method to achieve this is a gated entrance to the parking lot. For an individual to pass through a gate to the parking area, a security guard must approve the person for entry. The guard may be physically present in a guardhouse, or the approval may occur through a remote camera.

In place of a security guard, proximity cards and readers may be used. A proximity card, also known as a swipe card, is similar in size to a credit card and is swiped at the gate to gain entry. A *proximity reader* is a transponder that recognizes the presence of a proximity card and then sends a radio signal to a mechanism that opens the gate.

Fencing

Fencing is placed around property or selected buildings or areas within a building to create a physical gate or cage. Fencing is *not* the most secure option as it can often be easily breached. However, it can help deter some intruders from accessing a facility.

Lighting

Lighting is a strong preventative measure and provides a deterrent to individuals who otherwise would be able to sneak past other security measures, such as guards and security cameras. Security lighting should be considered for the perimeter of your business, as well as vital areas that may be vulnerable to attacks, such as storage areas, power distribution centers, and side doors. Lighting can be programmed to remain on indefinitely, turn on and off at regular intervals through automatic timers, or turn on through motion detection.

Alarms

Installing alarms to trigger notification of unwanted activity can serve as a detective control in your physical security plan. Loud, audible alarms notify a potential intruder, as well as individuals in the area, that the person's presence is detected. Noise-detection sensors can be used to trigger alarms in breach events that have audible sound, such as a window breaking or a door being forcibly opened. Alarms can also be fitted with motion-detection capabilities.

Audible alarms may provide a deterrent when sounded, but keep in mind that attackers may test response time from an alarm notification. Tying alarms with other measures, such as notification to appropriate personnel, increases efficiency of this type of control. Conversely, silent alarms can provide you with stealth notification to track and catch the person breaching a secured area.

Barricades

Barricades are physical obstructions to a passage. There are many different categories of barricades, and they may be permanent or temporary. Some barricades, such as Jersey walls, prevent vehicular traffic from getting too close to a building. **Jersey walls** are tee-shaped walls usually made of concrete to prevent vehicles from passing, as shown in Figure 5-2A. Jersey walls offer multiple configuration options and can be anchored in place, moved, and rearranged at will. Another example of a barricade is bollards. **Bollards** are vertical cylinders permanently installed to prevent vehicles from passing. They may be retractable to either allow or deny passage, as shown in Figure 5-2B. Bollards allow foot traffic to pass while preventing vehicular traffic.

Personnel

Inside personnel can serve as physical controls in a facility, as well. Often, security guards can be effective security assets for an organization. A security guard stationed at the entrance of a facility is able to control who physically enters the property. To be granted entrance by a guard, an individual must present valid credentials. This practice prevents unauthorized people from walking into the facility unchecked. Additionally, the presence of security guards can deter would-be intruders, potentially eliminating a threat before it starts.

In addition to security guards, the following personnel-related concepts can serve as physical controls for an organization:

- *Robot sentries* are autonomous devices used for monitoring and reporting intruder detection. With advances in artificial intelligence and use of wireless technologies, these devices often provide facial recognition capabilities with GPS accuracy.

- *Reception* personnel can serve as control largely in part to their workspace. A reception desk is also a barrier. While it provides a location for welcoming visitors, it also acts as a barrier to prevent unauthorized entry.

- *Two-person integrity*, also known as *two-person control* or the *two-person rule*, is a control method that requires two people, each with a unique key, to unlock a door or enter a code to provide access. This is a control technique that provides security by requiring the presence of two authorized people at all times, with each person simultaneously performing a specific task.

Figure 5-2 Common barricades include Jersey walls (A) and bollards (B).

A

B

Screen Filters

2.7

Screen filters, also known as *privacy filters*, attach to a computer monitor and prevent visibility of onscreen information from any person who is not sitting directly in front of the screen. These filters are made of polarized sheets of plastic and placed directly over the computer screen. Additionally, filters help improve glare and can protect LCD screens from scratches. Screen filters are especially helpful for users who work on laptops, since those users often cannot protect the physical location of where they are sitting, such as on a plane or in a meeting. Screen filters are also available for tablets as well.

Identification Badges

2.7

Many organizations require all employees to wear company-issued identification badges. Most badges include a photograph of the employee as well as the person's name or employee number. In a large organization, it is unlikely any single person will know every employee in the organization. Badges show that a person belongs in the building.

Even if employees are not required to wear badges, it is not uncommon for guests to be required to wear badges. Not only does a guest badge indicate a person is approved to be on the premises, a badge also serves to inform employees this person is an outsider. Guest access to facilities should be monitored, and areas that are only for employees should be clearly identified.

Smart Card

2.4, 2.7, 3.4, 3.7, 3.8

A **smart card** is a card that contains an embedded circuit or chip that stores information used to authorize or authenticate a person's identity and access to resources or physical locations. **Smart card authentication** employs the use of digital certificates to authenticate a person's identity, encrypt data transfer, and allow for digital signatures. The use of certificates to process smart card information for authentication uses a more complex configuration to prove identity. The Institute of Electronic and Electrical Engineers (IEEE) 802.1X authentication protocol is the designated standard to confirm identity. **IEEE 802.1X** is a wireless networking standard that provides more security than other standards by employing port-based security. IEEE 802.1X opens the required ports for access, and a user's identity is determined by the user's credentials or card's certificate. This information is then confirmed by a specialized authentication server.

A *common access card (CAC)* is a smart card that contains security information about the user stored on a microchip similar to microchipped credit cards. It is most commonly used for active duty and reserve military personnel, Department of Defense (DoD) employees, and authorized contractors. CACs operate using personal identity verification (PIV). **Personal identity verification (PIV)** is a US governmental standard for smart cards. A CAC displays a photograph of the user and can store 144kb of data on an integrated circuit chip. CACs are used for authentication and to ensure logical and physical security access to resources. These cards are inserted into a CAC reader to authenticate and determine if a person should be allowed access. CACs are not used instead of passwords; rather, they are often used in conjunction with one another.

Token

2.7, 3.7

A *token* is a device used to gain access to a resource. Tokens can be either hard or soft. A *hard token* is a physical device that often resembles a USB device in size and appearance and has ROM storage that can store a certificate or unique identifier. Hard tokens reveal alphanumeric values at fixed intervals that are used to gain access to a location or network. A software token, or *soft token*, is software that contains authenticating measures. Soft tokens are often accessed from a smartphone app or computer program.

A **secure token** is a device that stores information to authenticate a person's identity. Secure tokens take on the responsibility for issuing, validating, and canceling a token. For example, when a user logs in and authenticates, the authentication service will issue a token that is stored locally. For each subsequent transaction, the client includes a token in its request, and the authentication service will validate the token and provide the appropriate response. Secure tokens as a solution provide adaptability for an organization. Since the authentication session information is stored locally at the client, the service only needs to validate each token. For added security, the authentication service can be configured to include expiration times to limit a token's availability.

Over the last decade, software tokens have grown in popularity among security professionals. Apps containing software tokens are an attractive option versus possessing physical tokens as they are less costly to implement, there is no battery to expire, and users seldom lose or are otherwise not in possession of their phones. However, hardware tokens are considered more secure than software tokens since they store the credentials on the device as opposed to having them rely on downloaded information.

A software token works similarly to a hardware token, but the shared secret must be provided to each user, usually through software configuration. However, configuring software can be time-consuming, so some software tokens use public key cryptography instead. Public key cryptography speeds up the authentication process because the token contacts a centrally located device and provides its internal private key. The public key of the server is then used to authenticate the token. Public key cryptography is also safer since the shared secret is not stored on the token, which can be stolen or copied.

The value generated for both hardware and software tokens is considered a one-time password. A *one-time password (OTP)* is valid for only one login or transaction, and it is often valid for only a short period. In most cases, the user must enter the characters along with a username and password. However, some systems require a physical connection by inserting a hard token into the computer's USB port. This type of token is sometimes called a *dongle*.

There are two primary standards that are used when creating tokens: HOTP and TOTP.

✚ 2.4

- HOTP stands for *HMAC-based One-Time Password*, and it relies on two specific pieces of data. The first piece of data is the *seed*. The seed is the secret key, which is known only to the token and the server that will validate the token for authentication. The second piece of data is a *counter*. The counter is a changing factor of information. Like a shared secret, the counter is stored in the token and the authenticating server.

- The TOTP, or *Time-based One-Time Password* is like HOTP in that they both use the shared secret. In this design, however, the changing factor is based on time. TOTP uses time in short increments, such as 30 or 60 seconds. This ensures the OTP is only valid for that time frame, while the HOTP is valid until used. While TOTP is often the more secure choice, it is important for companies to consider time synchronization issues between the server and device using the token and the need for the user to resynch the token to the server if the time expires.

Like CACs, tokens are an example of multifactor authentication. Tokens offer a great deal of security. If a token is lost or stolen, it cannot be used for authentication. The user's name and password are needed, as well as the token, to provide authentication.

Safes and Vaults

Protecting data on a network extends to securing items not commonly associated with computer systems and networks. It is important that a security plan includes effective security measures for archiving or destroying sensitive paper documents or storing items deemed important or valuable to the organization.

Often, employees leave documents open on their computers, which means they can be accessed by others. Those in charge of mailrooms or supply cabinets sometimes fail to lock them, making them vulnerable to unauthorized entry. In an effort to prevent unauthorized usage, security professionals should work with those in management positions to ensure policies are enforced that outline appropriate use and storage of supplies that could support impersonation, such as company letterhead and business cards. It is important that there are secure storage areas in which these items can be placed, including lockable file cabinets; supply closets; and safes, which can be walk-in vaults or small, self-contained units. Keep in mind, simple locks may be easy to break or pick, so if these are in open areas, you may want to limit the type of data stored in these storage cabinets or utilize a more secure lock type.

Protected Distribution and Cabling

Protected distribution, also known as *protected cabling*, refers to the act of securing computer networking or communication cabling through physical safeguards to prevent unauthorized access or damage. Often, a protected distribution system employs locked connection points and protective conduit through which cabling is pulled. Some systems also incorporate sensors to notify security personnel of attempted access.

Lock Access and Cable Locks

Locks on doors and equipment limit access to locations unless a person has a key to gain entrance. However, a determined individual may not be deterred by the lack of an authorized key. The type of locks used should provide the appropriate level of security needed to secure an area. It is important to consider how accessible the lock is to an intruder and the length of time needed to be unobserved to bypass the lock.

Key-based locks are still dominant in most cases, and a key serves as the security token to gain access to a secured area. A significant drawback of key-based locks is that they can be picked. Lock picking is a skill used by individuals who wish to gain unauthorized access. There is an abundance of lock picking tools and how-to videos that walk a person through opening a closed lock. Methods of lock picking include

- *raking*, which is pulling a lockpick quickly through a lock;
- *bump keys*, which are specially cut keys that can bypass security in a traditional pin-and-tumbler lock;
- smashing the lock with a hammer; or
- cutting the lock open.

However, there is a wide array of nontraditional locks available to be used in conjunction with key-based locks. In addition to providing more security, nontraditional locks can often provide reports of access. Examples of nontraditional locks include the following:

- Proximity door scanners are often used with swipe cards, such as on hotel-room doors. This type of lock can also utilize near-field communication, in which the user only needs to place an access card close to the reader.
- Biometric locks are configured to provide access for a specific set or list of users.
- Keyless door entry locks, such as those with PIN pads, can be reconfigured easily and quickly in the event an employee leaves the organization.
- *Electronic locks* are electromechanical and lock or unlock only when a wireless signal is transmitted. These locks are used in conjunction with swipe cards, soft tokens, or near-field communication.

Cable locks are chain-like locks in which the locking mechanism is integrated into the cable. They are often made of thick steel or Kevlar that is difficult to cut. These locks are often used to secure equipment to a location; for example, bicycle locks are a type of cable lock. Laptops are often protected using cable locks. Since laptops are small and portable, they are often targeted for theft. Incorporating cable locks into a laptop, then securing it to a fixed location, such as a desk, will stop someone from picking up the laptop and walking out.

Closed-Circuit Television (CCTV)

2.7

Closed-circuit television (CCTV) is a system in which video cameras transmit signals to a centralized monitoring location. These signals are not publicly broadcasted, so outsiders cannot intrude on the broadcast from outside the organization. CCTV is also known as *video surveillance*. It allows for security guards or other employees to monitor key areas for unauthorized access or activity. Similar to alarms, cameras and security systems can be activated by a motion sensor. This allows a security system to be employed more efficiently. For example, configuring cameras to begin recording when motion is detected eliminates a need to monitor areas continuously. This can be especially costly if cameras are recording areas where no activity occurs.

There are many choices for CCTV depending on a business's needs. Some of the important elements include movement and housing.

- CCTV cameras can be fixed or movable. Movable cameras have the ability to pan, tilt, and zoom, which is known as PTZ. Some cameras allow for 360 degrees of viewing.
- Camera housing should be considered, as a camera will need to be mounted. Common choices for mounting include domes and bullets for cameras that are visible. For cameras that are hidden and not visible, discreet installation should be used. For example, a camera can be placed behind a two-way mirror.

There are additional features to consider with CCTV cameras, including object detection. **Object detection** is a type of artificial intelligence technology that is able to identify preprogrammed objects. This enables surveillance equipment to recognize people or items without human intervention. Often, this technology is deployed in video surveillance systems to identify objects such as faces, pedestrians, computers, or weapons. When a surveillance system detects a predefined object, the object is highlighted in a colored circle or box for ease of visibility.

Mantraps

1.1, 2.7

A **mantrap** is a physical access control system used to trap a person between two sets of interlocking doors. When a mantrap is employed, once a person enters an area, a first set of doors close before a second opens. Often, the second set of doors is controlled by a security guard who visually identifies a person before opening the doors. Having a space between two sets of doors creates an air gap. An **air gap** is an area designed to be completely isolated from secure areas of a building or room.

Mantraps are often used as a physical defense to prevent tailgating. **Tailgating** occurs when an unauthorized person walks into a facility with, or right behind, authorized people to appear as if with them. A tailgating attack is an example of social engineering in which a threat actor convinces an employee to help the attacker gain entry into a restricted area controlled by electronic devices. The attacker gains the trust of the employee and when the electronic device is activated for entrance, the attacker enters with the employee. Being with authorized people usually makes others believe a person is authorized; as such, entry is often not questioned.

Turnstiles

A **turnstile** is a device with bars or other obstruction to alternately block an entryway and allow only one person to enter at a time. Examples of turnstiles include those found at the entrance of sporting venues and amusement parks. Revolving doors are another popular example of turnstiles. There are different designs ranging from a single bar or panel to multiple bars that entirely block the entryway. Turnstiles are at the entrances of many subways, amusement parks, and other public places. The device can be set up to scan a security card so only those having the proper card can pass.

Signage

A simple and inexpensive security solution is to post appropriate signs. For example, signs marked *Authorized Personnel Only* or *Restricted Area* may deter people from entering a secure area. Signage can help enforce security while increasing awareness by reminding people to report suspicious activity. Signs also reinforce that security cameras are in use and tailgating is not authorized.

Logs

A log can be used as a component of a comprehensive physical security plan. Entry logs are often used to track names, dates, and times that visitors enter and exit a building. Equipment logs identify the date and time an individual checked equipment out of the building. Logs do not provide a preventative solution on their own, but can be used in detective or recovery efforts. For example, if there is a current threat to a business, reviewing the *visitor logs* may help pinpoint a potential source of the threat. Often, recovery and analysis following a security incident are expedited by the additional information provided by logs. This information is also helpful for determining a cause of an incident.

IT Physical Controls

Most companies have dedicated server and networking infrastructure rooms, but many small businesses fail to consider the ramifications of locating critical equipment such as servers, switches, and routers in unsecured rooms. Physical controls are needed to protect IT components from unauthorized access or damage.

At a minimum, all equipment should be placed in a room that is not accessible to unauthorized staff, customers, or visitors. As a security practice, equipment should be physically isolated to prevent intrusions. This can be accomplished by incorporating an air-gap network and protecting data signals from outside interference.

2.7

Air-Gap Network

An **air-gap network** is a computer network designed to be completely isolated from other networks, including connections to the Internet. Air-gap networks are an example of *secure network architecture*, which is the deployment of network devices with security measures enabled. These networks offer a form of physical network segregation. **Physical network segregation** is the act of isolating or segmenting a network so it is not accessible to unauthorized personnel. Segregation is common in highly classified networks where prevention of unauthorized network access is of the highest importance. A true air-gap network has no connection to wired or wireless sources, nor does it allow data to be transmitted outside the network. This prevents hackers from accessing the network remotely.

However, air-gap networks are not without vulnerabilities. An example of a vulnerability is system updates that come from outside the network. Since all software and operating systems receive their updates from manufacturers' web pages, alternative means to updating the systems must be in place. It is not a wise practice for a secured network to connect to outside sources directly since doing so risks exposure to intruders. For this reason, updates are often conducted with the use of portable storage. Remember, portable storage devices represent a critical vulnerability, since connecting them to the air-gap network could introduce malware to the network. Only an authorized network technician or security administrator should have the ability to insert portable storage into a network device.

2.7

Data Signal Protection

Physical security also includes protecting data signals as they travel along the network. Data transmissions must be reliable as well as secure for both wired and wireless transmissions.

One of the potential threats to data signals is electromagnetic interference (EMI). EMI is interference between two electrical or electronic devices. This interference is the result of an electromagnetic disturbance and can affect the performance of a device. **EMI shielding** is a barrier placed around wires to block EMI from interfering with the electrical signals in the wires. An example of EMI shielding is a Faraday cage. A **Faraday cage** blocks electromagnetic signals and distributes them around the exterior of the cage, preventing the signals from reaching the protected equipment. It also helps with temperature issues and will not burn or contribute to smoke volume in the case of a fire.

All electronic equipment gives off some type of electromagnetic signals. These signals, known as **electromagnetic radiation (EMR)**, are emitted from printers, computers, monitors, microwaves, transmission lines, and other devices. Some are strong enough to interfere with other signals, resulting in data loss. These signals can also reveal data to hackers. A preventive measure against EMR hijacking is a **protective distribution system (PDS)**, which is a set of safeguards implemented to protect the data sent over this type of media. A PDS typically describes the measures used to protect unclassified data sent over electrical or fiber-optics telecommunication networks. Sending data through these networks is primarily used for low or medium threat locations. PDS can be as simple as using metal or polyvinyl chloride (PCV) pipe. A PDS can provide more significant levels of protection by using more advanced features, such as conduit constructed of a ferrous metal, buried lines between buildings on a campus area, and constant surveillance for the carriers between areas or buildings.

Another way to counter malicious use of EMR is employment of products manufactured under TEMPEST standards. **TEMPEST** is a National Security Agency (NSA) specification and North Atlantic Treaty Organization (NATO) certification that attempts to counter the act of spying on information systems through leaking electromagnetic emanations. The name *TEMPEST* is an acronym for *Telecommunications Electronics Materials Protected from Emanating Spurious Transmissions*.

Companies that deal with sensitive and confidential data may choose to protect their data transmissions with approved TEMPEST products and specifications. TEMPEST specifications detail both methods used for spying and for shielding equipment against spying. NSA and NATO recommends three levels of protection for data:

- NATO SDIP-27 Level A: The strictest standard, assumes a hacker is in immediate vicinity.
- NATO SDIP-27 Level B: Assumes a hacker is within a 20-meter radius of the transmissions.
- NATO SDIP-27 Level C: Assumes a hacker is within about 100 meters of free-space attenuation.

Temperature Control

The design and purchase of equipment with proper cooling mechanisms is important for physical security of assets. Heat is not a friend to electronic equipment. Materials used in equipment can suffer a decreased life if exposed to high operating temperatures, which increases the electrical resistance of the conductors, slows the speed of data, and negatively impacts performance. Constantly varying temperatures also can cause stress to systems. As materials heat up and cool down, they expand and contract, which can eventually damage components.

Server Rooms and Data Centers

The physical location of equipment is important when considering temperature control. In many businesses, servers and networking equipment are typically stored in a secured room called a *server room*. However, this centralized location also creates heat concerns. The close proximity of equipment results in the output of a great deal of heat in an enclosed area. In turn, the heat can damage the equipment running the network and the servers hosting data.

A **data center** is a facility specifically designed to store and manage vast quantities of data. It is considerably larger than a server room and can be located on- or off-site of the business. A data center is typically a specially constructed room that is equipped to handle great needs for power, cabling, and environmental controls. Data centers run vast amounts of servers and other networking equipment. All of this equipment generates a great deal of heat that, if not properly managed, can cause malfunctions or shutdowns of systems. Heat is one of the biggest environmental threats to data centers.

Hot and Cold Aisles

One way to control temperature in a data center or server room is the use of hot and cold aisles. **Hot and cold aisles** refer to a layout design in which server racks are arranged in rows with cold air entering the room on one side and hot air exiting the room on the other side, as shown in Figure 5-3. The fronts of the server racks face the cold aisles. Heating, ventilation, and air-conditioning (HVAC) outlets are located in the cold aisle. This allows the equipment to draw in the cold air through their fans. The backs of the server racks face the hot aisles. Hot air generated by the equipment is expelled into the hot aisle, where HVAC return inlets are located. Hot air is removed from the room, cooled by the HVAC system, and returned to the room in cold aisles.

A properly sized heating, ventilation, and air conditioning (HVAC) system should be incorporated into a server room. The American Society of Heating, Refrigerating, and Air-Conditioning Engineers (ASHRAE) offers recommendations for maintaining and monitoring server rooms. Its recommendations include

- ambient room temperatures ranging between 64–80 degrees Fahrenheit;
- ambient humidity between 40–60 percent; and
- a minimum of six temperature sensors per rack.

Monitoring temperature is critical. Racks holding equipment should be monitored separately from room temperature. When notification is sent that the server room is overheating, it may already be too late for the servers and network equipment located in the racks. Therefore, rack-mounted sensors should be used in addition to the room sensors.

3.1

There are many temperature-control products on the market. Select one that uses simple network management protocol (SNMP). SNMP protocol collects and organizes data on managed network devices by deploying agents on remote devices. SNMP agents communicate with devices called *managers*. A type of message sent by an agent is a *trap message*. The temperature sensor collects traps and sends alerts to the manager when temperature levels are not at acceptable conditions. Security and network analysts use special software to monitor the activities reported by SNMP. **SNMPv3** is the most recent version of SNMP and enables authentication as well as encryption.

2.7

Fire Control

Another serious threat to data of a business is fire. Obviously, fires can be destructive and quick action must be taken to extinguish any fire that may occur.

Special consideration should be given to fire suppression. There are different types of fires, each based on the fuel that feeds the fire. The type of fire, in relation to the materials that ignited to create the fire, is referred to as *fire class*.

- Class A fires are fed by combustibles such as paper, wood, and some plastics. Anything that leaves an ash is considered a Class A fire.
- Class B fires are fed by flammable or combustible liquid, such as gasoline or oil.

Figure 5-3 The use of hot and cold aisles is one method of managing temperature in a data center or server room.

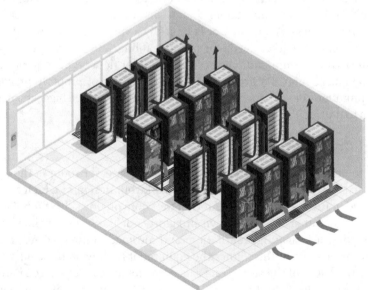

- Class C fires are energized electrical fires. This includes fires caused by outlets, circuit breakers, appliances, and wiring.
- Class D fires are fed by combustible metal, such as magnesium or titanium. This type of fire is more common in labs and industry than elsewhere.
- Class K fires are fed by cooking oil, animal fat, and grease.

Fire extinguishers are rated by fire class. Symbols on an extinguisher indicate its rating, as shown in Figure 5-4.

It is critical that IT personnel understand fire types and proper use of extinguishers *before* an actual fire emergency occurs. The fire-suppression equipment located in server rooms and data centers must be appropriate for the types of fire most likely to occur there. For example, electrical fires are more common in a server room than other types of fires. The fire-suppression equipment located in a server room must be appropriate for a Class C fire. IT personnel working in that area also must receive the proper training on how to use the fire-suppression equipment.

Fire-suppression systems that use water, such as standard building sprinklers, may cause damage to computers and network equipment. An alternative to water-based systems is systems that use FM-200. This is an environmentally friendly, water-less product created by DuPont. It is the preferred solution for many organizations such as governmental buildings, museums, and most telecommunication facilities. FM-200 is suitable for protecting facilities in Class A, B, and C fires.

Figure 5-4 Fire extinguishers are rated by the type of fire for which they should be used. Be sure to have an appropriately rated fire extinguisher for the types of fires that may be potentially encountered.

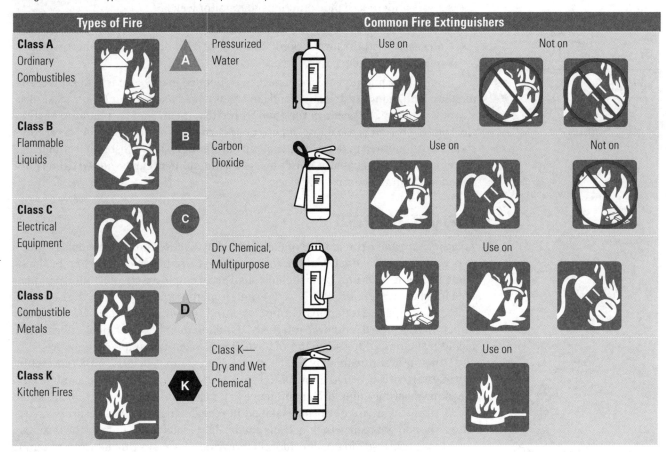

Goodheart-Willcox Publisher

FM-200 is a replacement for waterless fire-suppression systems that used Halon. Halon is a chemical that effectively extinguishes fire without damaging electrical systems. However, it is environmentally unfriendly. It is also potentially unhealthy for humans. The production and importation of Halon was banned in the United States in 1994, when the Clean Air Act Amendments of 1990 went into effect.

Water Control

 2.7

Water and electrical equipment are not compatible. It is important to consider damage to systems from a water source. Most people think of water damage caused by rainwater or river flooding. However, water damage can come from sprinklers, burst pipes, or even accidental spillage.

Unexpected water can quickly flood a room. In 2018, during a particularly cold week, a water pipe burst over the server room at the SPCA of Virginia Beach, VA. This water damaged a great deal of digital equipment and knocked out phone lines and electrical power.

In the previous example, by the time someone at the SPCA heard sounds associated with a water leak, it was too late. This is because unexpected water is much easier to avoid than it is to stop. The best way to protect equipment from water damage is with preventive planning. Proper maintenance of buildings and equipment is usually the responsibility of facilities management. However, IT personnel should conduct routine maintenance checks in areas such as server rooms. Other ways to control water is to install:

- sensors to monitor leaks inside cooling equipment and detect overflow;
- sensors underneath pipe junctions to monitor leaks;
- fluid-sensing cables that report potential leaks; and
- water sensors at the lowest point on the floor or under the floor where water would likely puddle.

 2.7

Computer equipment does not have to be flooded in order for it to fail. Therefore, moisture and humidity detection and control is equally important for physical security of equipment. If the air in the room is too dry, it can lead to a buildup of static electricity. If the air is too damp, it can cause corrosion to equipment. A server room should be monitored to determine moisture or humidity levels just as it is monitored for temperature. If necessary, humidifiers or dehumidifiers can be added to an HVAC system of humidity-control purposes.

Insider Threats

An *insider threat* is a threat to an organization that comes from an individual or group of people within the organization. Insider threats can be very costly to a business. Some insider threats may be malicious, such as an employee stealing information or uploading malware to the system. For example, in the summer of 2019, the Canadian financial company, Desjardins Group, admitted to being victimized by an insider threat. A disgruntled employee released 4.2 million members' personal information, including names, addresses, dates of birth, Social Security numbers, and more.

Other insider threats may be accidental. For example, in 2017, a US representative inadvertently revealed information from a classified report during a public congressional hearing about foreign influence in US elections. Employees who are not in the IT department are not usually skilled in recognizing potential security threats. Often, they do not realize their actions can be dangerous to the data or the business.

Many businesses do not consider their own employees as threats when planning defensive and preventive systems against potential hackers. In 2019, the security firm of Code42 released the *2019 Global Data Exposure Report.* A key finding in the report was that 69 percent of organizations admitted to suffering a data breach due to insider threats. Additional findings from the report are shown in Figure 5-5.

Most threats to a business and its data systems, including insider threats, are highly preventable through incorporation of physical and environmental measures such as those described in this chapter. In addition, it is critical that network users are highly trained in proper security measures and best practices.

Data Destruction

➕ 2.7

Data must be protected from unauthorized access, even when the data is no longer needed. Simply deleting data from media is not enough to stop a determined attacker from recovering deleted data. Even if you empty the Windows Recycle Bin, data still exists on the default storage device. Windows keeps track of the files on the media by using a technique called *pointers*. Each file contains pointers that identify its start and ending position on the disk, so Windows knows how to retrieve the file when requested. When a file is deleted, the pointers of the file are removed, and the sectors on the drive are marked as available. These sectors are holding the actual data. Nothing happens to these sectors unless another file overwrites that sector. Since the data remains stored until it is overwritten, it remains vulnerable to retrieval by unauthorized parties.

Destroying Paper-Based Data

➕ 2.7

Data printed on paper can be a security concern since it is easy to duplicate and remove from the premises. Discarding the paper in normal trash receptacles, even if they are locked, still presents the opportunity for an unauthorized user to retrieve the data. When paper-based data is no longer needed, the paper must be physically destroyed in order to provide the highest level of security. There are three approaches that will permanently destroy paper: burning, pulping, and shredding.

Burning the paper reduces it to ashes, which makes it impossible to reassemble this data. If a company has an incinerator, this is an easily accomplished task. However, since many companies do not have that option, there are other options to consider. An environmentally friendly security option to destroy the data is to consider pulping. **Pulping** is a process of putting paper in a tank of water and chemically removing the ink from the paper fibers. Once ink is removed, the paper can be broken down into pulp and processed to use as recycled paper. The third technique for paper destruction, shredding, is the process of reducing the paper to small strips to make it difficult to read. There are generally three types of cuts made to paper by a shredder. The type of cut selected depends on the level of protection needed.

- *Strip-cut shredders* slice the paper into long strips.
- *Crosscut shredders* slice the paper into short strips.
- *Micro-cut shredders* slice the paper into small bits similar to confetti; these types of shredders provide the most secure shredding.

▪ Use of social media platforms to send files or collaborate with colleagues	31%
▪ Clicking a live link that should not have been accessed (Chief Security Officers)	78%
▪ Clicking a live link that should not have been accessed (Chief Executive Officers)	65%
▪ Data breach within previous 18 months caused by employee action	50%
▪ Potential data leaks caused by departing decision-makers who consider company data as their own	72%

Source: code42.com

Figure 5-5 The *2019 Global Data Exposure Report* by security firm Code42 listed important findings regarding data security.

Combining the pulping and shredding options is perhaps the most secure way of destroying data. After removing the ink and breaking the paper down into pulp, letting the pulp fibers dry will turn it into unprocessed paper, which can then be shredded. Since the pulp was already stripped of all ink, there is no way to retrieve the data, even if someone had all the strips created by a shredder.

Destroying Data on Digital Media

✚ 2.7

As described previously, deleting files does not permanently remove the data from the media. Depending on the media type, there are techniques for destroying data. For magnetic hard drives, degaussing can be used. **Degaussing** rearranges magnetic fields by randomizing the patterns of magnetization. On a traditional drive, data is stored on the drive using magnetic fields. The degaussing process removes data from these magnetic fields. The result of this process is the data becomes unrecoverable, and the drive is no longer able to store information. However, degaussing will *not* work on solid-state drives (SSD) since the data is stored using integrated circuit assemblies.

Many times, a hard drive needs to be reused. In this case, physical destruction of the drive is not an option, and instead, the data must be purged from the media. **Data purging** refers to the removal of existing data from the drive. Examples include moving the data to a new device or erasing it completely from the existing drive. However, in many cases, data that has been purged can still be retrieved.

Disk Sanitization

✚ 2.7, 4.1

Sanitizing data or media is the best course of action to strengthen an organization's security posture. **Disk sanitization**, sometimes referred to as *disk wiping*, or *data sanitization*, is the irreversible and permanent removal of data from a storage device. Wiping a disk goes beyond simply marking files as deleted. It also performs a low-level format where the drive is overwritten with 0s and 1s. In many cases, this action is enough, but there are still advanced software programs that could recover the data. Most software programs are written to comply with the Department of Defense's standards for acceptable wiping. This standard is known as DoD 5220.22-M. This standard performs a three-step process:

- Step 1: All addressable locations on the drive are overwritten with binary zeros.
- Step 2: All addressable locations on the drive are overwritten with binary ones.
- Step 3: All addressable locations on the drive are overwritten with a random bit pattern.

With the advances in hard drive storage and technology, the DoD 5220.22-M standard has become outdated by comparison to some of the newer technologies. The National Institute for Standards and Technology (NIST) has created standards for disk sanitization in the categories of Clear, Purge and Destroy. The NIST standards also cover mobile devices, USB drives, servers, and emerging technologies. NIST maintains these standards in their document called *800-88 — Guidelines for Media Sanitization.*

Physical Destruction

In some cases, it may not be possible or desirable to sanitize a disk. The final option in this case is total physical destruction of the media. Physical destruction is just that, using a physical means to destroy the actual media. If the media is removable, physical destruction is the simplest solution, such as breaking a CD/DVD drive or crushing a portable flash drive. Additionally, physical destruction could include a

TECH TIP ⚙

 2.7

Many physical drives can be destroyed easily with a hard drive shredder, which uses metal gears or teeth to grind, break, or shred devices into small, recyclable pieces. If you contract with a third-party vendor, partner with a company that has high security standards, including chain of custody and certificate of destruction.

simple technique such as drilling a hole through the platters inside a hard drive, incinerating the hard drive, or using a crushing device to physically bend or break the hard drive, destroying the platters where the data is stored. Another option includes pulverizing the drive. Pulverizing a drive is accomplished by using a special machine that shreds the drive into small bits of media. If you frequently replace drives, this may be the most efficient means. Many reputable companies offer this service.

SUMMARY

Security Controls

- Security controls are tools or processes used to reduce risk to assets by slowing, minimizing, or stopping a threat.
- For physical controls, the three key goals for planning security measures are preventing a problem, detecting a problem, and recovering from a problem through corrective action.
- There are different types of controls including administrative, compensating, corrective, detective, deterrent, physical, preventive, and technical control.

Facility Security Controls

- Industrial camouflage is a concept in which a company designs a facility in a way that makes it unappealing or uninteresting to a potential attacker. Examples include installing limited or misleading identification and markings or choosing a location in a remote or mountainous area.
- A gated entrance to a parking lot and fencing around the perimeter can restrict access of who is able to enter. A security guard or proximity cards or transponders can be used to allow people access at the gate.
- Lighting is a strong preventative measure and provides a deterrent to individuals who may be able to sneak past other security measures, such as guards. It should be placed on the perimeter of the business as well as vital areas.
- Alarms trigger notifications of unwanted activity and can serve as a detective control in a physical security plan. Two types of alarms include audible and silent.
- Barricades are physical obstructions to a passage. There are many different categories of barricades, such as Jersey walls and bollards, and they may be permanent or temporary.
- Security guards can physically control who enters the property by checking valid credentials. They may deter would-be intruders, eliminating a threat before it starts. Additional inside personnel include robot sentries, reception personnel, and two-person integrity.
- Screen filters attach to a computer monitor and prevent visibility of onscreen information from nonusers. These are especially helpful for users who work on laptops.
- Many organizations require all employees to wear company-issued identification badges with the employee's name and photo on them. Other companies have employees carry a smart card, which contains an embedded circuit or chip that stores information used to authorize or authenticate a person's identity and access to resources or physical locations.

- A token is a device used to gain access to a resource. It can be a hard, soft, or secure token. Over the last decade, software tokens have grown in popularity among security professionals.
- It is important that a security plan includes effective security measures for physical items. Policies should be established for archiving or destroying paper and appropriate use and storage of supplies in a designated secure storage area.
- Protected distribution is the act of securing computer networking or communication cabling through physical safeguards. It often employs locked connection points, protective conduit, and sensors to notify security personnel of attempted access.
- Locks on doors and equipment limit access to locations unless a person has a key to gain entrance. Key-based locks are still dominant, but other locks include proximity door scanners, biometric readers, keyless door entry locks, electronic locks, and cable locks.
- Closed-circuit television (CCTV) is a system in which video cameras transmit signals to a centralized monitoring location. It allows for security guards or other employees to monitor key areas for unauthorized access or activity.
- A mantrap is a physical access control system used to trap a person between two sets of interlocking doors. It is often used as a physical defense to prevent tailgating.
- A turnstile alternately blocks an entryway and allows only one person to enter at a time. The device can be set up to scan a security card so only those having the proper card can pass.
- Posting appropriate signs is a simple and inexpensive security solution. It can help enforce security, increase awareness by reminding people to report suspicious activity, and reinforce that security cameras are in use.
- A log can be used as a component of a comprehensive physical security plan. Logs can be used in detective or recovery efforts as well as helpful for determining a cause of an incident.

IT Physical Controls

- Physical controls are needed to protect IT components from unauthorized access or damage. At a minimum, all equipment should be placed in a room that is not accessible to unauthorized staff, customers, or visitors. As a security practice, equipment should be physically isolated to prevent intrusions.
- An *air-gap network* is a computer network designed to be completely isolated from other networks, including connections to the Internet. It has no connection to wired or wireless sources nor allows data to be transmitted outside the network. This prevents hackers from accessing the network remotely.
- Data signals must be protected as they travel along the network. EMI shielding can help protect against electromagnetic interference. Two methods to protect data signals from malicious EMR include a protective distribution system (PDS) and employment of products under the TEMPEST standards.
- The design and purchase of equipment with proper cooling mechanisms is important for physical security of assets. Heat and varying temperatures can damage equipment. Keeping systems in controlled rooms can help ensure equipment will run properly.
- In many businesses, servers and networking equipment are typically stored in a server room. Another storage facility is a data center, which is a facility specifically designed to store and manage vast quantities of data. These rooms can overheat if the proper precautions are not taken.

Insider Threats

- An insider threat is a threat to an organization that comes from an individual or group of people within the organization.
- Some insider threats can be malicious, such as an employee stealing information or uploading malware to the system. Other insider threats may be accidental, as employees may not often realize their actions can be dangerous to the data or the business.
- Many threats to businesses and their data systems are preventable through incorporation of physical and environmental measures as well as with properly trained users.

Data Destruction

- Destroying paper-based data is important to decrease the risk of attackers finding physical copies of information. Destruction methods include burning, pulping, and shredding papers.
- Depending on the media type, there are techniques for destroying data. For magnetic drives, degaussing can be used. For hard drives being reused, the data must be purged from the media.
- Disk sanitization is the irreversible and permanent removal of data from a storage device. It marks files as deletes and performs a low-level format where the drive is overwritten with 0s and 1s. Sanitization is the best course of action to strengthen an organization's security posture.
- If sanitization is not possible or desirable, the final option is total physical destruction of the media. Physical destruction techniques include breaking a CD/DVD, drilling a hole through platters, incinerating a hard drive, and pulverizing the hard drive.

REVIEW QUESTIONS

1. Summarize security controls.
2. Identity different types of controls.
3. Define *physical security controls*.
4. Identify and explain five types of physical security controls.
5. A firm is constructing a new building and would like to establish permanent barriers to control vehicle access. What should be used?
6. A business wants to ensure that unauthorized people do not access certain parts of a building. Which physical security controls could they employ?
7. A business wants to be able to monitor who is in a building. What physical security controls could they employ?
8. A customer enters a bank foyer and is greeted by another set of doors. Employees "buzz" the doors open for customer access. What barrier did the bank install with this setup?
9. Briefly explain physical controls used within an IT system.
10. What is secure network architecture?
11. Identify the three levels of protection for data according to NSA and NATO.
12. Briefly explain how hot and cold aisles work.

13. List the ASHRAE recommendations for maintaining and monitoring server rooms.

14. List and describe the various fire classes and their corresponding suppression methods.

15. Describe measures to be taken to control water near computer equipment.

16. Explain examples of threats posed by insiders of an organization.

17. Summarize how most threats to a business can be prevented.

18. Compare and contrast methods of data destruction.

19. Which type of shredder provides the most secure shredding?

20. What are the three steps that the DoD 5220.22-M standard performs?

✚ SAMPLE SECURITY+ EXAM QUESTIONS

1. You create alerts to notify security administrators when an incorrect password is used for the Admin account on the server. Which security goal does this fulfill?

   A. Detecting a problem

   B. Preventing a problem

   C. Recovering from a problem

   D. Administering a problem

2. Your company is building a new facility and wants to prevent vehicles from having physical access near the building. Which of these solutions provides the *best* prevention of vehicle proximity?

   A. Install a PTZ camera

   B. Install bollards

   C. Install Jersey walls

   D. Require photo ID for all individuals parking their car near the building

3. You are concerned about unauthorized individuals gaining access to the server room. Which strategy is the *best* solution to prevent unauthorized access?

   A. Use a PTZ camera

   B. Install proximity card scanners on the server room door

   C. Hire a facility security guard

   D. Create strong access policies for employees

4. Jason and a group of coworkers took a break outside during working hours. When they reentered the facility, they were joined by another, unknown individual. This could have been prevented with _____.

   A. tailgating

   B. proximity cards

   C. CCTV

   D. mantraps

5. Which is the *best* method for protecting sensitive research data for a military contractor from being stolen?

    A. Place all the equipment in a server farm

    B. Use a FM-200 suppression

    C. Install the network as an air-gapped network

    D. Place bollards outside the building

6. Due to the vast amount of computer and network equipment running, which of the following is one of the biggest threats to most data centers?

    A. Unauthorized access

    B. Phishing attacks

    C. Heat-related issues

    D. AUP violations

7. Sparks fly from an outlet that computers are connected to, creating a small fire. Which fire extinguisher should be used to suppress the fire?

    A. Class A

    B. Class B

    C. Class C

    D. Class D

8. Your organization is concerned with security violations. Which strategy will *best* help the security team identify unwanted access?

    A. Motion detection sensors

    B. Fences

    C. Mantraps

    D. Natural barriers

9. The sales manager wants to ensure that confidential printed material is locked in the office after working hours in appropriate secured equipment. What should the sales manager use to secure the data?

    A. Cable locks

    B. File cabinet with key-based locks

    C. Infrared detection

    D. A safe

10. An employee left the organization and it was discovered that person had removed confidential information during their last week of employment. Which strategy should the company review for improvement?

    A. Separation of duties

    B. Onboarding procedures

    C. Clean desk policy

    D. Offboarding procedures

LAB EXERCISES

Lab Activity 5-1: Preventative Controls

In an earlier chapter, we reviewed the dangers of malware such as worms and root kits. One of the common sources for such malware is the use of mobile storage drives such as CD/DVDs, flash drives, and portable hard drives. One preventive control that can be implemented is to disable the computer's ability to recognize a removable drive, prevent read access, or prevent auto-running of such devices.

1. On a Windows computer, enter MMC into either the search box or in the **Run** dialog box. Then press the [Enter] key.

2. In the MMC, select **File>Add/Remove Snap-ins** to open the **Add or Remove Snap-ins** dialog box. Locate and select the Group Policy snap-in from the Available snap-ins: box, then click the **Add>** button to add the snap-in to the console. Click **OK** to return to the console.

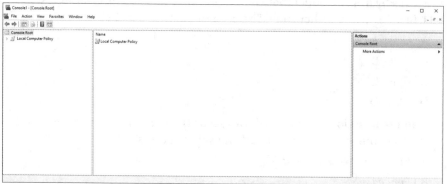

Goodheart-Willcox Publisher

3. Select **Local Computer Policy** and expand Computer Configuration.

4. Double-click on the **Administrative Templates** folder to open its contents.

5. In the subfolders, select **System**. From the resulting list click on **Removable Storage Access**.

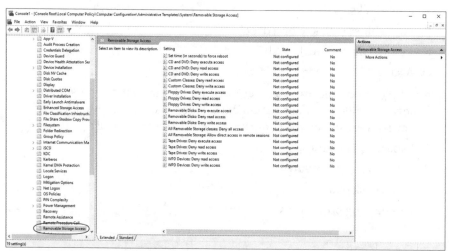

Goodheart-Willcox Publisher

In this section, you can choose to work with the specific type of removable devices, including CDs, DVDs, or removable disks. Alternatively, you can choose to apply settings to all removable disks.

6. To prevent a CD or DVD drive from being read, click on the **CD and DVD: Deny execute access** option. Setting the policy to **Enable** prevents the user from reading the contents of the disc. This is a good policy to enforce if you are concerned about someone copying information from a system to a writeable DVD. The same applies to the **CD and DVD: Deny write access** option.

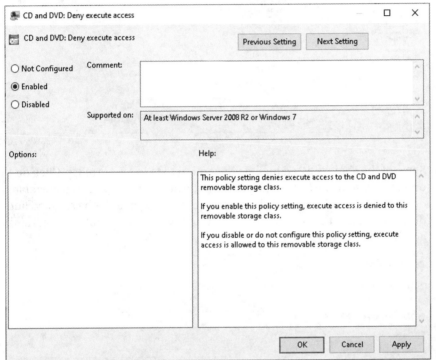

Goodheart-Willcox Publisher

7. Another threat can occur when a device contains executable files or scripts that run automatically. To mitigate this vulnerability, enable with **Removable Disks: Deny execute access** option.

8. If you would like to ensure all removable devices are blocked from access, select the **All Removable Storage classes: Deny all access** option. Enabling this option applies the settings to *all* removable storage devices. What is an advantage and disadvantage of this step?

9. Windows MMC can help prevent unwanted malware from running automatically by disabling the Windows AutoPlay feature. From your local policy template, click the left arrow in the tool bar to return one level in the snap-in. Scroll down to the **Windows Components** option and expand this folder. Double-click on the **AutoPlay Policies** option.

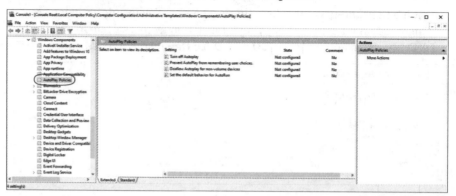

Goodheart-Willcox Publisher

10. Some of the choices listed include the option to turn off AutoPlay. Click on that option to review the settings. If you do not want any software on a portable drive running, which option should you select, and should it be enabled and disabled? Notice the Comment option. What type of comments do you think administrators should note here?

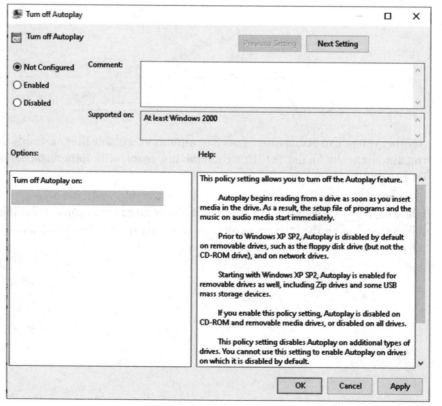

Goodheart-Willcox Publisher

11. Review this section. Which option and setting should you choose to prevent AutoPlay from running for a smartphone?

12. After closing the MMC, you would need to either restart the computer to apply any changes or force the changes by running the command **gpupdate /force**. Run that command from the Windows command line to see and document this option.

Lab Activity 5-2: Designing a Physical Security Plan

It is important to analyze physical security measures in an organization and identify areas of improvement. In this lab, you will use a drawing program, such as the freely available draw.io, to simulate a small business and identify locations where physical security could be improved by identifying the physical security measures.

1. From your browser, navigate to www.draw.io. If you have access to Microsoft Visio, you can use that option. Additionally, other free resources can be used if draw.io is unavailable.

2. Once the web page loads, you will be directed to select a default storage location. Choose a location as directed by your instructor. Then select **Create New Diagram**.

3. From the list of layout types, choose Other, and select **other/floor_plan.xml**, which resembles an office layout, as shown in the following screen capture. Then, click **Create**.

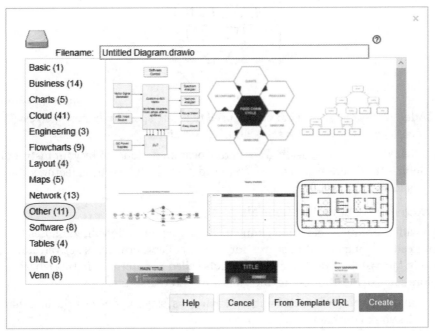

Goodheart-Willcox Publisher

Assume the business is an attorney's office, and it is located in a one-story, stand-alone building. Assume one of the offices will become a server room, and you have a maximum budget of 10,000 dollars.

4. Use the tools in the toolbox in the left-side pane to add security features. Text can be added using the **Text** tool from the General menu as shown in the following screen capture.

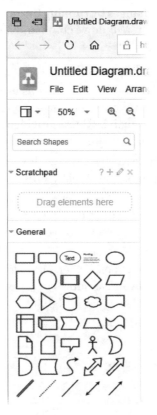

Additionally, the search bar can be used to locate specific shapes, such as security cameras, servers, safes, and, workstations.

5. When finished, save the diagram in the location designated by your instructor. Submit the diagram along with a report detailing what security features you would add to this office space.

Lab Activity 5-3: Detective Controls

Even with preventative solutions implemented, there may be vulnerabilities that go unnoticed. It is important to search for potential flaws or threats actively and continually. Microsoft purchased a suite of tools called Sysinternals. In this lab, you will explore some of the utilities included in the Sysinternals suite.

1. Conduct an online search using the keyword sysinternals. Select the link that takes you to the Microsoft web page.

2. On the left side of the page, expand the Downloads option; then expand the Security Utilities option.

3. From the expanded menu, select **Security Utilities.**

4. Click on **Autoruns.** This will take you to a dedicated page for this utility. From that page, select the **Run now option from Sysinternals Live.** It will appear in your task area; click the **autoruns.exe** link to launch.

5. This program will identify all programs that are starting automatically. Click on the **Logon** tab in the tool bar. How many programs are running automatically when you sign in? Were there any you were unaware of that are listed here?

6. Click on **Scheduled Tasks**. Sometimes a hacker will load a script that may disable important protections, such as turning off the firewall.

7. Right-click on one of the services and choose **Go to entry** from the shortcut menu. What happens when you choose that option?

8. Next, click on **Services**. Notice the services that are starting automatically. Minimize Autoruns.

9. How often do you think you should run this program? Explain whether or not you think it would be worthwhile to make it a scheduled task.

Lab Activity 5-4: School AUP

Most organizations will post the AUP on their website or direct users to its location at the login banner screen. A banner screen is displayed during the logon process and is often used for messages, announcements, or elements of the AUP. Locate your school's AUP, and fully read it. Then, answer the following questions.

1. Where did you find the AUP, and was it easy or difficult to locate?

2. Did you find the AUP easy to understand and follow?

3. What was something you read that you did not know before?

4. What changes would you make or recommend to this policy?

5. Share your reflections with your classmates.

CASE STUDY

Ramsay Malware and Air-Gapped Networks

An advanced form of malware called Ramsay was discovered in the spring of 2020 that specifically targets air-gapped networks. Three variants of Ramsay haves been discovered, each with new features and attack methods. The malware was first discovered in Japan and has been determined to have been launched against organizations using different attack vectors, including malicious RTF documents and a file masquerading as a 7zip installer. The primary aim of this malware is to gather Microsoft Word, PDF, and ZIP documents; encrypt the files; and place them in a hidden storage folder for future transfer. The malware is spread by searching networks and portable drives for all portable executable (PE) files, attaching to these files, and installing when an infected file is run. The method of exfiltration has not yet been determined, nor has the developer of this malware.

1. Based on the intended targets of air-gapped networks, what type of threat actor do you think is behind this malware? Expand on your reasoning.

2. What additional strategies could an IT department deploy to prevent this malware from reaching an air-gapped network?

3. It is possible that managers may incorrectly feel air-gapped networks are unlikely to become infected with malware. The Ramsay code illustrates that new threats could bypass existing security methods. Why is it important to share these announcements with non-IT management, even if your organization is not infected with Ramsay?

4. To what extent should a company avoid using the files associated with Word, PDF, and ZIP files? Explain why you think this would be an appropriate or inappropriate decision.

CHAPTER 6

Device Security

LEARNING OUTCOMES

- Summarize *hardening*.
- Identify and explain types of endpoint-protection tools used to protect host devices.
- Discuss securing a network through network hardening.
- Summarize techniques used for hardening a server.
- Identify and explain hardening techniques for operating systems.
- Recognize hardware system hardening techniques.
- Identify procedures used to harden applications.
- Explain three methods used for hardening a database.
- Discuss the importance of hardening external storage devices.

KEY TERMS

automated patch management service
blacklisting
blocked port
boot attestation
boot integrity
centralized patch management
client
closed port
database
data loss prevention (DLP)
disabled service
disk encryption
endpoint
endpoint detection and response (EDR)

endpoint protection
firewall
firmware
full-device encryption (FDE)
hardening
hardware root of trust
host
host intrusion-detection system (HIDS)
host intrusion-prevention system (HIPS)
host security
Measured Boot
next-generation firewall

Open Systems Interconnect (OSI) model
patch
patch management
salting
Secure Boot
self-encrypting drive (SED)
tokenization
Trusted Platform Module (TPM)
Unified Extensible Firmware Interface (UEFI)
whitelisting
Windows Registry

SECURITY+ CERTIFICATION EXAM OBJECTIVES

The following Security+ Certification Exam Objectives are covered in this chapter.

- 1.6: Improper or weak patch management
- 2.1: Data loss prevention (DLP)
- 2.1: Tokenization
- 3.2: Endpoint protection
- 3.2: Boot integrity
- 3.2: Database

- 3.2: Whitelisting
- 3.2: Blacklisting
- 3.2: Hardening
- 3.2: Self-encrypting drive (SED)/full disk encryption (FDE)
- 3.2: Hardware root of trust
- 3.2: Trusted Platform Module (TPM)

- 3.3: Next-generation firewall
- 3.8: TPM
- 4.4: Application whitelisting
- 4.4: Application blacklisting
- 4.4: DLP

OVERVIEW

Hardening user devices is a vital step in securing an organization's network against vulnerabilities and threats. This is accomplished through securing all networked devices, including user devices, servers, operating systems, applications, and databases. If individual devices are not secured, they present potential avenues of attack that can be exploited by cyber criminals. However, securing endpoint devices is a far more involved process than just installing antivirus software.

In this chapter, you will learn about methods for hardening devices on a network. In addition to hardening, topics include endpoint protection, such as antivirus software and firewalls; securing a network; server hardening techniques; methods for hardening operating systems and hardware; hardware hardening methods, including securing access to firmware and encrypting storage devices; and information about hardening applications, databases, and storage devices.

SECURITY+ NOTE

The CompTIA Security+ Exam will include scenario-based questions that require you to draw on experience and role-play as a security administrator. It is important to practice the concepts, utilities, tools, and methods discussed in this chapter so you can effectively prepare for those types of assessments.

Hardening

 3.2

Hardening is a security method that relies on tools, techniques, and actions to reduce IT vulnerabilities in an enterprise environment. Hardening incorporates proactive measures to ensure persistent security within a system by configuring options and system settings while simultaneously reducing the attack surfaces that attackers will attempt to exploit to gain access to the systems and data. Hardening is performed by configuring built-in system features; auditing systems for invalid and unnecessary files, users, and programs; and ensuring systems are patched on a regular basis.

Network devices are hardened, and in IT, devices on a network are referred to as hosts, clients, or endpoints. While all three terms generally refer to the same device, there are specific distinctions among them.

- A **host** is a device that is accessible over a network. Hosts can include computers, servers, printers, mobile devices, routers, or any device with network connectivity. Each host is uniquely identified with a host name and its own IP address on a network.

- A **client** is a device that requests and accesses services or resources from a server. The fundamental difference between a host and client is the ability to make requests to a server. For example, a router is a host, but it is not a client because it cannot request services. A typical workstation computer, however, can be a host and client, as well as an endpoint.

- An **endpoint** is any device that functions as a physical endpoint on a network. Endpoints can include most host types as well as portable smart devices and virtual machines. Clients and hosts have many diverse configurations, and each could have a large amount of vulnerabilities. Hardening these systems is critical to ensure there is a substantial reduction in vulnerabilities that could threaten an enterprise environment.

Several areas must be secured through hardening, and are based on the device or system, options and capabilities vary. Examples of locations where hardening is critical include the following:

- *Operating system hardening.* Hardening a device's operating system involves securing configurations, modifying default settings, and other features that could allow exploitation and intrusion.
- *Network hardening.* Hardening a network allows for secure protections by configuring network settings and devices to reduce potential security threats. Network hardening consists of many aspects, from using security appliances such as firewalls, to closing unnecessary ports of entry into systems.
- *Server hardening.* Servers are a critical component of networks since they provide access to needed services and data. Servers, both physical and virtual, must be configured and protected against open vulnerabilities and unauthorized access.
- *Application hardening.* Application hardening involves protecting an application from exploitation and being subject to tampering and intrusion.
- *Database hardening.* Databases contain data used by businesses for essential functionality. Hardening a database ensures data privacy is configured along with protections against exploits that could expose the data publicly.

Endpoint Protection

3.2

Securing endpoints should be a top priority for every organization. These devices are common vectors that provide avenues for hackers to launch attacks on a network.

Endpoint protection, also called *endpoint security*, is the practice of securing user endpoint devices on networks to prevent them from malicious activity and attacks. **Host security** is the methods used to secure an operating system, file structure, and applications used on a host from unauthorized activity or access. Every networked device, be it a router, server, computer, or printer, presents an entry point to a network. Threats to a network can originate from unpatched operating systems, unsecure system settings, and intentional or inadvertent user actions. IT administrators take precautions such as reviewing systems for unusual activity, errors, and warnings that may indicate a potential failure or suspect activity to prevent security accidents. In some cases, security administrators may want to analyze traffic flow on a single machine without making an effort to block traffic. Host devices are protected by a variety of endpoint-protection tools, such as endpoint detection and response utilities, antivirus software, firewalls, host intrusion systems, and data loss prevention techniques.

Endpoint Detection and Response (EDR)

3.2

Endpoint detection and response (EDR) is the tools and technology used to monitor devices continuously to identify malicious attacks on endpoint devices. EDR is an advanced technology that focuses on monitoring endpoint and network events through continuous monitoring and response to threats. It is an advanced security approach used to detect malicious activity on user devices.

Endpoint detection monitors events such as logins, running processes, and communication and forwards this information to a central database through a software agent installed on the endpoint. Analytic tools then analyze the database and perform investigation of its contents, providing reporting and alerting.

EDR focuses on threats and attacks that have evaded normal preventive measures. Endpoint response takes immediate action to mitigate an attack's spread and provide real-time forensic information. The combinations of these two techniques provides an efficient and timely response to remediate vulnerabilities.

Antivirus and Antimalware

Antivirus programs are software programs that search for, detect, and remove viruses on computer files stored or in computer memory. Antivirus programs focus on the traditional virus threats such as worms and Trojans.

Comparatively, *antimalware* is an encompassing program that detects malware-, spyware-, and virus-infected files and removes threats from an endpoint. Antimalware programs focus on recently created malware and exploits. Most products today offer protection for both types of threats. These protections offer specific safeguards for a myriad of vulnerabilities and threats that can affect endpoints.

Firewall

3.2, 3.3

A **firewall** is a network security tool that acts as a barrier or protection against unwanted data transfer at entry points by monitoring incoming and outgoing network traffic, as demonstrated in Figure 6-1. Firewalls are configured to allow selected traffic to flow in or out, or block all traffic on endpoint devices. A *host-based firewall*, also known as a *personal software firewall*, resides on an individual device and uses predefined policies and rules to filter traffic entering or exiting the host.

Typical firewalls focus on examining headers on data packets. Conversely, next-generation firewalls provide a higher level of analysis by exploring the data, or *payload*, inside the packet. A **next-generation firewall**, also known as a *next-gen firewall*, is a firewall that can run at all levels of the OSI model to monitor and filter traffic-based data inside packet headers or the packet's payload on header or application data. The **Open Systems Interconnect (OSI) model** is a conceptual framework that outlines how hardware and software function together to form a communications network. Next-generation firewalls provide more protection to endpoint devices than traditional firewalls because while firewalls block traffic based on port numbers, next-gen firewalls block traffic based on the traffic itself and the data it carries. This allows necessary ports to remain open to services and programs while blocking unwanted traffic.

TECH TIP

Firewalls can also be installed at the network level, as opposed to individual devices. There will be more discussion about network firewalls in a later chapter.

Host Intrusion Systems

3.2

A **host intrusion-detection system (HIDS)** is a security tool that passively examines and analyzes activity to and from an endpoint device and provides notifications of security threats. A HIDS is a useful tool for log analysis as it collects information regarding attempted intrusions but does not affect data flow.

Conversely, a **host intrusion-prevention system (HIPS)** is a security-monitoring program that monitors and analyzes incoming and outgoing traffic flow and immediately halts traffic if malicious activity is suspected. An HIPS expands on the HDS capabilities by its active involvement in the flow of data.

Data Loss Prevention (DLP)

2.1, 3.2, 4.4

Data loss prevention (DLP) is a security strategy that detects potential data breaches or exfiltration transmissions to ensure that sensitive, confidential, or critical data is not transferred outside the organization. Additionally, DLP software identifies sensitive or confidential data before it is leaked or sent from an endpoint. A DLP tool runs on the systems that protect and monitor data at rest (stored), in motion, or in use at an endpoint. This type of protection analyzes data regardless of application.

Figure 6-1 A firewall is a network security tool that acts as a barrier or protection against an unwanted data transfer.

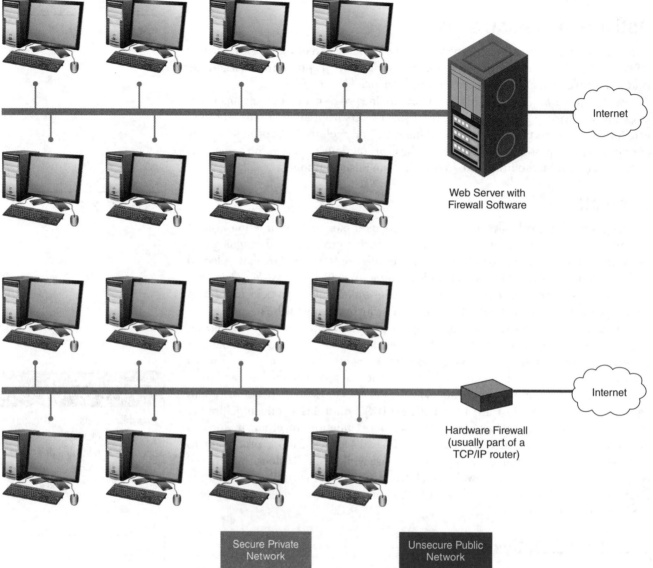

Goodheart-Willcox Publisher; (workstations) romvo/Shutterstock.com; (server) aShatilov/Shutterstock.com

Securing the Network

Network hardening is the process and steps used to secure a network by reducing the vulnerabilities present in network devices and management. Network security protection is dependent on network architecture, networking infrastructure equipment, and policies and procedures in place on the network. For example, if remote access through virtual private networks is allowed, security protections need to be established and configured to reduce or eliminate vulnerabilities associated with VPN connectivity.

Network hardening includes specialized equipment and software used to support network operations. Security methods include limiting nonessential access to networking equipment and utilizing group membership that supports network services including DHCP, IIS, and DNS. Routers and managed switches run their own operating systems, so best practices associated with specialized equipment are necessary, as is frequent, regular software or firmware updates. Physical security is also important, so networking devices should be stored or operating in a secure, locked location to prevent theft or tampering.

Securing a network through hardening includes using appropriate encryption levels and capturing and reviewing network traffic to identify anomalies in traffic operations. Traffic can be filtered through firewall rules to prevent unwanted network traffic. Wireless networking is also important to secure, such as creating guest access and using IEEE 802.1x, or *enterprise networking*, to ensure authentication of authorized users.

Hardening a Server

Servers are the workhorses of business operations. They provide the central storage, access, and coordination of resources to enable users to perform job duties. Servers are usually run on customized hardware or as a virtual machine located locally or in a cloud environment. Due to the sensitive nature of the data and services, it is critical to protect these systems using effective tools and procedures. Close attention must be paid to unique configurations, applications, and operating systems that are used by servers. For servers running in virtual environment, the physical host machine must also be hardened.

Server hardening uses some of the same concepts as host hardening. Updates must be installed and tested on a timely basis, and the principle of least privilege is necessary to follow to reduce security access to server resources. As with host operating systems, preventing unneeded services from running, removing unnecessary user accounts, configuring firewalls, and removing unneeded administrative shares are all necessary hardening steps.

Servers also have unique hardening aspects. These include implementing a least functionality approach. For example, a server running as a file server should not also function as a public-facing web server.

Servers should have multiple network interfaces that can be configured to separate traffic on a connection. Backups of critical files, configurations, and accounts should be performed on a daily basis. Auditing of servers is essential, especially to locate failed login attempts or file access. Additionally, administrator access should be strictly monitored, and all administrator accounts should be renamed from the default and configured with strong, secure passwords.

Operating System Hardening

 3.2

System hardening is the tools, techniques, and actions that reduce vulnerabilities and attack vectors in applications, networks, devices, and other aspects of computing. General hardening techniques include closing unused services and features that do not need to be running and removing unnecessary programs and access. Hardening also incorporates proactive measures to ensure persistent security within a system. If exploited, the vulnerabilities can lead to threats against the host and other systems on the network. Every operating system has its own unique configurations, but generally, these are the most common aspects of hardening a system.

Operating system hardening, also known as *OS hardening*, enables security personnel to configure an operating system securely while enabling timely periodic updates. Through securing of systems, attack surfaces for vulnerabilities are decreased. An *attack surface* is all points or areas of compromise in a system that allow hackers entry. An *attack vector* is the path a hacker uses to get into a system to commit an attack. If a system is exploited, vulnerabilities can lead to threats against the host and other systems on the network.

When a computer is purchased, the operating system default configurations often do not match the security requirements of the organization that purchased the system. A common method for establishing a base security implementation is to apply a *security template*, which includes groups of policies that can be loaded in one procedure. Security templates are commonly used in an enterprise environment to ensure an operating system includes hardening aspects before initial use.

Hardening techniques minimize an operating system's exposure to vulnerabilities and threats. OS hardening requires an understanding of functions needed by users and configuring security options and controls to enable those functions safely. Techniques can be used to remove inherent vulnerabilities and tighten security controls. Methods and procedures vary based on the OS type and version.

Services

A *service* is any program running in the background of an operating system that provides specific features and functionality. A service on a Linux host is a *daemon*. Some operating systems require services. For example, on a Windows host, the Local Session Manager service manages a user's session with the operating system. If the service stops, the operating system becomes unstable and unusable. Similarly, if a Linux host has a graphical interface, then the Display Manager (dm) service is required to run.

An *open service* is a service permitted to run on a computer. Some services are not essential for operating system processes but provide necessary functionality for the users. For example, services such as dynamic host configuration protocol (DHCP) is required for automatic IP assignments, and the cups service in Linux hosts is required to enable printing. Conversely, there are several services not necessary for functionality, such as FTP, which allows for file transfers; services that connect the host with an outside time provider; and services that allow remote access.

One of the primary security concerns with open services is that when a service runs, it becomes a potential avenue for a hacker to gain access to the system. It is critical that only services essential to operating a computer remain running and unneeded services be disabled. A **disabled service** is a locked service not permitted to run on a computer. For example, if you do not use Telnet or FTP, these services should be disabled from a default launch. If currently running, it should be stopped.

In Windows, services are managed from the PowerShell or graphical user interface (GUI), as shown in Figure 6-2. To manage a service in Windows, you can control its startup mode, status, and whether or not it logs on automatically to the operating system. A graphical interface is accessed through Task Manager. Click the **Services** tab in Task Manager, and then click **Open Services** or the **Services...** button at the top of the tab. In Linux, the **systemctl** command stops and starts services.

Ports

Ports not needed for daily use on a device should be disabled. *Ports* are virtual connections used by an operating system to allow IP protocol communication and traffic exchange. In TCP/IP, ports are identified by port numbers 0 through 65535.

TECH TIP

Many organizations have operating system hardening guides available at no cost. For example, many Windows 10 secure configuration guides are available online. Microsoft has also established secure baselines that can be downloaded as well as tools that can be used to configure Windows workstations.

✛ 3.2

TECH TIP

Windows services may also be accessed from Control Panel or the **Run** dialog box, provided the access has not been previously locked for security reasons.

✛ 3.2

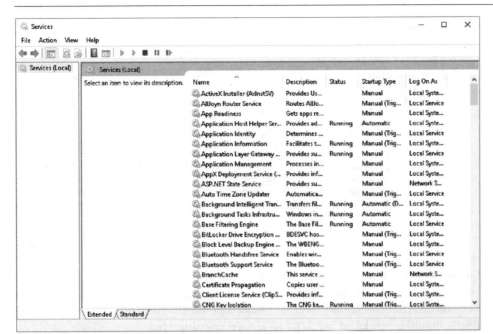

Goodheart-Willcox Publisher

Figure 6-2 In Windows, services are managed from the graphical user interface (GUI), which is accessed through Task Manager.

Ports are set to a specific state. A *port state* is the status of a port's visibility as to which services or applications are currently running. Port states are open, closed, and blocked.

- An *open port* is a communication port that actively accepts TCP or UDP connections. Ports required for communication must be open; however, open ports can be vulnerable if services using them are misconfigured or unpatched. Therefore, an unneeded port should be closed.
- A **closed port** is a communication port that does not have a process actively listening to it. If communication is sent through this port, the sender receives an automatic reply that the service is unavailable and attempted connections will be denied.
- A **blocked port** is a communication port that has been shut down so data cannot be transmitted through the port. All communication requests coming through blocked ports are ignored by a host system.

Hardening a System through Group Policies

Many features in an operating system can be restricted or configured by creating technical policies that are applied to any user who uses a computer. In Windows, this is accomplished through Group Policy management, as shown in Figure 6-3. Additionally, if an organization is using Active Directory, these policies can be pushed to endpoints through AD. Examples of policies used to help harden an operating system on endpoint devices include locking use of the command prompt, configuring local firewalls and web filters, requiring a password to log in or wake up a computer, and enforcing web browser settings. Password management, including the length, frequency of change, and history, are also settings applied through group policies.

Account Hardening

Security administrators should verify that only approved accounts exist on systems. Often, fake accounts are created to test software or policy enforcement and should

TECH TIP

Some port numbers must remain open to provide necessary protocol functionality. For example, HTTP uses port 80; HTTPS uses port 443; FTP uses port 21; POP3 uses either port 110 or 995; and IMAP uses either port 143 or 993.

Figure 6-3 In Windows, the Group Policy Editor is used to create and manage group policies.

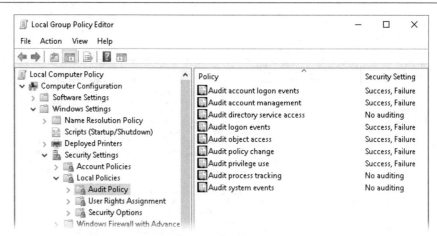

be removed or disabled if not actively used. The same is true for accounts of employees no longer with an organization. Root or administrator account privileges should be highly restricted and only given to authorized individuals, and accounts and privileges should be checked regularly to ensure unauthorized changes have not been made. An easy way to check local administrator group membership in Windows 10 is to run the PowerShell cmdlet syntax get-LocalGroupMember administrators, which returns a list of all members of the local administrator group. Administrators can check this list against known administrators to determine whether unauthorized administrators exist in a network. There will be more about PowerShell and command-line utilities later in this text.

Shared Folders

It is possible to share local folders on Windows and Linux systems, which enables other users to access and connect to the share remotely and view or edit files. However, a lack of oversight on shared folder settings can lead to unauthorized access if the folder sharing service is left vulnerable. Many times, shared folders allow *null access*, which lets a hacker connect to a remote shared folder without any valid account name.

Patch Management

✛ 3.2

Patch management is the process of deploying patches to networked devices to keep all devices up to date. A **patch** is an update provided by a vendor to correct errors or bugs in software or improve its operation. Often, patches apply enhanced security measures, and the errors or bugs resolved by patches represent security vulnerabilities. Applying patches, updates, and comprehensive collections of updates or enhancements, called *service packs*, is an essential function of hardening operating systems and applications.

Patch management is a systematic process that is used to acquire patches from software and operating system vendors, test and install the patches on related systems. This can be manual or through a centralized patch management server. *Manual patch management* is a method of navigating to vendor websites, downloading patches, and installing updates on individual workstations. **Centralized patch management** is a method of patch deployment that enables administrators to push updates to devices from a central point within a network. By centralizing patch management, an organization ensures patches are downloaded and installed on all systems.

An **automated patch management service**, also known as *auto-update*, is a program that automatically scans, downloads, and installs patches when available from the vendor. It is an automated service used to manage patches within an organization.

✚ **3.2**

Part of the patch management process is scanning and monitoring hosts to ensure the patches are downloaded and installed on the systems. Hosts with outdated updates represent a serious vulnerability to the security of a system and network.

One of the most common sources of cyberattacks results from *improper* or *weak patch management practices*. Three critical areas that must be continuously patched and monitored for updates include device firmware, applications, and operating systems.

✚ **1.6**

- **Firmware** is a read-only software program on a hardware device that provides instructions for the device to communicate with other hardware. Common examples include Basic Input/Output System (BIOS), Unified Extensible Firmware Interface (UEFI), and wireless router software used to configure and manage wireless networks. Routers, switches, computers, and many portable devices are updated only through occasional firmware patches. Failure to update devices can cause serious harm. The inability to update or patch firmware at regular intervals is a common weak configuration of patch management. If automatic updates are not incorporated for firmware, vendor updates must be monitored, tested, and patched manually and regularly to ensure the security of the devices on which firmware is installed.

- *Applications* include updates on browsers, software programs, games, and security tools. Weak patch management of applications often involves not knowing all the locations of an application's installation, resulting in outdated patches. In addition, not testing a patch before deployment has the potential to create problems on the devices on which the patch is installed. Patches for specific software applications, such as Adobe Reader and Google Chrome, are *third-party updates* and are typically delivered directly from the vendor. When third-party updates are released, an organization should first test the patch in a protected environment before it is distributed to networked devices.

✚ **3.2**

- *Operating systems (OS)* provide many potential attack vectors. Windows and Linux systems have commands that allow administrators to check on current versions or update systems. Weak patch configurations often include untimely updates. Another situation that can affect network security is failing to consider operating systems that exist on nontraditional devices, including tablets, mobile devices, switches, and routers.

Updating Windows

In Windows 10, updates are automatically downloaded and installed. However, a system may be configured manually. Most Windows updates are delivered on a monthly basis—commonly called *Patch Tuesday* in the IT industry, as shown in Figure 6-4. There may be urgent updates sent outside this scheduled time frame called out-of-band updates that may need to be addressed. Unlike home users, business versions of Windows offer more flexibility on scheduling the updates to allow administrators the ability to test and approve new updates. Windows also allows users to review and, if necessary, uninstall recently installed updates through Control Panel, as shown in Figure 6-5.

Updating Linux

In a Linux system, such as Ubuntu, updates can be installed from the command line or through the GUI. In the graphical interface select, **Edit**>**Software sources...** to

Figure 6-4 Microsoft has adopted Patch Tuesday as a standardized way to release patches and updates.

Updates are issued on Patch Tuesday

Figure 6-5 The updates that have been installed on a Windows machine can be viewed and, if needed, removed.

Click to uninstall   Select an update

Updates are grouped by publisher

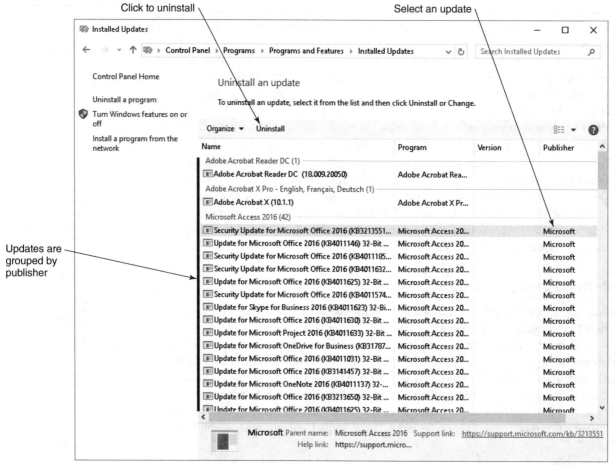

display the **Software Sources** dialog box. Click the **Updates** tab in the dialog box. In the **Automatic updates** area of the tab, check the **Check for updates** check box, and then select how often the computer should check for updates in the corresponding drop-down list. Finally, below the drop-down list, choose which option to use regarding how updates should be installed.

The **apt-get** command is used for installing updates on a command line. The **apt** command stands for *advanced packaging tool*. This command must be run as an administrator. To run the command as an administrator, use the **sudo** command with it. Enter sudo apt-get update to install updates.

Securing the Windows Registry

The **Windows Registry** is a hierarchical configuration database containing information, settings, options, and values for a given installation of the Windows operation system. Some system settings contained within the Registry apply to individual users while other settings apply to any user who logs on to the device on which the Registry is located.

To lessen the risk of vulnerabilities or attacks, administrators should harden the Registry. Hardening techniques for the Registry include limiting access to the Registry editing tool (**regedit.exe**) to authorized users, configuring Registry permissions to prohibit anonymous access, and disabling remote access to the Registry.

➕ **3.2**

Hardware System Hardening

Hardware hardening is the process of securing a system by reducing vulnerabilities related to the hardware and software integration. Securing computer hardware is one of the most important steps in securing a host system because if system hardware is corrupted or compromised, software- or application-based protections are irrelevant.

BIOS and UEFI Access

Computers use low-level software that controls the boot process. Prior to 2007, systems relied on a Basic Input Output System (BIOS) program. *Basic Input Output System (BIOS)* was chip-embedded firmware used to boot a computer and perform a Power-On Self-Test (POST). BIOS was one of the most important hardware components as it initiated the boot process and loaded the operating system. However, since 2007, systems have employed Unified Extensible Firmware Interface (UEFI) software. **Unified Extensible Firmware Interface (UEFI)** is a firmware interface that adds enhanced security measures to a boot process. Typically, these interfaces can be accessed during the boot process by pressing a key such as [F5], [Esc], or [Enter]. However, for the security of a device and the network to which it connects, these programs should not be accessible to anyone except IT staff. One effective method of ensuring only authorized personnel are able to access the booting firmware is to add an access password. By adding a password to the firmware interface, IT personnel can protect a device against unauthorized access and changes.

Boot Order

When a computer boots, it follows a predefined path to locate a bootable operating system. Normally an operating system is on the computer's hard drive. However, bootable operating systems can launch from removable media, such as an attached USB device, network attached storage (NAS) device, or CD/DVD.

A computer system can be reconfigured to search for operating system files on external media before its hard drive is searched, enabling the system to access files stored on the drive and bypassing previously configured permissions. To prevent this from occurring, boot order should be locked at the user level and only available through security settings such as a BIOS/UEFI password or through trusted boot operations.

Chassis Locks and Alarms

Included in hardening practices is securing computers by placing them in workspaces with physical case locks to prevent access to the hardware in the desktop unit. Often, cases are equipped with cylindrical locks similar to the one shown in Figure 6-6. For additional hardening practices, a sensor can be placed inside the case. If the sensor detects the case is open, the boot-up firmware (BIOS/UEFI) prevents the computer from starting, and administrators are alerted to a possible breach.

Boot Integrity

Boot integrity is the assurance that a computer is booting from a secure drive and running only authorized programs. Ensuring the security of bootable media represents the first step in securing computer hardware and networking infrastructure. There are three common elements to boot integrity: the use of UEFI and Secure Boot, Measured Boot with Trusted Platform Modules (TPMs), and boot attestation.

Figure 6-6 Locks can be used as physical protection to prevent access to hardware in a desktop unit.

UEFI

UEFI replaced the Basic Input/Output System (BIOS) firmware interface as the de facto booting firmware for desktop computers. By comparison, UEFI provides additional security by verifying digital signatures of all boot software, including drivers and an operating system. If a signature is invalid, the computer does not boot.

Boot security is achieved through a UEFI. **Secure Boot** is a feature of UEFI that ensures a computer uses only software trusted by a manufacturer for booting purposes. Secure Boot enables UEFI to check digital signatures. Typically, these signatures are stored in a Secure Boot database on a computer and can be deactivated by the user if untrusted software is needed. However, once deactivated, Secure Boot is difficult to reactivate without resetting the computer back to its original state.

Boot Attestation

Similar to Secure Boot, **boot attestation** is a mechanism that allows software to prove its identity. Attestation is usually performed after a boot-up using measurements generated through Secure Boot to verify software. The significant difference between Secure Boot and attestation is that Secure Boot verifies software it anticipates will run on boot-up, and attestation verifies software that is already running.

Measured Boot

Measured Boot is a boot feature that provides protection from rootkits and other malware that launch during an operating system boot process. When Measured Boot is employed, it verifies boot components, including firmware and drivers, and stores the information in a *Platform Configuration Register (PRC)* in a Trusted Platform Module (TPM). A **Trusted Platform Module (TPM)** is a chip located in a computer's hardware that runs authentication checks on hardware, software, and firmware. An example of an installed TPM is shown in Figure 6-7. Measured Boot does not validate or stop a boot process. Instead, each time a system is booted, Measured Boot compares boot components to stored information in the TPM to ensure no malware has been installed.

Typically, the starting point for a Measured Boot is a **hardware root of trust**, which is hardware that serves as a starting point in a chain of trust. A *chain of trust* is a series of trusted devices created as each hardware and software component of a computer system is validated. For example, UEFI and Secure Boot validate the integrity of boot software. Next, they validate software drivers. This process continues

3.2, 3.8

3.2

Figure 6-7 A Trusted Platform Module (TPM) is a chip located in a computer's hardware that runs authentication checks on hardware, software, and firmware.

until control is handed off to the operating system which helps to ensure only valid, trusted components are used during computer operation. While this process seems safe, imagine if a hacker implanted malware in boot software. In that scenario, the entire chain of trust could be compromised. Therefore, using hardware as a starting point in a chain of trust is safer since hardware cannot be compromised.

Disk Encryption

One hardening technique is disk encryption. **Disk encryption** is the process of converting all data on a hard disk into unreadable characters by applying a security key. It is a powerful hardening setting used to protect a hard drive's contents. Encrypting a drive ensures that data cannot be read by unauthorized personnel.

Full-device encryption (FDE), also called *drive encryption*, is a technology that renders data stored on a hard drive unreadable without an encryption key to unlock it. Encryption is particularly important on mobile devices as they are more likely to be stolen or lost than a traditional desktop computer. Therefore, encryption should be a high priority on mobile technologies. For security purposes, encryption should be used. Without encryption, if a password is cracked, account data can be accessed.

Similarly, **self-encrypting drives (SEDs)** are storage drives that automatically encrypt stored data. SEDs are in nontraditional hosts, such as multifunction devices, point-of-sale (PoS) systems, and other devices for which encryption must be guaranteed.

Opal Storage Specification is a set of SED specifications for encrypting and securing SEDs. These drives operate by performing an authentication process as soon as a device is powered. In the event of authentication failure, a drive can be programmed to deny access or delete all data.

Application Hardening

Applications are daily components of a user's work environment. The use of productivity, communication, design, and social tools are an essential tool for users to perform their duties. However useful, applications also represent the potential for unauthorized data access or system intrusion into hosts and potentially the enterprise network. To protect against unwanted attacks, these apps must be hardened to lessen or prevent security attacks. Software programs and apps installed on computers and devices should be under periodic review to confirm if the software is in use and following company policies.

Application hardening consists of using procedures and techniques to eliminate vulnerabilities in an application or its interaction with the operating system or user.

- For an application under development, secure coding practices can decrease vulnerabilities.
- For deployed applications, default accounts and passwords should be changed to ensure appropriate file permissions are assigned to reduce the possibility of unwanted access.
- Verification of security certificates can ensure authenticity and integrity of updates from the appropriate vendor.
- Installation of firewalls can prevent unwanted access.
- Installation of antimalware programs can ensure malicious files are not embedded in software.
- Encryption of data used in an app can help ensure confidentiality.
- All programs should be completely removed from the systems when no longer used or needed.

- **Whitelisting** is the process of specifying a list of approved applications or executable software permitted to run on a device or network. Any software not included on an application whitelist is denied permission to run. The automatic denial of applications is called *implicit deny*, or *deny-by-default*.
- **Blacklisting** is the process of specifying a list of unapproved applications or executable software that is not permitted to run on a device or network. By comparison, blacklisting is less restrictive than whitelisting because while whitelisting only allows listed programs to run, blacklisting permits all programs *except* those listed.

✚ 3.2, 4.4

Database Hardening

✚ 2.1, 3.2

A **database** is a structured, organized collection of data. A database enables collection of raw data as well as the organization, access, and review of data in an electronic format. The data is often the end goal for many hackers and protection of a database and its management platform is essential. *Database hardening* is the actions and procedures used to secure or enhance the security of a database. Methods for hardening a database often include the following:

- *Tokenization.* **Tokenization** is a method of protecting data by replacing it with tokens. The token is a random value, which represents original data, and the actual data is stored in a secured vault. This process uses a tokenization provider that handles the data replacement. There is no mathematical relationship between the token and the actual data, and the process is irreversible. This process adds security to a database since it prevents sensitive data from being stored on the business network.
- *Hashing.* In computing, a *hash* is a mathematical algorithm used to map or transform data into a fixed length. This process replaces the usable data with a hashed value. This is a one-way function; it is extremely unlikely for a hacker to reverse-engineer a hashed value back to its original content. Hashing is typically used for password storage in databases.
- *Salting.* When passwords are stored, a computed value, called a *hash*, is what is actually stored in most systems. To make a hash unbreakable, a salt is added to the password. Adding a random value is salting. **Salting** is a process that adds additional insignificant data to the end of data to create a different hash value. This adds another layer of security to the hashing process.

External Storage Devices

External storage devices should be protected in the same manner as internal hard drives. External storage devices include external hard drives, USB drives, network-attached storage (NAS) devices, servers, and cloud-based storage services. The importance of protecting these devices and services is due in part to synchronization with a primary drive. If an external device is infected with malware, a primary drive can be at risk due to synchronization.

Security administrators should pay attention to the insertion and removal of USB devices. This is especially important on devices where confidential or critical information could be stored. Data can be easily withdrawn and covertly by small devices placed in pockets. Similarly, USB devices can be used to insert malware into the system. One method for eliminating this potential risk is by employing USB data blockers. A *USB data blocker* is a device that prevents unauthorized transfer of information as well as the installation of malware to a device.

SUMMARY

Hardening

- Hardening is a security method that relies on tools, techniques, and actions to reduce IT vulnerabilities in an enterprise environment. It incorporates proactive measures to ensure persistent security while simultaneously reducing the attack surfaces.
- Network devices are hardened, and in IT, devices on a network are referred to as hosts, clients, or endpoints.
- Several areas must be secured through hardening, and are based on the device or system. Locations where hardening is critical include operating system, network, server, application, and database.

Endpoint Protection

- Endpoint protection is the practice of securing user endpoint devices on networks to prevent them from malicious activity and attacks. Endpoint-protection tools include EDR, antivirus software, firewalls, host intrusion systems, and DLP.
- Endpoint detection and response (EDR) monitors devices continuously to identify malicious attacks on endpoint devices. It focuses on threats and attacks that have evaded normal preventive measures.
- Antivirus programs search for, detect, and remove viruses on computer files stored or in computer memory, while antimalware detects malware-, spyware-, and virus-infected files and removes threats from an endpoint.
- A firewall acts as a barrier against unwanted data transfer at entry points by monitoring incoming and outgoing network traffic. It is configured to allow selected traffic to flow in or out, or block all traffic on endpoint devices.
- HIDS passively examines and analyzes activity to and from an endpoint device and provides notifications of security threats. Conversely, HIPS monitors and analyzes incoming and outgoing traffic flow and immediately halts traffic if malicious activity is suspected.
- Data loss prevention (DLP) detects potential data breaches or exfiltration transmissions to ensure that sensitive, confidential, or critical data is transferred outside the organization. It runs on the systems that protect and monitor data at rest, in motion, or in use at an endpoint.

Securing the Network

- Network hardening is the process and steps used to secure a network by reducing the vulnerabilities present in network devices and management. It includes specialized equipment and software used to support network operations.
- Physical security is also important, so networking devices should be stored or operating in a secure, locked location to prevent theft or tampering.
- Securing a network through hardening includes using appropriate encryption levels and capturing and reviewing network traffic to identify anomalies in traffic operations.

Hardening a Server

- Servers run on customized hardware or as a virtual machine. Therefore, close attention is paid to unique configurations, applications, and operating systems used by servers.
- Server hardening uses some of the same concepts as host hardening, such as installing and testing updates and following the principles of least privilege.
- Servers also have unique hardening aspects. These include implementing a least functionality approach. Servers should have multiple network interfaces that can be configured to separate traffic on a connection.

Operating System Hardening

- Operating system hardening enables security personnel to configure an operating system securely while enabling timely periodic updates. This decreases the attack surfaces for vulnerabilities.
- A security template establishes a base security implementation. It is used in an enterprise environment to ensure an operating system includes hardening aspects before initial use.
- Hardening techniques minimize an operating system's exposure to vulnerabilities and threats and tighten security controls.
- OS hardening techniques include disabling nonessential services and ports, incorporating restrictions through group policies, managing accounts effectively, removing unneeded folder shares, incorporating sound patch management strategies, and securing the Windows Registry.

Hardware System Hardening

- Hardware hardening is the process of securing a system by reducing vulnerabilities related to the hardware and software integration. Securing computer hardware is one of the most important steps in securing a host system.
- Hardware hardening techniques include creating BIOS and UEFI access passwords, configuring boot order, using chassis locks and alarms, ensuring boot integrity, and encrypting a device's hard drive.

Application Hardening

- Applications must be hardened to lesson or prevent security attacks. Software programs and installed apps should be under periodic review to confirm if the software is in use and following company policies.
- Application hardening techniques include securing codes, changing default accounts and passwords, verifying security certificates, installing firewalls and antimalware programs, encrypting data, removing programs that are no longer in use, and whitelisting and blacklisting applications.

Database Hardening

- A database is a structured, organized collection of data. Database hardening is the actions and procedures used to secure or enhance the security of a database.
- Methods for hardening a database often include tokenization, hashing, and salting.

External Storage Devices

- External storage devices should be protected in the same manner as internal hard drives.
- The importance of protecting external storage devices and services is due in part to synchronization with a primary drive. If an external device is infected with malware, a primary drive can be at risk due to synchronization.
- Security administrators should pay attention to the insertion and removal of USB devices. One method for eliminating potential risks from USBs is employing USB data blockers.

REVIEW QUESTIONS

1. Summarize *hardening*.
2. State the difference between a host, a client, and an endpoint.
3. Identify and explain three endpoint-protection tools used to protect host devices.
4. Which type of firewall can run at all levels of the OSI model?
5. Discuss securing a network through network hardening.
6. Summarize techniques used for hardening a server.
7. Identify and explain hardening techniques for operating systems.
8. Which type of port does not have a process actively listening to it?
9. What is the difference between manual patch management and centralized patch management?
10. List three critical areas that must be continuously patched and monitored for updates.
11. How do you update Linux?
12. Identify hardware system hardening techniques.
13. Which keys can be used to access the UEFI during the boot process?
14. Briefly explain the three common elements to boot integrity.
15. Define a *full-device encryption (FDE)* and its importance on mobile devices.
16. Identify procedures used to harden applications.
17. What is a database?
18. Explain three methods used for hardening a database.
19. Explain the importance of hardening external storage devices.
20. Define a USB data blocker.

➕ SAMPLE SECURITY+ EXAM QUESTIONS

1. Which statement *best* describes operating system hardening?
   A. Uninstalling older programs
   B. Patching systems to potential vulnerabilities in the operating system
   C. Installing a packet filtering firewall
   D. Creating a system baseline

2. Which of the following should be ensured before shutting down a service?

    A. The service startup-type is set to manual.

    B. Other services depend on this service running.

    C. Components are needed for this service to run.

    D. The service is located in the c:\windows\system32 directory.

3. Which security technique will help ensure security policies are in place on new host devices?

    A. Account hardening

    B. Centralized patch management

    C. Security templates

    D. DLP

4. Which of the following is *not* a technique used in account hardening?

    A. Removing unnecessary shares

    B. Limiting membership of the Administrator group

    C. Ensure only authorized users have access to the root password

    D. Verify current employees to active user accounts

5. Which of the following features is provided by Secure Boot in UEFI?

    A. It prevents another O/S from running outside the set boot ord.

    B. It offers chassis locks and alarms.

    C. It provides full-device encryption.

    D. It ensures only trusted software is used during the boot process.

6. Only pre-approved applications are available to be run if _____ is employed.

    A. whitelisting

    B. digital signature verification

    C. blacklisting

    D. a host firewall

7. Which security technique specifically helps prevent network attacks?

    A. Virtualizing servers

    B. Utilizing EDR

    C. Blocking specific services on a non-standard port

    D. Monitoring traffic with a HIDS

8. _____ is a security method in which sensitive data is replaced with random bits to prevent the sensitive information from being stored on the network.

    A. Salting

    B. Hashing

    C. Tokenization

    D. FDE

9. Which of the following should be hardened to prevent changes to the host by altering system settings?

   A. BIOS

   B. HIPS

   C. Firmware

   D. Registry

10. Sebastian needs to incorporate a security device that can monitor traffic that looks for data such as Social Security numbers and block the transmission. Which security tool should Sebastian use?

    A. HIDS

    B. Next-generation firewall

    C. Antimalware

    D. SED

LAB EXERCISES

Lab Activity 6-1: Windows Host Services

It is easy to see all the services installed and running on a host using Windows PowerShell. You can also view which ones are installed, but not running.

1. Applying what you have learned, launch Windows PowerShell.

2. Enter get-service. All installed services are listed whether they are running or not.

3. To view only the running services, enter: get-service | where-object {$_.status -eq "running"}.

4. You can also look for running services starting with just a specific letter. To find only services beginning with the letter W, enter: get-service w*.

5. Compare the PowerShell get-service cmdlet to the command **net start**, which is used at a normal command prompt. How is the PowerShell cmdlet more helpful?

Lab Activity 6-2: Startup Programs and Scheduled Tasks

In Windows, an easy way to locate startup programs is to run a Microsoft utility called msconfig. The Task Scheduler should also be examined for commands set to execute at a specific time.

1. Click the Windows **Start** button, and then enter msconfig in the search bar. Select msconfig.exe or System Configuration in the search results to launch the System Configuration utility.

2. In the System Configuration utility, click the **Startup** tab. In Windows 10, click the **Open Task Manager** link. In older versions of Windows, the startup information is accessed directly in the System Configuration utility.

3. From the startup tab select a program in the list, and right-click and choose the **Disable** button to prevent the program from loading, as shown. In older versions of Windows, uncheck the check box for a service to disable it.

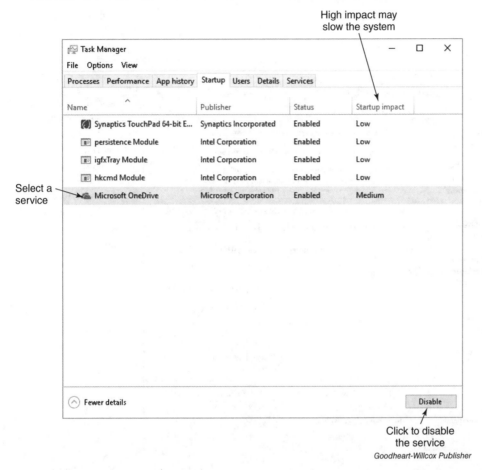

High impact may slow the system

Select a service

Click to disable the service

Goodheart-Willcox Publisher

4. Close the Task Manager and the System Configuration utility.

5. Enter task scheduler in the Windows search bar. Select the Task Scheduler application in the search results.

6. The initial view is a dashboard that allows you to view information on tasks, including recently run tasks. How many tasks ran in the last 24 hours? The last hour?

7. Click **Action>Display All Running Tasks** in the pull-down menu. A new window is displayed that shows all tasks currently running. Click the **Close** button after viewing the tasks.

8. In the left-side pane, expand the Task Scheduler Library tree, as shown. You can view scheduled tasks for various components, such as Microsoft; those scheduled through the event viewer; or other programs, such as Apple.

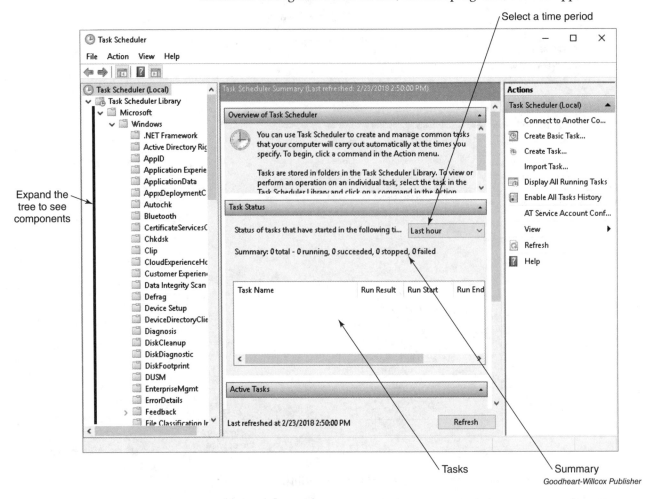

Goodheart-Willcox Publisher

9. Expand the Microsoft branch, and then expand the Windows branch. Scroll down to find the DiskCleanup branch, and select it. Information for this specific component is displayed. When was the last time this program ran?

10. With the DiskCleanup branch selected, click the **Actions** tab in the middle view. The path to the actual executable program is displayed.

11. Click the **General** tab. Can the program run if the user is not logged on? Will it run hidden (not visible to the logged-in user)?

12. Close the Task Scheduler.

Lab Activity 6-3: Audit Policy

Suppose your sales manager is working on a bid proposal and wants to track everyone who opens the file or changes its content. These events can be audited to help protect the integrity of the data in the bid proposal. Note: this exercise is based on Windows 10, and you will need administrative access to the system.

1. Create a new document in Microsoft Word, and add your name to the file.

2. Save the file as SalesBid in your working folder for this class, and exit Word. You will audit for users who are able to view and make changes to the file.

3. Click the Windows **Start** button, and enter group policy in the search box. Select **Edit group policy** in the results to open the Group Policy Editor application.

4. In the left-hand pane, expand the tree **Computer Configuration**>**Windows Settings**>**Security Settings**>**Local Policies** and select the Audit Policy branch.

5. In the right-hand pane, double-click Audit object access. The **Audit Object Access Properties** dialog box is displayed, as shown.

Goodheart-Willcox Publisher

6. Check the **Success** check box, and then click the **OK** button. Editing and saving the word-processing file is a "success event."

7. Close the Group Policy Editor.

8. Launch File Explorer, navigate to your working folder, right-click on the SalesBid document, and click **Properties** in the shortcut menu.

9. In the **Properties** dialog box, click the **Security** tab, and then click the **Advanced** button.

10. In the **Advanced Security Settings** dialog box, click the **Auditing** tab. Click the **Continue** button in the middle of the tab to acknowledge the warning.

11. Click the **Add** button at the bottom of the tab. A new dialog box is displayed for adding an auditing entry. You first need to select the principal, which is the user to audit.

12. Click the **Select a principal** link. In the new dialog box that is displayed, click in the **Enter the object name to select:** text box, enter everyone, and click the **OK** button.

13. Click the **Type:** drop-down arrow, and click **Success** in the list. Also, check **Modify, Read & execute,** and **Write** check boxes, as shown. Then, click the **OK** button. If you get any errors regarding enumeration, just click through them.

Goodheart-Willcox Publisher

14. Click the **OK** button to exit the **Advanced Security Settings** dialog box, and then the **OK** button to exit the **Properties** dialog box.

15. Open the SalesBid document in a word processor. Add today's date, and save and close the file.

16. Applying what you have learned, open the Event Viewer, and display the security log.

17. Applying what you have learned, open the **Filter Current Log** dialog box.

18. Enter the event ID 4660, as shown. Then, click the **OK** button to show only those events with this code.

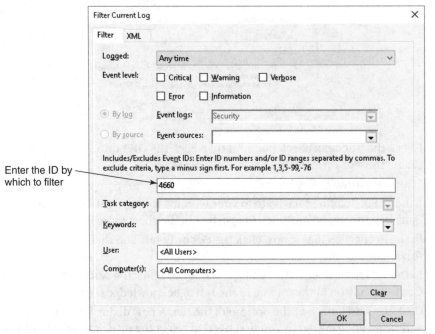

Enter the ID by which to filter

Goodheart-Willcox Publisher

19. Select the event in the middle pane of the Event Viewer. Look at the details for the event in the **General** tab at the bottom of the middle pane. The **Security ID:** entry is the user who changed the file. The program used to access the file is also listed. For example, if Microsoft Word was used to modify the file, the path to winword.exe will be given.

20. Close the Event Viewer.

Lab Activity 6-4: Windows Firewall

Microsoft Windows desktop and server operating systems have a built-in firewall. This is a software firewall that can be very useful.

1. Click the Windows **Start** button, and launch the Control Panel.

2. In the Control Panel, click **Windows Firewall** to display the firewall.

3. On the left, click **Turn Windows Firewall on or off**. On the new page, turn on the firewall for all types of network settings. Depending on your system, there may be two or three types.

4. Click the back button at the top of the Control Panel, and then click **Advanced settings** on the left. The **Windows Firewall with Advanced Security** window is opened, as shown.

Click to show
inbound rules

Click to create
a new rule

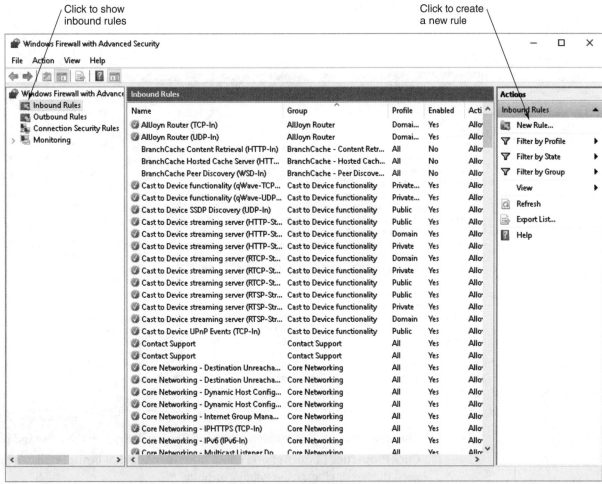

5. Click the Inbound Rules branch in the tree on the left. Then, in the **Actions** panel, click **New Rule...** to launch the **New Inbound Rule Wizard**.

6. On the first page of the wizard, click the **Port** radio button. This rule will control connections to a port. Click the **Next** button.

7. On the next page of the wizard, click the **TCP** radio button. Then, click the **Specific local ports:** radio button, and enter 23 in the corresponding text box. Click the **Next** button.

8. On the next page of the wizard, click the **Block the connection** radio button. This will prevent any inbound data from being sent to port 23. Click the **Next** button.

9. On the next page of the wizard, accept the default settings with the **Domain**, **Private**, and **Public** check boxes checked. Click the **Next** button.

10. On the final page of the wizard, enter No Telnet as the name. Click the **Finish** button. After finishing, you will notice the port now blocked in the inbound rules list, as shown.

New rule is created

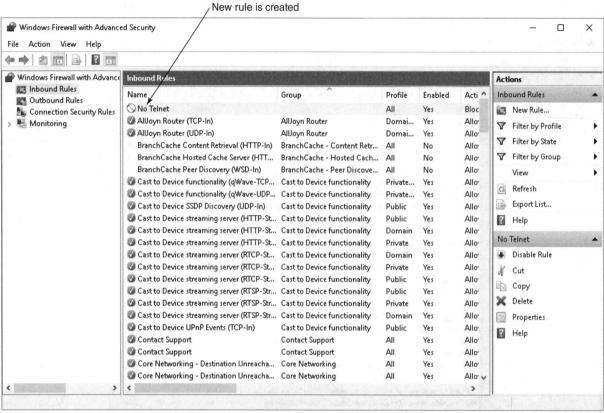

11. Click the Windows Firewall with Advanced Security branch in the left-hand pane.

12. Click **Properties** in the **Actions** pane. The dialog box that is displayed can be used to view or change the logging options.

13. On the **Domain Profile** tab, click the **Customize…** button in the **Logging** area of the tab.

14. In the **Customize Logging Setting for the Domain Profile** dialog box that is displayed, click the **Log dropped packets:** drop-down arrow, and click **Yes** in the list, as shown.

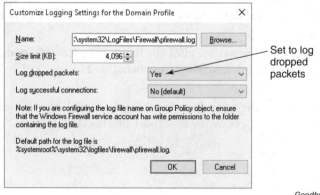

Set to log dropped packets

15. Click the **OK** button to close the **Customize Logging Setting for the Domain Profile** dialog box, and then click the **OK** button to save the settings and return to the **Windows Firewall with Advanced Security** window.

16. Close the **Windows Firewall with Advanced Security** window, and close the Windows Firewall.

CASE STUDIES

DDoS Attacks on Schools

In September of 2020, a DDoS attack was launched against Miami-Dade's public schools, targeting their online learning platform. This attack was launched during the first week school for students who were attending school virtually. Initially, the school district concluded the problems were from a software malfunction on a Cisco software connectivity switch, and that problem was remedied. The next day, most students and teachers were unable to access the virtual platform. They were eventually notified by Comcast, the district's Internet service provider, that they were also being impacted by a DDoS attack. Ultimately, a 16-year-old student within the Miami Dade public school system was arrested as a result.

1. What are some indicators that a second problem may have been occurring while the Cisco switch was repaired, and why do you think the school district's IT staff were unable to identify an in-progress attack?

2. What hardening techniques could have been performed by the school district to prevent the attack? What techniques could have been performed by Comcast?

3. Comcast's initial response to the outage was that there were no anomalies, but they later released an apology for the issues. Since the DDoS packets traversed Comcast's network infrastructure before reaching the Miami-Dade school systems, how responsible is Comcast for diagnosing, preventing, and resolving issues such as these? Explain your position.

4. The attack appeared to have been carried out using an open-source program called Low-Orbit Ion Cannon (LOIC), which is often used as a stress test. Security experts who have analyzed LOIC attacks indicated well-written firewalls can filter most ICMP and UDP traffic, and system logs can identify information related to LOIC attacks. How can some of the tools introduced in this chapter or previous chapters help identify or prevent similar attacks?

5. In 2019, there were 348 publicly disclosed cyberattacks on public schools, which tripled the number of attacks in 2018. In the summer of 2020, the FBI and renowned security experts issued warnings to K–12 schools planning to reopen with online environments. The warnings indicated a high potential for cyberattacks. Despite the warnings made to schools, Miami-Dade school district was victim of a successful target at the beginning of classes. What lessons can be learned from the Miami-Dade hack that can help other schools better prepare for cyberattacks?

Application Development and Security

LEARNING OUTCOMES

- Summarize application development.
- Discuss the software development life cycle and examples of SDLC models.
- Recognize tools for secure application development.
- Identify secure coding techniques.
- Differentiate between white-box and black-box testing for secure code reviews.
- Discuss various application vulnerabilities.
- List common types of application attacks.

KEY TERMS

agile model
API attack
application development
application programming interface (API)
application security (AppSec)
automation
binary
buffer overflow
buffer-overflow attack
camouflaged code
clickjacking
client-side request forgery
client-side validation
code reuse
code signature
code signing
compiler
cross-site request forgery (CSRF)
cross-site scripting (XSS) attack
data canary
data exposure
dead code
deference attack
deprovisioning
DevOps
directory traversal

DLL injection
domain hijacking
driver manipulation
driver shim
elasticity
fuzzing
HTTP header
infrastructure as code (IaC)
injection attack
input validation
integer overflow
integer overflow attack
integrity measurement
LDAP injection attack
library
load balancer
load balancing
man-in-the-browser (MITB)
manual code review
memory leak
normalization
null pointer exception
obfuscation
Open Web Application Security Project (OWASP)
pointer dereference error
privilege escalation

provisioning
race condition
refactoring
resilience
resource exhaustion
sandboxing
scalability
script
Secure Sockets Layer (SSL) stripping
server-side request forgery (SSRF)
server-side validation
session hijacking
shimming
software development kit (SDK)
software development life cycle (SDLC)
software diversity
SQL injection attack
static code analyzer
stored procedure
Structured Query Language (SQL)
typo squatting
version control
waterfall model
web application
web application firewall (WAF)
XML injection

SECURITY+ CERTIFICATION EXAM OBJECTIVES

The following Security+ Certification Exam Objectives are covered in this chapter.

+ 1.1: Typo squatting
+ 1.3: Privilege escalation
+ 1.3: Cross-site scripting
+ 1.3: Injections
+ 1.3: Pointer/object dereference
+ 1.3: Directory traversal
+ 1.3: Buffer overflow
+ 1.3: Race conditions
+ 1.3: Error handling
+ 1.3: Improper input handling
+ 1.3: Integer overflow
+ 1.3: Request forgeries
+ 1.3: Application programming interface (API) attacks
+ 1.3: Resource exhaustion
+ 1.3: Memory leak

+ 1.3: Secure sockets layer (SSL) stripping
+ 1.3: Driver manipulation
+ 1.4: Man in the browser
+ 1.4: Domain hijacking
+ 1.5: Predictive analysis
+ 1.5: File/code repositories
+ 2.3: Environment
+ 2.3: Provisioning and deprovisioning
+ 2.3: Integrity measurement
+ 2.3: Secure coding techniques
+ 2.3: Open Web Application Security Project (OWASP)
+ 2.3: Software diversity
+ 2.3: Automation/scripting

+ 2.3: Elasticity
+ 2.3: Scalability
+ 2.3: Version control
+ 2.5: Load balancers
+ 2.5: Scalability
+ 3.2: Input validation
+ 3.2: Secure cookies
+ 3.2: Hypertext Transfer Protocol (HTTP) headers
+ 3.2: Code signing
+ 3.2: Secure coding practices
+ 3.2: Static code analysis
+ 3.2: Dynamic code analysis
+ 3.2: Fuzzing
+ 3.2: Sandboxing
+ 3.3: Web application firewall (WAF)

OVERVIEW

Application development is the process of designing, programming, testing, and quality controlling applications. During the development of application code, measures should be taken to ensure the code is as secure as possible, making it difficult for a hacker to alter its intended functionality.

In this chapter, you will explore application development concepts, such as the phases of application development, software development life cycle models, secure DevOps and coding techniques, methods for reviewing code, and various vulnerabilities and threats that often plague applications.

SECURITY+ NOTE

While you do not have to be a programmer to sit for the CompTIA Security+ Certification Exam, awareness of threats posed by coding errors or ineffective application design is important. The exam might require you to view a few lines of code that define variables so you can recognize potential threats. It is helpful to be able to recognize programming functions, such as temporary storage of input data, numeric versus integer (int) data, and the definition of a string (str) of data.

Application Development

An *application*, or app, is a software program that runs on a computer or device to accomplish a defined task. **Application development** is the collective process of designing, programming, testing, and quality controlling a computer program to meet specific needs of a business. There are multiple types of application development, including web, mobile, and database programs.

An *environment* is the resources that host an application and is composed of software-based tools used by developers to create applications and software. Environments enable developers to create code without risking interaction with the computer on which they are working. There are multiple environments used in the application development process.

Application Development Environment (ADE)

An *application development environment (ADE)* is the hardware, software, and resources used to build software or web applications. This environment is used by the developers of the program in which code is created.

Test Environment

A *test environment,* also called the *QA environment,* is a controlled environment in which the components of the software are tested. The environment is used by testers to perform functional and nonfunctional testing. *Quality assurance (QA)* is a set of activities, procedures, or policies conducted to avoid or prevent mistakes in the development of an application as well as problems in the delivery of the application to users. QA is an important part of the application development process because it actively seeks to prevent errors.

Testing generally happens in a sandbox environment. **Sandboxing** is the act of running software in an isolated environment, called a *sandbox,* that is separate from other programs so if errors occur, they will not spread to other programs. Sandboxing is a security control and assures that if an error or security issue occurs in the testing, it will not affect other programs on a host or network.

Staging Environment

A *staging environment* is a pre-production environment used to ensure quality control before application deployment. *Quality control (QC)* is the action of checking an application to ensure it meets expectations. The staging environment is a configuration of software and hardware on which developers test code to ensure it functions as intended. *Staging* involves running simulations of production situations by using copies of existing data and setups to run performance tests. The staging portion of the application development process enables developers to test applications thoroughly and implement updates in a safe manner. Developers can view the live impacts of actual data while still operating in a protected setup, reducing risks after implementation of code.

Production Environment

A *production environment* is the setting in which an application is used by the intended audience. It is a real-time setting where applications are loaded on similar hardware used by the organization to run the program. Production environments are considered to be the final step in application development.

Software Development Life Cycle

The process of developing software applications should follow the standards set forth in a software development life cycle (SDLC) model. **Software development life cycle (SDLC)** is a conceptual process used to create, deploy, and maintain a software application. SDLC is also called a *software* or *application development process.* Through the application of SDLC, software development costs are lower, time to market increases, and the resulting product is of high quality. The steps in SDLC vary, but most life cycles include

- development;
- testing;
- staging;

- production; and
- quality assurance.

Three commonly used types of SDLC models are waterfall, agile, and DevOps.

Waterfall Development Model

The **waterfall model** is a development life cycle model that follows a sequential process in which each step is completed before moving to the next step. In a waterfall model, a developmental step cannot be attempted until the preceding step is completed. For example, a developer cannot move to step 2 unless step 1 is complete. Visually, each step is staggered under the previous one, making a stair-step, or waterfall, design, as illustrated in Figure 7-1.

This model is advantageous in environments where a predictable approach to requirements is defined and not subject to change. Small organizations or businesses are more apt to use a waterfall cycle, and projects using this model commit to an end goal by following a structured process. This methodical process allows for easy transfer of data between stages.

However, this model has disadvantages in certain situations. Unexpected changes or revisions could result in delays and possibly force an organization to restart the process. Because each step is completed in order, the next step in development cannot progress until the current step is finished. In addition, the waterfall model delays testing until after coding, which could result in significant delays if major errors or discrepancies are found and need correction.

Gathering and Analyzing Requirements

The first step in developing an application is to *gather and analyze requirements*. It is part of the planning process to find answers to why an application is needed and

Figure 7-1 The waterfall model is a development life cycle model that follows a sequential process, meaning each step is completed before moving to the next step of the cycle.

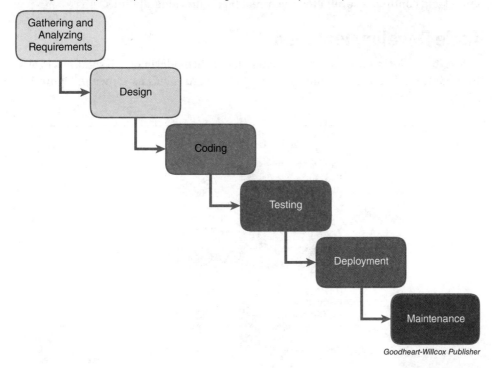

Goodheart-Willcox Publisher

which problems it will solve. This step not only includes gathering and analyzing information from customers, experts, and others who can assist in defining the goals for the project but also planning how to use that information to build an application to achieve the established goal. Once these requirements are established, they serve as the model for development.

Design

Design is the process of turning the planning results into specifications for the product. It is the creation of a blueprint for building the application and helping a programmer stay on target.

Coding

Coding is the process of writing code that makes the application work. In this phase, a developer uses the blueprint developed in the design phase to create the application.

Testing

Testing the code is the stage in which an application is thoroughly tested. Recall that software is tested in a testing environment to prevent any unexpected interactions with the system on which a tester is working.

Deployment

An application *deployment* is the release of software to the end-users. This occurs when the final product is published and put into the users' hands.

Maintenance

Maintenance is the final phase of the waterfall development model and refers to updates and patches for an application. After a program is released, developers are still responsible for ensuring it is safe, secure, and current. Programs must be maintained and continually evaluated to correct bugs and vulnerabilities.

Agile Development Model

The **agile model** is a software development life cycle model in which solutions evolve through team member collaboration and follow core values as shown in Figure 7-2.

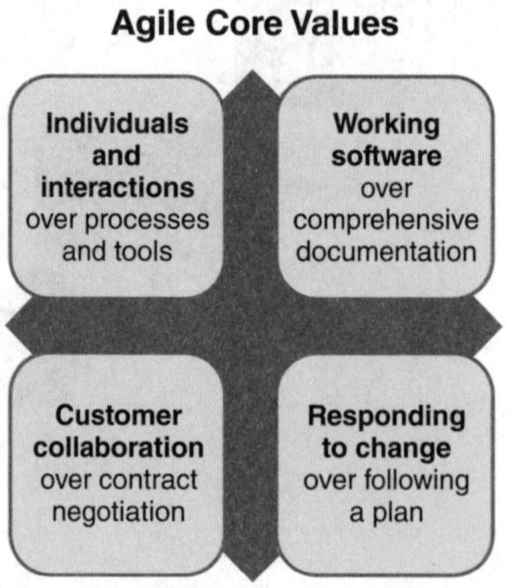

Figure 7-2 The agile model is a software development life cycle model in which solutions evolve through team member collaboration and follow four core values.

Agile Core Values

Individuals and interactions over processes and tools

Working software over comprehensive documentation

Customer collaboration over contract negotiation

Responding to change over following a plan

Goodheart-Willcox Publisher

The agile model was created to overcome the sequential nature of the waterfall model and, instead, use a model where work is completed in an ongoing, collaborative format. Agile development enables the ability to perform a number of diverse tasks simultaneously instead of having to follow a sequential path.

In an agile development model, work is broken into blocks, called *iterations*, as shown in Figure 7-3. When an iteration is complete, work is collectively evaluated and modified if needed before employees move to the next iteration. The project continues to move through each iteration until everyone agrees project goals are met. When a group consensus is reached, an application is deployed.

The agile development model offers advantages, such as rapid, continuous delivery of software and increased communication between developers and stakeholders. Changes or testing corrections are handled rapidly and do not require a restart of the process.

Disadvantages of the agile model include potential of a project going off-track if goals are not clearly defined. Additionally, if documentation is not emphasized or updated, particularly if many changes occur, maintenance of records is often difficult.

DevOps

DevOps, short for *developer operations*, is a philosophy that incorporates security concepts in the collaboration among developers, managers, and other IT and operational staff from development through production and support. It is a process of moving applications from the development and testing phases to deployment as quickly as possible while advocating for better communication between the developmental and business units. DevOps follows the agile SDLC model. In fact, DevOps is often called *agile operations*.

DevOps often follows a principle known as infrastructure as code. **Infrastructure as code (IaC)** is management of hardware and software through machine-readable files as opposed to physical configuration. In an infrastructure-as-code environment, the operations team uses a system's starting point as a baseline and creates scripts that will make configuration changes from the baseline. The scripts automate reconfiguration, removing the need for manual intervention.

Automation is a key principle in DevOps. **Automation** is the use of technology to perform processes without human intervention. In DevOps, automation starts with code development through production. The use of automation in IT processes is called *automated courses of action*.

Automation of common tasks can be an invaluable asset by providing security and efficiency on repetitive tasks. Commands can run independently, but it is

✚ 2.3

Figure 7-3 In the agile development model, each stage is broken down into cycles, called *iterations*.

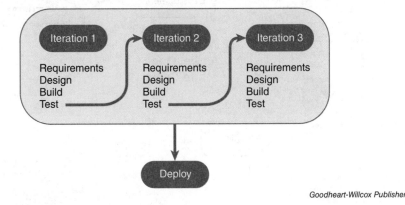

possible to make errors and it is less efficient to perform these tasks manually. Executing scripts through graphical utilities is more efficient.

A better option is to create scripts. **Scripts** are custom files containing commands and functions to be processed in order. Scripts provide for a higher level of security since they are often pretested for any configuration errors. Scripts can run singularly or be programmed to run automatically or triggered by an alert or action.

In some environments, changes may happen quickly. Relying on manual intervention could result in security threats, loss of data, or other performance issue. By automating courses of action, responses occur via automatic scripts. For example, if a physical drive runs low on space, a script could be triggered to run when there is 15 percent of space available by moving or deleting files.

Security automation is the automatic handling and processing of security-related tasks to identify vulnerabilities without human intervention. In the DevOps environment, security automation incorporates security directly in the development and testing of code, which allows for frequent and automatic testing of security and functionality. *Secure DevOps (DevSecOps)* is a further extension of DevOps that addresses the security issues in code quality and reliability. In a DevSecOps model, security analysts do not wait until a program is complete before conducting security testing; rather, they provide input at all levels of development and create threat models to help predict where an application could be vulnerable to malicious attacks.

DevOps follows a life cycle that has a goal of shortening development and delivering a quality product. Stages in the life cycle include monitoring, validation, testing, integration, delivery, and deployment, as illustrated in Figure 7-4.

 2.3

- *Continuous monitoring (CM)* is reviewing each phase of DevOps. This process uses automatic monitoring tools that help ensure the health, performance, reliability, and integrity of an application through all of its life cycle stages.

- *Continuous validation (CV)* is validating the performance of an application at every stage. Continuous validation ensures that when a program enters the testing stage, testers are receiving only stable versions of the application code, which leads to increased efficiency of testing.

- *Continuous testing (CT)* is a testing practice that uses automated and integrated testing throughout an application's life cycle. Automated testing validates functionality based on established objectives. It occurs more frequently, in a shorter duration, and at lower cost. Additionally, CT provides feedback at many levels to quickly address problems.

1.5

- *Continuous integration (CI)* is a development practice that requires the automatic integration of code into a code repository multiple times each day.

Figure 7-4 DevOps follows a seven-step life cycle that has a goal of shortening development and delivering a quality product.

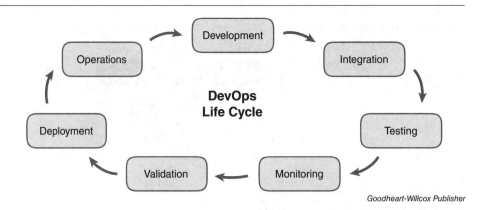

Goodheart-Willcox Publisher

Continuous integration ensures security is implemented at each stage by eliminating problematic code being recycled into projects. However, code repositories can be a source of an attack if threat actors are able to access them, and for security reasons, code repositories should be locked.

- *Continuous delivery (CD)* is a state of being able to deploy a version at any time and for any platform. The process is enabled through automated building, testing, and delivery, and updates to code.
- *Continuous deployment (CD)* is a process of deploying software for use but continually providing updates to enhance the program. Customers have the advantage of using the software early but opting in to get updates as they become available.

Secure Application Development

Application development should be performed in a way to ensure *application security*. **Application security (AppSec)** is the process of developing software that is free from vulnerabilities before it goes into production. AppSec is a process that happens *during* development of an application, not *after*. The best security defense is to embed the elements of security in all aspects of software development, from design to implementation.

Development Resources

There are many resources required for application development in an enterprise environment. In order to control security of resources, both provisioning and deprovisioning are necessary. **Provisioning** is the practice of providing access and resources to network services needed for employees to complete their jobs. Provisioning is often a company-wide process that involves the procurement, deployment, and management of multiple types of IT system resources. **Deprovisioning** is the removal of resource access from team members when those resources are no longer required.

Software Diversity

One method of software attacks occurs through predictive analysis. *Predictive analysis*, also called *predictive analytics*, is the examination of data, statistical modeling, and machine learning techniques to quantify the likelihood of a future cyber threat. Attackers use known coding patterns and usage to predict functionality, such as where in memory program information is located. Programs that are created using consistent methods increase the vulnerability of attackers being successful in attacks against the software. Consider the methods of software distribution. If a program were delivered on CD or via electronic downloads, each user would get an identical copy of the code. If the code were exploited, a massive attack could be launched on all users of the software. One method of improving the defense of these attacks is to implement *software diversity*.

Software diversity is the practice of transforming software into different forms before deployment. This is a development process that preserves the original code but adds a strong enough degree of uncertainty, so program implementations are different from other computer systems, or they perform differently when they are executed. This increases the uncertainty of finding potential targets that can be located and possibly breached. Diversification of the application enables the

TECH TIP

If done correctly, predictive analysis can also be a valuable source of threat intelligence. Security professionals can enable automation to pour over data to help determine trends, vulnerabilities, and attack vectors.

software to adapt to customer requirements or execution environments. This process makes it costly or time prohibitive to launch these types of attacks.

2.3

There are two methods of software diversity that can be used: compiler-based diversification or binary-based diversification. *Compiler-based diversification* is a diversification method that implements diversity through individualized distribution of software. A **compiler** is a program that converts code from a programming language into machine language. Diversifying through a compiler enables diversification to occur automatically because it avoids making changes in source code, instead making transformations of intended and unintended code sequences without impacting the functionality of the program execution. Compiler programs perform high-entropy transformation, which provides increased randomness of change but is performed on smaller or granular units of code. This forces many code changes to be randomized independently, which would cause an attacker significant time to discover the location of each code unit.

2.3

A second method of code diversity is binary-based diversification. *Binary-based diversification* is a diversification method in which diversity is implemented by rewriting binary files. In terms of software, a **binary** is a file in which content must be interpreted by a program or hardware processor that knows in advance how the file is formatted. Binary code works by encoding the data content with the binary digits of 0 and 1. Binary diversity is commonly referred to as *binary rewriting. Binary rewriters* are tools that accept a binary executable as input and produce a changed and improved executable as output. Binary rewriters have many advantages over compiler diversity, since they can work with a complete software application including libraries. Additionally, binary rewriters can often find optimizations missed by compilers and work for code produced from *any* source language or compiler. Random program binaries make it difficult for an adversary to take control of the program execution and launch successful attacks.

2.3, 2.5

Scalability

Scalability is the ability of a program to cope with increased loads, such as customers and new features, and continue functioning as needed. If an app has not been developed in a way to be scalable over time, the program may become dysfunctional. Ensuring scalability strengthens a program's **resilience**, which is the ability of a system to recover from a disruption in an acceptable amount of time.

Scalability is often enhanced or reduced by the presence or absence of load balancing. **Load balancing** is the distribution of processing needs over multiple servers. Load balancing is often referred to as *scheduling*. A **load balancer** is a network device that sends requests to various servers on a network based on predefined factors. The incorporation of load balancing techniques supports scalability because load balancing enables a system to increase or decrease processing needs as needed without interruption.

2.3

Elasticity

Elasticity is an application's ability to change resources dynamically as needs change. It is similar to scalability in the sense that they both refer to the ability to adapt to change dynamically, but where scalability is focused solely on expansion to accommodate potential future needs, elasticity focuses on the expansion or reduction in capacity to meet current demand. In the general sense, there are two types of elasticity: time-based and volume-based.

- *Time-based elasticity* is the automatic shutdown of resources no longer used or needed, such as a program that needs to accommodate additional users but only during working hours.
- *Volume-based elasticity* is a process in which the scope of a program scales to match its demand, such as a shared database program that has many infrequent and irregular users.

Integrity Measurement

Integrity measurement is a measurement and identification of changes made to a system as compared to its baseline. A *secure baseline* is a defined set of objectives and statistics that all applications must meet. In application development, baselines are used to set goals and measure success, similar to the function of baselines in assessing an environment's security. Baselining allows for comparison and analysis of the state of application or system after each development step to record changes and status of the program. Baselining enables fast remediation of problems and can reduce troubleshooting and programming time. If there are deviations from the baseline, it may be from coding errors, or an unapproved change, or failure to document code that should have been in the baseline.

Version Control

Version control, also called *source control*, is a method of tracking changes to a file. It is a tool used to reduce the time spent on development and increase successful deployment rates. Controlling versioning in application development enables engineering teams to collaborate on the most recent and up-to-date versions of source code despite frequent changes made to it. Version control software tracks individual changes made by each contributor to a project and disables the possibility of conflicting work.

However, without change management, a change to code could be damaged by a future change or open the application to vulnerabilities. *Change-management software* optimizes change management and provides a way to standardize documentation of requests and resolutions. It also provides an audit trail to determine who requested the change and who performed the requested operation.

TECH TIP

Version control is best managed with application tools specific to this purpose. The software can be local, distributed, centrally managed, or hosted in an online location for easier accessibility and backup. Some popular programs include free options, such as Git and Mercurial, or paid subscriptions, such as Vault and Fossil.

Secure Coding Techniques

Secure coding is the process of developing an application using techniques to help prevent the introduction of vulnerabilities that create security issues. Secure code is necessary to prevent an application from coming under attack by a threat actor.

When looking for best practices for secure coding, OWASP is a reliable source. The **Open Web Application Security Project (OWASP)** is a nonprofit organization that provides unbiased information about application security.

Many consider the *OWASP Top 10 Most Critical Web Application Security Risks* a must-read document. It is released periodically after extensive research and a public comment period. This list identifies the most commonly found and exploited vulnerabilities. In addition to security threats, it includes suggestions for prevention and mitigation. However, developers should not stop with this document. New threats and vulnerabilities can appear at any time, and developers must stay up to date with the newest issues.

Error Handling

Error handling is measures taken to ensure an application is able to respond to or recover from an error, as opposed to locking up or crashing. Applications that shut down unexpectedly can potentially expose a network to hackers. Similarly, applications that produce error messages often reveal too much information to hackers, such as an error message noting an incorrect password. To help handle errors, proper and secure coding measures should be incorporated to ensure an application can withstand, or recover from, an error. This can involve adding specific error-handling lines of code or performing extensive proofreading to ensure no errors exist within the code.

Improper error handling refers to software created without error handling capabilities. Without the ability to trap errors, underlying structure is left exposed to a hacker. For example, suppose an application does not have error handling and a hacker enters 50 characters in a text field designed to allow 25. Without the capability to handle such an error, the program could react in a number of ways, including crashing or issuing an operating system command line, which could be used to access a network or individual devices.

Input Validation

Input validation, also called *form validation*, is a programming configuration in which an input field rejects any characters that do not match its function or could cause a malfunction. For example, you may want users to enter only numbers in a given field. In this case, *proper input handling* rejects characters that are not numbers.

Improper input handling refers to a lack of input validation features in an application. Improper or nonexistent input handling features put an application at risk for malicious activity. For example, consider a form that incorporates text fields for user input. Without input validation, a user could enter a string of text that equates to a direct command to be executed by the server on which the form is stored.

Performing input validation helps prevent injection attacks. An **injection attack** is an attack in which a hacker is able to supply input that exploits a vulnerability in an application. Injection attacks result from intentional improper input. Improper input validation, as well as improper error handling, are indicative of deficiencies and poor design.

Input validation takes place in one of two locations. Validation that takes place in a browser is *client-side validation*. Validation that takes place on the server is *server-side validation*.

- **Client-side validation**, also called *client-side execution*, is an input validation for which user input is confirmed by a client web browser. Client-side validation is typically faster than server-side validation, but it is also more susceptible to attack. Designing validation checks for client-side validation should be thorough, and if a mistake is discovered it must be corrected on every device using that code version.

- **Server-side validation**, or *server-side execution*, is an input validation for which user input is confirmed by a server. This method of validation is slower than client-side validation due to the amount of processes handled by a server. Server-side validation is often more secure because it guarantees that only properly formatted input arrives at the server.

Whenever a user inputs data into a program, the program is susceptible to an attack. Input validation verifies that input generated by a user is appropriate and safe. Input validation implements safeguards to control the type and amount of data entered in a form, which can help prevent vulnerabilities.

Normalization

✛ 2.3, 3.2

Normalization is the process of organizing data in a database to reduce redundancies and improve performance. Data reduction allows databases to consume less disk space, which in turn increases performance. Data normalization enables data to be stored in one location only, which limits an attacker's access to just one database. Data that appears to be in multiple locations only refers to the original form. This also provides security since monitoring of database traffic only occurs in one location.

Normalizing data within code is a similar concept to normalizing a database. If multiple lines of code are repeated verbatim or rendered redundant by additional code, an application may not run effectively. With that in mind, it is important to review the code to make sure it is as streamlined as possible. This not only ensures the application will run smoothly but also reduces the overall footprint and file size of the program.

Obfuscation

✛ 2.3, 3.2

Obfuscation is the act of masking something to make it unclear. A *code obfuscator* is a tool that makes source code difficult to read. *Source code* is a program before it is compiled. *Compiled code* refers to code that has been translated into a language used by a CPU. If a hacker is able to read the source code, the program is vulnerable to a successful hack.

It is not enough simply to make source code unreadable to a hacker through compilation. Compiled code can be translated and reverted back to source code by running the code through a *program decompiler*. The act of decompiling code is called *reverse engineering*. Reverse engineering can be prevented by employing **camouflaged code**, which is code written in a way that makes it difficult for someone to read or interpret.

Code Reuse

✛ 2.3, 3.2

Code reuse is the practice of using existing code in a new application. Reusing code eliminates the need to write new code, resulting in lower development costs. Code reuse allows developers to work with tested code, which reduces the potential for the introduction of new vulnerabilities. However, reuse can also introduce dead code. **Dead code** is source code that is no longer used. Dead code wastes computational time and memory as well as increasing attack surfaces of an application.

It is common for programmers to use third-party libraries to pick up code written by others. A **library** is a collection of programming code used in software development. By using a library, a programmer does not to have to start from scratch when writing code. Libraries can also help eliminate dead code.

✛ 2.3

Libraries are often available to outside developers through software development kits (SDKs). A **software development kit (SDK)** is a collection of software development tools in one installable package. SDKs are a common method of secure application development and deployment.

It is common for programmers to use code written by others by accessing SDKs for code that applies to their projects. For example, a company like Facebook or Twitter provides an SDK to Apple iOS developers. In the SDK are common utilities found on the platform, such as login abilities and ad deployment. In this way, developers do not have to rewrite common functions. Instead, they can spend their time on the specific functionality of the app they are creating.

Security personnel must document use of SDKs so if a flaw or vulnerability is revealed in SDK code, the IT team can make necessary updates. If the used SDKs are not documented, it would be virtually impossible to apply important security updates. It is also important to test these libraries thoroughly in order to ensure no data is exposed.

When code reuse is in practice, it should be confirmed that the code is actually from the person or organization where it supposedly originated. The originator of a code is verified through code signing. **Code signing** is adding a code signature to an application. A **code signature** is a digital signature placed on code to verify its authenticity and integrity. A code signature verifies the originator of the code.

✛ 2.3, 3.2

Memory Management

Memory management is policies created, procedures enforced, and actions taken to allocate, distribute, and remove system memory. Managing memory includes assigning information such as variables in memory and clearing information from memory when no longer needed. The main purpose of memory management protection is to ensure a process is not accessing memory from an area it has not been allocated to use. This prevents malware or other applications from accessing the stored data. Data that remains in memory can also be a security risk; if it is not removed, there is the potential that other programs would be able to access this information. Memory is a shared resource that should be monitored to ensure programs that need memory can get it. When a program does not release memory no longer needed, memory cannot be reallocated to another program. Some programs, such as Java and Ruby, have a feature called *garbage collection* that can automatically deallocate memory when it is no longer needed. Other programs such as C++ do not have this functionality, and memory must be manually deallocated.

✛ 3.2

Secure HTTP Headers

An **HTTP header** is a block of data composed of fields that contain information used in an HTTP transmission. Headers normally include details about the client browser, requested page, and web server, among other topics. Adding security headers can help prevent Cross-Site Scripting (XSS) and other code-injection attacks by defining content sources that are approved, or prevent clickjacking threats, drive-by downloads, and other threats. The OWASP Security Headers Project outlines methods for increasing header security and restricting browser vulnerabilities.

✛ 3.2

Secure Cookies

Cookies are small text files saved on a computer for use with web browsers and websites. Cookies that are set with a secure flag or attribute are considered *secure cookies*. The purpose of secure cookies is to prevent unauthorized parties from accessing or reviewing cookie information. Secure cookies are only sent over secure or encrypted transmission sessions, such as HTTPS, to prevent hackers from eavesdropping, stealing, or altering cookie information.

✛ 2.3, 3.2

Stored Procedures

A **stored procedure** is a prepared SQL code that can be saved and reused when accessing databases and executing tasks. **Structured Query Language (SQL)** is a programming language used for managing a database that contains multiple linked tables. This technique prevents hackers from inserting commands into an application by forcing the program to use predefined procedures as opposed to a hacker entering malicious user input for the execution and manipulation of data. The stored procedure prevents the execution of SQL injection attacks.

Secure Code Review

Secure code review is a process that helps identify vulnerabilities that could put a program at risk in later stages of development. This review takes place during the development stage of SDLC when code is under development. Developers can identify problems and fix them before the later stages of SDLC occur.

Secure code review applies white-box testing and black-box testing. Both types of testing are used in the development process to identify security issues.

White-Box Testing

➕ 3.2

One approach to secure code review is *white-box testing*, which is a manual code review. A **manual code review** is the process of reading source code, line-by-line, to locate and identify vulnerabilities. Manual reviews locate inconsistencies within a program's source code. This adds a human level of analysis and critical thinking but can be a time-consuming and tedious process.

Black-Box Testing

➕ 3.2

In addition to manual testing, automated testing is used. Secure coding review uses *black-box testing*, which is the use of automated tools to check code. Examples of black-box testing include static code analysis, dynamic code analysis, and fuzzing.

Static code analysis is debugging source code before running the code. A **static code analyzer** is a tool that analyzes code for known vulnerabilities and errors, such as using unsafe libraries and input validation, buffer overflow, or injection errors.

Dynamic analysis is testing code after the program is run. It is essentially the opposite of static analysis, which tests a program without running it. The goal of dynamic analysis is to locate errors or bugs while the program is running in an effort to replicate the user experience. The nature of application code makes it difficult for a human to parse, meaning it can be difficult to locate every possible error. Running the program and looking for errors can be a safeguard against human oversights.

➕ 3.2

Fuzzing, also called *fuzz testing*, is an automated testing technique in which a program attempts to find coding errors or bugs in implantation of code, such as invalid, unexpected, or misconfigured data. Fuzzing is used for critical programs where security is an issue for malicious attacks.

The goal of a fuzz test is to test all input possibilities that could make a program crash. For example, a name-input field is tested by entering numbers, special characters, and large values; pressing function keys; and input of non-text characters. Doing so verifies that vulnerabilities are not exposed due to common or accidental keystrokes that a hacker might attempt.

➕ 3.2

TECH TIP ⚙️

Cross-platform development is common for app development, especially since it assists in developing an app to run on multiple platforms, including Android, Apple iOS, and Windows. Each revision of code is thoroughly tested and reviewed on a specific platform as code is often different and handled separately on each platform.

Application Vulnerabilities

Despite efforts taken to secure an application's code, there are still inherent vulnerabilities that happen. For example, if a computer does not have the hardware capabilities of running a specific program, doing so can lead to resource exhaustion. **Resource exhaustion** occurs when computer resources required to execute actions are depleted, preventing action from occurring. Exhaustion of resources causes programs or systems to lock up or shut down, most commonly resulting in a denial of service (DoS).

➕ 1.3

Integer Overflow

An **integer overflow** is a condition in which an arithmetic operation results in a number that is too large to be stored in the memory space allocated for the result. An *integer* in programming is a data type that stores a numeric value. An integer overflow can be exploited by an integer overflow attack. An **integer overflow attack** is an attack that occurs when an attacker alters a variable's value to something outside the variable's intended range.

Buffer Overflow

A *buffer* is part of the physical memory in a system used for temporary storage of data. A **buffer overflow** occurs when there is more data in the buffer than it can handle. This causes the remaining data to spill over into an adjacent area of memory. This can cause a system to crash, especially if it overwrites essential data in an adjacent memory location or leaves the system vulnerable to an attack.

A **buffer-overflow attack** is a cyberattack in which a hacker exploits a buffer overflow, resulting in extra data written to memory outside of the buffer. In some cases, the overflow may crash the program. However, a hacker could have the extra input include executable instructions in this location and overwrite another area in memory, as illustrated in Figure 7-5. When that type of entry is written into RAM, the computer executes the command. The impact of buffer overflows is often an application crashing or service interruption, resulting in a significant amount of lost time to restoring access.

There are different options for protecting against a buffer overflow. For example, a limit can be set for the data-entry box. Another interesting method to prevent overflow is for the programmer to use a data canary. A **data canary** is a known value placed at the end of the assigned buffer space. If a data canary remains the same, a buffer overflow has not occurred.

Pointer Dereference

In coding, a **pointer dereference error**, also called an *object deference*, is a vulnerability that occurs when a value has not been obtained from the correct area. A *pointer* is a variable in memory that stores the address of another variable and redirects, or points, the memory to the appropriate location, as illustrated in Figure 7-6. One type of pointer dereference issue is called a null pointer exception. A **null pointer exception** is a type of error that occurs when a value of NULL is stored in a valid memory area. Hackers can use buffer overflows to cause pointer dereference or null pointer errors to occur by overwriting or manipulating the memory storing the values. Dereference errors that are intentionally triggered are known as **dereference attacks**.

Figure 7-5 A buffer-overflow attack is a cyberattack achieved by a hacker exploiting a buffer overflow, resulting in extra data written to memory outside of the buffer.

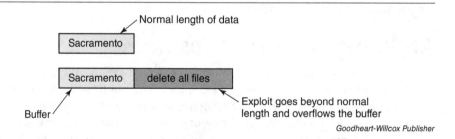

Goodheart-Willcox Publisher

Figure 7-6 A *pointer* is a variable in memory that stores the address of another variable and redirects, or points, the memory to the appropriate location.

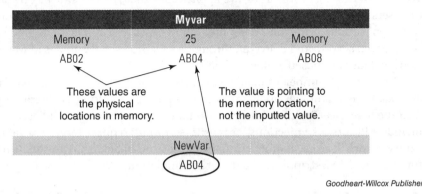

Goodheart-Willcox Publisher

Race Conditions

1.3

A **race condition** is a software vulnerability in which two simultaneous lines of executable code, called *threads*, attempt to access a shared resource. For example, consider a situation in which two threads of execution attempt to access memory at the same time. As one thread attempts to retrieve its own memory location value, the other thread will have overwritten the value as its own, making it irretrievable to the first thread. A *race condition attack* is one that exploits the existence of a race condition and takes advantage of a gap in time between the initiation and execution of a service.

The existence of race conditions can create time-of-check to time-of-use bugs. *Time-of-check to time-of-use (TOCTOU)* is a race condition in which an incident or attack occurs in the time between software verifying the state of a resource and actually using the resource. This creates a potential security vulnerability because if a hacker accesses and manipulates a file or resource between the time of check and time of use, that manipulated file will be used putting the application, client, and network at risk.

1.3

Imagine a scenario in which a banking application pulls contact information from a database to send information about accounts to customers. In the time between the application checking and using the database, a hacker accesses the database and changes the contact information within it so any banking information goes to the hacker's machine. If the application does not recheck the database's status, it will pull the manipulated contact information and send banking information directly to the hacker.

Memory Leak

1.3

A **memory leak** is a vulnerability that occurs when memory allocated for a program is not freed when the program is completed. A memory leak can be the result of a programmer creating and storing values in memory and neglecting to delete the information after allocated memory is no longer needed. In addition to inherent vulnerabilities, this type of error results in decreased memory for other uses, program crashes, or RAM exhaustion, which violates the principle of availability. In addition, a hacker could intentionally create a memory leak and crash the program by launching a denial of service attack.

TECH TIP

Software applications purchased from a reputable source are issued licenses that dictate how an application is to be used by an organization. When software is used outside the scope of its license, the purchasing organization has committed a *license compliance violation* and can be held accountable. A common example of a license compliance violation is the overuse of an application by multiple deployments that exceed the number of permitted installations.

Application Attacks

Web applications, or *web apps*, are applications that run dynamically through web browsers as scripts without requiring software to be installed. Unlike traditional software applications stored on a computer's hard drive, web applications are housed on remote web servers and delivered through a web browser. Examples of web applications include web-based e-mail such as Gmail.

There are a number of challenges faced in protecting web applications from attacks. Many, but not all, application attacks rely on exploiting a vulnerability within form-field or user-input interfaces. Commonly encountered application attacks include API attacks, injections, cross-site scripting, request forgeries, data leak or exposure, privilege escalation, clickjacking, session hijacking, typo squatting, directory traversal, SSL stripping, and driver manipulation.

Application Programming Interface (API) Attacks

An **application programming interface (API)** is a set of tools and programs that enables interactions between applications and components and provides communication between a client and server. For example, if you navigate to a website that requests a location, an API in your browser determines your physical location, not the website or browser itself. APIs are typically used to control access to hardware devices in addition to software functionality and integration of web technologies and applications.

Due to their widespread use, APIs are often targets of attackers. An **API attack** is the use of malicious code or exploitation of vulnerable code within an API. Typically, these attacks occur when API commands are entered to redirect control of tasks. Moreover, if authentication is not properly employed or managed, an API attack can access data sources outside the programming interface that were not the original target of the initial request.

API communications for HTTP and HTTPS can be observed, intercepted, and manipulated using common open-source tools. According to Internet vendor Akamai, 83 percent of web traffic is API traffic, making API environments valuable targets.

 1.3

Injection Attacks

An *injection attack* is malicious code inserted into a web application to cause an unexpected outcome. It is an attack in which a hacker is able to supply input that exploits a vulnerability in an application. This is one of the most common application attacks and enables a threat actor to modify software commands. There are two common types of injection attacks: DLL injection, SQL injection, LDAP injection, and XML injection.

DLL Injection

A **DLL injection** is a technique used to insert code into a running program, forcing the program to load a Dynamic Link Library. A *Dynamic Link Library (DLL)* is a library of reusable code that can be used by more than one program at a time. In a DLL injection, an attacker rewrites code in the DLL, which impacts all applications that regularly call on it. The best defense against DLL injection attacks is to ensure that an untrusted process does not get administrator access to the application. Additionally, antimalware programs should be kept updated as they provide protection against malicious code.

1.3

1.3

SQL Injection

An **SQL injection attack** is a code-injection technique in which a hacker inputs SQL-formatted commands in a user-input field. When submitted, the command executes and performs the desired actions. For example, in an SQL injection, commands called *SQL statements* could be injected to tell the database to show all tables, the fields in the tables, and the data values stored in the tables, as illustrated in Figure 7-7.

LDAP Injection

An **LDAP injection attack** is an injection attack in which an attacker exploits web applications that use constructed Lightweight Directory Access Protocol (LDAP) statements. In normal operations of web applications that use LDAP, user input is accepted and queried against a database using a back-end LDAP statement. During an injection attack, the LDAP interpreter that would normally grant permission for database queries is spoofed into granting permission without providing a password. This is accomplished through arbitrary queries entered by the user. Queries such as /ldap-search?user=* fool the LDAP interpreter into trusting the user and displaying all user accounts in the directory.

XML Injection

An **XML injection** is an attack method in which a hacker inserts script with the goal of compromising logic of an XML application. *Extensible Markup Language (XML)* is a markup language similar to HTML designed to store or transport information. In this type of attack, actors insert XML statements into user input fields, resulting in unexpected commands that can lead to security exploits. XML injections can lead to data disclosure as well as impact the ability to interact with any back-end of an external system.

Cross-Site Scripting

XSS attacks are one of the top 10 threats to websites. XSS stands for cross-site scripting. A **cross-site scripting (XSS) attack** is a widespread attack method in which hackers inject client-side scripts into pages of a trusted website, as shown in Figure 7-8. A user can be the victim of an XSS attack by clicking on a malicious link created by an attacker or visiting a page that has injected code. Once on the fake site, scripts download unknowingly into a user's computer. At this point, the attacker can

Figure 7-7 An SQL injection attack is an attack in which a hacker injects SQL-formatted commands, instead of data, as input in an effort to perform actions.

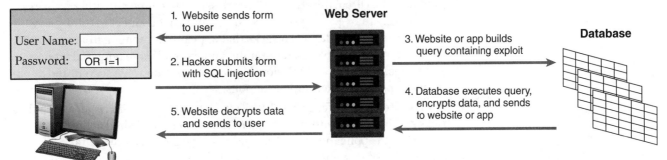

Goodheart-Willcox Publisher; (computers) romvo/Shutterstock.com; (servers) Sujith RS/Shutterstock.com

Figure 7-8 A cross-site scripting (XSS) attack is a widespread attack method in which hackers inject client-side scripts into pages of a trusted website.

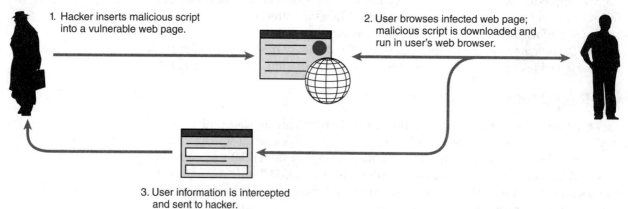

1. Hacker inserts malicious script into a vulnerable web page.

2. User browses infected web page; malicious script is downloaded and run in user's web browser.

3. User information is intercepted and sent to hacker.

Goodheart-Willcox Publisher; (people) Rawpixel.com/Shutterstock.com

gain control of the user data entered. Protecting against an XSS attack must be completed in the web application itself.

A common defense against XSS attacks is the deployment of a web application firewall. A **web application firewall (WAF)** is a specific firewall used to protect web applications by filtering and monitoring HTTP traffic between applications and the Internet. WAFs not only help prevent XSS attacks, but also injection and cross-site request forgery (CSRF) attacks.

Request Forgery

A *request forgery* is an attack in which a hacker is able to impersonate and forge a malicious session with a server. Request forgeries can occur on a client, server, or through cross-site requests.

- A **client-side request forgery**, also known as *universal cross-site scripting (UXSS)*, is a type of attack that exploits vulnerabilities on a client's device. Often, attackers target gaps in security in a browser or browser extension to create a condition where cross-site scripting is possible. This type of attack negatively impacts a browser by bypassing or disabling security features. UXSS attacks differ from traditional XSS attacks since the attacker is not targeting a web application or its server to inject malicious scripts. Instead, UXSS attacks originate from the client and exploit vulnerabilities in browser extensions to create an XSS environment.

- A **server-side request forgery (SSRF)** is an attack in which an attacker is able to access a server, which is used to generate HTTP requests to a desired or targeted website. Often, the attacker forces a server to connect to other websites or to external third-party systems. SSRF exploits that connect to third-party systems can cause additional attacks that appear to be coming from the third party, leading to legal issues, reputation damage, and more potential attacks. These attacks exploit trust relationships established between servers and applications to perform unauthorized actions.

- A **cross-site request forgery (CSRF)**, also referred to as *XSRF*, is an attack that tricks a web browser into executing an unwanted or undesired action by manipulating an application to which a user is logged in. In a CSRF attack, a user authenticates to a website as normal, such as logging into an online banking website, as shown in Figure 7-9. The attack then runs a script already on the

Figure 7-9 In a CSRF attack, a malicious script is on the user's computer, and once the user successfully logs in to a website, the script uses the established trust relationship to send commands to the web server.

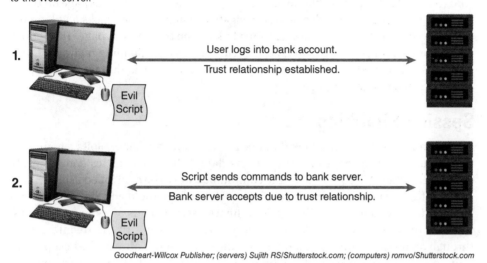

Goodheart-Willcox Publisher; (servers) Sujith RS/Shutterstock.com; (computers) romvo/Shutterstock.com

client's computer, originating from a link in an e-mail or instant message. The script sends malicious HTTP requests to the website. For example, the script may tell the bank to transfer money immediately to the hacker's account.

Data Exposure

Data exposure occurs when sensitive, personal, or confidential data is accidentally exposed to users. Data exposure is different from a data breach because exposure is not caused by a threat actor intentionally attempting to access or steal data. Exposure often is the result of unprotected database information, weak or no encryption, or coding flaws. It is important that the collection and use of data is identified, tracked, and protected throughout all stages of its life cycle, including data-in-transit, data-at-rest, and in data-in-use. Appropriate security measures are needed to protect the confidentiality and integrity of the data so it is not exposed, obtained, or manipulated by unauthorized individuals.

Privilege Escalation

Privilege escalation is the act of exploiting a coding error, design flaw, or oversight to gain elevated access to data that would normally be restricted. There are two types of privilege escalation attacks:

- *Vertical privilege escalation* involves a user exploiting the system to gain access to data above the currently assigned account permissions. For example, a part-time employee gaining access to a manager's account would constitute vertical privilege escalation.

- *Horizontal privilege escalation* involves a user accessing a different user's account to access restricted data for that other user. For example, a part-time employee accesses another employee's account because the second employee has access to files or programs the first employee does not. This would constitute a horizontal privilege escalation.

 2.3, 3.2

 TECH TIP

Ensure that data privacy policies established by your organization are verified when checking for potential data exposure. This should be identified in the SDLC so managers, programmers, and testers are aware of what is and is not acceptable during the coding and testing processes.

 1.3

Clickjacking

Clickjacking is a malicious attack that occurs when a user is tricked into clicking a concealed link. This is possible through a script loading a transparent page on top of the actual web page to which the user navigated. When the user clicks a link on the desired web page, the click is actually on a link on the transparent page. The actions of the transparent page are instead executed, such as downloading malware. Click-jacking is considered a form of hijacking because the user's action was intercepted and redirected to another page.

Session Hijacking

A **session hijacking** is an attack that occurs when an attacker exploits a computer session and gains access to a system or its data. When two parties communicate over the Internet, it is common for the communication to be controlled using session controls that include establishing a session with cookies and using SSL/TLS. Once a user authenticates to create the session, the web server sends a session token. Ses-sions are hijacked when a hacker intercepts a session token. Tokens are intercepted through prediction, sniffing, or stolen through a cross-script attack. The best preven-tative steps are to ensure client machines are using up-to-date antimalware software and system updates.

✈ 1.1, 1.4

Typo Squatting

Typo squatting, also called *URL hijacking*, is a social engineering attack in which a hacker registers a web domain name that is similar to a trusted website to take advantage of users making a typographical mistake when entering a web address. For example, a hacker could register a domain using a misspelling of a popular website domain, such as Google, and change the spelling with the hopes that users will incor-rectly enter the website URL. Another technique is to use the legitimate second-level domain, but with a different top-level domain. For example, the top-level domain for the Internal Revenue Service's website (www.irs.gov) is .GOV. A hacker may register irs.com. If a user accidentally enters the address using the .COM top-level domain to navigate to the IRS website, the web browser will be redirected to the fake and malicious site where the hacker is able to install malware, collect data, or participate in other malicious actions directed at the user. The previous example is also a form of domain hijacking. **Domain hijacking** is an attempt to transfer the ownership or registration and control of the domain from the rightful owner.

Not all sites that are similar to trusted sites contain malicious code. Sometimes competitors may try to take advantage of the similarity to attract business. However, typo squatting can just as easily be used for drive-by downloads.

✈ 1.3

Directory Traversal

Directory traversal is an attack in which hackers get beyond the web server's root directory and execute commands. For example, the root directory of a Win-dows-based web server running IIS is **Inetpub\wwwroot**. Locking web users into this environment is a critical task that keeps them out of sensitive directories, such as the Windows directory. Path traversal allows a hacker to bypass the wwwroot folder and access the directory. The best way to check for a directory traversal threat is to use a web-application scanner.

SSL Stripping

Secure Sockets Layer (SSL) stripping is an attack in which a threat actor removes encryption protection of an HTTPS transmission without user knowledge. *Hypertext Transfer Protocol Secure (HTTPS)* is an extension of the Hypertext Transfer Protocol (HTTP) that provides a high level of security through encryption using Secure Sockets Layer/Transport Layer Security (SSL/TLS). An HTTPS request is completed in three steps:

1. A user sends an unsecured HTTP request.

2. The server responds via HTTP and redirects the user to the HTTPS protocol.

3. The user sends a secure HTTPS request and the secure session will begin.

In an SSL stripping attack, a threat actor intervenes during step 3, when an HTTPS request is sent from the user to the secure site. The attacker intercepts the HTTPS request, forwarding it to the original site. Since the connection is still encrypted, the hacker downgrades HTTPS to standard, unencrypted HTTP, which will display requested content in an unencrypted form.

SSL stripping is a specific type of man-in-the-browser attack. A **man-in-the-browser (MITB)** attack is an Internet threat that infects a web browser and covertly modifies web pages, transaction content, or preferences. To help websites combat and protect against these types of attacks, the *HTTP Strict Transport Security (HSTS)* standard was developed.

Driver Manipulation

Driver manipulation is a type of attack in which a threat actor accesses and modifies device drivers within an operating system in an effort to bypass security measures or take control of a device. *Drivers*, or *device drivers*, are software programs that provide the necessary software for devices to interact with a computer system. Drivers enable the interaction between the operating system and hardware devices such as printers and USB drives. There are two main techniques for driver manipulation: shimming and refactoring.

Shimming is the practice of using a driver shim to force a program to run on a program for which it was not intended. A **driver shim** is a library of compiled code that translates commands so a program can run on multiple platforms. Shimming is a common practice in software development and is what enables one program to run on multiple operating systems. For example, if an operating system needs to call a legacy driver, the request can be sent to a driver shim for the old version. When code attempts to call the original driver, it is instead sent to the shim code. However, shimming can also be used maliciously when a shim is written to bypass a driver entirely and instead perform a different function altogether.

Refactoring is the process of modifying or restructuring existing code without changing any external behavior. Like shimming, refactoring is a normal process for improving nonfunctional aspects of software, such as making it less complex. However, refactoring can also be used maliciously, such as refactoring a driver to identify potential vulnerabilities and modify code in an effort to exploit those vulnerabilities. Since external behavior does not change, refactoring can be performed without any indication that it is occurring.

SUMMARY

Application Development

- Application development is the collective process of designing, programming, testing, and quality controlling a computer program to meet specific needs of a business. Examples include web, mobile, and database programs.
- An environment is the resources that host an application and is comprised of software-based tools used by developers to create applications and software. This enables developers to create code without risking interaction with the computer.
- Multiple environments are used in the application development process: application development environment, test environment, staging environment, and production environment.

Software Development Life Cycle

- Software development life cycle (SDLC) is a conceptual process used to create, deploy, and maintain a software application. By using the SDLC model, software development costs are lower, time to market increases, and the resulting product is of high quality.
- The steps in an SDLC life cycle include development, testing, staging, production, and quality assurance.
- Three commonly used types of SDLC models are waterfall, agile, and DevOps.

Secure Application Development

- Application security (AppSec) is the process of developing software that is free from vulnerabilities before it goes into production. It is a process that happens *during* development of an application, not *after*.
- The best security defense is to embed the elements of security on all aspects of software development, from design to implementation.
- Secure application development includes development resources, software diversity, scalability, elasticity, integrity measurement, and version control.

Secure Coding Techniques

- Secure coding is the process of developing an application using techniques to help prevent the introduction of vulnerabilities that create security issues. It is necessary to prevent an application from coming under attack by a threat actor.
- When looking for best practices for secure coding, OWASP is a reliable source. It is a nonprofit organization that provides unbiased information about application security.
- Secure coding techniques include error handling, input validation, normalization, obfuscation, code reuse, memory management, secure HTTP headers, secure cookies, and stored procedures.

Secure Code Review

- Secure code review is the process that helps identify vulnerabilities that could put the program at risk in the later stages. It takes place during the development stage of SDLC.
- Secure code review applies white-box testing and black-box testing. Both types of testing of are used in the development process to identify security issues.

- White-box testing is a manual review, which is the process of reading source code, line-by-line, to locate and identify vulnerabilities.
- Black-box testing is the use of automated tools to check code. Examples of black-box testing include static code analysis, dynamic code analysis, and fuzzing.

Application Vulnerabilities

- Despite efforts taken to secure an application's code, there are still inherent vulnerabilities that happen. One example is resource exhaustion, which occurs when computer resources required to execute actions are depleted, preventing action from occurring.
- Additional application vulnerabilities include integer overflow attack, buffer overflow attack, pointer deference, race conditions, and memory leak.

Application Attacks

- Web applications are applications that run dynamically through web browsers as scripts without requiring software to be installed. These are housed on remote web servers and delivered through a web browser.
- There are a number of challenges faced in protecting web applications from attacks. Many application attacks rely on exploiting a vulnerability within form-field or user-input interfaces.
- Commonly encountered application attacks include API attacks, injections, scripting, request forgeries, data leak or exposure, privilege escalation, clickjacking, session hijacking, typo squatting, directory traversal, SSL stripping, and driver manipulation.

REVIEW QUESTIONS

1. Summarize application development.
2. What is quality assurance (QA) and why is it an important part of the application development process?
3. What term defines the act of running software in an isolated environment separate from other programs so that if errors occur, they will not spread to other programs?
4. Discuss the software development life cycle and examples of SDLC models.
5. Briefly explain each step of the waterfall development model.
6. Identify advantages and disadvantages of the agile development model.
7. Identify and explain three tools for secure application development.
8. State the difference between a compiler-based diversification and binary-based diversification.
9. List two types of elasticity.
10. Identify secure coding techniques.
11. What topics are covered in the *OWASP Top 10 Most Critical Web Application Security Risks*?
12. Which type of validation occurs when user input is confirmed by a server?
13. Explain secure code review and in what stage of SDLC it occurs.

14. Differentiate between white-box and black-box testing for secure code reviews.

15. Explain three types of black-box testing.

16. Discuss various application vulnerabilities.

17. Define a *buffer* and a *buffer overflow*.

18. Briefly explain a time-of-check to time-of use (TOCTOU).

19. List common types of application attacks.

20. Identify and explain four types of injection attacks.

✚ SAMPLE SECURITY+ EXAM QUESTIONS

1. Which of the following is used to reuse code within an application?

   A. SDK

   B. NoSQL

   C. Compiler

   D. SDLC

2. In which threat does an application obtain a value from an unexpected area of memory?

   A. Deprovisioning

   B. Pointer dereference

   C. Injection attack

   D. Buffer overflow

3. What is an exploit in which more data can be entered than the program can accept?

   A. Data canary

   B. RAM scraper

   C. Buffer-overflow attack

   D. Immutable server

4. Which testing mechanism will ensure the system can run effectively in an overloaded environment?

   A. Garbage collection

   B. Dynamic analysis

   C. Stress testing

   D. Buffer-overflow testing

5. Which of the following is a specific testing method on web applications?

   A. Probing

   B. Clickjacking validation

   C. Fuzzing

   D. Deep analysis

6. Which attack method exploits the trust relationship between the web server and the client?

   A. SQL injection

   B. Directory traversal

   C. CSRF

   D. Buffer overflow

7. Git is an example of a _____.

   A. backdoor to other code

   B. code repository

   C. certificate authority

   D. Linux server

8. Which technique minimizes the storage of data in a database?

   A. Normalization

   B. API

   C. SQL

   D. Using buffers

9. Administrators must be able to track changes across multiple versions of an application. Which will help with this function?

   A. Sandboxing

   B. Immutable servers

   C. Continuous integration

   D. Change Management System

10. Which of the following is a threat to databases?

   A. Buffer-overflow attack

   B. Injection attack

   C. Directory traversal

   D. Cross-site scripting (XSS) attack

LAB EXERCISES

Lab Activity 7-1: Buffer-Overflow Attack

Richard Enbody of Michigan State University has posted an article providing an overview of a buffer-overflow attack in which the hacker does not need to know the password to log in. Note: if this article is no longer available, search for a different buffer-overflow simulation and share with your classmates.

1. Launch a web browser, and navigate to a search engine.

2. Enter the search phrase michigan state university buffer overflow. In the list of results, select the article entitled *Security in CS1: Buffer Overflow*. This is a brief article that includes a simulation on how a buffer-overflow attack works.

3. Read the article. Take note of the comparison between a normal login process and a buffer-overflow attack.

4. Download the demonstration. This is a PowerPoint file.

5. Once the PowerPoint file is downloaded, open it and run the slide show. You may be asked to enable content in order for the slide show to run.

6. Describe what vulnerabilities occurred and what preventative measures could have been taken.

Lab Activity 7-2: Web-Application Scanner

A web-application scanner looks for vulnerabilities in a website. This software tool should be used to fully test a website before it goes live to the public.

1. Launch a web browser, and navigate to a search engine.

2. Enter the search phrase burp suite and select the site for the software. Is this a free or commercial product?

3. On the Burp Suite web page, tools are offered to automate custom attacks on a web server. What is the advantage of a tool like this having the capability of offensive hacks?

4. Navigate to a search engine, enter the search phrase netsparker, and select the site for this software.

5. Describe this software and how you would incorporate it into your SDLC.

Lab Activity 7-3: OWASP Website

OWASP is a great resource for security information related to web development and security risks. Its website provides much useful information. Getting to know the website is beneficial to anyone working in web development.

1. Launch a web browser, and navigate to the OWASP website (www.owasp.org). Does the layout of this site look familiar to you?

2. Click the **About OWASP** link in the menu. What are the four core values of the organization?

3. Locate and read the code of ethics. Which points do you feel are related to keeping this project open source? Discuss your choices with the class.

4. Investigate other menu entries. OWASP hosts annual security conferences. What is this annual event called? When and where is the next conference in the United States?

5. Click the link to the conference in the United States. If the list of topics for the next conference is posted, which topics are most interesting to you?

6. Click the **Chapters** link in the menu. Where is the local chapter nearest to your hometown?

7. Return to the home page. At the top of the page, click the **Top 10** link.

8. On the next page, click the newest **OWASP Top 10** link in the Quick Download section, as shown. You may choose to download a PDF version or view a wiki version.

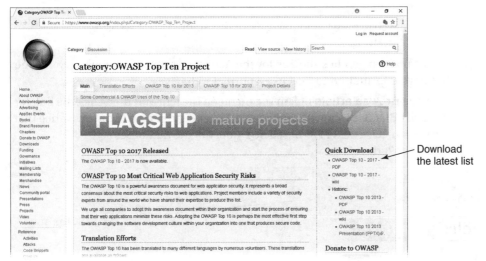

Download the latest list

9. In the document, locate the chart showing the differences between the current OWASP Top 10 and the previous release. How many changes were there?

10. Locate the Top 10 list. This provides a brief description of each threat. Details of each threat appear on the following pages.

11. Locate the details for the number one item. On each of the detail pages, the threat agents and attack vectors are identified. These are the "who" and "how" of the exploit. Each detail page also includes a section that helps identify if your site could be vulnerable to this threat as well as sample scenarios.

12. Review all detail pages to gauge how a company might use this information.

13. Locate the risk factor summary toward the end of the document. Look at the Impacts column. How many of the technical impacts are severe?

14. Look at the Attack Vectors column. How many of the attack vectors are easy to exploit?

15. What are your overall impressions of the document? What did you find that you feel would be particularly useful for security administrators?

Lab Activity 7-4: SQL Injection

A poorly programmed website can be vulnerable to SQL injection attacks. The company Acunetix produces a vulnerability scanner to check for security risks in web applications. It maintains a website for testing its scanner, which can be used to simulate attacks.

1. Launch a web browser, and navigate to the Acunetix test website (www.vulnweb.com).

2. On the main page, click the link for the Acuart test (testphp.vulnweb.com). The test page is formatted to look like a normal web page.

3. Click the **Browse artists** link in the menu on the left, and then click the link for the artist **Blad3**, as shown. Look at the address bar in your browser. Notice that the website has run a PHP-based SQL query of the database: artists.php?artist=2.

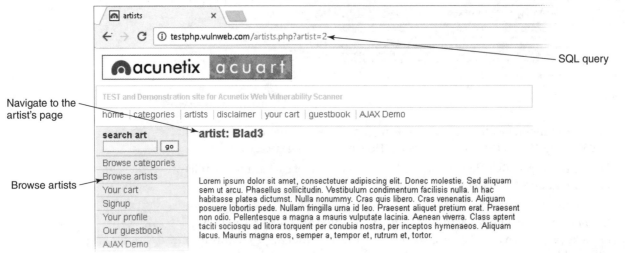

SQL query

Navigate to the artist's page

Browse artists

Goodheart-Willcox Publisher

4. Click in the browser address bar, and change the query to artists.php?artist=–1 UNION SELECT 1,pass,cc FROM users WHERE uname='test'. This looks for an artist record that does not exist (–1) as database records usually do not have negative numbering and extracts data from the database. The **UNION** command is used to join the attack (SELECT 1,pass,cc FROM users WHERE uname='test') with the original query (artists.php?artist=–1). The resulting data are displayed on the web page. In this way, hackers can extract data from the website's database.

5. Navigate to a search engine, and enter the search phrase sql injection test site. See if you can locate another simulator that demonstrates SQL injection attacks. Experiment with the simulator, and discuss your findings with your classmates.

CASE STUDY

Third-Party SDKs

In November of 2019, Facebook and Twitter began investigating reports from security researchers about select third-party software development kits (SDKs) that allow code developers access to collect user data without knowledge or permission. One of the malicious SDKs in question could allow outside developers to exploit a vulnerability in mobile infrastructure and access personal data, including e-mail address and recent posts to Twitter. This information could then be used by data monetization companies for targeted advertisements. Twitter acknowledged the code could allow for the possibility of a customer's Twitter account to be controlled by others but had no evidence these actions occurred. This vulnerability and others, such as the Cambridge Analytica's improper use of Facebook data for political purposes, has led to increased scrutiny of third-party SDKs and libraries.

1. What concerns do you have regarding the potential for third-party developers to access user data?

2. To what extent should social media or networking platforms and SDK owners be responsible for vulnerabilities in code taken from a library?

3. Explain whether you would or would not classify this as a cyberattack and why.

4. What recommendations would you make to support best practices and reduce vulnerabilities?

Mobile Devices and Embedded Systems

LEARNING OUTCOMES

- Summarize employee use of mobile devices.
- Explain types of mobile device connection methods.
- List examples of management tools used to implement secure mobile solutions.
- Summarize techniques for securing mobile devices.
- Discuss ways to enforce and monitor mobile devices used by employees.
- Define *embedded system* and its components.
- List and explain common constraints of embedded systems.
- Discuss embedded systems security.
- Summarize industrial control systems (ICS) and the use of SCADA.
- Explain the Internet of Things (IoT).
- List and discuss examples of embedded systems applications.

KEY TERMS

application management
Arduino
Bluetooth
bring your own device (BYOD)
carrier unlocking
cellular
cellular network
choose your own device (CYOD)
company-owned, personally enabled (COPE)
conditional access
containerization
context-aware authentication
custom firmware
drone
embedded system
enterprise mobility management (EMM)
facility automation
field-programmable gate array (FPGA)
firmware OTA update
hardware security module (HSM)
hotspot

impossible travel time restriction
industrial control system (ICS)
jailbreaking
microSD HSM
mobile application management (MAM)
mobile content management (MCM)
mobile device management (MDM)
multifunction printer (MFP)
multimedia messaging service (MMS)
password management
password vault
push notification
push notification service
Raspberry Pi
real-time operating system (RTOS)
remote wipe
rich communication services (RCS)
rooting
screen lock
Security Enhancements for Android (SEAndroid)

short messaging service (SMS)
sideloading
smart device
smart meter
smart sensor
static code
storage segmentation
system control and data acquisition (SCADA) system
system on a chip (SoC)
tethering
time-based login
unified endpoint management (UEM)
USB On-the Go (USB OTG)
virtualization
Voice over IP (VoIP)
vulnerable business process
wearable technology
Wi-Fi ad-hoc network
Wi-Fi Direct
zero-level formatting

SECURITY+ CERTIFICATION EXAM OBJECTIVES

The following Security+ Certification Exam Objectives are covered in this chapter.

+ 2.1: Hardware security module (HSM)
+ 2.4: Static code
+ 2.4: Push notifications
+ 2.4: Phone call
+ 2.6: Embedded systems
+ 2.6: System control and data acquisition (SCADA)/industrial control system (ICS)
+ 2.6: Internet of Things (IoT)
+ 2.6: Specialized
+ 2.6: Voice over IP (VoIP)
+ 2.6: Heating, ventilation, and air-conditioning (HVAC)

+ 2.6: Drones/AVs
+ 2.6: Multifunctional printer (MFP)
+ 2.6: Real-time operating system (RTOS)
+ 2.6: Surveillance systems
+ 2.6: System on a chip (SoC)
+ 2.6: Constraints
+ 3.3: HSM
+ 3.5: Cellular
+ 3.5: Wi-Fi
+ 3.5: Bluetooth
+ 3.5: USB

+ 3.5: Mobile device management
+ 3.5: Mobile devices
+ 3.5: Enforcement and monitoring of:
+ 3.5: Deployment models
+ 3.7: Time-based logins
+ 3.7: Impossible travel time/risky login
+ 3.7: Lockout
+ 3.8: Password vaults
+ 3.8: HSM
+ 3.8: Conditional access
+ 4.4: MDM

OVERVIEW

Digital security concerns are not limited only to traditional computing devices such as desktop computers or servers that run on businesses' networks. Security issues should be addressed for nontraditional systems, such as mobile, embedded, or specialized systems that connect to digital networks. The rise in mobile and embedded systems presents unique challenges to maintaining the security posture of an enterprise environment. Additional layers of security are needed to support mobile and embedded equipment as well as to mitigate risks associated with continuous connections that mobile and embedded systems provide.

This chapter explores concepts associated with mobile and embedded systems as well as methods for securing them. You will learn about various mobile devices and their connection methods; tools and methods for managing, securing, and monitoring mobile devices; embedded systems, their constraints, and how to secure them; and Internet of Things (IoT) devices.

SECURITY+ NOTE

Internet of Things (IoT) devices may be vulnerable to new or expanded threat vectors due to their status as an emerging technology. It is important for security administrators to be aware of new technologies used by their network and the people logged in to those networks. For example, an employee's smartwatch may not be connected to an organization's network, but if hacked, the watch could become a Bluetooth-based attack vector.

Mobile Devices

Traditional personal computers have long been the norm for businesses. However, in today's workplace, mobile devices such as smartphones, laptops, and tablets are the preferred tools for employees. Using these devices, workers can access company information when traveling or working from home, maintaining professional efficiency and workflow.

As technology changes, so do networked devices. In today's workforce, mobile devices surpass desktop computers as the standard of technology. Companies that previously provided personal computers for each employee may now provide laptops. This means the need for strong planning, implementation, and monitoring is a crucial and necessary component of security strategy.

An organization must have a plan to implement secure mobile solutions. For all instances of employee mobile device use for business purposes,

- employees should sign an Acceptable Use Policy (AUP) indicating they understand and will abide by those policies; and
- employees must be clear that those who do not abide by those policies will be disciplined depending on the violation.

To help build and maintain a security plan for mobile devices, companies often categorize devices into five distinct categories:

3.5, 4.4

- *BYOD.* **Bring your own device (BYOD)** is a strategy that allows employees, partners, and other personnel to use their personal devices to conduct business and connect to an organization's networks. While most people consider smartphones to be the emphasis of BYOD, companies consider all digital devices, including smartwatches, tablets, and laptops, as part of BYOD.
- *CYOD.* **Choose your own device (CYOD)** is a strategy in which a company selects the type of devices approved for connection to their network, but the employee chooses and owns the device. In this business model, the company and IT security team evaluate the risks and benefits of personal devices and, based on their testing and analysis, select devices they can adequately support and defend on their network. For successful secure deployment, the company often limits device options to specific models and operating systems.
- *COPE.* **Company-owned, personally enabled (COPE)** is a strategy in which a company owns and provides a device for an employee's work. In this scenario, an employee must use the employer-issued device for company business. However, employees have permission to access personal accounts on the device, including banking and social media. Company-owned devices enable the IT team to focus support and security protection to a specific model or platform, which reduces the managerial overhead of supporting various devices. In addition, contents on a COPE device technically belong to the organization, not the employee. Management has complete right of access to any information on the device. The device belongs to the company, and the employee in possession of the device can be required to return it at any time.
- *Corporate-owned.* A corporate-owned device is one in which an employer purchases, owns, and controls the content on an employee-issued device. The device is for professional use only. A corporate-owned model is challenging as it can be impossible to determine if a device is used according to guidelines. However, installing web filters and monitoring software can identify a device that is not used for business purposes.
- *VDI. Virtual desktop infrastructure (VDI)*, also known as *virtual mobile infrastructure (VMI)* or *virtual desktop environment (VDE)*, is a popular mobile deployment for many organizations. These environments operate through **virtualization**, which is a means of managing or presenting computer resources virtually as opposed to physically. The device accesses servers rather than stores data. Since data is stored on a secure server, if a device is lost or stolen, data is not at risk. VDI makes it convenient to push updates for applications on the server rather than on each individual mobile device. To ensure secure deployment of a VDI system, strong passwords are required to access servers and enforce policies, as is *full-device encryption*, which is a technology that renders data stored on a hard drive unreadable without an encryption key to unlock it.

Mobile Connectivity

Mobile devices use a variety of connection methods to communicate with other devices. Each connection method poses potential for security vulnerabilities for the devices or the network.

Cellular

⬦ 3.5

Mobile devices require a cellular connection. **Cellular** is a network technology that enables communication through mobile devices by using a system of stations and transceivers that make up a cellular network. A **cellular network** is a type of wireless network in which transmissions are distributed over groups of geographic areas called *cells*. The level or generation (4G, 5G, etc.) identifies the speed and characteristics of communication. Due to the nature of cellular traffic and networks, reliability of coverage and transmission can be negatively affected in rural areas. Before subscribing to a mobile service, a coverage assessment is necessary to confirm all employees will have connectivity.

Bluetooth

⬦ 3.5

Bluetooth is a wireless connection that enables mobile devices to share data via short-range, ad-hoc communication sessions. Devices that communicate via Bluetooth are paired to enable transmission. While security threats are possible with Bluetooth communication, an attacker needs to be within 30 feet of a device to communicate successfully. This often makes Bluetooth an unappealing option for hackers. Bluetooth connections should be disabled on devices when not in use to avoid potential vulnerabilities as well as unnecessary power drain.

Tethering is the use of an Internet-enabled device to share an online connection with a connected device through Bluetooth or Wi-Fi. Employees who use this connection method put the organization at risk for data loss or the introduction of malware to the device.

⬦ 3.5

USB

⬦ 3.5

Universal Serial Bus (USB) is an industry standard that specifies the protocols, connectors, and cables that are required for transmission. This may be a non-wireless option with mobile devices to transfer data between devices. USB communications requires a USB port and a device or appropriate cable to facilitate communication. A *USB connection* is a common computer connection that uses a Universal Serial Bus (USB) connector to transfer data. USB is often used for network connectivity, particularly with mobile devices, but should be used sparingly. When mobile devices are connected to a computer via USB, a synchronization process typically starts automatically. If one of the devices has a malware infection, this synchronization process could put the other device at risk.

One way to avoid data being transferred without permission is to disable transfer tools such as USB OTG. **USB On-the Go (USB OTG)** is a USB connection that enables multiple mobile devices to be connected without using a computer. By using USB OTG, a mobile device functions as not only a computing device but also a storage device, making data transfer from one mobile device to another quite simple. From a security perspective, this is problematic due to the possibility of sensitive date being transferred to unauthorized devices. Therefore, disabling USB OTG is a secure preventive measure for avoiding potential data loss. Disablement of USB OTG can be enforced through mobile device management programs.

Wi-Fi

Wi-Fi is a wireless connection that uses radio waves instead of copper-core or fiber-optic cable. Wi-Fi connections require central devices called *routers* to enable and provide communication. Transmissions are conducted on a 2.4- or 5-GHz frequency. Configuration of wireless networks can include secured, authenticated access or open, unencrypted access.

Wi-Fi connections should always be password-protected and only for use by employees on company property. Employees should not use public unsecured Wi-Fi connections, such as hotspots, for work-related tasks as company data could be hacked. A **hotspot** is a publicly accessible, often unsecured, Internet access point.

Wi-Fi Direct is a wireless connection that allows device-to-device communication without the use of a centralized network. It works by having one of the devices acting as an Access Point (AP) and the other device communicating using Wi-Fi Protected Setup (WPS) and WPA/WPA2 encryption. The setup is similar to Bluetooth connections where no intermediary device is required, but Wi-Fi direct provides higher speed and more versatility. There are security concerns when a device is connected to a network and another device simultaneously as malware from a device could affect a network.

A Wi-Fi network can also run in ad-hoc mode. A **Wi-Fi ad-hoc network** is a wireless network in which two or more devices connect to one another directly instead of communicating through a wireless router or access point. As with Wi-Fi direct, WPA2 encryption can protect the data and transmissions, but devices may be vulnerable to security threats if simultaneously connected to a network.

Management Tools

The use of mobile devices by employees in an organization requires tools to manage that use. The following tools can assist an IT administrator to implement secure mobile solutions.

- **Mobile device management (MDM)** is a set of software tools that provides a single management platform to control, modify, and secure devices remotely. MDM is necessary for enterprise mobility management (EMM).
- **Enterprise mobility management (EMM)** is an enterprise organization's processes and policies for operations of mobile devices used in the business. MDM and EMM are often combined to create a comprehensive security solution for mobile devices.
- **Unified endpoint management (UEM)** is a class of software tools that provides management for various types of endpoints, including mobile devices, PCs, and Internet-enabled devices. Management of endpoint devices is provided by a single platform using the network and the Internet remotely.
- **Mobile application management (MAM)** is a solution that provides specific functionality by enabling administrators to lock or disable apps and the data stored within them. A popular use case of a MAM is configuring it on corporate e-mail. A MAM solution can restrict features such as copy and paste to prevent data shared with other apps. A MAM platform provides additional benefits including software delivery and updates as well as configuration of policies on work-related apps. This includes distributing apps or software updates to mobile devices, and removing apps as necessary. Settings can be configured to allow only enterprise-approved apps the ability to run on mobile devices.

- **Mobile content management (MCM)** is a solution that enables a company to have control over mobile devices, device content, and how devices access data located on company systems. Employers can control access by considering the type of device and its available storage, screen resolution, memory, and processor usage. Content management goals include maximizing performance and access to content. Using a content management system as part of an MDM environment can help provide secure data access.
- **Application management** is the download, distribution, and control of apps through centralized tools and services. By enforcing application management, an organization knows which apps exist on its mobile devices and can prevent employees from downloading their own applications. One way to prevent employees from downloading apps to a company-owned device is to require an administrator password for all downloads.
- **Password management** is controlling the methods in which users create passwords to gain access to a company network. It is one of the simplest methods of protecting mobile data and ensuring the secure deployment of mobile devices. A program is installed on the device that enables a user to create, as well as store, passwords in a location called a password vault. A **password vault** is a repository for passwords protected by a master password. The downside to a vault is that it must be installed on each device for which it is used.

Securing Mobile Devices

Employees using mobile devices for business purposes pose security risks to an organization. Some of the risks are inherent vulnerabilities resulting from careless use of a device. Other risks are external threats to security.

Most security precautions can be configured using mobile device management (MDM). MDM tools can provide control over devices that connect to an organization's network. MDM gives an administrator the ability to perform many tasks, one example being granting conditional access. **Conditional access** is the configuration and control of devices to determine if access is granted to services or locations. Conditional access can be based on various criteria such as type of device or device OS.

3.8

Physical Security

Physical security is a concern for mobile devices used by employees. An obvious security risk is that mobile devices are subject to being lost, damaged, or stolen. Employees may be careless and leave their phone in a car or forget it at lunch in a restaurant. A lost or stolen device is vulnerable as confidential data can be hacked by the finder of the device. In any event, the company must replace an unrecovered business device. Purchasing insurance through the cell phone carrier can help in these situations.

Theft refers to the unauthorized taking of a device. Typically, a thief resets a stolen device back to factory settings, disabling location tracking. Once this reset occurs, there is little a user can do to locate the device.

Smartphones are frequently among the most-stolen items. *Apple picking* is the act of grabbing a smartphone or other mobile device from a user's bag or hands. The term comes from the frequent theft of Apple products as owners are using them. While theft cannot always be prevented or avoided, strategies can help secure an organization's data or locate a device in the event it is lost or stolen.

- From a mobile device management standpoint, few security tools are as useful in secure deployment of mobile devices as a remote wipe. If a device is lost or stolen, data should be deleted to prevent compromise of secure information.

Remote wipe is a remote-erase feature that, when activated, returns a device to its original factory settings. It includes deletion of *all* data on a device. Remote wipe benefits the employer by preventing access to data on a device and the potential for the security issues data leakage could expose.

- Some devices have a feature that locks a lost or stolen device indefinitely until a device is found. When locked, the device will disable all payment options and will not display notifications or alerts. To unlock the device, a user must verify personal identity. If a strong authentication is in place, it mitigates the risk of unapproved access to the device. Together, the ability to erase and lock a device remotely are known as a *kill switch*.

- Geolocation and global positioning system (GPS) tagging can be configured on a mobile device management system. *Geolocation* identifies the physical or geographical location of a device by using GPS coordinates or IP address assignment. *Global positioning system (GPS)* is a wireless connection method that enables a device called a *GPS receiver* to communicate and receive information from global navigation satellite systems (GNSS). Using geolocation can help locate a missing device. With mobile geolocation features, configuration settings can provide information relevant to current location of the device. Administrators can require location tracking with an MDM and prohibit the user from disabling this function. This can assist in locating a missing device.

- *GPS tagging*, also known as *geotagging*, is the act of including GPS information to media, such as photos taken from a mobile device. Through geotagging, a person's location is identified from information tagged to photographs or videos the person might take, revealing the location of the person and device.

- GPS is used for geofencing. *Geofencing* is the creation of a virtual fence or boundary using geographic coordinates. Once boundaries are established, the device uses a mobile communication method such as cellular or Wi-Fi to activate a programmed action when the device enters or exits the boundary. This provides security by ensuring mobile devices are accessed only in known, pre-approved geographical areas.

Cameras and Microphones

Mobile devices often have built-in cameras and microphones. This enables real-time, face-to-face communication through digital means. However, these same features also open the device to unauthorized surveillance. If a device is infected with malware, hackers can remotely activate cameras and microphones to spy on others. The same is true for desktop computers with built-in cameras or webcams. The best way around this vulnerability is to

- limit the number of apps that can access a camera or microphone;
- monitor each device for *unauthorized camera use*;
- use lens covers to obscure the view of a built-in camera;
- review app permissions regularly; and
- scan devices for *recording microphones*, which are device microphones that enable remote recording.

Authentication

Authentication prevents risky sign-in. A *risky login* is an unauthorized attempt to access an account. To avoid risky logins, a *zero-trust model* should be applied so logins and devices are verified each time an employee attempts to sign in. A **screen lock** is a security setting that requires authentication to access a device's home screen. This helps support the goal of confidentiality by only allowing access to employees or authorized personnel. Authentication measures used by screen locks are typically a password, PIN, or unique swipe pattern. Each of these is not without risk, however, as passwords and PINs can be cracked, and swipe patterns can be seen on a device if the screen is not wiped clean.

Biometric authentication uses unique body characteristics to provide authentication for a user. Common biometrics on devices include fingerprints and facial recognition screening. Screen locks that incorporate biometrics often rely on fingerprint, retinal, or facial recognition to unlock a device. Administrators can configure the MDM to incorporate this type of authentication to allow only the authorized user access to a device.

Devices can be configured to require two-factor authentication when login is attempted. When an employee logs in to a device, *push notification authentication* validates a user by sending a request to the mobile device. A code is sent via SMS message on a mobile device, as an e-mail, or a phone call. The code is required before login can be completed, which adds an extra level of security. For companies that prefer not to use push notification authentication, an authentication app can be installed on mobile devices to generate security codes independently.

Context-Aware Authentication

Context-aware authentication is a configuration setting that uses situational information—such as location, identity, and time of day—to verify a user. Context-aware authentication allows IT administrators to consider other factors for authenticating users by using context clues. Examples of context-based authentication factors include identifying the machine used to log in; reviewing the device's IP address, location, and time; and reviewing a user's historical browsing habits. Two popular examples of context-aware authentication are time-based logins and impossible travel time restrictions.

- A **time-based login** is a procedure that enables authentication of a user by either detecting the user's presence at a pre-established time or accounting for an interval of time for the user to travel to another location. In this example, the authenticating context is the time of day and the user's presence. If a user arrives outside the predefined time interval, authentication and access are denied.

- An **impossible travel time restriction** is a safeguard that prevents access to a user if the system detects the user traveled between two locations faster than anticipated. If a user signs in to a network at one location and later attempts to sign in at a new location, the system calculates how long it should take to travel between the two locations. If the travel time is too short, the user cannot sign in a second time.

Lockout

Devices should have a lockout period. After a specified number of attempts to log in, the device should lock out additional attempts. This helps to prevent a brute force or dictionary attack. Additionally, devices should automatically lock after a predefined duration of time. This eliminates the possibility of data being stolen from an unattended device.

3.5

2.4, 3.5

3.5

3.7, 4.4

3.7

✚ 3.5, 4.4

Storage Segmentation

Storage segmentation is the separation of company or organization data from personal data on a mobile device. This adds a layer of security to both data types and ensures there is no mixing between them. Storage segmentation is often accomplished using **containerization**, which is the separation of various data types into separate storage pools, called *containers* or *lockers*, so storage can be managed separately. Containerization establishes virtual barriers that help hinder malware from accessing company data.

✚ 3.5, 4.4

Push Notification

A **push notification** is a message or alert that appears on a mobile device without user interaction. These notifications are sent by push notification services, and they appear automatically on a device's screen, even if a user is running a different application. **Push notification services** is a system in place to send notifications to devices. Managing push notifications centrally through MDM enables an organization to control notifications sent to employees' devices, ensuring all employees are receiving the same notifications within a short time span.

✚ 2.1, 3.3, 3.5, 3.8

MicroSD Hardware Security Module

Some mobile devices have the ability to use memory cards, such as microSD cards, to transfer data. However, the data encryption provided by many mobile devices is a light software-based encryption method that is vulnerable to cracking. To help facilitate the security of data, organizations can mandate the use of a **microSD HSM**, which is a lightweight security solution that implements cryptographic key management in a microSD card. A **hardware security module (HSM)** is a cryptographic device that stores or manages encryption keys and performs cryptographic functions. The HSM found in a microSD HSM is engineered specifically for use in a mobile device.

✚ 3.5

SEAndroid

Security Enhancements for Android (SEAndroid), is an Android-specific security tool that prevents apps or processes from accessing data and resources they are not allowed to access. SEAndroid identifies and addresses critical gaps in Android security features by using a mandatory access control (MAC) model that allows privileges based on policies that control which users and apps are able to access files and resources. SEAndroid can also protect the integrity of applications and data while preventing both privilege escalation and app-based data leakage.

Enforcement and Monitoring

Mobile devices have specific security vulnerabilities that require enforcement and monitoring of policies. Often, vulnerabilities related to mobile devices are the result of users unknowingly making uninformed decisions. Other vulnerabilities stem from a lack of depth in user knowledge of the device. To prevent uninformed decision or incomplete knowledge from causing a security issue, it is necessary to establish policies and provide education and awareness to employees on the inherent vulnerabilities of devices and best practices for using them responsibly.

Employees using mobile devices can create security vulnerabilities for an organization when they are careless in mobile connections. Secure mobile solutions must be implemented through enforcement and monitoring of mobile connection practices. In general, devices used for business purposes should restrict connections of a device. For laptops, security restrictions can be set on a laptop's local policy that prevents the computer from recognizing external devices.

External Media

In general, mobile devices should be configured to restrict connection to external media. Connecting a mobile device to an unauthorized peripheral or computer puts the device at risk for malware. Additionally, if an employee connects a mobile device to third-party media, there is no way of knowing how secure the media is, which creates a security vulnerability for not only the device in question but also an organization's network once that device reconnects to it.

Third-Party App Stores

Third-party app stores are application marketplaces that only offer third-party apps. *Third-party apps* are applications created by developers rather than the vendor of the platform for which an app was originally created. For example, Android devices come with a Google Chrome app built-in, but the Google Play store may offer other web browsers as available downloads. In this example, the other web browsers are third-party apps.

Sideloading is often used to download third-party apps on a device. **Sideloading** is the process of installing applications from one device to another instead of using an official app-distribution method. The act of sideloading presents a vulnerability because there is no accountability for the source of downloaded programs from third-party locations or software.

Sideloading or downloading a third-party app can introduce malware to a device, enabling an attacker to take over. Employees should be prohibited from downloading apps to devices used to connect to company networks. The best measure to enforce app policies, including app approval and versions, is to use a mobile application manager (MAM) that provides the monitoring capabilities of apps used on devices and the ability to add, update, or remove apps as necessary. Additionally, a mobile device management (MDM) system can be used to configure strict settings to prevent access to third party stores or sideloading methods.

Text-Message Threats

Text messaging is a tool for threat actors to infiltrate an organization. Threat actors send a text with photos, links, or other information similar to phishing messages through e-mail. The same rules apply to text messages as e-mail: employees should not open or respond to text messages from people they do not know. One click on a link could infect a device or network.

- **Short messaging service (SMS)** is a text-messaging service that limits messages to 160 characters. While SMS communications are generally safe, threat actors can conduct social engineering attacks through SMS messages. These messages can infect a device or network. A good practice is to monitor SMS communication to ensure no threat actors have penetrated the system.
- **Multimedia messaging service (MMS)** is a messaging service that allows for photo, video, or audio to be included in a message. Employees with MMS-capable devices should be cautious about which messages they open as malware can be sent to a device through MMS similar to the way in which malware is sent through e-mail with an attachment.

- **Rich communication services (RCS)** is a mobile device communication protocol with more features and options than SMS. RCS includes features beyond text messages, including improved group chats, transmit in-call multimedia, and the ability to send read receipts and GIFs. However, a security concern is RCS does not support end-to-end encryption, which protects messages in transit. This means that if two devices are communicating on a network through RCS, messages could be intercepted and read by a hacker with relative ease.

Mobile Payments

A popular feature of mobile devices is the ability to use them to make mobile payments. Using mobile-payment software puts a smartphone at risk for malware. Employees should not have permission to make personal mobile payments using devices intended for business. If permission is granted an employee to use an app, a mobile-payment app should be researched for its privacy and data-sharing actions before downloading and be regularly updated. Users should also carefully read the permissions of any app installed to see what else the app is tracking or collecting.

Bypassing Device Restrictions

Mobile devices can be configured to bypass built-in limitations such as modifying an operating system on iOS devices. Employees should not have administrative rights to modify devices. Only members of an IT department should configure mobile devices.

In general, bypassing device restrictions often results in disabled security measures and creates a serious vulnerability. However, some Android manufacturers provide support for customization so security measures are not lost.

Three common bypasses include jailbreaking, rooting, and unlocking.

- **Jailbreaking** is the process of allowing an iOS device to bypass device restrictions. Jailbreaking is typically conducted to sideload apps, modify an operating system, or grant administrator privileges.
- **Rooting** is the process of bypassing device restrictions on an Android device to access administrator-level privileges. The difference between rooting and jailbreaking is that iOS devices are designed to be used as-is, whereas Android devices permit modifications to the operating system.
- **Carrier unlocking** is the legal process of disconnecting a phone from a wireless provider's network. Most phones are locked to the network of the provider from which a device was purchased. However, if a person or organization chooses to switch to a different wireless provider, devices can be unlocked so they may work on a new carrier's network without interruption. Employees should have no reason to perform this activity and only authorized members of an organization should be permitted to unlock a company-owned device.

Custom and Unauthorized Firmware

Firmware is a read-only software program on a hardware device that provides instructions for the device to communicate with other hardware. **Custom firmware**, also known as *after-market firmware*, is firmware modified by a third party to provide new features or access previously locked-down functionalities. In an effort to ensure secure deployment of mobile devices, an organization should block installation of custom or unapproved firmware. One way of enforcing firmware-centric policies is to handle all firmware updates in-house by the IT department. However, in cases where this is not feasible, security professionals should monitor downloads on off-site devices for firmware downloads that do not match with known updates.

Often, devices receive push notification of availability of a new version of firmware for download from the manufacturer. A **firmware OTA update** is a patch or system update for a mobile device distributed through a wireless provider as an over-the-air (OTA) update. Apple often pushes updates in this manner, especially since Apple is the sole creator and modifier of iOS. However, since Android devices are customizable, it can be difficult to determine if an update is legitimate or malicious. OTA updates should be performed by an IT staff member rather than an individual user.

 3.5

Embedded Systems

 2.6

An **embedded system** is a combination of hardware and software contained within a larger device used to complete a specific task. It is a microprocessor-based computer system designed for specific functions within a larger system. The purpose of an embedded system is to control a device and enable interaction from a user. It may or may not be programmable.

Embedded systems have low processing capability and handle a limited amount of data compared to a computer. These systems often rely on smart sensors to provide them with data needed to perform actions. A **smart sensor** is a device that receives, interprets, and computes data from its physical surroundings to perform predefined functions or actions based on specific input. A popular deployment of smart sensors is to monitor a system for maintenance problems and send alerts when needed.

An embedded system has three components: hardware, operating system, and application software. The hardware includes *system on a chip*, the operating system is a *real-time operating system* (RTOS), and the software is *firmware*. Hardware is needed for performance and security, and software is needed for features.

System on a Chip (SoC)

 2.6

System on a chip (SoC) is an integrated circuit that includes all fundamental computing components including a central processing unit (CPU), memory, storage, and input/output ports all on a single chip. This makes SoC an efficient method of deploying or supporting devices that are typically portable or small, such as the SoC inside a mobile device.

Real-Time Operating System (RTOS)

 2.6

Embedded systems require an operating system. A **real-time operating system (RTOS)** is an operating system designed specifically for the SoC in an embedded system. An RTOS runs indefinitely on systems that need less memory than normal operating systems such as Windows. It runs slow on big tasks but responds quickly and effectively and does not need to be rebooted periodically as with a traditional OS.

There are security implications of the RTOS that must be noted.

- *Shared memory* is unmanaged in RTOS systems, meaning invalid or malicious content could crash a system if data is altered before it is processed.
- Due to lack of shared-memory arrangement, a denial of service (DoS) attack could occur if memory is monopolized by a single process or task that prohibits additional system functionality.
- RTOS systems transfer information through messaging queries validated at a system level, rather than safe or legitimate sources.
- RTOS systems are easily attacked via code injection in which a threat actor places malicious code into a system to launch attacks.

Firmware

Firmware is used to operate hardware that has a single purpose such as flash memory devices. It helps device hardware run properly and is typically stored in the flash ROM. Most internal components of computers and peripheral devices have firmware stored on them. Without firmware, these components would fail to function.

Constraints of Embedded Systems

Embedded systems are optimized to meet programming constraints. However, since these systems are present in specialized equipment, their architectures differ from those of standard computers. Common constraints of embedded systems include the following:

✚ 2.6

- *Power.* The design of embedded systems results in a low-capacity battery in an effort to adhere to specified size and weight requirements of the device or system. This results in significantly less power than standard devices.
- *Computation.* Devices with embedded systems tend to have limited computational processing abilities. This limitation hinders the ability to run typical applications, including those used to defend against attacks or encrypt data stored on the device.
- *Networking.* Embedded systems are typically incapable of high-speed networking, instead utilizing a wireless connection method. This not only leaves data transfers susceptible to interception but also can have a negative impact on the delivery of critical real-time data.
- *Cryptography.* Cryptography is a technique used to secure information by using codes that only the intended recipient can process and understand. Due to the minimal available hardware and processing power of embedded-system devices, cryptographic protections are generally not possible, resulting in readable data.
- *Inability to patch.* It can be difficult or impossible to install patches and updates on embedded systems. Outdated or unpatched software often results in holes or backdoors in device security.
- *Authentication.* Due to the minimal power and storage capabilities of embedded systems, a lack of authentication measures and industry standards for authenticating users exists. However, authentication must be incorporated, when possible, to prevent hackers from gaining root access to devices.
- *Range.* Embedded systems are limited by distance. Due to *attenuation*, which is the loss of signal over distance, embedded systems must remain close in proximity to their respective connection point; otherwise, they will become inoperable or unreliable.
- *Cost.* A significant constraint on embedded systems is the ability to provide functionality and security measures needed while also remaining cost-effective. In addition to the cost of designing, developing, and implementing a system, maintenance of an embedded system also requires cost.
- *Implied trust.* An important constraint of embedded systems is trustworthiness. *Security* and *trust* are used interchangeably, even though fundamentally different. A system can be secure, but if a system can be bypassed, it is not trustworthy. In order for a system to be trusted, it must act as anticipated, be secure, and have the ability to identify errors or attempts at intrusion.

Security of Embedded Systems

The reliance on embedded systems is widespread, especially when one considers how prevalent these systems have become. However, the ability to secure them is difficult due to their relatively small size and limited computing resources. Embedded systems are susceptible to

- potential for attack replication due to the similarity among embedded system devices, and
- malware threats in remotely deployed systems that use a direct Internet connection with no firewalls.

In many cases, updating a device's firmware is the best method for establishing and maintaining security of hardware and embedded devices, but updating embedded system firmware can be difficult. Embedded systems are relatively inexpensive so replacing them is sometimes more efficient than updating firmware. An embedded system's *lifespan* is generally around 15 years. However, this creates a need to foresee potential threats a decade in advance due to embedded systems having a significantly longer lifespan than traditional workstation computers.

Aside from replacing entire control units, methods for maintaining the security of embedded systems include the following.

- Segment networks so only those with a definite need have access to embedded systems.
- Enable administrative monitoring of connections to embedded systems.
- Integrate third-party security management companies or applications.
- Change default credentials, such as usernames, passwords, and access PINs, whenever possible.

Industrial Control System (ICS)

✛ 2.6

An application of embedded systems is industrial control systems. **Industrial control system (ICS)** is an umbrella term that describes various types of systems, tools, and instrumentation used to operate or automate industrial processes. ICSs support critical infrastructure systems such as transportation, energy, manufacturing, and water treatment industries.

Security implications associated with ICSs are more complicated than simply downloading and applying the latest security patches, as commonly administered for typical network devices. Instead, these systems incorporate uniquely customized hardware and software solutions that require vendor configuration of the systems and testing of security enhancements and updates.

✛ 2.6

Industrial control systems are typically managed using a system control and data acquisition (SCADA) system. A **system control and data acquisition (SCADA) system**, also known as *supervisory control and data acquisition system*, is an embedded system used to monitor an interface with controls for machines and equipment in an industrial process. SCADA gathers real-time data and analyzes it for use in monitoring and controlling industrial equipment, as shown in Figure 8-1.

SCADA systems provide real-time data that enables management to make information-driven decisions. This includes continuous monitoring for vulnerability updates or patches, ensuring compliance to industry standards, and enforcing physical security policies.

Figure 8-1 A supervisory control and data acquisition (SCADA) system is hardware and software used to monitor an interface with the controls for machines and equipment in an industrial process.

Leo Pakhomov/Shutterstock.com

As an industrial automation control system, SCADA assists when human intervention is not a practical solution for control. There are situations where an industry is remote, difficult to reach, or unsafe/impractical for humans to reach such as the following:

■ *Facilities.* SCADA systems are used in facilities for monitoring, controlling, and automating management tasks. **Facility automation** is the digital transformation to automatic or electronic control for monitoring of systems crucial to facility operation, such as lighting; surveillance; energy management; heating, ventilation, and air-conditioning (HVAC) systems; and temperature control.

■ *Manufacturing.* SCADA systems used in manufacturing collect and analyze tasks such as real-time production data, regulate robots, and manage just-in-time manufacturing.

■ *Energy.* This industry sector often relies on SCADA implementations to monitor power grids, redirect power from excess capacity, restore power during outages, and track data for trend analysis.

■ *Logistics.* This industry deploys SCADA systems for planning and managing the flow of goods, services, and people to a destination. It is also used for monitoring warehouse activities, such as shipping and receiving. SCADA is also used to monitor storage containers.

■ *Water and sewage.* SCADA systems used in this industry monitor reservoir levels, regulate water flow, and manage treatment plants in addition to other important tasks.

SCADA is not a perfect solution and is susceptible to vulnerabilities introduced by its users. Intentional and unintentional changes or introduction of malicious malware by users can affect a network and cause major security issues.

✚ 2.6

Internet of Things (IoT)

The *Internet of Things (IoT)* incorporates embedded computing technology into non-traditional devices to enable network communication Internet connectivity. IoT devices, also called *connected devices*, are often included in discussions about pervasive computing. *Pervasive computing*, also called *ubiquitous computing,* describes devices with embedded microprocessors that allow for continuous connection to networks.

While most IoT devices are designed for consumer use, there are many IoT applications in industry called *Industrial Internet of Things (IIoT)*. This term, coined by General Electric, focuses on connecting devices in health care, transportation, and energy firms. Consider the significant influence IoT has had on the airline industry. Passengers use apps to book, manage, and track flight reservations as well as store boarding passes.

Distribution companies are large adopters of IoT. For example, UPS incorporated sensors into its vehicles. These sensors capture over 200 points of data each day that helps the company reduce vehicle emissions, fuel consumption, idle time, and other important functions.

IoT devices are often portable, inexpensive, and security is often overlooked. The expansiveness of IoT devices make their inherent security vulnerabilities especially problematic. The largest security implication is often privacy. Many devices do not have adequate security controls, such as requiring secure passwords. Moreover, most users are unaware of the extent to which data is collected, sold, or used by organizations. Therefore, both users and security administrators should make an effort to understand how much and how often data is collected. Administrators should also make an effort to encrypt the transfer of IoT data whenever possible; otherwise, data is susceptible to interception or manipulation.

Some IoT devices do not have individual user profiles. Instead, they have hardcoded embedded accounts, meaning the user cannot log out, enhance security, or change a password. These devices also tend to have *weak default* parameters—including configurations, settings, and passwords that are unable to be changed—which make them vulnerable to hacking. Additionally, devices' web interfaces, if they have one, may not have adequate security measures. This lack of interface often makes it difficult, if not impossible, to patch IoT devices, rendering them susceptible to attacks. Strategies used to offset the risks of in-home smart devices include the following.

- If possible, always change default passwords or access PINs of smart devices. Devices often do not have unique default passwords, so the chances are high of an attacker being able to guess or locate the password to your device.
- The incorporation of a web-application firewall can help prevent web-based attacks. A *web-application firewall (WAF)* is a specific firewall used to protect web applications by filtering and monitoring HTTP traffic between applications and the Internet.
- IoT devices, like most computing hardware, operate through firmware. Establish and follow a process for updating device firmware automatically as well as routinely searching for updates from manufacturer websites.

IoT devices have a variety of applications at multiple levels of society. However, some of the most prevalent and well-known applications are consumer-grade, in-home smart devices and wearable technology.

Smart Devices

Smart devices are electronic devices capable of performing important processes such as autonomous computing operations and context-aware functions. Examples include smart thermostats and in-home digital assistants. Smart devices often run in one of two modes:

- *autonomous computing*, which occurs when smart devices work independently without direct commands from a user; or
- *context-aware computing*, which employs sensors such as GPS data to connect to networks.

Smart devices, while convenient, present an avenue of attack for a potential hacker if the individual device, or the network to which it connects, is unsecured. Home or small-office networks often have the capability of establishing isolated guest networks that can be used to connect all IoT devices. Connecting IoT devices on their own network segment separate from other computing equipment reduces the ability of hackers to access computers and other personal devices.

Consider Samsung's SmartThings line of products. SmartThings enables home automation by controlling items such as lighting, radios and entertainment devices, door locks, and security alarms. Additionally, they can monitor a home for water leaks or other threats.

However, hackers can exploit device vulnerabilities and take control of their functionality. Research has found that many apps used to perform one specific function, such as monitoring battery level, can also eavesdrop on important network security functions, such as changing a password or PIN.

Wearable Technology

A popular use of IoT is wearable technology. **Wearable technology**, or *wearables*, is a type of IoT device worn by a consumer that houses a minicomputer for performing specific functions. Wearable technology includes smartwatches, such as the Apple Watch and Samsung Gear; glasses, such as Google Glass; and even some medical devices, such as Fitbit.

IoT devices in general can constitute a security threat. A simple solution for security administrators is not to allow employees to connect smart devices to the organization's network, or create a separate Wi-Fi network segment for employees' devices.

In many secure facilities, such as testing centers or military facilities, wearables are prohibited to prevent sensitive data from being captured. Wearables typically store data on the device itself, so if the device is stolen, the data is also stolen. There is currently little to no regulation or set of compliance standards for wearable technology, so devices often are left unpatched and use unsecured wireless connections, making them vulnerable to data interception.

The health-care industry is a large adopter of wearable devices. *Medical wearables* are IoT devices that operate autonomously and noninvasively through biosensors to perform a specific medical function, such as monitoring a user's heart rate, ECG measurement, or blood pressure as shown in Figure 8-2. Medical wearables have transformed the way doctors and patients exchange information. However, the use of embedded wireless systems creates significant vulnerabilities in these devices.

Updating firmware in wearables can be difficult. Many devices are dated and require firmware to be updated manually as opposed to auto updates. Some devices are simply too old and unable to update firmware at all, leaving them vulnerable to recently developed software attacks.

Figure 8-2 The health-care industry incorporates IoT devices into medical equipment to perform specific functions, such as monitoring a user's heart rate.

A significant security implication in wearable devices is a lack of authentication and encryption, making data storage and transfer susceptible to capture or manipulation. At times, a device and the information stored on it may not be the target of a given attack. If a device transmits information to a doctor's office through an unencrypted method, the recipient network can also be at risk. For example, if a user has a smart watch that transmits blood pressure information to the user's doctor, it is possible for a hacker to gain access to the device and use it to infiltrate the doctor's network, exposing terabytes of personal information such as Social Security numbers, personal addresses, and health information.

Embedded Systems Applications

Embedded systems are everywhere and in practically everything that we use. In fact, most people interact with at least one embedded system on a daily basis. Embedded systems are prevalent in specialized applications, such as in the following:

- vehicles
- drones
- multifunction printers
- aircraft
- surveillance systems
- medical systems
- Raspberry Pi devices
- field-programmable gate arrays (FPGAs)
- Arduino devices

Vehicles

 2.6

Modern automobiles typically have dozens of embedded electronic systems. Some are obvious, such as in-car entertainment systems and remote keyless entry. Other systems work behind the scenes, such as antilock brakes, airbag deployment, and autonomous emergency braking. The system of computing devices in a vehicle is called a *controller area network (CAN bus)*, as illustrated in Figure 8-3. A CAN bus allows microcontrollers to communicate with each other without a host computer.

Figure 8-3 Modern automobiles typically have dozens of computer-controlled electronic systems throughout the vehicle.

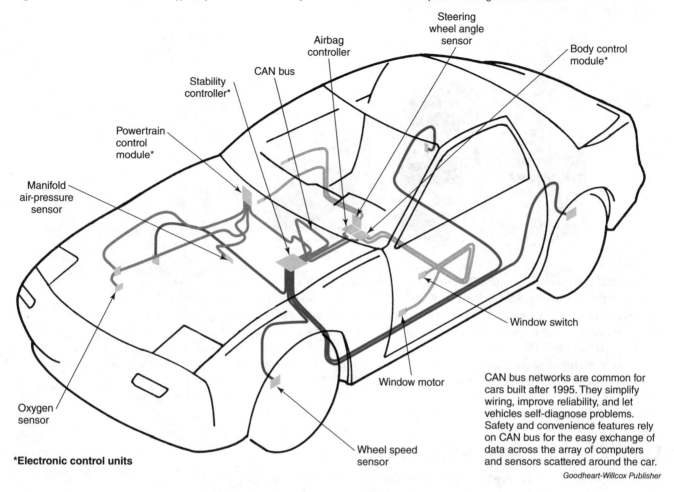

Steering
wheel angle
sensor

Airbag
controller

Body control
module*

CAN bus

Stability
controller*

Powertrain
control
module*

Manifold
air-pressure
sensor

Window switch

Window motor

Oxygen
sensor

Wheel speed
sensor

*Electronic control units

CAN bus networks are common for cars built after 1995. They simplify wiring, improve reliability, and let vehicles self-diagnose problems. Safety and convenience features rely on CAN bus for the easy exchange of data across the array of computers and sensors scattered around the car.

Goodheart-Willcox Publisher

As vehicles become more reliant on embedded systems, manufacturers have prioritized developing and improving digital-security features. Another security implication of note is the reliance of software written by third parties and used in automotive systems. Although there have not been widespread attacks on vehicles, demonstrations have shown it is possible to attack running vehicles from various attack vectors. The inherent vulnerabilities of Internet-enabled vehicles and third-party software makes it imperative for automotive manufacturers to ensure rigorous security protocols are in place in every vehicle.

Drones

+ 2.6

A **drone**, often called an *unmanned aerial vehicle (UAV)* or *uncrewed aerial vehicle*, is an unmanned, remote-controlled robot that can fly autonomously using an RTOS or controlled remotely by an operator. Many drones operate through Raspberry Pi hardware or a custom-designed system built by a user.

Drones perform a variety of tasks from agricultural operations of spraying fertilizer to delivering emergency medical supplies. They are frequently used for aerial photography and videography, especially in locations that are difficult for a person to access. Their embedded video systems produce high-power, high-quality video imaging which makes them suitable for surveillance.

Security implications of embedded software in UAVs include a vulnerability to malware, such as a Trojan, or signals beamed into the control stream of the drone. In addition, drones are vulnerable to hacking and hijacking. Often, source code for the systems in drones is available online, making it available for a hacker to inject malicious instructions using radio waves. The altered code can send data streams to an unauthorized person, tell a drone to navigate to a designated location, or cause the system to malfunction.

UAVs can be used for cyberattacks using Bluetooth sniffing to intercept communication, steal data, or perform radio-based scanning of access cards. Drones can also be configured to establish a malicious Wi-Fi network. Drones configured to broadcast malicious Wi-Fi connectivity are called *carrier drones*.

Protecting systems from rogue drones involves applying technological configurations and hardening. Deploying radar, or sound-wave detection, to scan for drones is important. Data transmissions should be unidirectional (drone to receiver) and protected. Devices should be centrally configured to prevent connections to unauthorized Wi-Fi networks.

Multifunction Printers

 2.6

A commonly overlooked area in which data can be at risk are output devices, such as printers, copiers, and fax machines. A **multifunction printer (MFP)**, often called a *multifunction device (MFD)*, is an output device that uses embedded systems to perform printing, faxing, copying, scanning, and e-mail functions.

Most people do not consider the security implications of these seemingly safe devices. Multifunction printers are connected to an organization's network, so they must be secured just as any other end device would be secured. In fact, due to embedded systems that help an MFP function, an IT team may consider dedicating more time and attention to a network printer than to a workstation. Consider the number of people who are able to connect with a multifunction printer. The large number of connections to a printer equates to a large number of different attack vectors. To help protect against a hacking attack on an MFP, a security team should use only secure or encrypted file transfer protocols, such as HTTPS and SNMPv3, instead of their unsecured counterparts whenever possible.

One possible solution for lessening the security risk of an MFP is to limit which printers are available to specific users. For example, suppose your organization has a department that handles sensitive employee information, such as payroll. This department should have its own printer on its own network segment to reduce the number of connections and potential attack vectors on this printer. Additionally, rather than printing over the Internet, an MFP can be configured to restrict printing to predefined subnetworks over a virtual network connection. This helps to secure the transfer of data to the printer.

Multifunction printers in enterprise environments should be configured to require user credentials in order to create or retrieve a print job. A user's credentials often consist of a **static code**, which is an authentication and access password or PIN that is unique to the individual and does not change automatically. The requirement of a static ensures that the only people using a printer are those authorized to do so.

Often, when an MFP is discarded, steps are not taken to remove or wipe the hard drive. This is a **vulnerable business process**, which is a set of activities by a business that can be easily exploited by a threat actor. Before discarding a MFP, the hard drive should be destroyed, sanitized, or encrypted with zero-level formatting. **Zero-level formatting** is a process in which new data is written over existing data to destroy the existing data.

 2.4

TECH TIP

Many printers have built-in auditing functions that enable you to verify information about the print job, including the time, number of pages, login names, IP address, and user who requested the print.

+ 2.6

Aircraft

There are many embedded components of an aircraft, each with a specific task. Many of these systems have straightforward functionality, such as door locking and opening mechanisms, while others are significantly more advanced. Everything from flight controls and navigation to radio communication with air traffic control is processed by an embedded system. Examples of critical embedded systems within an aircraft include the following:

- The *Integrated Modular Avionics (IMA) system* is a network of processors and sensors that provide management of navigation, guidance, and fuel management.
- Aircraft radio devices rely on secure embedded systems to enable coordination and communication from air traffic control (ATC) towers.
- A flight control system is an embedded system that enables a plane's flight operations, including take-off, landing, and autopilot operation.
- An aircraft's *flight data recorder*, commonly referred to as a *black box*, is a device that interacts with and records data provided by other components.

The most significant security implication with embedded systems in an aircraft is the vulnerability to attacks. Aircraft manufacturers, airlines, and the aviation industry must make extensive use of protective systems to guard against hacking of their systems. A cyberattack could result in catastrophic outcomes, such as disrupting information and changing data that would result in the pilot making decisions based on erroneous information. Cyber-based threats are not limited to hacks to the airplane itself; attack vectors include the airlines' operations networks and communication systems located in airports. Threats are not specific to large aircraft; smaller planes are especially vulnerable as they are often not protected by a strong physical security environment.

Consumers use on-board Wi-Fi to obtain Internet access and entertainment systems. While on-board Wi-Fi is separate from the internal network of components employed by the aircraft, there is a possibility of hacking among connected passenger devices. The open nature of the airplane's Wi-Fi makes hacking a serious risk to users of the Internet access. Therefore, unless Internet access is essential, users should avoid connecting to the public Wi-Fi signal.

+ 2.6

Smart Meters

A **smart meter** is a digital electricity meter that records information such as electrical or water consumption by a residence or organization in predefined intervals. Smart meters enable greater transparency in usage than their precursors provided and allow real-time reporting to a central system. This enables providers to record usage for billing purposes without having to visit each meter site. Security implications to consider and address with the usage of smart meters include privacy issues and cyberattacks.

- Since smart meters enable real-time recording of usage, concerns surrounding consumer privacy are prevalent. By transmitting real-time data, anyone reviewing the usage of a given meter could easily detect behavioral patterns of a building. For example, if much of an organization's electricity is used from 9:00 a.m. to 5:00 p.m., it can be assumed those are typical working hours for employees. This information can be used negatively against the organization by scheduling an attack outside of working hours.
- Cyberattacks can be a physical alteration of smart meters and injection of high frequency noise, which can prohibit the communication on the line. Because

meters are connected to power grids, attacks can cause outages or total electrical loss for geographic areas. Additionally, smart meters can be reprogrammed to provide fraudulent information, forcing consumers to pay more for access than actually used.

Surveillance Systems

Surveillance equipment utilizes embedded systems in camera and recording equipment. With the help of embedded vision technology, surveillance systems monitor critical infrastructure to prevent loss or detect damage. If a smart camera detects a problem, it can notify an administrator to take action to counter the issue.

Through use of advanced algorithms, intelligent video can reduce the amount of false positives that often occurs with surveillance systems. *Intelligent video* is digital video-recording technology integrated with analytical software. Advanced surveillance systems are not limited to traditional camera installations but used with mobile security robots and many outdoor settings such as landmarks.

As with all surveillance systems, security vulnerabilities include weak password management. Unnecessarily open ports and port forwarding can enable an unauthorized person to communicate between various network addresses. Often, security personnel are able to connect to a surveillance system remotely; as such, the enabling of remote connection makes the cameras susceptible to hacking if their systems are public-facing.

Often, attackers search for surveillance systems, as they are typically unpatched and extremely vulnerable access points to a network. Surveillance systems should be configured on a separate network segment or virtual connection to deter threat actors installing malicious content or stealing data.

Medical Systems

The application of embedded systems for the medical profession provide patient monitoring data in real-time. Defibrillators, glucose monitoring machines, dialysis machines, and infusion pumps transmit data so medical staff can provide immediate care and life-saving assistance. In addition, patient records can be electronically updated and shared with medical staff for diagnosis and health-care maintenance.

While much of the security of the devices resides with the manufacturer in the design of the embedded medical systems, medical practices must also incorporate appropriate cyber defenses, particularly in handling secure and sensitive data and maintaining equipment, including patches. In the United States, the Food and Drug Administration has issued best practices and other information for medical communities as it applies to devices and reporting.

A life-threating security implication lies in the ability of a hacker to cause a device malfunction. This could result in risks to the patient that could include death. Other serious threats include the possibility of a data breach, or the prevention of obtaining the data from the medical device.

Raspberry Pi

Raspberry Pi is a low-cost, single-board computer the size of a credit card and powered by a system on a chip (SoC), as shown in Figure 8-4. It plugs into a monitor and uses a keyboard to enable a user to explore programming in languages such as Python or Scratch. These inexpensive devices are often used in educational settings for learning computer science and can be used for gaming, IoT management, and surveillance cameras, or to replace desktop workstation computers.

Figure 8-4 A Raspberry Pi is a low-cost, single-board computer the size of a credit card and powered by a system on a chip (SoC).

Security implications associated with Raspberry Pi include the use of default passwords and user accounts on Pi operating systems. If defaults are not changed, a device can be subject to a hacker stealing credentials. Raspberry Pi devices should be hardened using firewalls and disabling unneeded ports or services.

 2.6

Field-Programmable Gate Array (FPGA)

A **field-programmable gate array (FPGA)** is a programmable hardware circuit used to carry out logical operations. It is *field-programmable* because consumers can program and reprogram multiple times. However, re-programmability is also a security implication as a cyber criminal can steal the chip and program for personal advantage. FPGA is used as a core for safety-critical embedded systems such as those in aerospace or auto industries.

 2.6

Arduino

Arduino is an open-source platform used for creating electronics projects. It relies on a simplistic single-board microcontroller and an associated software application that runs on a computer. The software is used to write code and then uploaded to the actual board.

Arduino can be used by anyone who wants to create an interactive environment such as interaction with a smart TV or the Internet. Due to its open-source nature, *all* levels of developers, from novice to expert, have the ability to manipulate or create new Arduino programs.

2.6

VoIP

Voice over IP (VoIP) is a networking protocol used to deliver voice traffic over standard network connections by enabling the use of existing networking infrastructure to build a telecommunication network. A primary security implication with VoIP is a lack of encryption, meaning an attacker can capture and replay VoIP packets. VoIP systems also face attack vectors similar to networks, including DDoS attacks and malware. Techniques for protecting VoIP systems and data include secure protocols such as Secure Real Time Protocol (SRTP), configuring multiple VLANs to separate voice from data traffic, and maintaining security updates.

SUMMARY

Mobile Devices

- In today's workplace, mobile devices are the preferred tools for employees. Mobile devices allow workers to access company information from virtually anywhere while maintaining professional efficiency and workflow.
- Companies that previously provided personal computers for each employee may now provide laptops or other mobile devices. Due to the increasing use of mobile devices, the need for strong planning, implementation, and monitoring is a crucial and necessary component of an organization's security strategy.
- To help build and maintain a security plan for mobile devices, companies often categorize devices into five categories: BYOD, CYOD, COPE, corporate-owned, or VDI.

Mobile Connectivity

- Mobile devices use a variety of connection methods to communicate with other devices.
- Mobile devices require a cellular connection, which is a network technology that enables communication by using a system of stations and transceivers that make up a cellular network. The level or generation identifies the speed and characteristics of communication. Before subscribing to a mobile service, a coverage assessment is necessary to confirm all employees will have connectivity.
- Bluetooth is a wireless connection that enables mobile devices to share data via short-range, ad-hoc communication sessions. Devices communicating via Bluetooth are paired to enable transmission. Bluetooth connections should be disabled on devices when not in use to avoid potential vulnerabilities as well as unnecessary power drain.
- Wi-Fi uses radio waves instead of copper-core or fiber-optic cable. Wi-Fi connections require routers to enable and provide communication. Transmissions are conducted on either a 2.4-GHz or a 5-GHz frequency. Configuration of wireless networks can include secured, authenticated access or open, unencrypted access, as well as password protected Wi-Fi connections.

Management Tools

- The use of mobile devices by employees in an organization requires tools to manage that use.
- The following tools can assist an IT administrator to implement secure mobile solutions: MDM, EMM, UEM, MAM, MCM, application management, microSD HSM, SEAndroid, and password management.

Securing Mobile Devices

- Some risks posed by employees using mobile devices are inherent vulnerabilities resulting from careless use of a device. Other risks are actual outside threats to security.
- Most security precautions can be configured using mobile device management tools, which can provide control over devices that connect to the network of an organization. MDM gives an administrator the ability to perform many tasks, one example being granting conditional access.

- Additional techniques for securing mobile devices can include implementing protocols to secure physical security, cameras and microphones, authentication, context-aware authentication, lockout, storage segmentation, and push notification.

Enforcement and Monitoring

- Mobile devices have specific security vulnerabilities that require enforcement and monitoring of policies. These vulnerabilities are often results of users unknowingly making uninformed decisions or from a lack of depth in user knowledge of the device.
- To prevent uninformed decisions or incomplete knowledge from causing a security issue, it is necessary to establish policies and provide education and awareness to employees on the inherent vulnerabilities of devices. It is also important for organizations to train employees on best practices for using mobile devices responsibly.
- Some policies and educational topics that employees can learn about include external media, third-party app stores, text-message threats, mobile payments, bypassing device restrictions, and custom and unauthorized firmware.

Embedded Systems

- An embedded system is a combination of hardware and software contained within a larger device used to complete a specific task. Its purpose is to control a device and enable interaction from a user.
- Embedded systems have low processing capability and handle a limited amount of data compared to a computer. These systems often rely on smart sensors to provide them with data needed to perform actions.
- An embedded system has three components: hardware, operating system, and application software. The hardware includes system on a chip, the operating system is a real-time operating system (RTOS), and the software is firmware. Hardware is needed for performance and security, and software is needed for features.

Constraints of Embedded Systems

- Embedded systems are optimized to meet programming constraints. However, since these systems are present in specialized equipment, their architectures differ from those of standard computers.
- Common constraints of embedded systems include power, computation, networking, cryptography, inability to patch, authentication, range, cost, and implied trust.

Security of Embedded Systems

- The ability to secure embedded systems is difficult due to their relatively small size and limited computing resources. Embedded systems are susceptible to attack replication and malware threats in remotely deployed systems that use a direct Internet connection with no firewalls.
- Updating a device's firmware is the best method for establishing and maintaining security of hardware and embedded devices. However, simply replacing the embedded system is sometimes more efficient than updating firmware.
- Additional security methods include segment network, enable administrative monitoring of connections, integrate third-party security management companies or applications, and change default credentials.

Industrial Control System (ICS)

- Industrial control system (ICS) is an umbrella term that describes various types of systems, tools, and instrumentation used to operate or automate industrial processes. ICSs support a variety of critical infrastructures.

- ICSs are typically managed using a system control and data acquisition (SCADA) system, which is an embedded system used to monitor an interface with controls for machines and equipment in an industrial process. SCADA gathers real-time data and analyzes it for use in monitoring and controlling industrial equipment.

- SCADA assists when human intervention is not a practical solution for control. There are situations where an industry is remote, difficult to reach, or unsafe/impractical for humans to reach.

Internet of Things (IoT)

- The Internet of Things (IoT) incorporates embedded computing technology into nontraditional devices to enable network communication Internet connectivity. Some of the most prevalent and well-known applications are consumer-grade, in-home smart devices and wearable technology.

- While most IoT devices are designed for consumer use, there are many IoT applications in industry called Industrial Internet of Things (IIoT). This term focuses on connecting devices in health care, transportation, and energy firms.

- IoT devices are often portable, inexpensive, and security is often overlooked. The expansiveness of IoT devices make their inherent security vulnerabilities especially problematic. Therefore, both users and security administrators should make an effort to understand how much and how often data is collected. Administrators should also make an effort to encrypt the transfer of IoT data whenever possible.

Embedded Systems Applications

- Embedded systems are everywhere and in practically everything that we use. In fact, most people interact with at least one embedded system on a daily basis.

- Embedded systems are prevalent in various specialized applications including vehicles, drones, multifunction printers, aircraft, smart meters, surveillance systems, medical systems, Raspberry Pi devices, field-programmable gate arrays (FPGAs), and Arduino devices.

REVIEW QUESTIONS

1. Summarize employee use of mobile devices.

2. Explain each of the five categories mobile devices are typically divided into by companies.

3. Explain four types of mobile device connection methods.

4. State the difference between Wi-Fi Direct and Wi-Fi ad-hoc network.

5. List examples of management tools used to implement secure mobile solutions.

6. Summarize techniques for securing mobile devices.

7. What techniques can be used to protect against camera and microphone vulnerabilities?

8. What is a risky login and what model can be used to avoid it?

9. Discuss three ways to enforce and monitor mobile devices used by employees.

10. Explain three common bypasses.

11. Define *embedded system* and its components.

12. What device do embedded systems rely on to provide data needed to perform actions?

13. What are the security implications of the real-time operating system (RTOS) that must be noted?

14. List and explain three common constraints of embedded systems.

15. Discuss embedded systems security.

16. Summarize industrial control systems (ICS) and the use of SCADA.

17. Explain the Internet of Things (IoT).

18. List two modes that smart devices often run.

19. How can an organization protect its network from attacks from wearables?

20. List and discuss four examples of embedded systems applications.

➕ SAMPLE SECURITY+ EXAM QUESTIONS

1. Which of these security vulnerabilities represents the largest security risk associated with wearable IoT devices?

   A. Location identification

   B. Malware

   C. SCADA infection

   D. SoC

2. An organization plans to lock down apps installed on mobile devices to prevent data loss. Which technology would help them achieve this goal?

   A. COPE

   B. MCM

   C. MMS

   D. MAM

3. Which strategy provides the employer the *most* control over the use of employees and smart phones?

   A. BYOD

   B. Drive encryption

   C. COPE

   D. CYOD

4. Which of these attack methods is often used against an RTOS?

   A. DoS

   B. Code injection

   C. Port forwarding

   D. Re-programmability

5. Which of the following is *not* a concern regarding a smartphone used as BYOD?

   A. The user engaged in jailbreaking or rooting the device.

   B. The user accessed confidential information on the device.

   C. Sideloaded apps have been installed.

   D. Containerization has been configured.

6. Which of the following will help with security issues regarding IoT devices?

   A. Ensure device firmware is regularly updated.

   B. Purchase devices only from reputable vendors.

   C. Do not allow the devices access to the Internet.

   D. Allow only administrators to use IoT devices.

7. A user installed an app using a third-party app store. Which presents the biggest risk to this action?

   A. The app uses location settings.

   B. The app may contain malware.

   C. The app developer is not known.

   D. The app may not work properly.

8. Which is a vulnerability associated with Wi-Fi Direct?

   A. It transmits at a higher speed.

   B. There is no encryption option possible for communications.

   C. The device can become infected with malware.

   D. It provides geotagging of all transmissions.

9. Which of the following is the *best* solution to protecting sensitive data on an app on a smart phone?

   A. Geofencing

   B. Preventing USB OTG access

   C. Using biometric authentication

   D. Using containerization with the app

10. What is *not* true about SCADA systems?

    A. They collect and report real-time data.

    B. They are the core of many critical infrastructure systems.

    C. They are used exclusively with infrastructure of the United States government.

    D. Their reliance on databases and web interfaces present vulnerabilities.

LAB EXERCISES

Lab Activity 8-1: Mobile Device Management

Mobile Device Manager Plus offers a free management platform for companies who wish to manage up to 25 devices within an organization. It supports Android, iOS, and Chrome OS. In his lab, you will install and explore an MDM interface.

1. Launch a web browser and navigate to a search engine. Conduct a search using the phrase ManageEngine Mobile Device Manager Plus. Navigate to the

ManageEngine website and search for the free edition. Download and follow the prompts for installation. Once installed, launch the management program.

2. Open a JavaScript-enabled browser and enter the following into the web address bar: http://localhost:9020. This should launch the management page in the browser. Note the default username and password fields are automatically filled in. Log in to the management interface.

3. The weak password should be immediately changed. Click on the **Admin** menu at the top of the page. Under Global Settings, choose **User Administration**. The only default user listed should be admin. Under the Action heading, select the **Action** button. The **Action** button is the one that looks like three dots. From the resulting menu, choose **Change Password**. Create a secure password for this app and click change.

4. In order for devices to be managed, they must first be enrolled. From the main menu, select **Enrollment**. View the different options for enrolling Apple, Android, Windows, and Chrome devices. Consider how the quick and advanced enrollment options differ and the level of security provided to an organization.

5. Next, click on **Device Mgmt**. Creating groups can allow easier management of devices. Groups can be created by geographic location, functional purpose, or business departments. Create a new device group called Sales Team. For the time being, leave the group empty, as devices can be added later. Select **Create Group>OK** to finalize the creation.

6. Next, select the **Action** button under the Action heading and choose **Associate Profile**. Review the options available to you in this section before closing the menu.

7. From the left side of the screen, select **App Repository**. Click **Add App>Apple Store App**. In the search bar, enter one. You should see an automatically generated list of apps. From that list, select **Microsoft OneDrive**. Take note of the store ID and category before selecting **Save**.

8. Add more apps from the various types listed (Android, Windows, and Chrome), and note the differences in installation for each app type.

9. Next, select Groups & Devices from the left side of the interface. Under the Action heading for the Sales Team group, select **Action>Distribute Apps**.

10. The Microsoft OneDrive app should be listed in the window. Select this app so it can be distributed. Notice the options of Silent Install, Distribute to App Catalog, and Notify users by e-mail upon distributing the app. Review the template that will be e-mailed by selecting **Configure App Distribution Mail Template**, and consider how you might customize it for an organization.

11. Review other features under Manage, specifically **Automate App Updates** and **Device Compliance**. Consider how they can help provide security and compliance to an organization.

12. Click on **Content Management**. From this area, you can deploy documents to devices. Either create a simple test document or choose one from your computer. Follow the prompts to drag and drop a document into this platform.

13. Return to **Groups and Devices**. Under the Action heading for the Sales Team group, select **Action>Distribute Document**. Under **Available Documents**, choose the file you uploaded into the platform, and click **Select**.

14. This MDM platform has a geofencing option as well. From the Device Management menu, select **Fence Policy** under the Geofencing heading. From the resulting screen, select **Create Policy**.

15. Under Define Compliance Rule, choose **Create Fence**.

16. For the Fence Name, enter Acceptable work area. Search for your city, and select it from the list. Notice the latitude and longitude will be auto filled upon your selection. Change the Fence Radius to 25 miles and click **Create**.

17. Under Define actions for non-compliant devices heading, choose **Immediately** from the Select frequency drop-down menu. Next, select **Notify** from the Select action type drop-down menu, and select **Send e-mail to admin** from the Select action drop-down menu. Add an e-mail to the list and review the default script. Then, select **Create Policy**. Note, if no mail server is configured, the policy will not be able to be created.

18. From the main menu, choose **Reports**. Notice the Security Reports available, along with App, Hardware, and Enrollment Reports. Consider how these reports will help with security management of the mobile platform.

19. Review other options this program offers, and when finished, remove it from your computer.

Lab Activity 8-2: Printer Security

You can set security measures to prevent users from printing to network printers. Manufacturers of MFPs have offered various options to offer security for their devices.

1. Click the Windows **Start** button and enter devices and printers in the search box. Select the **Devices and Printers** application in the list of results.

2. Click **Add a printer** at the top of the **Devices and Printers** window. A wizard is launched to guide you through the process of adding a printer.

3. In Windows 10, click **The printer I want isn't listed**, and in the new window, click the **Add a local printer or network printer with manual settings** radio button followed by clicking the **Next** button.

4. In the next screen on the wizard, click the **Use an existing port:** radio button, and select **LPT1: (Printer Port)** in the corresponding drop-down list. Click the **Next** button to continue.

5. Scroll through the list of printers, and select **Generic** in the **Manufacturer** column and **Generic/Text Only** in the **Printers** column, as shown. Click the **Next** button to continue.

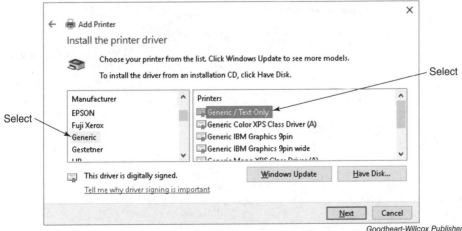

Goodheart-Willcox Publisher

6. On the next screen of the wizard, accept the default printer name by clicking the **Next** button.

7. On the next screen of the wizard, click the **Do not share this printer** radio button, and then click the **Next** button.

8. On the final page of the wizard, uncheck the **Set as the default printer** check box, and then click the **Finish** button. The printer is installed and appears in the **Devices and Printers** window.

9. Right-click on the printer in the **Devices and Printers** window, and click **Printer properties** in the shortcut menu.

10. Click the **Security** tab in the **Properties** dialog box. A list of authorized users and their printing privileges appears here. By default, what is the default printing privileges for all users? Suppose you do not want guest users to print to this printer. The Everyone special identity includes the Guest user. Therefore, the permissions for Guest need to be changed.

11. Click the **Add...** button. In the dialog box that is displayed, enter Guest in the **Enter the object names to select** text box, and then click the **OK** button. If a dialog box appears asking you to select one of several guest users, select the one named Guest. The Guest user is added.

12. Click **Guest** in the list in the **Properties** dialog box, and check the **Deny** check box for **Print** in the **Permissions for Guest** area, as shown. Remember, an explicit deny always takes precedence over an explicit allow.

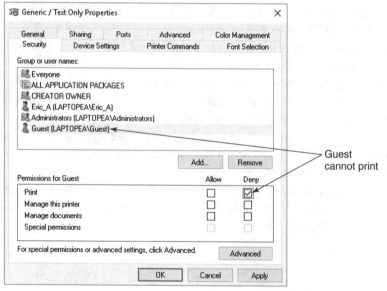

Guest cannot print

Goodheart-Willcox Publisher

13. Click the **OK** button to save the changes. Anyone logged in as the Guest user will now not be able to print to the Generic printer.

14. Launch a web browser and navigate to a search engine. Research MFPs to discover built-in security options that are offered. Do you feel one product superior than others from a security standpoint? Share your findings with your class.

CASE STUDY

IoT Data Breach

In December of 2019, Washington-based IoT provider Wyze announced a significant breach of personal data from 2.4 million customers. The data was exposed to hackers when an employee copied the data to a new database where the company was exploring new options to obtain data easily. Some of the data revealed included: usernames, e-mail addresses, connected cameras, SSID information, login information, and personal health information including height, weight, gender, bone density, bone mass, daily protein intake, and additional health information.

1. What are your thoughts on data and personal privacy related to IoT?

2. This data breach illustrates that despite local precautions of users, their data is vulnerable when stored on a third party's servers. What if anything can users do to protect their data?

3. Should IoT manufacturers be subject to HIPAA compliance as health care providers if they collect and store medical information? Defend your response.

4. The United States Senate has a bill in committee called the Internet of Things Cybersecurity Improvement Act of 2019 that calls for increased regulation on IoT devices and security. Do you feel governmental regulation is warranted for IoT devices, or should the industry develop its own guidelines? Provide a detailed argument for your opinion.

Introduction to Cryptography

LEARNING OUTCOMES

- Discuss cryptography and its role in enterprise security.
- Summarize encryption.
- List and explain examples of limitations of cryptography.
- Discuss symmetric encryption.
- Discuss asymmetric encryption.
- Explain hybrid cryptography.
- Summarize hashing.
- Summarize steganography.
- Discuss key stretching as it relates to passwords.
- Recognize types of password attacks.
- Identify and explain types of cryptographic attacks.
- Summarize quantum cryptography.

KEY TERMS

Advanced Encryption Standard (AES)
algorithm
asymmetric encryption
bcrypt
birthday attack
block cipher
Blowfish cryptography
brute-force attack
cipher suite
ciphertext
collision
cryptographic attack
cryptoperiod
data-at-rest
Data Encryption Standard (DES)
data-in-transit
data-in-use
dictionary attack
downgrade attack
elliptical-curve cryptography (ECC)
encryption key
entropy
hash table

hash-based message authentication
    code (HMAC)
hashing
high resilience
homomorphic encryption
hybrid cryptography
key exchange
key length
key pair
key strength
key stretching
key-stretching algorithm
lightweight cryptography
LM hash
low latency
man-in-the-middle attack
nonce
NTLM hash
pass-the-hash attack
Password-Based Key Derivation
    Function 2 (PBKDF2)
password cracker
password spraying

perfect forward secrecy (PFS)
plaintext
post-quantum cryptography
pre-shared symmetric key (PSK)
private key
pseudo-random number generator
    (PRNG)
public key
quantum communication
quantum computing
quantum cryptography
rainbow table
resource vs. security constraint
Rivest Cipher 4 (RC4) cryptography
Security Account Manager (SAM)
security through obscurity
session key
steganography
stream cipher
substitution cipher
symmetric encryption
transposition cipher
Triple DES (3DES) cryptography
Twofish cryptography

SECURITY+ CERTIFICATION EXAM OBJECTIVES

The following Security+ Certification Exam Objectives are covered in this chapter.

- ✚ 1.2: Password attacks
- ✚ 1.2: Cryptographic attacks
- ✚ 1.3: Pass the hash
- ✚ 1.4: Man in the middle
- ✚ 2.1: Masking
- ✚ 2.1: Encryption
- ✚ 2.1: At rest
- ✚ 2.1: In transit/motion
- ✚ 2.1: In processing
- ✚ 2.1: Hashing

- ✚ 2.5: Crypto
- ✚ 2.8: Key length
- ✚ 2.8: Key stretching
- ✚ 2.8: Salting
- ✚ 2.8: Hashing
- ✚ 2.8: Key exchange
- ✚ 2.8: Elliptical curve cryptography
- ✚ 2.8: Perfect forward secrecy
- ✚ 2.8: Quantum
- ✚ 2.8: Post-quantum

- ✚ 2.8: Ephemeral
- ✚ 2.8: Modes of operation
- ✚ 2.8: Cipher suites
- ✚ 2.8: Symmetric vs. asymmetric
- ✚ 2.8: Lightweight cryptography
- ✚ 2.8: Steganography
- ✚ 2.8: Homomorphic encryption
- ✚ 2.8: Common use cases
- ✚ 2.8: Limitations
- ✚ 4.1: Password crackers

OVERVIEW

Cryptology secures information by using mathematical algorithms to mask data so only intended recipients can process and understand it. Encrypting data is an essential part of data and network security. If all physical security controls fail and an unauthorized person is able to log on to a network, all unencrypted data is susceptible to theft, exposure, or manipulation. In a sense, cryptography is a last line of defense in data protection.

This chapter will explore introductory topics in cryptography and encryption, including limitations of cryptography, symmetric and asymmetric encryption, hybrid cryptography, hashing, steganography, key stretching, password attacks, and cryptographic attacks.

SECURITY+ NOTE

Roughly 12 percent of the Security+ Certification Exam is composed of questions regarding encryption. Therefore, it is an important topic to understand, particularly the difference between cryptography and hashing and how they work together to provide secure communications. Additionally, it may be helpful to memorize various acronyms listed in this chapter as they are not usually defined on certification exams.

Cryptography

An organization must protect the security of its data and communications. Securing data is a critical action, and one way to protect it is through the application of cryptography. *Cryptography* is a technique used to secure data by converting it into a form only the intended recipient can process and understand. The prefix *crypt* is derived from the Greek word *kryptos* meaning hidden or secret, and the suffix *graphy* meaning writing. Over time, methods of cryptography have evolved. Modern cryptography uses mathematical concepts and sets of rule-based concepts and calculations to convert the message into a format that hides the message.

Unencrypted data can be read by anyone. If *unencrypted data* is stolen, it can be read by an unauthorized person and security is at risk. However, if *encrypted data* is stolen, it can only be read by the person who was supposed to see it in the first place. To help prevent cryptography from being cracked and data accessed, a diverse set of cryptographic methods should be employed so if one level of cryptography is breached, other levels will remain to enforce protection.

 2.5

Cryptography is important to enterprise security as it protects data in its three common usage states:

- **Data-in-transit**, also called *data-in-motion*, is data transmitted across a network during a session. A *session* is an established communication over a network between two parties.
- **Data-at-rest** is data that is being stored on a computer or network.
- **Data-in-use**, also called *data-in-processing*, is data actively being used by computer or system memory.

In addition, cryptography supports data confidentiality, integrity, authentication nonrepudiation, and obfuscation.

Confidentiality

An obvious reason for using cryptography is to protect confidentiality of data. *Confidentiality* is the condition of being private or secret. By nature, cryptographic encryption supports protecting data. This means that depending on other needs, most modern cryptographic algorithms automatically support confidentiality. Confidentiality is important to an organization for maintaining its security posture.

Integrity

Cryptography is used to protect integrity of all data at rest, in transit, and in processing. *Integrity* refers to an unchanged, unimpaired, or unaltered state. Integrity means ensuring data is not changed or altered when it is stored or transmitted to another destination. Cryptographic encryption helps support data integrity by masking data until it reaches the intended recipient.

Authentication

Authentication is the process of validating or verifying identity. It may not be enough to obscure or protect the data; adding the element of a user providing and validating their credentials may require a cryptographic function that supports authentication. Unauthorized persons must be restricted from accessing confidential data.

Nonrepudiation

Nonrepudiation is the assurance that an individual or group of people cannot deny the validity of something. Essentially, nonrepudiation proves beyond doubt that a user did send the message rather than a third party.

Obfuscation

Obfuscation is the act of masking data so it is unclear or unintelligible but still usable. Obfuscation does not *transform* data; it merely makes interpretation difficult and provides protection against threat actors. This is the same fundamental principle as cryptography: securing data by converting it into a form only the intended recipient can process and understand.

It is important not to confuse obfuscation with obscurity. **Security through obscurity** is a flawed concept that a system is secure as long as only authorized people understand how the security functions. This is a flawed concept because secrecy is the primary method of security.

Encryption

Cryptography applies the concept of encryption. *Encryption* is a data protection technique that includes changing information from its original form, **plaintext**, to a disguised or encoded format called **ciphertext**. Only the intended receiver can *decrypt* the data, which is the process of changing ciphertext back to its original plaintext so it can be read.

Messages are encrypted or decrypted using algorithms. An **algorithm** is a set of procedures resulting from a mathematical formula. In simple terms, algorithms, also called *ciphers*, are formulas used to disguise plaintext, into something unreadable and then back into readable text. Two common ciphers are transposition and substitution.

- A **transposition cipher** is a cryptographic algorithm in which letters are rearranged within each word in the text. For example, *poottrsasniin* is a transposition of the word *transposition*. Deciphering a transposition cipher does not require access to a key. It only requires the thought process of rearranging the letters to form a logical word or phrase.

- A **substitution cipher** is a cryptographic algorithm in which each letter or character of a word is replaced by a different letter or character. Well-known substitution ciphers include Caesar, ROT13, polyalphabetic, Vigenère, and XOR, as shown in Figure 9-1. A *polyalphabetic substitution* cipher mixes a number of cipher alphabets in the cryptogram so each plain text letter is continuously changed.

To ensure encryption is thorough enough so only the intended recipient of a message is able to decode it, an encryption key is used. An **encryption key** is a random string of alphanumeric characters used to encrypt or decrypt a message. **Key strength** is the resilience of the key used to resist attack. The strength of a key is enhanced or reduced by the key's randomness, length, and lifespan.

- *Randomness* means there is no pattern to the numbers; they are random. **Entropy** is the degree of randomness with which a key is generated. Entropy is important to the security of a key because it makes a key less predictable. *Predictability* is a cryptographic limitation by which an encryption key can be easily guessed. A **pseudo-random number generator (PRNG)** is a number-generation algorithm that creates a sequence of numbers that appear to be randomly generated but is actually based on the same starting number. Pseudo-random number generators should not be used to create keys since the numbers they produce are not truly random.

- **Key length**, or *key size*, is the number of bits in a cryptographic algorithm's key. The size of a key can be a cryptographic limitation as short keys can be broken easier than long keys.

- **Cryptoperiod** is the span of time for which a key is authorized for use. A key may be *ephemeral*, which means it is for single use. Conversely, a key may also be *static*, which means it is for use over a defined period of time. Controlling longevity protects a key from compromise.

Ciphers adhere to specific *modes of operation*, which specify how a given cipher handles data. Three modes of operation include the following:

- An *authenticated mode of operation* is a particular operational modality in which ciphers are authenticated. An authentication code is generated that verifies the message was not manipulated at any point during its transmission. An example of a widely adopted authentication encryption mode standard is Galois counter mode (GCM).

+ 2.1

+ 2.8

+ 2.8

Figure 9-1 There are various techniques that can be used for a substitution cipher. In Example A, each letter in the alphabet is substituted with the letter preceding it by three alphabetical places. In Example B, the Vigenère cipher uses a table of the alphabet written 26 times in 26 rows. In each row, the alphabet is shifted to the left by one.

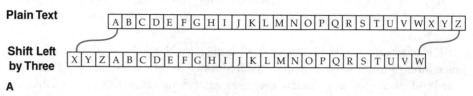

Plain Text

| A | B | C | D | E | F | G | H | I | J | K | L | M | N | O | P | Q | R | S | T | U | V | W | X | Y | Z |

Shift Left by Three

| X | Y | Z | A | B | C | D | E | F | G | H | I | J | K | L | M | N | O | P | Q | R | S | T | U | V | W |

A

A	B	C	D	E	F	G	H	I	J	K	L	M	N	O	P	Q	R	S	T	U	V	W	X	Y	Z
B	C	D	E	F	G	H	I	J	K	L	M	N	O	P	Q	R	S	T	U	V	W	X	Y	Z	A
C	D	E	F	G	H	I	J	K	L	M	N	O	P	Q	R	S	T	U	V	W	X	Y	Z	A	B
D	E	F	G	H	I	J	K	L	M	N	O	P	Q	R	S	T	U	V	W	X	Y	Z	A	B	C
E	F	G	H	I	J	K	L	M	N	O	P	Q	R	S	T	U	V	W	X	Y	Z	A	B	C	D
F	G	H	I	J	K	L	M	N	O	P	Q	R	S	T	U	V	W	X	Y	Z	A	B	C	D	E
G	H	I	J	K	L	M	N	O	P	Q	R	S	T	U	V	W	X	Y	Z	A	B	C	D	E	F
H	I	J	K	L	M	N	O	P	Q	R	S	T	U	V	W	X	Y	Z	A	B	C	D	E	F	G
I	J	K	L	M	N	O	P	Q	R	S	T	U	V	W	X	Y	Z	A	B	C	D	E	F	G	H
J	K	L	M	N	O	P	Q	R	S	T	U	V	W	X	Y	Z	A	B	C	D	E	F	G	H	I
K	L	M	N	O	P	Q	R	S	T	U	V	W	X	Y	Z	A	B	C	D	E	F	G	H	I	J
L	M	N	O	P	Q	R	S	T	U	V	W	X	Y	Z	A	B	C	D	E	F	G	H	I	J	K
M	N	O	P	Q	R	S	T	U	V	W	X	Y	Z	A	B	C	D	E	F	G	H	I	J	K	L
N	O	P	Q	R	S	T	U	V	W	X	Y	Z	A	B	C	D	E	F	G	H	I	J	K	L	M
O	P	Q	R	S	T	U	V	W	X	Y	Z	A	B	C	D	E	F	G	H	I	J	K	L	M	N
P	Q	R	S	T	U	V	W	X	Y	Z	A	B	C	D	E	F	G	H	I	J	K	L	M	N	O
Q	R	S	T	U	V	W	X	Y	Z	A	B	C	D	E	F	G	H	I	J	K	L	M	N	O	P
R	S	T	U	V	W	X	Y	Z	A	B	C	D	E	F	G	H	I	J	K	L	M	N	O	P	Q
S	T	U	V	W	X	Y	Z	A	B	C	D	E	F	G	H	I	J	K	L	M	N	O	P	Q	R
T	U	V	W	X	Y	Z	A	B	C	D	E	F	G	H	I	J	K	L	M	N	O	P	Q	R	S
U	V	W	X	Y	Z	A	B	C	D	E	F	G	H	I	J	K	L	M	N	O	P	Q	R	S	T
V	W	X	Y	Z	A	B	C	D	E	F	G	H	I	J	K	L	M	N	O	P	Q	R	S	T	U
W	X	Y	Z	A	B	C	D	E	F	G	H	I	J	K	L	M	N	O	P	Q	R	S	T	U	V
X	Y	Z	A	B	C	D	E	F	G	H	I	J	K	L	M	N	O	P	Q	R	S	T	U	V	W
Y	Z	A	B	C	D	E	F	G	H	I	J	K	L	M	N	O	P	Q	R	S	T	U	V	W	X
Z	A	B	C	D	E	F	G	H	I	J	K	L	M	N	O	P	Q	R	S	T	U	V	W	X	Y

B

Goodheart-Willcox Publisher

- *Unauthenticated mode of operation* is an encryption mode that provides the secrecy of encryption but does not include any authentication measures to verify there was no tampering of the transmission. Cipher block chaining (CBC) is an example of an unauthenticated mode of operation.

- *Counter mode (CTR) of operation* is an encryption mode that mandates both the sender and receiver of a message access a counter, which generates a new value each time a cipher block is exchanged. Counter mode is sometimes abbreviated as *CTM*.

2.8

Cryptography Limitations

Modern cryptography is essential for the security posture of an organization. However, it does have its limitations. For example, a weak key is a common limitation because weak keys are easily decrypted. In addition, encryption is typically not a fast process, often taking hours to complete, so if speed is essential, consideration must be given to how quickly a given cipher encrypts data.

Keys are an essential component of the cryptographic process. However, an important limitation in cryptography is that keys do not last forever. NIST recommends instilling time limits, called *cryptoperiods*, on keys used for encryption. Cryptoperiods are defined by various factors such as operating system usage, classification and volume of data to be protected, and personnel rotation. The longer a key is used, the greater the potential for the key to become compromised.

Despite NIST recommendations for cryptoperiods, some vendors tend to reuse keys in an effort to reduce the costs associated with generating and storing keys and the digital certificates used to create them. Key reuse is problematic and creates unnecessary vulnerabilities. For example, the reuse of a cracked key puts a system at risk for unauthorized access.

Additional common limitations to cryptography include its presence in low-power devices, devices with low latency, and highly resilient cryptography.

Low-Power Devices

 2.8

Low-power devices, such as mobile phones and tablets, are those with significantly less power than traditional computing devices, such as a computer or server. This becomes problematic when one considers the *computational overhead*, or excess usage of time, memory, and bandwidth, of employing cryptographic functions. In low-power devices, cryptography is limited to methods that use minimum resources. This can present a challenge when an organization attempts to transmit sensitive data to employees who use these devices. A **resource vs. security constraint** is a limitation in providing cryptography based on the demands of the algorithm compared to available power.

Techniques such as lightweight cryptography are used to ensure data is protected while transmitting to these devices. **Lightweight cryptography** is an encryption method that uses a small footprint so that it can meet standards while accommodating low-power devices and/or low computational complexity.

 2.8

Low Latency

 2.8

Low latency describes processing data with minimal delays. Like devices with limited power, applications that require low latency rely on encryption that has minimal computational overhead. Since time is a critical aspect of this need, it is important to use fast encryption methods or methods that use limited resources, such as homomorphic encryption. **Homomorphic encryption** is an encryption method in which data is converted into ciphertext that can be analyzed, searched, and modified without the need to decrypt the information, as illustrated in Figure 9-2.

High Resilience

 2.8

High resilience is the ability to recover from failure or lack of resources quickly. For a cryptographic system to have high resilience, it must be able to provide normal operations without changes or disruption. A system requiring high resilience must employ cryptographic systems that have strong encryption keys and enhanced processing power to provide computations.

Symmetric Encryption

 2.8

Symmetric encryption is an encryption method that uses a single key to encrypt and decrypt data. With symmetric cryptography, each device in the exchange must

Figure 9-2 Homomorphic encryption is an encryption method in which data is converted into ciphertext that can be analyzed, searched, and modified without the need to decrypt the information.

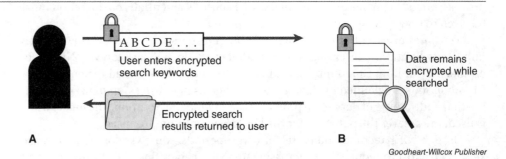

Goodheart-Willcox Publisher

have the same secret key for that transaction. The key used in symmetric cryptography is a pre-shared symmetric key. A **pre-shared symmetric key (PSK)**, also called a *secret algorithm*, is a secret value previously shared between two parties.

A **key exchange** is the process in which the cryptographic key is exchanged, or shared, between a sender and a receiver. This exchange must occur in a secure manner so only those two participants know the key. Ideally, a key exchange should enable perfect forward secrecy. **Perfect forward secrecy (PFS)** is a cryptographic security feature in which a key is changed from one encrypted conversation to another conversation or is changed after a message is sent. Imagine a scenario in which a hacker steals an encryption key. With PFS, a hacker can only read one message with the stolen key. Old or future messages cannot be decrypted because they key changes too frequently.

Symmetric Algorithm Types

Ciphers are often bundled into suites. A **cipher suite** is a combination of message authentication code, encryption, and authentication algorithms used with Transport Layer Security (TLS) and Secure Sockets Layer (SSL) for connections between a browser and server. It is important that the algorithms used in a given suite are secure, as are the keys used within them. Weak cipher suite implementations cause browser connections to become unsecure, meaning any data transmitted over a web browser, including financial or personal information, can be intercepted and decrypted.

There are two cipher suites associated with symmetric encryption: block cipher and stream cipher.

- A **block cipher** is a cipher that encrypts blocks of data in a fixed size at one time. The fixed size is usually of 64 or 128 bits. This makes this algorithm fast and capable of processing large quantities of data at one time.
- A **stream cipher** is an algorithm that encrypts each bit of data at one time by repeatedly taking one character and replacing it with another. It encrypts each bit of data at one time. This method is best for data that is smaller than 64 bits in total. Due to its speed, stream ciphers are usually employed in low-latency devices. Additionally, stream ciphers are often found as hardware solutions such as in the chips of credit cards.

Symmetric Encryption Standards

There are common symmetric encryption standards that have been used to encrypt data. Examples include the following:

- Data Encryption Standard
- Advanced Encryption Standard
- Triple DES

- Rivest Cipher
- Blowfish
- Twofish

Data Encryption Standard (DES)

In the United States, the first major symmetric cryptography algorithm was DES. The **Data Encryption Standard (DES)** is a symmetric-key algorithm that requires keys to be 56 bits in length. This bit length offers 70 quadrillion possible combinations. Although that sounds like it would be difficult to find the key used, a persistent brute-force attack could break this key. A **brute-force attack** is an intensive attack that tries every possible combination of letters, numbers, and special characters to determine the key, as shown in Figure 9-3.

As computing power increased over time, keys created with DES became easier to discover. As such, DES encryption weakened and is considered a deprecated algorithm. *Deprecated* is a term to describe a key or cipher that is no longer recommended for use. DES was effectively replaced by AES.

Advanced Encryption Standard (AES)

The **Advanced Encryption Standard (AES)**, also known as *Rijndael encryption*, is a symmetric block cipher that requires 128-, 192-, or 256-bit keys. In AES, data is transformed by steps including substitution and transformation. The data is first placed in an array, and then the cipher transforms the data over multiple rounds. The number of rounds is based on key length.

AES employs 10 rounds of transformation for 128-bit keys, 12 rounds for 192-bit keys, and 14 rounds for 256-bit key lengths. Today, AES is the official US governmental standard for cryptographic encryption.

Triple DES (3DES)

Triple DES (3DES) cryptography is a symmetric-key block cipher that employs DES encryption but uses two or three keys for a much stronger algorithm. Data is encrypted using the first key, decrypted using the second key, and re-encrypted with the third key. 3DES has been widely used in many implementations, particularly in industries that use it for financial transactions and credit card payments. Due to known vulnerabilities, NIST will retire this algorithm, and it will be disallowed after 2023.

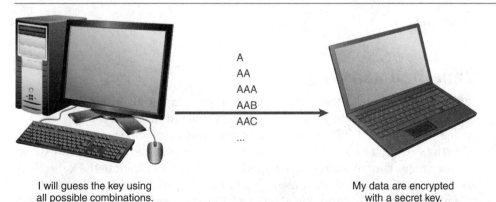

A
AA
AAA
AAB
AAC
...

I will guess the key using
all possible combinations.

My data are encrypted
with a secret key.

Figure 9-3 A brute-force attack is an intensive attack that tries every possible combination of letters, numbers, and special characters to determine the key.

Goodheart-Willcox Publisher; (devices) romvo/Shutterstock.com

Rivest Cipher 4 (RC4)

Rivest Cipher 4 (RC4) cryptography is a stream cipher characterized by a variable-size cipher and a random algorithm based on permutation. In mathematics, *permutation* is the act of arranging numbers into a specific order or set. The order of the digits in a permutation matters. For example, assume the combination for a lock is 123. The combination must be entered in that order for the lock to be opened.

Blowfish and Twofish

Blowfish cryptography is a free symmetric cryptographic encryption originally designed to replace the DES cipher. Only 64 blocks of data are encrypted at one time, which makes it a fast cipher. **Twofish cryptography** is a block cipher that encrypts data in 128-bit blocks and key sizes up to 256 bits and is the successor to Blowfish. It was a finalist when NIST conducted a contest to replace the official DES standard. Twofish is fast on 32-bit CPUs and 8-bit CPUs, which includes smart cards and embedded chips.

Asymmetric Encryption

2.8

Asymmetric encryption is an encryption method that uses two mathematically related keys, a public key and a private key, to encrypt and decrypt data. A **public key** is a key that does not need to be protected. A **private key** is an encryption key that does need protection.

When using asymmetric cryptography, data cannot be decrypted without use of both a public and private key. The receiver's device is the only device able to decrypt data since the receiver is the only person with the private key. For example, suppose a user is sending encrypted information, such as a password, to a server. When asymmetric cryptography is used, a public key is obtained from the receiver, in this case, the server, as shown in Figure 9-4. Data is encrypted at the user's machine with the public key and then sent. The receiver then uses its private key to decrypt the data.

If anyone were to intercept the data, the contents of the transmission would not be readable as the private key is at the remote site. If a private key is exposed or released, the key pair must be replaced. A **key pair** is a public and private key used in combination for asymmetric encryption. The larger the value is for a private key, the harder it is to crack.

Asymmetric cryptography is used with such security protocols as SSL/TLS, SSH, the VPN transport protocols (PPTP, L2TP, SSTP), and IPSec. There are several asymmetric algorithms in use, including

- Diffie-Hellman;
- elliptical curve;
- RSA; and
- DSA.

Diffie-Hellman

Diffie-Hellman (DH) was the first asymmetric cryptographic algorithm developed. It was created to combat the issue of secure encrypted symmetric keys being attacked during transmission. Diffie-Hellman algorithms are divided into *groups*, which determine the strength of a key. Higher group numbers offer more secure transmissions, but they require more additional computing processes to generate the keys. There are many groups that are often identified by their key such as DH-768 and labeled by a group number. For example, DH Group 1 uses keys of 768 bits, although many vendors suggest avoiding this group due to its small key.

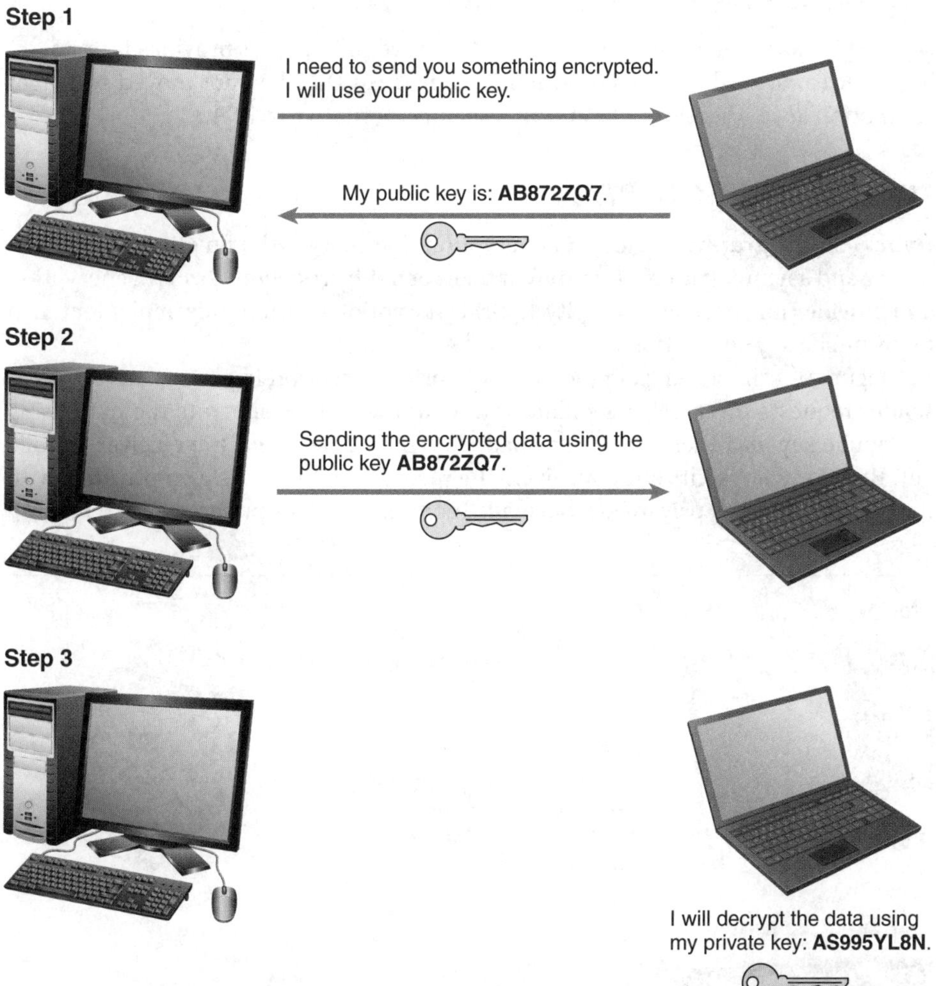

Step 1

I need to send you something encrypted. I will use your public key.

My public key is: **AB872ZQ7**.

Step 2

Sending the encrypted data using the public key **AB872ZQ7**.

Step 3

I will decrypt the data using my private key: **AS995YL8N**.

Goodheart-Willcox Publisher; (devices) romvo/Shutterstock.com

Figure 9-4 Asymmetric cryptographic algorithms use two keys, a public key and a private key, to encrypt and decrypt data. A message is encoded with the public key and decoded with the private key.

Diffie-Hellman Ephemeral (DHE) is employed when an ephemeral key is used in a key exchange. An *ephemeral key* is a temporary key that is used once. Another DH variant is the *Elliptic-Curve Diffie-Hellman (ECDH)*, which uses elliptical-curve cryptography. When ECDH is combined with an ephemeral key, it is known as *Elliptic-Curve Diffie-Hellman Ephemeral (ECDHE)*. Since ephemeral keys are not reused, their use enables perfect forward secrecy.

Elliptical-Curve Cryptography

2.8

Elliptical-curve cryptography (ECC) is an encryption method based on numbers located on an elliptical curve rather than using prime numbers. ECC employs smaller keys when compared to other cryptographic models but provides equivalent security. This makes ECC a better choice for low-power devices that do not have the computational power to work with very large prime numbers. Today, ECC is used in many applications including HTTPS, Apple's iMessage, proving ownership of bitcoins, and more.

Rivest-Shamir-Adleman (RSA)

Rivest-Shamir-Adleman (RSA) is a popular algorithm based on factoring large numbers into their prime number values. RSA encryption is used in browsers, virtual private network communications, and other secure implementations.

Digital Signature Algorithm (DSA)

Digital Signature Algorithm (DSA) is an alternative to RSA that provides faster signing. DSA is currently less secure than RSA because DSA has not moved to longer encryption keys. Therefore, DSA is not a secure alternative to RSA.

Hybrid Cryptography

Hybrid cryptography is a form of encryption that merges the functionality of symmetric and asymmetric cryptography. It takes benefits from both forms of encryption and provides for speed and security. Hybrid encryption is commonly implemented in many public key encryptions.

Figure 9-5 shows an example of how hybrid encryption is performed. First, the sender requests the receiver's public key. Next, the sender encrypts the data using the public key *and* encrypts the payload of its private key with the receiver's public key. Both keys are sent to the receiver. The receiver first uses its own private key to decrypt the sender's private key payload. Then, the sender's private key can be used

Figure 9-5 Hybrid cryptography is a form of encryption that merges the functionality of symmetric and asymmetric cryptography.

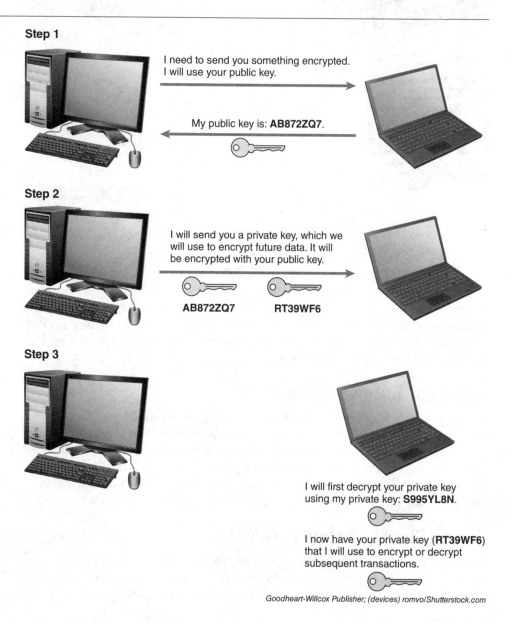

Step 1

I need to send you something encrypted. I will use your public key.

My public key is: **AB872ZQ7**.

Step 2

I will send you a private key, which we will use to encrypt future data. It will be encrypted with your public key.

AB872ZQ7   **RT39WF6**

Step 3

I will first decrypt your private key using my private key: **S995YL8N**.

I now have your private key (**RT39WF6**) that I will use to encrypt or decrypt subsequent transactions.

Goodheart-Willcox Publisher; (devices) romvo/Shutterstock.com

to decrypt subsequent data. This process is used to send the private key to a remote site securely. Once the receiver has the private key from the remote site, communication can occur with a pre-shared symmetric key.

In many hybrid implementations, the sending device does not send its own private key; instead, it creates a temporary symmetric key known as a session key. A **session key** is a symmetric key that verifies its integrity and is used for the duration of a session between a sender and receiver. Session keys verify the integrity of the sessions for which they are created and are discarded when the session is closed.

Hashing

 2.1, 2.8

Hashing is a mathematical function that creates a value based on the data. The value created by hashing is a *hash* or *hash value*. Hashing is *not* an encryption function; rather, it is a one-way process for uniquely identifying data. Hashing has many purposes in computing, and regarding security, its intended use is to ensure data integrity, not confidentiality.

One use of hashing is to ensure a file has not been manipulated in transit, as shown in Figure 9-6. If the original hash value is known, it can be compared to the hash value computed after the file is downloaded or received. If both hashes match, the downloaded file is shown to be identical to the original file, meaning it has not been altered or corrupted. The computed hash value, or output, is known as a *message digest*. The larger the digest, the more secure the hash. Any changes to the file, even something as small as changing the case of a letter in the file, will result in a new hash value for the file.

There are several hashing algorithms available and used today, including the following:

- *Message Digest Version 5 (MD5)* was developed by RSA and creates a 128-bit hash.
- *Secure Hash Algorithm (SHA)* was developed by the National Security Agency (NSA); SHA-1 produces a 160-bit hash; other variations include SHA-256 and SHA-512.
- *RACE Integrity Primitives Evaluation Message Digest (RIPEMD)* was developed by Cosic Research of the Catholic University of Leuven in Belgium; RIPEMD-160 produces a 160-bit hash.

> **TECH TIP**
>
> In addition to free utilities online, commands are used to generate hash output. In Windows, the command syntax **certutil** and **get-filehash** are used to view hash output. In Linux, you can use the command syntax **md5sum** or **sha256sum**.

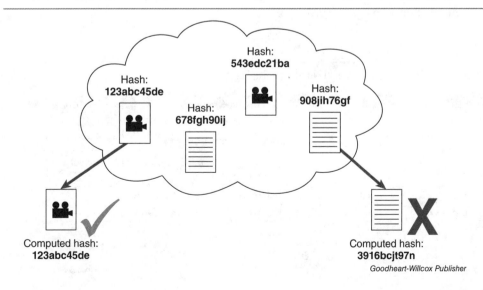

Figure 9-6 Hashing is a mathematical function that creates a value based on the data. It can be used to verify the integrity of a file that is transferred.

Goodheart-Willcox Publisher

Most hashing programs take any size input and produce an output of a fixed length. Notice in Figure 9-7A, the MD5 hashing algorithm computed a hash value for a simple word and the result was represented by 32 hex digits. In Figure 9-7B, the sentence is considerably longer than a single word, but the outcome or resulting message digest is still just 32 bits.

Another function of hashing is HMAC. **Hash-based message authentication code (HMAC)** is a message-authentication code that employs a cryptographic key as well as a hash in order to authenticate the sender. HMAC adds an authentication function as well as creating a hash by using two inputs: the message and a secret key. The sender and receiver use a pre-shared secret key that is not used anywhere else. When data is transmitted, the key and message are hashed together and sent along with the message. Once the receiver receives the message, it generates its own HMAC by using its copy of the secret key and hashing algorithm. This HMAC should match the one sent by the client. If it matches, the receiver knows the file was unaltered and came from the expected sender.

Steganography

Steganography provides a similar purpose as cryptography. **Steganography** is the practice of hiding a file, text, image, or video inside another file. The larger the host file, the easier it is to hide something in it. This is what makes pictures or video files an obvious choice to embed hidden data. However, it is important to note that steganography *hides data* from the user, whereas cryptography *masks data* to ensure its confidentiality and privacy.

What makes steganography an interesting security practice over encryption is that users do not know anything is different about a file.

Key Stretching

Often, the goal of a threat actor is to uncover a password. **Key stretching** is the process of making passwords longer, more complex, and harder to crack. A **key-stretching algorithm** is an algorithm that intentionally limits the ability of an attacker to decode passwords by requiring increased time to create a digest.

One example of key stretching is to take a password, perform a hash, hash the password hash, and repeat the process a desired number of times. This process makes the password more resilient to brute-force attacks since it is strengthened by multiple hashes. A more common example of key stretching is the addition of either salt or a nonce to a password.

2.8

TECH TIP

Although audio, video, and image files are often the first choice in hiding data with steganography, data can also be hidden in common network protocols by changing payload and header data and changing the structure of packet transmissions.

2.8

Figure 9-7 Most hashing programs take any size input and produce an output of a fixed length.

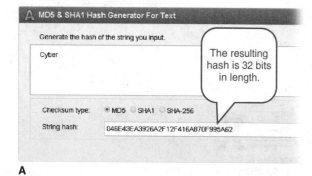

A

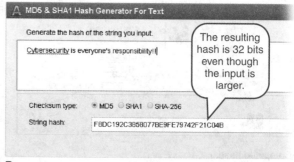

B

- *Salting* is the use of a random value, called a *cryptographic salt*, to make a hash unique. Consider the password *2@taT1ME*. Salting this password involves adding random numerical values, such as *742B*. The resulting stored password in this example would be *2@taT1ME742B*.

- A **nonce** is an arbitrarily chosen, unique number used only once in communication. The word *nonce* comes from the phrase *number used once*. Unlike a salt, a nonce does not necessarily have to be random or kept secret, provided it is not reused with the same key.

Popular examples of key stretching include the bcrypt and PBKDF2 algorithms.

Bcrypt

Bcrypt is a cipher based on the Blowfish block cipher with a nonce added to the password. The Linux operating system stores passwords separate from the user account information. Linux passwords are stored in a file called shadow in the etc folder (/etc/shadow). As in Windows, the passwords are hashed. Hashing can be done with MD5-crypt, bcrypt and sha256, or sha512 crypt. However, unlike the Windows operating system, Linux distributions, often called *distros*, use cryptographic salt. The encryption algorithm varies based on which distro is in use, but most use bcrypt.

PBKDF2

Password-Based Key Derivation Function 2 (PBKDF2) is a key-stretching technique in which a pseudorandom function, such as a hashing operation, and a salt is added to an input password. PBKDF2 is based on public-key cryptography standards (PKCS). Due to its resilience, PBKDF2 is especially resistant to rainbow attacks and dictionary attacks.

Password Attacks

There are two primary methods hackers use in an attempt crack passwords: online and offline.

- An *online attack* is one in which a hacker attempts various password attempts at a login screen. Online attacks are often very time-consuming; as such, they are impractical and not often used.

- An *offline attack* is one in which the attacker obtains a file of password values and loads the file into the attacking computer. Then, the attacker can compare the stolen password values with self-created values.

Common password attacks include dictionary attacks, brute-force attacks, rainbow tables, plaintext/unencrypted passwords, pass-the-hash attacks, and password spraying.

Dictionary Attack

A **dictionary attack** is a software-based password-cracking method that uses a list of words and their precomputed hash values to determine a user's password. Most of the words on the list are found in a dictionary, which is where the name originates. The program compares a user's password hash to the ones found in the dictionary list. If there is a match, the plaintext password of the hash is revealed.

A dictionary attack generates log data indicating many unsuccessful login attempts to user accounts. It is likely an attacker focuses on high-level privileged accounts such as Administrator, root, or webadmin, and attempts to log in to these accounts would be evident in the logs.

Brute Force

✚ 1.2

Another method that is more time-consuming, but ultimately more successful, is a brute-force attack. A *brute-force attack* is an intensive attack that tries every possible combination of letters, numbers, and special characters to determine the key. On an average computer, this type of attack could take years, depending on the size and complexity of the stored passwords. It also requires many CPU processing cycles.

To speed up the process of brute-force attacks, hackers use hash tables. A **hash table** is a data set that contains cracked passwords with preconstructed hashes for every password entered into the table. The passwords included in a hash table are more complex than words found in a dictionary. The table allows a password-cracking program to search quickly through the list for a password that was already cracked. A hash table can lead to fast cracking. However, the trade-off is the creation of an exceptionally large file for the hash table.

Most brute-force attacks increase the bandwidth and decrease performance since the systems will be running continuously in an attempt to identify the password. Just as with dictionary attacks, log entries showing unsuccessful attempts will be an indicator of a possible attack. If this is an online attack, and account lockout restrictions have been set, there will be a high number of accounts locked out due to invalid password attempts.

Rainbow Table

✚ 1.2

A rainbow table is another tool for cracking passwords and is more complex than a hash table. A **rainbow table** is a precomputed table of calculations used to speed up the password cracking process by using a hashing function and reduction function.

A rainbow table is needed for each hashing function. For example, one rainbow table is needed for Windows passwords, and another table needed for the database program MySQL.

Rainbow table files are quite large, and log data could indicate unsuccessful login attempts. Indicators of a successful attack would show potential unauthorized access to data, unusual source IP addresses, and unauthorized activities. Rainbow tables are often bought and sold between hackers.

Plaintext/Unencrypted

✚ 1.2

A *plaintext password* is one that is unencrypted. A password stored in plaintext is clearly visible and readable by anyone who uses packet sniffing tools to view data transmissions.

An account using a compromised plaintext password can be flagged by logins outside usual locations as noted by IP addresses. Unauthorized access, data content changes, and deletions to an account are often indications of a compromised account. Viewing the transfer of account and password information in a packet sniffing program can help to discover he presence of a plaintext password.

Pass the Hash

✚ 1.3

A **pass-the-hash attack** is an attack in which a hacker intercepts or steals a message digest, sends it to a remote system, and is authenticated as an acceptable user. By obtaining both a valid username and a hash digest, the hacker is able to log in to the system easily, with no need for brute force. There is no single defense against this type of attack, so diligence and defense-in-depth are vital, as is the use of firewalls, intrusion-prevention or intrusion-detection systems, IPSec, secure patching methods, and least privilege.

On a local Windows computer, user accounts and passwords are stored in the SAM database on the machine. **Security Account Manager (SAM)** is the local database of users and groups on a Windows system. The Windows operating system encrypts passwords using one of two hashing mechanisms: LM or NTLM.

LM hash, or *LAN Manager hash*, is an old (pre-Windows NT) method of encrypting local passwords. One of the encryption methods used to create the hash is DES, which is weak and not difficult to break. There are many issues with LM hash, as shown in Figure 9-8, including the following:

- Password-length limitation
- Longer passwords are divided into two halves, which allows each half to be broken separately.

An LM hash is considered much weaker than an NTLM hash. An **NTLM hash**, or *New Technology LAN Manager hash*, is Microsoft's most recent password-encryption method. It is the successor to Microsoft's LM hash and is created simply by using a hashing algorithm.

TECH TIP

The Windows SAM file is located in the **C:\Windows\ System32\config** folder, but it is not accessible after the operating system is booted.

Password Spraying

+ 1.2

Password spraying is a cryptographic attack that attempts to access a large number of user account names with just a few commonly used passwords. Most network administrators configure account lockout policies in their security settings to prevent unlimited attempts to crack a user's password. Brute-force attacks can quickly generate account lockouts with their repeated attempts at breaking the password. Password spraying, however, tries to crack the passwords of accounts using just a few commonly used passwords, such as *Password1, Summer2020*, etc. After limiting to a few guesses, typically between three and five passwords, if no match is made, the attacker moves to the next account and tries the technique again. This allows the hacker the ability to remain undetected by not locking out accounts.

Although password spraying attacks can occur on any system, they are used often on single sign-on (SSO) accounts due to the reach of potential assets if the hacker is successful. Some indicators of this attack are a high number of authentication attempts within a short period of time, and the likelihood of a high failure rate on specific IP addresses.

Cryptographic Attacks

+ 1.2

Cryptographic attacks are attacks attempting to break the secrecy of encrypted data or discovering the value of the private encryption key used to mask the data. There are various attack methods to run against cryptosystems. Some use advanced

---

Figure 9-8 LM hash is an old (pre-Windows NT) method of encrypting local passwords. One of the encryption methods used to create the hash is DES, which is weak and not difficult to break. This is one of the many issues with LM hash.

Condition	Security Issue
Uses DES encryption.	Easily cracked.
Password limited to 14 characters.	Since there are 95 printable ASCII characters, there is a finite number of possible password combinations, which is 95^{14}.
Passwords longer than seven characters are divided into two halves.	Each half can be attacked on its own, which reduces the possible combinations to 95^7.
Does not use a cryptographic salt.	Lacks security of additional random value on the password.

Goodheart-Willcox Publisher

mathematic principles, others include those that target algorithm weaknesses, attempt to intercept transactions, or force hashing collisions. Others methodically target the cryptographic algorithm with data inputs in attempts to discover the secret information.

Cryptographic attacks are either passive or active. *Passive attacks* often involve intercepting and eavesdropping on the communication channel. These are hard to identify since there is no noticeable disruption to services and performance. *Active attacks* are typically more noticeable since they actively attempt to crack encryption methods. Indicators of active attacks vary by the type of attack method, but some common changes in processing and unusual activities may be related to a potential cryptographic attack. Some of these symptoms include modification of information in an unauthorized manner, initiation of unintended or unauthorized information in transmissions. Another indictor may include alteration of authentication data such as the originator name, or timestamp of request, unauthorized deletion of data, higher than normal CPU processing, and denial of access of information.

Commonly encountered cryptographic attacks include birthday, collision, and downgrade attacks.

 1.2

Birthday Attack

A **birthday attack** is a cryptographic attack that attempts to exploit the birthday paradox. The *birthday paradox* is a mathematical theory that states in a set of randomly chosen people, some pair of them will have the same birthday. For example, in a room of 23 people, there is a 50 percent chance that two people have the same birthday. However, as the number of people in a room is increased to 70, the probability of a pair having the same birthday increases to 99.9 percent.

A birthday attack has more success when there is a higher likelihood of collisions. If there is a high number of collisions, the attacker will try to exploit the probability that there will be multiple results with the same output. Some of the indicators include the same IP address used repeatedly in unsuccessful attempts to access the system and multiple IP addresses used to try and crack the encryption. Logs may also provide data in reference to the attempted access. Birthday attacks are a form of brute-force attacks and will often generate a noticeable increase in traffic and drop in performance of the system where the encrypted data is located.

 1.2

Collision Attack

Hashing relies on the creation of unique, uncrackable hash digests. However, it is possible for a hash not to be unique. A **collision** is an error in which two different inputs produce the same message digest. Collisions are exploited by an application that compares two hashes; this exploitation is called a *collision attack*. Both MD5 and SHA-1 are found to generate collisions, and as such, neither hashing algorithm is recommended for most applications.

In a collision attack, the hacker must be in control of the input to the hash function. As with birthday attacks, a great deal of traffic is generated in an attempt to duplicate the hash digest to crack the encryption. This should have an impact on network bandwidth and performance. Successful attacks could result in unauthorized data usage and possibly deletion or alteration of data. Log data could help identify the location of the hacker, or attempted hack.

 1.2

Downgrade Attack

A **downgrade attack** is an attack in which a hacker forces a system to switch to a lower or less-secure cryptographic standard. In this cryptographic attack, the hacker is not attempting to break encryption keys, but instead is forcing the system to revert to an older, less-secure cryptographic system. For example, *SSL stripping* is a type of downgrade attack. Imagine a scenario in which a client wants to exchange information with a web server using the HTTPS protocol. However, during the transmission, a hacker forces the communication to use HTTP. Since HTTP is an older, unencrypted, and less-secure version of SSL/TLS, this action constitutes a downgrade attack. Downgrade attacks make networks far more susceptible to attack, exploitation, or penetration.

Downgrade attacks often require the hacker to be able to intercept and modify the network traffic. In a downgrade attack, the client initiates communication with the server to begin the negotiation of cipher usage. The hacker will intercept and drop this request and instead terminate the current connection. The client will try again with a lower version of SSL/TLS requested. This may result in delays due to the multiple attempts a client computer will make to generate the connection. This attack is also considered to be a **man-in-the-middle attack**, which is a network attack in which legitimate communication is intercepted and a fictitious response is forged and sent to the sender. This type of attack can be confirmed by viewing the transactions using network packet sniffers.

+ 1.4

Password Cracking

+ 4.1

A **password cracker** is a device or application that recovers a password stored on a system or compares potential passwords against hashes. Some of the programs are specifically designed for Windows, others for Linux, and some have variants for both operating systems. Common programs include John the Ripper, Cain & Abel, hashcat, and Hash Suite, as shown in Figure 9-9. Each tool offers different features, such as speed, hybrid accounts, and the number of algorithms supported.

Cracking passwords is not just for logon accounts. For example, a hacker may be running Aircrack-ng. This is a Wi-Fi password-cracking tool that targets WEP and WPA passwords. The best defense against password cracking is the use of strong passwords combined with salting and hashing actions.

Quantum Cryptography

+ 2.8

Quantum computing is a new area of computer science that uses quantum theory to enable computing bits to exist in more than one state. Traditionally, computing bits exist in one of two states: 0 or 1 (off or on). However, quantum theory percepts that matter can exist in multiple states simultaneously. Based on this thinking, quantum computing allows quantum bits, or *QuBits*, to exist in any combination of 0 or 1. The ability of QuBits to exist in varying states of on or off enables faster computational operation and less power consumption than computers that function without them. The theory that drives quantum computing can be applied to cryptology to help strengthen encryption endeavors.

Until recently, most encryption techniques were based on mathematical solutions. However, **quantum cryptography** is a cryptographic science in which quantum mechanics is used to encrypt data. Quantum cryptography relies on *quantum key distribution (QKD)*, which is the use of quantum communication to share a key between two parties. **Quantum communication** is digital communication that uses photons, or tiny particles of light, to transfer data along fiber-optic lines. The benefit of quantum communication is the inherent difficulty to crack. Photons are able to represent multiple combinations of 1s and 0s, making it nearly impossible to decode. Additionally, since data transfers exist in a quantum state, any access to the state will result in a signal change. This is due to a quantum mechanical statement known as

+ 2.8

Figure 9-9 A password cracker is a device or application that recovers a password stored on a system or compares potential passwords against hashes. Hash Suite is one of the many password cracking tools available.

the *no-cloning theorem*, which states that the perfect duplication of an unknown, arbitrary quantum state is impossible. Due to this impossibility, if anyone were to attempt to read data encoded through quantum cryptography, the quantum state would be altered, making eavesdropping easily detected.

 2.8

Computers in the future are projected to be based on quantum mechanics and will have the capability to very easily discover and break the long keys used in today's mathematical encryption codes. **Post-quantum cryptography**, sometimes referred to as *quantum-proof cryptography*, *quantum-safe cryptography*, or *quantum-resistant cryptography*, is cryptographic measures that are intended to be secure against attacks generated from a quantum computer.

SUMMARY

Cryptography

- Cryptography is a technique used to secure data by converting it into a form only the intended recipient can process and understand. It uses mathematical concepts and sets of rule-based concepts and calculations to convert the message into a format that hides the message.

- In enterprise security, cryptography is important as it protects data in its three common usage states: data-in-transit, data-at rest, and data-in-use.
- Cryptography also supports data confidentiality, integrity, authentication, nonrepudiation, and obfuscation.

Encryption

- Encryption is a data protection technique that includes changing information from plaintext to ciphertext. Only the intended receiver can decrypt the data.
- Messages are encrypted or decrypted using algorithms, or ciphers. Two common ciphers used are transportation and substitution.
- An encryption key is a random string of alphanumeric characters used to encrypt or decrypt a message. It is used to ensure encryption is thorough enough so only the intended recipient of a message is able to decode it.
- Ciphers adhere to specific modes of operation, which specify how a given cipher handles data. Three modes of operation include authenticated, unauthenticated, and counter mode.

Cryptography Limitations

- An important limitation in cryptography is that keys do not last forever. The longer or more often a key is used, the greater the potential for the key to become compromised. NIST recommends instilling cryptoperiods on keys used for encryption.
- Additional common limitations to cryptography include its presence in low-power devices, devices with low latency, and highly resilient cryptography.

Symmetric Encryption

- Symmetric encryption is an encryption method that uses a single key to encrypt and decrypt data. Each device in the exchange must have the same secret key for that transaction.
- A key exchange is the process in which the cryptographic key is exchanged or shared between a sender and a receiver. Ideally, a key exchange should enable perfect forward secrecy (PFS).
- A cipher suite is a combination of message authentication code, encryption, and authentication algorithms used with TLS and SSL for connections between a browser and server. Block and stream ciphers are two suites associated with symmetric encryption.
- Common symmetric encryption standards used include DES, AES, Triple DES, RC4, Blowfish, and Twofish.

Asymmetric Encryption

- Asymmetric encryption is an encryption method that uses two mathematically related keys, a public and a private key, to encrypt and decrypt data.
- Data cannot be decrypted without use of both a public and private key. The receiver's device is the only device able to decrypt data since the receiver is the only person with the private key.
- Asymmetric cryptography is used with such security protocols as SSL/TLS, SSH, the VPN transport protocols (PPTP, L2TP, SSTP), and IPSec.
- There are several asymmetric algorithms in use, including Diffie-Hallman, elliptical curve, RSA, and DSA.

Hybrid Cryptography

- Hybrid cryptography is a form of encryption that merges the functionality of symmetric and asymmetric cryptography. It takes benefits from both forms of encryption and provides for speed and security.
- In many hybrid implementations, the sending device creates a temporary symmetric key known as a session key. These keys verify the integrity of the sessions for which they are created and are discarded when the session is closed.

Hashing

- Hashing is a mathematical function that creates a value based on the data. It is *not* an encryption function; rather, it is a one-way process for uniquely identifying data.
- Hashing has many purposes in computing, and regarding security, its intended use is to ensure data integrity. One use is to ensure a file has not been manipulated in transit.
- Several hashing algorithms are used today including MD5, SHA, and RIPEMD. Most hashing programs take any size input and produce an output of a fixed length.
- Hash-based message authentication code (HMAC), another function of hashing, is a message-authentication code that employs a cryptographic key as well as a hash in order to authenticate the sender. It adds an authentication function as well as creating a hash by using two inputs: the message and a secret key.

Steganography

- Steganography is the practice of hiding a file, text, image, or video inside another file. The larger the host file, the easier it is to hide something in it.
- Steganography hides data from the user, whereas cryptography masks data to ensure its confidentiality and privacy. Unlike cryptography, in steganography, users do not know anything is different about a file.

Key Stretching

- The goal of a threat actor is to uncover a password. Key stretching is the process of making passwords longer, more complex, and harder to crack.
- One example of key stretching is to take a password, perform a hash, hash the password hash, and repeat the process a desired number of times. A more common example is the addition of either a salt or a nonce to a password.
- A key-stretching algorithm is an algorithm that intentionally limits the ability of an attacker to decode passwords by requiring increased time to create a digest. Bcrypt and PBKDF2 algorithms are two popular examples.

Password Attacks

- An online attack is one in which a hacker attempts various password attempts at a login screen. An offline attack is one in which the attacker obtains a file of password values and loads the file into the attacking computer. These are two primary methods hackers use to attempt cracking passwords.
- Common password attacks include dictionary attacks, brute-force attacks, rainbow tables, plaintext/unencrypted passwords, pass-the-hash attacks, and password spraying.

Cryptographic Attacks

- Cryptographic attacks are attacks attempting to break the secrecy of encrypted data or discovering the value of the private encryption key used to mask the data. These attacks are either passive or active.

- A birthday attack is a cryptographic attack that attempts to exploit the birthday paradox. The birthday paradox is a mathematical theory that states in a set of randomly chosen people, some pair of them will have the same birthday.
- A collision is an error in which two different inputs produce the same message digest. Collisions are exploited by an application that compares two hashes; this exploitation is called a collision attack.
- A downgrade attack is an attack in which a hacker forces a system to switch to a lower or less-secure cryptographic standard. The hacker is forcing the system to revert to an older, less-secure cryptographic system.

Quantum Cryptography

- Quantum computing uses quantum theory to enable computing bits to exist in more than one state. This quantum theory percepts that matter can exist in multiple states simultaneously. The theory that drives quantum computing can be applied to cryptology to help strengthen encryption endeavors.
- Quantum cryptography is a cryptographic science in which quantum mechanics is used to encrypt data. It relies on quantum key distribution (QKD), which is the use of quantum communication to share a key between two parties.
- Computers in the future are projected to be based on quantum mechanics and will have the capability to very easily discover and break the long keys used in today's mathematical encryption codes.

REVIEW QUESTIONS

1. Discuss cryptography and its role in enterprise security.
2. Explain *security through obscurity* and why it is a flawed concept.
3. Summarize encryption.
4. Briefly explain each of the three modes of operation.
5. List and explain examples of limitations of cryptography.
6. Discuss symmetric encryption.
7. Which cipher suite encrypts blocks of data in a fixed size at one time?
8. Which symmetric encryption standard is characterized by a variable-size cipher and a random algorithm based on permutation?
9. Discuss asymmetric encryption.
10. Briefly explain four types of asymmetric algorithms.
11. Explain hybrid cryptography.
12. Summarize hashing.
13. Summarize steganography.
14. Discuss key stretching as it relates to passwords.
15. Which algorithm is a key-stretching technique in which a pseudorandom function and a salt is added to an input password?
16. Explain four types of password attacks.
17. State the difference between an online attack and an offline attack.
18. Identify and explain types of cryptographic attacks.
19. Explain a password cracker.
20. Summarize quantum cryptography.

➕ SAMPLE SECURITY+ EXAM QUESTIONS

1. Which type of cipher is being used to replace APPLESAUCE with PLACSPUEEA?

   A. Caesar cipher

   B. Transposition cipher

   C. Monolithic cipher

   D. Polyalphabetic cipher

2. If a cipher key is discovered, what cryptology concept will prevent this key from being used to read future encrypted data with that key?

   A. Confusion

   B. Diffusion

   C. Perfect Forward Secrecy

   D. Obfuscation

3. You set up an encryption key for your web server transactions. Which of these will help increase the strength of a key?

   A. A key generated with PRNG

   B. A key generated with steganography

   C. A key protected by obfuscation

   D. A key that has a low value of entropy

4. Which cryptographic method would you select to send secure information that does not involve knowing any information prior to the encryption?

   A. Asymmetric cryptography

   B. Symmetric cryptography

   C. Twofish

   D. Steganography

5. Which of the following is an asymmetric encryption standard?

   A. RC4

   B. 3DES

   C. Diffie-Hellman

   D. ECC

6. If you have the unencrypted text and the encrypted text, what type of hack could be performed?

   A. Chosen plaintext attack

   B. Replay attack

   C. Known plaintext attack

   D. Chosen cipher attack

7. Which statement is not true about hashing?

   A. The same algorithm must be used by sender and receiver.

   B. A hash digest can be reverse engineered.

   C. MD5 is no longer considered secure.

   D. A hash that can be duplicated is called a collision.

8. Which is true about password encryption and Linux operating systems?

   A. Linux stores encrypted passwords in the **/etc/pwd** file.

   B. Linux does not salt their passwords unlike Windows encrypted passwords.

   C. Most Linux distributions use bcrypt to encrypt their passwords.

   D. Linux stores encrypted passwords in the same file as the user names.

9. What is true about hashing collisions?

   A. They occur when two different hashing algorithms produce the same output.

   B. They occur when it is mathematically possible to generate a reverse hash.

   C. They occur when two of the same inputs can produce two different hash outputs.

   D. They occur when two different inputs can generate the same message digest.

10. What is the best way to protect e-mail from snooping?

   A. Implement quantum encryption

   B. Use Open PGP

   C. Hash the e-mail content with SHA-256

   D. Use hybrid encryption

LAB EXERCISES

Lab Activity 9-1: Practicing Legacy Cryptography with the Vigenère Cipher

The Vigenère cipher is based on multiple substitution ciphers. A keyword is selected to determine how the message is encrypted and decrypted. Without the keyword, the cryptogram is very difficult to decode.

1. To encrypt a phrase, such as *meet at dawn*, the first step is to remove the spaces:

   meetatdawn.

2. A keyword needs to be selected that is shorter than the phrase. For this example, use the word *phones*.

3. Write the message. Underneath it, write the keyword. Repeat the keyword until you run out of letters in the message:

   meetatdawn
   phonesphon

4. Match the first letter in the message to the letter below it. This determines which row to use in the cipher matrix. For example, the letter M matches up with the letter P.

5. Using the matrix in Figure 9-1, move across the top row to the letter M. Then, move down in that column to the row that begins with the letter P (left-hand column). The letter in the cell at the intersection of the M column and the P row is the encoded letter. In this case, it is the letter B.

6. Repeat the process for the remaining letters. When done, the cryptogram should be: blsgelshka.

7. Decrypt this phrase: j jiiou laerfvs. The key is *beach*. Remember, the message uses the first row, and the key uses the first column. What did you get?

8. Challenge! Decrypt this phrase: b mzrd lxjiit wtar. The key is *rheat*, but it is encrypted with a transposition cipher. You must first decode the key, and then use it to decode the message.

Lab Activity 9-2: Viewing Cryptographic Methods

In this lab, you can view several methods of encryption and see the results of differing key lengths and encryption. In this lab, you will download and use the open source program called Cryptool. It can be found at www.cryptool.org.

1. Navigate to the Cryptool website. Locate, download, and install Cryptool1 to your local device.

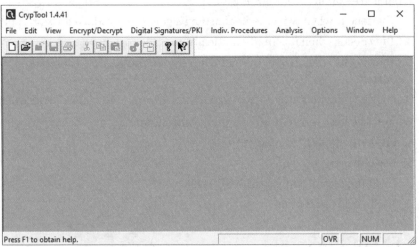

Goodheart-Willcox Publisher

2. When the program opens, select **File**>**New** to open a blank window. In the Unnamed1 window, enter the following phrase: This is a secret message. Next, select **Encrypt/Decrypt**>**Symmetric (modern)**>**RC4**.

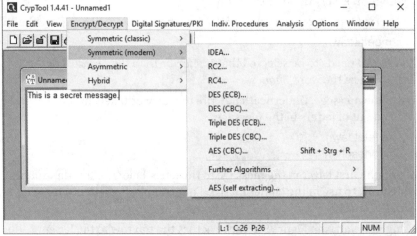

Goodheart-Willcox Publisher

3. In the Key Entry: RC4 window, select a Key length of 24 bits, and enter the following key: A1 B2 C3. Notice the key value is in hexadecimal. When you click **Encrypt**, the encrypted text appears. The encrypted text is also displayed as a hexadecimal output in the second column as well as in ASCII format in the third column of this window.

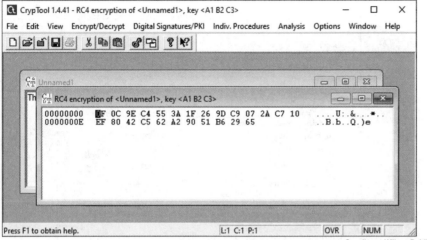

If a given ASCII character is not displayable, the character will be represented with a period (.). Highlight the hexadecimal text to see the corresponding ASCII text.

4. Close the encrypted text from Step 3, and open a new window. In the Unnamed2 window, enter the following text: Education. Select **Encrypt/Decrypt**>**Asymmetric**>**RSA Encryption**.

5. A public key is needed, so select the default user, Bob. Select **Encrypt** to view the encrypted output of Education.

6. Verify the encrypted output by selecting **Encrypt/Decrypt**>**Asymmetric**>**RSA Decryption**. Next, enter the key from Bob's information (1234) and click **Decrypt** to see the decrypted output of Education. Close the windows.

7. Cryptool also provides a random number generator. Select **Indiv. Procedures**>**Tools**>**Generate Random Numbers**. Leave the default options in place, including the values for Seed and the Length of output in bytes. Select **Generate Output** to view the results. You may have to move your mouse or press random keys on your keyboard to generate the value. Leave this output window open and repeat the process. Compare the two files. Note any patterns or similarities you notice, then close the windows.

8. The Cryptool program can also be used to test the effectiveness of passwords. Select **Indiv. Procedures**>**Tools**>**Password Quality Meter**. In this demonstration, you will be able to see how different programs apply quality measurement. Each tool is based on a different algorithm. For the first attempt, enter the following text: password. As you enter the text, the Password quality based on assumptions (and password entropy in bit) box will display the password quality. In this

example, notice most of these algorithms determine the entropy as fairly low (or predictable), as shown in the following screen capture.

Password Quality Meter ✕

Description

It is not possible to exactly determine and quantify the security of passwords. But it is possible to estimate the security of passwords based on certain assumptions.

Below you can see four implementations of password quality meters, helping you to estimate the security of your password.

Password input

Please enter your password here. The password quality is shown in percent and updated with every key stroke.

Password: | password |

☑ Show password   Password length: | 8 |

Password quality based on assumptions (and password entropy in bit)

KeePass:		29 % (37 bit)
Mozilla:		30 %
PGP:		31 % (39 bit)
CryptTool:		22 % (28 bit)

Resistance against dictionary attacks (evaluates only the first 32 characters)

Compliant with password guidelines:
- No (Password contains too few digits: 0/1)
- No (Password contains too few special characters: 0/1)

Reconstruction from words, sequences and patterns:
Found: assword
Patterns: -
Sequences: -
Keyboard sequences: -
Dictionary words [1,648,594]: ass, ssw, sword

| Password guidelines | | Cancel |

Goodheart-Willcox Publisher

Now, change the password to the following: P@SSw0rd1. In this output, one algorithm registers a much higher quality than the others.

9. Password entropy can be determined using another tool in Cryptool. From the Tools menu, select **Password Entropy**. The following window will display.

Password Entropy ✕

Description

This dialog computes a random password.

The password entropy describes how hard it is to guess the password. The password alphabet defines which characters are used to create the password. The combination of entropy and alphabet yield the password length.

Input parameters for password generation

Entropy: | | bit

Alphabet: | ABCDEFGHIJKLMNOPQRSTUVWXYZ |

☑ Use current text alphabet | Text options |

☐ Don't use confusable characters (written transmission)

☐ Don't use confusable characters (telephonic transmission)

☐ Use alphabet for WLAN passwords (64 characters)

Generated password

Password length: | | characters

Password example: | |

| Generate password | Measure password quality | Close |

Goodheart-Willcox Publisher

In the Password Entropy box, select **Text options**. Next, select the checkboxes next to Lowercase letters and Special characters, and then select **Apply**. Enter 16 in the Entropy: box and select **Generate password**. Note the password displayed in the Password example: box. Select **Measure password quality** to view the strength of the password. Now generate a password using 48 bits of entropy and compare the result to the 16-bit password. Select **Measure password quality** to compare the strength of the 48-bit password to that of the 16-bit password.

Lab Activity 9-3: Steganography in Practice

It is quite easy to hide text in an image file. In this activity, you will visually compare two image files to see if a hidden message can be detected. Then, you will hide a message in an image file.

1. Obtain the two images for this lab from your instructor.
2. Open each image file in an image viewer. Can you tell which one contains a hidden message? If so, how?
3. Launch a web browser, and navigate to the Steganography Online website (stylesuxx.github.io/steganography). Google Chrome is recommended for this activity. If this site is not available, search for online steganography tools, and select a website to use. Be aware, however, that you may not be able to decode the hidden message in the file from the student companion website.
4. Click the **Decode** tab on the web page. Then, click the **Browse...** button, navigate to your working folder, and open the Bison01.png image file. Once the image is displayed on the web page, click the **Decode** button. Is there a hidden message in this image? If so, what is it?
5. Applying what you have learned, try decoding the Bison01.png image file. Is there a hidden message in this image? If so, what is it?
6. Click the **Encode** tab on the web page. Then, click the **Browse...** button, and open the Bison01.png image file. You will add a hidden message to this image.
7. Click in the text box that contains the text Enter your message here. Enter This is a top-secret message for *your name* in the text box, and click the **Encode** button. The web page will display a binary representation of the message and two new images. The bottom image contains your hidden message.
8. Right-click on the bottom image, click **Save image as...** in the shortcut menu, and save the image as MyMessage.png in your working folder.
9. Applying what you have learned, use the website to decode the message in the MyMessage.png image file.

Lab Activity 9-4: Hash Output

It is easy to generate hashes using Windows PowerShell. Hashes can be generated with the default algorithm or an algorithm can be specified. Additionally, there are websites that can be used to generate hashes. You need Windows 10 to complete this activity.

1. Create a file using a word processor. Type the following in exactly as written: I want a career in cybersecurity.
2. Save the file with the name career in your working folder, and then close the file.
3. Open PowerShell and navigate to your documents folder where you saved the career file.
4. Enter get-filehash career.docx. Be sure to enter the file extension that matches your file. What is the default algorithm used?

5. Enter get-filehash career.docx -algorithm sha1. Compare this digest to the previous one. This time, the command forced the SHA-1 algorithm to be used.

6. Enter get-filehash career.docx -algorithm md5. This forces the MD5 algorithm to be used, as shown. What do you notice about the three different hash digests?

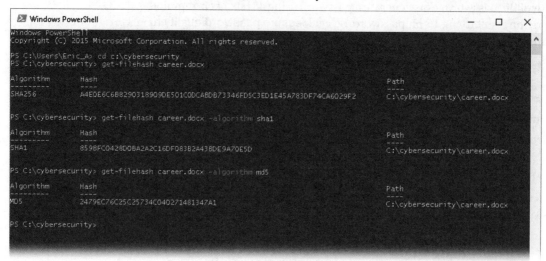

Goodheart-Willcox Publisher

7. Launch a web browser, and navigate to the OnlineMD5 website (www.onlinemd5.com).

8. Click the **Browse...** button on the page, navigate to your working folder, and select the career file.

9. Click the **MD5** radio button, and note the hash (file checksum) that is generated.

10. Repeat the process for SHA-1 and for SHA-256. Write down the SHA-256 hash digest.

11. Open the career document, add your name at the end of the file, and save the file.

12. Reload (refresh) the web page, then generate a new SHA-256 hash digest for the file. What happened?

Lab Activity 9-5: Linux Passwords and Hashes

The file containing Linux passwords can be easily viewed by the root user. It is also easy to see the hash Linux creates for a file based on the algorithm used.

1. Sign into Linux as the root user.

2. Enter cd /etc to change to the etc directory.

3. Enter ls shadow to list the file containing the user passwords. The nano text editor can be used to open this file and view its contents.

4. Enter nano shadow to open the shadow file.

5. Scroll through the file to see the user accounts that are in this system. Notice the hash of each password is not displayed. Instead, an * appears in place of the hash. To view file hashes, use the Linux command appropriate to the hash you want to calculate.

6. Press [Ctrl][X] to exit the file. If prompted, do not save any changes.

7. Enter cd ~ to move to the home directory.

8. Enter nano to create a new, blank file.

9. In the file, enter cybersecurity as the text, press [Ctrl][X], and when prompted press [Y] to save the file. Name the file MyFile.

10. Enter md5sum MyFile to view the MD5 hash of this file. Provide a screenshot.

11. Enter sha256sum MyFile to view the SHA256 hash. Provide a screenshot.

CASE STUDY

Hashing Concerns

Recently, devices from Google, Amazon, Apple, and Samsung were found to be susceptible to a Wi-Fi vulnerability in which hackers can eavesdrop on wireless communications. This vulnerability resulted from the use of an all-zero encryption key found in Wi-Fi chips produced by Broadcom and Cypress. A wide range of devices was impacted, including Kindles; Amazon Echo Dots; MacBooks; iPhones, Google Nexus, and Samsung Galaxy smartphones; and Raspberry Pi minicomputers.

This vulnerability has been labeled *Kr00k*, which is a reference to not only the all-zero encryption key, but also a previous hack called *Krack*. The Kr00k attack occurs when a disassociated device is disconnected from Wi-Fi or roams into a new access point. After disassociation occurs, the session key stored in the devices' NIC is cleared and reset to zero. This results in decryption with data remaining in plaintext. Attackers can force a dissociation of the device by sending an unencrypted, unauthenticated management frame.

Since most traffic is encrypted with TLS, some researchers have downplayed the impact of Kr00k but have recommended patching devices nonetheless.

1. The number of affected devices is currently unknown since not every wireless and IoT device was tested. What could an organization do to ensure the safety of the equipment it is using?

2. Explain the extent to which you think manufacturers are lacking in their testing of Wi-Fi chips. Is there too much reliance on defense-in-depth strategies such as TLS to help mitigate potential threats? Elaborate on your answer.

3. Patching mobile devices can be difficult for an organization as a whole as many of them are unable to be centrally managed. How can you ensure that devices connecting to your business are fully patched?

4. Github currently houses a number of utilities created to allow users to test their equipment. Which devices would you recommend testing using these tools and why?

5. Mobile device management and using COPE or CYOD strategies provide tighter controls over mobile devices. What other strategies should you consider to prevent unauthorized, potentially vulnerable devices from connecting to your business network?

Public Key Infrastructure

LEARNING OUTCOMES

- Explain public key infrastructure.
- Summarize the importance of digital certificates.
- Compare and contrast two trust models used in PKI.
- Discuss certificate management.
- Differentiate among certificate types.
- Identify and explain various certificate formats.
- Summarize certificate attributes.
- Explain PKI management and the procedures used to manage keys.
- List common cryptographic transport protocols.
- Identify types of block cipher operational modes.
- Discuss crypto service providers.

KEY TERMS

blockchain
Canonical Encoding Rules Certificate (CER)
certificate authority (CA)
certificate chaining
certificate management
certificate revocation list (CRL)
certificate-signing request (CSR)
Cipher Block Chaining (CBC)
common name (CN)
Counter Mode (CTR)
cryptographic modules
cryptographic service provider (CSP)
digital certificate
digital signature
Distinguished Encoding Rules (DER)
distributed-trust model
Electronic Codebook (ECB)

Galois/Counter Mode (GCM)
hierarchical-trust model
Hypertext Transfer Protocol Secure (HTTPS)
intermediate CA
key escrow
object identifier (OID)
Online Certificate Status Protocol (OCSP)
path validation
Personal Information Exchange (PFX)
pinning
PKCS#7
PKCS#12
PKI management
Privacy Enhanced Mail (PEM)
Public Key Cryptography Standards (PKCS)

public key infrastructure (PKI)
public ledger
registration authority (RA)
root certificate
Secure Multipurpose Internet Mail Extension (S/MIME)
Secure Real-Time Protocol (SRTP)
secure shell (SSH)
Secure Sockets Layer (SSL) protocol
SSH key
SSL decryptor
SSL/TLS accelerator
SSL/TLS handshake process
Transport Layer Security (TLS)
trust model
X.509

SECURITY+ CERTIFICATION EXAM OBJECTIVES

The following Security+ Certification Exam Objectives are covered in this chapter.

+ 2.8: Digital signatures
+ 2.8: Blockchain
+ 3.1: SSH
+ 3.1: Secure/multipurpose Internet mail exchanger (S/MIME)

+ 3.1: Secure real-time protocol (SRTP)
+ 3.1: Hypertext transfer protocol over SSL/TLS (HTTPS)
+ 3.1: IPSec

+ 3.3: SSL/TLS
+ 3.7: Certificates
+ 3.7: SSH keys
+ 3.9: Given a scenario, implement public key infrastructure.

OVERVIEW

In the previous chapter, you learned about using cryptographic algorithms for securing data to protect its confidentiality. However, when using the Internet or exchanging information in large organizations, it is not realistic to exchange pre-shared symmetric keys. Additionally, when using asymmetric encryption, it can be difficult to know the organization you contacted is the same one providing you the public key to use to encrypt your data.

In this chapter, you will learn not only about public key infrastructure (PKI), but also important related concepts, such as digital certificates; certificate, management, types, and formats; and common cryptographic protocols used for cryptographic implementation; various types of block cipher modes; and crypto-service providers.

SECURITY+ NOTE

PKI consists of many elements that work together across systems and the Internet. Each component of PKI has a distinct responsibility and role that defines how it fits within Public Key Infrastructure. Pay close attention to how these components work with each other to provide encryption and integrity. Additionally, ensure you comprehend the standards used by digital certificates and the benefits provided by digital signatures.

Public Key Infrastructure

 3.9

Public key infrastructure (PKI) is a set of policies, hardware, and procedures necessary for creating, distributing, managing, storing, or revoking public keys used in digital certificates. The process combines hardware, software, and trusted third parties to establish ownership and, thus, integrity of a public key used in digital certificates.

A concern of a public key is its authenticity. A digital signature can confirm a key is valid and from an authorized source. A **digital signature** is a computed value used to validate the sender of a digital file, such as an e-mail or document. Digital signatures are created using encryption to provide confidence that no one has tampered with the file during transmission. Digital signatures provide the assurance that users who exchange e-mails, documents, or other information are who they claim to be. A signature ensures integrity of the file to which it is applied.

2.8

Digital Certificate

3.7

A **digital certificate** is an electronic file digitally signed and used to verify that a public key belongs specifically to that person or entity. The purpose of using a digital certificate is to ensure trust or confidence in the information received. A digital certificate exchanged between users is a sign of personal trust between the parties.

Digital certificates are issued by third parties, and each certificate contains information about its purpose and owner, as well as information about the key. Certificates verify the authenticity of a key hosted online by including the digital signature of the entity that signed the certificate. Digital certificates include

- a public key;
- identified information about the person issuing the certificate; and
- digital signature(s).

Certificate Authority

A **certificate authority (CA)** is a trusted third-party source that issues and validates digital certificates. A CA is an important part of verifying a key's security. While certificates are widely available to an individual or organization that needs one, an individual or organization cannot simply generate a digital certificate on their own. Certificates are created and distributed by a certificate authority.

When obtaining a certificate, a public certificate authority can be used or it can be produced privately using an in-house authority.

- A *public CA* is a well-known company that provides services to issue and manage certificates in exchange for a fee. Going through an established, well-known company can be advantageous when producing a certificate as these certificate authorities are often the most secure and reputable. Another advantage is certificates managed by public CAs are easily accessible to clients who need access. Examples of public CA companies include GoDaddy, VeriSign, Thawte, and DigiCert.
- An *in-house CA*, or *private CA*, is a CA that creates and maintains certificates for itself or its own company. An in-house CA is often an inexpensive choice when companies are just issuing certificates to employees and company applications and services. In this case, it is easy to deploy certificates to users.

Certificate-Signing Request (CSR)

To apply for a digital certificate, a certificate-signing request is completed. A **certificate-signing request (CSR)** is a request for a digital certificate that contains an applicant's public key, additional identification information, and integrity protection. A CSR is signed with an organization's private key and submitted to a registration authority.

A **registration authority (RA)** is an authority that verifies a certificate-signing request and informs a certificate authority to issue the digital certificate. It accepts the request for a certificate and verifies a person's identity to ensure the party making the request is authorized by the organization requesting the service.

After an organization proves its identity to the RA, the request is processed and sent to an intermediate CA. An **intermediate CA** is a subordinate certificate authority that manages specific needs, such as confirming identities and processing requests.

Once the intermediate CA processes and approves a request, the approval is sent to a CA to issue a digital certificate in the organization's name. The CA can be online or offline. *Online certificate authorities (online CAs)* are CAs connected directly to a network. Conversely, *offline certificate authorities (offline CAs)* are CAs *not* connected directly to a network.

In order for the CA to provide verification systems, the CAs must be online and available. However, one excellent reason to have an offline CA is security. If a CA is used infrequently or for specific times or purposes, it is safer to keep the CA offline where it is not vulnerable to attacks.

The CA then authorizes a certificate

- in person;
- through e-mail; or
- via internal documents.

Trust Model

A concern of a public key is that a key is authentic and from an authenticated source, so trust must be involved. A **trust model** is the relationship between parties. If it is a direct trust, the parties know each other and trust the key. A third-party trust is a relationship in which each individual party involved in a key trusts a third-party that the key is authentic.

PKI uses various trust models to distribute digital certificates. The first trust model is a **hierarchical-trust model**, which is a trust model in which there is just one master CA, known as the *root CA*. The root CA signs *all* digital certificates it issues, as shown in Figure 10-1. By signing the certificates, root CAs are providing their verification that the digital certificate is authentic.

In a company that issues its own certificates within the organization, having a single CA sign all the certificates is acceptable. On a large-scale model, such as the Internet, this can be limiting due to the volume of requests going to just one CA. An alternative to the hierarchical model is a distributed-trust model. A **distributed-trust model** is a trust model in which the workload of signing certificates is distributed among several intermediate CAs as shown in Figure 10-2. Any of the intermediate authorities can validate a signature because the certificate was issued from a higher-level and trusted root CA.

Certificate Management

Certificate management is the processes, procedures, and steps taken to ensure digital certificates are current and stored properly. Certificates serve as the foundation of encryption. Improper management of certificates and keys can lead to attackers cracking the encryption, rendering an entire encryption system useless. Two important topics associated with certificate management are revocation and certificate repositories.

Figure 10-1 A hierarchical-trust model is a trust model in which there is just one master CA, known as the root CA.

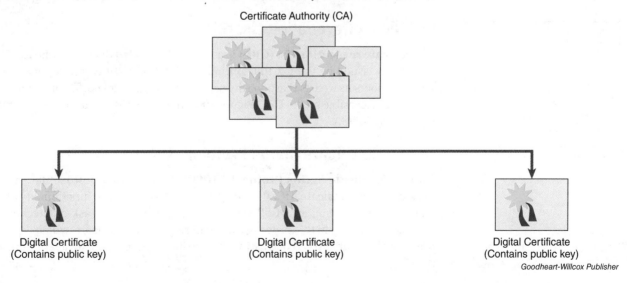

Certificate Authority (CA)

Digital Certificate
(Contains public key)   Digital Certificate
(Contains public key)   Digital Certificate
(Contains public key)

Goodheart-Willcox Publisher

Figure 10-2 A distributed-trust model is a model in which the workload of signing certificates is distributed among several intermediate CAs.

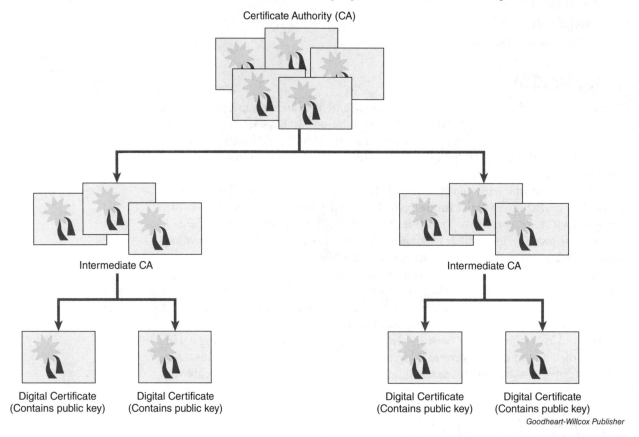

Goodheart-Willcox Publisher

Revocation

A certificate is revoked when there is a security concern. *Revocation* occurs when a certificate containing a public key is revoked, invalid, or no longer considered safe. For example, if a private key held by Amazon were exposed, it would be a reason to revoke the digital certificate from Amazon. In Windows, **path validation** is the process of verifying a digital certificate is safe and not revoked. This process involves validating the chain of certificates in the issuance path. There are two ways for a browser to check the revocation status of the certificate: a CRL and using an OCSP.

Certificate Revocation List (CRL)

➕ 3.9

A **certificate revocation list (CRL)** is a list of all canceled digital certificates. A CRL is typically issued by the CA that initially issued the certificates. The list contains serial numbers as well as reasons why certificates were revoked. The list appears in a file that is accessible by the URL. Figure 10-3 shows the CRL location for a certificate from Comodo RSA.

Online Certificate Status Protocol (OCSP)

➕ 3.9

Online Certificate Status Protocol (OCSP) is an Internet protocol for obtaining the status of a certificate. OCSP is an alternative to a CRL. The functionality of OCSP relies on CAs creating an OCSP server, which performs the task of checking for a revoked certificate. In this process, the client requests a certificate, which is provided from a web server. Instead of trusting the certificate automatically, a request is made

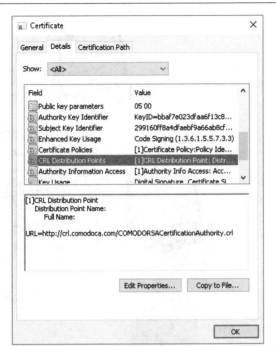

Figure 10-3 A certificate revocation list (CRL) is a list of all digital certificates that have been canceled.

to the OCSP inquiring on the certificate's status. The OCSP will respond to the client with the requested information.

This method, while effective, can cause significant bandwidth requests to the OCSP for a busy website. To handle this, OCSP stapling is a preferred method. *OCSP stapling* is a standard for verifying a certificate's revocation status in which the web server in question will request the certificate status for its own website. Once the OCSP responds with the status, the information can be cached for a designated period of time. When a client requests subsequent certificates from the website, the web server responds with the certificate and cached OCSP response. The web server will periodically query the CA and its OCSP to update its cached information.

Once the CA verifies a certificate, the user's browser is notified that the certificate is valid, and the browser should find the certificate in its own store. Once the browser has a valid certificate, information can be exchanged safely.

Certificate Repository (CR)

A *certificate repository (CR)* is a centralized, publicly accessible database of certificates. CRs assist in certificate management to enable viewing the status of a digital certificate. CRs also provide revocation information, expiration date, and certificate status. A repository can be configured to run locally or as a server-based storage component connected to a CA's network.

Certificate Chaining

Certificate chaining is the act of linking one certificate to another to establish trust between them. If the certificate is present in the local operating system, the computer can trust the public key provided in the certificate.

Figure 10-4 outlines how a public key is verified using certificate chaining. In the scenario depicted, Trey wants to log in to an Amazon account to do some shopping. The web browser asks Amazon's web server for Amazon's public key for data to be

Figure 10-4 Certificate chaining is the act of linking one certificate to another.

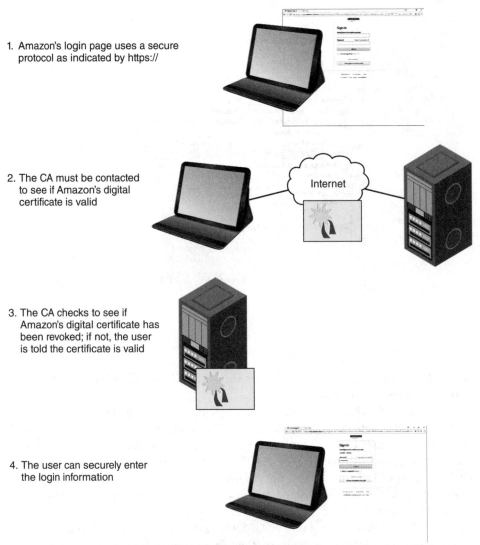

1. Amazon's login page uses a secure protocol as indicated by https://

2. The CA must be contacted to see if Amazon's digital certificate is valid

3. The CA checks to see if Amazon's digital certificate has been revoked; if not, the user is told the certificate is valid

4. The user can securely enter the login information

Goodheart-Willcox Publisher; (server) aShatilov/Shutterstock.com; (laptop) romvo/Shutterstock.com

encrypted. Before Amazon's public key can be received, Trey's browser must trust that the certificate from Amazon, which contains the public key, is actually from Amazon. To provide this validation, Amazon's web server returns a certificate signed by a CA, which is itself signed by another certificate. This is an example of certificate chaining.

Pinning

3.9

One concern about the process of contacting a CA is the possibility that information provided to a client can be compromised in an attack. When a certificate is compromised, it should be marked as invalid.

One way to ensure the public key provided is valid is to employ certificate pinning, also known as public key pinning. **Pinning** is the process of associating a host or client application with an *expected* certificate or public key. Pinning can occur when an application is developed or the first time a client acquires a site's public key or certificate. When a key is pinned during application development, the certificate or public key is preloaded into the application. When acquired the first time, it is *key continuity* and is safe, provided the site was not compromised when the key was acquired.

The pinning process is complete when the client requests the certificate that contains the public key. If this information is the same, the client can trust the public key. The entire certificate can be pinned or, more likely, the public key is pinned. This way, if the certificate expires, the public key is still used, and the app will not need to be updated with a new certificate pinned in its code.

Whether or not pinning occurs, it is important that a certificate is checked for revocation that may have occurred after the certificate and public key were published. In the example shown in Figure 10-4, the certificate presented by Amazon includes the public key, which contains information about the issuer of the CA. The request is sent to the CA. Before the CA validates the key, it must make sure the certificate Trey presented was not revoked by Amazon before its scheduled expiration date. A revoked certificate can no longer be trusted.

Certificate Types

There are multiple types of digital certificates available. In general, there are three main certificate types:

- root
- domain
- hardware and software

Root Digital Certificate

A **root certificate** is a certificate that reflects the highest point in the chain of trust for certificate authorities. A root certificate is signed by an issuing CA. For example, root certificates from CAs that are trusted by Microsoft and Apple for their operating systems are sent to client computers to be placed in their own store of trusted certificates. In Windows operating systems, the Windows Root Certificate program enables trusted root certificates to be distributed automatically during the Windows update process.

Domain Digital Certificate

A *domain digital certificate* is one issued from a web server to a client or user. These types of certificates not only ensure a web server's authenticity but also ensure the connection to the server is encrypted. Four examples of domain digital certificates are domain validation (DV), extended validation (EV), wildcard, and subject alternative name (SAN).

Domain Validation (DV) Certificate

Domain validation (DV) certificate is a certificate issued to entities after the applicant proves control of a domain. The applicant must prove ownership or administrative rights to the domain in question in order to obtain the certificate. DV certificates verify that the domain is controlled by an appropriate entity, but they do *not* imply or indicate any level of security or encryption.

Extended Validation (EV) Certificate

Extended validation (EV) certificate is a certificate that verifies legal entities of the certificate owners. EV certificates provide a level of assurance since the owner of the website must pass a thorough and globally standardized identity verification process. EV certificates display the legal identity and other legal information as part of the credentials.

Wildcard Certificate

A *wildcard certificate* is a certificate used to verify a domain and its subdomains, provided the subdomains exist within the primary domain to which a certificate is issued. For example, if a domain is called acme.com, a certificate issued to *.acme.com would apply to manufacturing.acme.com and marketing.acme.com. Wildcard certificates are often cheaper and more convenient options than creating certificates for all subdomains.

Subject Alternative Name (SAN) Certificate

Subject Alternative Name (SAN) is a certificate that allows multiple host names to be protected by a single certificate. The certificate for DigiCert shown in Figure 10-5 is a good example of an SAN. This certificate would be valid for any of the URLs listed in the field. A company does *not* need a SAN certificate if it is using a wildcard, such as *.acme.com, because that certificate would apply to any of the first-level domains. However, if the company has other names, such as acme.com and acme.net, then the SAN certificate can include those names.

Hardware and Software Digital Certificate

A *hardware or software digital certificate* is a certificate that relates specifically to hardware or software. These certificates validate the authenticity of a user as well as the software programs and services that user operates. Examples of these certificates include machine, e-mail, user, code signing, and self-signed.

Machine

A *machine certificate*, or *computer certificate*, identifies a computer on a network. This type of certificate is helpful when a network service, such as Microsoft Active Directory Services, uses machine authentication to verify and identify a computer used to access the network.

Figure 10-5 A Subject Alternative Name (SAN) is a certificate that allows multiple host names to be protected by a single certificate.

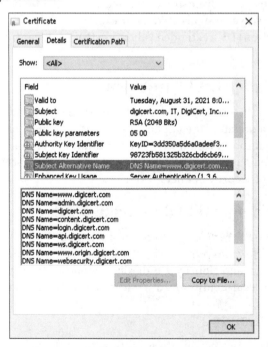

E-Mail

An *e-mail certificate*, also called a *SMIME certificate*, is used to encrypt and digitally sign e-mail. These certificates ensure messages are encrypted before being transmitted. It also verifies digital signatures placed in e-mail messages.

User

A *user certificate* is created for an individual user and often referred to as a *personal certificate*. This type of certificate is used to identify a specific user. These certificates can be used for signing documents, e-mail, and other electronic correspondence, such as contracts. For example, to ensure integrity, many colleges require that individuals providing references digitally sign the reference letters they submit.

Code Signing

A *code-signing certificate* is used by software developers to ensure users the code received and being used has not been altered or compromised by a third-party entity. Any executable code can use a digital certificate to prove identity. A common use of code-signing certificates is with device drivers installed on operating systems.

Self-Signed Digital Certificate

A *self-signed digital certificate* is one signed by the company itself. Self-signed certificates are easy to make and do not cost the company any additional money. However, these certificates are also less secure because they do not provide confirmation of identity besides what is offered by the issuing company.

Certificate Formats

Digital certificates are verified using a cryptographic function. By using a digitally signed certificate, you can be assured that a public key belongs only to the entity you want, and it has not been altered. **X.509** is the format used for public certificates to ensure consistent formatting. There are a number of different certificate encodings and file extensions associated with the X.509 format. *Encoding* refers to the act of storing human readable values in a manner that the computer can understand. These various certificate formats define or restrict the usage of the certificates for specific purposes. Some of the common extensions for the different certificate encodings include DER, CER, PEM, PFX, PKCS, PKCS#7, and PKCS#12.

- **Distinguished Encoding Rules (DER)** is a certificate that encodes the public key in binary code. This type of certificate uses the extension of .der and is commonly used by Java programs.
- **Canonical Encoding Rules Certificate (CER)** is a certificate format that can have its data encoded by DER or using Base64. *Base64* uses the ASCII character set to change the data. CERs contain only public keys, which are stored for SSL encryption.
- **Privacy Enhanced Mail (PEM)** is a certificate type that provides integrity and confidentiality to e-mail messages. PEM is the most common of the certificate extensions.
- **Personal Information Exchange (PFX)** is a certificate type used to create certificates for authentication. PFX files are commonly found in Windows and contain both a certificate and the corresponding public key.

- **Public Key Cryptography Standards (PKCS)** is a set of standards devised and published by RSA Security. While there are several standards included in PKCS, two well-known ones are PKCS#7 and PKCS#12.
- **PKCS#7** is used to sign or encrypt messages under a PKI and is often used for single sign-on (SSO). Files formatted with the PKCS#7 standard will have an extension of p7b or p7c.
- **PKCS#12** is a standard that defines a file format used to store private keys along with their corresponding public key certificate. Files associated with the PKCS#12 standard will use the .p12 extension.

Digital signatures must identify a name to each object type. An **object identifier (OID)** is a numeric value that identifies the application or service for which the certificate is used. Inside a certificate, this information is placed in a property field called Enhanced Key Usage. Figure 10-6 shows an example of an OID for a certificate from Verisign.

⊹ 3.9

Certificate Attributes

A digital certificate contains a variety of added information called *certificate attributes*. A certificate's attributes often include details about the issuer, algorithm, lifespan, and key type. The information used in the certificate can do more than document details, however. Some certificates may require a review of its attributes to see if values match in order to be authorized for use. For example, an X.509 certificate has several fields, one of which provides the attributes for the complete or distinguished name of an object. A *distinguished name* is composed of multiple attribute-value pairs including a common name. A **common name (CN)** is the fully qualified domain name (FQDN) of the web server that is to receive a certificate, as shown in Figure 10-7.

⊹ 3.9

PKI Management

PKI management is managing certificates, authorizing keys, storing keys, and other tasks to safeguard keys. One task of particular importance is key handling. *Key handling* is the methods and procedures used to manage keys and includes the following:

- *Escrow.* **Key escrow** is a process in which keys are managed by a trusted third party, such as a certificate authority. In an escrow situation, a private key is divided in half. Each half is then encrypted and delivered to the escrow organization, which stores each half separately. Each half is requested from the escrow organization by an end-user and reassembled for decryption. This process eliminates the possibility of an end-user losing a private key.
- *Expiration.* Keys have built-in expiration dates that prevent attackers from stealing keys and being able to decrypt data over extended periods of time.
- *Renewal.* Often, users will let keys expire only to create new keys. Instead of going through this time-consuming process, keys can be renewed, much like a

TECH TIP ⚙

Security administrators should identify which types of keys should be stored using key escrow. Some keys that should be considered are those used for SSH management, full disk encryption, and other critical services. Keep in mind, storing keys outside of the organization creates an additional vulnerability to consider.

Figure 10-6 An object identifier (OID) is a numeric value that identifies the application or service for which the certificate is used.

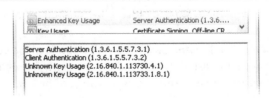

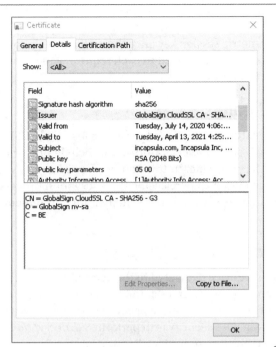

Figure 10-7 A common name (CN) is the fully qualified domain name (FQDN) of the web server that is to receive a certificate.

Goodheart-Willcox Publisher

library book. Through renewal, both public and private keys can be reused, and new keys do not have to be created. However, key renewal should be used sparingly, as the use of one key over extended periods of time makes it vulnerable to theft, misuse, or cracking.

- *Revocation.* Some keys may need to be taken out of use prior to their expiration date. *Revocation* occurs when a certificate containing a public key is revoked, invalid, or no longer considered safe. For example, if a contract with a vendor is terminated, the vendor's key will need to be revoked. After a key is revoked, the certificate authority should be notified, and the key should be entered on the certificate revocation list. Once a key has been revoked, it cannot be reinstated as active.

Cryptographic Transport Protocols

Recall that cryptography is used to protect not only data-at-rest and data-in-use but also data-in-transit. This means that cryptography should be strong enough to secure data transmitted across networks without being intercepted and cracked. Common transport protocols that enable cryptography include SSL, TLS, HTTPS, SSH, S/MIME, SRTP, and IPSec.

SSL/TLS

 3.3

When a client goes to a website where confidential or personal information must be entered, the site should encrypt the sensitive information. A popular secure transport protocol of PKI is the SSL protocol. The **Secure Sockets Layer (SSL) protocol** is a protocol that provides authentication and encryption between two computers. SSL was developed by Netscape to transmit sensitive information with encryptions. Today, SSL is implemented as part of the enhanced security protocol of TLS. **Transport Layer Security (TLS)** is a cryptographic protocol designed to provide security between networked computers. TLS is the successor to SSL, as SSL alone is no longer considered secure.

The **SSL/TLS handshake process** is an encryption process that includes verification of digital certificates based on asymmetric encryption. This handshake process results in a symmetric session key once the verification is completed. This entire transaction adds processing overhead to each request, which can result in a decline in performance, particularly on a busy web server.

SSL/TLS Accelerators

An **SSL/TLS accelerator** is a dedicated device or installed SCSI or PCI card that is connected to the web server. Accelerators often include one or more coprocessors to facilitate SSL/TLS processing. In this configuration, all encryption processing is offloaded to the accelerator, thus releasing the encryption processing from the web server's CPU. This increases overall performance for the remainder of web server transactions.

SSL Decryption

An **SSL decryptor** is a device dedicated to the decryption of SSL traffic. Firewalls are used to help a business protect confidential and sensitive data from being stolen or exposed. However, firewalls can only inspect unencrypted data. One method to protect data and maintain data security is to perform *SSL decryption*. In SSL decryption, a decryptor device, typically a firewall, will intercept the user's request for the public key from a website. The firewall acts as a proxy and generates its own public key for the user. When the user sends data, it is encrypted with the proxy's public key. The data is then decrypted with the proxy's private key. If the data meets company standards, the transaction will be encrypted with the original public key from the server, and the proxy will request the public key from the intended web server. The SSL decryption process is illustrated in Figure 10-8.

TECH TIP

Since an SSL decrypting firewall is internal, the resulting certificate can be placed on all end-user computers.

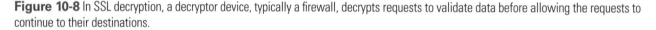

Figure 10-8 In SSL decryption, a decryptor device, typically a firewall, decrypts requests to validate data before allowing the requests to continue to their destinations.

User

This firewall is the proxy. It has its own public and private keys.

External web server G-W.com

1. The user contacts G-W.com for the public key.
2. The firewall (proxy) intercepts the request and provides its own public key.
3. After digital certificates are checked, the user encrypts the data with the proxy's public key.
4. The proxy server decrypts the data with its private key.
5. If the data is compliant, the proxy server requests the public key from G-W.com.
6. The typical encryption process then occurs between the proxy and external web server.

Goodheart-Willcox Publisher; (workstation icon) romvo/Shutterstock.com; (server icons) aShatilov/Shutterstock.com; (wall icon) beboy/Shutterstock.com

HTTPS

✚ 3.1

In a web browser, the address bar normally shows the HTTP protocol in use as http:// followed by the website address. When SSL/TLS is in use, the address bar shows https:// followed by the website address. **Hypertext Transfer Protocol Secure (HTTPS)**, sometimes referred to as *Hypertext Transfer Protocol over SSL/TLS*, is an extension of the Hypertext Transfer Protocol (HTTP) used for secure communication over the Internet. The *S* indicates a secure connection. The browser should also display an icon, typically a lock, in or near the address bar to indicate a secure connection, as shown in Figure 10-9.

SSH

✚ 3.1, 3.7

Secure shell (SSH) is a secured protocol used to provide remote administrative management of servers, routers, switches, and other devices. In SSH, the actual encryption used is based on a negotiation between the client and the server or device being used. SSH relies on the usage of SSH keys to provide the ability to create encrypted sessions by using a number of encryption technologies including symmetric and asymmetric cryptographic functions, and hashing. **SSH keys** are pairs of access credential keys used by the SSH protocol to confirm a person's identity.

S/MIME

✚ 3.1

Secure Multipurpose Internet Mail Extension (S/MIME) is an e-mail signing protocol used to increase the security of e-mail transactions. S/MIME is used to

- prove the identity of the sender through use of digital signature;
- encrypt the e-mail content between the parties; and
- ensure there is secure document sharing across networks.

SRTP

✚ 3.1

Secure Real-Time Protocol (SRTP) is a secure extension to the Real-Time Transport Protocol (RTP) for protecting Voice over IP (VoIP) communications. Networks do not send only data packets; they also are used to send voice transmissions using VoIP. The actual voice content is handled by RTP, which by itself, offers no security. Anyone who can use a packet sniffer could listen to the phone call. SRTP provides confidentiality of the voice data by encrypting its content. SRTP uses AES as its default cipher. In addition to encryption of the data, SRTP uses an algorithm over the packet's payload and parts of its header. SRTP also creates an authentication tag that is used to validate the payload content thus providing integrity.

Icon indicates a secure connection

Secure protocol

Figure 10-9 Hypertext Transfer Protocol Secure (HTTPS), sometimes referred to as *Hypertext Transfer Protocol over SSL/TLS*, is an extension of the Hypertext Transfer Protocol (HTTP) used for secure communication over the Internet.

Goodheart-Willcox Publisher

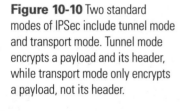

IP Security

IP Security (IPSec) is a security protocol that can be used to encrypt and secure data traveling over computer networks using the TCP/IP protocol. In essence, IPSec uses cryptographic functions to provide data integrity and confidentiality for IP traffic. IPSec also can provide authentication of data traffic over a TCP/IP network. When the IP suite was developed, security of the traffic was not considered necessary. The TCP/IP protocol suite does not include any built-in mechanisms for securing transmissions on a network. When the need became clear, the IPSec framework was developed to provide network security protocols to protect data in transmissions.

IPSec is part of an open standard in the Internet Protocol version 4 (IPv4) protocol suite. The two protocols used by IPSec that make it a secure encryption transmission method are Authentication Header and Encapsulated Security Payload. *Authentication Header (AH)* is an IPSec protocol that enables data integrity and authentication while protecting against replay attacks. *Encapsulated Security Payload (ESP)* is an IPSec protocol that enables confidentiality, data integrity, and authentication.

IPSec was developed by the Internet Engineering Task Force (IETF), an open community of researchers, manufacturers, and professionals who collaborate to ensure the Internet architecture runs smoothly and adapts to changes in technology. Specifically, IPSec has four goals.

- *Confidentiality:* data is encrypted and only available to the intended recipient.
- *Integrity:* data has not been changed or tampered with during transit.
- *Data authentication:* the sender is verified as who they say they are.
- *Protection against replay transmissions:* each packet is verified to be unique and not a duplication of previously sent data.

IPSec relies on negotiations between the sender and receiver to establish mutual authentication and encryption keys. Together, senders and receivers are known as *peers. Mutual authentication* occurs when both peers agree that the other is who they claim to be. This provides assurance to each person's identity before transmitting data securely.

There are two standard modes of IPSec implementation:

- *Tunnel mode* encrypts a payload and its header, which contains routing information. Tunnel mode is typically used for virtual connections because it provides a greater degree of security than transport mode does.
- *Transport mode* only encrypts a payload, not the header, as demonstrated in Figure 10-10. Transport mode is often used for a connection that uses another type of security, so only the payload needs to be protected.

Figure 10-10 Two standard modes of IPSec include tunnel mode and transport mode. Tunnel mode encrypts a payload and its header, while transport mode only encrypts a payload, not its header.

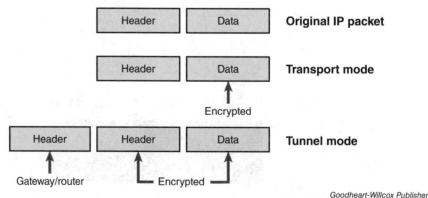

Goodheart-Willcox Publisher

Validating and Securing Network Transmission

One of the challenges in protecting data traveling over the Internet or any other computer network is ensuring the data is transmitted safely. Consider logging into an e-mail provider or online banking service. For successful login, your credentials must be encrypted and decrypted solely by the provider. Fortunately, there is a secure process used to exchange encrypted information and ensure connection to a valid site. This process involves the use of digital certificates and security keys. Another important aspect of verifying validity of information is ensuring the information is not altered from its original state.

Block Cipher Operational Modes

Knowing the amount of data that can be processed at one time is an important factor in determining how to implement cryptography. Some algorithms that operate using a *stream cipher* encrypt each bit of data at one time. Stream ciphers are best for data smaller than 64 bits in total. A stream cipher is often a solution for hardware that does not require complex encryption. However, for faster and more capable processing of large quantities of data, it is better to use algorithms that operate using block cipher modes of operation.

A *block cipher* encrypts blocks of data in a fixed size at one time. The fixed size is usually 64 or 128 bits of data, making it faster and better able to process large amounts of data than stream ciphers.

Block ciphers are often implemented in devices that need low latency processing. *Latency* is the amount of time a package of data takes to reach its destination. Therefore, *low latency* refers to a brief period of time between inputting data into an algorithm and receiving a coded output. Since blocks of data are encrypted sequentially, speed of processing the encryption is important. The faster the processing, the lower the latency.

A *block cipher mode of operation* is a cryptographic algorithm that uses a block cipher to provide encryption or confidentiality. A *mode of operation* specifies the way in which an encryption process will occur. Block cipher modes of operation include Electronic Codebook (ECB), Cipher Block Chaining (CBC), Counter Mode (CTR), and Galois/Counter Mode (GCM).

Electronic Codebook (ECB)

Electronic Codebook (ECB) is a cryptographic mode in which a message is divided into blocks with each block separately encrypted using the same key. However, ECB is not a secure cryptographic procedure as there is a concern that identical blocks of plaintext will produce identical blocks of ciphertext, thus making ciphertext easy to decipher, as illustrated in Figure 10-11.

Cipher Block Chaining (CBC)

Cipher Block Chaining (CBC) is an encryption mode in which randomization is performed on a key. CBC prevents identical blocks of ciphertext from generating. With CBC, a preceding cipher block is used as input for a subsequent block after using XOR with the next unit of plaintext. Since the first block of text does not have any ciphertext, there needs to be a process to add some randomness to this block. This is accomplished using an initialization vector. An *initialization vector (IV)* is a randomly generated number or variable added to an encryption key every time there is a transmission. On the second and subsequent passes, the key will include the previously encrypted cipher block of text.

Figure 10-11 Electronic Codebook (ECB) is a cryptographic mode in which a message is divided into blocks with each block separately encrypted using the same key.

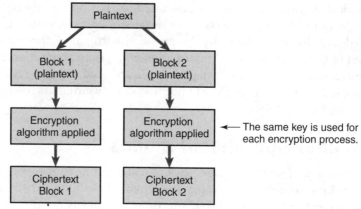

Goodheart-Willcox Publisher

2.8

Blockchains

A **blockchain** is a list of records—called *blocks*—that are linked together using cryptography. Blockchain was developed to serve as the public ledger for the Bitcoin cryptocurrency network. A **public ledger** is a record-keeping system that details the representation of blocks in a chain while preventing its contents from being edited without authorization.

Each block in a chain represents a digital record about transactions, such as the purchaser, date, time, and dollar amount of purchase. Purchaser information is stored using a digital signature in lieu of a user's name. The chain of blocks references the public database where blocks are stored. Blocks are created and added to the chain in chronological order, meaning new blocks are added to the end of the chain.

Each block in a chain has a unique hash value created from its own block and the block directly behind it, as illustrated in Figure 10-12. If a hacker were to alter a block, the resulting hash would change, along with the hash of every block in sequence. The recalculations needed to perform these operations would be an enormous undertaking and require an improbable amount of computing power.

Counter Mode (CTR)

Counter Mode (CTR) is a block cipher mode of operation that mandates both the sender and receiver of a message access a counter, which generates a new value every time a cipher block is exchanged. Counter mode is sometimes abbreviated as *CTM*. CTR begins by creating blocks of plaintext. In the first block, two values are used as a randomly generated nonce and a counter that begins with zero. The value of the

Figure 10-12 In a blockchain, each block has a unique hash value created from its own block and the block directly behind it.

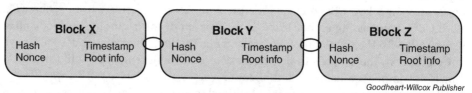

Goodheart-Willcox Publisher

nonce and the counter are then encrypted with an encryption key. This value is then XOR'ed with the plaintext to create the ciphertext. In subsequent blocks, the same process will occur, but the counter will increment by one each time.

Galois/Counter Mode (GCM)

Galois/Counter Mode (GCM) is a process that encrypts and processes message authentication codes (MACs). GCM is a widely adopted cryptographic mode in which high throughput rates are achieved. Its high performance is the primary reason GCM has been so widely adopted. GCM not only encrypts plaintext, but also generates an authentication code to verify that a message was not tampered with at any point during its transmission. GCM employs a counter, similar to CTR/CTM, but adds a string of plaintext to the transmission that lists network protocols in use.

Crypto Service Providers

To protect data throughout the encryption process, you need to select the cryptographic algorithm that best suits your implementation and system requirements. Once you choose the algorithm, a cryptographic service provider is used to implement your selection. A **cryptographic service provider (CSP)**, or *crypto service provider*, is a hardware- or software-based library that implements coding or decoding functions so that an encryption algorithm is executed. A CSP contains the implementation of cryptographic standards and algorithms and is necessary to provide encryption and decryption services in systems. The CSP manages the **cryptographic modules**, which are combinations of hardware, firmware, and software that perform cryptographic functions. Cryptographic modules, or *crypto modules*, perform the actual encryption functions, such as authentication, encryption, decryption, random number creation, and digital certificate creation.

The US federal government provides the *Federal Information Processing Standard (FIPS) Publication 140-2*, which defines the minimum security requirements for cryptographic modules in information technology hardware and software. Validated modules for these standards were approved through a joint venture between federal agencies for the United States and Canada.

Information technology components and software choose the CSP that works for their product. The primary reason encryption is used is to provide confidentiality of data. The CSP needs to support encryption for files, disk drives, and e-mails. However, in some cases, the reason for encryption is to provide high integrity. These cases result in using a CSP that employs hashing to provide the verification of data from its original source to the destination or to guarantee nonrepudiation.

In other uses, there are products specific for devices that have lower power needs, such as with mobile or IoT devices, and light-weight modules for devices that have low latency that need quicker encryption and decryption processing. These types of devices typically use smaller keys and symmetric encryption. Another reason for using encryption may be to ensure high resiliency. High-resiliency encryption may need to provide a higher degree of protection against attacks. Large key sizes are common with this CSP.

It will always be a challenge for goals of a system to provide the best cryptographic function within the constraints of the system. Providers must balance the type of encryption, processing time, and other factors against the desired outcome of the resource in question.

TECH TIP

In Windows 10, CSP provides three management services: confirming signatures for Windows files, adding and removing Trusted Root Certification Authority certificates on the computer, and retrieving root certificates from Windows updates.

SUMMARY

Public Key Infrastructure

- Public key infrastructure (PKI) is a set of policies, hardware, and procedures necessary for creating, distributing, managing, storing, or revoking public keys used in digital certificates.
- PKI process combines hardware, software, and trusted third parties to establish ownership and, thus, integrity of a public key used in digital certificates.
- To ensure the authenticity of a public key, a digital signature is used to confirm a key is valid and from an authorized source. A signature is created using encryption.

Digital Certificate

- A digital certificate is an electronic file digitally signed and used to verify that a public key belongs specifically to that person or entity.
- The purpose of using a digital certificate is to ensure trust or confidence in the information received. It is a sign of personal trust between the parties.
- Digital certificates are issued and validated by third parties, usually a certificate authority (CA). They include a public key, identified information about the person issuing the certificate, and digital signature(s).
- To apply for a digital certificate, a certificate-signing request (CSR) is completed.

Trust Model

- A trust model is the relationship between parties. Two common trust models PKI uses are hierarchical-trust model and distributed-trust model.
- The hierarchical-trust model is a trust model in which there is just one master CA, known as the root CA. The root CA signs all digital certificates it issues. This model is common in small companies that issue their own certificates.
- A distributed-trust model involves the workload of signing certificates being distributed among several intermediate CAs. Any of the intermediate CAs can validate a signature because the certificate was issued from a higher-level and trusted root CA.

Certificate Management

- Certificate management is the processes, procedures, and steps taken to ensure digital certificates are current and stored properly. Two important topics associated with certificate management are revocation and certificate repositories.
- Certificates are revoked when there is a security concern. Revocation occurs when a certificate containing a public key is revoked, invalid, or no longer considered safe.
- A certificate repository (CR) is a centralized, publicly accessible database of certificates. CRs assist in viewing the status of a digital certificate, revocation information, expiration date, and certificate status.
- Certificate chaining is the act of linking one certificate to another to establish trust between them. If the certificate is present in the local operating system, the computer can trust the public key provided in the certificate.
- To ensure a public key provided is valid is to employ certificate pinning. Pinning is the process of associating a host or client application with an expected certificate or public key.

- Whether or not pinning occurs, it is important that a certificate is checked for revocation that may have occurred after the certificate and public key were published.

Certificate Types

- There are multiple types of digital certificates available. In general, there are three main certificate types: root, domain, and hardware and software.
- A root certificate reflects the highest point in the chain of trust for certificate authorities. A root certificate is signed by an issuing CA.
- A domain digital certificate is one issued from a web server to a client or user. These types of certificates ensure a web server's authenticity as well as the connection to the server is encrypted. Four examples of these certificates include DV, EV, wildcard, and SAN.
- A hardware or software digital certificate validates the authenticity of a user as well as the software programs and services that user operates. Examples include machine, e-mail, user, code signing, and self-signed certificates.

Certificate Formats

- Digital certificates are verified using a cryptographic function. This allows a user to be assured that a public key belongs only to the entity wanted, and it has not been altered.
- X.509 is the format used for public certificates to ensure consistent formatting.
- Various certificate formats define or restrict the usage of the certificates for specific purposes. Some of the common extensions for the different certificate encodings include DER, CER, PEM, PFX, PKCS, PKCS#7, and PKCS#12.

Certificate Attributes

- A digital certificate contains a variety of added information called certificate attributes. It often include details about the issuer, algorithm, lifespan, and key type. Attributes are also used to see if values match in order to be authorized for use.
- A distinguished name is composed of multiple attribute-value pairs including a common name. A common name (CN) is the fully qualified domain name (FQDN) of the web server that is to receive a certificate.

PKI Management

- PKI management is managing certificates, authorizing keys, storing keys, and other tasks to safeguard keys.
- Key handling is an important task in PKI management. It is the methods and procedures used to manage keys. Methods and procedures include escrow, expiration, renewal, and revocation.

Cryptographic Transport Protocols

- Cryptography is used to protect data-at-rest, data-in-use, and data-in-transit. Cryptography should be strong enough to secure data transmitted across networks without being intercepted and cracked.
- Common cryptographic transport protocols include SSL, TLS, HTTPS, SSH, S/MIME, SRTP, and IPSec.
- One of the challenges in protecting data is ensuring the data is transmitted safely. To ensure the connection is safe, the process involves the use of digital certificates and security keys as well as ensuring the information is not altered from its original state.

Block Cipher Operational Modes

- A block cipher encrypts blocks of data in a fixed size at one time, usually 64 or 128 bits of data. This makes it faster and better able to process large amounts of data than stream ciphers.
- A block cipher mode of operation is a cryptographic algorithm that uses a block cipher to provide encryption or confidentiality.
- Block cipher modes of operation include Electronic Codebook (ECB), Cipher Block Chaining (CBC), Counter Mode (CTR), and Galois/Counter Mode (GCM).

Crypto Service Providers

- A cryptographic service provider (CSP) is a hardware- or software-based library that implements coding or decoding functions so that an encryption algorithm is executed.
- A CSP manages the cryptographic modules. These modules perform the actual encryption function.
- The primary reason encryption is used is to provide confidentiality of data. The CSP needs to support encryption for files, disk drives, and e-mails.
- For devices with lower power needs, these devices typically use smaller keys and symmetric encryption. Another reason for using encryption may be to ensure high resiliency. High-resiliency encryption may need to provide a higher degree of protection against attacks. Large key sizes are common with this CSP.

REVIEW QUESTIONS

1. Explain public key infrastructure.
2. How is a digital signature created and what assurance does it provide?
3. Summarize the importance of digital certificates.
4. Briefly explain the process of a certificate-signing request (CSR).
5. Compare and contrast two trust models used in PKI.
6. Discuss certificate management.
7. What are two ways for a browser to check the revocation of a certificate?
8. What term defines the process of associating a host or client application with an *expected* certificate or public key?
9. Differentiate among three main certificate types.
10. Explain the four types of domain digital certificates.
11. Which hardware and software digital certificate is also known as a personal certificate?
12. Identify and explain seven common extensions for certificate formats and encoding.
13. Define an *object identifier (OID)*.
14. Summarize certificate attributes.
15. Explain PKI management and the procedures used to manage keys.
16. List common cryptographic transport protocols.
17. Explain an SSL/TLS accelerator and an SSL decryptor.
18. What is the fixed size of data for a block cipher?

19. Identify four types of block cipher operational modes.

20. Explain crypto service providers.

⊹ SAMPLE SECURITY+ EXAM QUESTIONS

1. Which is *true* about the Electronic Codebook (ECB) algorithm?

   A. It uses a weak key.

   B. Each block of data is encrypted with the same key.

   C. Each block of data is encrypted with a random key.

   D. It uses an initialization vector when encrypting each block of data.

2. Which is the *best* method to reduce bandwidth when checking if a certificate is revoked?

   A. Use a CSR

   B. Self-sign the certificate

   C. Implement OCSP with stapling

   D. Use a CRL

3. Which of the following actually performs the encryption of data?

   A. Crypto modules

   B. CA

   C. Digital certificate

   D. CRL

4. What does a customer need to provide the RA so they can issue a digital certificate?

   A. CSR

   B. CRL

   C. Digital signature

   D. Domain validation

5. Which provides the highest level of assurance that verifies the legal entities of the certificate owners?

   A. Wildcard digital certificate

   B. Extended validation (EV) certificate

   C. Subject alternative name

   D. Domain validation certificate

6. What is the highest level of trust in PKI?

   A. RA

   B. Digital certificate

   C. Root CA

   D. Intermediate CA

7. Which method allows a third party to store a copy of a private key?

   A. Key archiving

   B. Key escrow

   C. Offline CA

   D. Distributed-trust model

8. Where is a revoked digital certificate listed?

   A. Shadow file

   B. NSA

   C. CRL

   D. PKI

9. What security protocol should be used for providing confidentiality of voice data?

   A. WPA2 with CCMP

   B. SSH

   C. IPSec

   D. SRTP

10. Which is *true* about a distributed-trust model?

    A. Only root CAs can validate signatures.

    B. Both root CAs and intermediate CAs can validate signatures.

    C. It is not recommended for large-scale models of signature validation.

    D. There are no root CAs.

LAB EXERCISES

Lab Activity 10-1: Certificate Authorities and Certificates

Secure websites are critical to online retail businesses. To ensure customers know a site is secure, most retail websites display a seal or logo of the certificate authority that issued the digital certificate used on the site.

1. Launch a web browser and navigate to a search engine.

2. Enter the search phrase online certificate authority. What are the names of some of the companies listed? Are there any free resources?

3. Navigate to the Godaddy website (www.godaddy.com). Notice the address bar in the browser shows the HTTPS protocol in use, and an icon such as a padlock is displayed to reinforce this.

4. Look for the option to buy an SSL certificate, and click the button.

5. Locate another source to purchase a certificate. Some choices include Thawte, Digicert, and Comodo. Compare to determine if anything is different or better between the vendors.

   When transmitting confidential information, it is critical to ensure the web page is using SSL/TLS and the certificate is valid. This can be verified from most browsers' address bar. This activity uses Google Chrome, but the process for other browsers is similar.

1. Launch Chrome, and navigate to a website where security is important. Any site where a login is used, such as Amazon.com, should work.

2. Look at the browser's address bar. You should see https:// as part of the website's address. To the left of that, you should see the word secure and a closed lock.

3. Click the word **Secure** once. A dialog box is displayed, as shown. Under the certificate, it should indicate valid. Click the **Valid** link, and you are directed to the actual certificate used to validate this site. From there you can review details such as issuer, expiration, date, and more.

Operating systems are populated with many certificates from the CAs. These are seen in the browser as intermediate authorities. Which certificates an operating system has along with the contents of the certificates can be viewed using a web browser. This activity uses the Chrome web browser.

1. Launch Chrome.

2. Click the **Customize and Control Google Chrome** button in the upper-right corner of the window and click **Settings** in the drop-down menu.

3. In the upper-left corner of the new screen, click the **Main Menu** button, and then click **Advanced** to expand this section.

4. In the expanded **Advanced** area, click the **Privacy and Security** link.

5. On the new screen, scroll down, and click **Manage Certificates**. The **Certificates** dialog box is displayed.

6. Click the **Intermediate Certification Authorities** tab in the dialog box. This tab displays the certificates that are loaded into Chrome. The column headers can be used to sort the certificates. For example, to view the certificates by expiration date, click on the **Expiration Date** header.

7. Locate a certificate that has CA in its name and double-click it to display information about the certificate in a new dialog box.

8. The **General** tab in the dialog box displays basic information including purpose of the certificate and dates it is valid.

9. Click the **Details** tab, as shown.

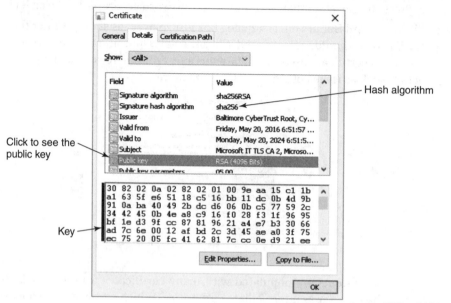

Goodheart-Willcox Publisher

10. Which hashing algorithm is being used?

11. Click Public Key in the list. The key is displayed in the lower part of the dialog box. Look how long this key is!

12. Click the **Certification Path** tab. Who issued this certificate?

13. Close all open dialog boxes and Chrome.

Lab Activity 10-2: EFS File Encryption and Certificate Creation

EFS is the Encrypting File System found in Microsoft Windows. You can use it to encrypt a folder or file. The folder will be accessible to you because you are the user who encrypted it. If another person logs on and tries to use the folder, that person will not have access to the private key.

1. Launch Windows file explorer.

2. In your working folder, create a subfolder named Payroll.

3. Right-click on the Payroll folder, and click **Properties** in the shortcut menu.

4. On the **General** tab of the **Properties** dialog box, click the **Advanced...** button. The **Advanced Attributes** dialog box is displayed, as shown.

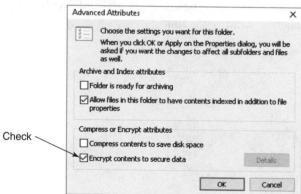

Goodheart-Willcox Publisher

5. Check the **Encrypt contents to secure data** check box, and then click the **OK** button.

6. Click the **OK** button in the **Properties** dialog box to apply the encryption. Historically, in Windows 7, the folder name is displayed in green to indicate it is encrypted. In Windows 10, this same display option can be enabled.

7. Open Windows Control Panel and click the **User Accounts** link.

8. On the User Accounts page, click the **Manage your file encryption certificates** link to launch a wizard. The wizard will step you through the process of creating a backup of the recovery key. It can also be used for managing certificates. Click the **Next** button to continue.

9. On the second page of the wizard, click the **Use this certificate** radio button. There should be a certificate listed below it that was issued by you. Click the **Next** button to continue.

10. On the next page of the wizard, make sure the **Back up the certificate and key now** radio button is on, and then click the **Browse…** button. Navigate to your working folder and enter a descriptive name such as PayrollPrivateKey.

11. In the wizard, enter a secure password in the **Password:** text box, and reenter it in the **Confirm password:** text box. Then, click the **Next** button. The file is saved as soon as you click this button.

12. On the next page of the wizard, click the **Cancel** button, or choose **I'll update my encrypted files later.** If you wanted to update previously encrypted files, you could continue with the wizard.

13. Using Windows file explorer, navigate to your working folder to verify the backup file was created. The file will have a .pfx file extension. Provide a screenshot.

14. From your **Start** menu, enter certmgr. When the option Manage Computer Certificates appears, press [Enter]. Click **Yes** on the User Account Control warning.

15. Expand **Trusted People** under the Certificates list, and then expand **Certificates**. You should see the certificate you just created. Double-click to open and click on details. Record the Cryptographic Cipher used and Expiration Date.

16. Choose **Edit Properties**. For the Friendly name, enter your name and make sure the purpose is only for Encrypting file system. Create a screenshot.

17. Close all open windows.

CASE STUDY

Key Escrow

In 2019, the founder of QuadrigaCX, Canada's largest cryptocurrency exchange, died unexpectedly. Due to a single point of failure, the exchange no longer had access to the information and money stored within it. While access to the founder's laptop was available, neither the password for accessing the exchange nor a recovery key could be located. As a result, approximately $190 million in cryptocurrency remains unavailable to the investors.

1. Describe what type of regulations regarding key escrows you think should be required.

2. In your opinion, to what extent should key escrows be protected from hackers or governmental overreach?

3. To what extent do users have a responsibility to ensure any financial institution or business has a provision for key recovery in place?

4. List other solutions you think could be implemented in businesses to prevent a situation like this from occurring.

CHAPTER

11

Command-Line Interface Management

LEARNING OUTCOMES

- Define *command-line interface*.
- Explain how to use the Windows command prompt.
- Discuss elements of Windows PowerShell.
- Examine elements of the Linux operating system.
- Identify examples of Linux commands and their purposes.
- Explain the Linux help and other command options.
- Summarize the primary usage of Python.
- Define *OpenSSL*.

KEY TERMS

alias
append
arp command
batch file
cat command
chmod command
cmdlet
command prompt
command-line interface (CLI)
current directory
device driver
dig command
distro
forked

grep command
hard link
hexadecimal numbering system
home directory
ifconfig
ipconfig command
logger command
Linux
method
nslookup command
object
open-source software
OpenSSL
pathping command

ping command
piping
process
property
provider
Python
route command
service
shell
switch
symbolic link
tracert command
wildcard character
Windows Management
    Instrumentation (WMI)

 SECURITY+ CERTIFICATION EXAM OBJECTIVES

The following Security+ Certification Exam Objectives are covered in this chapter.

- 4.1: Network reconnaissance and discover
- 4.1: tracert
- 4.1: nslookup/dig

- 4.1: ipconfig/ifconfig
- 4.1: ping/pathping
- 4.1: arp
- 4.1: route

- 4.1: File manipulation
- 4.1: PowerShell
- 4.1: Python
- 4:1 OpenSSL

OVERVIEW

Management of operating systems is an essential technical skill needed by all security professionals. Administrators will find that using the command line provides greater control, as opposed to relying on a GUI, when managing operating systems such as Windows, Linux, and macOS. Working from the command line, often called the terminal or shell, provides access to commands and functionality that is not available through graphic utilities embedded in each major operating system.

In this chapter, you will learn how to execute commands, navigate file systems, and obtain additional information to achieve advanced functionality.

SECURITY+ NOTE

While completing the CompTIA Security+ Exam, you will be presented with output generated from command-line programs to analyze. As you learn commands throughout this book, take note of both the output and information provided.

Command-Line Interface

 4.1

All major desktop and server operating systems provide the ability to manage their systems using a command-line interface (CLI). A **command-line interface (CLI)** is a text-based user interface that executes actions within the computer by entering textual commands instead of employing a mouse or touch screen. Security personnel must be able to navigate major operating systems, including their respective command-line interfaces in order to harden the network against intrusions and obtain information to actively prevent and respond to system attacks. A command-line interface is an important tool for assessing an organization's or network's security posture. *Security posture* is the actions, philosophies, and strategies for ensuring the security of an organization's software, hardware, network, and data. Two major operating systems that make heavy usage of their command-line interfaces are Microsoft and Linux.

In Microsoft operating systems, there are two command-line interfaces. The first is the original shell, which is often referred to as the *command prompt* or *command line*. The second is an advanced command-line interface called *PowerShell*. Generally, a **shell** is software that provides a direct method of running commands to the kernel. A *kernel* is the core of any given operating system. Most shells allow users to run commands directly from a command-line interface. In addition to advanced commands, PowerShell also offers the ability to create scripts.

As with the Microsoft operating system, Linux operating systems have their own shells that act as command interpreters used to execute other programs. Similar to PowerShell in Windows, the shell in Linux also can be used as a programming language to create scripts. Linux offers its users the opportunity to choose the type of shell they wish to run. The shell most commonly used is the Bourne-Again Shell (Bash). While other shells offer the same basic functionality as Bash, they also have unique features. Some other popular Linux shells include enhanced C shell (Tcsh) and Korn shell (Ksh).

Regardless of the interface type, managing systems from the command-line interface offers more options and flexibility when running commands than when using a graphical interface. In many cases, using the shell is the only way to run a command to obtain data. Consider the Windows command **ipconfig**, which provides information about network addresses and related configurations. There is no equivalent command built into the Windows graphical interface.

Becoming skilled at shell interfaces is an important skill to develop. Many of the advanced security and troubleshooting tools are used in the shell. For example, neither the Ubuntu Server Linux distribution nor Microsoft-branded Server Core, has a graphical interface.

Windows Command Prompt

The Windows **command prompt** is a command-line interface for entering commands manually. Command prompt grew out of the original Microsoft computer operating system: Disk Operating System (DOS). PC computers used DOS or MS DOS (Microsoft DOS) as the operating system until the release of Windows 95. Beginning with that release, the command-line interface acted as an application on the system. The CLI was no longer the operating system; rather, Windows was the operating system and the command line, or command prompt, was one of its applications. Today, the command line still provides substantial commands for managing a computer system and its resources.

Entering Commands

In Windows 10, the command prompt is located in the **Start** menu in **All Apps**>**Windows System**>**Command Prompt**. The actual program file is cmd.exe. When an application is launched, it appears in a window, as shown in Figure 11-1. All commands at the prompt must be entered using the keyboard and executed by pressing the [Enter] key.

Important commands used to assess the security posture of an organization include the following:

- **ping**
- **tracert**
- **pathping**
- **nslookup** and **dig**
- **arp**
- **route**
- **ipconfig**

4.1

Ping

The **ping command** is a command-line tool used to test the connection between two networked devices. The syntax for **ping** is the command name followed by either an IP address or a host name, such as ping 192.168.103.17 or ping server1. You can also test an Internet connection to a website by using the domain name, such as ping g-w.com. The **ping** command can simulate a DoS attack by sending out multiple requests, and the resulting strain on a network can provide security administrators insight into how a network would handle such an attack.

Figure 11-1 The Windows command prompt is a command-line interface for entering commands manually.

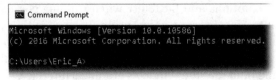

Tracert

The **tracert command** is a command-line utility that displays the path a data packet takes across a network. Figure 11-2 shows the results of a **tracert** command to the Google home page. The syntax of this command is the command name followed by a device name, IP address, or domain name, for example tracert server16, tracert 192.168.22.9, or tracert g-w.com. Tracert can be used by security administrators to verify data packets are not following a spoofed or malicious route.

You may see entries on your path showing asterisks (*). This means a remote router is not replying with requested information. Like **ping**, the **tracert** command relies on the ICMP (Internet Control Message Protocol), to which some routers do not respond.

Pathping

The **pathping command** is a TCP/IP utility that provides information about network latency and identifies the hops between the source address and the destination address. *Latency* is a delay in data transfer between two devices. **Pathping** functions as a combination of ping and tracert and executes its operation by sending ICMP requests to each hop. The **pathping** command can be run by entering the **pathping** command followed by an IP address or DNS name.

Nslookup and dig

The **nslookup command** is a command-line tool used to locate information related to the domain name system (DNS). **Nslookup** queries a network's local DNS server by default to obtain IP information from a named host or named host information. For example, if you wanted to obtain the IP address of the Microsoft.com Internet domain, the syntax would be nslookup Microsoft.com.

The **nslookup** command can be used by security administrators to verify DNS configurations are correct and secure. When the results of an **nslookup** command contain a nonauthoritative answer, it means the responding DNS server is not the original, or authoritative, source of the DNS record. For example, if you enter nslookup Microsoft.com on your home or business network, the result is not an originally created entry Microsoft.com; rather, the results show an answer returned from a local temporary cache lookup.

The **dig command** is the Linux command-line equivalent to the Windows-based **nslookup** command. The acronym **dig** stands for *digital information grouper* and performs the same function as **nslookup**, though it has more functionality than **nslookup**.

4.1

4.1

4.1

```
C:\>tracert google.com

Tracing route to google.com [172.217.7.206]
over a maximum of 30 hops:

  1    1 ms    <1 ms    <1 ms  192.168.0.1
  2    7 ms     7 ms     7 ms  10.11.0.1
  3    9 ms     9 ms    10 ms  100.127.41.28
  4    7 ms     8 ms     8 ms  100.120.124.26
  5   13 ms    13 ms    15 ms  ashbbprj01-ae2.rd.as.cox.net [68.1.0.242]
  6   13 ms    12 ms    14 ms  98.182.1.86
  7   14 ms    15 ms    15 ms  108.170.240.97
  8   12 ms    12 ms    13 ms  216.239.54.109
  9   11 ms    14 ms    16 ms  iad30s10-in-f14.1e100.net [172.217.7.206]

Trace complete.
```

Figure 11-2 The **tracert** command is a command-line utility that displays the path a data packet takes across a network.

ARP

The **arp command** is a command-line tool used to view and modify entries in the Address Resolution Protocol (ARP) cache. The syntax for this command varies depending on the results being sought. For example, to view mappings from IP addresses to MAC addresses, you would enter arp -a. The results of this syntax include dynamic entries of local devices on a network. A *dynamic entry* is one generated automatically with no administrator intervention. *Static entries*, or those that are manually configured, can be created by entering arp -s followed by a specific IP and MAC address, for example arp -s 192.168.103.33 00-aa-23-1b-c4-e8.

The ARP command can be used by security administrators to determine if an ARP poisoning attack has taken place. Evidence of an ARP poisoning attack presents itself as two different IP addresses sharing the same MAC address.

Route

The **route command** is a command-line tool that enables a user to view the local routing table and make changes if necessary. To view the local routing information, enter the command syntax route print. The resulting output will list recognized network adapters as well as IPv4 and IPv6 default route tables. The results list helps in determining the security posture of an organization by providing insight into whether a network's default gateway has been poisoned and allowing a user to reset the information if poisoning has occurred.

IPConfig

The **ipconfig command** is a command-line tool that displays all devices connected to a network. The **ipconfig** command can be used to refresh DHCP and DNS settings. From a security standpoint, **ipconfig** can be used to verify that configuration settings are secure.

Switches

Most commands can be altered using built-in options called switches. In a command-line interface, a **switch** is a modifier added to a command to enforce specific parameters and help limit or narrow the possible results. In most cases, a switch is preceded by either a hyphen (-) or a forward slash (/). For example, running the **ipconfig** command displays essential information about network connections on a computer, such as the IP address, subnet mask, and default gateway. The **ipconfig** command is one of the most basic networking commands available and is an essential security tool. It provides information about the host's network adapter and its TCP/IP settings. Since malware attacks can often change these settings, it is important to ensure their addresses are accurate.

By adding the /all switch, a user can also obtain information about the computer's default MAC, DNS, and DHCP addresses, as well as IP lease information. Switches are not case-sensitive and are used with most commands.

Piping

Piping is the act of directing the results of one command into the input syntax of another command. This enables a user to run multiple commands simultaneously, provided the commands are separated with a pipe symbol. For example, in the dir | more entry, **dir** is the first command, which is a list of all the files and additional directories in that location. The pipe symbol sends the directory listing to the **more** command, which results in the screen output of the **dir** command pausing until the user advances it to see one new line at a time, as demonstrated in Figure 11-3. The

Figure 11-3 The **dir** command lists all the files and additional directories in a given location.

```
C:\windows\system32\cmd.exe

C:\Windows>dir | more
 Volume in drive C is Windows
 Volume Serial Number is 387C-E23F

 Directory of C:\Windows

11/01/2019  09:41 AM    <DIR>          .
11/01/2019  09:41 AM    <DIR>          ..
04/11/2018  06:38 PM    <DIR>          addins
01/13/2019  04:11 AM    <DIR>          appcompat
07/10/2019  04:34 PM    <DIR>          apppatch
11/07/2019  06:17 PM    <DIR>          AppReadiness
10/17/2019  02:31 PM    <DIR>          assembly
04/04/2018  04:19 AM           133,096 avrcpctrlr.dll
04/04/2018  04:19 AM           125,928 avrcpio.dll
10/09/2019  07:50 PM    <DIR>          bcastdvr
04/11/2018  06:34 PM            67,072 bfsvc.exe
04/11/2018  06:38 PM    <DIR>          Boot
04/11/2018  06:38 PM    <DIR>          Branding
10/09/2019  02:26 AM    <DIR>          CbsTemp
08/14/2018  08:21 AM             2,338 comsetup.log
04/11/2018  06:33 PM            35,138 Core.xml
04/11/2018  06:33 PM            35,138 CoreSingleLanguage.xml
08/14/2018  08:13 AM                12 CSUP.txt
04/11/2018  06:38 PM    <DIR>          Cursors
01/13/2019  08:30 PM    <DIR>          debug
08/14/2018  08:26 AM            30,483 diagerr.xml
04/11/2018  06:38 PM    <DIR>          diagnostics
08/14/2018  08:26 AM            30,483 diagwrn.xml
04/12/2018  04:15 AM    <DIR>          DigitalLocker
-- More --
```

dir command can also be helpful in quickly locating information hidden or located in subdirectories.

Another useful command compatible with piping is the **findstr** command. This command can extract character data from the output of the first command. For example, if an administrator wants to view default DHCP settings quickly using ipconfig, ipconfig | findstr "DHCP" is entered. Similarly, the administrator can locate IPv4 configuration information by entering ipconfig | findstr "IPv4".

Most commands have a built-in help feature to identify additional options or parameters of the command. To access the help, add a forward slash (/) after the command and then a question mark (?). For example, dir /? provides additional options for the **dir** command, as shown in Figure 11-4.

While some commands work without a space between the command and the switch options, most commands will not. It is good practice to include a space after each command keyed if you are adding additional switches.

File and Directory Commands

Some of the most used commands in the command prompt are employed for file and directory management and navigation. These commands include **md**, **cd**, **dir**, **del**, and **rd**.

The command to create a new directory or subdirectory is **md**. This is short for *make directory*. For example, md Data creates a directory called *Data*, which is located within the current directory. The **current directory** is the directory in which a user is working, and it is reflected in the command prompt. Directory names are case-sensitive, meaning the case used when the name of the directory is first entered will be matched in the actual directory name. Therefore, the directory name could be Data, data, or DATA, depending on how it was entered in the command.

TECH TIP

The **systeminfo** command is an effective tool for locating IP and MAC addresses and identifying installed network adapters. It also provides information about installed patches, booting location, and hardware versions and information.

Figure 11-4 The /? option can be used to display help for most commands, such as the **dir** command shown here.

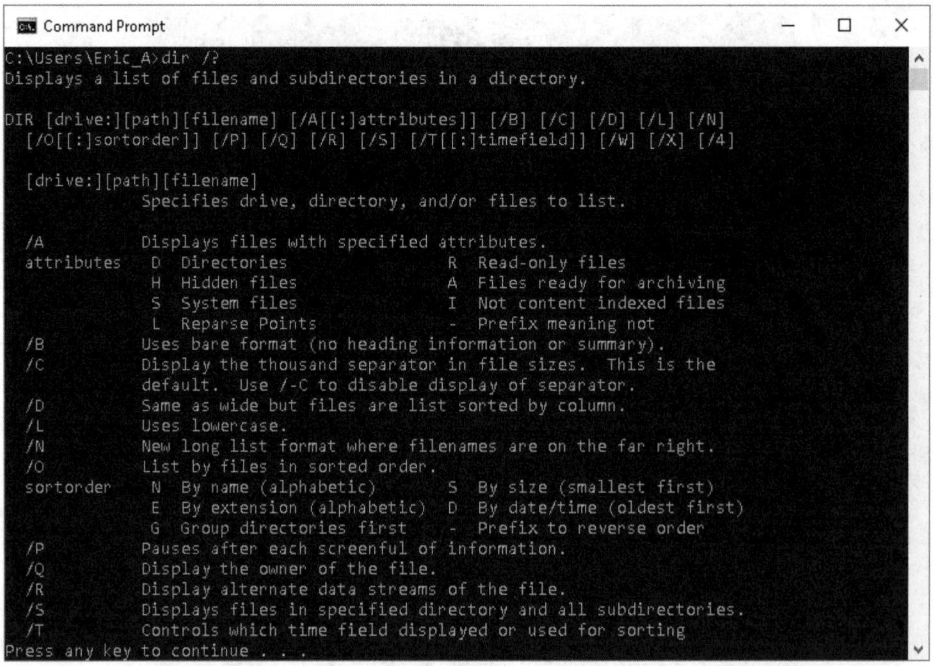

Goodheart-Willcox Publisher

When a directory is created, two indicators are generated within it that appear as dots, as shown in Figure 11-5. These symbols are called *markers*. Markers exist in every directory and subdirectory, and they cannot be deleted. A marker consisting of a single dot (.) refers to the current directory. A marker consisting of two dots (..) refers to the parent directory from which the current directory branches. A *parent directory* is a directory that is above the current directory in a file-system hierarchy.

Remember, the current directory refers to the directory in which you are working and is reflected in the command prompt. For example, in Figure 11-4, the current directory is Data. When a command is entered, Windows executes it based on the

Figure 11-5 Markers exist in every directory and subdirectory, and they cannot be deleted.

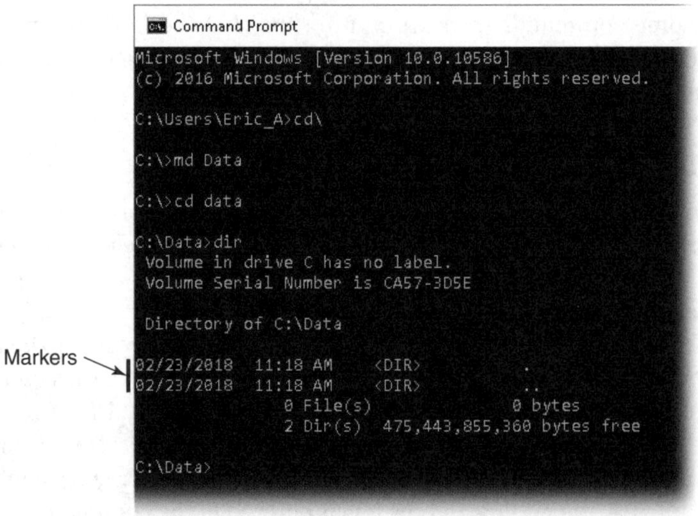

Goodheart-Willcox Publisher

current directory. The **cd** command (change directory) allows you to assign another directory as the current directory. For example, cd Programs makes the Programs subdirectory the current directory. Entering cd \Programs\Apps changes the focus of the command line to the Apps subdirectory located in the Programs directory off the root. *Root* is the highest-level directory in a file system. In the previous example, the first backslash tells Windows to go to the root. From there, it looks for the Programs directory and then for the Apps subdirectory. You can also use the backslash key (\) or parent directory marker (..) as shown in Figure 11-6.

Unlike when using Windows File Explorer, when you change to a directory using the command prompt, the contents are not immediately displayed. You must "ask" to see the files and subdirectories using the **dir** command. This is short for *directory listing*. The **dir** command is a very powerful command when combined with some of its switches. For example, the **/s** switch tells the command to search not just the current directory but all of its subdirectories as well. The command can also be filtered to display only certain file types, or the files can be displayed sorted by name, date created, file extension, or size. This can be helpful when searching for malicious or inappropriate files.

Wildcard characters can be used with the **dir** command. A **wildcard character** is a character used to represent one or more unknown characters in a string of text. The question mark wildcard (?) represents a single unknown character. The asterisk wildcard (*) represents any number of unknown characters. Wildcards are used to help in searches and identify specific files, programs, and features. Examples include the following:

- Dir B*.* displays all files in the current directory with a file name that starts with the letter B, contains any other characters, and has any file extension.
- Dir *.pdf displays all files in the current directory with the .pdf file extension, regardless of each file's name.
- Dir Day0?.txt displays all files in the current directory with the .txt file extension that have names beginning with Day0 and contain one other character, such as Day01.txt, Day02.txt, and Day03.txt, but not Day03A.txt.

The command to delete files is **del** and both the file name and extension must be included. To delete a single file, enter del *filename.extension*. Similar to the **dir** command, the question mark and asterisk wildcards can be used in place of unknown characters. For example, del *.exe deletes all files with a .exe file extension in the current directory. The command to delete an entire directory is **rd**. This is short for *remove directory*. For example, rd data deletes the directory named data. By default, the **rd** command will not allow you to remove a directory if it contains any files or subdirectories. In addition, the current directory cannot be deleted.

Host Management

There are many commands that help in managing a system or remote host from the command line. For example, the **tasklist** command provides a snapshot of all tasks currently running on a host. *Tasks* represent individual actions taken by an operating system. For example, if the Google Chrome web browser is running, you will see

cd\	Changes the current directory to the root directory of the drive.
cd..	Moves up one directory (to the parent directory). For example, if the current directory is c:\data\Jan\budget and cd.. is entered, the new current directory would be the c:\data\Jan directory.

Figure 11-6 The **cd** command allows a user to assign another directory as the current directory.

Goodheart-Willcox Publisher

an instance of it in the task list. The **tasklist** can be used to determine if there is any malware or other suspicious software running.

The **/fi** switch is used to filter the search of the running tasks. You can filter by memory usage, process status, services using a process, and more. For example, entering tasklist /fi "memusage gt 20000" will filter all running tasks to show only those that are using more than 20 megabytes of memory.

The format of the results returned by the **tasklist** command can be changed using the **/fo** switch. To see the results as a list, enter tasklist /fo list. When using this format, it may be best to combine it with the **more** command. This allows you to manually control scrolling of the list.

Viewing Processes and Services

In addition to tasks, both processes and services run on a computer, and each has its own distinctions. A **process** is an actively running computer program. An example of a process is the CPU opening the web browser after a user has selected it. A **service** is a program that runs in the background of an operating system to provide specific features and functionality. A service uses a system port as a means of entering or exiting the system, but it does not interact with the desktop.

If you are searching for specific processes that are running, you can combine the **tasklist** command with the **find** command. For example, enter tasklist | find "MicrosoftEdge" to see if Microsoft Edge is running, as shown in Figure 11-7. The quotation marks are required around the name of the process.

The **tasklist** command will *not* identify running services. Enter net start to see the services that have started. By viewing these services, you can identify if there are any services that may make the host vulnerable to a hacking attempt. For example, you may find an unapproved virtual private network (VPN) client running. You can then take measures to disable or stop them from running. Enter net stop and the name of the service to stop it from running.

Stopping a task from running at the command prompt is accomplished by using the **taskkill** command. You can stop a process by its image name or by the processor identification (PID) number. The *image name* is the name of the process. The *PID* is a unique number assigned by the operating system to identify that specific process. Some processes run more than once, so you may need to use the PID to be accurate.

Suppose you want to terminate the Notepad application. You can do that by using the **taskkill** command with the /im (image name) or /pid switch. For example, enter taskkill /im notepad.exe to terminate the Notepad application by its image name.

Figure 11-7 By combining the **tasklist** command with the **find** command, you can look for a specific process that is running, such as Microsoft Edge.

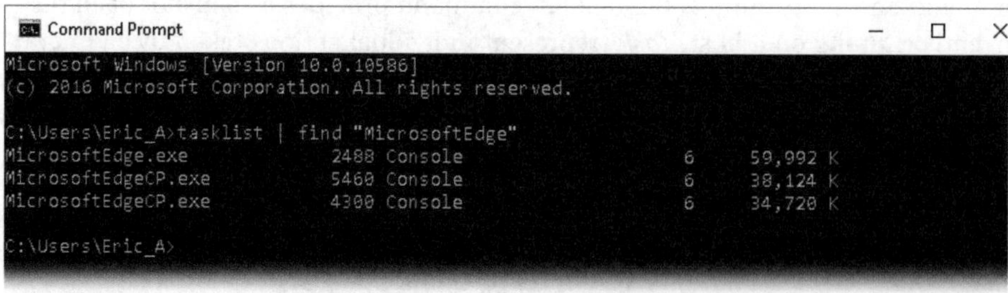

Viewing Device Drivers

It is also possible to view installed device drivers through the command-line interface. A **device driver** is a software program that instructs a piece of hardware how to operate. The **driverquery** command is used to view installed drivers. The **/si** switch can be added to see which drivers are digitally signed by the manufacturer. A digitally signed driver is identified as an authorized driver from the manufacturer. Because drivers provide specific instructions directly to hardware, they are a source of potential malware. A list of drivers can be exported to a comma-separated values (CSV) file. For example, enter driverquery /si /fo csv >drivers.csv to create a list of signed drivers and export it to a CSV file named drivers. Depending on how many drivers are installed, it may take a few seconds to generate the file. Figure 11-8 shows an example of a driver list in a CSV file opened with a spreadsheet program.

Batch Files

A **batch file** is a single file in which a command, series of commands, or set of instructions to be processed in sequence is listed. There are many times when a command, or series of commands, needs to be run more than once. The process of running commands multiple times can be automated using batch files. Batch files are created with Notepad or a plain-text editor and saved with the .bat file extension. To run the batch file, simply enter the name of the file at the command prompt. When running a batch file, the file extension does not need to be entered, but you must either be in the same directory as the batch file or otherwise specify the appropriate file path.

Any command-line program can be included in a batch file. In addition, there are some specific commands primarily used in batch files. Consider the example illustrated in Figure 11-9. A batch file issues the **echo** and **ipconfig** commands. The **echo** command displays two messages and the values of both the computer name and date variables. The @echo off entry in the first line of the batch files suppresses the word echo from appearing when the **echo** command is used. Then, the **ipconfig** command is run.

Figure 11-8 A list of drivers can be exported to a comma-separated values (CSV) file and opened in spreadsheet software, such as Microsoft Excel.

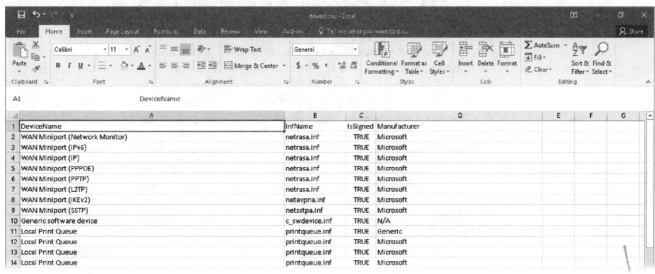

Goodheart-Willcox Publisher

Figure 11-9 Batch files can be used to automate tasks by combining several commands.

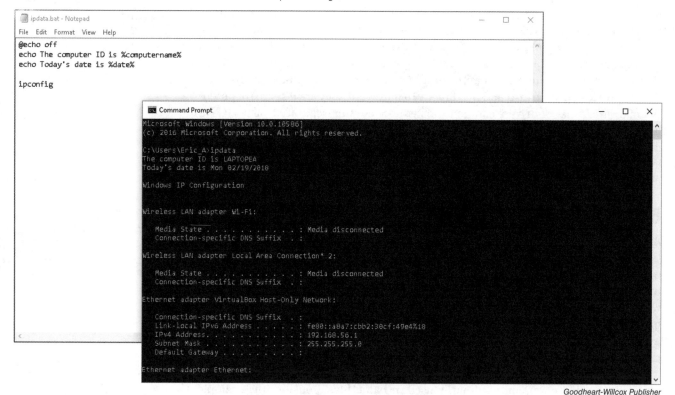

Goodheart-Willcox Publisher

Using Command Prompt Effectively

When used effectively, command prompt can be a powerful tool. For example, results from a command issued in cmd.exe can be saved directly to a file. To redirect the output from the screen to a file, use the right chevron character (>). For example, dir > Files.txt will save the directory listing to a file named Files.txt in the current directory.

The data output from a command is appended into the existing file by using two right chevrons (>>). To **append** data means to add the data to an existing data set. For example, ipconfig >> pcdata.txt adds the output of the **ipconfig** command to the bottom of the existing pcdata.txt text file. If the file specified does not exist, it will be created.

There may be times when the output from a command needs to be used in a file type other than plain text. The **clip** command can be combined with another command to direct the output to the system clipboard. For example, ipconfig | clip will send the output of the **ipconfig** command to the clipboard. At first glance, it appears nothing has happened, but if you launch a word processor, you can see the data on the clipboard, as shown in Figure 11-10. The [Ctrl][V] key combination can be used to paste the data into the document.The **title** command can be used to change the title bar of the Windows command prompt. This can help document the machine used when taking a screenshot, since the machine name is included in the title bar. System variables can be used in the title. For example, entering title %computername% %date% will display the host's computer name and the current date in the title bar. The title bar resets for the next session of the command prompt.

The **color** command can change the color of a command prompt for easier viewing using two hexadecimal digits, as shown in Figure 11-11. The **hexadecimal numbering system** is a base-16 numbering system that uses 16 characters (0–9, A–F) to represent numbers. The first hexadecimal digit in the **color** command

Figure 11-10 The output of a command-prompt command can be directed to the system clipboard and then used in a document.

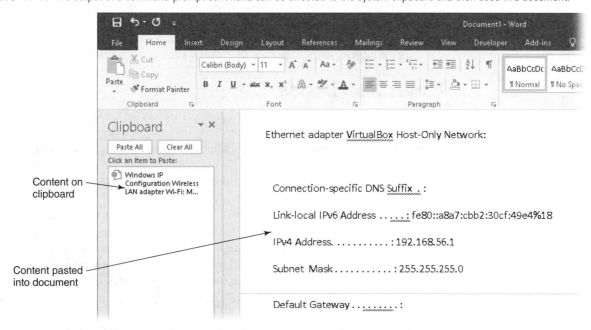

Figure 11-11 The color of the command prompt can be changed using hexadecimal numbers.

Hex Digit	Color	Hex Digit	Color	Hex Digit	Color	Hex Digit	Color
0	Black	4	Red	8	Gray	C	Light Red
1	Blue	5	Purple	9	Light Blue	D	Light Purple
2	Green	6	Yellow	A	Light Green	E	Light Yellow
3	Aqua	7	White	B	Light Aqua	F	Bright White

specifies the background color. The second hexadecimal digit specifies the text color. For example, entering color 1F produces bright white text on a blue background. As with changing the title, the colors reset for the next session of the command prompt.

Windows PowerShell

 4.1

PowerShell is a powerful command-line shell integrated with Windows.NET technology, which is a platform used for building apps. Microsoft made its transition to PowerShell with the release of Windows XP, and beginning with Windows 7,

PowerShell became integrated into the operating system. PowerShell can take the place of cmd.exe, as most commands used in cmd.exe work equally as well in PowerShell. It is important for security technicians to be skilled in understanding and operating PowerShell. Many hackers use it to create scripts for launching cyberattacks, so a security plan should include how to prevent attacks from this threat vector.

PowerShell Basics

PowerShell treats everything as an object. An **object** is a self-contained resource that stores information about itself in properties and provides program code used to interact with it. For example, a file or folder is an object, as are users, groups, servers, computers, and services.

Data, such as a service name, is embedded into objects. Data embedded into an object is a **property**. Objects also contain *methods*. A **method** is a set of instructions that specifies an action to be performed on an object. For example, the kill method is used to end a running process. Suppose Notepad is running. The command syntax (Get-Process Notepad).Kill() identifies the Notepad program and stops it from running in one command. Figure 11-12 shows examples of data categorized as properties and methods. Output from cmd.exe is text. In PowerShell, the output from a command may *look* like text, but it is actually an object, which allows output results to be piped.

PowerShell was designed for use by network administrators. In addition to some very powerful command-line programs, PowerShell provides the ability to create your own variables and scripts. PowerShell does not just manage the file system or run commands; it can manage a wide array of systems, including

- processes;
- services;
- event logs;
- Windows Management Instrumentation (WMI);
- Active Directory; and
- Windows registry files.

Microsoft made PowerShell open source in 2016. **Open-source software** is software that has unlocked source code that can be modified by anyone. Microsoft's move to make PowerShell open source allows an administrator to run PowerShell on Linux and Macintosh operating systems. This reduces the amount of time and effort needed for administrators to develop scripts and manage systems by using one powerful interface.

Figure 11-12 PowerShell treats everything as an object. Each object contains properties and methods.

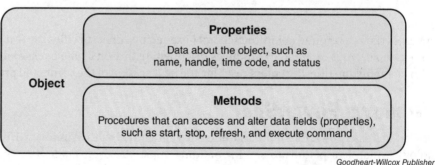

Goodheart-Willcox Publisher

PowerShell Commands

Cmdlets (pronounced *command-lets*) are programs inside PowerShell. There are over 100 cmdlets included in PowerShell. PowerShell is also extensible, which means cmdlets can be added to the PowerShell interface. For example, administrators can manage virtual environments with VMWare and cloud environments with Amazon's AWS tools in Windows PowerShell. Cmdlets and their options are not case sensitive in PowerShell. In addition to the cmdlets, the commands used with the command prompt are available in PowerShell, such as **cls** and **md**. However, the actual commands are replaced with cmdlet equivalents, but for easier transition between the interfaces, these commands are available from an alias for the original command. An **alias** is an alternate name for designating a file or fields. PowerShell aliases include Linux commands along with command-prompt commands.

PowerShell cmdlets use a specific syntax called *verb-noun syntax*. The command is a verb or action that acts on the noun. For example, **get-childitem** is a cmdlet. Get is the verb, or the action. The noun on which the verb will act is childitem. When run in a directory, the **get-childitem** cmdlet will list all the items (child objects) in the directory.

PowerShell Help

In PowerShell, the **get-help** cmdlet is used to display help. The syntax for this command is get-help, then the name of the cmdlet. For example, entering get-help get-service will display help for the **get-service** cmdlet, as shown in Figure 11-13.

In recent versions of PowerShell, expanded help files are no longer included on the basic installation of PowerShell, as indicated in the Remarks portion of Figure 11-13. The expanded help files are accessed online using the -online switch and can also be downloaded using the **update-help** cmdlet.

Figure 11-13 Help is accessed in PowerShell with the **get-help** cmdlet.

```
Windows PowerShell                                           —   □   ×

Windows PowerShell
Copyright (C) 2015 Microsoft Corporation. All rights reserved.

PS C:\Users\Eric_A> get-help get-service

NAME
    Get-Service

SYNTAX
    Get-Service [[-Name] <string[]>] [-ComputerName <string[]>] [-DependentServices] [-RequiredServices] [-Include
    <string[]>] [-Exclude <string[]>] [<CommonParameters>]

    Get-Service -DisplayName <string[]> [-ComputerName <string[]>] [-DependentServices] [-RequiredServices] [-Include
    <string[]>] [-Exclude <string[]>] [<CommonParameters>]

    Get-Service [-ComputerName <string[]>] [-DependentServices] [-RequiredServices] [-Include <string[]>] [-Exclude
    <string[]>] [-InputObject <ServiceController[]>] [<CommonParameters>]

ALIASES
    gsv

REMARKS
    Get-Help cannot find the Help files for this cmdlet on this computer. It is displaying only partial help.
        -- To download and install Help files for the module that includes this cmdlet, use Update-Help.
        -- To view the Help topic for this cmdlet online, type: "Get-Help Get-Service -Online" or
           go to http://go.microsoft.com/fwlink/?LinkID=113332.

PS C:\Users\Eric_A>
```

Goodheart-Willcox Publisher

Advanced PowerShell Commands

PowerShell offers the ability to manage local and remote systems. It includes many commands to aid in networking, security, Hyper-V virtualization, and Active Directory management for Microsoft servers. By adding additional parameters or piping multiple commands for a task, you can retrieve important information. Some helpful tools are introduced in this section to help you become comfortable with the PowerShell interface. There are many more cmdlets to explore than those presented here. Future chapters will explore additional cmdlets to manage security and networks as well.

When in PowerShell, you are working in environments called providers. A **provider** is a program that organizes data in specialized groups to be easily viewed and managed. Think of a provider as a layer that allows for focusing on managing a specific data store using the same commands, similar to a driver for an operating system. By switching between providers, you can exclusively manage multiple environments, such as the registry, file system, Active Directory, and more. For example, when working in the file system, running the **get-childitem** cmdlet displays subdirectories and files. However, if you are in the Active Directory provider, the **get-childitem** cmdlet displays user objects. The different providers allow access to different information stores. Use the **get-psprovider** cmdlet to see the providers installed on a system, as shown in Figure 11-14.

Each provider has a shortcut to access its environment. In the output for the **get-psprovider** cmdlet, the Drives column indicates the shortcut for each provider. For example, enter either cd hklm: (HKey-Local Machine) or cd hkcu: (HKey-Current User) to access the registry. In the Windows registry, there are specific sections that contain data called *hives*. To return to the file system provider, enter c: to access the file system, which is the default provider.

Regardless of provider, use the **get-childitem** cmdlet to list the items. This cmdlet is similar to the command prompt **dir** command. Notice in the example in Figure 11-15, the date listed is the LastWriteTime. However, more data is tracked on each file than what is displayed by default. To see additional properties, enter the following syntax: get-childitem | get-member.

You can query and view data in these additional properties. For example, suppose you want to see the files in the order they were last accessed (opened), which may be different from the last time the file was saved. Enter get-childitem | sort-object lastaccesstime to see this output. The results can be limited by using the -include switch, which adds items to the list. Conversely, the -exclude switch removes items from the results.

Obtaining a computer's IP address from PowerShell is easy. The **get-netipaddress** cmdlet provides this information. To see the information presented in a column format, combine the cmdlet with the **format-table** cmdlet using the pipe symbol.

Figure 11-14 The **get-psprovider** cmdlet lists providers installed on a system. The **Drives** column indicates the shortcut for each provider.

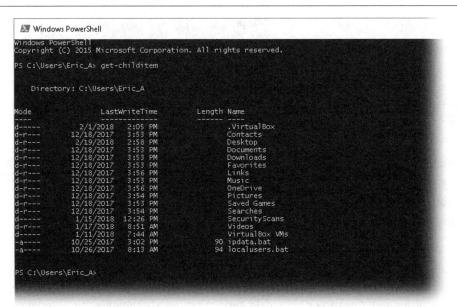

Figure 11-15 The **get-childitem** cmdlet lists items in the default environment.

The **get-wmiobject** cmdlet provides information about hardware installed in the computer. **Windows Management Instrumentation (WMI)** is the infrastructure in Windows for managing data and operations. When using this cmdlet, a class is specified for the search. WMI *classes* represent the resources to be managed. For example, entering get-wmiobject win32_bios returns attributes of the system's basic input/output system (BIOS). A computer system's *basic input/output system (BIOS)* is a set of instructions built into the computer's firmware that monitors and controls input and output operations. Figure 11-16 shows additional WMI object data.

Even with filtering, you may still retrieve more information than desired or needed. Objects can be filtered further according to desired specifications. For example, suppose you want to view only services that are stopped. You can sort by stopped services, but it is easier to issue the **where_object** cmdlet, which displays only stopped services. The **where_object** cmdlet analyzes each object in a list based on a condition. The specified condition is enclosed in curly brackets. For example, enter get-service | where-object {$_.status -eq "stopped"} to show only services whose status equals stopped. In this command string, $_. is a variable representing the current object being processed. The variable is the property of that object. In this example, the property is status. Figure 11-17 shows additional operators used to test conditions.

Suppose you need to find all Google services that are running. Enter the following syntax, get-service | where-object {$_.displayname –match "goog"}.

Class	Meaning
win32_computersystem	Properties related to a computer running Windows
win32_environment	System environmental variables
win32_logicaldisk	Storage device on a system
win32_networkadapter	Network adapter installed
win32_networkadapterconfiguration	Configuration of a network adapter
get-help get-wmiobject –examples	Provides help examples for the cmdlet

Figure 11-16 Windows Management Instrumentation (WMI) is the infrastructure in Windows for managing data and operations. There are many options for WMI object data.

Goodheart-Willcox Publisher

Figure 11-17 There are many operators that can be used in conjunction with the **where_object** cmdlet to test conditions.

Operator	Meaning
-contains	Contains
-eq	Equal to
-ge	Greater than or equal to
-gt	Greater than
-le	Less than or equal to
-lt	Less than
-match	Matches using regular expressions
-ne	Not equal to
-notcontains	Does not contain
-notmatch	Negated matching using regular expressions

The resulting list includes any service from Google that is currently running on the system. Notice you do not need to enter the full name for Google. Not having to enter a full name for a service can be helpful if a service happens to use an abbreviated name.

PowerShell also provides an easy way to send the data output to a file or HTML format. The data can be stored in CSV format, converted to HTML, or saved in a plain-text file. There are three different cmdlets to do this. For example, the following are used to send the output from the **get-service** cmdlet to a file:

- get-service | export-csv *filename*.csv
- get-service | convertto-html >*filename*.html
- get-service | out-file *filename*.txt

While many commands discussed previously will also function in the PowerShell interface, they also have cmdlet equivalents. These equivalents are outlined in Figure 11-18.

PowerShell Scripts

For automating tasks, PowerShell does not use batch files. Instead, commands are placed into scripts, which are similar to batch files. A *script* is a custom file containing commands and functions to be processed in order. Scripts can be more powerful than batch files due to the advanced use of cmdlets and their methods.

As with batch files, creating a script does not require knowledge of any special programming language. Scripts are created using Notepad or any plain-text editor. Scripts in PowerShell have a .ps1 file extension. Make sure to change the editor's default file extension to .ps1 when saving the file. To run a script, enter ./ and the script's name. If the script is not in the current directory, the complete path to the script file must be entered. For example, to run a script titled fileconversion that exists in the current directory, enter ./fileconversion. However, if the fileconversion script were in a different directory labeled utilities, enter ./utilities/fileconversion.

TECH TIP

The PowerShell Integrated Scripting Editor (ISE) is a user-friendly interface that allows the same functionality of running any PowerShell cmdlets, but it allows for easier navigation in locating appropriate commands. The ISE interface is often used for learning syntax and placing commands into the built-in editor, which increases the efficiency of creating a script.

Figure 11-18 Many command prompt networking commands have PowerShell cmdlet equivalents.

Networking Command	PowerShell cmdlet Equivalent
Ipconfig	Get-netipaddress
Ping	Test-connection
Nslookup	Resolve-dnsname
tracert	Test-netconnection

Goodheart-Willcox Publisher

Automation is often used in security as a form of system control for actions that do not require intervention, such as reporting or monitoring. The use of automation strategies in a data-security process is often referred to as an *automated course of action*. Automation increases a system's *resilience*, meaning the system is able to return to normal operation after an interruption.

Scripts provide a powerful method of automation. They are created to accept input from the administrator, run at default or scheduled times, provide continuous monitoring, and respond to security vulnerabilities quickly through automation or manual intervention. For example, suppose you want to verify that certain operating system patches called hotfixes were installed. The basic cmdlet is get-ciminstance -classname win32_quickfixengineering. A system administrator can place the aforementioned command in a script and prompt a user for the computer name to verify, or manually validate, the configuration of networked machines. Scripts can be configured to take immediate action. For example, a script can be created to search for a specific process running, such as a keylogger or other malware, and immediately end the process if found and create a file logging the affected computers' names.

The PowerShell environment may need to be configured to allow running of scripts. To determine the current script execution status, use the **get-executionpolicy** cmdlet. This cmdlet will identify the current policy for the system. The four policies are:

- restricted (no scripts can be run)
- all signed (only scripts signed by a publisher can be run)
- remote signed (downloaded scripts must be signed by a trusted publisher)
- unrestricted (no restrictions, all PowerShell scripts will run)

The **set-executionpolicy** cmdlet is used to change the policy. For example, set-executionpolicy allsigned will change to that policy. Before the policy is changed, you are prompted to accept or reject the change, as shown in Figure 11-19.

Introduction to Linux

Most desktop and laptop personal computers use either the Windows operating system or macOS. However, a great deal of network servers, including many web servers, actually run a Linux distribution. **Linux** is an open-source computer operating system derived from the UNIX operating system. The Linux operating system is a versatile and powerful operating system that is the choice of many IT departments. Linux is also open source, which allows it to be freely modified. Open source offers a great deal of flexibility for customized Linux environments. Some versions of Linux are created with built-in hacking tools, and many hackers find that Linux is an easier platform for launching attacks. Therefore, it is important for security technicians to have a fundamental understanding of working with the Linux shell.

Figure 11-19 A policy may need to be changed to allow scripts to be run. You will be prompted to accept or reject the change.

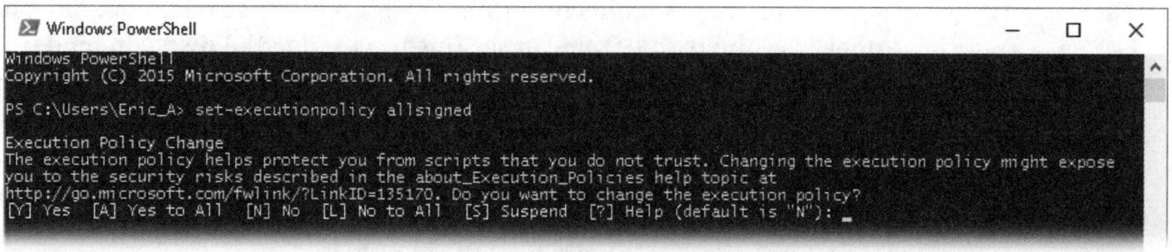

Linux Basics

As you have learned, Linux was derived from the UNIX operating system. UNIX was developed by AT&T Bell Labs in the 1970s. UNIX underwent many changes but remained a primarily proprietary operating system. There was significant interest in a free version of UNIX, and this came to fruition when Linus Torvalds, a software engineer from Finland, developed a kernel and released it as open source under the name of Linux. The development of an open-source kernel resulted in a number of Linux distributions being created or forked. **Forked** is a term for a program that has been modified to create an entirely new development branch that is a separate program. Open-source software can be legally forked without permission.

Linux is licensed under the GNU project, sponsored by the Free Software Foundation. The GNU project was created to give computer users freedom in development and use of software. Users can freely run GNU software, share it, study and review its code, and even modify it. Releasing Linux under the GNU General Public License has allowed others to adapt it to their own versions of Linux.

A **distro**, or *distribution*, is a unique operating system based off a Linux kernel and package management system. A distro typically includes a Linux kernel, tools and libraries licensed under GNU, and a package-management system. A *package-management system* is a collection of software tools for various functions, such as using, installing, configuring, and removing application programs on the Linux operating system.

There are hundreds of Linux distros available today. Some are commercial. Many are for special purposes, such as for superusers, home users, or by hardware or service applications. Hardware or service applications include distros for laptops, gaming, servers, routing, and hacking.

Linux Shell

With many distros available for Linux, the graphical user interface (GUI) can vary from one to another. However, the command-line interface (CLI) provides a common interface and offers an efficient way by which to manage the operating system.

Like Windows, the Linux command-line environment is called the shell and is a command-language interpreter that executes commands from direct keyboard entry or a program. Through the Linux shell, a user can interact with the operating system. Bash is the most popular shell. Bash is freeware found in most Linux distros developed by the Free Software Foundation and released under the GNU license.

In Linux, the command-line interface typically reflects your login name and a symbol. The symbol will be either a dollar sign ($) or a pound sign (#). When the symbol is $, you are logged in as a regular user. When the symbol is #, it reflects the user is logged in as a superuser with root privileges ({root}), as shown in Figure 11-20. Some commands can only be run as a superuser.

Linux Commands

When you first log in to Linux, the working directory is set to your home directory. A **home directory** is a directory where a user stores personal files. Most home directories have the path L. You can see this by entering the **pwd** command, as shown in Figure 11-21. The **pwd** command stands for print working directory. Similar to Windows, Linux also requires a space after each command. However, unlike the Windows shell, the shell interface in Linux *is* case-sensitive. Additionally, in Linux, directories are separated by a forward slash (/) instead of a backslash (\) as they are in Windows.

The **cd** command (*change directory*) does just what it implies; it changes the current directory where you are located. For example, cd /Documents changes from the

Figure 11-20 The command-line prompt in Linux indicates the level at which a user is logged in. A dollar sign ($) indicates the user is signed in as a regular user, and a pound sign (#) indicates the user is signed in as a superuser.

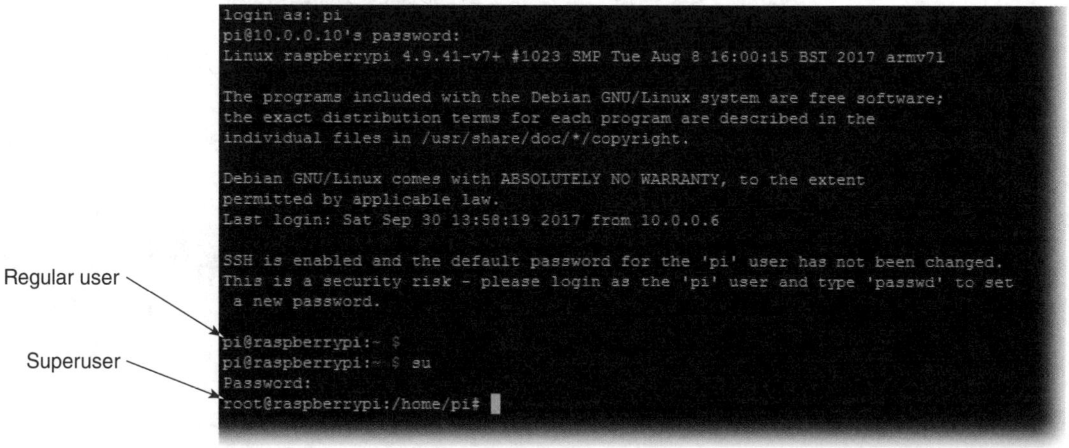

Regular user

Superuser

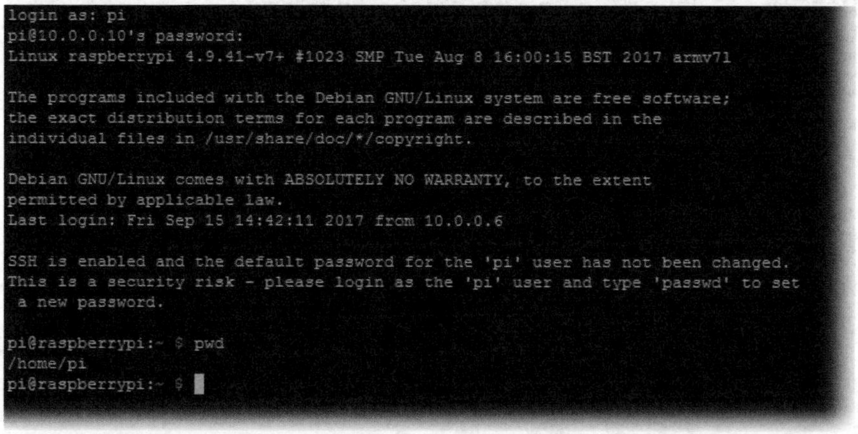

Figure 11-21 The home directory in Linux is typically /home/*UserName*.

current directory to the subdirectory named Documents. Other examples of using the **cd** command, as well as other basic commands, are shown in Figure 11-22.

Viewing Files and Directories

To view the files in a directory, enter the **ls** command, as shown in Figure 11-23. In this example, directories are shown in blue. This makes it easier to distinguish directories from files. The command **ls** is short for *list*. The real power of the **ls** command, as with many CLI commands, is adding switches to increase functionality.

When you run the **ls** command, it may not be obvious what the information represents, as shown in Figure 11-24. At the top of the list is the total number of files in this directory. The first character in an individual file or folder listing specifies the type of the file. A hyphen (-) means it is a normal file. A D means it is a directory. An S means it is a socket file. An L means it is a link file. A *socket file* is a file that allows a user to pass information between different applications, similar to piping a command. An L means it is a link file. A *link file* is a part of a file system that allows a user to access one file from multiple locations, similar to a shortcut created in Windows.

The next nine characters comprise field 1. This specifies the file permissions. Permissions are discussed in detail in Chapter 3. The character after field 1 is field 2,

Figure 11-22 There are many useful commands in a Linux command shell.

Command	Description
cd..	Navigates to the parent directory
cd /	Changes to the root folder
cd ~	Changes to the root of your home directory
rm	Removes files or directories
mkdir	Makes or creates a new directory
cp	Copies files from one location to another
mv	Moves or renames a file
echo	Sends information back to the screen
clear	Clears the screen of all information

Goodheart-Willcox Publisher

Figure 11-23 The **ls** command in Linux lists the files in a directory.

```
login as: pi
pi@10.0.0.10's password:
Linux raspberrypi 4.9.41-v7+ #1023 SMP Tue Aug 8 16:00:15 BST 2017 armv7l

The programs included with the Debian GNU/Linux system are free software;
the exact distribution terms for each program are described in the
individual files in /usr/share/doc/*/copyright.

Debian GNU/Linux comes with ABSOLUTELY NO WARRANTY, to the extent
permitted by applicable law.
Last login: Fri Sep 15 15:09:26 2017 from 10.0.0.6

SSH is enabled and the default password for the 'pi' user has not been changed.
This is a security risk - please login as the 'pi' user and type 'passwd' to set
 a new password.

pi@raspberrypi:~ $ pwd
/home/pi
pi@raspberrypi:~ $ ls
Desktop    Downloads  Pictures  python_games  Videos
Documents  Music      Public    Templates
pi@raspberrypi:~ $ 
```

Goodheart-Willcox Publisher

Figure 11-24 The information returned by the **ls** command lists the type of file; permissions for the user, group, and anyone else who accesses it; links to the file; owner, size, and group of the file; date last modified; and name.

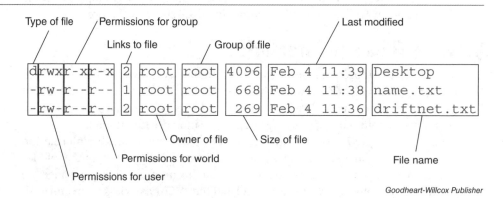

Goodheart-Willcox Publisher

which indicates how many links to the file exist. After field 2 is field 3, which displays the owner of the file. In Figure 11-24, the owner of the file is root. Field 4 specifies the group of the file. In this example, the group is also called root. Field 5 is the size of the file. Field 6 shows the date and time when the file was last modified. Field 7 is the last column and lists the actual name of the file.

Links

Links allow you to work with a single file but have access via different files. If data is changed in a file, the change is reflected in both the original file and the linked file. There are two types of links: *hard links* and *symbolic links*, as shown in Figure 11-25. A **hard link** points directly to the original data. This allows you to point to a single file instead of creating multiple ones. A **symbolic link** is one made to another *link*, not directly to the original data. The primary difference between a hard link and soft link is that with a hard link, the data must be on the same file system and partition. A symbolic link does not have that restriction.

In Linux, the **ln** command is used to create both type of links. To create a hard link, simply enter ln *file1 file2*, substituting the two desired files for *file1* and *file2*. To create a symbolic link, add the **-s** switch, for example ln -s *file1 file2*. Be aware, however, if you delete the original data file, the link will be broken. If you try to view the contents via the symbolic link, an error will be received. This is because the link is trying to reference the data in the originally linked file.

Linux Help and Command Options

Most Linux commands can provide help on a command and its switches. Add the **-help** switch to display help. For example, ls -help will provide help on the **ls** command. This switch also provides the syntax or usage information of the command. Linux also contains built-in commands. To view additional help on a shell's built-in commands, enter the **help** command followed by the name of the shell command.

Many executable programs also include a formal piece of documentation called a manual, or man page. You can view this documentation using the **man** command, as shown in Figure 11-26. In this example, the man page for the **ping** command is displayed. The **ping** command is used to test the connectivity between the user's computer and a specified destination IP address. To exit or quit the man page, press the [Q] key.

Piping

The pipe symbol is used as a command option in Linux the same way as it is in a Windows command or PowerShell prompt. The symbol tells Linux to send the output of one command to another command. For example, entering ls | nl first creates a list using the **ls** command, and then sends the list to the **nl** command to create a numbered list.

The **head** and **tail** commands are used to limit the view of the output. The **head** command displays the first part of a file. The **tail** command displays the last part of a file. The **-n** switch for either command specifies the number of lines to display. If you do not specify a number, the command will display ten lines by default. The **head** and **tail** commands are useful when a list is piped to them. This shortens the list display, as shown in Figure 11-27.

4.1

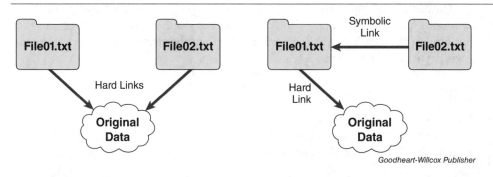

Figure 11-25 A hard link is direct to the original data, while a symbolic link points to another link.

Goodheart-Willcox Publisher

Figure 11-26 The **man** command helps a user view the executable programs documentation.

```
PING(8)                    System Manager's Manual: iputils                    PING(8)

NAME
       ping - send ICMP ECHO_REQUEST to network hosts

SYNOPSIS
       ping [-aAbBdDfhLnOqrRUvV46] [-c count] [-F flowlabel] [-i interval] [-I
       interface] [-l preload] [-m mark] [-M pmtudisc option] [-N node
       info option] [-w deadline] [-W timeout] [-p pattern] [-Q tos] [-s pack
       etsize] [-S sndbuf] [-t ttl] [-T timestamp option] [hop ...] destina
       tion

DESCRIPTION
       ping uses the ICMP protocol's mandatory ECHO_REQUEST datagram to elicit
       an ICMP ECHO_RESPONSE from a host or gateway.  ECHO_REQUEST datagrams
       (``pings'') have  an  IP and ICMP header, followed by a struct timeval
       and then an arbitrary number of ``pad'' bytes used  to  fill  out  the
       packet.

       ping  works  with both IPv4 and IPv6. Using only one of them explicitly
       can be enforced by specifying -4 or -6.

       ping can also send IPv6 Node Information Queries (RFC4620).  Intermedi
       ate hops may not be allowed, because IPv6 source routing was deprecated
       (RFC5095).

OPTIONS
       -4      Use IPv4 only.

       -6      Use IPv6 only.

       -a      Audible ping.

       -A      Adaptive ping. Interpacket interval adapts to  round-trip  time,
               so  that  effectively  not more than one (or more, if preload is
               set) unanswered probe is present in the network. Minimal  inter
               val is  200msec  for  not super-user. On networks with low rtt
               this mode is essentially equivalent to flood mode.

       -b      Allow pinging a broadcast address.

       -B      Do not allow ping to  change  source  address  of  probes.   The
               address is bound to one selected when ping starts.

       -c count
               Stop  after  sending  count  ECHO_REQUEST packets. With deadline
               option, ping waits for count ECHO_REPLY packets, until the time
Manual page ping(8) line 1 (press h for help or q to quit)
```

Goodheart-Willcox Publisher

Figure 11-27 The **tail** command can be used to shorten a list to include only a specified number of items at the end of the list.

```
pi@raspberrypi:/ $ ls
bin  boot  dev  etc  home  lib  lost+found  man  media  mnt  opt  proc  root  run  sbin  srv  sys  tmp  usr  var
pi@raspberrypi:/ $ ls | tail -n 5
srv
sys
tmp
usr
var
pi@raspberrypi:/ $
```

Goodheart-Willcox Publisher

Output can be piped to multiple commands. Each subsequent command takes its output from the previously run command. For example, you can create a list of commands, shorten it to the first ten, and then number the list, by entering the following syntax: ls | head | nl.

 4.1

Cat

The Linux-based **cat command** is a utility used to view and create files, display contents of multiple files simultaneously, or redirect the contents of multiple files into a single file. Cat is short for *concatenate*, which means linking items together in a series. The basic syntax is cat test, which displays the contents of a test file. To combine the contents of multiple files, list the files you wish to combine with the cat command, then insert a greater-than symbol followed by the new file's name. For example, to create a file named NewFile with the contents of Test1 and Test2, use the command syntax cat test1 test2 > newfile.

Grep

The **grep command** is a helpful utility used to search for plaintext data. It is useful for printing the lines from a file or input stream that match an expression. For example, if you need to locate all files containing the word Linda that are located in the /passwd subdirectory of the /etc directory, enter the following syntax: grep Linda /etc/passwd.

Data can also be piped to the **grep** command. For example, the results of the command syntax, ifconfig | grep 192 shows only the lines in the output of the **ifconfig** command that contain the string 192.

Chmod

4.1

The **chmod command** is a Linux-based command that enables a user to change file and folder permissions. Recall from Chapter 3 that there are three types of permissions: read (r), write (w), and execute (x). Permissions are assigned to three entities: the user, the user's default group, and others. Permissions can be assigned in one of two modes: symbolic or octal.

In *symbolic mode*, the command syntax for adding or removing permissions is either a plus or minus sign. Additionally, permissions can be set at user, group, or other levels using the initials u (user), g (group), or o (other). Permissions can also be assigned for all users using the initial a. For example, if you want to assign rwx permissions to TestFile1 for a default group, then the command syntax would be chmod g+rwx testfile1. In this example, the + is adding the rwx permissions. If the goal were to remove those same permissions, the syntax would be chmod g - rwx testfile1.

In *octal mode*, numbers are used to represent permissions. Each number represents the binary value of the desired permission, as shown in Figure 11-28. Octal numbers can be combined to apply permissions for users, groups, and everyone else on a system. When combining octal-based permissions, the first number applies to the user, the second number applies to the group, and the third number applies to everyone else. For example, if you wanted to assign all permissions to the users, read permissions for the group, and no permission for everyone else for TestFile1, the command syntax used is chmod 740 Testfile1.

Octal Value	Binary Equivalent	Resulting Permission
0	000	No permission
1	001	Execute permission
2	010	Write permission
3	011	Write and execute permissions
4	100	Read permission
5	101	Read and execute permissions
6	110	Read and write permissions
7	111	Read, write, and execute permissions

Figure 11-28 In octal mode, each number represents the binary value of the desired permission.

Goodheart-Willcox Publisher

Viewing Running Processes

A *process*, or running program, is viewed with the **ps** command. Each process has a unique identifier called a processor ID (PID), as shown in Figure 11-29. On a server, it is helpful to see which user is running the processes. This action can be accomplished by adding the **–u** switch. Also, the **grep** command can be used to look for processes by using keywords. For example, ps | grep bash will look for any process that contains the string bash. The **top** command is even more detailed. **top** displays statistics about processes and resources and will run until you press the [Q] key to end the command.

4.1

TECH TIP

In computing, a network interface card verifies that the packets it receives are correct. Any packets that do not belong to the NIC are dropped. However, if you need to capture or analyze *all* traffic flowing through the interface, promiscuous mode must be enabled. This can be accomplished by entering ifconfig *adapter name* promisc, where *adapter name* is replaced with your actual adapter name. To disable promiscuous mode, place a hyphen before promisc. (-promisc)

Viewing Network Configuration

As with Windows command line programs, Linux offers a great deal of commands to view network configuration information. The most visible of these commands is **ifconfig**, which is the Linux equivalent of the Windows **ipconfig** command. Like **ipconfig**, the **ifconfig** command returns information about network adapters and related TCP/IP information. The results of the **ifconfig** command are shown in Figure 11-30.

Figure 11-29 The **ps** command lists the processes that are currently running in Linux.

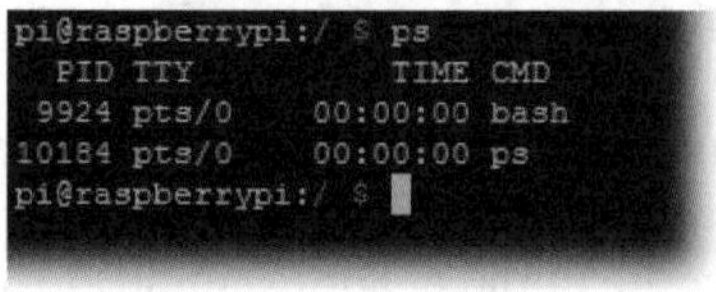

Goodheart-Willcox Publisher

Figure 11-30 The **ifconfig** command is the Linux equivalent of **ipconfig** and displays information about network adapters and related TCP/IP information.

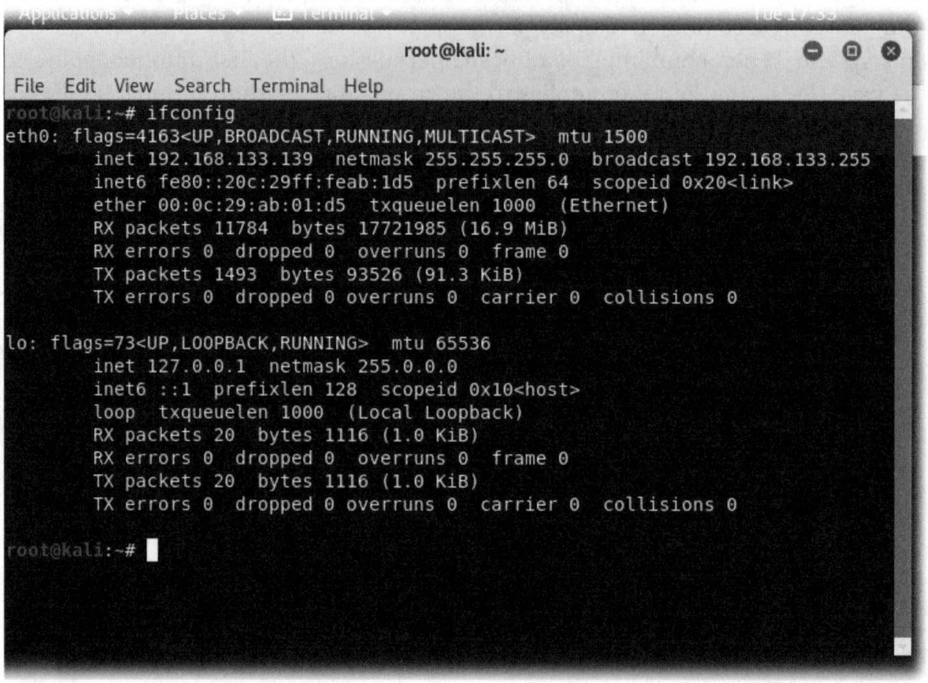

Goodheart-Willcox Publisher

The **ifconfig** command returns similar information as get-netipaddress, but it also provides other helpful information, such as the status of packets being sent to (TX) and from (RX) the network adapter. Additionally, **ifconfig** is used to monitor security on a network by looking at the number of packets moving to and from a device. If a device that does not normally see a great deal of traffic suddenly has a high number of packets, it would be a cause for additional monitoring or investigation.

The **ip** command is similar to **ifconfig**, but it is much more powerful and has more capabilities, such as configuring or modifying routing, tunneling, and creating or deleting IP addresses. An important switch for the **ip** command is –route, which allows a user to view the default router, as shown in Figure 11-31. Since it is possible for a hacker to change the settings on a default router, it is important to monitor the routing information closely.

In Linux, you can also use the **ping** command; however, the command will continue pinging the destination until you manually stop the command by pressing [Ctrl][C]. The **traceroute** command replaces **tracert** from Windows, but you can still use **nslookup** for DNS or the command **dig**, for example dig ubuntu.com.

Logger

✛ **4.1**

The **logger command** is a Linux-based command that enables an administrator to make notes in the syslog log file located in the **/var/log** directory. This command is installed in most Linux distributions by default and enables security personnel to communicate securely within a log file. **Logger** also enables users to test the functionality of log files to ensure they have not been manipulated.

The syntax consists of the **logger** command followed by the comment to be added to the log. For example, if a security administrator wanted to add a note to the log file requesting a review of the DHCP log for unauthorized changes, the command syntax would be something similar to logger review dhcp log for unauthorized

---

Figure 11-31 The **ip** command is similar to **ifconfig**, but it is much more powerful and has more capabilities, such as configuring or modifying routing, tunneling, and creating or deleting IP addresses.

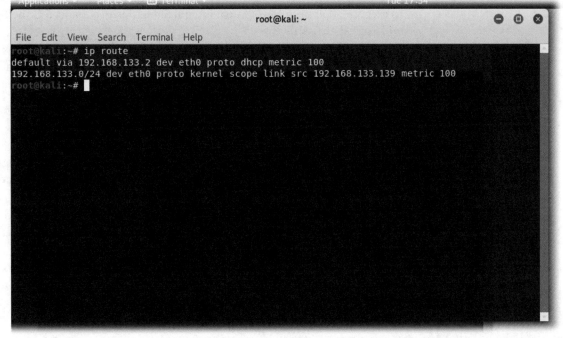

Goodheart-Willcox Publisher

changes. Once run, the command will insert the note along with a timestamp and the user's name to the end of the log file.

Python

4.1

Python is a versatile programming language often used for web, mobile app, and desktop app development. It is often a choice for administrators to create scripts to perform tasks. Python is not installed on Windows by default but is found in many Linux distributions. It is free and can be downloaded on any platform. As with PowerShell, Python has a text or script editor that is used to create scripts, which are saved with a .py extension.

OpenSSL

4.1

OpenSSL is an open-source command-line tool used by network administrators for cryptographic management. OpenSLL is typically used to create Secure Sockets Layer (SSL) certificates and verify cryptographic algorithms, which are used to ensure the confidentiality and integrity of key exchanges.

SUMMARY

Command-Line Interface

- A *command-line interface (CLI)* is a text-based user interface that executes actions within the computer by entering textual commands instead of employing a mouse or touch screen.
- In Microsoft operating systems, there are two command-line interfaces: original shell and PowerShell.
- Linux operating systems have their own shells that act as command interprets to execute other programs: Bourne-Again Shell (Bash), enhanced C shell (Tcsh), and Korn shell (Ksh).
- Managing systems from the command-line interface offers more options and flexibility when running commands than when using a graphical interface.

Windows Command Prompt

- The Windows command prompt is a command-line interface for entering commands manually.
- When entering a command, all commands at the prompt must be entered using the keyboard and executed by pressing the [Enter] key. Key commands used to assess the security posture of an organization include: **ping, tracert, pathping, nslookup** and **dig, arp, route**, and **iconfig**.
- In a command-line interface, a *switch* is a modifier added to a command to enforce specific parameters and help limit or narrow the possible results. It is often preceded by either a hyphen (-) or a forward slash (/).
- *Piping* is part of the interface that refers to the act of directing the results of one command into the input syntax of another command. This enables a user to run multiple commands simultaneously, provided the commands are separated with a pipe symbol.

- Some of the most used commands are employed for file and directory management and navigation. These commands include **md**, **cd**, **dir**, **del**, and **rd**.
- The **tasklist** command gives you a snapshot of all tasks currently running on a host and helps a user manage all of the tasks running in a system.
- Both processes and services run on a computer. A *process* is an actively running computer program. A *service* is a program that is run in the background of an operating system to provide specific features and functionality. These can be combined with task commands to find or stop tasks.
- It is possible to view installed device drivers through the command-line interface by using the **driverquery** command.
- Batch files are a way to automate tasks using the Windows command prompt by combining several commands into a single script.
- When used effectively, command prompt can be a powerful tool. Command output can be directed to a file or the system clipboard instead of the screen, and the command prompt window can be customized to suit your preferences.

Windows PowerShell

- Windows PowerShell is a powerful, open-source, object-based command-line shell integrated with Windows.NET technology that can be used to manage a system.
- PowerShell treats everything as an object. Objects are embedded with data (known as properties) and contain methods, which are actions performed on the data.
- *Cmdlets* are programs inside PowerShell. There are over 100 cmdlets included in PowerShell, but more cmdlets can be added. In addition, it is important to remember PowerShell cmdlets use a specific syntax called *verb-noun syntax*. The command is a verb or action that acts on the noun.
- In PowerShell, the **get-help** cmdlet is used to display help. In recent versions of PowerShell, expanded help files are no longer included on the basic installation of PowerShell. The expanded help files are accessed online using the -online switch and can also be downloaded using the **update-help** cmdlet.
- Advanced PowerShell command options can be used to manage networking, security, Hyper-V virtualization, and the Active Directory for Microsoft servers.
- Providers are programs that organize data in specialized groups to be easily viewed and managed. By switching between providers, you can exclusively manage multiple environments.
- PowerShell uses scripts to automate tasks, similar to batch files, for the command prompt. Scripts can be more powerful than batch files due to the advanced use of cmdlets and their methods.

Introduction to Linux

- Linux is an open-source operating system that was derived from the UNIX operating system. Due to its open-source nature, a number of Linux distributions have been created or *forked*.
- A *distro* is a unique operating system based off a Linux kernel and package management system that typically includes a Linux kernel, tools and libraries licensed under GNU, and a package-management system.

- Due to the multiple variations of the program, the command-line interface (CLI) provides a common interface and offers an efficient way by which to manage the operating system.
- The Linux command-line environment is called the shell and is a command-language interpreter that executes commands from direct keyboard entry or a program.

Linux Commands

- When you first log in to Linux, the working directory is set to your home directory, or a directory where a user stores personal files.
- Linux commands are case sensitive and can be used to manage files, directories, networking environments, and other operating system functionality.
- The **cd** command (*change directory*) does just what it implies; it changes the current directory where you are located.
- The **ls** command, short for *list*, allows you to view the files in a directory. The real power of the **ls** command, as with many CLI commands, is adding switches to increase functionality.
- Links allow you to work with a single file but have access via different files. A hard link points directly to the original data. A symbolic link is one made to another link, not directly to the original data. The **ln** command is used to create both type of links.

Linux Help and Command Options

- Most Linux commands can provide help on a command and its switches by adding the **-help** switch. Entering the **help** command followed by the name of the shell command helps you view additional help on a shell's built-in commands.
- The pipe symbol is used to tell Linux to send the output of one command to another command. The **head** and **tail** commands are used to limit the view of the output.
- The **cat** command is used to view and create files, display contents of multiple files simultaneously, or redirect the contents of multiple files into a single file. It is short for concatenate, which means linking items together in a series.
- The **grep** command is a helpful utility used to search for plain-text data. It is useful for printing the lines from a file or input stream that match an expression.
- The **chmod** command allows a user to change file and folder permissions. Permissions are assigned to three entities: the user, the user's default group, and others. They can also be assigned in one of two modes: symbolic or octal.
- A process can be viewed with the **ps** command. Several commands can be used to view running processes including **-u** switch, **grep** command, and **top** command.
- The most visible of the Linux commands is **ifconfig**, which returns information about network adapters and related TCP/IP information.
- The **logger** command is a Linux-based command that enables an administrator to make notes in the syslog log file located in the **/var/log** directory. It enables security personnel to communicate securely within a log file as well as enables users to test the functionality of log files to ensure they have not been manipulated.

Python

- Python is a versatile programming language often used for web, mobile app, and desktop app development. It is often a choice for administrators to create scripts to perform tasks.

OpenSSL

- OpenSSL is an open-source command-line tool used by network administrators for cryptographic management. OpenSSL is typically used to create Secure Sockets Layer (SSL) certificates and verify cryptographic algorithms.

REVIEW QUESTIONS

1. Define a *command-line interface (CLI)*.

2. What is a *security posture*?

3. Summarize how to use the Windows command prompt.

4. Explain how to launch the Windows command prompt in Windows 10.

5. Explain each of the seven main commands used to assess the security posture of an organization.

6. Which command would you enter at the command prompt to stop a task running?

7. Which command is placed in a batch file to display two messages and the values of both the computer name and date variables?

8. Identify and explain two elements of Windows PowerShell.

9. How is the syntax of a PowerShell cmdlet constructed?

10. List and explain the purpose of two advanced PowerShell commands.

11. If you want to run a script titled fileconversion that exists in the current directory, what would you enter?

12. List and explain three elements of the Linux operating system discussed in the chapter.

13. Different versions of Linux are referred to as _____.

14. On a Linux system, how can you determine if you are logged in with superuser rights?

15. Identify three Linux commands and their purposes.

16. What is the purpose of the **cd ~** command in Linux?

17. Compare a hard link to a symbolic link.

18. Explain the Linux **help** command and one other command option discussed in the chapter.

19. Summarize the primary usage of Python.

20. What is *OpenSSL*?

SAMPLE SECURITY+ EXAM QUESTIONS

1. You are searching for a specific Excel file you believe contains proprietary company information. Which of the following Windows command prompt entries will assist in locating all Excel files on the computer?

   A. find *.xlsx /s

   B. dir *.xlsx /s

   C. locate *.xlsx /s

   D. dir *.xlsx /more

2. Which command identifies the local networking configuration specifically for IPv6 configuration information?

   A. ipconfig /ipv6

   B. ipconfig | findstr "IPv6"

   C. ipconfig /all

   D. ipconfig /v6

3. When using the Windows command prompt, which of the following entries will direct the output to an existing file named results.txt?

   A. ipconfig /output results.txt

   B. ipconfig > results.txt

   C. ipconfig >>results.txt

   D. ipconfig /results.txt

4. Which of the following is a PowerShell cmdlet?

   A. **getservice**

   B. **get-service**

   C. **get_service**

   D. **services-get**

5. Using PowerShell, you need to create a list of all files in a directory with a name that begins with the letter D, and you want to save the list in a file named discovery.txt. What is the correct entry for doing this?

   A. get-childitem d*.*

   B. get-childitem d*.* > discovery.txt

   C. get-childitem d*.* | out-file discovery.txt

   D. get-childitem d*.* | export discovery.txt

6. The Linux shell entry ls | lh | nl returns an error. What is the correct command entry?

   A. ls -lh -nl

   B. ls -lh | nl

   C. ls -lh | Nl

   D. ls -Lh | Nl

7. Which of the following will help monitor your system for specific dangerous files without direct intervention?

   A. A cmdlet

   B. The **get-process** command

   C. Bash

   D. A script

8. You need to determine which program is using the majority of the CPU time on the computer. You are concerned this program might be malware. Which Linux command is best suited for this task?

   A. **grep**

   B. **cal**

   C. **echo**

   D. **ps**

9. Which of the following is a *false* statement?

   A. Linux commands are case sensitive.

   B. Windows command prompt commands are not case-sensitive, but PowerShell cmdlets are.

   C. PowerShell can be installed on Linux.

   D. PowerShell aliases include Linux commands along with command-prompt commands.

10. Which of the following would identify if a computer is being directed to the correct router on a Linux host?

   A. ifconfig

   B. ip gateway

   C. ip route

   D. ls

LAB EXERCISES

Lab Activity 11-1: Command Prompt Options

There are two modes to the command-line interface. It can be run in normal mode or as an administrator.

1. Click the Windows **Start** button, and enter cmd in the text box. This is perhaps the easiest way to launch the command prompt, but it is also located in the **Start** menu itself.

2. The command prompt is running in normal mode. In the command prompt window, enter exit. As soon as you press the [Enter] key, the window is closed.

3. Click **Start**>**All Apps**>**Windows System** and locate the **Command Prompt** icon.

4. To run the command prompt as an administrator, right-click on the **Command Prompt** icon, and click **Run as Administrator** in the shortcut menu.

5. If prompted, click the **Yes** button to continue, or enter appropriate credentials. Notice the title bar indicates the command prompt is being run as an administrator, as shown.

6. Enter dir. The **dir** command lists files and folders in the current directory.

7. Enter dir /? to display help for the **dir** command. Review the options available. Which switch would you use to perform a directory listing and include the subdirectories?

8. Enter dir /s /p. This combines two switches with the command. Describe the function performed by this entry. Note: the result of this command can be long. After you have viewed enough to determine the command's purpose, press the [Ctrl][C] key combination to exit the command. This key combination cancels any command prompt command (but does not exit the command prompt application).

9. Enter cls. The **cls** command clears the screen. This command allows you to clean up the command prompt display.

10. Enter tasklist. This command is similar to running the task manager in the graphical interface.

11. The task list may be longer than one page (screen). To advance the page one line at a time, enter tasklist | more.

12. Press the [Enter] key to show each next line, or press the [Ctrl][C] key combination to exit the command.

13. Press the [F7] key. The commands previously used in this session of the command prompt are displayed in a pop-up box. You can navigate the list with the arrow keys. Press the [Enter] key to execute the highlighted command.

14. Press the [Esc] key to exit the history.

15. Enter exit. This closes the command prompt window.

Lab Activity 11-2: Navigational Commands

Navigating directories using a command-line interface is much different from navigating folders using a graphical interface. It is important to understand how commands are used to navigate through directory structures.

1. Applying what you have learned, launch the command prompt as a regular user.

2. The command prompt should indicate Users\YourUserName. This means the current directory is your personal Users folder. If not, enter cd\users\YourUserName using your valid username.

3. Enter md Practice. This creates a directory named Practice from your current location. It is a subdirectory of your personal Users folder. However, you have simply created the folder, not navigated to it.

4. Enter cd practice. The command prompt should now reflect that you have moved to the Practice directory. Notice that even though the directory was named with an uppercase *P*, this is ignored by the **cd** command.

5. Enter copy c:\windows*.exe. This copies all executable files (with the .exe file extension) from the Windows directory to the current directory, which is your Practice directory.

6. Enter dir s*.*. This displays only the files in the current directory that start with the letter S.

7. Enter cd.. to return to the parent directory of Practice. This is your personal user folder.

8. Enter rd practice. You should receive an error. Why did this happen?

9. Enter rd /? to display the help for the **rd** command. Which switch allows a directory to be deleted even if it contains content?

10. Enter rd practice /s. When prompted, confirm yes or y to delete the Practice directory.

11. Enter cd practice. You should receive an error stating the path cannot be found. This is because the Practice directory no longer exists.

12. Enter exit to close the command prompt.

Lab Activity 11-3: Commands in Batch Files

A batch file can be used to issue several commands in sequence. This is an effective means of simplifying several tasks.

1. Click **Start>All apps>Windows Accessories>Notepad** to launch Notepad.

2. Add the following text to the file.

```
@echo off
Title: %computername% %date%
echo Local users on %computer name%
echo
net user
```

3. Click **File>Save As…**, navigate to your personal Users folder, and save the file as localusers.bat. Be sure to enter .bat as the file extension, not the default .txt extension.

4. Applying what you have learned, launch the command prompt. If needed, navigate to your personal Users folder where the batch file is saved.

5. Enter localusers. The batch file is run, and the output should look similar to what is shown here.

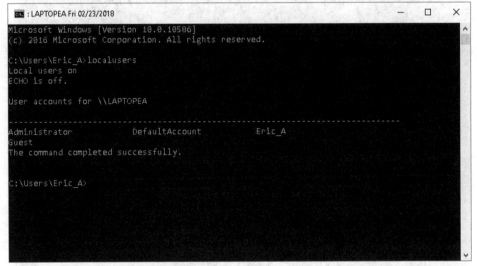

Goodheart-Willcox Publisher

Lab Activity 11-4: PowerShell Cmdlets and Aliases

PowerShell has many commands and aliases. It is easy to list all the commands and aliases in PowerShell for quick reference.

1. Click **Start>All apps>Windows PowerShell>Windows PowerShell**. The PowerShell window is displayed. There are visual cues that allow you to differentiate this from the command prompt. The default background is blue, the title bar states PowerShell, and there is a PS on the prompt.

2. Enter alias. Common command-prompt commands along with Linux commands are displayed with their new PowerShell cmdlet, as shown. Look for some of the commands you have used at the command prompt and find their PowerShell equivalents.

3. To view the cmdlets, enter get-command | more. Remember, the **MORE** command allows you to advance the list one line at a time and the [Ctrl][C] key combination cancels the command.

4. To narrow the search, the list can be filtered by verb or noun choices. Try these options:

   > get-command -verb get
   > get-command -noun disk
   > get-command -noun network*

5. Enter 7*3. What happens?

6. Enter get-se and press the [Tab] instead of the [Enter] key. You can continue pressing the [Tab] key until the command you want appears. Then, press the [Enter] key to execute the command.

7. Enter get-service | sort-object status. This will run the **get-service** cmdlet, and then that output is sorted by the status column.

Goodheart-Willcox Publisher

Lab Activity 11-5: Help for PowerShell Cmdlets

In PowerShell, a separate command is used to access help files. It is important to understand how to use help, including how to access expanded help online.

1. Click **Start**>**All apps**>**Windows**, right-click on the **Windows PowerShell** icon, and click **Run as administrator** in the shortcut menu. When prompted, click the **Yes** button or enter the proper credentials to run the program.

2. Enter get-help get-service. Note: if you receive a message about downloading updated help files, enter N for no. What is the alias for this cmdlet?

3. Press the up arrow on the keyboard once to return to the previous command. At the end of the command, add the -online switch (get-help get-service -online). If you have an active Internet connection, the default web browser is launched and the online help options with more detail is displayed, as shown.

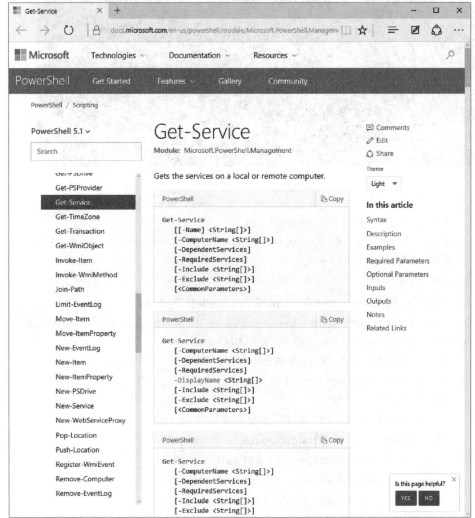

Goodheart-Willcox Publisher

4. Read the information on the online help page. What would you enter to find all services that start with the letter *S*?

5. What would you enter to sort *all* services by status?

6. Close the web browser and return to the PowerShell window.

7. Enter update-help. This cmdlet will install the expanded help files on the computer, as shown. It may take a few minutes to complete the download.

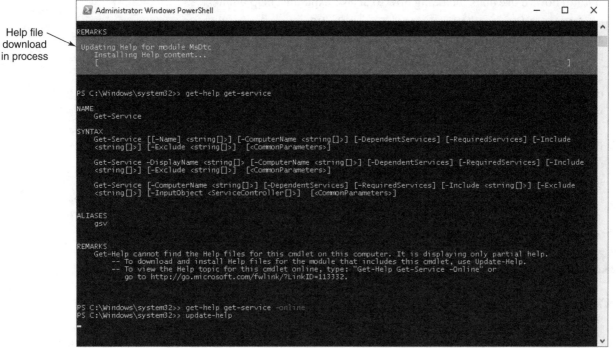

Help file download in process

Goodheart-Willcox Publisher

8. After it finishes, enter get-help get-service -examples. This will display the examples you saw in the online help.

9. Enter get-help get-service —detailed. This will display the full, expanded help that you saw in the online help.

10. Enter exit to close the PowerShell window.

Lab Activity 11-6: Advanced PowerShell Cmdlet Options

PowerShell has many useful commands, or cmdlets. Many of these cmdlets have options that can extend the usefulness of the command.

1. Click **Start>All apps>Windows PowerShell>Windows PowerShell.**

2. Run the **get-childitem** cmdlet to see all files starting with T, but excluding those with a .dll file extension:

   get-childitem c:\windows\t*.* -exclude *.dll

3. View the items in the Windows folder in order by file size:

   get-childitem c:\windows*.* | sort-object length

4. View the installed printers in a column list:

   get-wmiobject win32_printer | format-table

5. Export the list of all processes to an HTML view:

   get-process | convertto-html >process.htm

6. Open the HTML file in the default web browser:

   invoke-item process.htm

7. List all files in the Windows folder greater than 20,000 bytes in size and sorted by name:

get-childitem c:\windows | where-object {$_.length –gt 20000} | sort-object {$_.name}

Lab Activity 11-7: PowerShell Scripts

PowerShell scripts are similar to batch files. They are created in a plain-text editor and saved with a .ps1 file extension.

1. Launch Notepad or any plain-text editor.

2. Save the file as RunningServices.ps1 in your personal Users folder.

3. Enter the following in the script file. The pound sign or hash tag (#) is used in a script file to indicate a comment. Anything after the pound sign is not executed.

#This is my script -- *your name*
#To insert some blank lines on the screen add empty quotation marks ""
#To insert text on the screen, place the text between quotation marks
""

"Open Running Services--Report generated on " + (get-date)
""

get-service | where-object {$_.status -eq "running"}

4. Save the file, and exit Notepad.

5. Applying what you have learned, launch PowerShell and run it as an administrator.

6. Applying what you have learned, change to your personal Users folder where the RunningServices.ps1 script file is saved.

7. Enter .\runningservices to run the script, as shown. Note: if you receive an error that runningservices is not a recognized cmdlet, it is likely the policy needs to be changed to allow scripts to run.

Goodheart-Willcox Publisher

8. Enter set-executionpolicy unrestricted, and confirm you want to change the policy.

9. Enter .\runningservices, and the script should now run.

10. Enter set-executionpolicy restricted, and confirm you want to change the policy. This returns the system to the safer policy for scripts.

Lab Activity 11-8: Linux Commands and Switches

As with Windows command-line commands, many Linux commands have switches. To be proficient in using Linux, it is important to know how to use command switches.

1. As directed by your instructor, launch Linux and access the shell.

2. Are you logged in as a superuser or regular user? How can you tell?

3. Enter the **pwd** command. What is your home directory?

4. Change to the etc directory by entering: cd /etc.

5. Enter ls -lh, as shown. The H stands for *human readable format*.

```
drwxr-xr-x   2 root root     4.0K Jan 18  2017 rsyslog.d
-rw-r--r--   1 root root      12K Aug 19  2015 RTIMULib.ini
drwxr-xr-x   2 root root     4.0K Sep  7 15:00 samba
-rw-r--r--   1 root root     4.1K May 17 11:59 securetty
drwxr-xr-x   4 root root     4.0K Sep  7 14:55 security
drwxr-xr-x   2 root root     4.0K Sep  7 14:46 selinux
-rw-r--r--   1 root root      11K Apr  5 20:07 sensors3.conf
drwxr-xr-x   2 root root     4.0K Sep  7 15:24 sensors.d
-rw-r--r--   1 root root      19K Dec 26  2016 services
drwxr-xr-x   2 root root     4.0K Sep  7 15:08 sgml
-rw-r-----   1 root shadow    940 Sep  7 15:37 shadow
-rw-r--r--   1 root root       73 Sep  7 14:47 shells
drwxr-xr-x   2 root root     4.0K Sep  7 14:59 skel
drwxr-xr-x   2 root root     4.0K Sep  7 16:12 ssh
drwxr-xr-x   4 root root     4.0K Sep  7 15:06 ssl
-rw-r--r--   1 root root      771 Jul 27 22:17 staff-group-for-usr-local
-rw-r--r--   1 root root       16 Sep  7 14:59 subgid
-rw-------   1 root root        0 Sep  7 14:47 subgid-
-rw-r--r--   1 root root       16 Sep  7 14:59 subuid
-rw-------   1 root root        0 Sep  7 14:47 subuid-
-r--r-----   1 root root      669 Jun  5 12:22 sudoers
drwxr-xr-x   2 root root     4.0K Sep  7 15:05 sudoers.d
-rw-r--r--   1 root root     2.7K Sep  7 15:05 sysctl.conf
drwxr-xr-x   2 root root     4.0K Sep  7 15:05 sysctl.d
drwxr-xr-x   5 root root     4.0K Sep  7 14:47 systemd
drwxr-xr-x   2 root root     4.0K Sep  7 14:46 terminfo
-rw-r--r--   1 root root        8 Sep  7 14:47 timezone
drwxr-xr-x   2 root root     4.0K Sep  7 15:30 timidity
drwxr-xr-x   2 root root     4.0K Jul  5 20:31 tmpfiles.d
drwxr-xr-x   3 root root     4.0K Sep  7 14:59 triggerhappy
-rw-r--r--   1 root root     1.3K Mar 16  2016 ucf.conf
drwxr-xr-x   4 root root     4.0K Sep  7 14:47 udev
drwxr-xr-x   2 root root     4.0K Nov 25  2016 udisks2
drwxr-xr-x   3 root root     4.0K Sep  7 15:02 ufw
drwxr-xr-x   2 root root     4.0K Sep  7 14:46 update-motd.d
-rw-r--r--   1 root root     1018 Jan 23  2017 usb_modeswitch.conf
drwxr-xr-x   2 root root     4.0K Jan 23  2017 usb_modeswitch.d
-rw-r--r--   1 root root       51 Jan 13  2017 vdpau_wrapper.cfg
drwxr-xr-x   2 root root     4.0K Sep  7 14:53 vim
drwxr-xr-x   3 root root     4.0K Sep  7 15:30 vnc
-rw-r--r--   1 root root     4.9K Mar 18 14:12 wgetrc
drwxr-xr-x   2 root root     4.0K Sep  7 15:24 wildmidi
drwxr-xr-x   2 root root     4.0K Sep  7 15:13 wpa_supplicant
drwxr-xr-x  11 root root     4.0K Sep  7 15:29 X11
drwxr-xr-x  10 root root     4.0K Sep  7 15:24 xdg
drwxr-xr-x   2 root root     4.0K Sep  7 15:08 xml
drwxr-xr-x   2 root root     4.0K Sep  7 15:24 xpdf
pi@raspberrypi:/etc $
```

6. Enter ls -lt. This lists the directory by modified time.

7. Enter ls -ltr. Adding r to the end of the switch reverses the order. Notice the differences in the directory listing.

8. Enter ls -R. Remember, commands are case sensitive, so be sure to enter an uppercase R. This command switch allows you to search the current directory and all others recursively. Recursively in this case means it will search the current directory and all subdirectories.

Lab Activity 11-9: Linux Command Help

The help system in Linux can assist in learning how to use commands. Access help to see a description of the command and its available switches.

1. Launch Linux, and access the shell.

2. Enter the **clear** command to clean the screen display.

3. Enter cd / to navigate to the root directory.

4. Enter ls -help to view the help screen for the **ls** command.

5. Try running the **ls** command with the **-x** switch and then with the **-X** switch. What is the difference between the two switches? Look carefully at the output to see the difference.

6. Enter cd ~, and then enter pwd. What is the working directory?

7. Applying what you have learned, display help for the **rm** command. What is the command to use to remove empty directories?

8. Investigate these system commands in Linux: **uptime**, **last**, **free**, and **du -h**. What information does each provide? Try each of the commands. Pipe the **du -h** command to the **more** command. Describe how each command is useful to a security technician.

CASE STUDIES

PowerShell and Linux "Hacking" Videos

In 2019, YouTube sparked outrage by removing legitimate educational security videos that involved ethical hacking techniques, including those involving the use of Linux and Microsoft PowerShell methods. After responding to the many complaints over their actions, YouTube restored many of the videos and referred users to their "Harmful and Dangerous Community Content Policy." Many professionals complained the policy was too broad and provided no clarity on how certain videos are flagged. While the controversy appears to have been resolved, the concern about these "ethical videos" remains.

1. Explain the extent to which you agree with the following statement: *While these instructional videos may provide resources for ethical hackers, YouTube's response was justified due to the overwhelming number of cyber threats that may have occurred due unknowingly to the use of the tools in the videos.*

2. If a hacker is arrested and found to have used or accessed videos that were related to the hack in question, how liable should YouTube or the video poster be? Elaborate on your response by considering other hosted activities and whether those are held to a similar standard.

3. If such videos were banned or instead available on the darknet, a culture of backroom sharing and interactions with less ethical individuals could occur. How could those resulting interactions impact the ability of security professionals to combat threats?

4. Many of the videos hosted on YouTube do not always have disclaimers regarding legal liabilities or ethical responsibility. If YouTube or similar sites required this, what type of difference could this make to the availability or usability of the videos?

LEARNING OUTCOMES

- Define *secure network design*.
- Summarize out-of-band management (OOBM).
- Identify types of network devices used to provide security for a network.
- Explain security devices commonly encountered in a network.
- Identify elements included in network architecture security.
- Discuss where security devices can be placed.
- Explain types of deception technology.
- Recognize basic network segmentation designs.
- Summarize microsegmentation.

KEY TERMS

access control list (ACL)
active-active configuration
active-passive configuration
affinity scheduling
aggregation switch
aggregator
anomaly
anomaly monitoring
antispoofing
authentication header (AH)
BPDU guard
broadcast storm
Challenge Handshake Authentication
    Protocol (CHAP)
configuration management (CM)
content filter
correlation engine
deception technology
demilitarized zone (DMZ)
DNS sinkhole
Dynamic Host Configuration Protocol
    (DHCP) snooping
east-west traffic
encapsulating security payload (ESP)
Extensible Authentication Protocol
    (EAP)

extranet
fake telemetry
flood guard
forward proxy server
guest network
heuristic-based monitoring
honeyfile
honeynet
honeypot
Hypertext Markup Language version 5
    (HTML5)
in-band
Internet Key Exchange Protocol
    version 2 (IKEv2)
intranet
IP Security (IPSec)
IP spoofing
jump server
Layer 2 Tunneling Protocol (L2TP)
loop prevention
MAC filtering
MAC flooding
microsegmentation
Microsoft Challenge Handshake
    Authentication Protocol (MS-
    CHAP)

NAT gateway
network address translation (NAT)
network interface card (NIC) teaming
network segmentation
network TAP
non-persistence
north-south traffic
out-of-band
out-of-band management (OOBM)
packet-filtering firewall
Password Authentication Protocol
    (PAP)
Point-to-Point Tunneling Protocol
    (PPTP)
port mirroring
port security
protocol
proxy firewall
proxy server
Quality of Service (QoS)
reverse proxy server
round-robin scheduling
Secure Socket Tunneling Protocol
    (SSTP)
security configuration management
    (SCM)

security zone
signature-based monitoring
stateful firewall
stateless firewall
transport mode

tunneling
tunnel mode
unified threat management (UTM)
   device
virtual IP (VIP) address

virtual local area network (VLAN)
virtual private network (VPN)
VLAN access control list (VACL)
VPN concentrator
zero trust

 SECURITY+ CERTIFICATION EXAM OBJECTIVES

The following Security+ Certification Exam Objectives are covered in this chapter.

+ 1.4: Media access control (MAC) flooding
+ 2.1: Configuration management
+ 2.1: Geographical considerations
+ 2.1: Secure Sockets Layer (SSL)/ Transport Layer Security (TLS) inspection
+ 2.1: Deception and disruption
+ 2.5: Network
+ 2.5: Non-persistence
+ 3.1: IPSec
+ 3.3: Load balancing
+ 3.3: Network segmentation
+ 3.3: Virtual private network (VPN)
+ 3.3: Out-of-band management
+ 3.3: Port security
+ 3.3: Jump servers

+ 3.3: Proxy servers
+ 3.3: Network-based intrusion detection system (NIDS)/network-based intrusion prevention system (NIPS)
+ 3.3: HSM
+ 3.3: Sensors
+ 3.3: Collectors
+ 3.3: Aggregators
+ 3.3: Web application firewall (WAF)
+ 3.3: Stateful
+ 3.3: Stateless
+ 3.3: Unified threat management (UTM)
+ 3.3: Network address translation (NAT) gateway

+ 3.3: Content/URL filter
+ 3.3: Open-source vs. proprietary
+ 3.3: Hardware vs. software
+ 3.3: Appliance vs. host-based vs. virtual
+ 3.3: Access control list (ACL)
+ 3.3: Route security
+ 3.3: Quality of Service (QoS)
+ 3.3: Implications of IPv6
+ 3.3: Port spanning/port mirroring
+ 3.8: EAP
+ 3.8: Challenge Handshake Authentication Protocol (CHAP)
+ 3.8: Password Authentication Protocol (PAP)

OVERVIEW

The security of a computer network often relies on the successful implementation of a secure design that includes a wide array of devices with built-in security features. A network cannot function without infrastructural devices such as bridges, switches, and routers, and those devices can be secured; however, it is ideal to include additional devices designed to protect a network, such as firewalls, intrusion-detection systems, and monitors that record suspect events.

In this chapter, you will explore common vulnerabilities that can affect the operation of network devices. Additionally, you will learn about necessary configurations that enable security teams to enhance network security and monitor activity on connected devices to prevent or deny attacks.

SECURITY+ NOTE

Topics that comprise the Implementation domain in the CompTIA Security+ SY0-601 Exam Objectives account for one-fourth of the certification exam questions, illustrating the importance of this area to security professionals, network specialists, and organizations. It is important to understand the role of the network devices fully, as well as their vulnerabilities and methods of protection. As you review the content, be sure to make note of appropriate design principles and locations of networking devices and zones and how they impact network security.

Secure Network Design

Secure network design is the process of designing a network to include measures to support network security. *Network security* is the policies, procedures, and techniques used to eliminate or monitor unauthorized access or intrusion to a computer network and its devices. It focuses on protection of the infrastructure and architecture of the network through the application of software and hardware solutions.

Infrastructure is the components that make up a network. Infrastructure is the hardware and software that enables communications between devices, application, and users.

Architecture is the design of the network and placement of the components. Secure network architecture requires strategic placement of devices. Placement is dependent on the purpose of the device, its resilience, and where or how it interacts with the network.

Quality of Service (QoS) is a set of technologies that enable a network to run priority applications and deliver as expected despite limited capacity or connectivity. It focuses on reducing *latency*, which is a delay in packet delivery; *jitter*, which is variance in latency; and error rates. QoS also optimizes bandwidth. Network reliability is achieved through QoS technologies differentiating among devices for processing and data flows as well as enabling an administrator to assign priority order and bandwidth limitations for packets. QoS is of particular importance to applications reliant on real-time packet delivery, such as VoIP applications and video conferencing.

On Windows machines, QoS is installed by default with network connections beginning with Windows XP. This can be toggled on or off through the QoS Packet Scheduler, as shown in Figure 12-1.

Figure 12-1 Quality of Service (QoS) is a set of technologies that enable a network to run priority applications and deliver as expected, despite limited capacity or connectivity.

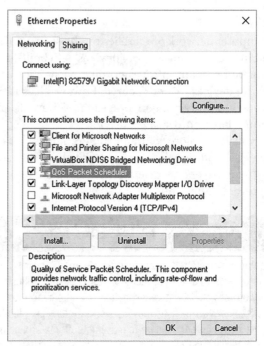

Goodheart-Willcox Publisher

Out-of-Band Management (OOBM)

 3.3

Secure network design relies on the ability to perform out-of-band management. **Out-of-band management (OOBM)** is a method of remotely managing and controlling infrastructure using an interface separate from the primary connection. Managing devices remotely enables administrators to maintain control through dedicated alternative access methods that do not rely on the LAN. This means that administrators can manage devices from anywhere, and in the event LAN connectivity fails, administrators can continue management of devices through OOBM.

A primary reason for incorporating out-of-band management is security. Public-facing devices that handle Internet traffic, such as routers, switches, and firewalls, should not be accessible to arbitrary access or management. Out-of-band management can be accomplished using the following:

- *Modem.* Connecting a modem to the console port of a networked device is a traditional method of enabling OOBM. However, it requires a dedicated phone line and modem for each device managed, so scalability is drastically limited. Additionally, due to bandwidth constraints, only a few devices can be accessed simultaneously, and securing modem lines can be difficult to achieve.
- *Terminal server.* Terminal servers are devices with low-speed serial interfaces that connect to various devices in a remote location. A terminal service is most useful when there are a number of devices requiring management. Terminal access is possible through a separate network, usually through an Ethernet connection.
- *Separate management network.* Devices can be placed on a network separate from the main network. It is important, however, to ensure these devices cannot be accessed from the main network. This is often accomplished using a virtual local area network (VLAN).

Network Devices

Networks have standard devices, also known as *appliances* or *hardware*, that enable functionality and communication on a network. Devices are classified by functionality in the seven-layer *Open System Interconnection (OSI)* reference model. When configured properly, network appliances provide security for a network.

Hub

A *hub* is a network device that connects multiple nodes and local area networks together. Hubs are the most basic of all networking devices because they only connect networking devices with identical protocols. In computing, a **protocol** is an industry-accepted standardized format that allows communication between devices. Protocols exist in all layers of the OSI model and will be discussed in more detail in a later chapter.

Hubs do not have filtering or addressing capabilities and can only distribute packets to connected devices. In addition to functioning as a basic connection point, hubs can also be used as repeaters by amplifying signals before sending data packets. Hubs operate at the physical layer (layer 1) of the OSI model. As a secure networking practice, hubs should *not* be used in enterprise networks because they do not offer enhanced security protection.

Bridge

A *bridge* is a hardware or software device used to join two separate networks or network segments to enable communication. Bridges operate at the data link layer (layer 2) of the OSI model, so all connections made to a given bridge must use the same DLL protocol, such as Ethernet.

When networks are connected, the risk of malware and attack increases. Suppose one network connected to a bridge is secured while another connection is not. This connection establishes an unsecured link between the two networks and puts them both at risk. The steps for securing bridges are comparable to those used to protect other network equipment.

Switch

A *switch* is hardware that connects devices on a network and is responsible for managing traffic within a network or subnet. It relies on packet switching to receive and transmit data to its appropriate destination. Switches operate on either the data link layer (layer 2) or the network layer (layer 3) of the OSI model. *Layer-3 switches* are switches that also provide routing capabilities in addition to their normal tasks. Switches perform largely the same function as hubs, but they distribute traffic much more efficiently and are often referred to as *intelligent hubs*.

Often, multiple switches are needed to connect devices. In a typical network setup, switches are connected to each other in a *daisy-chain* manner, meaning after the primary switch, each subsequent switch is plugged into the one ahead of it. This connection can often increase the time needed to navigate traffic on a network. To combat this situation, switch aggregation is employed in a multiple-switch environment. An **aggregation switch** is a networking device used to combine multiple network connections in a single switch, as illustrated in Figure 12-2. Switch aggregation is a preferred method for increasing network performance and availability.

Configurations for enabling security in a switch include the following.

 3.3

Port Security

Port security is a traffic-control feature that prevents unknown or unauthorized devices from forwarding packets. It also enables a security administrator to configure

Figure 12-2 An aggregation switch is a networking device used to combine multiple network connections in a single switch.

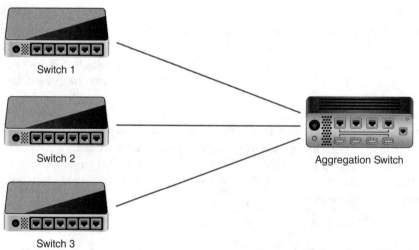

Switch 1

Switch 2

Switch 3

Aggregation Switch

Goodheart-Willcox Publisher; (switches) Ulvur/Shutterstock.com

individual ports to allow a specific number of MAC addresses. A common way of enabling port security is through MAC filtering. **MAC filtering** is an access control method by which a MAC address is used to determine access to a network.

Do not rely on MAC filtering to deter a competent hacker. MAC addresses can be spoofed or faked, which may allow a hacker access through the MAC filter. There are many tools to spoof MAC addresses, including utilities such as Nmap and SMAC. In addition, Windows stores MAC addresses in the registry, and with the proper permissions, addresses can be changed in the registry as well. Port security often includes the following.

Loop Prevention

Loop prevention is the incorporation of protocols that prevent a switch from creating a continuous loop of traffic that ultimately floods the switch with needless packets. Data packets originating from the same source and traveling to the same destination are able to traverse the network using different active paths, which provides redundancy in data transmission. A *network loop* occurs when data sent across a network amplifies itself using the multiple paths instead of stopping at its destination. Network loops are often caused by misconfigured servers and can lead to broadcast storms. A **broadcast storm** is an accumulation of a high volume of traffic on a network in a short period of time. Broadcast storms, sometimes called *broadcast radiation*, often utilize the majority of a network's bandwidth and can eventually cause a network to fail if it is not resolved.

Loop prevention can be enabled in switches by using Spanning Tree Protocol (STP) or Rapid Spanning Tree Protocol (RSTP). For additional loop prevention, switches transmit *Bridge Protocol Data Units (BPDUs)*, which are frames of data containing information about STP/RSTP. However, some attacks generate spoofed BPDUs that can cause DoS or MITM attacks. DoS and MITM attacks generated from spoofed BPDUs can be prevented by enabling a BPDU guard on a switch. A **BPDU guard** is a switch feature that uses STP/RSTP to prevent BPDUs from being accepted on a given port. If an attacker attempts to send a BPDU message, the guard will shut down the message and not allow the request to be used in calculating routes and traffic flows.

DHCP Snooping

Dynamic Host Configuration Protocol (DHCP) snooping is a layer-2 security technology built into a switch that prevents unauthorized DHCP servers from assigning IP addresses to clients. It is a series of techniques that help improve the security of DHCP infrastructure. In essence, DHCP snooping enables the dropping of messages from untrusted servers or from devices whose MAC addresses do not match MAC addresses known to be valid. DHCP snooping enables port security by dropping requests to decline or release IP addresses that are transmitted over port numbers that do not match the ports used in DHCP configuration.

Flood Guards

A **flood guard** is a firewall-type feature that limits the amount of memory a switch can use to store data for each port. If that memory fills, alarms alert administrators or the port is automatically disabled.

Switches are vulnerable to MAC flooding, so the incorporation of a flood guard is often needed. **MAC flooding** is a network attack in which multiple MAC addresses are assigned to one physical port on a switch. In a MAC flooding attack, the threat actor sends Ethernet frames in a large, persistent number. Each frame has its own physical sender address, and the switch becomes overwhelmed with the number of requests until it does not have enough memory to store the MAC information. The memory depletion results in legitimate addresses being pushed out of the switch's memory, and the switch begins functioning as a hub—sending all data to all ports regardless of intended destination—in an effort to locate a legitimate response. A common indicator of a MAC flood is decreased network speed; since all data is sent to every host, speed and performance are noticeably decreased.

Routers

A *router* is a device that forwards data packets between computer networks and operates at the network layer of the OSI model. Routers are an integral part of most networking environments, and without them, data would be limited to traveling just within the local subnet. They play an active role in moving traffic, as shown in Figure 12-3. Networked routers communicate with each other, searching for updates to routing information so they can adjust the information they receive.

Route Security

⊹ 3.3

Like switches, routers must be secured in order to prevent exploitation of vulnerabilities. Route security can be accomplished by taking the following precautions:

- Regularly patch all router firmware and the router's operating system.
- Secure routers with strong passwords that are difficult to guess.
- Only use SSH for remote access.
- Back up all router configuration information.
- Ensure that only traffic that should be on the subnet is allowed.
- Remind users about security access and responsibilities with a router banner.
- Have a plan to check for updates to firmware, and install only patches directly from the manufacturer as third-party patches may not be reliable.

Passwords should be encrypted if the router software allows. Additionally, access levels should be limited only to those who need access, and security changes should be applied to routers for both console and remote access modes.

Router configurations and logs should be maintained by using a system log (syslog) server. Ensure change logs are updated anytime a change is made, indicating what was done and by whom.

Figure 12-3 A router is a device that forwards data packets between computer networks and operates at the network layer of the OSI model.

Goodheart-Willcox Publisher; (computers) romvo/Shutterstock.com;
(laptop) Jemastock/Shutterstock.com; (router) RealVector/Shutterstock.com

Access Control Lists (ACLs)

3.3

Routers manage traffic using **access control lists (ACLs)**, which are lists of permissions associated with network objects that control which devices are allowed on a given subnet. Therefore, it is essential that ACLs remain accurate; otherwise, unnecessary traffic will exist on the subnet. ACLs provide two important types of security:

- *File system security* refers to security functions in an ACL that protect files managed by an operating system.
- *Database security* refers to security functions in an ACL that protect database systems.

A significant security concern associated with routers is IP spoofing. **IP spoofing** is the creation of a fake IP address that matches a local IP address so malicious external traffic appears to be originating from inside the network. To counter, an ACL can be configured to employ antispoofing measures. **Antispoofing** is a technique that identifies and protects against IP spoofing by blocking inbound traffic originating from a suspect network address. For example, if the network is using the 192.168.x.x private IP address range, an entry in the ACL may be:

    deny ip 192.168.0.0 0.0.255.255 any

This will block any inbound traffic using 192.168 in the first two octets from entering a network.

Load Balancer

2.5, 3.3

Load balancing is a technology that evenly distributes processing needs over multiple servers. A *load balancer* is a network device that sends requests to various servers on a network based on predefined factors and operates at either the transport or application OSI layer (layer 4 or 7). Load balancers provide resilience to a network by performing as their name implies: they balance the processing load on a network among servers. Various scheduling protocols are used to distribute processes among servers, including the following:

- **Round-robin scheduling**, also known as *cyclic executive scheduling*, is a scheduling protocol rotation in which the amount of time permitted for a process to run is applied to each process in equal amounts and in circular order without priority.
- **Affinity scheduling** is a scheduling protocol that distributes loads based on which device is best capable of handling a given load. This type of scheduling ensures processes are handled in the most efficient manner possible.

Many networks employ multiple load balancers, called a *cluster*, to help further distribute requests and tasks. **Active-passive configuration** is an operational modality in which one load balancer is responsible for distributing network traffic while a second balancer operates passively unless the first balancer fails. Active-passive configuration enables uninterrupted services because the passive balancer automatically operates in the event of failure on the part of the active balancer, much like a failover.

3.3

Active-active configuration is an operational modality in which all load balancers are actively operating. This configuration allows all balancers to work cooperatively and combine network traffic. However, in the unlikely event all load balancers in an active-active configuration fail, network traffic can be compromised.

Load balancing can often be achieved through NIC teaming. **Network interface card (NIC) teaming** is the act of combining network interface cards (NICs) to function as one logical NIC called a *bond*. Once teamed, the connected NICs appear as one adapter and share the same IP address. NIC teaming increases network bandwidth,

improves performance, and provides load balancing and fault tolerance by incorpo-rating redundant NICs.

Another feature of load balancing is *session persistence*, also known as a *sticky connection*, which is a configuration that directs a client's requests to the same back-end web or application server for either the duration of the client's session or the time it takes to complete a task or transaction. Session persistence improves perfor-mance and availability of resources. It also creates an identifying attribute to a user, such as a cookie or their IP address. For example, a user sends a request to a server. If session persistence is configured, all requests in this transaction will be sent to just one server. Servers cache live data and pre-cache information it believes may be requested. If one server is handling an entire transaction, session persistence accel-erates the transaction. However, without session persistence, it is possible subse-quent transactions in a sequence are sent to a different server, which degrades efficiency of operations.

The servers to which load balancers transmit traffic are often given **virtual IP (VIP) addresses**, which are IP addresses that do not correspond to physical network devices. These addresses are combined with specific port numbers to identify vari-ous servers. VIPs can be configured to accept different types of data, and the same IP address can be used, provided different port numbers exist for each server.

Load balancing provides security advantages for a network. For example, load balancers exist between a router and server, so if they detect an attack or malware, traffic can be halted before it reaches its intended destination. They can also mask identifying packet headers in HTTP packets, which eliminates the possibility of a hacker identifying information about a network.

Proxy Server

Another example of a network appliance is a **proxy server**, which is a server that functions as a gateway between a local network and the Internet. The inclusion of a proxy server provides security by hiding the identity of either the client or server, depending on the type of proxy server used. Generally, proxy servers operate at the application layer of the OSI model.

Proxy servers are either forward or reverse. A **forward proxy server**, or *forward proxy*, is an Internet-facing proxy server used to intercept and forward requests from a local network to the Internet, typically through a firewall, on behalf of the user. For example, one type of forward proxy server is one that operates between an external web server and a client computer in order to check memory for recent requests and whether the request is already stored in cache.

When a client makes a request for an Internet resource, the request is sent to the forward proxy server, which is configured with settings that will be used to allow the request to continue to the Internet. The forward proxy can manage requests from multiple clients and track them, so responses received from the Internet are sent back to the requesting client. Since the proxy server is making the Internet request, client identities are hidden from the Internet. A forward proxy server acts as a sin-gle point of access and control, making it easier to configure and enforce security policies.

A **reverse proxy server** is an internal-facing proxy server that sits behind a fire-wall, processes incoming requests from the Internet, and routes them to the correct internal server. This process is transparent to the clients. Reverse proxies hide the identities of the servers, adding to the security of the transactions. Reverse proxy servers also provide additional features such as load balancing, which ensures a sin-gle server is not overloaded from too many requests.

Jump Server

A **jump server**, also known as a *pivot server* or *jump host*, is a network appliance used to access and manage devices in a separate security zone. A **security zone** is a segmented section of a network and contains systems that have limited access to the internal network. Because jump servers are accessed from less-secured zones, a client computer must use SSH to connect before launching an administrative task or using the server as a connection point to other servers.

The purpose of a jump server is to bridge communication between local computers and other servers. Notice the configuration in Figure 12-4. In this scenario, the admin in the local area network never connects directly to the web server, as doing so could expose elements of the PC's security zone. Instead, the admin connects to the jump server, which securely communicates with the web server, thus never exposing the local network.

One important caveat to jump servers is the ripple effect caused if the server is compromised. If a jump server is accessed by unauthorized users, any device that connected to it can also be accessed. Therefore, great care should be taken to harden jump servers against unauthorized access.

Aggregator

An **aggregator** is a device or service provider used to consolidate and serve multiple other devices or users with either its own functionalities or by forwarding transmissions in a compressed or more efficient way. Aggregators deliver connectivity between carrier networks and mobile service providers by combining devices and services into one circuit that is easy to use and manage.

Security Devices

Traditional networking hardware provides basic security through built-in protocols and encryption. However, devices specifically designed to protect a network often provide a greater degree of security. Security devices commonly encountered in a network include the following.

Firewalls

A *firewall* is a network security tool that acts as a barrier or protection against unwanted data transfer at entry points by monitoring incoming and outgoing network traffic. It is a first line of defense for a network. Firewalls can be *host-based*,

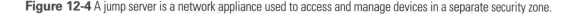

Figure 12-4 A jump server is a network appliance used to access and manage devices in a separate security zone.

Admin workstation
on local LAN

Jump server
running SSH

Web server

which are installed on individual machines, or *network-based*, which are located at the entry and exit points of a network.

A network firewall sits between two networks and can be a physical network device or a software solution, as shown in Figure 12-5. *Physical firewall* devices are located between a server and other networks; any data entering or exiting the network *must* pass through this appliance. *Software firewalls* are commonly used to protect communication to and from the devices on which they are installed. Software firewalls can be employed in a virtualized environment. Often, a combination of physical and virtual firewalls are used to build multiple security layers in the event a threat actor escapes a virtual host. In this scenario, if a virtual firewall is breached, the physical firewall still provides a barrier that the actor must penetrate to access or exit the real network.

✚ 3.3

Firewalls can be proprietary or open-source. A *proprietary firewall*, also called a *commercial firewall*, is owned by an entity and usually offers advanced capabilities, updates, and round-the-clock vendor support and maintenance. However, proprietary

Figure 12-5 A network firewall sits between two networks and can be a physical network device or a software solution.

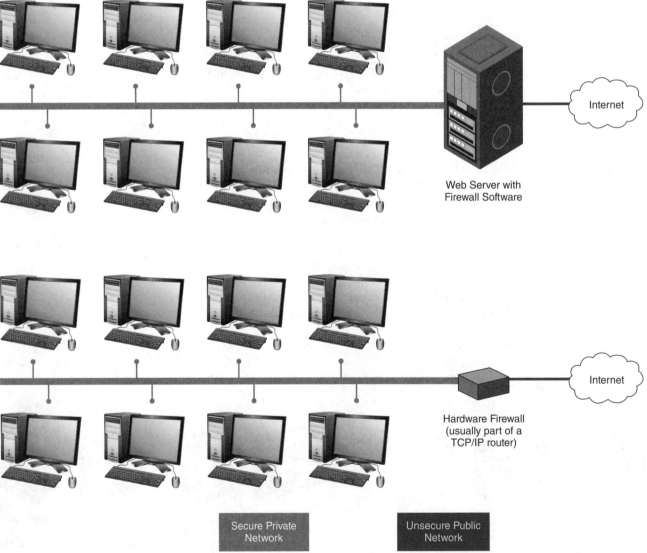

firewalls can also be expensive solutions. Some well-known proprietary firewalls include Check Point Firewalls and Cisco systems.

An *open-source firewall* is created by a community and distributed with a license that allows a user to access source code. It can be free or less expensive than proprietary firewalls, and there are many reputable options. However, support may be limited or nonexistent. Instead, many of these types of firewalls have strong user support through blogs and forums. One popular example of an open-source firewall is the Linux-based **iptables** utility.

There are basic types of firewalls designed to control flow of traffic, including the following.

Packet-Filtering Firewall

Packet filtering is a technique used to monitor and control incoming and outgoing data packets for a given network. A **packet-filtering firewall** is a firewall that examines all data packets and either forwards or drops them based on predefined rules that designate where a packet can go. Rules are often based on network addresses, ports, or protocols, such as Internet Control Message Protocol (ICMP). Packet-filtering firewalls are often considered a network-layer device because the data in the header is examined by the firewall. This includes source and destination IP addresses.

A packet-filtering firewall works by reading the header of each packet. After evaluating the header content, the firewall will either allow (accept) or deny (drop) the packet. Figure 12-6 shows a packet with a destination port of 23 being examined at the firewall. Since the firewall has a rule to block data to port 23, the packet is dropped. When data is transmitted, packets are either TCP or UDP packets. Firewalls must be configured to determine which protocols or ports are blocked and allowed.

Stateful Firewall

 3.3

A **stateful firewall** is a firewall that monitors packets over an established period of time and accepts only packets that were previously tracked. In essence, stateful firewalls record the state of a connection and make packet-filtering determinations

Figure 12-6 A packet-filtering firewall examines all data packets and either forwards or drops them based on predefined rules that designate where a packet can go.

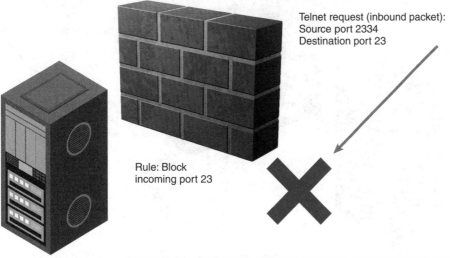

Telnet request (inbound packet):
Source port 2334
Destination port 23

Rule: Block
incoming port 23

Goodheart-Willcox Publisher; (server) aShatilov/Shutterstock.com; (wall) beboy/Shutterstock.com

based on that connection. Each packet that enters or exits the firewall is analyzed. If a packet matches an active connection that was previously tracked, it is allowed through the firewall. This prevents a packet from being manipulated to appear as if it were part of a larger transmission. It does not stop the packets that originate a conversation.

A stateful firewall does not limit analysis to just the packet header. It also inspects the state of the traffic entering and exiting the firewall. Stateful firewalls maintain a *state table* of previous packets. In Figure 12-7, a packet is inbound for port 80, which is not blocked. However, since the packet is a reply, the firewall searches the state table. It does not find the source IP address (192.168.101.55) in the state table. This means the packet has not previously been through the firewall. Therefore, the packet is dropped. In general, stateful firewalls do a better job at blocking unwanted traffic than stateless firewalls.

Stateless Firewall

✚ 3.3

A **stateless firewall** is a firewall designed to protect networks based on static information, such as source and destination addresses or ports. Stateless firewalls simply inspect information and either allow or deny packets based on specified rules. Packet-filtering firewalls are stateless because they filter based on static information. Since packet-filtering firewalls often allow replies through the firewall automatically, stateless firewalls are easily bypassed by hackers that manipulate a packet header and add the word *reply*.

A stateless firewall is also known as an ACL. If the ACL does not address the type of data in question, the firewall rejects the packet due to an *implicit deny clause*. This clause states that if a given action, transmission, or process is not explicitly permitted, traffic is denied. Implicit deny is not manually configured; by default, there is an implicit deny all at the end of every ACL.

Proxy Firewall

A **proxy firewall** is a network security device that protects a network by filtering a packet's data as well as its header. It also filters application protocol information

Figure 12-7 A stateful firewall monitors packets over an established period of time and accepts only packets that were previously tracked.

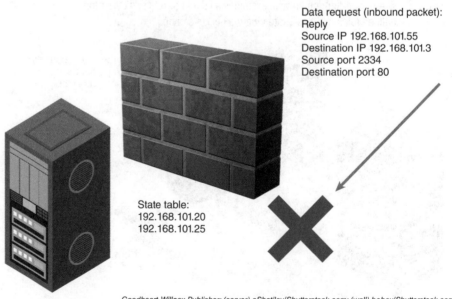

Data request (inbound packet):
Reply
Source IP 192.168.101.55
Destination IP 192.168.101.3
Source port 2334
Destination port 80

State table:
192.168.101.20
192.168.101.25

Goodheart-Willcox Publisher; (server) aShatilov/Shutterstock.com; (wall) beboy/Shutterstock.com

such as HTTP or FTP. The firewall acts as a *proxy*, which is an intermediary device. It is linked to the client with one connection and to the server with another connection. Proxy server firewalls are the most advanced firewalls and are more common on network segments.

Proxy server firewalls are often used by organizations to block websites based on the URL or content. For example, many businesses block social media URLs for security or productivity reasons. The URL is blocked by a proxy server firewall that reads the content requested.

Web Application Firewall (WAF)

A *web application firewall (WAF)* is a specific firewall used to protect web applications by filtering and monitoring HTTP traffic between applications and the Internet. Web servers host web services and pages for user access. Due to the applications and data that reside there, there are some very specific attacks on web servers including XSS attacks. WAFs not only help prevent XSS attacks, but also injection and cross-site request forgery (CSRF) attacks.

Content Filter

A **content filter**, also called a *URL filter*, is software- or hardware-based technology often incorporated in a firewall to monitor Internet traffic and prevent access to blacklisted websites, files, and services. Content filters can help maintain network security by preventing users from navigating to websites known to be malicious in nature. They can also prevent users from downloading files from unapproved sources or sites that could open a computer and network to attacks and malware.

Unified Threat Management Device

A **unified threat management (UTM) device** is an all-in-one security device that enables a network to be managed using one appliance. Consider the owner of a small- to medium-sized business exploring, purchasing, and configuring the security solutions for a network. This process may involve a great deal of equipment, configuration, time, and money. However, installing a unified threat management appliance can simplify managing a network's security.

Network Intrusion Detection

Security practices are necessary to block network threats and attacks. To detect intrusions, specialized network appliances, such as an intrusion-detection system (IDS), are used.

An *intrusion-detection system (IDS)* is a hardware- or software-based security tool used to detect an attack on a network. Three components comprise the IDS.

- *Sensors* are hardware appliances that generate events to trigger the IDS.
- A *console* monitors security events and sends out an alert to the sensors.
- The *engine* records events identified by the sensors and records them in a database.

Intrusion-detection systems are managed by in-band or out-of-band methods, as shown in Figure 12-8. **In-band** is a management method in which an IDS is connected to the network and manages devices using common protocols of the network. **Out-of-band** means that the IDS has an access server connected to a management port on each device.

Figure 12-8 Intrusion-detection systems are managed by in-band or out-of-band management methods.

Management Method	Connection Type	Attack Blocking	Path of Data Flow	Security Implications
In-Band	Connected directly to network and evaluates original data	Able to block attacks in progress	Routes traffic directly through the device	Used with firewalls, intrusion-prevention systems, honeypots, and threat detection
Out-of-Band	Connected to a port on each device	Unable to block attacks in progress	Receives copy of data	Forensic analysis with data loss protection, intrusion-detection systems, and forensic packet recording

Goodheart-Willcox Publisher

 3.3

An *inline IDS* is connected to a network and actively monitors and stops malicious traffic. A *passive IDS* is connected to a switch through a port that receives a copy of network traffic. Passive means to *monitor* but *not* take action when encountering an incident. There are two basic types of IDS.

- A *host-based intrusion-detection system (HIDS)* protects the host, such as a computer on which it is installed. It is a software application that detects attacks as they happen on the host.
- A *network-based intrusion-detection system (NIDS)* monitors the network on which it is installed including any subnetworks. It is a software application that detects attacks as they happen on the network.

There are different types of monitoring used when examining network traffic. Examples are as follows.

 3.3

Anomaly Monitoring

Anomaly monitoring is a method that detects anomalies in a network's traffic statistics. An **anomaly** is a deviation from expected network activity. Network activity is collected and compared to a baseline. Activity that varies from the baseline could be a concern for network security. For example, suppose the baseline shows that around 2 p.m. on most days the network traffic hovers around 30 percent of bandwidth. Then, one day around this time, network traffic is 70 percent utilization, which is a significant deviation from the baseline that bears further investigation to see if there is a threat.

 3.3

Signature-Based Monitoring

Signature-based monitoring is a method that examines network traffic or searches for patterns to compare against a predefined signature database. This is similar to how antimalware software works in that signatures are stored, frequently updated, and used to compare activity. For example, the intrusion-detection system may find a pattern of characters in data packets that match known attack patterns. These packets are flagged as a potential intrusion.

 3.3

Heuristic-Based Monitoring

Heuristic-based monitoring, also known as *behavioral-based monitoring*, is a method in which scanning is applied to normal processes to determine if a threat exists. *Heuristic* refers to an approach to problem solving. This type of monitoring does not depend on predefined standards or policies. Instead, it relies on continuous monitoring and applies artificial intelligence to determine if specific traffic will harm a system.

Intrusion-Prevention Systems

In addition to *detecting* intrusions, network appliances can *prevent* intrusions. An *intrusion-prevention system (IPS)* is a hardware- or software-based security-monitoring tool that monitors and analyzes incoming and outgoing traffic flow and immediately halts traffic when malicious activity is detected. Similar to an IDS, an IPS can be host-based (HIPS) or network-based (NIPS). Where an IDS can only notify an administrator of an intrusion, an IPS can actively prevent intrusions from happening.

Other Network Security Devices

Additional network security devices are shown in Figure 12-9.

Network Architecture Security

Secure network architecture is the deployment of network devices with security measures enabled. A network's design can strengthen or secure it from threat actors. Elements of the design should include the following.

Security Zones

A common mistake is to build a single network to which all users have access. It is far more secure to build multiple security layers, or zones, as network partitions

Figure 12-9 Additional examples of security devices commonly encountered in a network.

Device	Function(s)	Notes
Hardware security module (HSM)	• Cryptographic device that stores or manages encryption keys and performs cryptographic functions • Encrypts communication to prevent it from being intercepted and read	• Often installed as a plug-in card or external device attached to computer or server
SSL inspector	• Intercepts traffic, decrypts it, and scans it for malicious files • Creates secure connection between web browser and client so files can be transferred securely	• Placed between the client and server inspect Secure Sockets Layer (SSL) and Transport Layer Security (TLS) traffic
Security gateway	• Blocks malicious content and packets in real time • Provides added layer of enhanced security	• Functions at application layer of OSI model • Operates much like a firewall
Media gateway	• Converts one form of media into another	• Often called a *softswitch* • Enables different technologies and networks to communicate with each other
Security information and event manager (SIEM)	• Supports organizational security through real-time collection and compilation of log data • Produces analyzed results and reports	• Collects information from multiple security devices • Reports on events as they happen

Goodheart-Willcox Publisher

with users' access abilities determined by need. In networking, a *security zone* is a segmented section of a network and contains systems that have limited access to the internal network. In simple terms, security zones help isolate areas of a network that require public access from those that do not. Additionally, security zones help isolate or quarantine an attack in the event a breach occurs. Security zones are typically separated from the network using a layer-3 security device, such as a firewall.

The inclusion of security zones helps divide a network and increase resilience in the event a breach occurs. There can be multiple security zones in a network, and depending on the data needing protection, each security zone can have several security layers within it. Each zone contains a layer called a *trust zone* that enables sharing of resources and communication to higher- or lower-level security zones. For example, a web server may be in a high-security zone but needs to communicate with application servers in lower-level zones to ensure data is pushed to those who need it. Despite the servers operating in different zones, they can communicate effectively through the trust zone. Examples of security zones include the following.

⊹ 3.3   Demilitarized Zone (DMZ)

A **demilitarized zone (DMZ)** is a segment of a network that allows some public access and borders a private network where the public access is blocked. A DMZ is also called a *screened subnet* or a *perimeter network*. A DMZ is typically used for public-facing servers including web servers, FTP servers, or other servers that require public access. Be sure to place only those servers that *need* public access in the DMZ, as all data stored in the DMZ is exposed to the Internet.

A DMZ is created by developing borders between different networks. Borders are established by using firewalls, as shown in Figure 12-10. In this example, users in the public domain can have access to the web and e-commerce servers located in the DMZ.

Figure 12-10 A demilitarized zone (DMZ) is a segment of a network that allows some public access and borders a private network where the public access is blocked.

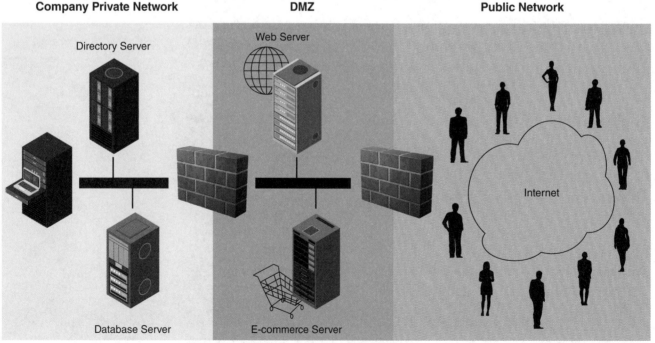

The type of traffic and hosts that enter the DMZ are filtered by a public-facing firewall. Another firewall then borders the DMZ and the company's private network. This firewall locks down the limited amount of traffic allowed into the DMZ. Servers such as directory servers and databases should *not* be accessible from the public domain.

Network Address Translation

Network address translation (NAT) is a method of remapping an IP address so a device with a private address can be used on a public network such as the Internet. *Private IP addresses* are not assigned to individual users or organizations but are available for use by anyone in a private internal network. Packets transmitted with a private IP address are dropped when they reach a router, meaning private IP addresses cannot be used on the Internet. NAT effectively replaces a private IP address with a public IP address—called an *alias address*—by modifying the network address information in the IP header of data packets in transit. When a packet is returned to NAT software, the process is reversed, and the packet is sent to the correct computer.

NAT enables many devices on a private network to share a single gateway to the Internet. A **NAT gateway** is a managed service that bridges the connection between a local network and the Internet by translating IP addresses from private to public or vice versa. When a packet is bound for the Internet, it is sent to a NAT gateway where a public IP address is assigned to the transaction. NAT maintains a table of the requesting private IP and port number but places only the public-facing IP address on the packet in the public network. In this sense, a NAT gateway functions similarly to a firewall by only allowing Internet traffic to reach a network if a device requested it. If the data is unsolicited, the packets are dropped.

 3.3

Intranets and Extranets

An **intranet** is a private Internet environment for an organization's internal use only. Intranets are a great resource for businesses because they provide a secured environment for forms, information, tools, services, and applications shared among employees.

3.3

An **extranet** is a type of intranet that can be partially accessed by authorized users outside an organization. An example of when this environment may be useful is to allow an approved vendor, such as a supplier, access to the intranet. There may also be a case where a vendor or other partner needs access to company data. Collaborating on projects is another potential application for an extranet.

3.3

Guest Network

A **guest network** is an open network that is separate from a primary network and allows anyone to gain access without permission. The use of a guest network enables an organization's visitors, such as presenters, contractors, or vendors, to access network resources or the Internet without allowing them to reach secured data or devices.

Zero Trust

3.3

Zero trust is a security model in which no one from inside or outside the network is trusted by default, and all users attempting to access network resources are required to verify their identities. In zero trust architecture, the assumption is that attackers can be located inside *and* outside the network, so by default, no device is trusted automatically.

Establishing zero trust requires administrators to identify or define a *protect surface*, which comprises a network's most critical and valuable data, assets, applications, and services (DAAS). Once the protect surface is identified, data flows are identified and analyzed to determine usage patterns and optimal data flow. After data flow has been determined, a security zone is built around the protect surface by implementing a next-generation firewall as a segmentation gateway. Once the protect surface has been securely isolated, the entire zero trust architecture is continually monitored through evaluation of security logs and analytics and modified as needed.

Network Segregation

Network segregation is the act of isolating a network so it is not accessible to unauthorized personnel. It relies on the development and enforcement of communication rules to prevent data transfers between critical systems and less-sensitive systems. In essence, segregation isolates various areas of a network so an unauthorized user cannot access everything. Often, networks are segregated using *air-gap networks*, which are computer networks designed to be completely isolated from other networks, including connections to the Internet. For example, a network within a governmental institution, such as a prison, may be isolated or physically segregated from other networks or the Internet.

Due to the lack of Internet connection, air-gapped networks do not receive regular, automatic patch updates, which creates a potential vulnerability. Security administrators must have alternative plans in place for maintaining up-to-date security patches and software upgrades. This often includes copying downloaded patches and drivers to removable storage and inserting the device into the air-gapped network. The removable storage device used to transfer these updates should be secured between uses, as malware can be introduced through the device.

2.1

Geographical Considerations

Geography of a network is determined by devices and nodes and the distance between them. Because of the constraints in speed and distance, the geography of a network dictates the technology, hardware, and media used to connect nodes. For example, devices more than 100 meters (328 feet) apart from one another cannot be connected directly by Category 6 (Cat 6) Ethernet cable because of technological constraints of Cat 6 cabling.

Nodes can be located in the same building as other devices or spread over distance.

- *Intrabuilding geography* are devices that are networked within the same building, such as employee workstations in an office setting.
- *Interbuilding geography* are nodes that are networked in different buildings in the same general location such as two branches of a bank or offices sharing the same metropolitan area.
- *Distant remote buildings* are devices that are networked with a significant amount of distance between them, such as an employee or contractor accessing an office server while working from overseas or in another country.

2.1

Configuration Management (CM)

Configuration management (CM) is the process of maintaining computers, servers, and applications in a preferred, consistent state to ensure a system's performance remains as efficient as possible despite changes made over time. CM is an essential function that enables repetition of processes implemented for dependability and ensures that if a system crashes, a technician can replicate the environment and restore services quickly. An ideal CM process serves as a roadmap to correlate business and security needs with configuration settings that enable IT staff to manage a system through various device life cycles.

Security configuration management (SCM) is the management and control of configurations for an information system with the goal of enabling security and managing risk. SCM actively works to identify not only misconfigured devices but also unexpected or unusual changes to critical areas of a system, such as registry keys or database files. SCM tools enable network administrators to know if unauthorized changes are occurring. These tools monitor, compare, and analyze network activity to detect breaches and determine if unapproved changes were made. SCM tools rely on the following to help detect unauthorized activity or changes.

Diagrams

Network diagrams help define or outline a network's organization and infrastructure. Often, logical diagrams are created first. *Logical deployment diagrams* summarize resources on a network as well as the network's *physical topology*, which is the physical arrangement of computers, devices, and cabling in a network environment. These diagrams emphasize connections between devices. This information is important to SCM tools because if a device is discovered unexpectedly, it could indicate malicious intent, such as a rogue device. A logical diagram identifies data workflows and communication needs while providing an understanding of how data is stored, shared, and protected. These diagrams lead to a deeper understanding of a business's data, including identifying potential vulnerable environments or unprotected data.

After logical diagrams are created, physical diagrams are made. *Physical deployment diagrams* identify the exact location of security appliances, such as firewalls, IPSs, and routers. These diagrams can help identify network boundaries between trusted and untrusted networks. Additionally, physical diagrams provide a holistic, big-picture view of all security appliances, configurations, and potential gaps in coverage. After both diagrams are created, ensure that they match; otherwise, connections are likely to be overlooked.

Baseline Configuration

A *baseline* is a starting point that represents normal operational performance and is used to make data comparisons. Creating a baseline enables the tracking of performance, disk activity, memory usage, and other points of reference. Familiarity with baselines enables possible early indication or detection of security concerns, such as increased network or web traffic or radical changes to a number of foreign website visits, all of which could be potential indicators of malicious activity or malware.

Standard Naming Conventions

A *standard naming convention* is a set of rules that dictates how account or device names are established. Standardizing the creation of names enables easy identification of network equipment, such as servers, routers, and switches. This standardization helps to locate and identify equipment quickly, which is useful to ensure accuracy of security configurations and response to vulnerabilities and threats.

Internet Protocol (IP) Schema

Internet protocol (IP) schema is a conceptual model that defines or outlines the process by which IP addresses are distributed to networked devices. Well-designed IP schema helps prevent creation of overlapping or duplicate subnets, duplicate host addresses, wasted IP address space, and unnecessary complexity. Additionally, configuration management tools incorporate an organization's IP schema to determine whether IP addresses are legitimate, so it is important that an addressing plan be comprehensive in design.

IP addressing should be treated carefully, especially for configuration routes. One configuration error can disable data flow, deny services, direct traffic to incorrect locations, or cause SCM tools to sound a false alarm. An important decision to make regarding IP schema is the incorporation of IPv6.

Internet Protocol version 6 (IPv6) is the most recent version of the Internet Protocol (IP). IPv6 offers a wealth of benefits, the most obvious being the 128-bit address and the massive amount of available IP addresses for expansion. The virtually inexhaustible quantity of addresses can eliminate the need for using private IP addresses. In turn, the lack of private IP addresses eliminates the need to configure and maintain NAT services on a network. Additionally, using IPv6 offers mandatory IPSec-provided authentication as well as improved capabilities in carrying voice, video, and data traffic.

In order to incorporate and realize the full benefits of IPv6 in an organization, all network devices must support IPv6. Despite the ratification of IPv6 in 2017, administrators have been slow in some cases to take advantage of IPv6's scalability and security features due to a reliance on the familiar usage of IPv4. If not already using IPv6, companies must prepare a strategy for implementing an upgrade, including plans for ensuring devices can support IPv6 and how best to handle addressing of devices such as Domain Name System (DNS) and Dynamic Host Configuration Protocol (DHCP) servers.

Non-Persistence

Non-persistence is actions taken and configurations implemented to ensure unwanted data is not retained when new devices are added, and instead, a clean disk image is used. Non-persistent installations do not retain user data, personalized settings, or changes made to the device, which enables IT staff to start a device from a clean, generic state. This helps maintain consistent management of devices because it guarantees all devices are installed with the same features, settings, and restrictions.

Consider a scenario in which changes made to an installation image corrupt data. If a non-persistent version exists, a faulty image can be restored to the settings in the non-persistent image, allowing you to roll back to a known operational state, much like rolling back a device driver. Examples of non-persistent installations are listed in Figure 12-11.

Placement of Security Devices

Security devices are placed at the border of or inside the network. Devices at the network border help prevent malicious traffic from gaining access to and traversing a network. Conversely, devices inside the network monitor and analyze network traffic. Sometimes security devices are located in both places for additional security and defense-in-depth.

- *SSL accelerators.* SSL accelerators are typically hardware cards installed in a web server and contain dedicated processing capabilities for handling SSL/TLS transactions. Large networks may install dedicated SSL/TLS hardware modules as virtual SSL/TLS servers in addition to a proxy server that sits between a user and web server. The accelerator handles the generation of SSL keys during an SSL connection and increases performance of web server transactions.

Figure 12-11 Non-persistence is actions taken and configurations implemented to ensure unwanted data is not retained when new devices are added and instead, a clean disk image is used.

Tool	Description	Usage
Revert to known state	Restores device to secure state	Revert to known state restores a device to a known stable setting.
Last known good configuration	Undoes recent alterations that negatively impacted security	Last known good configuration is a rollback technique that restores a device to a previous configuration known to be secure.
Live boot media	Bootable image stored on USB or optical media	Live boot media temporarily establishes a non-persistent client used to access a remote network securely.

Goodheart-Willcox Publisher

- *Taps.* A **network TAP**, also called a *port TAP*, is a networking device installed inside a network to monitor traffic. The word *TAP* is an acronym for *test access port.* The role of each tap is to obtain raw information. Therefore, the locations of sensors are important; for example, you might want sensors monitoring traffic from a switch to a router or traffic from the router to a specific IP address. TAPs and sensors can look for specific protocol traffic, such as TCP or HTTP, or they can monitor activity including logons, logoffs, file access, and USB insertion.

- *Port mirrors.* **Port mirroring** is a method of traffic monitoring in which data packets are copied from one switch port to another. Port mirroring, also known as *Switched Port Analyzer (SPAN)* or *port spanning,* does not alter or modify the original data in a packet; it only copies the information from one port to another. When mirroring ports, the monitoring computer is connected to a mirror port, where all network traffic is viewed. The monitoring computer can be a dedicated workstation or a secondary machine running protocol analysis software.

- *Sensors.* A *sensor* is a network device used to monitor a network for intrusion. Sensors should be placed inside the network where they will have the ability to view as much information as possible. Look at the example in Figure 12-12. Placing a sensor in Zones A or B enables the monitoring of traffic between the Internet and internal network or between the Internet and DMZ. However, neither zone is conducive to monitoring traffic between all areas of the network. Therefore, Zone C would be an ideal placement for a sensor, as it views all traffic between the Internet, DMZ, and internal network.

- *Collectors.* A *collector* is hardware that gathers information about network traffic. Similar to a sensor, a collector should be placed in a location where it can gather the largest-possible data stream.

- *Filters.* A *content filter*, also called a *URL filter*, is a software- or hardware-based technology used to block unwanted or malicious traffic moving to and from the Internet. The location of these devices is important to ensuring no traffic is able to traverse a network unchecked. Filters should be placed inside the network, where they can allow or block as much information as possible.

- *Aggregation switch.* An *aggregation switch* is a networking device used to combine multiple network connections in a single switch. An aggregation switch should be placed between routers and servers so they can identify and stop attacks directed at servers or applications.

Figure 12-12 A sensor should be placed inside the network where it will have the ability to view as much information as possible.

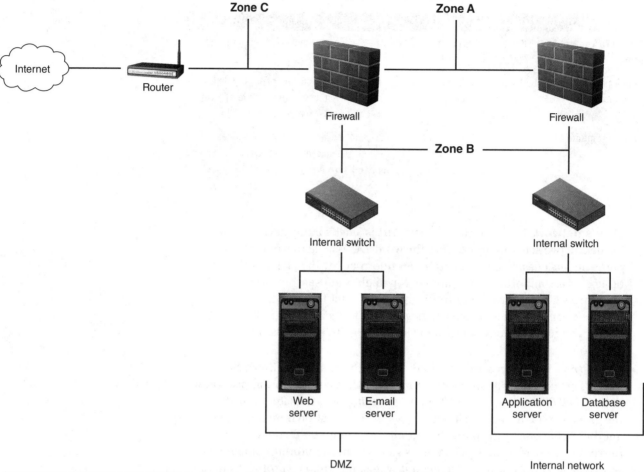

Goodheart-Willcox Publisher; (router) RealVector/Shutterstock.com; (wall) beboy/Shutterstock.com; (internal switch) ridjam/Shutterstock.com; (servers) Denis Rozhnovsky/Shutterstock.com

- *Correlation engine.* A **correlation engine** is a software application that has been programmed to understand relationships. Correlation engines collect data from various sources and use predictive analysis to discover malicious activity. They can also analyze the events and return valuable information, such as identification of patterns, times, and suspicious IP addresses. Like other types of data collectors, correlation engines are best located inside the network so they can collect as much data as possible.

- *DDoS mitigator.* A *DDoS mitigator* is a device that identifies and prevents distributed denial of service (DDoS) attacks in real time. Like sensors and filters, DDoS mitigators should be placed in a location that enables them to monitor the largest-possible stream of data.

Deception Technology

Deception technology is security tools and techniques designed to prevent a threat actor who has already breached a network from doing any damage. Deceptive devices are typically distributed as decoys that mimic authentic network assets. The principle of deception technology is to strengthen an organization's security posture by deceiving, detecting, and mitigating attacks. Deception, detection, and mitigation are accomplished by making attackers think they have successfully breached network security and gained access to devices that are, in actuality, irrelevant to organizational operations.

Deceptive technology can, and often does, mimic legitimate technology assets in the organization, which entices a criminal to attempt to exploit the asset. These devices are monitored, and when an attack is detected, protection can quickly be deployed to similar assets. Examples of deception technology include the following.

Honeypot

A **honeypot** is a computer or server loaded with files or applications that appear to be authentic and placed in a network zone with limited security. It is a decoy device with imitations of authentication data files and intentionally configured with vulnerabilities so it can be attacked and easily compromised. A **honeynet** is a network intentionally established and configured to be vulnerable to attract attackers and study their methods. Honeynets are often composed of two or more honeypots. The logic behind incorporating an easily attacked device or network is so threat actors reveal their attack techniques, which can be analyzed to determine how secure the real network is to such an attack.

Honeyfile

A **honeyfile** is a fake file located on a network folder share. Honeyfiles act as bait and are designed to detect and observe hackers accessing a network with the intention of modifying, copying, or stealing data from the network. When honeyfiles are accessed, an alarm is triggered that notifies administrators of the activity.

Fake Telemetry

The incorporation of fake telemetry is another security technique that employs deception. *Telemetry* is the recording, reading, and transmission of information from remote locations. Therefore, **fake telemetry**, also called *deception telemetry*, is false data recorded through simulations. Telemetry data is often desired by hackers as it provides insider information about how resources and services are accessed in an organization. Similar to honeyfiles, fake telemetry can alert administrators to an intrusion before damage or data loss can occur.

DNS Sinkhole

A **DNS sinkhole** is a DNS server used to prevent the resolution of host names of specific URLs. When a DNS server is contacted, it responds by returning an IP address assigned to the URL. Similarly, when a DNS sinkhole is contacted, it responds with a false IP address, which adds a layer of protection to the network security. If a malicious URL is requested, the request is forwarded to a fake or deceptive site. The deceptive site can be a customized website created to indicate the request was forwarded and denied because of malicious content, as illustrated in Figure 12-13.

Network Segmentation

Network segmentation is the act of dividing a network into smaller sections, called *network segments* or *subnetworks*, to separate data to reduce its exposure. Segmenting a network enables organizations to divide network infrastructure and data centers logically. Network segments can help restrict access for an attacker as well as reduce the attacker's ability to traverse entire enterprise environments. There are basic network segmentation designs including the following.

Figure 12-13 A DNS sinkhole is a DNS server used to prevent the resolution of host names of specific URLs.

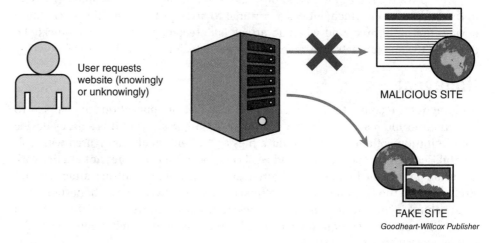

MALICIOUS SITE

FAKE SITE

Goodheart-Willcox Publisher

3.3

TECH TIP

VLAN 1 is the default VLAN name on switches. By default, all the switch ports are in VLAN 1. Traffic not sent with VLAN tags is sent through a VLAN called a *native VLAN*. Unless explicitly defined, the native VLAN is VLAN1. This can open security vulnerabilities since VLAN 1 was not designed as a data VLAN.

Virtual Local Area Network (VLAN)

One method for segmenting network traffic in a network is to incorporate virtual local area networks. A **virtual local area network (VLAN)** is technology that enables remote users to be grouped logically even when connected to different switches. Figure 12-14 shows an example of how a VLAN is organized. Hosts can be located anywhere on the local area network. VLANs are often created on network switches by assigning devices based on the physical switch port or the MAC address.

VLANs create virtual subnets, which allow a VLAN to be secured further with VLAN access control lists. A **VLAN access control list (VACL)** is a permission set that provides access control for packets traveling into or out of a VLAN. Each VLAN can be configured with a unique VACL.

One of the security benefits of a VLAN is that it limits the broadcast of packets to that network only, allowing traffic from each group to be separated. In networks, broadcast traffic does not pass through routers, so network sniffing would be limited only to the devices on a given VLAN. For example, in Figure 12-14, the research department traffic is separated from the administration traffic on the network. The executive traffic is also isolated from the other two departments.

Virtual Private Network (VPN)

A **virtual private network (VPN)** is a virtual network connection that provides a way to encrypt data traveling through unsecured public networks, such as the Internet. While the security in VPNs is strong, security professionals must still guard against the possibility of a hacked or stolen laptop configured with this option.

There are two common implementations of VPN configurations: remote access and site to site. A *remote-access VPN* allows a user to connect to a network using a remote client's Internet connection. This is a popular method for allowing users to work from home or any other Internet connection.

3.3

Figure 12-14 A virtual local area network (VLAN) is technology that enables remote users to be grouped logically even when connected to different switches.

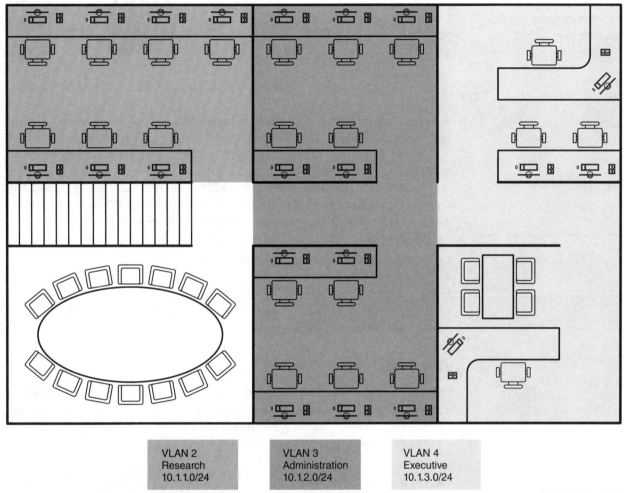

VLAN 2
Research
10.1.1.0/24

VLAN 3
Administration
10.1.2.0/24

VLAN 4
Executive
10.1.3.0/24

Goodheart-Willcox Publisher

A *site-to-site VPN* allows an organization to connect static or fixed sites to each other using the Internet as the communication platform. This type of VPN enables users to access resources on the remote location securely.

Site-to-site VPNs are commonly set up with a **VPN concentrator**, which is a device that collects VPN connections and delivers traffic to the appropriate VPN node. Concentrators enable secure VPN device creation and delivery of messages between nodes in a VPN. In addition to their routing capabilities, VPN concentrators also

- provide support for additional traffic tunnels;
- allow the system to authenticate users, encrypt, and decrypt data; and
- ensure delivery of data from one site to another.

With the release of Windows 10, Microsoft enables a feature called *always-on VPN*, which automatically connects the client to a default VPN when Internet access

3.3

Figure 12-15 Tunneling is the process of using a virtual private network (VPN) to encrypt data before transmitting it across a remote connection.

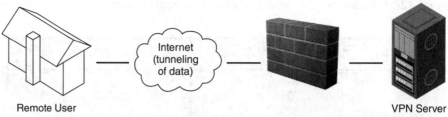

Remote User

Internet (tunneling of data)

VPN Server

Goodheart-Willcox Publisher; (wall) beboy/Shutterstock.com; (server) aShatilov/Shutterstock.com

is recognized outside the corporate network. This type of VPN ensures all traffic is sent to the company network securely. Another assurance with an always-on VPN is that users will not be able to drop the VPN connection when the device is not physically attached to the company network.

Tunneling is the process of using a VPN to encrypt data before transmitting it across a remote connection, as illustrated in Figure 12-15. When using a VPN, two options can be used depending on which traffic you are protecting.

 3.3

- A *full tunnel* is a VPN that routes all traffic over the VPN.
- A *split tunnel* routes only some traffic over the VPN, while allowing other traffic to connect to the Internet directly.

An advantage to a split tunnel is the reduction in bandwidth needed for traffic, while a full tunnel will allow network and security administrators more control and security over all data transmissions.

VPN Protocols

Data on a VPN connection is encrypted, which protects data traveling across a public network. When creating the connection, security parameters are set, such as the security encryption protocol. These protocols include the following:

- PPTP
- L2TP
- SSTP
- IKEv2
- HTML5

Point-to-Point Tunneling Protocol (PPTP) is a networking protocol for connecting to VPNs. PPTP is the most outdated of the tunneling protocols. Originally created by Microsoft, PPTP supports many Windows clients. It provides data confidentiality in the form of encryption but does not support integrity. That is, there is no guarantee data is not modified in transit. Authentication, or verifying the sending user, is not supported in this protocol. Ports associated with PPTP include TCP 1723 and 47.

 3.3

Layer 2 Tunneling Protocol (L2TP) is a tunneling protocol used by Internet service providers to enable operation of a VPN over the Internet. L2TP supports Microsoft clients running Windows 2000 and newer. Unlike PPTP, integrity, along with confidentiality and authentication, *are* supported. When using L2TP with Internet key exchange traffic, UDP port 500 must be configured to allow inbound traffic.

Secure Socket Tunneling Protocol (SSTP) is a VPN tunneling protocol that provides support for traffic over an SSL/TLS-encrypted connection. It supports authentication, integrity, and confidentiality. SSTP uses port 443, which is an additional security benefit because it is easier for traffic to pass through proxy servers and firewalls without having to open any additional ports. Support for SSTP began with Windows Vista Service Pack 1.

Internet Key Exchange Protocol version 2 (IKEv2) is a tunneling protocol that uses the IPSec tunneling protocol over UDP on port 500 to establish a security association. **IP Security (IPSec)** is a security protocol that can be used to encrypt and secure data traveling over computer networks using the TCP/IP protocol suite. IPSec allows for strong encryption and authentication protocols. It cannot be used on clients prior to Windows 7 or Microsoft server operating systems prior to Server 2008R2. In addition to supporting confidentiality, integrity, and authentication, IKEv2 provides significant support for wireless mobility users who move between access points. The key elements of IPSec include AH and ESP.

■ **Authentication header (AH)** is a security feature used to authenticate the sender and determine if there are any changes to the data during transmission. If the data must use NAT, it cannot use AH.

■ **Encapsulating security payload (ESP)** is an alternative to AH that authenticates the header as well as encrypts the data. When selecting ESP, data travels on the network in one of two modes: tunnel mode or transport mode. **Tunnel mode** is an IPSec mode that encrypts the IP header of the original packet. This allows for travel through NAT devices. This makes tunnel mode the common choice when setting up site-to-site VPNs. **Transport mode** is an IPSec mode that encrypts only the data and ESP information, not the original packet. This mode is more commonly used with remote-access VPN.

Hypertext Markup Language version 5 (HTML5) is the fifth revision of the HTML standard. In addition to functioning as a web-browsing standard, HTML5 can be used as a secure remote access solution. Remote desktop client solutions running HTML5 offer secure connections without requiring browser plug-ins. By offering secure connections natively as opposed to via plug-ins, the attack surface within both the browser and machine is decreased substantially.

Using HTML5 provides a pure browser solution, which enhances security since it does not require any additional software to be installed in the browser. An HTML5 RDP solution offers a secure gateway solution that eliminates the need to configure a VPN with SSL security and allows users the ability to have a remote connection in a secure manner.

VPN Authentication

After choosing a protocol, the next setting to make for a VPN is the method of authentication. Typically, users are authenticated through a form of *identity and access management (IAM) service*, which facilitates the management of digital identities. There are several IAM services to choose from for authentication, including the following:

■ Password Authentication Protocol (PAP)

■ Challenge Handshake Authentication Protocol (CHAP)

■ Microsoft Challenge Handshake Authentication Protocol (MS-CHAP)

■ Extensible Authentication Protocol (EAP)

Password Authentication Protocol (PAP)

Password Authentication Protocol (PAP) is an unencrypted password-based authentication protocol that uses Point-to-Point Protocol (PPP) to validate users. Historically, PAP was commonly used for dial-up systems in which transmissions had a guaranteed path to the destination. However, it should *not* be used for modern networks. Since PAP is not encrypted, the username and password are sent in plaintext, which is a significant vulnerability for any system.

3.3

3.1

3.3

3.8

3.8

Challenge Handshake Authentication Protocol (CHAP)

Challenge Handshake Authentication Protocol (CHAP) is a protocol in which an authenticating server sends a challenge to a client after the client establishes a connection to the server. With CHAP, a client and server must have a previously identified shared secret. In this case, the shared secret is the user's password. The client converts the challenge and the secret to a value using a one-way hash function, which is sent to the VPN server. The VPN server then confirms that the value matches the values calculated by the server. If both values match, access is granted. If the values do *not* match, hash functions are employed. This process is illustrated in Figure 12-16. At any time during the session, the server may periodically send a challenge to the client to confirm identity. This occurs behind the scenes without any knowledge of this transaction by the user.

Microsoft Challenge Handshake Authentication Protocol (MS-CHAP)

Microsoft Challenge Handshake Authentication Protocol (MS-CHAP) is Microsoft's version of the Challenge Handshake Authentication Protocol. Some differences between CHAP and MS-CHAP is that MS-CHAP includes a session ID in the challenge, and the password does not need to be stored in clear text, but can be encrypted. A *session ID* is a unique numerical identifier that a server assigns to a user for the duration of the user's visit, or session, to the server. The response from the client includes the session ID, username, and user password, as shown in Figure 12-17. There are significant vulnerabilities with MS-CHAP, however. For example, due to MS-CHAP's reliance on the outdated DES encryption, brute force attacks are possible. Therefore, it is suggested a more secure method of data transmission be used.

3.8

Extensible Authentication Protocol (EAP)

Extensible Authentication Protocol (EAP) is an authentication protocol framework that outlines secure transport and usage of information. This may include data from smart cards and biometric data. EAP is frequently used for authentication within a wireless network. There are two sub-protocols of EAP:

- *Lightweight EAP (LEAP)* was developed by Cisco based on the CHAP protocol and designed for use with wireless networking. Windows does not natively support LEAP. Cisco now recommends against its use, as it has been found to be cracked.

Figure 12-16 Challenge Handshake Authentication Protocol (CHAP) is a protocol in which an authenticating server sends a challenge to a client after the client establishes a connection to the server.

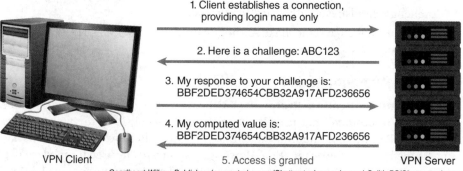

1. Client establishes a connection, providing login name only

2. Here is a challenge: ABC123

3. My response to your challenge is: BBF2DED374654CBB32A917AFD236656

4. My computed value is: BBF2DED374654CBB32A917AFD236656

VPN Client

5. Access is granted

VPN Server

Goodheart-Willcox Publisher; (computer) romvo/Shutterstock.com; (server) Sujith RS/Shutterstock.com

Figure 12-17 In a Microsoft Challenge Handshake Authentication Protocol (MS-CHAP), a session ID is included in the challenge and the password does not need to be stored in clear text, but can be encrypted.

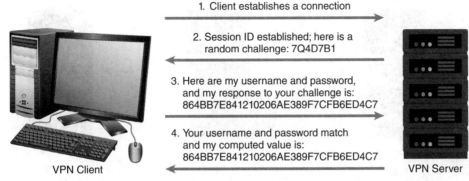

1. Client establishes a connection

2. Session ID established; here is a random challenge: 7Q4D7B1

3. Here are my username and password, and my response to your challenge is: 864BB7E841210206AE389F7CFB6ED4C7

4. Your username and password match and my computed value is: 864BB7E841210206AE389F7CFB6ED4C7

VPN Client

VPN Server

5. Access is granted

Goodheart-Willcox Publisher; (computer) romvo/Shutterstock.com; (server) Sujith RS/Shutterstock.com

- *Protected EAP (PEAP)* fully encloses or, *encapsulates*, EAP. It works with the Transport Layer Security (TLS) protocol. Transport Layer Security (TLS) is a transport protocol that encrypts all data sent between a VPN and an Internet connection to prevent third parties from intercepting packets. PEAP was jointly created by Microsoft, Cisco, and RSA Security.

Microsegmentation

✛ 3.3

Microsegmentation is a security technique that enables administrators to split a network's attack surface by logically dividing the network into segments based on individual workloads. The main difference between segmentation and microsegmentation is that while segmentation is typically a north-south traffic control, microsegmentation instead focuses on limiting east-west traffic. **East-west traffic** is traffic that flows from one server to another within an organization's data center. Conversely, **north-south traffic** is the flow of traffic from an organization's data center to an outside location, as illustrated in Figure 12-18.

In many networks, security administrators have focused a great deal of their security defenses on the north-south route by configuring firewalls and intrusion-detection systems. In most cases, little attention has been focused on the lateral movement of data within the network, and this lack of attention presents a serious network vulnerability. This lack of attention was the catalyst for the development of microsegmentation.

Most traffic in virtualized data centers is composed of east-west traffic. Therefore, if a threat penetrates perimeter firewalls, attackers can move throughout the network, launch attacks, and access data with only a handful of precautions that could identify or stop the attack. A malicious script could run on the web server and exploit the back-end database server, and there is no protection within the data center to monitor this exchange.

One area that has seen a huge increase in microsegmentation is in the virtualization of servers in data centers. In a virtualized network, it is not feasible to use traditional security appliances on servers, primarily due to the high requirements of management and potential for performance degradation. Instead, this type of environment needs to be protected by approaching security based on workload

Figure 12-18 East-west traffic flows from one server to another within an organization's data center, while north-south traffic flows from an organization's data center to an outside location.

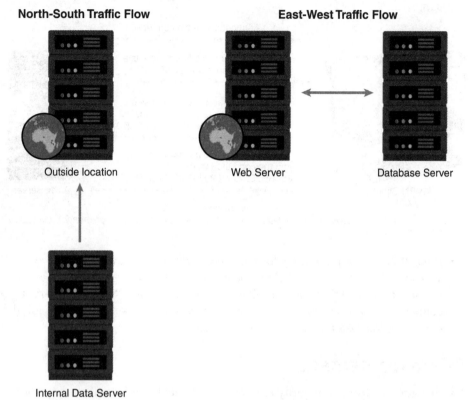

characteristics, not physical device. This is possible in a virtual computing environment using a hypervisor. A hypervisor can see *all* the traffic. Therefore, it is possible to establish intelligent policies to monitor security criteria for all services, databases, and web servers within a data center instead of individual machines. In virtualization, microsegmentation enables the creation of secure zones within the network to divide a data center into distinct security segments and deploy security policies to provide application-level security controls. This additional layer of control adds more protection and resistance to attacks.

For example, in Figure 12-19, if a malicious script is executed at the web server, the intelligent policies running on virtualized firewalls and services evaluates that traffic flow before entering the database server and exploiting or stealing information.

Figure 12-19 One area that has seen a huge increase in microsegmentation is in the virtualization of servers in data centers.

East-West Traffic Flow

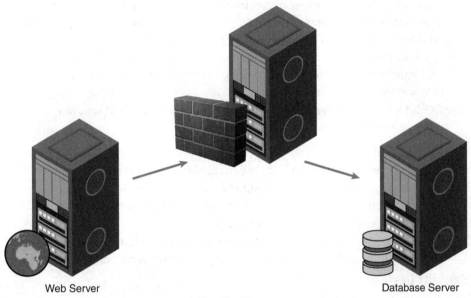

Web Server

Database Server

Data center using intelligent management.

Goodheart-Willcox Publisher; (wall) beboy/Shutterstock.com; (server) aShatilov/Shutterstock.com

SUMMARY

Secure Network Design

- Secure network design is the process of designing a network to include measures to support network security.
- Network security is the policies, procedures, and techniques used to eliminate or monitor unauthorized access or intrusion to a computer network and its devices.
- Through the application of software and hardware solutions, network security focuses on the protection of the infrastructure and architecture of a network.

Out-of-Band Management (OOBM)

- Out-of-band management (OOBM) is a method of remotely managing and controlling infrastructure using an interface separate from the primary connection. This enables administrators to maintain control through dedicated alternative access methods that do not rely on the LAN.
- A primary reason for incorporating OOBM is security. Public-facing devices that handle Internet traffic should not be accessible to arbitrary access or management.
- OOBM is accomplished using modems, terminal servers, and separate management network.

Network Devices

- A network has standard devices that enable functionality and communication.
- Devices are classified by functionality in the seven-layer Open System Interconnection (OSI) reference model. When configured properly, network appliances provide security for a network.
- Types of network devices used to provide security for a network include a hub, bridge, switch, router, load balancer, proxy and jump server, and an aggregator.

Security Devices

- A firewall acts as a barrier or protection against unwanted data transfer at entry points by monitoring incoming and outgoing network traffic. It is a first line of defense for a network. Firewalls can be host- or network-based.
- A unified threat management (UTM) device is an all-in-one security device that enables a network to be managed using one appliance. A UTM can simplify managing a network's security.
- An intrusion-detection system (IDS) is used to detect an attack on a network. It is managed by in-band or out-of-band. Two basic types of IDS are HIDS and NIDS.
- An intrusion-prevention system (IPS) monitors and analyzes incoming and outgoing traffic flow and immediately halts traffic when malicious activity is detected. An IPS can actively prevent intrusions from happening.
- Additional security devices include HSM, SSL inspector, security and media gateways, and SIEM.

Network Architecture Security

- Secure network architecture is the deployment of network devices with security measures enabled. A network's design can strengthen or secure it from threat actors.
- Elements of the design should include security zones, a zero-trust model, network segregation, geographical considerations, and configuration management (CM).

Placement of Security Devices

- Security devices are placed at the border of or inside the network. Sometimes security devices are located in both places for additional security and defense-in-depth.

- Examples of elements used to help strengthen security devices include SSL accelerators, taps, port mirrors, sensors, collectors, filters, an aggregation switch, a correlation engine, and a DDoS mitigator.

Deception Technology

- Deception technology is designed to prevent a threat actor who has already breached a network from doing any damage. It is typically distributed as a decoy that mimics authentic network assets.
- A honeypot is a computer or server loaded with files or applications that appear to be authentic and placed in a network zone with limited security. It imitates authentication data files and is intentionally configured with vulnerabilities so it can be attacked and easily compromised.
- A honeyfile is a fake file located on a network folder share. It acts as bait and is designed to detect and observe hackers accessing a network with the intention of modifying, copying, or stealing data from the network.
- Fake telemetry is false data recorded through simulations. It can alert administrators to an intrusion before damage or data loss can occur.
- A DNS sinkhole is a DNS server used to prevent the resolution of host names of specific URLs. When a DNS sinkhole is contacted, it responds with a false IP address, which adds a layer of protection to the network security.

Network Segmentation

- Network segmentation is the act of dividing a network into smaller sections to separate data to reduce its exposure. Two main network segmentation designs include VLAN and VPN.
- A virtual local area network (VLAN) is technology that enables remote users to be grouped logically even when connected to different switches. VLANs are created on network switches usually by assigning devices based on the physical switch port or the MAC address.
- A virtual private network (VPN) is a virtual network connection that provides a way to encrypt data traveling through unsecured public networks. Two common implementations of VPN configurations: remote access and site to site.
- When creating the VPN connection, security parameters are set. These include security encryption protocols and authentication methods.

Microsegmentation

- Microsegmentation is a security technique that enables administrators to split a network's attack surface by logically dividing the network into segments based on individual workloads.
- Microsegmentation focuses on limiting east-west traffic, which is traffic that flows from one server to another within an organization's data center.
- One area that has seen a huge increase in microsegmentation is in the virtualization of servers in data centers using a hypervisor. Therefore, it is possible to establish intelligent policies to monitor security criteria for all services, databases, and web servers within a data center.

REVIEW QUESTIONS

1. Define *secure network design*.

2. State the difference between infrastructure and architecture.

3. Summarize out-of-band management (OOBM).

4. Briefly explain three elements used to accomplish out-of-band management.

5. List types of network devices used to provide security for a network.

6. Identify and explain two configurations used for enabling security in a switch.

7. List techniques used to accomplish route security.

8. Briefly explain an access control list.

9. Explain four security devices commonly encountered in a network.

10. Which type of firewall monitors packets over an established period of time and accepts only packets that were previously tracked?

11. Explain three types of monitoring used to examine network traffic.

12. Identify elements included in network architecture security.

13. Identify and explain four examples of security zones.

14. What five elements do security configuration management (SCM) tools rely on to help detect unauthorized activity or changes?

15. Summarize where security devices should be placed.

16. Explain four types of deception technology.

17. Identify and explain two basic network segmentation designs.

18. List types of VPN protocols.

19. Explain four IAM services used for authentication.

20. Summarize microsegmentation.

✛ SAMPLE SECURITY+ EXAM QUESTIONS

1. Which of the following security measures can be easily bypassed by the nmap tool?

    A. NAT

    B. MAC Filtering

    C. Loop prevention

    D. DHCP snooping

2. Which solution *best* helps in preventing performance issues as the result of MAC flooding?

    A. Implement a firewall at the switch.

    B. Prevent rebroadcast of MAC addresses through all ports.

    C. Implement a flood guard to limit available switch memory for the CAM table.

    D. Incorporate MAC filtering on the switch.

3. Which *best* describes the security concern with DHCP snooping?

   A. A hacker can obtain lease information to a specific client.

   B. A hacker can intercept and change DHCP leases for a client.

   C. An unauthorized DHCP server will lease IP addresses on a subnet.

   D. The attack will exhaust the available IP addresses in a scope.

4. In order to maintain availability, which of the following features can help with performance by equally distributing requests to devices in an ordered manner?

   A. Affinity scheduling

   B. Active-passive configuration

   C. Session persistence

   D. Round-robin scheduling

5. Which device reviews inbound requests from the Internet and routes them to the appropriate internal server?

   A. Reverse proxy server

   B. Jump server

   C. Forward proxy server

   D. Load balancer

6. Which firewall technique allows packets that match an active connection?

   A. Virtual firewall

   B. Network-based firewall

   C. Stateful firewall

   D. Packet-filtering firewall

7. Which firewall is *best* suited to filter and monitor HTTP traffic?

   A. Proxy firewall

   B. Web application firewall

   C. Host firewall

   D. Content filtering

8. Which networking device is commonly used for forensic analysis and is unable to stop an active attack?

   A. Jump server

   B. UTM

   C. In-band IPS

   D. Out-of-band IDS

9. The security zone designed only for employees of a business or organization is a(n) _____.

   A. DMZ

   B. intranet

   C. extranet

   D. zero trust

10. Which is a key difference between CHAP and MS-CHAP authentication?

   A. Passwords must always be encrypted in CHAP but not MS-CHAP.

   B. Biometric information is supported in MS-CHAP but not in CHAP.

   C. A session ID is included in an MS-CHAP handshake but is omitted in a CHAP handshake.

   D. There is no shared secret in MS-CHAP.

LAB EXERCISES

Lab Activity 12-1: Changing a MAC Address

In this lab, you will demonstrate the ability to change or spoof a MAC address using a Kali Linux distribution.

1. Log into Kali Linux and open a terminal window.

2. Run the **ifconfig** command and record your current MAC address. In Linux, the MAC address is often recorded as the *ether* or *physical address*. Use the address for either the eth0 or WLAN adapter.

3. Verify the MAC address by running the following command syntax. You may have to substitute your adapter name for *eth0* if it differs. Remember, Linux commands are case-sensitive.

   macchanger eth0 –s

   Generate a screen capture of the command output and submit it with this lab.

4. Before the MAC address can be changed, the adapter must be taken offline. Additionally, the user must have root privileges. If necessary, change to the root user before executing the following syntax:

   ifconfig eth0 down

5. To assign a new MAC address, use the following syntax:

   macchanger eth0 -r

   Record your new MAC address and generate a screen capture to submit with this lab.

6. Spoofed addresses can be specified to assigned statically similarly to how an IP address can be assigned statically. Change your MAC address again using the same syntax as in Step 5. However, instead of using the **–r** switch, use the following syntax:

   -m fc:25:3f:17:d2:7a

   Generate a screen capture to submit with this lab.

7. If a valid MAC vendor is required, the following syntax can be used to view available network card vendors:

   macchanger -l

   Which company was used for the fake address in Step 6?

8. Reset the MAC address to the default setting by using the following syntax.

   macchanger -p

   Generate a screen capture of the result to submit with this lab.

9. Re-enable your network adapter using the following syntax:

   ifconfig eth0 up.

   Remember, you may have to substitute your adapter name for *eth0* if it differs.

Lab Activity 12-2: VPN Client Configuration

VPN provides a way to connect remote users to a network securely. A VPN can be easily configured in Windows. The ability to create a VPN is built into the operating system. In this lab, you will utilize the Windows VPN feature to configure a new client.

1. Click **Start>Settings** in Windows 10 to display the Settings window.

2. Click **Network & Internet** to display the **Network & Internet** windows. Click **VPN** on the left side of the window.

3. Click the **Add a VPN connection** button on the right side of the window. A new window is displayed, as shown.

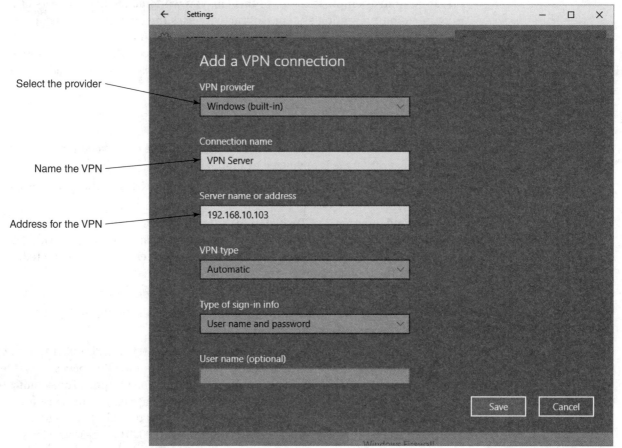

Goodheart-Willcox Publisher

4. Click the **VPN provider** drop-down arrow, and select **Windows (built-in)** from the list of options.

5. Click in the **Connection name** text box, and enter VPN Server.

6. Click in the **Server name or address** text box, and enter 192.168.10.103.

7. Click in the **VPN type** drop-down menu. Notice the available options. Click **Automatic** in the drop-down list.

8. Leave the remaining default options, and click the **Save** button to create the VPN. The new VPN is listed on the right side of the **Network & Internet** window.

9. Right-click on VPN connection you created, and select **Properties** from the shortcut list.

10. Click on the **Security** tab. Which of the drop-down options would you choose to provide the highest degree of security?

11. Assume the VPN connection requires the use of a smart card for multifactor authentication. To configure this requirement, select the **Use Extensible Authentication Protocol (EAP)** option. Click **Properties** and locate the option for **Microsoft: Smart Card** as shown. Click **OK** to save your settings.

Lab Activity 12-3: Snort Rules for Intrusion Detection

An intrusion-prevention system (IPS) not only detects malicious or suspicious behavior but also takes action to stop the problem. Snort can be used as an active scanner (intrusion prevention). In this lab, you will practice the concepts of using an intrusion-prevention system. This activity uses the open-source program Snort. Make sure this is downloaded and installed before beginning.

Snort uses a special configuration file named snort.conf. It is located in the /snort/etc directory. It is configured with basic settings, but the file can be edited if you need any customized changes.

1. In a Linux terminal window, enter cd /etc/snort.

2. Enter ls, and locate the configuration file.

3. Enter nano snort.conf to open the configuration file in a text editor. The configuration file is organized by numbered steps.

4. The default network is set to "any." In configuration Step 1, what is the variable used to store the default network?

5. In configuration Step 7, which rule deals with the domain name system? Snort has many preconfigured rules, but you can create your own custom rule. Next, you will create a rule that sends an alert to the screen if a ping is detected. Close the snort.conf file.

6. Enter cd /etc/snort/rules to change to the folder where snort rules are located.

7. Enter sudo nano local.rules to open the default rules file. This file is empty until rules are added to it.

8. Enter alert icmp any any -> any any (msg:"Ping Detected!";sid:1000001;) into the text file. Be sure to enter this exactly as shown, including the spaces. This rule is for ping attempts. The any any indicates any IP and any port. The -> indicates an inbound direction. The message text (msg) will appear on the console screen when a ping is detected. The sid is the identifier for the rule. It must be unique and start with this number. All SIDs lower than 1000001 are reserved for snort.

9. Press the [Ctrl][X] key combination and then the [Y] key to save the file. When prompted for the file name, accept the name local.rules. For the rule file to be used, the snort.conf file must be checked to make sure this rule is set to run, and not remarked as ignore.

10. Enter cd /etc/snort to change to the snort folder.

11. Enter sudo nano snort.conf to edit the configuration file.

12. Scroll down to configuration Step 7.

13. Locate the line that reads #site specific rules. Make sure there is *not* a pound sign or hash tag (#) in front of this line: include $RULE_PATH/local.rules.

14. Save and exit the configuration file. Now the rule can be tested.

15. Enter sudo snort -c /etc/snort/snort.conf -A console -l /var/log/snort -i eth0. The -c specifies the console file, -A shows the alerts on the screen, -l is the log file location, and -i is for the network interface.

16. Open a new terminal window, and enter ifconfig to identify your local IP address.

17. Ping the host using your local IP address.

18. Switch to the terminal window in which Snort is running. Watch for the alert to be displayed. If you do not see the alert, open another terminal, and ping the IP address of another computer on your network.

19. Stop the ping and Snort by pressing the [Ctrl][C] key combination in each terminal window.

20. Enter cd /var/log/snort to change to the Snort log directory, and then enter ls -lh to view the logs in the directory. Using the date and time, identify the most recent log you created.

21. Enter sudo snort -r *xx*.log.*nnn*$, substituting *xx* and *nnn* to match the log file you created. Review the information in the log. Create and save a screenshot.

22. Launch a web browser, and navigate to a search engine. Search for snort users manual, and open a reliable link to the manual. The rule you created just set the option to display a screen alert. Other actions can be taken. Using the manual, identify what you would use for an action for the following scenarios.

    A. Log the packet

    B. Ignore the packet

    C. Block and drop the packet

Lab Activity 12-4: Honeypots

A honeypot is a decoy server set up to attract hackers away from the live server. Most honeypots are deployed on Internet-facing networks or in the demilitarized zone (DMZ). In this activity, you will simulate an environment that uses a honeypot. This activity uses the free student version of HoneyBOT, currently located at atomic-software-solutions.software.informer.com. Make sure this is downloaded and installed before beginning on one machine and ensure nmap is downloaded and available on a second machine.

1. Launch the machine in which HoneyBOT is installed.

2. Launch HoneyBOT.

3. Click **View>Options** in the pull-down menu. Enter the alias -DemoServer. Create and save a screenshot. Apply the settings.

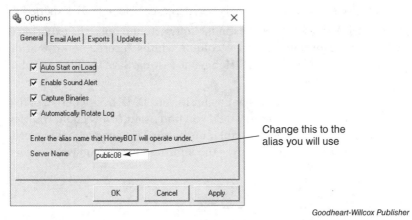

Goodheart-Willcox Publisher

4. Record the IP address of your computer. You will need this information to probe this machine from the other machine.

5. Start the HoneyBOT by clicking the **Start** button on the toolbar. If multiple network adapters are detected, you can leave the default **All Adapters** selected.

6. Launch the second machine. Ensure nmap/zenmap is installed. It can be downloaded for free at www.nmap.org. You will send some commands to the first machine. Using the software tools you learned in previous labs, perform the following.

   A. Launch ZenMap, which is the graphical interface for Nmap. When it opens, enter the IP address of the first virtual machine in the **Target** text box. Select an intense scan on the DemoServer, and then click the **Scan** button.

   B. Ping the DemoServer.

7. Return to the DemoServer computer, and click the **Stop** button to end the honeypot server collecting information.

8. In the left-hand pane of HoneyBOT, expand and select the Ports branch in the tree. How many ports were targeted during the scans? Look at the status bar at the bottom of the screen. How many records are listed? Create and save a screen capture.

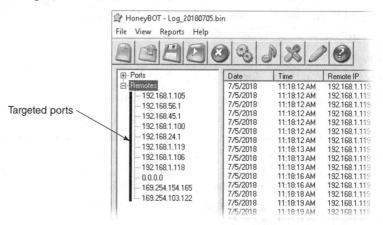

Targeted ports

Goodheart-Willcox Publisher

9. Expand the Remote branch. Find the remote machine that had some entries, and double-click one of the entries. Review the type of information contained in this capture.

10. Click **File**>**Export** in the pull-down menu. The data are automatically exported in a CSV format, and the file is saved in the c:\HoneyBOT\Exports folder.

11. Launch Microsoft Excel or similar software, and open the exported CSV file. Adjust the formatting such as column widths. Insert a new row at the top and add the title DEMO Server: Honeypot Testing. Save the file and submit it to your instructor.

12. Suppose you tracked this honeypot in your DMZ over a period of five days. What type of information would you find useful? How could you view the data in a spreadsheet to gain useful information? Do you feel this is worth the time to run a honeypot and analyze the information? Defend your answer.

CASE STUDY

Attacks on Unnamed Agencies

Cyberattacks can impact any organization or governmental system. In 2020, an unnamed US federal agency was attacked via two command and control (C&C) points established by a hacker. Although not confirmed, analysts believe hackers may have obtained user credentials and passwords by exploiting a known vulnerability identified in early 2014. This vulnerability allowed attackers to retrieve files and passwords remotely and was found to have been exploited at multiple federal agencies.

The attack enabled the hacker to review e-mail messages and documents for passwords and navigate the network to locate additional sensitive or valuable information. This attack was revealed by the US Department of Homeland Security (DHS) as a warning of poor digital security practices. The analysis report, AR20-268A, is available for review on the US Cybersecurity and Infrastructure Security Agency (CISA) website.

1. Why do you think the DHS revealed specific information such as details of the attack but chose not to release the specific agency that was breached?

2. Why do you think many agencies neglected to patch network systems despite a known vulnerability? What recommendations can be put in place to mitigate these risks moving forward?

3. One of the IP addresses used in the attack, 185.86.151.223, was used multiple times during the attack and reconnaissance phases. Which security systems or measures in this chapter could have been used to alert or block this IP address?

4. The attackers created a persistent Secure Socket Shell (SSH) and mounted a file share to drop files and reduce their visibility in the system. One of the recommendations made following this attack was to use an Enterprise Firewall and jump server for remote access How can these recommendations help against another similar type threat?

5. In its analysis report, CISA makes recommendations for preventing similar attacks in the future. Do you think these recommendations are sufficient? What risks is CISA taking by posting its recommendations publicly?

Secure Network Administration

LEARNING OUTCOMES

- Discuss items that are important to secure network administration.
- Explain three security items used to assess network security.
- Identify command-line utilities used for network reconnaissance and discovery.
- Discuss common network attacks.
- Identify tools and utilities used to investigate network incidents.

KEY TERMS

bandwidth monitor
Cuckoo
curl
DNS attack
DNS poisoning
DNS Security Extensions (DNSSEC)
dnsenum command
Domain Name System (DNS)
Dynamic Host Configuration Protocol (DHCP)
exploitation framework
file integrity monitor (FIM)
File Transfer Protocol (FTP)
File Transfer Protocol/SSL (FTPS)

hping command
ICMP echo request
Internet Mail Access Protocol (IMAP)
IP Flow Information Export (IPFix)
IP scanner
MAC cloning
monitoring service
netcat command
NetFlow
netstat command
network access control (NAC)
network administration
network security assessment

nmap
packet replay
packet sniffer
Post Office Protocol (POP)
scanless
Secure File Transfer Protocol (SFTP)
sFlow
sn1per
System Health Agent (SHA)
tcpdump command
theHarvester
universal resource locator (URL) redirection
URL redirection attack

 ## SECURITY+ CERTIFICATION EXAM OBJECTIVES

The following Security+ Certification Exam Objectives are covered in this chapter.

- + 1.4: Address resolution protocol (ARP) poisoning
- + 1.4: MAC cloning
- + 1.4: Domain Name System (DNS)
- + 1.4: Distributed denial of service (DDoS)
- + 1.4: Malicious code or script execution
- + 3.1: Protocols
- + 3.1: Use cases
- + 3.3: DNS
- + 3.3: Network access control (NAC)
- + 3.3: Out of band management

- + 3.3: Monitoring services
- + 3.3: File integrity monitors
- + 4.1: nmap
- + 4.1: hping
- + 4.1: netstat
- + 4.1: netcat
- + 4.1: IP scanners
- + 4.1: curl
- + 4.1: the harvester
- + 4.1: sn1per
- + 4.1: scanless
- + 4.1: dnsenum
- + 4.1: Nessus

- + 4.1: Cuckoo
- + 4.1: SSH
- + 4.1: Packet capture and replay
- + 4.1: Exploitation frameworks
- + 4.3: SIEM dashboards
- + 4.3: Log files
- + 4.3: syslog/rsyslog/syslog-ng
- + 4.3: journalctl
- + 4.3: nxlog
- + 4.3: Bandwidth monitors
- + 4.3: Netflow/sFlow
- + 4.3: Protocol analyzer output

OVERVIEW

Network services are essential programs that provide functionality to users on networks, including logging in, accessing the Internet, and requesting files or resources. Many of these services have existed for some time, and as such, a number of vulnerabilities have been identified. Therefore, proper administration of a network, particularly the secure administration of a network, is vital to maintaining data integrity and availability.

In this chapter, you will explore essential and secure network administration topics, including secure protocols, establishing a secure DNS, and continual monitoring of a network. You will also learn about vulnerabilities with common network services and methods for assessing network security. Additionally, common network attacks and tools for investigating network incidents will be covered.

Secure Network Administration

Network administration is the operational tasks that provide ongoing support, management, and maintenance to enable a network to run efficiently. Often, administration tasks include the

- design, installation, and assessment of a network;
- creation of regular backups;
- development of documentation to enable maintenance, such as diagrams and schematics;
- implementation of authentication measures;
- ongoing troubleshooting and user assistance; and
- installation of security devices, such as sensors and intrusion-detection and intrusion-prevention systems.

After a network is designed, it is the responsibility of IT and security professionals to continue working to ensure it stays secure. The proper administration of a network is vital for its ongoing security; without it, devices and the data stored on them are vulnerable to attack and compromise.

Secure Protocols

In computing, a *protocol* is an industry-accepted standardized format for transmitting data. Protocols enable network communication between devices. A protocol is similar to a rule that everyone must follow.

There are many protocols used in networking, but not all were created with security in mind. A *secure protocol* is one that has additional built-in security enhancements, such as encryption. Figure 13-1 lists protocols that provide security enhancement as well as their common services and uses.

3.1

Figure 13-1 A secure protocol is a protocol that has additional built-in security enhancements, such as encryption.

Protocol	Network Service	Usage
Secure Real-Time Transport Protocol (SRTP)	Voice and Video	Provides encryption, authentication, and integrity to VoIP and video conferencing data; secure alternative to Real-Time Transport Protocol (RTP)
Network Time Security (NTS)	Time Synchronization	Provides security and authentication to key exchanges through incorporation of TLS; secure alternative to Network Time Protocol (NTP)
Secure Multi-Internet Mail Extension (S/MIME)	E-mail Services	Enables encryption of e-mails to protect unwanted access and interception
Hypertext Transfer Protocol, Secure (HTTPS)	Web Services	Encrypts information transmitted over the Internet to increase security of data transfers; secure alternative to Hypertext Transfer Protocol (HTTP)
Secure File Transfer Protocol (SFTP) and File Transfer Protocol/SSL (FTPS)	File Transfer	Ensures data is transferred using a private, safe stream of data; secure, encrypted alternatives to File Transfer Protocol (FTP)
Lightweight Directory Access Protocol, Secure (LDAPS)	Directory Services	Provides encryption to directory information data, including usernames and passwords; secure alternative to Lightweight Directory Access Protocol (LDAP)
Secure Shell (SSH)	Remote Access	Provides a secure channel over which applications such as remote login and command-line execution is conducted; secure alternative to Telnet
Domain Name System Security Extension (DNSSEC)	Domain Name Resolution	Provides encryption to information distributed through the Domain Name System; security-enhanced alternative to DNS
Simple Network Management Protocol version 3 (SNMPv3)	Routing and Switching	Provides security, authentication, and privacy to network devices, systems, and applications, particularly routers and switches
IP Security (IPSec)	Subscription Services	Establishes encrypted connections between networked devices and allocates subscription-based updates, such as antivirus signatures and IDS/IPS definitions

Goodheart-Willcox Publisher

Dynamic Host Configuration Protocol (DHCP)

Dynamic Host Configuration Protocol (DHCP) is a network management protocol used to assign an IP address automatically when a client connects to a network. DHCP employs *dynamic addressing*, which is the automatic assigning of addresses, as opposed to *static addressing*, which is the manual configuration of network addresses. In dynamic addressing, when a workstation is powered on, it requests an address from a DHCP server. The DHCP server receives the request and assigns the device an IP address from the DHCP pool of addresses. IP addresses are leased for a preconfigured time, after which the process of requesting an IP address starts over.

Domain Name System (DNS)

Domain Name System (DNS) is a hierarchical, decentralized protocol that maps a domain name to a corresponding IP address. With DNS, a user is able to enter a URL with a domain name in a browser. The browser then checks the domain name against its DNS server, which maps or translates the domain name to the correct network address. Without DNS, network users would be forced to memorize not only domain names but also their corresponding IP addresses.

If you are using a network with Microsoft servers, storing the DNS information in the Active Directory provides additional protection and security to data access, as well as the transfer of data between DNS servers.

File Transfer Protocol (FTP)

File Transfer Protocol (FTP) is a protocol that enables the transmission of files between devices connected over the Internet. When data is transferred across network media, it must be protected. A common practice for securing file transfers is to connect to remote connections from a host. Additionally, some web servers offer the ability to download files instead of providing HTTP services. Two secured variations of FTP include the following:

- **Secure File Transfer Protocol (SFTP)**, also known as *SSH File Transfer Protocol*, is a secure alternative to FTP that uses a single channel to transmit and receive data. SFTP was designed as an extension of SSH to provide security file transfers and uses a Secure Shell to encrypt and transmit data.
- **File Transfer Protocol/SSL (FTPS)** is an extension to File Transfer Protocol (FTP) that has SSH functionality with an added second channel for secure transmissions. FTPS is more widely known, but it is less secure than SFTP.

 3.1

Secure Shell (SSH)

Secure shell (SSH) is a secure protocol used to provide remote login and secure transmission of data to remote devices. Most devices are managed remotely, which requires administrators to have a secure method of connection to those devices to protect the confidentiality of data, integrity of authentication, and device configurations and settings. SSH provides security through the public key encryption of data transmitted during a session.

SSH is a replacement for the much older, deprecated Telnet protocol, which provided remote connection capabilities but transmitted data in plaintext.

Any network service can be secured using SSH scripting environments, such as PuTTY, which is a free, open-source SSH terminal emulator. SSH-enabled shells function as secured command-line interfaces (CLIs) that can be used to connect to remote devices over unsecured networks such as the Internet. This secure connection also enables CLIs to function as a tool for assessing organizational security. For example, assume you were working at a Windows machine but needed to check configuration of a UNIX server in a different building. You can open an SSH client, such as PuTTY, and enter the command lines needed to check the server as though you were sitting at the UNIX server. The commands entered are sent securely from the Windows PC to the UNIX server, and the results displayed on the Windows PC. In Linux, SSH is accessed directly from the terminal window.

3.1

4.1

Lightweight Directory Access Protocol, Secure (LDAPS)

Lightweight directory access protocol, secure (LDAPS) is a secure protocol that provides access to network directory databases containing information about authorized users, user rights and privileges, and other organizational information. Historically, data accessed using standard LDAP had no built-in security to protect confidentiality of information as it is transmitted in plaintext. This presented security vulnerabilities, since most directories include sensitive information. To mitigate the vulnerabilities of traditional LDAP, LDAPS was developed as a secure alternative that encrypts data through the SSL protocol.

3.1

3.1

E-Mail Protocols

There are two general protocols used in e-mail messaging: POP and IMAP. **Post Office Protocol (POP)** is a legacy e-mail protocol that enables users to retrieve incoming e-mail messages. The most recent iteration of POP is *POP3*. A user's e-mail client connects to a POP3 server and downloads messages to the user's computer. After messages are downloaded, they are deleted from the POP3 server. *Secure Post Office Protocol (POP3S)* is a secure equivalent to POP that provides an encrypted process for e-mail clients to retrieve mail from the remote server.

Internet Mail Access Protocol (IMAP) is a more recent and advanced e-mail protocol that enables mail to be stored on and accessed from a server. IMAP is considered a remote e-mail protocol because, while it functions in the same manner as POP, messages are not deleted from the mail server; nor are they downloaded to the user's computer. IMAP can be configured securely by using *IMAP over SSL/TLS (IMAPS)*.

The *Simple Mail Transfer Protocol (SMTP)* is a communication protocol that enables transmission mail servers to distribute e-mail messages over the Internet. SMTP is the oldest e-mail protocol but is still widely used as a backbone in e-mail transfers between servers. There is no native security layer within SMTP, so security must be configured manually to ensure e-mail messages are encrypted. Securing SMTP can be accomplished by configuring an SSL connection or employing secure ports such as port 465 or 25025 instead of default port settings. Security extensions can also be used, such as SMTP authentication (SMTP AUTH), which requires client authentication on submission servers.

3.3

DNS

Domain Name System (DNS) is a hierarchical, decentralized service that associates domain names to corresponding network IP addresses. On both Windows and Linux workstations, the operating system allows for the temporary storage of DNS requests and resolutions in the local DNS cache. The *local DNS cache* is a temporary storage location on the computer to improve DNS lookup performance.

TECH TIP

In Windows, you can view the local DNS cache using CMD or PowerShell with the syntax, **ipconfig/displaydns** or **get-dnsclientcache**. To clear the cache from the CMD or PowerShell interface, you can use the command syntax **ipconfig/flushdns** or **clear-dnsclientcache**.

Domain Reputation

A *domain reputation* is a score or level of reliability assigned to an organization's domain. DNS servers build models of domains known to be legitimate as well as those known to be malicious. These models are then used to calculate a reputation score for a new domain to determine if it is trustworthy. There are models that provide assurance scoring on domain. They consider many factors including public availability of information, SSL vulnerabilities, and SSL certificate consistency of information.

E-mail service providers also view a domain's reputation and decide on the trustworthiness of e-mails originating from that site. A company with a poor domain reputation can be indicative of frequent or prolonged attacks and lead to customers and partners forgoing use or recommendations of the domain.

Security issues that can hurt a domain's reputation include a recent domain registration or registration in an offshore country. Failure to make information publicly available through a Whois lookup can increase suspicion of the domain.

1.4

DNS Attacks

A **DNS attack** is a cyberattack in which vulnerabilities within the Domain Name System are exploited. DNS servers are critical elements of network communication as they enable communication through device name instead of IP address. Unfortunately, because of their importance, DNS servers are among the most frequently attacked devices. If a DNS server's information is corrupted, especially one from an Internet service provider (ISP), the corrupted data will likely be sent to other DNS servers. Data can be corrupted through hacking or mistakes and can have a significant impact. Examples of attacks on DNS devices include the following.

Domain Hijacking Attack

Domain hijacking is an attempt to transfer the ownership or registration and control of the domain from the rightful owner. Public domain names are registered with the Internet Corporation for Assigned Names and Numbers (ICANN), which ensures no duplication of domain names and identifies the lawful registrar of the domain. Domain hijacking attacks are often performed against the ICANN registration so attackers can use a domain for their own purposes, such as tricking users into thinking they were on a legitimate site to steal or collect information from users. Companies may not be aware of the attack until after it is successful, often when they find fraudulent data on their websites, or their login credentials can no longer be used to manage the domain.

✛ 1.4

DNS Poisoning Attack

DNS poisoning occurs when an entry is embedded in the victim's local DNS cache that redirects a legitimate URL to an incorrect IP address. DNS poisoning is often the result of malware or manipulation of the local host's file, which is used to prepopulate the local DNS cache when a computer is booted. The host's file is an attractive target because it will automatically add information to the DNS cache when the computer starts.

✛ 1.4

The local DNS cache improves system performance by resolving future requests locally. However, the local DNS cache is vulnerable to DNS poisoning. It is not required to use a local DNS cache, but many system administrators do not block its use since it increases the retrieval time for web page loading. To prevent its use, administrators can configure a policy that disables the local DNS caching service.

DNS databases are also vulnerable to poisoning actions. DNS servers on a network store records with information about device names and IP addresses. DNS databases can become quite large, so tables are organized into smaller units called *zones*. Multiple DNS servers are located on networks to provide performance and redundancy of information should a DNS server become unavailable. A server used by a company to store records of resources for their business are called *authoritative DNS servers*.

DNS poisoning may not always be obvious, especially to a user requesting a domain name. If an attacker created a page mimicking the official domain, users may not be aware of the redirection and could provide login credentials or other personal and confidential information on these pages. One method of discovery is to monitor DNS activity to locate abnormal actions, such as a single source querying your DNS server for multiple names with no resolution. The lack of resolution indicates the requests are not attempting to resolve names, but instead are searching for a specific target. Another indicator of DNS poisoning could include unusual or unexpected content on the redirected web page.

There are several actions you can take to protect a system from DNS poisoning, including the following:

- Install antimalware programs on clients to help prevent DNS cache hijacking. *DNS cache hijacking* is an attack that involves inserting malicious or invalid entries into the cache.
- If using Microsoft Server, store the DNS database in the Active Directory to gain additional security protections.

- Limit who has privileges to configure the DNS environment and records.
- Require multifactor authentication for users who maintain DNS records.
- Review DNS server logs and audit DNS records for unauthorized changes regularly.
- Consider not hosting the local DNS client cache.

- Consider configuring **DNS Security Extensions (DNSSEC)**, which is a suite of specifications that requires all responses from a DNS server be digitally signed to ensure they come from an authorized source.

URL Redirection Attack

A **URL redirection attack** is a network attack that redirects a user from a valid web page to a malicious copy, often for phishing campaigns. These attacks are typically accomplished by an attacker gaining access to a domain and configuring a URL redirection. **Universal resource locator (URL) redirection**, also called *URL forwarding*, is a technique used to reroute one domain to another. Often, redirection is intentionally performed by website administrators to give a legitimate web page more than one URL address.

Usually, URL redirections go unnoticed until an administrator reviews site traffic or analytics. Redirection attacks can be prevented through stringent practices such as installation of a web application firewall (WAF), website scanners, and maintenance of up-to-date software and code.

DNS Amplification Attack

A *DNS amplification attack* is an application-layer distributed denial of service (DDoS) attack that uses publicly accessible DNS servers to overwhelm a different computer system with DNS-style response traffic. DNS amplification attacks are accomplished by sending DNS lookup requests using a spoofed target address. When the queried DNS server responds, records are sent to the target's address, not the hacker's. This floods the target's DNS with requests and denies service to valid user requests. Despite the victimized device being connected to a private network, the attack is likely occurring at a public-facing DNS server. Unfortunately, that means not much can be done to prevent a DNS amplification attack.

Network Access Control (NAC)

Network access control (NAC), also known as a *host health check*, is a network solution that unifies endpoint security by verifying that a host meets minimum standards before it is allowed to connect to a network. Network access control is an effective tool in the identification and correction of systems that do not have sufficient security installed. By conducting host health checks, NAC helps prevent unsecure devices from infecting other network nodes or creating additional vulnerabilities on a network. NAC standards require that a host

- is running an operating system with the latest security patches installed;
- has up-to-date antivirus signature files;
- has a firewall that is turned on; and
- is an approved device.

Network access control relies on agents to collect data and report to access servers. An *agent* is software or code that searches for vulnerabilities in the client. Some agents may run at system boot, while others can be persistent, constantly checking for vulnerabilities. Most antivirus programs are a type of persistent agent. There is also an *agentless* option, such as with Microsoft and the Active Directory. In this case, when a user logs on or off the domain, NAC runs from the server holding the Active

Directory, also known as a domain controller. This eliminates the need to download any software to the host device.

NAC follows a four-step process, as illustrated in Figure 13-2.

1. The client self-assesses its security posture using a **System Health Agent (SHA)**, which is a program that performs a self-check on the client. The self-assessment is called a Statement of Health (SoH).

2. The SoH is sent to a Health Registration Authority (HRA), which is a server that enforces security policies on a network. The HRA also employs antivirus and patch management services to ensure the most recent configurations are used.

3. The client is issued a health certificate if approved by the HRA. If it is not approved, the client is connected to a quarantine network, where its configurations are corrected before it can connect to the network. If the configuration cannot be corrected, the client is denied access to the network.

4. The client's health certificate is submitted to network servers to verify its security configurations are acceptable for network usage.

NACs can be categorized as dissolvable or permanent. A *dissolvable NAC* is one in which the client logs in remotely and downloads and runs the agent. A *permanent NAC* is one in which the agent stays installed on the client at all times.

NAC typically quarantines and, later, reconnects clients using one of two methods:

- The client is leased an address from a DHCP server that connects it to the quarantine network. Later, the client is leased an IP address that reconnects it to the live, production network.

- The Address Resolution Protocol (ARP) table is modified so the client first connects to the quarantine network. This method is often used by attackers to gain access to a network.

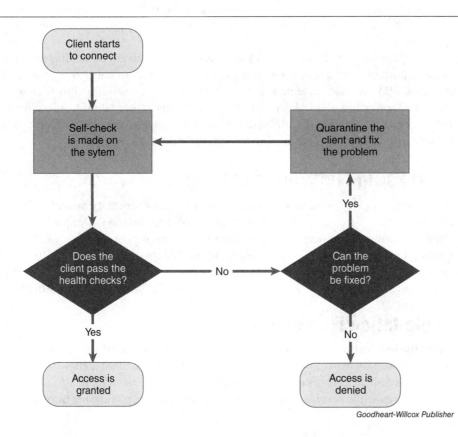

Figure 13-2 Network access control (NAC) unifies endpoint security by verifying that a host meets minimum standards before it is allowed to connect to a network.

Goodheart-Willcox Publisher

➕ 3.3

Monitoring Services

Monitoring services are software-based utilities that continually observe an individual device or network as a whole for hardware errors, interruptions, or performance anomalies and notify an administrator in the event an error or outage is detected. *Network security monitoring* is the collection, analysis, and management of warnings and indications that assist in detecting and responding to network breaches. It involves the use of a continuously running system that watches a network for performance issues or failing devices. Often, businesses will protect and manage their IT systems through network monitoring services. If issues are detected, administrators are alerted by SMS, e-mail, or phone call so immediate action can be taken. Network security monitoring tools often include features such as the following:

- network-level threat detection
- monitoring of queries for secure data
- detection of suspicious behavior
- threat-feed integration
- automated security alerts

➕ 3.3

File Integrity Monitoring

A **file integrity monitor (FIM)**, also called a *file integrity check (FIC)*, is a security control or process that monitors changes made to files stored on a computer and validates the integrity of software, including the operating system. With an FIM, files are examined to see what changes were made, when, and by whom. For example, the Windows program System File Checker (**sfc.exe**) can check the integrity of Windows system files for corruption by comparing the original file against running copies. If an incorrect version is found, the utility replaces the impacted file. The results of the scan are saved in a *component-based servicing file*. This log is usually stored with the name **CBS.log** and identifies files that were scanned, restorations from backups, or if a repair could not be attempted.

An FIM can be a critically useful tool, but it needs advanced intelligence to put context around changes, or it could generate a great deal of alerts due to many file changes. FIM solutions use baselines or a known good state for files that will be examined and change intelligence to notify administrators when needed. An FIM helps companies protect their infrastructure and remain compliant with many regulatory compliance standards including SOX, PCI-DSS, and HIPAA.

Assessing Network Security

A **network security assessment** is an audit or review of security measures in place on a computer network conducted to identify or locate previously unknown vulnerabilities. Similar to vulnerability assessments discussed previously in this text, it is vital that network security be assessed to determine its susceptibility to attack. Various security tools, techniques, and methods are proactive actions used to evaluate individual areas of a network to determine vulnerability and its resistance to attacks.

➕ 4.1

Exploitation Frameworks

Exploitation frameworks are software packages that contain apps and tools used to analyze and replicate attacks during vulnerability assessments. These frameworks provide exploit structures and monitoring tools to confirm organizational security and defenses while revealing at-risk devices, data, and applications. *Organizational* *security* is sustained levels of security in communicational and information management practices without sacrificing the confidentiality, integrity, and availability of data.

Exploitation frameworks are frequently used when testing network configurations. One such example is Metasploit, which contains scripts used to scan and discover services and vulnerabilities, as well as a number of exploits used to hack targeted devices.

Another valuable framework is the Browser Exploitation Framework (BeEF). BeEF is a pen testing utility that targets exploitation of web browser and web apps. This offensive security tool enables the tester to assess security posture by using client-side attack vectors in the browser.

Packet Capture and Replay

Packet capture is the interception of a data packet as it crosses a specific network point in real time. **Packet replay**, also known as *traffic replay*, is a review of previously captured data packets. Replaying the contents of data packets can help identify suspicious traffic, confirm IDS/IPS alerts, and investigate security incidents. After packets are replayed, they are either stored as part of an ongoing investigation or discarded.

A **packet sniffer** is a tool that uses a network interface card (NIC) to capture raw data traveling on network media and replay it for analysis. In many cases, a packet sniffer can also analyze traffic by including the protocol used in the transmission. Packet sniffers that offer insight into protocols used are *protocol analyzers.*

Depending on the type of utility and its configuration, a packet sniffer may see only the traffic coming to and from the host computer, or it may see all traffic on the network segment. Packet sniffers can intercept traffic on both wired and wireless networks. The biggest difference between intercepting wireless traffic as opposed to wired is that wireless traffic can only be viewed one channel at a time per NIC. To sniff multiple channels, additional network cards must be configured to monitor different channels.

Packet sniffers can only read unencrypted data. Encrypted data will appear illegible. For that reason, encrypting data is the best defense against a hacker who may be using a sniffer to view data transmitted on the network. As a security administrator, you can use a sniffer to uncover a great deal of information that will allow you to check for potential security threats and vulnerabilities.

One of the best-known packet capture and replay tools is a free, graphical open-source program called Wireshark, previously called Ethereal. Wireshark can be installed on Windows and Linux platforms and provides many options for sorting, reviewing, and analyzing network traffic. Wireshark captures can be reviewed in real-time or saved and analyzed at a later point. Figure 13-3 shows the default view of a network capture.

Not all packet sniffers or protocol analyzers operate through third-party software. The Linux **tcpdump command** is a text-based solution that functions as a packet sniffer and allows users to capture and analyze packets to view data as it is collected, as well as its protocol and direction of datagram. The **tcpdump** command is included in many Linux distributions, collects the same data as Wireshark, and can be customized to filter traffic based on IP addresses and protocols, among other types of data. When using **tcpdump**, a user can direct output to a capture file and review it in a graphical manner by opening the saved file in Wireshark. Figure 13-4 shows an example of **tcpdump** recording ARP requests and network-time protocol information.

4.1

4.1

4.1

Figure 13-3 Wireshark is a packet capture and replay tool that provides many options for sorting, reviewing, and analyzing network traffic.

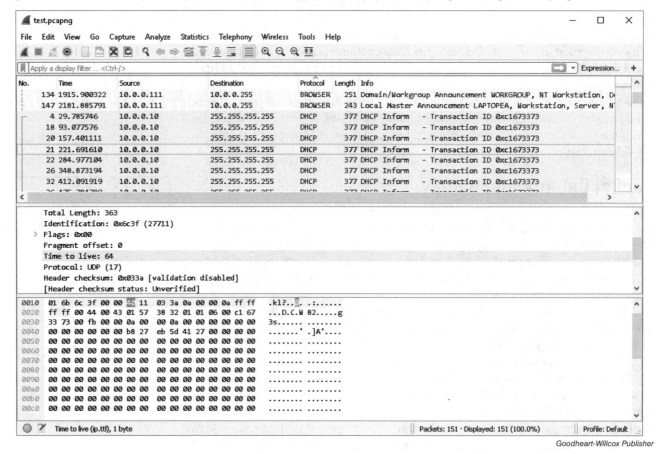

Goodheart-Willcox Publisher

Figure 13-4 The **tcpdump** command is a text-based solution that functions as a packet sniffer and allows users to capture and analyze packets to view data as it is collected, as well as its protocol and direction of datagram.

```
09:39:14.123970 ARP, Request who-has kali tell _gateway, length 46
09:39:14.124035 ARP, Reply kali is-at 00:0c:29:ab:01:d5 (oui Unknown), length 28
09:39:14.124320 IP 66.85.78.80.ntp > kali.34927: NTPv4, Server, length 48
09:39:19.173564 ARP, Request who-has _gateway tell kali, length 28
09:39:19.173767 ARP, Reply _gateway is-at 00:50:56:fb:2e:68 (oui Unknown), length 46
09:39:46.326853 IP kali.46244 > 66.85.78.80.ntp: NTPv4, Client, length 48
09:39:46.378131 IP 66.85.78.80.ntp > kali.46244: NTPv4, Server, length 48
```

Goodheart-Willcox Publisher

4.1

4.3

A lightweight network utility called *tcprelay* can be downloaded and used to replay traffic saved with the **tcpdump** command. Tcprelay operates as a TCP tunnel by listening to traffic on a specific port and forwarding all traffic to a remote host and port. Forwarding traffic to a remote host enables traffic to be logged for additional review later.

Protocol analyzer output can be collected, saved, and analyzed in a variety of ways. Often, output is used to support investigations of security incidents. Protocol analyzers allow users to sort data by time, protocol, node address, and other fields based on packet information, enabling the isolation of data from different perspectives and refinements. For example, if a rogue device is suspected on a network, an administrator can use Wireshark to filter queries moving to and from an IP address of a suspect device. With this information, administrators can see what types of packets are moving to or from the device with that IP address. Wireshark also offers the ability to generate built-in reports that provide useful information when investigating a suspected security incident. Figure 13-5 shows a report that details source and destination addresses collected during packet capture including the packet count for each address.

IP Scanners

4.1

An **IP scanner** is a tool that searches a network for IP addresses and other relevant information regarding network devices. While relatively simple in nature, an IP scanner can provide important information in terms of assessing network security. For example, unauthorized devices such as malicious access points or storage devices that would have gone unnoticed otherwise are identified during an IP scan. Some IP scanners offer enhanced features, such as the ability to access shared folders, scan MAC addresses, and disconnect devices remotely.

Network Reconnaissance and Discovery

One of the first steps in obtaining detailed network information is gathering adequate information about the network and structure through network reconnaissance. *Network reconnaissance* is testing for potential vulnerabilities and gathering information about the organizational structure of a network. *Network discovery* is the process of identifying devices connected to a network. It often involves a host sending messages over a network looking for responses or discoverable devices.

During network reconnaissance, network discovery is performed using passive or active tools. *Passive tools* are those used to obtain information without alerting a target or user to the actions. *Active tools* are those that interact directly with a network and its hosts to collect additional data. The amount of information obtained through reconnaissance helps security personnel identify potential weaknesses in

---

Figure 13-5 Report detailing sources and destination addresses collected during packet capture.

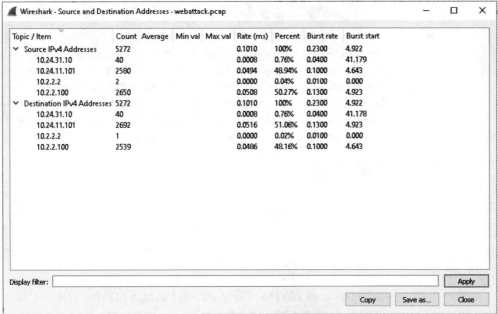

Topic / Item	Count	Average	Min val	Max val	Rate (ms)	Percent	Burst rate	Burst start
∨ Source IPv4 Addresses	5272				0.1010	100%	0.2300	4.922
10.24.31.10	40				0.0008	0.76%	0.0400	41.179
10.24.11.101	2580				0.0494	48.94%	0.1000	4.643
10.2.2.2	2				0.0000	0.04%	0.0100	0.000
10.2.2.100	2650				0.0508	50.27%	0.1300	4.923
∨ Destination IPv4 Addresses	5272				0.1010	100%	0.2300	4.922
10.24.31.10	40				0.0008	0.76%	0.0400	41.178
10.24.11.101	2692				0.0516	51.06%	0.1300	4.923
10.2.2.2	1				0.0000	0.02%	0.0100	0.000
10.2.2.100	2539				0.0486	48.16%	0.1000	4.643

their network's security. The following command-line utilities can be used for network reconnaissance and discovery.

Netcat

The **netcat command** is a versatile utility that can read and write data using the TCP/IP protocol suite. Netcat is used for network reconnaissance and discovery as well as assessing network security. It can perform a wide array of functions, including listening and scanning system ports and transferring files using the TCP protocol.

Nmap

Nmap is a text-based protocol analyzer that scans networks; discovers hosts, services, and port information; analyzes the results to identify open ports; and creates educated guesses on the operating systems in use. Scanners such as nmap can be a valuable tool for assessing network and organizational security because they not only scan a network to discover hosts but also provide analysis of data packets they intercept.

Netstat

The **netstat command** is a helpful utility for conducting network reconnaissance. **Netstat** is a command-line utility that allows you to view TCP and UDP connections, routing tables, and other network interface and protocol statistics. The results of **netstat** can be filtered to view ICMP, IPv4, and IPv6. With this command, you can see statistics and ports that are open, closed, or listening to incoming sessions. This may provide clues to the source if you are under attack. The Windows version of the **netstat** command has the switches shown in Figure 13-6. As a command, **netstat** will also work on Linux-based systems, but it has largely been replaced by the **ss** command.

The syntax for the **netstat** command is to preface each switch with a dash (–). However, the interval value is not preceded by a dash. Multiple switches can be combined, for example:

    netstat –a –n 20

The output screen lists data in columns: Proto (name of protocol), Local Address (the IP address and the port number), Foreign Address (the IP address and port number of the remote computer), and State. Figure 13-7 explains the different values listed in the State column. There are different states of connections on the output. Due to the way TCP/IP communicates with other hosts, connections cannot be immediately closed. Packets may arrive out of order or be transmitted after the connection has been closed. This can result in a delay in closing the session.

Curl

Curl, short for *client URL*, is a network reconnaissance and discovery command used to transfer data to and from a server using various protocols to request information and analyze the resulting information. For example, you can use **curl** to request the header information from a website, which can provide version and other useful information as noted in Figure 13-8. Curl can be used to perform a variety of commands quickly, such as downloading files and web pages, transferring files securely, and looking up directory information through LDAPS. This enables quick and safe network administration when needed.

4.1

4.1

TECH TIP ⚙️

Nmap returns port status, including whether a port is open, closed, filtered, or unfiltered. Administrators explicitly set open and closed settings, but a filtered status is returned when a packet is prevented from reaching the port, and an unfiltered status implies the port is accessible but unable to provide a current port state.

4.1

4.1

Figure 13-6 Netstat is a command-line utility that allows you to view TCP and UDP connections, routing tables, and other network interface and protocol statistics.

Switch	Definition
a	Active: this switch lists all active connections, which includes the listening ports. netstat –a
e	Ethernet statistics: this switch lists statistics of the Internet connection, which includes the number of packets that were sent, received, errors, etc. netstat –e
n	This switch lists the connections in numerical or IP form; instead of seeing a web address by name, it is listed by its IP address. netstat –n
o	Owning process: this switch shows the active connection along with the process identification (PID) number. netstat –o
p	Protocols: this switch allows you to filter through the different protocols. netstat –p tcp (in place of TCP can be any of the protocols: IP, IPv6, ICMP, ICMPv6, TCP, TCPv6, UDP, UDPv6)
r	Routing table: this switch is the same as the **route print** command. netstat –r
s	Statistics: this switch lists statistics for each protocol (differs from the **e** switch). netstat –s This switch can be combined with the p switch to identify a specific protocol. netstat –sp udp
f	Fully qualified domain name: this switch displays the entire name of a foreign address. netstat –f
Interval	Use this value to give the computer a specific amount of time (in seconds) between the probing of active connections. netstat –an 20

Goodheart-Willcox Publisher

Figure 13-7 There are different states of connections on the output.

Connection State	Definition
Established	Both hosts are connected.
Closing	The remote host has agreed to close its connection.
Listening	The local host is waiting to handle an incoming connection.
Syn_rcvd	A remote host has asked to start a connection.
Syn_sent	The local host has accepted to start a connection.
Last_ack	The local host needs to obliterate (erase from memory) the packets before closing the connection.
Timed_wait	The local host has closed the connection, but it is being kept around so any delayed packets can be matched to the connection and handled appropriately; they will time out within four minutes.
Close_wait	The remote host is closing its connection with the local host, but it is being kept around so any delayed packets can be matched to the connection and handled appropriately; they will time out within four minutes.
Fin_Wait 1	A client is closing its connection.
Fin_Wait 2	Both hosts have agreed to close the connection.

Goodheart-Willcox Publisher

Figure 13-8 Curl is used to transfer data to and from a server using various protocols to request information and analyze the resulting information.

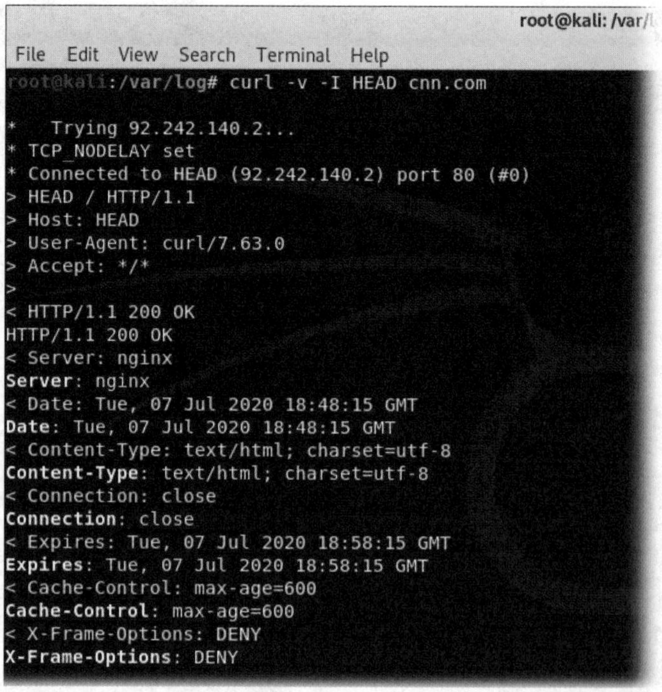

Goodheart-Willcox Publisher

DNSenum

An easy to way to test one's ability to access DNS information is the Kali Linux **dnsenum** command. The **dnsenum command** is a network reconnaissance command that displays DNS information and retrieves DNS servers and entries within an organization. Using the **dnsenum** command, administrators can determine what information is publicly accessible and how best to lock it from access. For example, Figure 13-9 shows results provided by **dnsenum** in which every type of DNS server for the targeted website is visible, including names and e-mail servers.

hping

The **hping command**, or *hping3 command*, is a network reconnaissance command that is used to scan and analyze ports, conduct network security audits, and test firewalls. Additionally, **hping** can provide analysis of TCP/IP traffic. **hping** is inspired from the **ping** command, which uses the ICMP protocol to send echo commands. However, **hping** supports TCP, UDP and ICMP, which provides increased functionality when compared to the traditional **ping** command.

hping is a versatile tool, and it can provide a wealth of information pertinent to assessing organizational security. Security administrators can use **hping** to learn how to analyze packets so they can better understand malicious packets from hackers, test firewalls by crafting packets that should be blocked, and use the command for advanced **traceroute** tracking.

In Figure 13-10, **hping** is testing whether port 80 is open on the IP address indicated. The count value (**-c**) indicates only one attempt is sent, and the **-v** switch provides the verbose output, which refers to additional details about what the computer is doing or loading.

Figure 13-9 The **dnsenum** command displays DNS information and retrieves DNS servers and entries within an organization.

```
Name Servers:
_____

c.ns.buddyns.com.                    5        IN      A       116.203.6.3
f.ns.buddyns.com.                    5        IN      A       103.6.87.125
h.ns.buddyns.com.                    5        IN      A       119.252.20.56
j.ns.buddyns.com.                    5        IN      A       185.34.136.178
g.ns.buddyns.com.                    5        IN      A       192.184.93.99


Mail (MX) Servers:
_____

aspmx.l.google.com.                  5        IN      A       172.217.197.27
alt1.aspmx.l.google.com.             5        IN      A       64.233.186.26
alt2.aspmx.l.google.com.             5        IN      A       209.85.202.26
aspmx2.googlemail.com.               5        IN      A       64.233.186.27
aspmx3.googlemail.com.               5        IN      A       209.85.202.26
aspmx4.googlemail.com.               5        IN      A       172.253.120.27
aspmx5.googlemail.com.               5        IN      A       172.217.218.27
```

Goodheart-Willcox Publisher

Figure 13-10 The **hping** command is used to scan and analyze ports, conduct network security audits, and test firewalls.

```
root@kali:~# hping3 -c 1 -V -p 80 192.168.133.2
using eth0, addr: 192.168.133.143, MTU: 1500
HPING 192.168.133.2 (eth0 192.168.133.2): NO FLAGS are set, 40 headers + 0 data bytes
len=46 ip=192.168.133.2 ttl=128 id=54155 tos=0 iplen=40
sport=80 flags=RA seq=0 win=32767 rtt=7.3 ms
seq=0 ack=60975573 sum=8a2c urp=0


--- 192.168.133.2 hping statistic ---
1 packets transmitted, 1 packets received, 0% packet loss
round-trip min/avg/max = 7.3/7.3/7.3 ms
root@kali:~#
```

Goodheart-Willcox Publisher

Scanless

Scanless is a Python-based command-line utility that performs port scanning on websites using a variety of online scanning tools, as shown in Figure 13-11. Online port scanning tools offer results similar to traditional scans and can provide useful information beyond open ports, including running services and OS fingerprinting, which can be valuable information for assessing organizational security. **Scanless** requires Python in order to run and provides anonymity, as the user's IP address is not used or displayed.

Harvester

An important Linux-based command for conducting network reconnaissance is **the-Harvester**, which is a command-line utility that gathers information such as e-mails, subdomains, employee names, IP addresses, and open ports from public sources, among other data. Due to the variety of information it collects, **theHarvester** is often used in the early stages of a penetration test as a form of intelligence gathering. When performed correctly, **theHarvester** will show a user important information about not only a network and the devices connected to it but also the users of those devices. For

Figure 13-11 Scanless is a Python-based command-line utility that performs port scanning on websites using a variety of online scanning tools

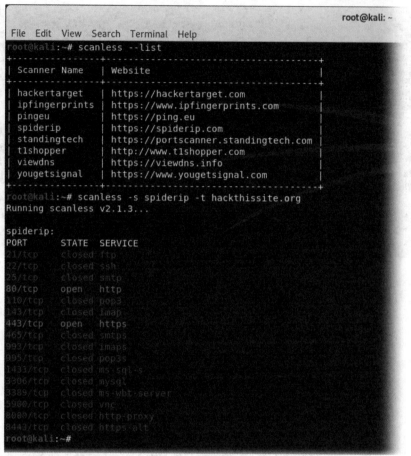

example, Figure 13-12 shows the first 100 responses of a search run in **theHarvester** for LinkedIn accounts of Apple employees.

Sn1per

Sn1per is an automated network reconnaissance tool that collects data during vulnerability assessments and penetration tests. Sn1per can collect a great deal of information relevant to organizational security assessments, including WHOIS records, HTTP headers, DNS, TCP, and UDP port enumeration. Typically, a user would have to use multiple tools to obtain this information.

Sn1per also provides for other functionality, such as assessing anonymous LDAP and FTP access. Additionally, it offers several configuration options for customizing how it searches and reports vulnerabilities.

Cuckoo

Cuckoo, also known as *Cuckoo Sandbox*, is an open-source automated malware analysis system. It enables an administrator to place a file in its protected environment to analyze how malicious files operate when executed. Often used in vulnerability assessments or penetration tests, Cuckoo can analyze files from Windows, Linux, Android, and macOS platforms. The output from the Cuckoo application includes a

Figure 13-12 theHarvester gathers information such as e-mails, subdomains, employee names, IP addresses, and open ports from public sources, among other data.

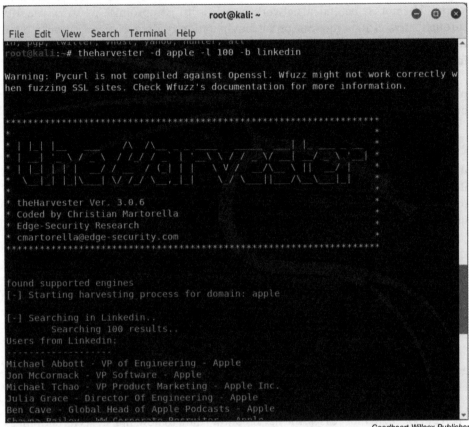

detailed report summarizing information about what a file did when it was executed, such as file creation, memory dump, screen recording or captures, and network traffic dump. This information is valuable to security administrators for assessing the security posture of an enterprise environment because it reveals how specific files or programs behave on a network, which enables IT staff to apply preparation or preventive measures.

Nessus

 4.1

Nessus is a proprietary vulnerability scanner used for obtaining information about vulnerabilities within devices in an organization. It was created by Tenable, Inc. and provides both free and commercial options. Nessus provides an easy-to-use interface and can discover a great deal of information. It can be used to scan for viruses and other malware, missing patches, expired or revoked security certificates, and much more.

In addition to functioning as a vulnerability scanner, Nessus also functions as an information resource, as it provides over 450 compliance and configuration templates that enable security administrators to audit configuration compliance against CIS benchmarks or other best practices. Additionally, Nessus provides valuable reporting on regulatory compliance including HIPAA. Reports can be customized for specific needs, including customized views such as reporting by specific vulnerabilities or by host.

Network Attacks

Network attacks are attempts to gain unauthorized access to an organization's network. The motive behind a network attack is to compromise network security through surreptitious monitoring or manipulation of data. Network attacks often target equipment or services that provide the backbone of a company's network infrastructure in an effort to gain access and perform exploits.

Network attacks can be launched from remote connections, malicious software placed in the network through deceptive or social engineering attacks, or an insider of the organization. Common network attacks include the following.

✛ 1.4

ARP Poisoning

Address Resolution Protocol (ARP) poisoning is an attack in which a spoofed Address Resolution Protocol (ARP) message is sent onto a LAN and causes network traffic to be sent to the attacker. This process is similar to the previously referenced NAC quarantine method in which an ARP table is modified.

In an ARP poisoning attack, a user is directed to a hacker's computer instead of the location the user was attempting to reach. This often happens on routers using default settings. The data sent to the router goes to the hacker instead of the router. In most cases, after intercepting the data and reading the content, data is then sent to the legitimate router. ARP poisoning is often accomplished through software that scans a subnet for IP and MAC addresses of hosts. After hosts are identified, the hacker selects the desired target and sends ARP packets containing the hacker's MAC address and the target's IP address. Then, any packet destined for the target's IP address is sent to the hacker's machine instead. The process is illustrated in Figure 13-13.

It may not always be readily noticeable that a default gateway's MAC address has been poisoned. In most cases, the hacker allows data to flow, but steals its content as it passes through the hacker's device. One method of detecting this attack is to view the MAC addresses in the ARP cache. If two different IP addresses share the same MAC address, this may indicate a poisoning attack.

Figure 13-13 ARP poisoning is an attack in which a spoofed ARP message is sent onto a LAN and causes network traffic to be sent to the attacker.

1. Tyrese's computer issues an ARP request looking for a MAC address.

4. Tyrese's computer receives the ARP reply appearing to be from 192.168.1.55, but it is really from 192.168.1.95, which is the hacker's computer.

Who has 192.168.1.55? Reply to 192.168.1.25.

2. Alice's computer replies to the ARP request since that is her IP address.

192.168.1.25

192.168.1.55

192.168.1.95

3. The hacker has been eavesdropping, intercepts the ARP reply, and changes it.

Goodheart-Willcox Publisher; (people) Rawpixel.com/Shutterstock.com; (computers) romvo/Shutterstock.com

Preventing ARP poisoning is possible through static ARP entries, which ensure IP addresses are always assigned to specific MAC addresses. Another possibility is to use network switches that support *dynamic ARP inspection (DAI)*. This technique validates ARP packets on a network, intercepts all ARP requests, verifies the IP to MAC addresses for validity. If the addresses are valid, the request is forwarded; otherwise, the ARP request is dropped.

MAC Cloning

+ 1.4

MAC cloning, also known as *MAC spoofing*, is an attack in which a threat actor configures a host using the MAC address of a different, validated host. A machine configured with the MAC address of another legitimate host overwrites the entry in the Content Addressable Memory (CAM) table, and data destined for the original host is instead sent to the attacker. Indicators of this attack method include the loss of expected traffic. Additionally, a MAC cloning attack can be seen by a protocol analyzer that assesses the flow of information in a network.

Denial of Service (DoS) Attacks

Recall that *denial of service (DoS) attacks* are cyberattacks that prevent rightful users from accessing systems. DoS attacks do not steal or destroy data. Rather, they are intended to prevent access. Often, DoS attacks are conducted against DNS servers, but all devices on a network are susceptible to DoS and DDoS attacks.

In a *distributed denial of service (DDoS) attack*, many hosts contribute in attacking the victim. Most often, those hosts are under the control of malware. The hosts, then, are known as bots. *Bot* is a shortened form of *robot*. Hosts are considered bots when their actions are controlled by another device. DDoS attacks can occur in any environment where users are denied the ability to access a resource or service.

DoS and DDoS attacks are capable of crippling a network by targeting different areas within it. Depending on the desired outcome, an attacker may target specific services or devices, or an attacker may use a botnet to shut down an entire network. For example, an attack can target *network applications*, which are the services or applications that run at the top layer of the OSI model (the Application layer); *operational technology (OT)*, which is the equipment located in a network, such as cameras, sensors, and other smart objects; or the network itself, which often incorporates a botnet spamming servers with illegitimate requests.

+ 1.4

Regardless of an attacker's target, there are many types of denial of service attacks that can be launched, including the following.

Smurf Attack

A *Smurf attack* is a DoS attack in which a system is overrun by spoofed ping messages. Ping messages use the sub-protocol of Internet Control Message Protocol (ICMP) for communication. For this reason, this type of attack is also known as a *ping flood*. When a target host is pinged, it essentially asks, "Are you there?" several times. Each question generates a response from the target host. In a Smurf attack, the victim's system is overwhelmed attempting to reply to all of the "Are you there?" questions.

Fraggle Attack

A *fraggle attack* is a DoS attack in which a system is overrun by a large amount of spoofed UDP traffic to the broadcast address within a network. Fraggle attacks are similar in practice to Smurf attacks. The difference is that fraggle attacks use UDP to conduct the attack instead of TCP.

SYN Flood

The other type of DoS attack is a SYN flood. A *SYN flood* is a DoS attack in which the perpetrator sends multiple SYN requests with the goal of rendering the target system unresponsive to real traffic. Essentially, a SYN flood involves the hacker exploiting a vulnerability in the three-way handshake by not closing the handshake. Recall the normal process is as follows:

1. SYN by sender
2. SYN/ACK by receiver
3. ACK by initial sender

In a SYN flood, the attacker sends a SYN, which the target answers with a SYN/ACK. Instead of closing the handshake with an ACK, the hacker sends another SYN, to which the target again replies, as shown in Figure 13-14. This cycle repeats throughout the attack.

Protecting Against DoS Attacks

Unfortunately, DoS attacks happen quite frequently. However, if a company has the right preventive plan in place, DoS attacks can be resolved quickly. This was the case in the 2018 attack against GitHub, the popular developer platform. The GitHub attack registered traffic that was measured at 1.35 terabits per second, an incredibly high volume of data. At the time, this was the largest recorded DoS attack ever recorded. Although the attack was massive, GitHub only suffered minimal disruptions as they had a mitigation program in place that sent all traffic from GitHub to a service, which essentially scrubbed all malicious traffic and only directed legitimate traffic back to GitHub.

Mitigation programs to stop or minimize the effect of denial of service attacks involve a plan of action that can be taken to protect the network. Mitigation plans should include regular software updates, blocking known suspicious IP addresses, and training staff to recognize the symptoms and traffic from an attack. It can involve different tools in a network such as an intrusion-detection or intrusion-prevention system; firewalls; and specialized software, such as applications from Cloudfare, Incapsula from Imperva, and SiteLock. Many cloud vendors also offer specialized software to protect servers running in their cloud systems.

Figure 13-14 A SYN flood occurs when the perpetrator sends multiple SYN requests with the goal of rendering the target system unresponsive to real traffic.

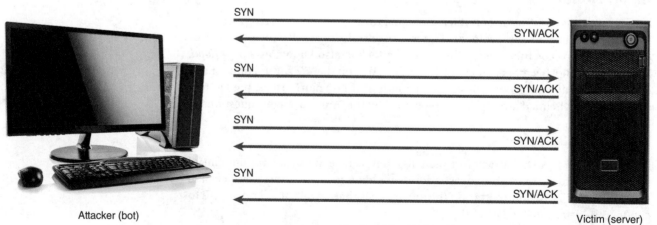

Attacker (bot)   Victim (server)

Goodheart-Willcox Publisher; (computer and server) Denis Rozhnovsky/Shutterstock.com

Much of the protection against DoS attacks takes place on edge routers. An *edge router* is a router that separates the internal network from the public network. However, mitigating a DoS—and, by extension, a DDoS—attack should start within the network. As evidenced by the attack on GitHub, more advanced protection is often necessary to defend against large attacks. Most attacks originate outside the network, so this is the logical place to implement security measures defending the network from these attacks. In addition to contracting with outside security vendors, other security appliances can be used to prevent DoS attacks through special configurations and access control lists.

During a normal three-way handshake, when the target receives a SYN packet, the transmission control block (TCB) functionality in TCP/IP stores a TCB SYN-RECEIVED state. This indicates the session is only halfway completed. Since a SYN flood never completes this process, the TCB cannot change the status to ESTABLISHED, as shown in Figure 13-15. If a SYN flood occurs, TCB statuses remain open and will eventually exhaust the memory of the target.

If a source IP is not faked, or *spoofed*, the IP can be blocked in the firewall. However, many DoS attacks occur with spoofed IP addresses. One way to overcome a DoS attack from spoofed addresses is to limit the total number of sessions. This prevents the system from being overloaded with traffic.

Other preventive measures can be taken to minimize DoS attacks. For example, a client can be configured with antimalware software to prevent the host from running programs as part of a larger botnet. It is also possible to turn off ICMP at the host through a host firewall. This prevents the host from responding to ICMP requests. However, turning off ICMP prevents legitimate uses of the **ping** and **tracert**

Figure 13-15 Since a SYN flood never completes a session, the TCB cannot change the status to ESTABLISHED.

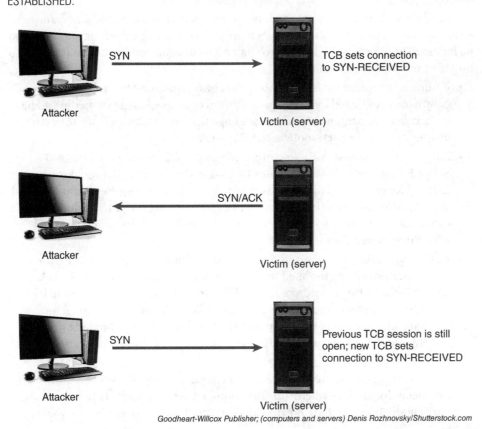

Goodheart-Willcox Publisher; (computers and servers) Denis Rozhnovsky/Shutterstock.com

commands. Finally, routers must be configured to limit the forwarding of broadcast traffic on a network.

DHCP Attacks

DHCP servers are frequent targets of attack. Many times, these attacks come in the form of rogue DHCP servers. A *rogue DHCP server* is a spoofed DHCP server used to launch an attack in which the client's TCP/IP information, including the default gateway, come from an attacker. When this occurs, the client is assigned false gateways or DNS information that can ultimately lead to pharming sites or man-in-the-middle attacks. Rogue DHCP servers can be prevented by enabling DHCP snooping on a network switch.

DHCP is also vulnerable to a *starvation attack*, which occurs when forged packets requesting addresses are sent to the DHCP server. A starvation attack can exhaust the available supply of IP addresses for lease, denying legitimate users the ability to connect on the network. One possible mitigation strategy against a starvation attack is to configure network switches to limit the number of allowed MAC addresses originating from a client.

Malicious Code and Script Execution

✚ 1.4

Scripts are small programs that can be run to perform a variety of automated tasks. Network administrators often use scripts to perform a variety of management tasks. However, scripts are also a popular vector to launch malware or other destructive intent, such as stealing data or denying access. There may be some indicators of malicious script execution. For example, the discovery of malware, unusual performance, or unexpected networking or disk activity could indicate that a malicious script has been executed. Additionally, unanticipated system configuration changes, documents, or file activity could be the result of malicious scripts.

Unlike traditional programs, scripts do not need to be compiled and can run in a variety of environments, including Python, PowerShell, and Bash. Scripts can also be included in Microsoft Office macros using Visual Basic for Applications (VBA) to provide functionality within the file.

- Python is a popular tool for scripting. It is easy to use and has a large library of commands employed by developers. Python continues to grow rapidly and has unfortunately become a standard language used in malware creation, particularly in the creation of remote access Trojans.

- PowerShell scripts are easy to write, and PowerShell includes an Integrated Script Editor (ISE), shown in Figure 13-16. The PowerShell ISE provides an easy method for creating scripts for those with limited knowledge of commands and options. Microsoft has built-in protections for running scripts by using a script execution policy, which prevents scripts from running if they are not signed with a digital signature.

- Bash is a popular command-line shell used in Linux distributions. Creating scripts in Bash allows the shell to execute commands from these scripts. As with other scripting environments, scripts written in bash are often used by customizing and automating administrative tasks. Malicious code can be written using bash to perform a variety of attacks including changing firewall settings, downloading, and installing executables, or creating malware from scripting tools.

- *Macros* are scripts written using Microsoft's Visual Basic software and stored in Microsoft documents. Microsoft Office applications typically do not allow files, particularly those that are downloaded, to run if they have embedded macros.

Figure 13-16 The PowerShell ISE provides an easy method for creating scripts for those with limited knowledge of commands and options.

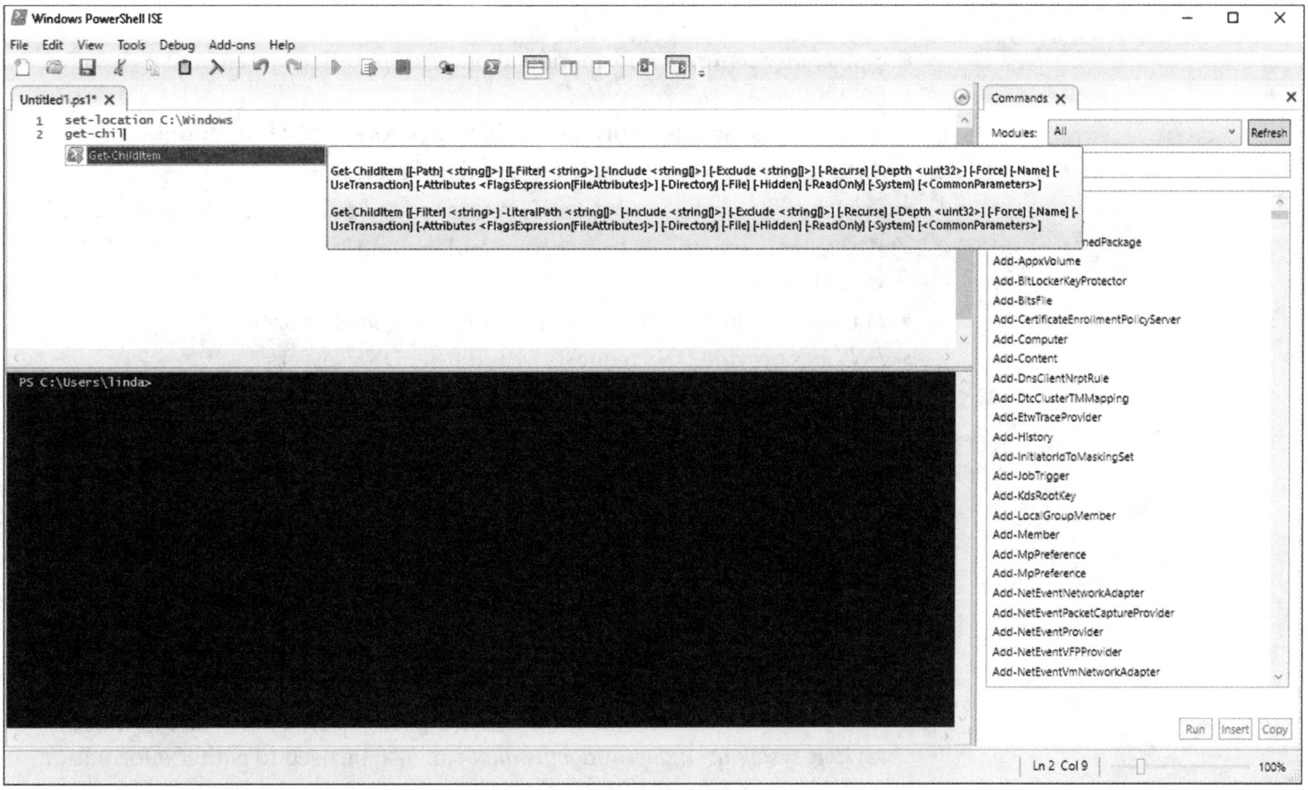

Goodheart-Willcox Publisher

Malicious files with embedded macros are often transmitted via e-mail as an attachment or downloaded from the Internet.

Investigating Network Incidents

A *network incident* is an event or occurrence that is not part of normal operations of a network and disrupts the network's connectivity or usability. Network incidents are wide-ranging and can vary from an unplugged cable to an unauthorized person gaining access to data. When a network incident is discovered, it should be investigated using appropriate tools and utilities such as the following.

SIEM Dashboard

A *SIEM dashboard* is a tool that summarizes data and transforms it into useful information to provide simple security monitoring. SIEM tools are useful in investigating network incidents by monitoring a system for anomalies in critical hardware operations and collecting data from sensors installed on a network. SIEM dashboards highlight trends in activities, including changes in network traffic. The data collected from dashboards can then be evaluated against baseline data as part of an investigation for threats and breaches.

4.3

Log Files

A *log file*, also called an *event log*, is a record of events that occur during server or computer operation. A *log* is accumulated data about a system and its services, time and dates of user actions, and other activities that affect the security of an organization.

Event logs can be useful when investigating an incident by providing critical information about computer and network operations. Examples of event logs include the following:

- *System logs* generate information about the operating system and its components.
- *Network logs* include information about network services or devices.
- *Application logs* detail events triggered by applications.
- *Security logs* can be used to track events related to configurations.
- *Web logs* are created by web servers and include information about websites visited by each user.
- *PowerShell logs* list PowerShell providers accessed by users.
- *DNS logs* provide DNS requests to and from DNS servers.
- *Authentication logs* record login and authentication attempts.
- *Dump files* record data about services and applications and are often generated automatically after a system crash.
- *Voice over IP (VoIP) logs* contain relevant data to VoIP sessions.
- *Call manager logs* provide details and diagnostics about calls placed over a network.
- *Session initiation protocol (SIP) logs* detail information about the SIP process in VoIP sessions.
- *System logging protocol (syslog)* is a standard event logging protocol used to send system and event log information to a specific server and aggregated multiple logs in one central location. Variations or equivalents of syslog, notable *rsyslog, syslog-ng, nxlog*, and *journalctl* can also be used to gather information about logs.

Bandwidth Monitors

Bandwidth monitors are network tools that allow administrators to monitor and analyze inbound and outbound network traffic and usage. The information obtained from monitoring bandwidth usage enables administrators to track which hosts are using the most bandwidth.

Bandwidth monitors are also helpful with investigating performance issues and incidents. Through bandwidth monitoring, security staff are able to identify an excessive or unusual amount of traffic from a host, which could be indicative of malware; CNC software; content streaming; or users illegally downloading content, stealing files, or copying and sending data to cloud locations.

Netflow

NetFlow is a network protocol created by Cisco that collects IP traffic as it flows in and out of a network interface card and allows for monitoring of the network in real time. The purpose of NetFlow is to analyze active IP traffic through session sampling and determine where data is going and how much traffic is created as a result.

NetFlow is used by IT security professionals to investigate network security incidents by creating an understanding of network traffic in a system. NetFlow helps IT professionals determine where traffic originates as well as its intended destination, volume, and path taken on a network. NetFlow is not a packet sniffer; instead, it is used for the monitoring of data to develop traffic flow analysis. It is also helpful as a security tool, as data generated by NetFlow can help detect changes in traffic behaviors that could help identify anomalies that may indicate a security breach.

sFlow

sFlow, short for *sampled flow*, is a proprietary packet sampling protocol that enables the capture of packet metadata, such as statistics, infrastructure, and routing information. It was developed to offer similar services to NetFlow on non-Cisco platforms. Since sFlow is not restricted only to IP traffic, it can collect, monitor, and analyze traffic from OSI layers 2–7. The collection of upper-layer data allows for the reporting of detailed visibility into traffic analysis since it can identify VLANs and MAC addresses.

Both Netflow and sFlow can be helpful for monitoring traffic and intrusion detection. These tools enable complete network surveillance with alerts for suspicious activity. Additionally, these programs can create baselines of typical traffic and identify anomalies, such as those associated with Internet Control Message Protocol (ICMP) attacks.

IPFix

Since both Netflow and sFlow are proprietary, there is no standard or industry regulation for them to follow. To resolve the lack of overarching guidance, the Internet Engineering Task Force (IETF) developed a common universal standard for the export of IP flow information from networking devices. **IP Flow Information Export (IPFix)** is a network flow standard that provides for the export of the flow of information from routers, switches, firewalls and other devices located in the network infrastructure. IPFix is used for collection and analysis of data by exporting the information about network flows from devices.

ICMP Monitoring

Attackers often use well-known services to hide command and control communications common to many malware infections. One of the network protocols often used for attacks is ICMP. *Internet Control Message Protocol (ICMP)* is an OSI network layer protocol used to identify and control routing problems on a network. If errors are detected, ICMP packets are sent to inform endpoints about the error, which can instruct routers about potential route problems.

Additionally, ICMP is used to send **ICMP echo requests**, which are query messages sent to destination machines to establish connectivity. These messages are sent using the **ping** command, which sends ICMP echo requests with arbitrary data to make a connection and receive an ICMP echo reply using the same data. This is known as *ICMP tunneling*. The information flow in an ICMP tunnel is not controlled by any security mechanism, but this type of traffic is undetectable to proxy-based firewalls.

Attackers can exploit the use of ICMP and send unidirectional traffic, often in the form of ICMP type 0 replies, which is simply an echo reply notification, or type 3 replies, which translate to an unreachable destination. Programs such as NetFlow can help analyze ICMP traffic, including identifying unidirectional echo replies, unusual ICMP traffic that varies from baselines, repeated ICMP messages traveling to or from unexpected destinations, and messages traveling over extended periods of time. Additionally, NetFlow is capable of performing statistical analysis, including percentage of inbound vs. outbound ICMP requests and deviations from baseline ICMP packet sizes.

SUMMARY

Secure Network Administration

- Network administration is the operational tasks that provide ongoing support, management, and maintenance to enable a network to run efficiently.
- It is the responsibility of IT and security professionals to continue working on a network after it is designed to ensure the network stays secure. Proper administration of a network is vital for its ongoing security.
- Key items that are important in secure network administration include establishing secure protocols, DNS, network access controls (NAC), monitoring services, and file integrity monitoring.

Assessing Network Security

- A network security assessment is an audit or review of security measures in place on a computer network conducted to identify or locate previously unknown vulnerabilities. It is vital that network security be assessed to determine its susceptibility to attack.
- Exploitation frameworks are software packages that contain apps and tools used to analyze and replicate attacks during vulnerability assessments. They provide exploit structures and monitoring tools to confirm organizational security and defenses while revealing at-risk devices, data, and applications.
- Packet capture is the real-time interception of data packets that traverse a network. Packet replay is the review of previously captured data packets. This can help identify suspicious traffic, confirm IDS/IPS alerts, and investigate security incidents.
- An IP scanner is a tool that searches a network for IP addresses and other relevant information regarding network devices. It can provide important information in terms of assessing network security.

Network Reconnaissance and Discovery

- Network reconnaissance is one of the first steps in obtaining detailed network information. It is the testing for potential vulnerabilities and gathering information about organizational structure of a network.
- During network reconnaissance, network discovery is performed using passive or active tools. In addition, the amount of information obtained through reconnaissance helps security personnel identify potential weaknesses in their network's security.
- There are several command-line utilities that can be used for network reconnaissance and discovery. These include **netstat**, **curl**, **dnsenum**, **hping**, **scanless**, **theHarvester**, sn1per, Cuckoo, Nessus, **netcat**, and nmap.

Network Attacks

- Network attacks are attempts to gain unauthorized access to an organization's network. The motive behind a network attack is to compromise network security through surreptitious monitoring or manipulation of data.
- Network attacks can be launched from remote connections, malicious software placed in the network through deceptive or social engineering attacks, or an insider of the organization.

- Common network attacks include ARP poisoning, MAC cloning, denial of service (DoS) attacks, DHCP attacks, and malicious code and script execution.

Investigating Network Incidents

- Network incidents are events or occurrences that are not part of normal operations of a network and disrupt the network's connectivity or usability. They are wide-ranging and can vary in type of event or occurrence.
- When a network incident is discovered, it should be investigated using appropriate tools and utilities. These include a SIEM dashboard, log files, bandwidth monitors, NetFlow, sFlow, IPfix, and ICMP monitoring.

REVIEW QUESTIONS

1. List administration tasks often conducted when securing a network.
2. Identify and explain five items that are important in secure network administration.
3. Which secure protocol enables the transmission of files between devices connected over the Internet?
4. Identify and explain four types of DNS attacks.
5. What four items do NAC standards require a host be able to complete?
6. Explain three security items used to assess network security.
7. Define the **tcpdump** command and tcprelay.
8. List command-line utilities used for network reconnaissance and discovery.
9. What is the difference between passive tools and active tools used for network reconnaissance?
10. Briefly explain the **netstat** command.
11. Which command-line utility is used to scan and analyze ports, conduct network security audits, and test firewalls?
12. What tasks can be accomplished with the sn1per?
13. Briefly explain the **netcat** command.
14. Explain five common network attacks.
15. What are three common types of DoS attacks?
16. Explain four environments in which scripts can be executed.
17. Identify tools and utilities used to investigate network incidents.
18. Identify and explain types of event log files.
19. Define *NetFlow* and *sFlow*.
20. Briefly explain IPFix.

SAMPLE SECURITY+ EXAM QUESTIONS

1. Which protocol secures VoIP traffic on a network?
   A. VNC
   B. SRTP
   C. LDAPS
   D. S/MIME

2. A security administrator wants to test their vulnerabilities using known hacking tools. Which of the following should be taken to fulfill that goal?
   A. Run tcpdump to analyze traffic.
   B. Use theHarvester to locate known vulnerabilities.
   C. Install an exploitation framework.
   D. Use passive reconnaissance tools.

3. Which of the following tools would help identify a device and port used for access if you suspect an unauthorized connection on your network?
   A. Cuckoo
   B. Sn1per
   C. IPFix
   D. Netstat

4. You want to prevent a user from running personally created PowerShell scripts, but you also have to allow scripts developed by administrative to run. Which of the following methods would *best* accomplish this task?
   A. Set PowerShell script execution to support digitally signed scripts only.
   B. Prohibit use of PowerShell but allow the command prompt.
   C. Modify the default PowerShell scripting environment to use SSH only.
   D. Remote connect to the machine using SSH and run the scripts as needed.

5. Which of the following security tools would enable a company to analyze potential malicious traffic patterns from a Layer-2 switch?
   A. Nessus
   B. tcpreplay
   C. hping
   D. sFlow

6. Which of the following is indicative of a DHCP starvation attack?
   A. MAC addresses are linked to incorrect IP addresses.
   B. Legitimate users are unable to obtain an IP address.
   C. The default gateway issued via DHCP is poisoned.
   D. IP addresses are spoofed.

7. Which of these attacks is an attack on operational technology?
   A. ARP poisoning
   B. An attack targeting DNS servers
   C. A DDoS attack launched against security cameras
   D. URL redirection

8. Which is a characteristic of a malicious macro?

    A. The macro originates from an MS Word document.

    B. The macro runs from Python.

    C. The macro is created using PowerShell ISE.

    D. The macro is delivered using ICMP packets.

9. What is the concern regarding an attacker running a ping sweep?

    A. It denies service to DNS servers.

    B. Attackers can identify valid IP addresses in use on the network.

    C. It poisons the local DNS cache.

    D. It is the precursor to a DDoS attack.

10. Amir used his computer to access a compromised web page. Upon further investigation, it appeared that Amir's settings were compromised, not the web page in question. What is the *likely* cause of the corruption?

    A. Botnet

    B. DNS poisoning

    C. Spyware

    D. Watering hole attack

LAB EXERCISES

Lab Activity 13-1: Wireshark Basics

This activity requires Wireshark to be installed on your computer. When installing it, if prompted to install Winpcap, install that as well. Wireshark offers viewing in legacy mode, but for this activity, the normal mode will be used.

1. Launch Wireshark.

2. Once Wireshark launches, you can open a previous Wireshark capture (**.pcap** file), or you can double-click a network interface card (NIC) in the list at the bottom of the screen to begin capturing. The graph you see next to an NIC is depicting the network traffic.

3. After double-clicking an NIC, data are immediately displayed as they are captured. If you do not see data, and you are on a wired connection, minimize Wireshark, open a web browser, and ping your default gateway. If you are on a wireless connection, the wireless NIC has to support promiscuous mode (sees all packets transmitted).

4. Once you see data being captured, let it run for a few minutes. Then, click the **Stop capturing packets** button on the toolbar.

5. By default, information is listed sequentially, which is in the order it is seen. You can sort the view using the column headers. For example, to view all packets by a network source address, click the **Source** column heading.

6. Another very helpful feature is filtering out. For example, you may only want to see packets from a specific source address or protocol. To view packets by certain criteria, click in the display filter on the toolbar and enter the filter, as shown. For example, to see all DHCPv6 traffic, enter dhcpv6 in the display filter bar. Notice as you begin entering the filter, the text is red. Once you have

entered enough for the filter to be recognized, the text turns green. To clear the filter, click the X on the right-hand side of the filter.

Enter the filter

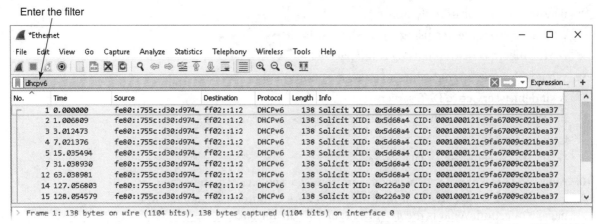

> Frame 1: 138 bytes on wire (1104 bits), 138 bytes captured (1104 bits) on interface 0

7. Clear any filters, and then enter a TCP filter. Find any packet with TCP in the Protocol column, and select it. Details for the packet are displayed in the middle and bottom areas of the Wireshark window. Notice the different lines displayed in the middle area. What is listed depends on what details are available for the selected packet. Click the triangle to the left of a line to show expanded information about that line. The details in the Frame line are just basic information such as the size of the packet. The Ethernet II line identifies data you would see placed in a frame, such as MAC addresses. The Internet Protocol Version 4 line shows addressing and TTL information. The Transmission Control Protocol line lists the detailed TCP information.

8. Expand the Transmission Control Protocol line, scroll down, and expand the Flags line. What flags are set in your example?

9. With the filter still set, look at the status bar in the lower right-hand corner of the Wireshark screen. The **Packets:** label shows the total number of packets in the capture. The **Displayed:** label shows how many packets are available with the current filter.

10. To save the capture, click **File>Save As...** to display a standard save-type dialog box. Name the file TestCapture, and save it in your working folder for this class.

11. Close Wireshark.

Lab Activity 13-2: UDP and TCP Information in Wireshark

Wireshark can be used to view the flags in TCP transmissions. Wireshark uses relative ISNs for simplicity. However, this can be changed to view the absolute ISN instead.

1. Applying what you have learned, launch Wireshark.

2. Click **File>Open...**, navigate to your working folder, and open the capture you created earlier.

3. Sort the view by protocol. Scroll down to entries using the TCP protocol. Look for one that shows a SYN transaction in the Info column. When you find one, double-click the entry to see the details.

4. In the top part of the details window, click the arrow next to Transmission Control Protocol to expand that section. What is the sequence number? What flags are set? Note the frame number for this transaction.

5. Close the details window to return to the main Wireshark window. Search for a SYN/ACK response. In terms of frame numbers, the response should be very close to the SYN packet.

6. Double-click the response that corresponds to the SYN packet you opened. Expand the Transmission Control Protocol section. What are the sequence and acknowledgement numbers? Note the frame number. Close the details window.

7. In the main Wireshark window, find the third part of the handshake. This should be the ACK packet. What do you expect the sequence and acknowledgement numbers to be? Which flags will be set to *on* (1)? Open the ACK transaction, and see if you were correct.

8. Choose **Edit>Preferences…** from the menu in the main Wireshark window. In the Preferences dialog box that is displayed, double-click **Protocols** on the left-hand side to expand it. Wireshark makes it easier to view the sequence and acknowledgement numbers since they can be quite large. You can change the default view to show the actual numbers, not the relative numbers.

9. Scroll down to find TCP, and click it. Note the default setting is to use relative numbers, as shown.

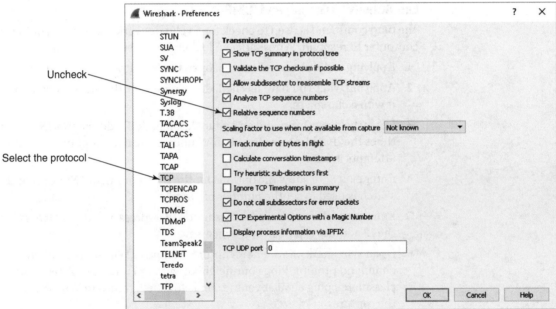

Goodheart-Willcox Publisher

10. Uncheck the **Relative sequence numbers** check box, and then click the **OK** button to save and close preferences.

11. Return to the first frame you identified (the SYN). What is the sequence number now?

12. Change to the SYN/ACK option. What are the sequence and acknowledgement numbers?

13. What do you believe the numbers will be for the ACK transaction? Open the ACK transaction to see if you were correct.

14. In the details window for the ACK transaction, scroll down further under Transmission Control Protocol. Notice the SYN/ACK sequence of events is displayed. RTT stands for round-trip time. Close the details window.

15. Select the first frame (SYN) in the main Wireshark window, but do not open it. Then, click **Statistics**>**Flow Graph** in the menu. A window is displayed that shows the entire conversation exchanged in this network request. It includes the transfer of data and possibly other transactions such as encryption. The top shows the IP addresses involved in the transaction; the left side indicates the times of each transaction. You can view this in other ways as well. If you see a FIN packet, that indicates the final transmission in the sequence.

16. At the bottom of the window, click the **Flow type:** drop-down arrow, and click **TCP Flows** in the drop-down list. This view makes it easier to see the sequence and acknowledgement numbers in the far right Comment column. Do you understand now why Wireshark shows relative numbers?

17. Click the **Save As...** button at the bottom of the graph window. A standard save-type dialog box is displayed that allows the graph to be saved as a PDF, PNG, BMP, JPEG, or TXT file. Save the graph as a PDF using your name as the file name.

18. Applying what you have learned, reset the TCP display to relative numbers.

19. Close Wireshark.

Lab Activity 13-3: Ping and ICMP

The **ping** command is used to check for a valid network address. It requires the target computer to respond. Wireshark can log ping requests.

1. Applying what you have learned, open the Windows Command Prompt.

2. Applying what you have learned, determine your IP address, and then exchange it with a classmate.

3. Enter the **ping** command and your classmate's IP address. Notice how many times the IP address is pinged. In Windows, the default number of ping attempts is four.

4. Enter ping /? to show the options for the **ping** command. Notice that the -n switch is used to set the number of pings.

5. Enter ping followed by your classmate's IP address and the switch -n 2. Notice the IP address is pinged only twice.

6. Open Wireshark. Start a new capture. Minimize Wireshark and return to the command prompt. Ping your neighbor with ten attempts. After verifying your classmate's ping against your target is finished, return to Wireshark and stop the capture.

7. Applying what you have learned, filter the display by ICMP.

8. Look at the ICMP packets. You should find the ten you sent, and the ten replies sent to your classmate, as shown.

9. Double-click a reply frame to open it. Expand the Internet Control Message Protocol area in the top of the details window, and then expand Data under that. Notice that Windows sends an alphanumeric sequence for the data during ping requests, as shown. The Linux version of the **ping** command uses

numerical values for the padding. This will be helpful in revealing the operating system being used in the ping transmissions.

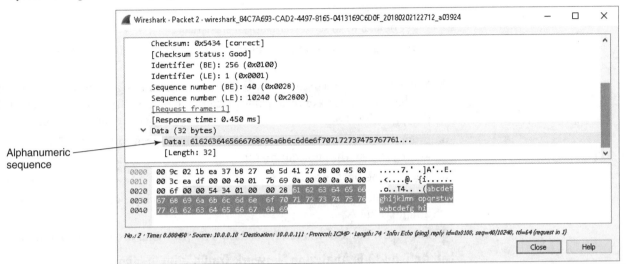

Alphanumeric sequence

Lab Activity 13-4: IP Scanner Software

A ping sweep can be done without using any special software. In this exercise, you will conduct a ping sweep of your current subnet. It uses the ICMP protocol to discover devices on a network. This exercise assumes a /24 subnet.

1. Applying what you have learned, open the Windows Command Prompt, run the **ipconfig** command, and note the network address of your subnet.

2. Enter the following command (all this is one command), substituting your network address for x.x.x.%x. For example, if your network address is 192.168.1.0, then enter 192.168.1.%x in place of x.x.x.%x.

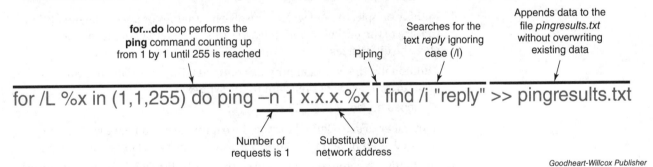

3. This command runs for a while as all hosts on the network are pinged. When the command is finished, open the pingresult.txt file with Notepad or other word processor. Review the valid addresses on your subnet.

4. Launch a web browser, and navigate to a search engine. Enter the search phrase portable apps ping sweep software. Compare some of the software features between the different programs.

5. Discuss with your classmates the benefits of using some of these programs as a security technician and the potential hacking risks they represent.

Lab Activity 13-5: Netstat Command

The **netstat** command is useful in examining network connections. A significant volume of data can be acquired using **netstat**.

1. Applying what you have learned, launch the Windows Command Prompt, and enter the **netstat** command. It will take a few minutes to collect and view the active connections.

2. Enter netstat -e to see a snapshot of statistics.

3. Enter netstat -a. How does the output with this switch differ from the command with no switches?

4. You may see a connection and wonder what it is running on the computer. This can be determine by entering netstat -o. The **-o** option displays the processor ID (PID) number. Locate any PID number from your netstat configuration.

5. From the Windows Taskbar, right-click an empty area and choose **Task Manager** from the shortcut menu.

6. Click on the **Details** tab.

7. Click on the **PID** tab to sort it from low to high. Each process running has a unique value.

8. Locate the number you referenced from Step 4. What program was running?

Lab Activity 13-6: Analyzing Network Traffic with tcpdump

Note: This lab requires use of Kali Linux.

1. Open Kali Linux and log in as root. Once logged in, open the Terminal.

2. Run the **tcpdump** command. Traffic on the default network card will begin displaying. After viewing traffic, press [Ctrl][C] to stop the capture and return to the terminal prompt.

3. You can configure the **tcpdump** command to view traffic from a specific port. To view this, you first need to ensure traffic will be moving in and out of the desired port. Open your web browser and navigate to www.yahoo.com. Next, return to the terminal and run the following syntax:

   tcpdump –nn –so port 80

   In this example, the **-nn** will not resolve hostnames or ports. The **-so** option sets the size of the packet to *unlimited*. Try the command without the **-nn** option to view the differences.

   Additionally, the **-v** option provides more detailed or *verbose* information. The order of switches is not relevant to the syntax:

   tcpdump -so -v port 80

   Remember to use [Ctrl][C] to stop the capture after you have viewed the required amount of traffic. Note: the order of the switches is not relevant.

4. The **tcpdump** command can be used to filter traffic from a specific IP address and further refine the search to view direction (source or destination). However, you need the target IP address. You can obtain an IP address by running the **nslookup** command. Use **nslookup** to obtain the IP address for Google.com.

5. Next, add Google's IP address to the end of the following command and run it:
   tcpdump host

6. Open your browser and navigate to www.google.com. Repeat Step 5 alternating between source direction by adding **-src** or **-dst** switched before the **host** portion of the command.

7. Keywords or terms can be extracted by adding grep to the command. For example, the **tcpdump -v | grep "length"** command returns results containing the word *length*. How can you use grep to assist in security concerns?

8. By default, **tcpdump** outputs data to the screen, but you can instead export results to a **.pcap** file and view the results using Wireshark or other packet analyzer programs that support **.pcap** files. Do so using the following syntax:

    tcpdump -w -c 50 test.pcap

    In this example, the **-c 50** switch will limit the results to 50 packets.

9. Open Wireshark. From the main interface, select **File>Open**. Scroll to locate the **test.pcap** file you created in Step 8 and choose **Open**. View the contents and verify that 50 lines of packets were captured. Close Wireshark.

10. Using the experience and knowledge generated by this lab, how can **tcpdump** be used in script development on a network?

Lab Activity 13-7: Configuring the PowerShell Scripting Environment

1. From a Windows computer, open PowerShell as an administrator by right-clicking PowerShell and selecting **Run as Administrator** from the shortcut menu.

2. Change to your personal home directory by running the following command, replacing *name* with your username:

    set-location c:\users\name

3. View the available script restriction policies by entering the following syntax:

    get-executionpolicy -list

    What is the current restriction policy?

4. Set the default policy to unrestricted using the following command syntax:

    set-executionpolicy -executionpolicy unrestricted

    Observe the security announcements regarding the risks to this decision and press [Y] to change the policy.

5. Open Notepad and enter the following commands, one per line:

    #Test PowerShell Script
    get-childitem

6. Save the script as testscript.ps1. It is very important to change the Save as type to **all files (*.*)** so the file extension is correctly assigned.

7. Return to the PowerShell window and enter .\testscript.ps1 followed by the [Enter] key. The script *should* execute a directory search. If note, consult your instructor.

8. Now, you will change the execution policy to test running scripts with other policies. Run the following command:

    set-executionpolicy -executionpolicy restricted

    Observe the security announcements regarding the risks to this decision and press [Y] to change the policy.

9. Input the following syntax, following by the [Enter] key.

    .\testscript.ps1

    What happened when you ran the script this time?

10. On your own, change the execution policy to All Signed. Rerun the script.

    In your own words, explain what happened on this execution.

11. Before exiting PowerShell, return the environment to the execution policy that was identified in Step 3.

Lab Activity 13-8: Exploring Security Tools in Kali

Note: This lab requires use of Kali Linux.

1. Open Kali Linux and log in as root. Once logged in, open the Terminal.

2. Using theHarvester, a technician can scrape e-mails or other company information. In this first example, you will search Microsoft for the first 100 results using Bing as a data source.

3. Enter and execute the following syntax. Review the data found.

    theHarvester -d Microsoft -l 100 -b bing

4. Review the data found. Repeat the command again, but change the data source to Google instead of Bing. What differences did you notice?

5. TheHarvester is a valuable tool for obtaining information that might be useful in reconnaissance. In this step, you will use theHarvester to search for people who have affiliated themselves with Microsoft on the LinkedIn platform. Enter and execute the following command syntax and review the results:

    theHarvester -d Microsoft -l 100 -b linkedin

6. TheHarvester can also be used to query for *all* information on a site using the -all switch. Re-execute the command from Step 5, but substitute -all for the linkedin portion of the command. Summarize the differences you see in the results. (Be aware, this command can take a few minutes to run using the **-all** switch because it is searching all data sources.)

7. The next security tool is **curl**, which is a simple tool that can be used to simulate a GET response from a URL. Enter and execute the following command syntax:

    curl -I cnn.com

    The -I switch limits the search only to document information. How can this be used in terms of reconnaissance?

8. Repeat the command from Step 7, but this time, include the verbose switch. Summarize the differences you see in results.

9. The final security tool to review is **dnsenum**, which reveals DNS information for a website. Enter and execute the following command syntax:

    dnsenum google.com

10. How can the **dnsenum** command be used to help secure a network? How can it be used for reconnaissance?

Lab Activity 13-9: Changing the Default Shell for a User in Kali

Note: This lab requires use of Kali Linux, and the user must be logged in as the root user.

1. In this example, we will add a user assigning the restricted shell for the user and modify an existing user. First, verify you are using the restricted shell. This can be verified by confirming the location of rbash, which is the restricted default shell.

2. Enter and execute the following command

    cat \etc\shells

    Verify the entry of rbash in this file, and record the folder location if it is located somewhere other than the default location (/bin/rbash). If the folder's location is *not* the default, use the location identified in the following steps.

3. Create a new user called Charlie. Assign Charlie the restricted shell using the following syntax:

    useradd Charlie -shell /bin/rbash

4. Verify the shell was assigned by running **cat /etc/passwd**. This will display a list of all users, including their default shells.

5. Using what you have learned, create a new user called Chelsey. Do not assign a shell. Then, run **cat /etc/passwd** to observe the default shell that was automatically assigned to her.

6. The command to change a user's shell is **usermod**, followed by the username and new shell designation. Using what you have learned in the previous steps, change Chelsey's default shell to rbash. Then, verify the change using the **cat** command on the passwd file. If you are unable to determine the correct command syntax, ask your instructor for help.

7. Enter and execute the following command to identify the logged-in user's current shell type:

   echo $SHELL

8. To delete users, use the **userdel** command followed by the username. For example, to delete the username Willcox, the command syntax is userdel Willcox. Use the **userdel** command to delete the users created in Steps 3 and 5.

CASE STUDY

Disinformation about Exploitation Frameworks

Many of the commands and tools used by exploitation frameworks can be used for ethical purposes, including penetration testing. Use of these tools can greatly help analysts to understand their networks, data flows, and security vulnerabilities. However, they also have the means to deliver cyberattacks against users and organizations.

Due to the potential for these frameworks to be used maliciously, a campaign to discredit the utility and value of these tools and paint the users as hackers was distributed throughout the United Kingdom in early 2020. Specific software programs, including Discord, Tor browser, virtual machines, Kali Linux, and Metasploit, were featured on a poster suggesting possession of these utilities implied dubious or potentially illegal computer activity. Reportedly created on behalf of the West Midlands Regional Organized Crime Unit, the campaign was quickly denounced by the UK's National Crime Agency.

1. Why do you think there is a stigma or false perception that using these tools indicates solely malicious activity?

2. This campaign was directed toward parents, which implies that students and teenagers are most often the users of these tools. To what extent could that inference suggest that students or teenagers are learning these commands to commit a criminal act?

3. In this chapter, you learned about theHarvester, which scrapes e-mails. While often used as a reconnaissance step in obtaining information, how do you think it can be useful as a defensive measure by an organization's security analyst?

4. Kali Linux issues a response suggesting the campaign had the opposite effect and was in reality encouraging students to explore and use these programs without adequate training. How likely do you think it is that this campaign would increase student curiosity among the tools and utilities referenced in the campaign?

5. Regardless of age, using these commands can have a serious impact if done incorrectly or with malice. How can schools, including your academic institution, promote ethical values and responsibility of usage?

Wireless Network Security

LEARNING OUTCOMES

- Define *wireless network security*.
- Discuss elements of establishing wireless installations.
- Explain advantages and vulnerabilities of various wireless connection methods.
- Recognize types of wireless vulnerabilities to consider and monitor.
- Identify potential threats to wireless security.

KEY TERMS

ANT
baseband
bluejacking
bluesnarfing
captive portal
cell
channel overlay
controller-based access point (controller-based AP)
Counter Mode with Cipher Block Chaining Message Authentication Code Protocol (CCMP)
disassociation attack
EAP over Transport Layer Security (EAP-TLS)
EAP Tunnel Transport Layer Security (EAP-TTLS)
EAP-Flexible Authentication via Secure Tunneling (FAST)

evil twin router
fat access point
infrared (IR)
jamming
narrowband (NB)
near-field communication (NFC)
open security
predictive site survey
pre-shared key (PSK)
Protected EAP (PEAP)
radio-frequency identification (RFID)
RADIUS Federation
Remote Authentication Dial-In User Service (RADIUS) server
replay attack
rogue access point (rogue AP)
session replay attack
Simultaneous Authentication of Equals (SAE)

stand-alone access point (stand-alone AP)
subscriber identity module (SIM) card
thin access point
Wi-Fi analyzer
Wi-Fi Protected Access (WPA)
Wi-Fi Protected Access II (WPA2)
Wi-Fi Protected Access III (WPA3)
Wi-Fi Protected Setup (WPS)
Wi-Fi survey
wireless access point (WAP)
wireless cracker
wireless LAN controller (WLC)
wireless local area network (WLAN)
wireless network security
wireless router
wireless site survey
Zigbee

SECURITY+ CERTIFICATION EXAM OBJECTIVES

The following Security+ Certification Exam Objectives are covered in this chapter.

- + 1.3: Replay attack
- + 1.4: Wireless
- + 2.6: Communication considerations
- + 3.3: Media access control (MAC) filtering
- + 3.4: Given a scenario, install and configure wireless security settings.

- + 3.5: Cellular
- + 3.5: Wi-Fi
- + 3.5: Bluetooth
- + 3.5: NFC
- + 3.5: Infrared
- + 3.5: Point to point
- + 3.5: Point to multipoint

- + 3.5: Global Positioning System (GPS)
- + 3.5: RFID
- + 3.8: EAP
- + 3.8: 802.1X
- + 3.8: RADIUS

OVERVIEW

Wireless networks offer the ability to connect devices through radio waves as opposed to hard-wired connections. Wireless networks can be configured in multiple modes, each offering differing connection methods and cryptographic algorithms. IT staff must be prepared to support all types of wireless configurations and configure appropriate security settings.

Wireless and mobile access present significant security challenges for network administrators because the risk of data interception is increased exponentially when communication is transferred wirelessly. Without robust security, it is much easier to intercept and manipulate data sent over radio waves than over a networking cable.

In this chapter, you will learn about different types of wireless connection methods as well as how wireless security concerns are addressed. Additionally, you will learn about methods to document and analyze your Wi-Fi signals, and the types of threats that are launched against wireless networks and technologies.

SECURITY+ NOTE

The prevalence of wireless connectivity has increased drastically over the last decade. As such, the CompTIA Security+ Certification Exam places heavy emphasis on its candidates understanding the inherent vulnerabilities and common attacks to wireless networks. Additionally, understanding the role of authentication in Enterprise Wi-Fi, along with consumer access points, is vital to obtaining a Security+ Certification.

Wireless Network Security

Wireless network security is the process of enabling security on a wireless local area network. It is a specific subset of network security that focuses on protecting mobile and other wireless devices from attacks or interception of data. A **wireless local area network (WLAN)**, or *Wi-Fi*, is a wireless networking technology that uses radio waves rather than a copper-core or fiber-optic cable. Wi-Fi communication technology operates on the unlicensed spectrum as defined in 1997 by the IEEE 802.11 standards. There have been several revisions to the original 802.11 standard as outlined in Figure 14-1.

The IEEE 802.11 standards were the foundation of wireless security protocols developed by the Wi-Fi Alliance. There have been a number of iterations to the Wi-Fi Alliance's security protocols, including WEP, WPS, WPA, WPA2, and WPA3. However, the two most common security protocols used by wireless networks today are WPA2 and WPA3.

Figure 14-1 The IEEE 802.11 standard is the basis of Wi-Fi and has been updated several times since its inception.

IEEE Standard	Year Released	Radio Frequency	Approximate Speed
802.11a	1999	5 GHz	54 Mbps
802.11b	1999	2.4 GHz	11 Mbps
802.11g	2003	2.4 GHz	54 Mbps
802.11n	2009	2.4 GHz or 5 GHz	54–600 Mbps
802.11ac	2013	2.4 Ghz or 5 GHz	450–1300 Mbps
802.11ax (Wi-Fi 6)	2019	2.4 GHz or 5 GHz	Up to 3.5 Gbps

Goodheart-Willcox Publisher

Wired Equivalent Privacy (WEP)

Wired Equivalent Privacy (WEP) is a deprecated standard used by legacy devices. One of the concerns with WEP is that it uses the same key to encrypt and decrypt data. If a passphrase is weak, easily determined, or revealed during a hacking attempt, the network and data could be accessed using that key. Due to its inherent security vulnerabilities, WEP is not recommended for wireless security.

Wi-Fi Protected Setup (WPS)

Wi-Fi Protected Setup (WPS) is a network security setting and standard for wireless networks. WPS was released in 2007 as a simple, fast method of securing wireless communication, specifically intended to help home users who have limited knowledge and skills on setup and security. There are three main methods for enabling WPS:

- *PIN method*: the user enters the personal identification number (PIN) located on the new device's router.
- *Push method*: the user pushes a button on the new device and access point, enabling the two devices to discover each other.
- *Near-field communications (NFC) method*: This short-range wireless method can be used to transfer network settings to the new device. No manual PIN entry is necessary.

However, WPS contains several design flaws. For example, there is no lockout policy on entered PINs, so a hacker could make an unlimited number of attempts to guess a PIN. Additionally, the PINs used in WPS are eight digits, but only seven of them are used. The eighth digit is a checksum value. If a hacker uses a brute-force computer program to generate and attempt PINs automatically, it will only take a matter of hours until access is granted. As such, WPS-secured devices are also not recommended for network usage.

Wi-Fi Protected Access (WPA)

Wi-Fi Protected Access (WPA) is a wireless security standard that replaced WEP and offers more security in terms of keys and user authentication. Where WEP used the same key for encryption and decryption, WPA instead uses Temporal Key Integrity Protocol (TKIP). Additional security enhancements made to WPA include the use of Extensible Authentication Protocol (EAP) and a pre-shared key (PSK).

Temporal Key Integrity Protocol (TKIP) is an encryption protocol used in wireless networking. TKIP generates a new key each time a packet is transmitted across a network. With TKIP-based encryption, the required length for a key is increased from 64 to 128 bits per packet, which makes the key much more difficult to crack.

Additionally, WPA also implements Extensible Authentication Protocol (EAP). *Extensible Authentication Protocol (EAP)* is an authentication protocol framework used frequently in wireless communication that outlines secure transport and usage of information. EAP employs a secure public key encryption system, which makes accessing a network far more difficult than with WPS or WEP.

Pre-shared key (PSK) is an authentication method used in WLAN security that requires a key value before granting access to an AP or wireless devices. PSK verifies users via a password or code commonly called a *passphrase*. PSK is fundamentally more secure than **open security**, also called an *open connection*, which is a wireless connection that requires no authentication and offers no encryption. Open connections are often located in public spaces such as cafés, airports, or other retail or dining establishments.

Wi-Fi Protected Access II (WPA2)

3.4

Wi-Fi Protected Access II (WPA2) is the second generation of WPA that provides stronger security protections and better control of network access. WPA2 took the existing security implementations of WPA and enhanced them, particularly in the areas of encryption and authentication.

3.4

The WPA2 cryptographic protocol replaced the RC4 cipher with AES encryption and added Counter Mode with Cipher Block Chaining Message Authentication Code Protocol. *Advanced Encryption Standard (AES)*, also known as *Rijndael encryption*, is a symmetric block cipher that requires 128-, 192-, or 256-bit keys. **Counter Mode with Cipher Block Chaining Message Authentication Code Protocol (CCMP)** is a wireless encryption standard designed to be used with wireless LANs. The biggest difference between CCMP and traditional Cipher Block Chaining (CBC) is that when CCMP attempts to reach the last block in its chain, the value of that block is appended with a MAC value. Not all devices may be able to support CCMP, however. In those situations, WPA2 with TKIP can be employed as a fallback.

WPA2 is currently the most widely used security option for WLANs. WPA2 provides multiple authentication techniques, including the following.

802.1X

3.4, 3.8

Businesses often use the IEEE 802.1X standard for authenticating users wirelessly. The *IEEE 802.1X standard*, also known as *enterprise Wi-Fi*, is a wireless networking standard that provides more security than other standards by employing port-based security. Specifically, it enables port-based authentication after a user's identity has been confirmed. It is not always convenient or safe to use the standard connection option of providing users with the passphrase for WLAN access because a passphrase can be easily shared with those who should not be accessing the network. Additionally, as employees join and leave the company, the security of the passphrase becomes weaker. With enterprise Wi-Fi, users do not need to be given a passphrase specifically for wireless access. Instead, they are authenticated through their network login names and passwords.

With the 802.1X standard, EAP is incorporated into data frames and used to provide authentication. In this process, the access point takes the role of a security guard. It passes the credentials and information between the client and authenticating server. In 802.1X, the client is known as the *supplicant*, and the AP is considered the *authenticator*. The 802.1X process is depicted in Figure 14-2.

1. The client (supplicant) sends a request packet for access.
2. The authenticator (AP) requests identity information from the client.
3. The authenticator (AP) sends this information to the authentication or RADIUS server.
4. The RADIUS server sends a challenge to the authenticator, which is then sent to the client.
5. The client responds with the challenge.
6. If the RADIUS server approves the challenge, the client will be granted access.

3.4, 3.8

Enterprise Wi-Fi, sometimes referred to as *WPA2 Enterprise*, provides security by implementing port-based authentication by opening ports for network access. It uses an authentication server called a RADIUS server to confirm the user's identity. A **Remote Authentication Dial-In User Service (RADIUS) server** is an identity and access authentication server that functions on both wired and wireless networks.

Figure 14-2 With the 802.1X standard, Extensible Authentication Protocol (EAP) is incorporated into data frames and used to provide this authentication.

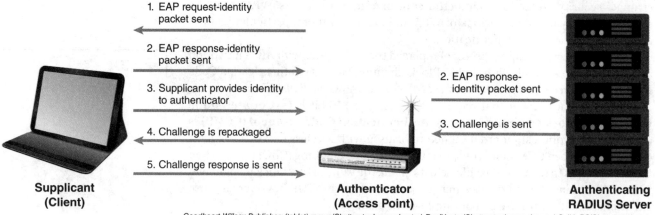

Goodheart-Willcox Publisher; (tablet) romvo/Shutterstock.com; (router) RealVector/Shutterstock.com; (server) Sujith RS/Shutterstock.com

A **RADIUS Federation** is a method where users can connect and authenticate to one network while using credentials from another network. The term *federation* refers to different computing entities adhering to standards in a collective manner. A user's credentials will be packaged by the local RADIUS server, which will then send it to the specified RADIUS server. The RADIUS servers work together to pass these credentials between the different systems.

PEAP

Protected EAP (PEAP) is an open-standard authentication protocol created jointly by Cisco, Microsoft, and RSA to protect EAP communications. PEAP uses a lightweight tunneling protocol to enable secure authentication.

EAP-FAST

EAP-Flexible Authentication via Secure Tunneling (FAST) is an authentication protocol created by Cisco to replace a previously unsecure version of EAP called Lightweight EAP (LEAP). EAP-FAST uses a lightweight tunneling protocol to enable authentication.

EAP-TLS

EAP over Transport Layer Security (EAP-TLS) is a protocol that provides certificate-based authentication. TLS is the security protocol used when connecting to a web server securely and is commonly used in wireless authentication. It offers strong security and is widely supported.

EAP-TTLS

EAP Tunnel Transport Layer Security (EAP-TTLS) is an extension of EAP-TLS that allows communication to be sent through a protected tunnel. EAP-TTLS helps reduce attacks such as man-in-the-middle attacks.

Wi-Fi Protected Access III (WPA3)

Wi-Fi Protected Access III (WPA3) is the newest generation of Wi-Fi security and provides advanced security protocols to the communication of wireless transmissions. It was designed to use the latest security methods, disallow the use of outdated legacy protocols, simplify Wi-Fi security, and increase cryptographic strength. WPA3 also maintains interoperability with WPA2 devices. There are two variations of WPA3: WPA3-Personal and WPA3-Enterprise.

- *WPA3-Personal* provides stronger protections to users by providing a more robust password-based authentication, even if users choose less recommended complexity choices in their passwords. This is possible due to a technology called SAE. **Simultaneous Authentication of Equals (SAE)** is a password-based security authentication method that replaced the PSK method used by WPA2. SAE allows for additional functionality that protects a password or passphrase from being easily cracked by off-site brute-force or dictionary-based attacks. WPA3 also offers an individualized encryption process in which users are unable to snoop on another's WPA3-personal traffic, even if they have the password and are connected to the Wi-Fi network.

- *WPA3-Enterprise* offers greater security for the enterprise networks. WPA3-Enterprise features an optional mode that uses 192-bit minimum-strength security protocols and cryptographic tools. Authentication encryption uses 256-bit Galois/Counter Mode Protocol (GCMP-256).

Devices capable of running WPA3 must connect to wireless networks also using WPA3 in order to take full advantage of all of WPA3's features. Likewise, WPA2 devices are still supported on WPA3 equipment, but not with the enhanced security offered.

Wireless Installations

The first step in building a secure wireless environment begins with decisions regarding equipment, placement, encryption, and protocol usage. It is important to know the location of your network infrastructure, including access points and their broadcast reach in order to secure them effectively. Important steps taken with wireless installations include conducting a site survey.

Site Survey

The first step in building a secure wireless network is to conduct a wireless site survey. A **wireless site survey** is the process of planning, designing, and documenting a wireless network environment. Site surveys identify signal ranges, lack of coverage areas—called *dead zones*, and **channel overlays**, which are overlapping channels that enable resiliency in a wireless network. Site surveys also identify areas of a network that will likely have more users than other areas, the number of devices likely to connect on each floor or in each room, and the materials used when walls and floors were constructed. There are two general types of site surveys: predictive and Wi-Fi.

Predictive Site Survey

A **predictive site survey**, also called a *wireless heat map*, is a visual representation of wireless signal strength, often depicted as a map, within a network, as shown in Figure 14-3. Depending on the software used to create it, a heat map is often generated by dropping access points at their installation point and signals being retrieved by the software. This information is then used to demonstrate coverage. Most heat maps provide continuous updates, while others can map connected devices in addition to showing coverage. Heat maps are an excellent tool to locate dead zones or unauthorized access points that may be malicious.

Using heat maps, network engineers can determine how strong a signal will be in a given location. Engineers can also determine how far a signal will extend outside an organization's physical setting. This information can provide insight into the

Figure 14-3 A predictive site survey, also called a *heat map,* is a visual representation of wireless signal strength within a network.

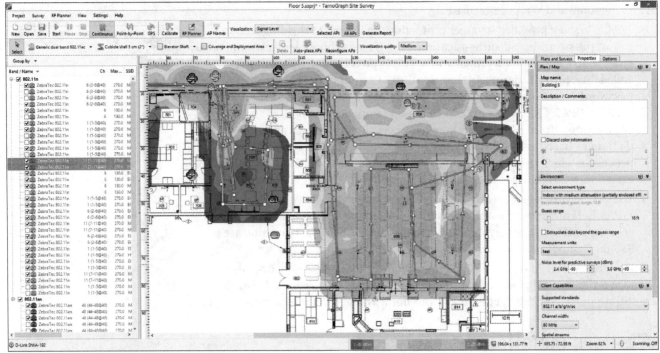

likelihood of unauthorized people using the organization's Wi-Fi signal to connect to the network, which could lead to attacks, such as wardriving.

Wi-Fi Survey

A **Wi-Fi survey** is a service that combines a predictive survey with analysis by a network engineer to determine what is needed to deploy a wireless network at a given location. Often, Wi-Fi surveys are conducted using **Wi-Fi analyzers**, which are devices used to locate wireless signals and signal strength in physical locations. Figure 14-4 displays the results of the Wi-Fi Analyzer App for Windows displayed in a graph. Notice that the Wi-Fi channels are included below each chart.

Wireless Access Point

A **wireless access point (WAP)**, also known as an *access point (AP)*, is a networking device that provides access to a connection between a wireless network and a physical cable-based network. Wireless security can be managed well, provided AP settings are configured correctly and placement was carefully considered. If a wireless network's range extends beyond the company's physical boundaries, this could make it easier for attackers to attempt to gain access.

One of the first steps in securing a wireless network is choosing the best type of AP to match the needs of the network. Depending on the deployment method and network architecture, an administrator has a number of options from which to choose when determining the correct type of access point. Each type of access point provides a unique set of security measures, and the needs of a network determine which type of AP to install.

Securing the wireless access points in a network, particularly stand-alone access points, is an essential protection mechanism to prevent unwanted access. Access points should have complex passwords provided strictly on a need-to-know basis.

3.4

3.4

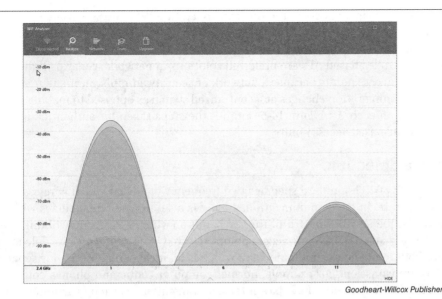

Figure 14-4 Wi-Fi analyzers are devices used to locate wireless signals and signal strength in physical locations and are often used in a Wi-Fi survey.

Goodheart-Willcox Publisher

Additionally, APs should be monitored for firmware updates, which should be downloaded and installed in a timely fashion. Wireless access points and controllers should also be physically secured to protect against tampering and theft.

Fat vs. Thin Access Points

A **fat access point** is a network device that exists independently from other network devices and can manage authentication, encryption, and other wireless functions. Fat APs are sometimes called *autonomous APs* because they do not rely on other devices to perform necessary functions. Fat APs contain all the necessary software to handle all aspects of the network, from configuration to encryption. Fat APs are often used in home or small-office networks due to their autonomy, but in large networks, such as those on college campuses, the amount of time spent configuring each individual AP would be too great. In these scenarios, the use of multiple thin access points is a better option. These type of access points present a weak security vector; they are individually configured and require vigilant maintenance and updates.

A **thin access point** is one that does not contain all the management and configuration functions found in fat APs. Its primary responsibility is to receive and transmit wireless data. The bulk of the configuration for thin APs is performed at a wireless connection switch, so each AP does not need to be configured manually. Not only does configuration at a switch save time, but it also ensures the same security settings are present on every access point. This reduces possible configuration errors or security vulnerabilities.

Stand-Alone vs. Controller-Based APs

Even though thin APs can be configured universally at a connection switch, both fat and thin access points are considered stand-alone access points. A **stand-alone access point (stand-alone AP)** is an access point that requires individual configuration but has appropriate functionality to accept data and forward it to the appropriate device. A simpler, more consistent option is to implement controller-based access points on a network.

A **controller-based access point (controller-based AP)** is an access point that receives and transmits wireless traffic and is managed by a wireless LAN controller (WLC). A **wireless LAN controller (WLC)** is a device that manages multiple access points in a network. The APs controlled by a WLC are sometimes referred to as *lightweight access points (LWAPs)* since they do not make any forwarding decisions. Instead, all data is forwarded to the WLC.

Controller-based APs are preferred solutions in network scenarios that contain multiple access points because a network or security administrator can make widespread configuration changes at a centralized switch as opposed to making multiple changes on each AP. Figure 14-5 outlines the steps taken for authentication using controller-based access points.

Band Selection

The IEEE 802.11 standard specifies two frequency bands on which wireless devices can operate. In telecommunication, a *band* is a set range of frequencies within the radio frequency (RF) spectrum. The two bands on which wireless networking operate is 2.4 GHz and 5 GHz. Some access points, referred to as *dual-band*, are able to operate both frequencies simultaneously, which is an ideal configuration for separating data transmission. For example, normal computer traffic and phones could travel on the 2.4-GHz band. More data-intensive transmissions, such as gaming or video streaming, can be handled more efficiently on the 5-GHz band.

Each of the RF bands is subdivided into segments called *channels*. A device can be set to use a specific channel within each frequency. Channels are measured by width, which identifies the amount of data or bandwidth that can be sent during transmission. Channel width is measured in megahertz (MHz), and the minimum channel width needed is 20 MHz.

An issue to consider is the possibility of interference from an overlapping channel. For example, in the 2.4-GHz band, there are 11 possible channels. Channels 1, 6, and 11 are the only channels that do not overlap. A specific problem with 2.4-GHz

Figure 14-5 A controller-based access point (controller-based AP) is an access point that receives and transmits wireless traffic and is managed by a wireless LAN controller (WLC).

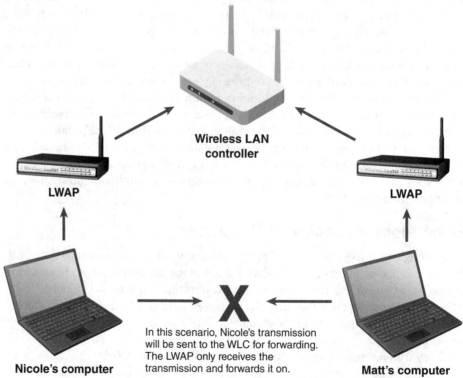

Wireless LAN controller

LWAP

LWAP

In this scenario, Nicole's transmission will be sent to the WLC for forwarding. The LWAP only receives the transmission and forwards it on.

Nicole's computer

Matt's computer

Goodheart-Willcox Publisher; (computers) romvo/Shutterstock.com;
(LWAPs) RealVector/Shutterstock.com; (WLAN controller) Aiiiza/Shutterstock.com

channels is that many devices operate on this frequency, including cordless telephones, microwave ovens, Bluetooth devices, and even some car alarms. These devices can affect wireless transmissions and availability.

The 5-GHz band has more channels than the 2.4-GHz band, but the 5-GHz band includes 23 channels that do not overlap. This reduces the possibility of using an overlapping channel. It also reduces interference from nearby channels. However, the 5-GHz channel is used in the United States by the military and many weather apps; therefore, the FCC requires any device using the 5.250 to 5.350, 5.470, and 5.725 frequencies to have a feature called DFS. *Dynamic frequency selection (DFS)* is a channel-allocation mandate that detects interference with military and weather radar and automatically shifts the frequency being used by the wireless device. This is needed to ensure critical radar applications are not disrupted.

Antennae Types and Placement

 3.4

Access points have one or more antennae built into the device. An antenna may be omnidirectional or unidirectional, as shown in Figure 14-6. *Omnidirectional* means it will send and receive in all directions. *Unidirectional* means it will only send and receive from one specific direction. Since a unidirectional antenna only transmits in one direction, the power of the transmission will be greater than if the same device transmitted in all directions. There is also less interference at the access point since the receiver must listen and respond to signals from only one direction. While there are strong benefits to unidirectional antennae, in many situations they are not flexible enough for establishing communication between a transmitter and receiver. For example, if there are receivers on opposite sides of a transmitter, a single unidirectional antenna will not provide coverage for both.

Placement of access points is an important consideration to ensure proper coverage. An AP using omnidirectional signaling should be placed in the center of the coverage area. With unidirectional antenna placement, ensure you are not too far from the host devices so the signal can provide adequate coverage. If you are trying to avoid individuals from connecting or attempting to connect in a specific physical area, you may need to move the AP or reduce the power on the AP so it cannot receive a connection in that specific location.

 3.5

Antenna type is often based on if the signal is point-to-point or point-to-multipoint. *Point-to-point* is a telecommunication method that describes a connection between two distinct points. An example of a point-to-point communication is a broadcast link between two businesses to send and receive data over long distances. *Point-to-multipoint* is a transmission method where one device or network is configured to transmit to multiple devices. A common example is an outdoor wireless

Omnidirectional Antenna

Unidirectional Antenna

Goodheart-Willcox Publisher

Figure 14-6 An omnidirectional antenna broadcasts in all directions, while a unidirectional antenna broadcasts in only one specific direction.

network where a wireless central base station is mounted on a building so multiple clients connect to it.

Captive Portal

3.4

A **captive portal** is web page a user must view when connecting to a wireless network before broad access to the network is granted. Typically, a captive portal enables a user to connect to access points, but to do anything more, the user must open a browser and accept the terms of service. This allows the operator of the WLAN the ability to present its acceptable use policy (AUP). If you have ever used public Wi-Fi at a library, airport, or restaurant, you likely had to agree to an acceptable use policy before accessing web pages. Essentially, you were "held captive" and could not access the Internet until agreeing to terms. There are commercial and open-source products available for creating captive portals.

Wireless Router

A **wireless router** is a device that has the same capabilities of an AP but also adds functionality to wireless connections to LANs or WANs. Wireless routers can serve as an access point, but an access point cannot function as a router. This is due to a router's ability to transmit data packets across large networks, such as the Internet. Routers maintain tables of information such as the locations and identifying information of other routers.

Wireless Connection Methods

There are multiple wireless communication methods used for interoperability between devices. Each method has advantages and vulnerabilities. Examples of wireless connection methods include the following.

Cellular

3.5

Cellular is a network technology that enables communication through mobile devices by using a system of stations and transceivers that make up a cellular network. A *cellular network* is a type of wireless network in which transmissions are distributed over groups of geographic areas. A cellular network transmits data from multiple transmitters called *base stations*. Each base station is allotted a portion of the overall bandwidth. The coverage provided by the base station is contained within a specified geographic area known as a **cell**. Figure 14-7 shows how cells are arranged to provide coverage. When a mobile user moves out of one cell, the base station performs a handoff to the next cell.

Cellular Generations

Terms such as 4G and LTE are often used when talking about cellular networks. The G stands for *generation*. Generational specifications are provided by the International Telecommunication Union (ITU). The original Internet connection was 2G. Most users today have a 4G or, depending on location, 5G connection. The 4G standard required providers to offer certain speeds. Long-Term Evolution (LTE) is the path used to provide 4G speeds. The top wireless providers have standardized 4G as their communication standard.

The latest generation of cellular connectivity is called *5G*, the rollout of which has already begun in major cities around the world. 5G networks are expected to provide larger channels for data speed, lower latency to improve response time, and ability to connect significantly more devices at one time.

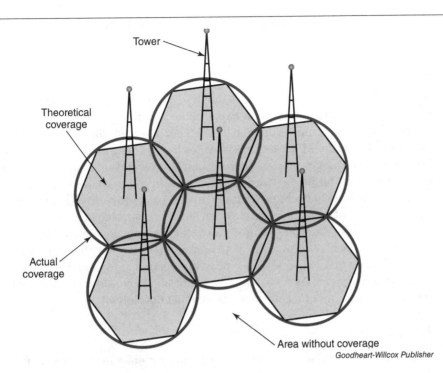

Tower

Theoretical
coverage

Actual
coverage

Area without coverage

Goodheart-Willcox Publisher

Figure 14-7 The coverage
provided by the base station
is contained within a specified
geographic area known as a cell.
When a mobile user moves out of
one cell, the base station performs
a handoff to the next cell.

With 5G rollout only recently occurring, there are still many unknowns regarding its security. However, 5G networks are increasingly based on software. Therefore, one important security implication to consider is the development of the 5G software. Flaws related to poor software development could pose a number of risks to the security of 5G.

 2.6

RF Spectrum

Cellular networks operate in licensed areas of the RF spectrum. The *radio frequency (RF) spectrum* is a range of frequencies by which radio waves operate and communicate. Within a given market, mobile carriers cannot transmit or receive data using the same frequencies. Mobile devices transmit a great deal of data, meaning a large spectrum of RF frequencies is desired. With many competing needs, including satellite transmissions, managing the spectrum can be a difficult process for the Federal Communications Commission (FCC). The FCC is tasked with freeing up additional space in the spectrum to help increase the amount of unlicensed space used to increase capacity of wireless technologies. To facilitate this task, the FCC offers incentives for television broadcasters to use less of the spectrum. It also returns unused spectrum from other governmental agencies.

SIM Cards

2.6

An important consideration regarding cellular is the reliance on subscriber identity module (SIM) cards. A **subscriber identity module (SIM) card** is an integrated circuit that stores a cellular device's international mobile subscriber identity (IMSI) number and related key. Together, an IMSI and its key are used to authenticate cellular subscribers on a given network.

Generally, SIM cards are secure, but they can be weaponized in a SIM swap attack. A *SIM swap attack* is a form of social engineering in which a person convinces a cellular carrier to switch a cellular number to a different SIM card. Once this is accomplished, all phone-based multifactor authentication practices are compromised. Unfortunately, in a SIM swap attack, the target does not have a lot of recourse.

However, security measures such as carrier PINs or passcodes can help prevent swap attacks.

WLAN

A *wireless local area network (WLAN)*, or *Wi-Fi*, is a wireless networking technology that uses radio waves rather than copper-core or fiber-optic cable and operates on the unlicensed spectrum as defined by IEEE 802.11 standard. Wi-Fi typically runs in *infrastructure mode*, which requires devices to send data to a central access point before the data moves on to its destination. However, Wi-Fi connections can also connect through ad hoc networking. *Ad hoc networking* is a type of connection in which two or more devices communicate with each other directly instead of going through a central device such as a router. Devices operating in ad hoc mode cannot connect to another network. Ad hoc networking is typically used in situations where users need to be able to transmit data among themselves without an Internet connection or external network. This type of connection, however, is not often recommended or necessary. As such, administrators should consider monitoring for these types of connections and enforcing a policy that disallows it.

Bluetooth

Bluetooth is a wireless connection that enables mobile devices to share data via short-range, ad hoc communication sessions. It is defined by the IEEE 802.15 standard. Devices using Bluetooth must be paired together to provide communication.

Bluetooth devices are often able to connect in an ad hoc fashion with minimal security, but device-specific options exist for enabling or limiting Bluetooth communication. Users can implement security measures to create "trust devices" through service- or device-level security, encryption, and use of PINs or passphrases. For example, the popular AirDrop feature on Apple devices allows users to share images, web pages, and other data via Bluetooth. The Bluetooth connection establishes a peer-to-peer wireless connection between the devices, both of which have established their own firewall, and messages are sent with encryption. Apple users can choose not to receive messages through AirDrop, receive AirDrop messages only from contacts, or receive AirDrop messages from any device in the near vicinity.

Near-Field Communication (NFC)

Near-field communication (NFC) is a wireless communication standard that facilitates transmissions using electromagnetic radio fields between devices of a very close proximity. NFC is limited to a radius of approximately four inches and is often used for contactless payment methods such as Apple Pay or Samsung Pay.

NFC enables devices to communicate through electromagnetic radio fields as opposed to the radio transmissions used by Wi-Fi. A user must bring the device close to the access point in order to connect using NFC. NFC is relatively secure, especially since devices must be close to transmit, but it can be vulnerable to frequency jamming, replay attacks, or man-in-the-middle attacks. For secure deployment, a connection must be configured properly and encryption employed.

ANT

ANT is a proprietary wireless technology that allows devices to communicate with each other wirelessly over short distances. It is designed for low-bit, low-power transmissions of small packets. It is like the low-energy version of Bluetooth, but Bluetooth is able to handle larger packets of data.

ANT is primarily used by sensors and many products in the sports, fitness, and health-care sectors. ANT devices are particularly vulnerable to jamming or DoS attacks, as well as intercepted data since encryption is not enabled by default and must be configured manually. To ensure secure deployment, encryption should be used and best practices should be applied when transmitting data.

Infrared

Infrared (IR) is a wireless communication technology that conveys data through infrared radiation. Infrared is a short- and medium-length communication option that uses electromagnetic energy at a wavelength longer than that of red light. It is a type of light that exists outside the visible light spectrum. Infrared operates using line-of-sight methods as opposed to radio waves. *Line-of-sight* refers to a connection that requires a broadcaster and receiver to be visible to one another with no interruption in the light between them. Some systems require an unobstructed access between transmitter (source) and receiver (destination).

There is also a very limited range in using this technology. These two aspects increase the security of using infrared communication and combined with fast speed make it an attractive option for development of new technologies. Additionally, infrared is often used when security is of top concern or when third-party interference is expected.

GPS

Global Positioning Systems (GPSs) are communication methods that enable a device called a *GPS receiver* to communicate and receive information from global navigation satellite systems (GNSSs). These satellites transmit microwave signals to the earth and the devices use their receivers to enable communication. GPS technology is used extensively in geographic information systems, which combine cellular networks for communication GPS information to provide mapping and location services. Security concerns for GPS range from privacy implications of locating people to the possibility of GPS coordinates being hacked in planes, boats, and cars.

Radio-Frequency Identification (RFID)

Radio-frequency identification (RFID) is a wireless technology that uses electromagnetic fields to automatically identify objects and track tags or smart labels that are attached to the objects. RFID is employed in many fields, including ID badges, inventory management, libraries, and supply chain management.

Narrowband

Narrowband (NB) is a radio communication method that utilizes a narrow set, or *band*, of frequencies within a given communication channel. In a sense, narrowband is the opposite of *broadband*, which uses wide bandwidth data transmissions. The difference between narrowband and broadband is further illustrated in Figure 14-8.

Narrowband connections are used for devices with short-range abilities, such as RFID connections and automotive keyless entry fobs. Narrowband is also employed in Narrowband IoT (NB-IoT) devices, which are able to transmit over an extended range while using little power.

Narrowband devices have a low network footprint and do not offer a major security risk on their own. The security implications arise from the scale of NB devices. There is a strong potential for coordinating denial of service (DoS) attacks by using a wide array of devices to send unplanned communication to victims.

Figure 14-8 Narrowband (NB) is a radio communication method that utilizes a narrow set, or band, of frequencies within a given communication channel.

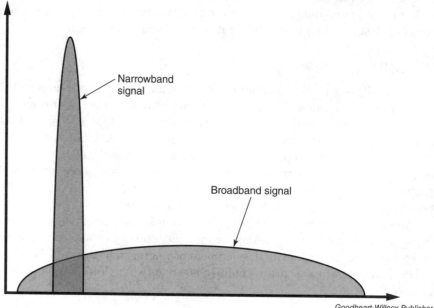

Goodheart-Willcox Publisher

2.6

Baseband

Baseband refers to a frequency's original range before it is converted through modulation. *Modulation* is the process of converting one frequency to another. For example, an audio signal transmitted on a radio frequency is modulated to a much higher, inaudible, frequency range used for radio broadcasts, cell phone conversations, and satellite transmissions. After the signal is transmitted, it is *demodulated* to the original baseband signal.

Security implications include vulnerabilities within flawed firmware. Some smartphones and IoT devices operate with baseband vulnerabilities that enable attackers to execute a memory corruptions attack over the air. Additional considerations include vulnerabilities that enable attackers to monitor communication, place calls remotely, or transfer large volumes of data.

2.6

Zigbee

Zigbee is a telecommunication network standard based on IEEE's 802.15.4 personal area network standard. It is considered an alternative to Wi-Fi and Bluetooth for some applications, including low-power sensors, such as the ones often found in home IoT sensors. For example, smart home devices, such as light bulbs that can be adjusted over wireless connections, are powered by Zigbee. Due to its prevalence in smart home and home automation appliances, security implications are important considerations to make when installing.

Some Zigbee security standards are based on features included by the manufacturer, so these standards likely vary from one device to another. The main security risks to Zigbee devices include theft of sensitive data, such as security encryption keys, from a node; theft of the node itself; unauthorized control of a node, such as from theft or replay attacks; and loss of the service through jamming and other interference attacks.

Wireless Vulnerabilities

Due to the nature of wireless connectivity, it is inherently vulnerable to interception or attack. While security precautions can and should be taken when installing and configuring a wireless network, vulnerabilities can open a network to potential risk due to the inability to control how Wi-Fi users configure their own devices. Important vulnerabilities to consider and monitor include the following.

Deprecated Protocols

Old wireless security protocols such as WEP and WPS are no longer recommended for use. However, depending on the device used to access a network, an organization may not be able to control the type of encryption used. Devices operating with *deprecated protocols*, or protocols that have been discouraged from usage, pose a significant risk to any network to which they connect. For example, WEP utilizes a straightforward cryptographic pattern, making it easy for attackers to break encryption. If a device is operating with WEP and connects to your network, data transmitted to and from the device is at risk. Similarly, WPS-enabled devices are at risk due to the possibility of an attacker cracking the access PIN with relative ease. For these reasons, only devices operating with robust, modern cryptography, such as WPA2 or WPA3, should be used to connect to a WLAN.

MAC Address Filtering

✚ 3.3

MAC address filtering is among the most common forms of access control on a wireless network. However, MAC filtering is inherently vulnerable due to the exchange between an AP and a wireless device. The initial exchange of information is typically unencrypted, so an attacker could intercept or monitor packets, record MAC addresses of approved devices, and use those addresses to trick an AP into thinking an attack is being carried out by an authorized device.

Additionally, the scope of managing multiple MAC addresses is large and can pose challenges. As new users are added to an organization and given permission to use an AP, the database of approved addresses needs to be updated. Furthermore, as old users leave, those addresses must be removed from the address database. This requires constant attention and updating that is often impractical, if not impossible, in large enterprise settings.

SSID Broadcast

The name of a wireless network is known as its *service set identifier (SSID)*. Smaller networks are usually configured as a *basic service set (BSS)*, which is a wireless network with a single access point. Large networks have multiple APs to allow for continuous coverage over a wider area; this configuration is called an *extended service set (ESS)*, as illustrated in Figure 14-9. When a network has multiple APs, all the APs have the same name.

You have likely noticed SSIDs appear on your phone or laptop when you are within coverage of a network. While broadcasting an SSID is convenient, it also represents a vulnerability. For example, if the SSID of a network includes the name of the organization that owns it, an attacker can easily identify a potential target. The easy solution to this problem is to prevent an AP from broadcasting the SSID. However, this can create connectivity problems for authorized users. Instead of preventing the SSID broadcast, it should be restricted so that only those who know it can connect to it. Another option is to create separate SSIDs or channels for employees and guests so data remains separated.

Figure 14-9 The name of a wireless network is known as its *service set identifier (SSID)*. Smaller networks are usually configured as a *basic service set (BSS)*, and larger networks with multiple APs use an *extended service set (ESS)*.

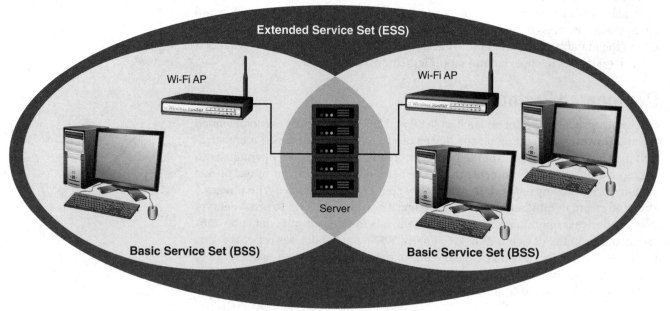

Goodheart-Willcox Publisher; (server) Sujith RS/Shutterstock.com; (computers) romvo/Shutterstock.com; (routers) RealVector/Shutterstock.com

Threats to Wireless Security

Transmissions on wireless networks do not follow set paths to and from their destinations. Except in a highly secured facility, there is simply no way to protect radio signals from interception. Furthermore, wireless networks, such as Bluetooth systems, NFC devices, RFID systems, and WLANs, are relatively easy to set up and deploy, which makes them targets for hackers. Examples of threats to wireless security include the following.

 1.3

Replay Attacks

A **replay attack** is an attack in which a hacker captures login credentials during an initial attack, stores them, and retransmits them at another time. The hacker could also capture encrypted information and send it later without breaking the encryption on the credentials. Replay attacks are low-tier man-in-the-middle (MITM) attacks since they require an attacker to intercept information in transit.

 1.3

Website owners often record users' interactions with their web pages. They record mouse clicks, moves, and input to analyze usability. However, if not secured properly, this information can be used maliciously. A **session replay attack**, also known as a *playback attack*, is a type of replay attack in which an attacker steals a session ID and reuses it to impersonate an authorized user. The fundamental difference between a session replay and standard replay attack is that a session replay essentially recreates a user's time spent on a website or application as opposed to just a login attempt.

1.4

Evil Twin

An **evil twin router** is an illegitimate router that carries the same SSID as the desired AP. Evil twin routers are considered a type of rogue router or rogue access point. A **rogue access point (rogue AP)** is an unauthorized access point that enables a hacker to circumvent network security. Evil twins are often used to commit MITM attacks by placing the rogue router near the target and providing a stronger signal so the victim connects to the evil twin by mistake. At this point, all traffic routes through the evil twin. A hacker can intercept and discover all data sent to and from the target. This process is illustrated in Figure 14-10.

Hackers can deploy networks with SSIDs that sound legitimate. One way to do this is to create an SSID that is the same as a legitimate one except for case, such as ACME_Network instead of ACME_NETWORK.

Bluejacking and Bluesnarfing

 1.4

Bluejacking is a Bluetooth-based concern in which somebody sends an unsolicited message, such as an advertisement, via Bluetooth. You may have had a retailer do this to you as you walked past a store in a mall. Bluejacking is usually just annoying, not a serious threat.

A more troubling attack is called Bluesnarfing. **Bluesnarfing** is a Bluetooth-based attack in which a hacker exploits a Bluetooth connection to steal data from a Bluetooth-enabled device. Hackers may be able to inject viruses and other malware into the device.

There are steps that can be taken to protect the data and device:

- The easiest protection is turning off Bluetooth when it is not in use.
- The risk of data being intercepted or for hijacking is high in public, crowded areas, so the user must be extra vigilant.
- Use the security measures offered on the device, from authentication to encryption.

Disassociation

 1.4

A **disassociation attack** is a form of a denial of service attack in which the hacker disconnects a user from their wireless network. This is done by sending a disassociation signal to the victim. A *disassociation signal* is one that deactivates a user from an access point. When the victim's computer is disconnected, it will typically attempt to reconnect to the current network automatically or search for a wireless network. If the hacker had also established an evil twin, the user's computer could unknowingly connect to the illegitimate AP, especially if the evil twin signal is stronger than the legitimate AP's. Within minutes, all traffic between the two devices can be intercepted and parsed using a program such as Ettercap or Wireshark.

Figure 14-10 An evil twin router carries the same SSID as the desired AP and provides a stronger signal, which means it will likely be the one to which a user connects.

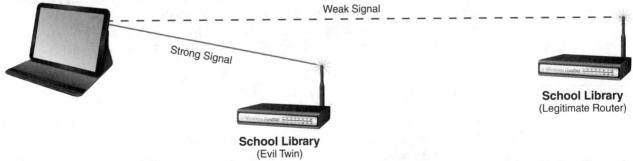

Goodheart-Willcox Publisher; (tablet) romvo/Shutterstock.com; (routers) RealVector/Shutterstock.com

Jamming

Jamming is intentionally interfering with wireless signals to prevent a transmission from being usable. *Jammers* are RF transmitters that block or scramble other RF signals. Jammers cannot determine which signals are undesirable and which are welcome, so it interferes with all signals, including Wi-Fi signals, cellular transmissions, and GPS communication. The Communications Act of 1934, later amended by the Telecommunications Act of 1996, is a federal law that prohibits the marketing, sale, and use of a transmitter designed to block, interfere, or jam wireless signals.

RFID Attacks

Radio frequency identification (RFID) tags function through an antenna that produces an electrical signal to power a transceiver in the tag. A popular use of RFID tags includes employee badges that can be detected by a proximity reader. RFID tags are small and can be placed in or on devices, and they are read when they near the proximity reader. This technology is very helpful when processing a large volume of scanning is necessary, for example, many employees entering a building, or a user checking out several items at the library.

RFID tags are passive or active. A *passive tag* does not have its own power source; it receives power from the reader. When the RFID tag is near the reader, the antenna in the tag forms a magnetic field. However, the range for these tags is about 15 meters, or roughly 50 feet, so outside of that range, the tag does not have power.

Active RFID systems use battery-powered RFID tags that continuously broadcast their signals. A common example of these is automobile tolling systems such as EZ-Pass. These tags have a range of approximately 150 meters, or roughly 500 feet.

RFID tags provide efficient services but are susceptible to attacks, particularly eavesdropping and replay attacks. *Eavesdropping* occurs when an unauthorized reader listens to transmissions between the RFID tag and the read to gain data that can be recorded and reused to gain access, steal data, or act on the communication by intercepting information or manipulating data.

Additionally, an attacker can swap an RFID tag with a duplicate tag that transmits false data and violates the integrity of the information. Administrators should review RFID tags to ensure the validity of each tag and corresponding reader.

> ## TECH TIP ⚙
>
> RFID-based automobile key fobs are popular methods of remote access. Hackers can monitor signals to obtain unique codes from a specific key fob or use a relay box to pick up the radio signal from an unused key fob to access a car. Key fobs can be stored in faraday bags to protect fobs when not in use.

NFC Attacks

Near-field communication (NFC) is a set of standards that establishes communication between devices in close proximity of each other. NFC devices are used often in retail, including contactless payment systems and rewards cards. The use of NFC in wireless networking is vulnerable due to the inherent properties of the technology itself. For example, if data sent from one device to another via NFC is unencrypted, a nearby device can intercept it. Additionally, if a hacker is close enough, it may be possible to tap a reader to a user's device and steal data. Hackers could corrupt the data being sent to the reader or interfere with the data being sent. The loss of phones with NFC payments can be prevented by having passwords or biometric locks on their systems.

Initialization Vectors (IVs)

An *initialization vector (IV)* is a randomly generated number or variable added to an encryption key every time there is a transmission. However, this is still not foolproof. In an IV attack, an attacker is able to learn the plaintext of a packet and can then compute the encryption key stream used by the IV. Once the key stream is found, any other packet using the same IV can be decrypted. There is a limit to the size of the IV, depending on the length of the WEP key. Therefore, it is possible for hackers to create tables of keys, which could be used to decrypt packets.

Wireless Crackers

A **wireless cracker** is a tool designed to break the encryption protections of a WLAN. An example of such a tool is Aircrack-ng. One of the primary features of this program is to crack passwords in the WPA handshake.

Administrators can use programs, such as Aircrack-ng, to determine if the network's encryption is strong or if a hacker could use the same tool to discover passwords. Once this information is known, the appropriate steps can be taken to harden the wireless networks and access points.

SUMMARY

Wireless Network Security

- Wireless network security is the process of enabling security on a wireless local area network. It mainly focuses on protecting mobile and other wireless devices from attacks or interception of data.
- WLAN, or Wi-Fi, is a wireless networking technology that uses radio waves rather than copper-core or fiber-optic cable.
- Wi-Fi communication operates on the unlicensed spectrum as defined by IEEE 802.11 standards. These standards were the foundation of wireless security protocols developed by the Wi-Fi Alliance.
- The Wi-Fi Alliance has had a number of iterations of wireless security protocols. These include WEP, WPS, WPA, WPA2, and WPA3. WPA2 and WPA3 are the two most common protocols today.

Wireless Installations

- The first step in building a secure wireless environment begins with decisions regarding equipment, placement, encryption, and protocol usage.
- It is important to know the location of a network infrastructure, including access points and their broadcast reach in order to secure them effectively.
- Important steps taken with wireless installations include conducting a site survey, which is the process of planning, designing, and documenting a wireless network environment. Two types of surveys include a predictive site and Wi-Fi survey.
- WAP is a networking device that provides access to a connection between a wireless network and a physical cable-based network. The needs of a network help determine which type of WAP, band selection, and antennae type and placement to install.

Wireless Connection Methods

- Cellular is a network technology that enables communication through mobile devices by using a system of stations and transceivers that make up a cellular network. Key elements of a cellular network are cellular generation, RF spectrum, and SIM cards.

- Wi-Fi runs in infrastructure mode but can also connect through ad hoc networking. Ad hoc devices cannot connect to another network and are used in situations where users need to be able to transmit data among themselves without an Internet connection or external network. However, ad hoc is not often recommended or necessary.
- Bluetooth enables mobile devices to share data via short-range, ad-hoc communication sessions. Bluetooth devices are often able to connect with minimal security, but device-specific options exist for enabling or limiting Bluetooth communication by establishing "trust devices."
- Near-field communication (NFC) facilitates transmissions using electromagnetic radio fields between devices about four inches apart. It is relatively secure, but NFC can be vulnerable to frequency jamming, replay attacks, or man-in-the-middle attacks.
- ANT allows devices to communicate with each other wirelessly over short distances. It is like the low-energy version of Bluetooth. ANT is particularly vulnerable to jamming, DoS attacks, and intercepted data since encryption must be configured manually.
- Infrared (IR) conveys data through infrared radiation. It operates using line-of-sight methods and has a very limited range. These two aspects increase the security of using IR communication and combined with fast speed make it an attractive option for development of new technologies.
- Global Positioning Systems (GPSs) are communication methods that enable a GPS receiver to communicate and receive information from a GNSS. Security concerns for GPS range from privacy implications of locating people to the possibility of GPS coordinates being hacked in planes, boats, and cars.
- Radio-frequency identification (RFID) uses electromagnetic fields to automatically identify objects and track tags or smart labels that are attached to the objects. RFID includes narrowband and baseband.
- Zigbee is an alternative to Wi-Fi and Bluetooth and is often found in smart home devices. Some Zigbee security standards are based on features included by the manufacturer. The main security concern of a Zigbee device is theft of sensitive data.

Wireless Vulnerabilities

- Due to the nature of wireless connectivity, it is inherently vulnerable to interception or attack. Vulnerabilities persist that can open a network to potential risk.
- Much of the vulnerabilities stems from the inability to control how Wi-Fi users configure their own personal devices.
- Important vulnerabilities to consider and monitor include deprecated protocols, MAC address filtering, and service set identifier (SSID) broadcasting.

Threats to Wireless Security

- Transmissions on wireless networks do not follow set paths to and from their destinations. There is simply no way to protect radio signals from interception, unless in a high security facility.
- Wireless networks, such as Bluetooth systems, NFC devices, RFID systems, and WLANs, are relatively easy to set up and deploy, which makes them targets for hackers.

- Examples of threats to wireless security include replay attacks, evil twin routers, Bluejacking, Bluesnarfing, disassociation attacks, jamming, RFID attacks, NFC attacks, initialization vector (IV) attacks, and wireless crackers.

REVIEW QUESTIONS

1. Define *wireless network security*.
2. Why is Wired Equivalent Privacy (WEP) not recommended for wireless security?
3. Identify the three main methods for enabling Wi-Fi Protected Setup (WPS).
4. Briefly explain five of the authentication techniques for Wi-Fi Protected Access II WPA2.
5. Define Wi-Fi Protected Access III (WPA3) and identify what it was designed to accomplish.
6. Identify elements of establishing wireless installations.
7. Briefly explain two general types of site surveys.
8. Differentiate between a fat access point and a thin access point.
9. Define *band*.
10. To ensure proper coverage, where should an AP be placed for omnidirectional and unidirectional signaling?
11. Explain advantages and vulnerabilities of four different wireless connection methods.
12. What is the latest generation of cellular connectivity and what is it expected to provide?
13. What is the radio frequency (RF) spectrum?
14. State the difference between narrowband and broadband.
15. What is the cause of wireless vulnerabilities?
16. Identify and explain types of wireless vulnerabilities to consider and monitor.
17. List potential threats to wireless security.
18. What type of wireless attack involves a hacker capturing login credentials during an initial attack, storing them, and retransmitting them at another time?
19. What steps can be taken to protect a device and data from Bluesnarfing?
20. Define *near-field communication (NFC)*.

✚ SAMPLE SECURITY+ EXAM QUESTIONS

1. Which of the following security methods would enable a hotel chain to require that guests enter their room information before being connected to the wireless network?

    A. WPA2-PSK

    B. 802.1X

    C. Captive portal

    D. WPA3-SAE

2. Which of the following would *best* enable you to identify any unauthorized devices on your network?

   A. Perform a wireless site survey.

   B. Analyze the network traffic.

   C. Put your Bluetooth device in discovery mode to determine other devices.

   D. Hide all known SSIDs and search for those broadcasting names.

3. Which of the following concerns specifically relates to 5G connections?

   A. It is more software dependent and vulnerable to attacks against code.

   B. It is more susceptible to DoS attacks than its predecessors.

   C. It uses a strong encryption, but a weak authentication method.

   D. It uses an unlicensed area of the spectrum.

4. In addition to changing the SSID and password information, what is the best thing to do to secure a router?

   A. Add shielding to the router.

   B. Install a captive portal.

   C. Use MAC address filtering.

   D. Keep firmware up to date.

5. Which of the following would be the most advanced encryption method for use in a business?

   A. WPA2—AES

   B. WPA3—SAE

   C. WPA3—Enterprise

   D. 802.1X

6. Why is MAC filtering not a true security measure?

   A. It is not possible to enter all MAC entries in the wireless router.

   B. A MAC address can be spoofed, thus bypassing the configuration.

   C. It is only a temporary measure.

   D. It only applies to Windows and Linux devices, not iOS-based tablets or smartphones.

7. In a situation where two routers have the same SSID, but not the same ESS, the routers are said to be:

   A. Incompatible

   B. Evil twins

   C. BSS devices

   D. Poisoned

8. What attack may a hacker use to force the user to connect to an evil twin?

   A. Jamming

   B. Replay attacks

   C. Bluejacking

   D. Disassociation

9. Which represents an attack of unwanted messages and texts via an open Bluetooth connection?

    A. Bluejacking

    B. Bluetexting

    C. Bluemessaging

    D. Bluesnarfing

10. When using the IEEE 802.1X standard authentication, which of the following is the computer referred to when trying to connect to the wireless network?

    A. Authenticator

    B. WNIC

    C. AP

    D. Supplicant

LAB EXERCISES

Lab Activity 14-1: Viewing Wireless Information with Netsh

Netsh is a command-line Windows program that allows you to view and configure networking protocols. In this lab, we will use it to view wireless information. You need access to a windows device with a wireless adapter to view this information.

1. Open the Windows Command Prompt with administrator access.

2. Enter the syntax netsh, which places you in the interactive mode of this command. Type ? and press the [Enter] key to see all available commands.

3. Run the **wlan** command to access the wireless local area network configuration page. Type ? and press the [Enter] key to see all available commands in this context.

4. Type show interfaces and enter. This displays the wireless interfaces on your system and their MAC address and status. Provide a screenshot of your results.

5. Use the syntax show networks to display a list of all wireless networks in your area. How many wireless networks were discovered? What authentication options did you see?

6. Use the **showwlanreport** command to obtain complete information. This command will create an HTML file. Note the location of this file.

7. Type and enter quit to exit.

8. Navigate to the file indicated in the **netsh showwlanreport** and open it with your default browser. How could this tool be useful to a security administrator?

Lab Activity 14-2: Exploring a Wireless Router's Configuration

Each wireless router vendor has its own interface and options. Essentially, all devices need similar configuration information. In this lab, you will use free simulators from tp-link to explore the configuration interface.

1. Launch a web browser, and navigate to a search engine.

2. Conduct a search using the phrase, tp-link emulators. At the time of this writing, the correct website was located at https://tp-link.com/us/support/emulator.

3. Choose the **Archer c3200** device. If you find multiple options, be sure to select the English version.

4. The basic setup screen is the default interface. Click on the **2.4G** icon in the upper right-hand corner of the interface. This provides an overview of the networks that have been created. Guest networks have been created; how can their use improve security of your wireless network?

5. Click on the **Wireless** tab from the left side of the screen. Explain whether you would or would not choose to use the default SSIDs that are displayed.

6. Change the 2.4-GHz SSID to Labrouter_1 and the password to A76qNR5!. For Wireless 5GHz-1, create the SSID of Labrouter_5GHz and use the password of A76qNR5!. Uncheck the enable box for Wireless 5GHz-2 and hide the SSID. Create a screenshot of your settings.

7. Click on the **Advanced** tab at the top of the screen and choose **Wireless Settings**.

8. View the security options from the drop-down menu. What is the default security? Which encryption algorithm is used? Is this the most secure option available?

9. Change the Security option to WPA/WPA2 Enterprise. Why is the password option not used in this mode?

10. Look at the options under Mode. How could the default option of 802.11bgn mixed open security vulnerabilities on your network?

11. Assume you are configuring this device in a lab room where there are other 2.4-GHz networks located. Which channel might you choose and why?

12. The transmit power has three options. Which choice would you select if you are trying to limit the coverage area? Why did you select your choice?

13. Change to the 5GHz-1 option on this page. Review the mode, Channel, and Channel Width options. What has changed on them and why?

Wireless	2.4GHz | 5GHz-1 | 5GHz-2

14. Click on the **Security** tab on the left-hand side of the screen. Choose **Access Control** in the sub menu. To add MAC filtering, select the **Add** option in the Devices in Blacklist menu. Add the device name: Lab computer, and the MAC address of AA:BB:CC:11:22:33. Take a screenshot of this before you click **Save**.

15. You can choose between Whitelist or Blacklist for MAC filtering. If this were an AP you were using in an open school lab where students can connect as needed, which option will likely be more useful to you? Explain your answer.

16. Locate the **Administration** option under **System Tools**. In this location, you could change the admin password. Notice there is an option to allow remote management. Is this something you would choose for your home router? Why or Why not?

17. Choose logout to simulate leaving the router. Close this page when completed.

Lab Activity 14-3: Router Security Vulnerabilities

Wireless routers are often overlooked in security planning. Many homeowners never change the security settings from the factory defaults. In businesses, routers may continue to be used after manufacturer support has ended.

1. Launch a web browser, and navigate to the Common Vulnerabilities and Exposures website (www.cve.mitre.org).
2. Locate the site's **Search CVE List** button and click it.
3. Enter the name Archer.
4. Scroll through the list looking at the descriptions. The entry in the **Name** column contains a number code. The first number is the year the vulnerability was revealed. The second number is an index number assigned to the event. How many reports were returned for the router you entered?
5. Select one of the results to read full information about the reported issue. What is the name of the CVE and its specific vulnerability?

Lab Activity 14-4: MAC Addresses

The first three octets of a MAC address indicate the hardware manufacturer. If you have this information, you can use a website to find the name of the manufacturer.

1. Launch the Windows Command Prompt and enter the **GETMAC** command to find the MAC address on your local machine. Note the first three octets.
2. Launch a web browser and navigate to the What's My IP website (www.whatsmyip.org).
3. Locate the **MAC Address Lookup** menu entry and click it.
4. In the text box, enter the MAC address of your local machine, as shown. You can enter just the OUI instead of the full address.

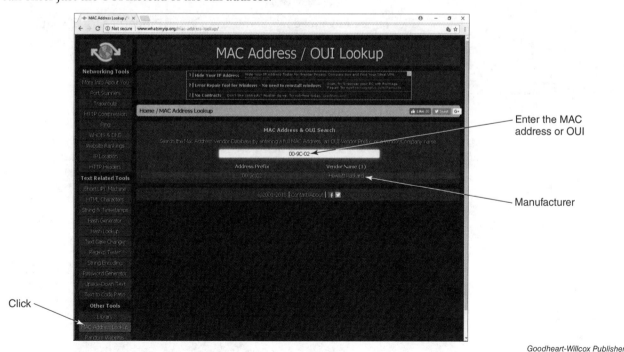

Goodheart-Willcox Publisher

5. Enter Netgear in the text box. Notice all the OUIs assigned to this vendor. You can search by other vendors as well, such as Dell or Intel.

6. If your network card supports this feature, you can change your MAC address in the properties of the network adapter. Open **Device Manager** and navigate to **Network adapters.** Expand the **Network adapters** section. Locate your network adapter and right-click to access properties.

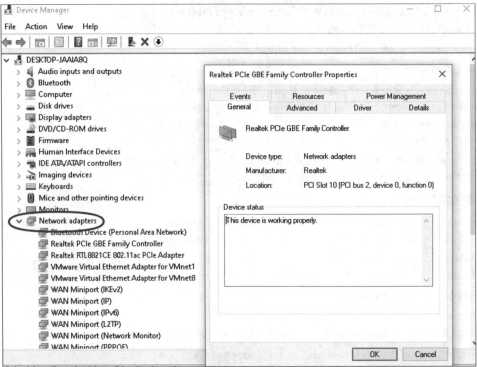

Goodheart-Willcox Publisher

7. Click on the **Advanced** tab. Scroll down in the **Properties** list. If your NIC supports this feature, you will see an option for Network Address. Add a valid hexadecimal address of 12 characters as shown in the following screen capture. Click **OK** to save.

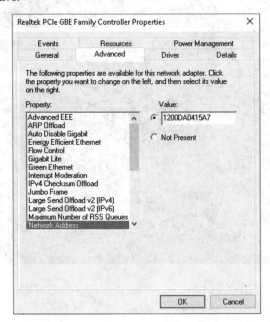

Goodheart-Willcox Publisher

8. Return to the command prompt, and run **getmac** again. Provide a screenshot of your spoofed MAC address.

9. After observing this change, return to the Network Address property, and select the **Not Present** option to use the default MAC address.

10. How can knowing the manufacturer of a MAC address aid you in securing your wireless network infrastructure or analyzing a possible attack?

CASE STUDY

Android Devices and Bluetooth Hacks

In February 2020, an advisory was issued that alerted Android users of a Bluetooth vulnerability that enabled phones to be hacked wirelessly without user knowledge. While the hacker would have to be within Bluetooth range, no user interaction to the device needs to occur, and the hacker can steal personal data and spread malware. The only Android devices found to be seemingly unaffected were devices running Android 10, as well as a handful of Google Pixel and certain Android One phones, depending on the software version installed. Unfortunately, the flaw is not easily patched unless mobile carriers have issued patches for specific Android devices. As of this writing, the problem is ongoing.

1. Based on this flaw, do you think Android users should avoid using Bluetooth-enabled devices, particularly in crowded areas, such as public transportation? Defend your response.

2. This hack only works if a hacker knows a device's Bluetooth MAC address, which is generally broadcasted in discovery mode. Many users are unaware of this setting and the risk it exposes. List strategies for educating Android users about Bluetooth settings and inherent vulnerabilities.

3. Android devices appear to be more prone to attacks, such as this Bluetooth vulnerability. Knowing this, explain whether you would recommend allowing or disallowing Android devices on your network. How can you keep these devices from infecting other hosts on the network?

4. Mobile devices are prime targets for hackers due to their widespread use and availability to both consumers and hackers alike. Since vulnerabilities and malware pose continual threats, many manufacturers no longer adequately support legacy devices from a security perspective. Rather, users are often instructed to upgrade their devices. Who has a greater responsibility in protecting the data in this scenario: the manufacturer of the older device or the user who does not upgrade to a newer device? What are some options that could help eliminate the use of older devices? Provide a detailed response.

Cloud Computing

LEARNING OUTCOMES

- Discuss advantages, disadvantages, and vulnerabilities of cloud computing.
- Identify components of the cloud infrastructure.
- Explain five common cloud models.
- Summarize two types of cloud service providers.
- Identify types of cloud services.
- Summarize cloud access security.
- List methods used for cloud security.
- Discuss types of cloud security controls.
- Summarize virtualization.

KEY TERMS

Anything as a Service (XaaS)
Clarifying Lawful Overseas Use of Data (CLOUD) Act
cloud access security broker (CASB)
cloud application security
cloud audit
cloud backup
cloud computing
cloud governance
cloud infrastructure
cloud instance
cloud model
cloud security
cloud security control
cloud service provider (CSP)
cloud storage
community cloud
container
container security

edge computing
Firewall as a Service (FWaaS)
fog computing
guest operating system
high availability (HA)
hosted service
host operating system
hybrid cloud
hypervisor
Infrastructure as a Service (IaaS)
managed security service provider (MSSP)
managed service provider (MSP)
microservice
next-generation secure web gateway (SWG)
off-premises model
on-premises model
personal cloud

Platform as a Service (PaaS)
private cloud
public cloud
reference architecture
resource policies
secrets management
Security as a Service (SECaaS)
security group
serverless architecture
services integration
Software as a Service (SaaS)
software-defined networking (SDN)
software-defined visibility (SDV)
thin client
transit gateway
uptime
virtual machine (VM) escape
virtual machine (VM) sprawl

SECURITY+ CERTIFICATION EXAM OBJECTIVES

The following Security+ Certification Exam Objectives are covered in this chapter.

+ 1.2: Cloud-based vs. on-premises attacks
+ 1.6: Cloud-based vs. on-premises vulnerabilities
+ 2.1: Data sovereignty
+ 2.1: Cloud access security broker (CASB)

+ 2.1: API considerations
+ 2.2: Summarize virtualization and cloud computing concepts.
+ 2.4: Cloud vs. on-premises requirements
+ 2.5: On-premises vs. cloud

+ 2.5: Cloud
+ 3.6: Given a scenario, apply cybersecurity solutions to the cloud.
+ 5.2: Cloud security alliance

OVERVIEW

Organizations of all sizes benefit from a cloud-based approach for the storage and access of data, features, and services. Cloud computing has become one of the most prevalent forms of data distribution, but it has several security concerns. For example, with data housed off-site in the cloud, what happens if the cloud provider is hacked? Security protocols must be in place to ensure that an incident in the cloud does not extend to a local network. Additionally, precautions must be made to ensure that in the event a cloud environment is compromised, the data within it remains secure.

Among the most important considerations to be made with cloud computing is that security is in place to allow only authorized users access while protecting data transmissions. In this chapter, you will explore aspects of cloud computing, including advantages and disadvantages to cloud environments; typical cloud infrastructure and models; cloud-based services and service providers; security in the cloud; and topics regarding virtualization.

SECURITY+ NOTE

For many businesses, the cloud provides vital services from redundancy to deployment of resources. Cloud computing is tested heavily on the CompTIA Security+ Certification Exam. Therefore, it is important to study the different services offered in cloud computing and their primary usage, including software, platform, and infrastructure. On the exam, you will likely be asked to evaluate scenarios to determine the correct solution for cloud computing.

Cloud Computing

Historically, organizations incorporated computers and related technology using an **on-premises model** in which an organization purchases hardware and software needed for business operations and uses them on-site. As businesses and their computer systems grow, the cost for additional assets and maintenance also grows, resulting in many organizations choosing to operate with a hosted service. A **hosted service** is a resource deployment method in which data servers, storage devices, and networking resources are utilized using a remote connection for which services are contracted. Cloud computing is an example of a hosted service.

Cloud computing is using remote servers on the Internet to host, access, and store data rather than using a personal computer or local server using a pay-per-use service model. An important aspect of cloud computing is collaboration and sharing of data by its users. This is considered an **off-premises model** in which an organization accesses and stores data in an off-site facility.

The term *cloud* was chosen as the name of this service because when network engineers were designing systems, they needed a conceptual way to identify a network for which they did not know all the details. They settled on a cloud as a symbol to represent the unknown network design elements, as illustrated in Figure 15-1. Today, most cloud-based services use a cloud symbol to illustrate their cloud connection to customers.

Advantages of the Cloud

There are many advantages of cloud over on-premises models, some of which are as follows.

Cost

Using a cloud model can save an organization money. In an on-premises model, an organization purchases hardware, maintains the equipment, and updates systems periodically or as needed. In a cloud environment, the company pays a fee to use the cloud vendor's equipment but does not incur equipment and maintenance costs on a regular basis.

Speed and Accessibility

The cloud advantage allows a vast amount of computing resources to be provisioned in minutes to provide rapid response to changing needs, including the need for more resources such as computing power, memory, and data storage. Cloud computing enables access anywhere there is Internet access and increased functionality for mobile devices, including smartphones. This accessibility allows access to users from any location without the need for further configuration.

+ 2.5

Cloud Backup and Recovery

A **cloud backup**, also called an *online backup* or *remote backup*, is a strategy of backing up data to an off-site, virtual, or cloud-based server as opposed to a local server. Backing up data stored in the cloud is much simpler than backing up data stored on a physical storage device. Cloud storage systems typically have automatic backups that copy data to the cloud location. Most responsible cloud vendors then replicate these backups to servers in other locations. This provides another level of redundancy to protect the data.

Figure 15-1 The term *cloud* was chosen for Internet-based services because network engineers needed a conceptual way to identify a network for which they did not know all the details. They settled on a cloud as a symbol to represent the unknown network design elements.

alexmillos/Shutterstock.com

Recovering data from the cloud is also simpler than recovering lost data from a hard drive. Because the data is stored on drives in the cloud, there is no need to locate saved backups; the data is immediately available for recovery.

Disadvantages of the Cloud

A significant disadvantage to cloud computing is uncertainty. Cloud concerns relate directly to honoring the core security principles of data protection: confidentiality, integrity, and availability.

Confidentiality

One of the most important concerns for many cloud users is preserving data privacy. *Data privacy* includes practices that assure a person's or company's data is respected and not shared with unauthorized parties. *Uncertainty* is a consideration that businesses must understand when they use a cloud. There is always a great deal of concern when a business entrusts its data to another company. When using the cloud, a *gatekeeper* takes control of data management. This leaves important questions unanswered, such as when data is available and who can access data.

Integrity

When data is not controlled by the owner, it is always a concern that the data might be manipulated. *Data integrity* is the assurance that data is not changed or altered when it is stored or transmitted to another destination. The information must maintain its consistency, accuracy, and trustworthiness at all times.

Availability

Availability means data can be accessed when needed. If the Internet is not accessible, cloud services cannot be used and a business could be halted. The cloud is dependent on access to the Internet and the reliability of an Internet connection.

Cloud Vulnerabilities

Cloud-based and on-premises models share similar vulnerabilities, such as the following:

- Poor authentication policies may allow user accounts to be compromised and stolen.
- Access control policies determine the rights or abilities a user has to use the services. If configured incorrectly, users could acquire more access and privileges than necessary.
- Outages, communication problems, and security vulnerabilities can be caused by *misconfigurations* or mistakes made by an IT staff.

However, there are vulnerabilities specific to cloud environments that do not exist in an on-premises model. One of the most obvious is that visibility is lost when infrastructure is controlled by another party. Cloud customers have to depend on the provider and cannot personally control operations.

- Risk is increased in the cloud due to cloud vectors. A *cloud vector* provides a new attack avenue that can originate through the cloud provider, its operations, and cloud-specific technologies and software. In particular, public clouds serve as a large target, increasing the lure of hackers to exploit the security of data in the cloud.

TECH TIP

Consider incorporating an extra level of redundancy when backing up your data. *Cloud-to-cloud backups* can help prevent data loss if an employee accidentally or intentionally deletes information. Additionally, check your service agreements with the cloud provider to determine length of time for which backups are maintained.

+ 1.2, 1.6

- *Shared service*, also called *multitenancy*, is an environment used in public clouds that allows multiple customers to share the hardware and resources of the cloud vendor. Such an environment requires strong measures to isolate customer data and services from others.
- A supply-chain attack on a cloud vendor is rare, but when it happens, the impact could be extreme, potentially exposing many customers' systems and data.
- Cloud-based vendors are more often the target of a denial of service attack compared to a local organization. When a platform begins to get low on resources, the automatic scalability of the systems will provide more resources, such as network bandwidth. This increase in bandwidth can actually strengthen the attack by increasing the attack vector. In a localized DoS attack, this would not occur automatically.

Cyberattacks follow data and resources, regardless of whether data is on-premises or cloud based. An on-premises network is susceptible to attacks that compromise on-site security. Local businesses are easily identifiable, and if a hacker wants to target a medical facility, physically locating a target and its network is an easy discovery. In a cloud computing environment, the cloud vendor offers anonymity and is difficult to physically locate.

Cloud Infrastructure

Cloud infrastructure consists of computing hardware, software, and other components necessary to provide the required infrastructure for delivering business operations from a remote location. Located in the cloud are physical servers, storage platforms, networking equipment, and applications to run the operations.

Servers

Physical servers are located in the cloud and serve as hosts for a business's local servers and services. Physical servers run virtualization technologies that allow multiple server operating systems to be installed and configured as virtual machines. *Virtualization* is a means of managing or presenting computer resources virtually as opposed to physically, allowing multiple customers to share applications.

3.6

An *instance* is a virtual machine in a cloud; the terms *virtual machine (VM)* and *instance* are used interchangeably. A **cloud instance** is a virtualized server installation within a cloud computing environment. Instances are installed, built, and operated using remote access to a cloud platform. Instances share the resources of several nodes and are far easier to scale than physical servers.

A cloud instance functions much in the same way as physical servers. However, cloud instances require dedicated computer resources that physical servers do not. While they require more resources, cloud instances are virtualized. Since instances are virtualized, they are independent of hardware, can be transferred easily from one node to another, and offer significantly more portability than a physical server.

3.6

Storage

Cloud storage is using remote servers hosted on the Internet to *store* data rather than *process* data. The service may be free or pay-per-use. Customers use the cloud storage service so they can store data at a location other than on their server or personal computers. Data centers protect the data and keep it secure. To protect storage security, policies must be in place.

- *Permissions.* Roles define who has permissions to access data and operations that can be performed.

- *Encryption.* *Encryption* is the process of converting data into unreadable characters by applying a security key. Encryption protects data from being read by unauthorized parties as well as protecting against brute force attacks.
- *Replication.* *Replication* is where data is stored virtually so it is accessible from multiple computers. This process improves reliability and ensures redundancy.
- *High availability.* **High availability (HA)** is the ability of a system to remain available with no interruption. It means that downtime is minimized and uptime is maximized. **Uptime** is a measurement expressed as a percentage of time that the cloud storage system is working and available.

Storage technologies, such as network-attached storage (NAS) and storage area networks (SANs), provide the storage capabilities for file storage, access, and data archival or backup. The benefits of cloud storage enable a flexible and efficient utilization of physical assets while allowing for rapid deployment of resources and virtual machines.

Data sovereignty is a concept that states digital data is subject to the jurisdiction and laws of the country where the storage device is located. If data is stored in a country other than where the business is located, there may be legal ramifications. For example, some countries do not permit businesses to store or back up data to servers located in other countries, and data may be accessible to local governmental regulations that differ from the country of residence. When using a cloud vendor, it is important to identify this information and adjust contracts to reflect business preferences.

The **Clarifying Lawful Overseas Use of Data (CLOUD) Act** is a federal law that provides oversight into data storage on cloud providers. Essentially, the CLOUD Act allows federal law enforcement to compel any US-based service provider to turn over requested data stored from any location. A subpoena or warrant is required for this request, but it applies to any location, both within the United States and other countries. The CLOUD Act modified the existing Stored Communications Act (SCA).

2.1

Hardware

2.2

Cloud hardware consists largely of networking hardware such as routers, switches, load balancers, and firewalls. It also includes a **transit gateway**, which is a transit hub used to interconnect a company's virtual private cloud (VPC) and on-premises network. A transit gateway acts as a cloud router and simplifies the network communication between locations. It also allows connections to each location, provides encryption, and prevents data from traveling over the Internet.

Applications

2.1, 2.2

Microservice, also known as *microservice architecture*, is a software application development method made up of reusable components used in a cloud-native application. This is an environment in which a single application is composed of many smaller independent services that communicate over well-defined application programming interfaces (APIs). An *application programming interface (API)* is a set of tools and programs that enables interactions between applications and components and provides communication between a client and server. An app built with micro-services architecture allows each component to be developed, deployed, and scaled without affecting functionality of other services in the app. Each microservice has its own unique set of capabilities and functionality. If the service gets too complex, it can be broken into even smaller services. Microservices offer more benefits than a monolithic application where everything must work together. Additional benefits to microservices include the following:

- Independent teams can work quickly to foster ownership of their services.
- Flexible scaling allows microservices to be scaled to meet demands as needed.

- Teams have more technological freedom since they can use the tools needed for their service, regardless of what other teams are using.
- Code can be reused by creating blocks of code that allow for use in other applications.
- Microservices are resilient to failure, which means if one component fails, the entire application is not necessarily affected.

Software-defined networking (SDN) is an approach to management of a network using the application of code. It allows a network to be managed consistently, regardless of the underlying network technology. SDN enables the network to be centrally controlled by software beyond the networking devices. Since networking infrastructure does not need to be proprietary software, SDN is a form of *infrastructure as code*, which is the management and provisioning of network infrastructure through machine-readable files instead of physical devices or tools. In a traditional environment, devices function in an autonomous manner and have limited understanding of the overall state of the network. Instead of managing each device, SDN focuses on interaction with the network through APIs rather than management tools, as shown in Figure 15-2.

Software-defined visibility (SDV) allows automation between software programs through a set of open, RESTful APIs, which allow them to interact directly. A *RESTful API* is software code based on a representational state transfer, which is an architectural style for developing web services. To achieve this goal, network traffic is collected and made available through pervasive monitoring or visibility framework. This allows apps using SDV the ability to receive traffic from this fabric to dynamically respond to events without waiting for administrator intervention. SDV allows devices on the network to interact with the visibility framework as needed.

Cloud Models

A **cloud model** is the way in which cloud infrastructure is provisioned for use. As illustrated in Figure 15-3, there are five common cloud models.

Private Cloud

A **private cloud** is a cloud-computing resource owned and managed by a single private organization. Services are exclusively for employees and members of the organization. This model provides the most security and control.

Figure 15-2 Software-defined networking (SDN) is an approach to management of a network using software applications and focuses on interaction with the network through APIs rather than management tools on each device.

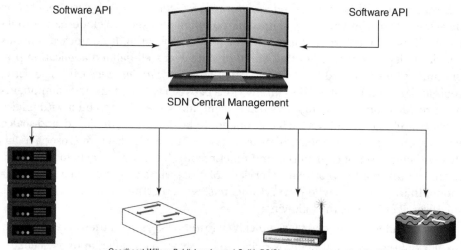

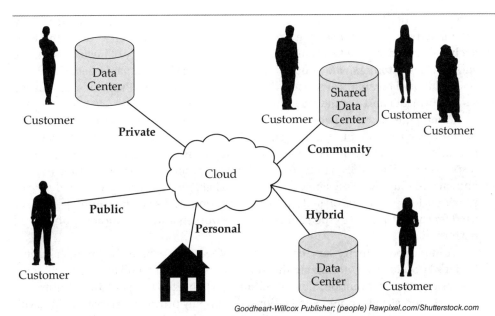

Figure 15-3 There are five basic cloud-deployment models: private, public, community, hybrid, and personal.

Goodheart-Willcox Publisher; (people) Rawpixel.com/Shutterstock.com

Public Cloud

A **public cloud** is a cloud-computing resource that provides services to anyone. Google cloud services such as Google Drive are free, but other solutions, such as Carbonite backup, require payment for use of services. Since the data is located in a shared space on a public cloud, security is a concern since it is easily accessible from any Internet connection.

Community Cloud

A **community cloud** is a cloud-computing resource shared by everyone in an affiliated organization and is not available to anyone outside of the organization. For example, a state community college system might create a community cloud. The cloud allows different campus locations to share resources with only faculty, staff, and students of the community college permitted to have access.

Hybrid Cloud

A **hybrid cloud** is a cloud model that combines public, private, or community clouds. Hybrid deployments are often unique to their purpose or the organization using them. For example, many schools use their own community cloud as storage systems but use Google for e-mail. This combines a private cloud with a public cloud.

Personal Cloud

A **personal cloud** is a cloud-computing resource that allows a user to manage their own cloud service to store files or offer services within a household. Personal clouds are often referred to as *home clouds* and are a popular option for many consumers.

Cloud Service Providers (CSPs)

A **cloud service provider (CSP)** is a vendor that provides IT services over the Internet. Cloud vendors can provide specific services as well as offer a full range of generalized services such as storage, business applications, or infrastructure. Cloud vendors remove the responsibility of creating and maintaining infrastructure for deployment of IT services from a business and provide these services for a fee. There are many types of cloud service providers. Some are focused on vertical markets, such as health care or education, while others support a variety of businesses at the same time. Customers who choose CSPs evaluate services available, security, costs, scalability, and reliability of services. Two common types of CSPs include a managed service provider and a managed security service provider.

A **managed service provider (MSP)** is a vendor that manages a customer's IT operations environment. A managed service provider takes care of the IT services and administration while enabling a company to focus on business. The primary responsibility of an MSP is to take care of the operations of the information systems and ensure that data and services remain available for the users. Managed service providers typically focus on systems administration. MSPs can be comprehensive or used for specific purposes such as backups, network monitoring, authentication, and performance.

A **managed security service provider (MSSP)** is a vendor that manages a customer's IT security environment. The MSSP is responsible for all aspects of IT security in terms of prevention, detection, and response to threats to the enterprise network, infrastructure, and applications. Commonly provided services include vulnerability scanning, managing firewalls and intrusion detection, endpoint protection, encryption, password management, and a host of other services that help protect an organization's security requirements. Many MSSP solutions offer 24-hour operations centers to ensure security solutions are continuously protecting the customer.

Although both types of vendors provide management services to an organization, they each perform unique functions. MSPs focus on typical IT *operations*, while MSSPs focus on *security* to keep an organization and its data safe.

Cloud Services

Cloud services are categorized as Infrastructure as a Service (IaaS), Software as a Service (SaaS), Platform as a Service (PaaS), and Anything as a Service (XaaS). There are also new and emerging services, such as Security as Service (SECaaS). These services deliver a variety of offerings including media streaming and online data storage.

Services integration is a system of cloud tools and technologies that connect systems, applications, data, and IT environments to provide real-time exchange of information. Deploying services integration allows data to be shared among services eliminating *data silos*, which isolate information to a specific service. Services integration allows improved communication, operational efficiency, and reduced operational costs.

Infrastructure as a Service (IaaS)

Infrastructure as a Service (IaaS) is a cloud-computing service in which a vendor provides the customer with virtualized infrastructure over the Internet. This is the most basic cloud service. IaaS infrastructure consists of servers, operating systems, storage, and other essential components outsourced to the IaaS provider. There are many advantages for IaaS, including

- load balancing;
- *scalability*, which is the ability of a program to cope with increased loads; and
- decreased hardware investment due to an organization renting equipment from the service provider.

Software as a Service (SaaS)

Software as a Service (SaaS) is a complete software distribution solution from the cloud that eliminates the need to install resources locally. SaaS is probably the most well known and visible of the cloud services to most end-users.

There are several advantages to using SaaS as an online-provided service. The vendor takes care of all services and eliminates the need for an organization or individual to

- install, configure, and maintain a local application;
- apply security patches to all installations of a given application;
- implement version upgrades; and
- provide *resilience*, which is the capacity to recover quickly from an undesirable situation, such as a system failure or natural disaster.

There are, however, disadvantages to using SaaS solutions. Disadvantages include

- the need to maintain an active and reliable Internet connection;
- dependence on the vendor to maintain the hardware and software; and
- compliance with vendor regulations or policies that govern data and physical storage locations.

It is important to keep in mind that even though an application is running from the cloud, all licensing rules for software usage still apply. Therefore, the vendor's End User License Agreement (EULA) must be reviewed to assure compliance to permitted usage.

Platform as a Service (PaaS)

Platform as a Service (PaaS) is a cloud service that allows a customer to develop, run, and manage their applications in the cloud. A business maintains control over its applications but does not have to manage or configure the infrastructure. Many companies turn to PaaS solutions to help implement their online presence as a cost-saving solution. PaaS applications are deployed as single units. By creating applications as single units, an organization is only charged when the application is called, rather than paying for an application to be readily available on demand.

Anything as a Service (XaaS)

Anything as a Service (XaaS) is a collective term that refers to the delivery of any service through the Internet. Cloud services initially focused on traditional services, such as SaaS and IaaS, but they have expanded to offer essentially any IT service through the cloud that has traditionally delivered through on-premises deployment. Cloud services are evolving, including Desktop as a Service (DaaS), Containers as a Service (CaaS), and Storage as a Service (STaaS).

Serverless Architecture

Serverless architecture is a cloud service that provides on-demand software and hosting on an as-used basis. It is also known as *serverless computing* or *function as a service (FaaS)*. These services offer the benefits of hosting applications without the need for server hardware and software. Serverless systems are similar to PaaS applications. However, where PaaS applications are deployed as single units, serverless architecture is an application built using individual, autonomous functions.

Security as a Service (SECaaS)

Security as a Service (SECaaS) is a business model that integrates security services into the infrastructure of an organization. A SECaaS vendor acts as a type of off-site gatekeeper for a network because it

- scans e-mail for viruses;
- hosts the network's firewall;
- looks for intruders and prevents their access to the network; and
- uses analytics to detect patterns of early warnings of potential threats.

Non-Cloud Services

On-premises computing provides IT services and processing of information at the company's location. Cloud computing provides the same services as on-premises computing via the Internet. While companies enjoy the advantages of the cloud, availability and latency can affect operations and performance.

There are non-cloud services that keep data close without reverting to a total on-premises approach. Edge computing and fog computing are two models that work within a local network to execute tasks typically processed in the cloud.

Edge computing is a model that collects information and processes it on devices that are close in proximity. The data remains on the device where it originated, which increases security. **Fog computing** is a decentralized model in which computing activities take place on devices that are not physically close but connected by a LAN. Fog computing is capable of processing more data than edge computing due to it having more resources through a LAN.

Both models use a local network to perform data analysis and intelligence instead of sending raw data to the cloud for processing. The key difference between these two options is where the actual processing occurs. Edge computing requests are processed on a device or sensor, and fog computing requests are processed in a fog node or IoT device, as illustrated in Figure 15-4.

Thin clients are computing devices that do not contain internal storage. They are often used as tools for protecting data and are good choices when combined with cloud computing. They connect to an enterprise network through network adapters

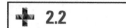

Figure 15-4 Edge computing is a model that collects information and processes it on devices that are close in proximity. Fog computing is a decentralized model in which computing activities take place on devices that are not physically close but connected by a LAN.

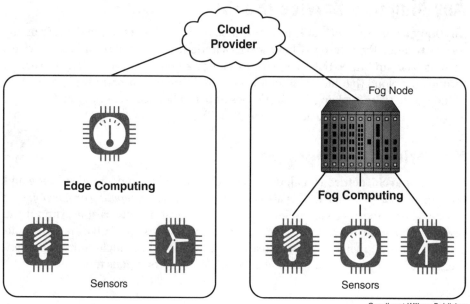

Goodheart-Willcox Publisher

and run a preconfigured interface that appears as a normal desktop operating system. Thin clients provide security as data is saved on a server rather than a local machine.

Cloud Access Security Broker (CASB)

2.1, 3.6

Organizations often add a **cloud access security broker (CASB)**, which is a set of services or software tools that enable an organization's enterprise security policies to extend to its data stored in the cloud. A CASB is located between the users and the cloud, as illustrated in Figure 15-5. It may be cloud-based or hosted at the customer's location. A CASB describes a set of security solutions organized around four main areas: visibility, compliance, data security, and threat protection.

- *Visibility* provides insight into how cloud services are used by enabling an individual to see which users are accessing data. A person can also view the type of device used to access the data as well as which apps users are running from the cloud and when they are run.
- *User compliance* with laws, such as HIPAA or SOX, is essential, as is compliance to internal policies. A CASB helps ensure a business is compliant with rules and regulations.
- *Data security* can be monitored and examined for proper use to help with data loss protection (DLP).
- *Threat protection* helps ensure an organization remains vigilant against threats. This includes both internal and external threats.

Cloud Security

Cloud security is the protection of data transmitted and stored in the cloud as well as methods used to protect against vulnerabilities and reduce attacks. Cloud security is a shared responsibility between a cloud vendor and its customers. The cloud vendor handles the security of the infrastructure, while the customer is responsible for the user layer. The user layer includes user behavior, apps, and data used on the cloud. Cloud security includes various methods, such as firewalls and segmentation.

Firewalls

A *firewall* is a network security tool that acts as a barrier or protection against unwanted data transfer at entry points by monitoring incoming and outgoing network traffic. When deployed in a cloud setting, firewalls provide protective defensive measures designed to stop or mitigate unauthorized access.

Cloud firewalls form virtual barriers around cloud platforms, applications, and cloud infrastructure. The same threats that can occur in on-premises equipment can also impact services located in the cloud. Installed firewalls base their decisions on Open Systems Interconnection (OSI) layers, such as block traffic by address (layers 2, 3), con-

3.6

> **TECH TIP**
>
> One of the most effective practices in securing your cloud is to incorporate multifactor authentication. This will ensure that only authorized personnel can log in to your cloud and access confidential data.

Figure 15-5 A CASB sits between the cloud and the users to provide secure connection and enforcement of polices.

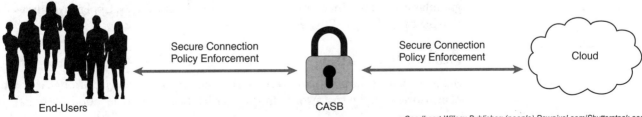

tent (layers 4–7), or deep packet inspection that can be provided by a next-generation firewall. Cloud-based networks can use firewalls as a barrier to monitor incoming and outgoing traffic at key devices. Working in the cloud, however, offers another solution called Firewall as a Service.

Firewall as a Service (FWaaS) is a method of delivering a firewall and other advanced security tools to the cloud environment. In this security method, the firewall appliance factor is eliminated by making security available everywhere throughout the cloud. This network security includes URL filtering, IPS, next-generation monitoring and more. FWaaS aggregates traffic from multiple sources, including on-site data centers, cloud infrastructure, mobile users, and branch offices. Security policies are applied and enforced across all locations and users. In addition, visibility and control of the networks is applied without deploying physical firewall appliances.

This type of security implementation can reduce costs and improve a business's total cost of ownership (TCO). Businesses do not have to invest in multiple security appliances, purchasing the physical technology and frequent upgrades of equipment, ensure adequate training, and maintain the systems and policies.

Next-Generation Secure Web Gateway (SWG)

3.6

A **next-generation secure web gateway (SWG)** is a cloud-based solution that can prevent malware, protect data, filter content, manage applications, and detect threats. They are similar to firewalls but next-gen SWGs provide advanced threat protection through such features as global threat intelligence, extended detection and response, advanced phishing protections, and remote browser isolation.

Security Groups

3.6

A **security group** is a virtual firewall solution that filters traffic entering and exiting a cloud environment. Security groups enable consistent configurations of security permissions for users, similar to an Active Directory. For example, as opposed to assigning user permissions individually, an administrator can establish security groups for each job function in an organization, assign rights and permissions at the group level, and add or remove users to their appropriate groups. This not only helps secure access to the cloud but also improves the efficiency of existing firewall configurations within cloud architecture.

Segmentation

3.6

Segmenting your network is a proven strategy that allows you to create different security policies or zones for your network needs. Confidential data can be segmented from public information through a unique set of policies and permissions. Lateral movement between the segmented networks can be controlled and monitored easier.

3.6

Within the cloud, internal segmented firewalls (ISFWs) and access control lists (ACLs) control user access. Typically, networks are segmented using layer-2 methods, such as VLANS, or layer-3 methods, such as IP addressing. However, it is important that firewalls have the capability of monitoring traffic on layers 4 through 7 of the OSI model as well. This is due to the ability of upper-layer firewalls to offer more granular control over network traffic than lower-layer devices. Upper-layer firewalls also have the ability to filter content.

Authentication

2.4

Authentication is the practice of verifying the identity of a valid user through a variety of measures including passwords and biometrics. Regardless of location, on-premises or cloud, a strong authentication process is vital for protecting the network and its data. Authentication is a vital security component to ensure that only authorized individuals are accessing network resources.

For on-premises models, authentication is handled by services. In Windows, this is a subsystem called Local Security Authority Subsystem (LSASS); in Linux, the equivalent program is called *lsassd*. Businesses using directory services, such as Microsoft's Active Directory, use Kerberos to perform the authentication process that allows network access. Kerberos also supports single sign-on, a popular authentication feature that reduces the need for multiple logins to access network resources. *Single sign-on (SSO)* is an authentication service that allows a user to use one login and password combination to access a set of services.

Authentication to a cloud environment is not as straightforward as in a physical network. One option for private cloud authentication is to take advantage of directory services or Kerberos. By taking advantage of these services, a private cloud essentially becomes an extension of the local, physical networking environment. If an external cloud is connected to a local network or private cloud using a Virtual Private Network (VPN), it is a representation of the local network and changes are not necessary.

High Availability across Zones

A critical need in the cloud environment is to provide functionality even if there is an outage. *Availability zones* are locations in a data center from which public cloud services operate. A *cloud region* is the actual geographic location where the cloud resources are located. Each region can contain more than one availability zone. Rather than selecting one zone for services, locating resources in different zones provides isolation from most types of physical infrastructure and software services failure. Therefore, it provides *high availability across zones*. By locating resources in multiple zones, you can provide a greater deal of redundancy since an outage in one location is unlikely to affect the other zone. To increase high availability, you can locate resources in different regions.

Cloud Native Controls vs. Third-Party Solutions

Cloud customers often wonder if they should utilize the tools created and provided by the host providing the cloud platform, or if they should seek out and invest in third-party offerings. While there is no one right answer, the best choice is to utilize the transition to cloud platforms as an opportunity to utilize tools on a needs-driven basis. This means adopting host-provided controls when needed but also seeking third-party options that best fit the requirements of the organization.

When comparing host-provided controls to those developed by a third party, verify that the third-party offerings are actually native to cloud-based usage. Some tools may be "cloud friendly" but not "cloud native." This means that while the tools will function in a cloud environment, they may not be able to function with application platform interfaces (APIs) used by cloud platforms.

The integration of applications and services from devices provides real-time information. APIs can present vulnerabilities that leave the systems and data vulnerable to attack including man-in-the-middle attacks, weak authentication, and lack of encryption. Incorporating API inspections will test the security of the API interactions in your cloud environment including testing authentication, user authorizations, and data flow between systems.

2.5

Cloud Security Controls

Cloud security controls are the processes that enable cloud architecture to protect against vulnerabilities and mitigate malicious attacks. It includes all the policies and guidelines that protect a cloud-computing environment.

Cloud governance is the policies and procedures used by an organization to manage its processes associated with the cloud. It assists an organization in protecting the security of cloud data and setting expectations for how the cloud is used. *Policies* are sets of rules that guide an organization in decision-making. *Procedures* are processes or step-by-step instructions needed to complete a task and the way in which the policies will be applied.

5.2

Frameworks provide guidance for cloud security for an organization. The *Cloud Security Alliance (CSA)* is a nonprofit organization that offers comprehensive frameworks for best practices in cloud security. One such framework is the CSA Cloud Control Matrix (CCM). The *CSA Cloud Control Matrix (CCM)* provides a series of controls designed to provide a fundamental security framework to cloud vendors and prospective cloud customers to assess the security risk of a cloud vendor. You can find controls on data center utilities, environmental conditions, physical controls, and how a cloud vendor handles human resources issues. The matrix is freely available for download. Each of the domains listed in the matrix is mapped to industry-accepted security standards, regulations, and other frameworks.

5.2

Another framework is the CSA Cloud Reference Architecture. The *CSA Cloud Reference Architecture* initiative enables security architects and organizations to leverage a common set of solutions to help manage their security needs between the company's IT department and the cloud provider. The architecture is a combination of a methodology and set of tools that allows security administrators to define protections that enable trust in the cloud.

A **reference architecture** is a document, or a set of documents, that provides recommendations of structures and integration of IT products and solutions. This document provides details about accepted best practices for specific technologies including cloud infrastructure. These documents are essential in providing companies guidelines to help develop appropriate solutions to improve efficiency, operations, and security.

3.6

Integration and Auditing

Integration into the cloud is a must for modern day business. However, moving data to the cloud necessitates an integration process to migrate data from on-site servers to the cloud. Integration tools can assist in the migration process as well as protect data. Cloud integration and cloud security complement each other.

A **cloud audit** is an independent examination of cloud service controls in terms of items such as privacy impact and performance. An audit helps an organization identify risks so changes can be implemented to protect against them.

3.6

Cloud computing provides resources on demand. To ensure the availability of resources, *dynamic resource utilization* is used to balance processing loads and ensure systems are not overwhelmed by low-priority requests. Virtual machines can be configured to allocate resources dynamically based on characteristics of a job or a user.

2.2, 3.6

Resource Policies

Managing a cloud environment can be a challenging practice, especially when it comes to protecting access to data and services to provide a high degree of security. Resource policies can help with this management process. **Resource policies** specify permissions for who can access and act on resources. They are often attached to a resource. *Resources* are items such as networks, applications, storage, services, and servers used for everyday activity.

Secrets Management

It is not enough to strengthen and limit access to the cloud. Data within the cloud must also be secured. In terms of cloud computing, a *secret* is an object that stores sensitive data. Examples of secrets include artifacts such as private encryption keys, credentials, privileged accounts, SSH keys, and other sensitive data. **Secrets management** is the practice of using specific tools, policies, and procedures for ensuring the confidentiality and availability of information through digital authentication. Secrets management can incorporate dedicated tools such as Secret Manager from Google cloud, use of the principle of least privilege, policies governing passwords and coding, and auditing. Challenges to managing these secrets include hard-coded credentials, lack of monitoring and control, and decentralized management in which multiple users and departments maintain their own sets of secrets.

Virtualization

Virtualization is a means of managing or presenting computer resources virtually as opposed to physically, allowing multiple customers to share applications. Cloud computing offers users multiple virtualization options by which software applications or entire computer systems are housed remotely. Networking in the cloud involves the use of virtual networks and virtual machines.

Virtual Network

3.6

A *virtual network* is one that connects virtual machines or devices to other machines or devices. A *virtual private cloud (VPC) endpoint* is a cloud configuration that enables users to connect to a VPC through secure channels. Endpoint policies can be configured to control access to resources in other cloud services.

The transfer of information along these networks, including to and from clients, must be secured against all threats, including eavesdropping, routing problems, and misconfigurations.

One way to provide security is to use public and private subnets. For example, you would create a network for a public-facing server, such as a web server. The back-end servers can be protected by using a private network that cannot communicate directly with the Internet, but instead must be routed through a network address translation (NAT) gateway.

3.6

Network IP addresses can be public or private. A *public IP address* is one that is provided by an Internet service provider (ISP) and identifies a device connected to the Internet. A *private IP address* is one that is used to assign devices within a local network. The distinction between public and private IP addresses is a common cybersecurity solution for cloud-based environments.

Most companies incorporate private IP addresses for use within the organization. However, in order to send packets across a public network, such as the Internet, a public address is needed. This means a public address is needed to access any information stored in a cloud environment. Additionally, public-facing servers, such as web servers, need to be located on a public network with a public address. A device with a private IP address can obtain a public address through NAT, which maintains tables of private IP addresses that are mapped dynamically to public addresses.

Servers located in cloud locations can also use private IP addresses to create private virtual subnets. Devices in the private virtual subnet can only access the Internet by using a NAT gateway that is located in a public subnet. As with a local private network, special attention needs to be addressed to the security of the private subnets to prevent unwanted traffic and access to the resources located in the private network.

Virtual Machines

In order to provide a virtualized environment, two operating systems are installed on a device: a host operating system and a guest operating system. A **host operating system**, or *host OS*, is software installed on a device that interacts with that device's hardware. There can only be one host OS installed on a device. This is due to the host OS being the underlying operating system that enables the computer to function. For example, if Windows 10 is installed on your computer, then Windows 10 is your host OS. Host operating systems are loaded first; otherwise, a computer will not boot.

A **guest operating system**, or *guest OS*, is software installed and running on a virtual system. The difference between guest and host operating systems is that a user can install and run multiple guest operating systems, but there can only be one host operating system. Most times, a guest OS is a different operating system than the host OS. A guest OS is typically used to run applications that are not compatible with the host OS, test functionality of applications in an isolated environment, or run multiple applications that may require different operating systems but the same hardware. Both host and guest operating systems are managed by a hypervisor.

A **hypervisor** is a software program that monitors and manages virtual operating systems. There are two types of hypervisors. A *type I hypervisor*, often referred to as a *native hypervisor*, is one that runs on computer hardware instead of an operating system. This type of installation is called a *bare metal hypervisor*. *Type II hypervisors* are those that run on the host operating systems, similar to a typical application, as illustrated in Figure 15-6.

Containers

A hypervisor is used to leverage virtualized physical hardware. Another option for leveraging virtualized hardware includes using a container. A **container**, also called an *application cell*, is executable software that contains applications and utilizes the host OS. Since it uses the host OS, a container does not need a guest OS. A container has dependencies and application code packaged in a way to enable it to execute quickly and reliably from the cloud, as illustrated in Figure 15-7.

Container security is processes, policies, and procedures implemented to ensure containers run as designed. Customers should be aware of cloud application security when using containers. **Cloud application security** is the policies and procedures that govern information exchanges that occur in cloud environments, such as Microsoft Office 365.

VM Sprawl Avoidance

Virtual machine sprawl is a significant concern in a virtual environment. **Virtual machine (VM) sprawl** occurs when deployment of virtual machines is abundant and improperly managed. In a virtual environment, it is possible for administrators to forget about VMs no longer needed. This can drain system resources or present an unattended attack vector. There are several methods for avoiding or preventing VM sprawl.

- VM creation should be limited, and policies should be established that require a sufficient need for a virtual machine. Additionally, when VMs are created, they should be done so consistently and with best practices in mind.

Hypervisor or Virtual Machine Monitor (VMM)

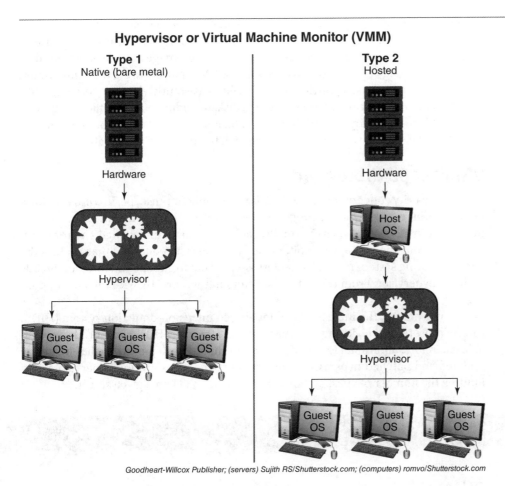

Type 1
Native (bare metal)

Type 2
Hosted

Goodheart-Willcox Publisher; (servers) Sujith RS/Shutterstock.com; (computers) romvo/Shutterstock.com

Figure 15-6 A type I hypervisor is one that runs on computer hardware instead of an operating system. Type II hypervisors are those that run on the host operating systems.

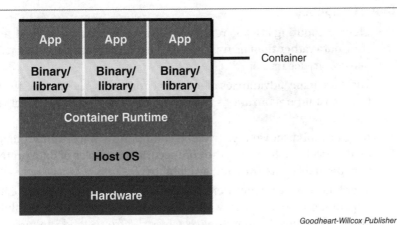

Goodheart-Willcox Publisher

Figure 15-7 A container has dependencies and application code packaged in a way to enable it to execute quickly and reliably from the cloud.

- Automated reporting should be implemented that continuously monitors resource usage and VM capacity and reports to administrators when thresholds are met. Through automated reporting, IT administrators can help curb VM sprawl before it gets too far out of hand.

- Monitor VM life cycles or establish time-based policies to eliminate VMs after they are no longer needed. Many VMs are only required for a brief time in order to test functionality. Once testing is completed, the VM should be removed in order to free up resources.

- Establishing a library or archive of VMs enables user to create secure VMs based on need. For example, an IT department is able to identify the purpose of a VM, and if a library exists containing a master image of a previously used VM, that image can be used to create a new VM while ensuring that limitations, including time-based policies, are enforced consistently. A *master image* is a file that contains a virtual copy of a storage disk, including bootable files. Images are able to be deployed much faster than hands-on configuration because an image does not have to be built from scratch but based off a template.

VM Escape Protection

2.2

Another security concern unique to VMs is virtual machine escape. **Virtual machine (VM) escape** occurs when a program breaks out of the virtual environment and interacts directly with a host. Normally, each VM runs in an isolated environment. In a virtual machine escape exploit, malicious code is run on a VM that enables the guest operating system to break out of its isolated environment and interact directly with the hypervisor. From there, the user can interact directly with the host operating system.

In many cases, the inclusion of a host-based intrusion-detection system (HIDS) can help protect a device against VM escape. However, HIDS are not always reliable. Therefore, additional layers of protection should be deployed, such as regularly updated and patched hypervisors, inclusion of sandboxes around hypervisors, and limiting the number of guest systems able to be installed on a given server.

SUMMARY

Cloud Computing

- Cloud computing is using remote servers on the Internet to host, access, and store data rather than using a personal computer or local server using a pay-per-use service model.

- There are many advantages of cloud over on-premises models. These include lower cost for organizations, faster speed and accessibility, and cloud backup and recovery.

- A significant disadvantage to cloud computing is uncertainty. Cloud concerns relate directly to honoring the core security principles of data protection: confidentiality, integrity, and availability.

- The cloud-based and on-premises models share similar vulnerabilities, such as poor authentication. However, there are unique cloud vulnerabilities and attacks that must be monitored, such as risk from cloud vendors.

Cloud Infrastructure

- Cloud infrastructure consists of computing hardware, software, and other components necessary to provide the required infrastructure for delivering business operations from a remote location.

- Elements included in the cloud infrastructure are physical servers, storage platforms, networking equipment, and applications to run the operations.

Cloud Models

- A cloud model is the way in which cloud infrastructure is provisioned for use. There are five common models.
- A private cloud is a cloud-computing resource owned and managed by a single private organization. This model provides the most security and control.
- A public cloud is a cloud-computing resource that provides services to anyone. Examples include Google Drive or Carbonite backup.
- A community cloud is a cloud-computing resource shared by everyone in an affiliated organization and is not available to anyone outside of the organization.
- A hybrid cloud is a cloud model that combines public, private, or community clouds. Hybrid deployments are often unique to their purpose or the organization using them.
- A personal cloud is a cloud-computing resource that allows a user to manage their own cloud service to store files or offer services within a household. It is often referred to as a home cloud and is a popular option for many consumers.

Cloud Service Providers (CSPs)

- A cloud service provider (CSP) is a vendor that provides IT services over the Internet. Vendors can provide specific services as well as offer a full range of generalized services such as storage, business applications, or infrastructure.
- Cloud vendors remove the responsibility of creating and maintaining infrastructure for deployment of IT services from a business and provide these services for a fee.
- Two types of CSPs include managed service provider (MSP) and managed security service provider (MSSP). Although they both provide management services to an organization, they each perform unique functions. MSPs focus on typical IT operations, while MSSPs focus on security to keep an organization and its data safe.

Cloud Services

- Cloud services deliver a variety of offerings including media streaming and online data storage.
- Cloud services are categorized as Infrastructure as a Service (IaaS), Software as a Service (SaaS), Platform as a Service (PaaS), and Anything as a Service (XaaS).
- There are also new and emerging services, such as Security as Service (SECaaS). Additional services include serverless architecture and non-cloud services.

Cloud Access Security Broker (CASB)

- Organizations often add a cloud access security broker (CASB), which is a set of services or software tools that enable an organization's enterprise security policies to extend to its data stored in the cloud. It is located between the users and the cloud.
- A CASB describes a set of security solutions organized around four main areas: visibility, compliance, data security, and threat protection.

Cloud Security

- Cloud security is the protection of data transmitted and stored in the cloud as well as methods used to protect against vulnerabilities and reduce attacks.

- Cloud security includes various methods. These include firewalls, next-generation secure web gateway (SWG), security groups, segmentation, authentication, high availability across zones, and deciding between cloud native controls vs. third-party solutions.

Cloud Security Controls

- Cloud security control is the process that enables cloud architecture to protect against vulnerabilities and mitigate malicious attacks. It includes all the policies and guidelines that protect a cloud-computing environment.
- Cloud governance is the policies and procedures used by an organization to manage its processes associated with the cloud. It assists an organization in protecting the security of cloud data and setting expectations for how the cloud is used.
- Cloud security controls include conducting cloud integration and auditing, establishing resource policies, and utilizing secrets management.

Virtualization

- Virtualization is a means of managing or presenting computer resources virtually as opposed to physically, allowing multiple customers to share applications.
- Cloud computing offers users multiple virtualization options by which software applications or entire computer systems are housed remotely. Networking in the cloud involves the use of virtual networks and virtual machines.

REVIEW QUESTIONS

1. State advantages and disadvantages of cloud computing.
2. Identify elements included in the cloud infrastructure.
3. Briefly explain the four policies used to protect storage security.
4. Differentiate between software-defined networking (SDN) and software-defined visibility (SDV).
5. Explain five common cloud models.
6. Summarize cloud service providers.
7. Identify types of cloud services models.
8. List the advantages of an Infrastructure as a Service (IaaS).
9. State the advantages and disadvantages of Software as a Service (SaaS) model.
10. Briefly explain a serverless architecture.
11. Explain edge and fog computing.
12. Summarize cloud access security.
13. Identify and explain three methods used for cloud security.
14. What is the Firewall as a Service (FWaaS) method?
15. Define a *cloud region*.
16. Identify and explain types of cloud security controls.
17. What is cloud governance?
18. Summarize virtualization.
19. List several methods used to avoid or prevent virtual machine (VM) sprawl.
20. Explain virtual machine (VM) escape.

SAMPLE SECURITY+ EXAM QUESTIONS

1. Woodland Electric is a regional electricity supplier serving a 200-square-mile area. A great many of the service technicians need access to data on a regular basis. Security of the information is important. What should Woodland Electric incorporate?

    A. A multitenant solution

    B. A private cloud

    C. XaaS

    D. SaaS

2. Barbara's Bookstore has many locations in the San Francisco area. Barbara decides on a public cloud for her data storage. Which of the following is *not* a benefit of using this solution?

    A. As Barbara's business grows, the cloud is easier to scale.

    B. The owner of the bookstore is not responsible for hardware and maintenance.

    C. Barbara can customize this environment to meet her needs.

    D. Skilled professionals will manage the system.

3. What do mobile app developers use to allow them to focus completely on the product, not the development environment?

    A. Community cloud

    B. Load balancing

    C. Sandbox

    D. PaaS solution

4. Which of the following statements relates to secrets management?

    A. Storage of SSH keys

    B. Auditing of confidential information

    C. Instance awareness

    D. Securing the VPC endpoint

5. A stand-alone package of software and embedded operating system that runs in the cloud is known as a(n)_____.

    A. bare mental hypervisor

    B. isolated VM

    C. emulated VM

    D. container

6. Which cloud solution processes data on the device where it was collected?

    A. A transit gateway

    B. Thin client

    C. Fog computing

    D. Edge computing

7. A company that wants to allow the cloud vendor to manage their entire cloud infrastructure would implement which of the following strategies?

   A. Managed services

   B. XaaS

   C. VPC

   D. Serverless architecture

8. A company wants to ensure data is available regardless of a potential disruption or outage. Which security measure will provide this objective?

   A. Resource policies

   B. VM segmentation

   C. High availability across zones

   D. Next-generation SWG

9. Which is *not* a feature provided by CASB?

   A. Ensures a business meets the requirements of governmental mandates such as HIPAA

   B. Provides data sovereignty

   C. Ensures only authorized users access data

   D. Integrates security with existing security solutions

10. Managing the deployed VMs and those that are no longer used helps with which security concern?

    A. VM Escape Protection

    B. VM Sprawl

    C. Application cells

    D. Hypervisor malware

LAB EXERCISES

Lab Activity 15-1: Installing VirtualBox

It is important to get an understanding of how to install and configure virtual machines. In this exercise, you will create the shell for an operating system in a VM. However, at this time, you will not install a guest operating system. You must have the permissions needed to install software to complete this exercise.

1. Launch a web browser, and navigate to the VirtualBox website (www.virtualbox.org).

2. Navigate to the downloads page, and download the latest version of VirtualBox for your host platform. For example, if your host computer is running a Windows operating system, download the version for Windows hosts.

3. Once the installer is downloaded, install the VirtualBox software on your host machine. Use the default settings for the installation.

4. Launch VirtualBox.

5. On the opening screen, click the **New** button on the toolbar to begin. A wizard will guide you through the steps of creating a virtual machine.

6. On the first page of the wizard, click in the **Name:** text box, and enter My Test OS, as shown. This will be the name of the virtual machine. Click the **Next** button.

7. The next page of the wizard asks you to set the amount of memory for the virtual machine. Click the **Next** button to accept the default setting.

8. The next page of the wizard asks if you wish to create a virtual hard disk for the VM. Click the **Create a virtual hard disk now** radio button, and then click the **Create** button.

9. You must now set up the virtual hard disk. On the next page of the wizard, click the **VDI (VirtualBox Disk Image)** radio button. Then, click the **Next** button.

10. On the remaining pages of the wizard, accept the default settings. When the wizard is finished, the main VirtualBox screen appears, and your VM is listed on the left, as shown.

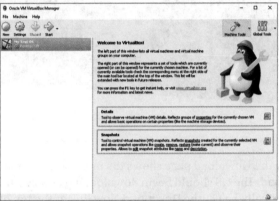

Goodheart-Willcox Publisher

11. With your VM selected in the list, click the **Settings** button on the toolbar. The **Settings** dialog box is displayed for your VM.

12. Click **General** on the left of the dialog box, and click the **Advanced** tab on the right. Notice the path to the VM is listed. You can also change settings such as sharing the clipboard and dragging and dropping between the host operating system and the VM.

13. Click **User Interface** on the left, and then the drop-down arrow next to the **Machine** button. The option for a snapshot is located here.

14. Click **Storage** on the left, and then click disk image branch under **Storage Devices**. This branch has an icon that looks like a CD/DVD. The name of this branch should be Empty because you have not yet loaded an operating system.

15. In this exercise, you will not be loading an operating system. If you were, the next step would be click the CD/DVD icon to the right of the **Optical Drive:** drop-down list, click **Virtual Optical Disk File…** in the drop-down menu, browse to the location of the ISO installation disk, and open the disk image. To load the operating system from a DVD, click **Host Drive** in the drop-down menu instead of the **Virtual Optical Disk File…** option.

15. Click the **Cancel** button to exit the **Settings** dialog box without making any changes. Then, close VirtualBox.

Lab Activity 15-2: Installing Ubuntu on VirtualBox

Virtual machines make up the computing environment within cloud computing. Often, administrators test new operating systems in virtual settings to see how their software interacts with the OS. In this lab, you will go through the process of installing Ubuntu, a Linux-based OS, on the VirtualBox software installed in the previous lab.

1. Open a web browser and navigate to the Ubuntu website (www.ubuntu.com). Select **Download>Ubuntu Desktop**.

2. Confirm that the Download page shows the most recent version of Ubuntu, and click **Download**. The OS should begin downloading as a **.iso** file; if it does not start automatically, select the **Download Now** link at the top of the page.

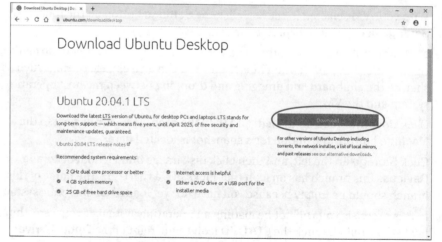

3. After Ubuntu has downloaded, open **VirtualBox** and select the **New** button. This should open the Create Virtual Machine dialog box.

4. In the Create Virtual Machine dialog box, name the OS Ubuntu Desktop, and select **Linux** from the **Type:** drop-down menu. Next, select **Ubuntu_64** from the **Version:** drop-down menu (Ubuntu_64 refers the 64-bit version of Ubuntu). Click **Next**.

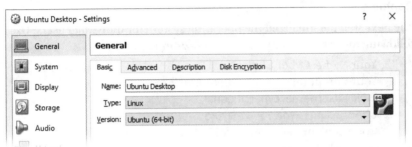

5. VirtualBox will prompt you to choose an amount of RAM to use with the virtual installation. Use the default recommendation for RAM and select **Next**.

6. You will now be prompted to create the VM hard drive. Ensure that the radio button next to **Create a virtual hard disk now** is selected, and click **Next**.

7. Designate an appropriate amount of space to use for the virtual hard disk (consult your instructor for specifics), and click **Create**.

8. Ensure that your Ubuntu file has finished downloading. If it has, you can proceed to Step 9; otherwise wait for the download to complete before moving forward.

9. You should see an Ubuntu OS in the left side of the VirtualBox Manager screen. Double-click it.

10. A pop-up menu will appear prompting you to select a start-up disk. Click the folder icon to browse the computer for the Ubuntu **.iso** file you downloaded previously. Locate and select the **.iso** file and click **Open**. The Ubuntu ISO file will now open in VirtualBox.

11. If the Ubuntu ISO file appears in the Select start-up disk menu, select **Start**. Otherwise, repeat Step 10.

12. Once the Ubuntu OS loads, select **Install Ubuntu**. The first window of the installation wizard will show selections for updated and third-party software for utilities. Ensure both checkboxes are selected, which will ensure Ubuntu has everything it needs to install and run, and click **Continue**.

13. Next, you should see the Installation type screen. Select the box labeled **Erase disk and install Ubuntu**. Since this is a blank virtual machine, nothing on your computer will be deleted. Remember, the point of VirtualBox, as well as other VM software, is to serve as a sandbox in which operating systems and applications can be tested. Click **Install Now**.

14. When prompted, click **Continue**. This ensures you understand that the virtual drive will be erased and the Ubuntu installation will proceed.

15. The wizard will prompt you to select a time zone that correlates to your present location. Select your time zone and click **Continue**.

16. You will not be able to use your standard keyboard until Ubuntu has finished installing. Therefore, you will need to enable the on-screen keyboard by clicking the person-shaped icon in the upper-right of the window. Then select **Screen Keyboard**. Be sure to choose the appropriate language before selecting **Continue**.

17. The next step personalized the operating system for individual users. Use the following information for your personalization options:

> Your Name: Cyber Student
> Your Computer's Name: cyber-VirtualBox
> Pick a username: cyberstudent
> Choose a password: P@$$w0rd
> Confirm your password: P@$$w0rd

18. Retain the default selection to require a password to log in and click **Continue**.

19. Over the next few minutes, as Ubuntu installs, tips and tricks will appear during the installation for your review. When installation is complete, a window appears alerting you that installation is complete and you need to restart your computer in order to use the new installation. Click **Restart Now**. This will only restart your virtual machine, not your entire computer. During restart, you may be prompted to remove the installation media; in this case, continue with the restart process as normal. When it restarts, log in with the user and password you created in Step 17.

Lab Activity 15-3: Creating Snapshots in Ubuntu

In this lab, you will create a snapshot using the Ubuntu installation you completed in the previous lab activity. A snapshot creates a saved version of the operating system and all current settings. You can revert back to snapshots at any time.

1. Log in to Ubuntu using the credentials you made in Step 17 of the previous lab. Once you have logged in and gained familiarity with Ubuntu, create a snapshot by selecting **Machine>Take Snapshot**. On the subsequent window, name the snapshot Original Settings. For the description, enter Default configuration after installation. Take a screenshot of your settings. Click **OK** to create the snapshot.

2. Change the background of your desktop by right-clicking the desktop and selecting **Change Background** from the shortcut menu. Select any picture different from your current background and click **Select**.

3. Click **Devices>Change Clipboard to Bidirectional**. Do the same for **Devices>Drag and Drop**. This will enable you to drag files between your host machine and VirtualBox.

4. You will not restore your virtual machine using the snapshot you created in Step 1. In order to do this, verify that the virtual machine is in a saved store or powered off. To do this, select **Machine>ACPI Shutdown**.

5. With the VM powered off, click **Machine Tools**>**Snapshots**, as shown.

6. A list of snapshots created in the VM will display. You should see one titled Original Settings. The current state of the VM indicates that changes have been made since that snapshot was created. Generate a screenshot of this window.

7. Select the **Original Settings** snapshot, and then click **Restore** on the toolbar. You will be prompted with a warning that includes an option to create a snapshot of the current state. Deselect the **Create a snapshot of the current machine state** option and click **Restore**.

8. The current state option changes after you restore the VM. Click the **Start** button on the main window in VirtualBox to launch Ubuntu. What happened to the changes you made prior to shutting down the VM?

9. Other than creating a snapshot after you first install Ubuntu, what are other examples of when you might want to ensure a snapshot is made? Provide two examples.

10. Power off your VM and close VirtualBox.

Lab Activity 15-4: Google SaaS Offerings

Most people are familiar with Gmail, Google's e-mail service. Google Docs is another popular Google app due to its being a free equivalent of Microsoft Word. However, Google has a number of SaaS offerings available with which most people are unfamiliar.

1. Launch a web browser and navigate to the Google home page (www.google.com).

2. Click the **Google apps** button located next to the **Sign in** button. A drop-down menu appears containing popular applications.

3. Click **More** at the bottom of the menu to expand it and show more apps.

4. Click **Finance** in the expanded menu. The finance page offers an overview of markets, currencies, and top stories affecting the markets and finance.

5. Select **Google apps**>**More**>**Even More**. A page is displayed that shows a complete set of Google services.

6. Scroll down on the page until you see the complete list of icons representing all the Google services. Select **Cardboard**. Summarize the purpose of Google's Cardboard service.

7. On the Google Cardboard page, open the menu and select **TiltBrush**. Watch the introductory video and provide your thoughts on the service.

8. Return to the page showing the expanded services from Google. Explore additional SaaS offerings. What else is of interest to you?

Lab Activity 15-5: IaaS Vendors

There are many websites that compare cloud vendors. As you look through these sites, take note of each vendor's strengths, costs, and potential disadvantages.

1. Open a web browser and conduct a search using the phrase cloud wars bob evans. Bob Evans has created a weekly Cloud Wars ranking. Evaluate the search results for a reputable source, and read one of his Cloud Wars articles. Which vendors are within the top ten?

2. Rackspace is an IaaS provider that sells multicloud solutions. Navigate to the Rackspace website (www.rackspace.com). Locate and select the **About** link. Read about some of the strengths and features of Rackspace, its employees, and its product offerings. Take particular note about the certifications possessed by Rackspace staff.

3. Navigate to the Google Compute Engine website (cloud.google.com/compute/). Search the site for pricing information. How does Google price this particular cloud product? What services are available in the free plan?

Lab Activity 15-6: Private Cloud

Personal clouds allow you to store files, including photos, videos, and music. You can then access these files from any Internet connection. There are many options for creating a personal cloud.

1. Launch a web browser, and navigate to the Amazon website (www.amazon.com).

2. Search for seagate personal cloud. What are some of the storage sizes available? Select one of these products, and review the product details. What are some of the other options or features of this product?

3. Navigate to a search engine, and enter the search phrase western digital my cloud home. Select a review of this product, and read the details. How does it compare in features and price to the Seagate product?

4. You do not need to buy specialized hardware to create a personal cloud. Navigate to the Tonido Server website (www.tonido.com). What platforms can be used to access this software?

5. Navigate to the FuguHub website (fuguhub.com). What are some of the unique features of this product? Compare this product to the Tonido product.

6. Using a search engine, look for other products or solutions for personal clouds. Summarize your findings, and offer a recommendation with justification for your choice.

Lab Activity 15-7: Cloud Vendor Terms of Service

All cloud vendors should have a terms of service agreement and most will also have an acceptable use policy. Dropbox is a popular provider of data storage. It has both a ToS and an AUP.

1. Launch a web browser, and navigate to the Dropbox website (www.dropbox.com).

2. Scroll to the bottom of the page, and click the **Privacy & Terms** link under the Support menu.

3. On the next page, click the **Terms of Service** tab to display the ToS. Notice there is also a tab for the acceptable use policy.

4. Read the ToS. For what reason would Dropbox view your content?

5. If you want to sue Dropbox over a ToS issue, and you live in Austin, TX, where will the case be heard?

6. Can you belong to a class-action lawsuit against Dropbox? A class-action lawsuit involves many users suing over the same claim.

7. Click the **Privacy Policy** tab at the top of the page and read the policy. Dropbox states it uses cookies and pixel tags. Click the **cookies and pixel tags** link within the document to learn how a pixel tag is used.

8. Scroll down in the privacy policy to locate the **Transparency Report** link, and click it. How does Dropbox respond to requests from law enforcement and governmental agencies?

9. Dropbox may store your data on servers located in foreign countries. Select the privacy policy tab and scroll down in the privacy policy to locate the link to www.privacyshield.gov and click it. What is the Privacy Shield? Have you ever considered that your data may be stored in foreign locations? Does this concern you? Summarize your findings.

Lab Activity 15-8: SECaaS Solutions

SECaaS has become a good option for companies and organizations who do not have in-house security experts. There are many solutions for SECaaS.

1. Launch a web browser, and navigate to the FireEye website (www.fireeye.com). Review the features and pricing for this SECaaS.

2. Navigate to the Sonicwall website (www.sonicwall.com). Review the features and pricing for this SECaaS.

3. Navigate to the Alert Logic website (www.alertlogic.com). Review the features and pricing for this SECaaS.

4. Navigate to the Qualys website (www.qualys.com). Review the features and pricing for this SECaaS.

5. Create a table to compare and contrast these four SECaaS. Which ones are specialized? Which ones are more generalized? What features does each offer? What pricing models are used?

6. Summarize your findings in a report.

CASE STUDY

Role of Cloud Computing and Pandemics

In early 2020, the COVID-19 pandemic caused a dramatic shift in US employment that resulted in many businesses establishing policies for employees to work remotely. One of the most heavily impacted areas was the use of Cloud computing. Conduct research on the impacts, both positive and negative, that COVID-19 had on cloud computing during the peak of its presence in the United States. Answer the following questions.

1. What are some of the long-term impacts COVID-19 will have on cloud services?

2. What are some of the long-term impacts COVID-19 will have on IT and cybersecurity in general?

3. Prepare a two-page report on this topic using research formatting required by your institution.

Governance, Risk, and Compliance

LEARNING OUTCOMES

- Discuss governance and its role in organizational security.
- Identify assets at risk for an organization.
- Summarize risk management.
- Discuss the role of risk analysis.
- Summarize four generally accepted responses to risk.
- Discuss data governance and its role in asset security.
- Identify personnel policies implemented by organizations to decrease risks.
- Recognize types of employee user training methods used by organizations.
- Summarize third-party risk management (TPRM).

KEY TERMS

acceptable use policy (AUP)
annualized loss expectancy (ALE)
annualized rate of occurrence (ARO)
asset
asset life cycle
asset management
background check
change control
change management
clean-desk policy
critical asset
data anonymization
data clearance
data compliance
data governance
data life cycle
data masking
data minimization
data owner
data retention policy
employment contract
environmental disaster

executive user
governance
heat map
information rights management (IRM)
inherent risk
intellectual property (IP)
IT asset management (ITAM)
job rotation
managerial control
mandatory vacation
man-made disaster
operational control
personally identifiable information (PII)
policy violation
privileged user
pseudoanonymization
qualitative assessment
quantitative assessment
residual risk
risk acceptance
risk analysis

risk assessment
risk avoidance
risk awareness
risk control self-assessment
risk impact
risk mitigation
risk posture
risk register
risk transfer
role-based awareness training
sender policy framework (SPF)
separation of duties
single loss expectancy (SLE)
social media analysis
supply chain attack
system administrator
system owner
third-party risk management (TPRM)
threat assessment
user
vulnerability assessment

SECURITY+ CERTIFICATION EXAM OBJECTIVES

The following Security+ Certification Exam Objectives are covered in this chapter.

+ 1.2: Supply-chain attacks
+ 2.1: Data sovereignty
+ 2.1: Tokenization
+ 2.1: Rights management
+ 4.1: Data sanitization
+ 4.2: Retention policies
+ 5.1: Compare and contrast various types of controls.
+ 5.3: Acceptable use policy
+ 5.3: Job rotation
+ 5.3: Mandatory vacation

+ 5.3: Separation of duties
+ 5.3: Clean desk space
+ 5.3: Background checks
+ 5.3: Nondisclosure agreement (NDA)
+ 5.3: Social media analysis
+ 5.3: Onboarding
+ 5.3: Offboarding
+ 5.3: User training
+ 5.3: Diversity of training techniques
+ 5.3: Third-party risk management

+ 5.3: Data
+ 5.3: Credential policies
+ 5.3: Organizational policies
+ 5.4: Multiparty
+ 5.4: IP theft
+ 5.4: Risk types
+ 5.4: Risk management strategies
+ 5.4: Risk analysis
+ 5.4: Disasters
+ 5.5: Explain privacy and sensitive data concepts in relation to security.

OVERVIEW

The function of cybersecurity and the security of enterprise environments is to ensure the data stored within those environments is protected. As organizations become more reliant on digitization of data, the need to protect information increases exponentially, particularly for personal or sensitive data. Organizations must have plans or policies enacted that secure not only information that is stored but also information that is being deleted or otherwise removed from a system. However, in any business or organization, risk is a natural consequence of the actions and decisions taken by a business and its employees. The potential for risk occurs on many levels, and managing, assessing, responding to, and even predicting risk are essential functions for any business. While frameworks can help develop guidelines in these areas, decisions on handling potential threats and liabilities must ultimately be made within an individual organization.

In this chapter, you will learn about data governance, as well as policies, management strategies, and training methods for ensuring compliance with regulations and laws protecting data and its dissemination. In addition, you will be introduced to many important topics associated with risk, including types; causes and likelihood; managing, assessing, responding to, and predicting the possibility of events and threats; and best practices.

SECURITY+ NOTE

Cybersecurity focuses on protecting data in all forms and locations. Expect to see scenarios and examples that test your understanding of data roles in an organization, along with policies and technical tasks that protect data. This understanding extends to how data is viewed, accessed, and stored outside the organization. Additionally, the CompTIA Security+ Certification Exam places significant emphasis on a candidate's knowledge of risk assessment and avoidance. Be prepared to encounter scenarios in which companies use specific software or tools to evaluate the types of risk faced.

Governance

Governance is the process of operating an organization. *Governance, Risk, and Compliance (GRC)* provides guidance for an organization to be strategic, manage risks, measure performance, and be compliant with business and government regulations.

It is how an organization is operated and controlled through documented policies and procedures applied in the operation of business to establish organizational security. *Organizational security* includes safeguards used to protect an organization. It focuses on people, policies, and procedures. *People* are the employees of the business. *Policies* are sets of rules that guide an organization in decision-making. *Procedures* are the processes, or step-by-step instructions, needed to complete a task and the way in which the policies will be applied.

Strategies

Governance guides an organization to be strategic through appropriate controls. Controls are written and implemented by managers to protect the organization and can be used to mitigate risks. *Security controls* are safeguards to minimize risks to assets of an organization. Security controls typically fall in one of three categories.

 5.1

- **Managerial controls** are security controls that use management or administrative processes to implement and measure performance as well as intervene and take corrective actions when needed. This represents the guidance, rules, and procedures for implementing controls within the enterprise.
- **Operational controls** are security controls implemented by people who carry out day-to-day operations of a business. It includes personnel security, physical security, and protection of data inputs and outputs. Controls in this category include training awareness and hardware and software system maintenance.
- *Technical controls* are security controls that use technology to automate device management for access and application of confidential data. Controls in this category include cryptography, authentication, authorization, and accountability.

 5.1

Control Types

Organizations can be proactive by applying different types of internal controls to protect a business. Internal controls are intended to protect organizational assets.

- *Deterrent controls* are those that attempt to dissuade attacks or violations from occurring. Examples of deterrent controls include laws and organizational policies.
- *Preventive controls* are those that attempt to avoid or prevent an incident from occurring. A firewall is an example of a control that prevents IT incidents.
- *Detective controls* are controls that identify existing problems with company processes. Examples of controls designed to detect problems include quality control and loss prevention.
- *Corrective controls* are controls that work to lessen or repair damage or restore resources after an undesired activity or event. Examples of corrective controls include virus quarantining, process termination, and system reboots.
- *Compensating controls* are those that provide alternative or contingency controls in the event a typical control is ineffective or unavailable. A compensating control is an action implemented to act as a backup control. For example, e-mail encryption is a compensating control for weak or ineffective data encryption because it ensures that an e-mail message is encrypted even if an attachment is not encrypted.
- *Physical controls*, or *physical security controls*, are tangible controls used to protect the physical assets of an organization. Physical controls include locks, mantraps, and surveillance cameras.

Credential Policies

Credential policies control the authentication process for an organization. Without these policies, unauthorized persons put the security of an organization at risk. Credential policies are necessary for the following.

- *Personnel.* Personnel are the individuals employed by an organization.
- *Third parties.* A third party includes outside businesses with which a company works. Third parties include vendors, supply chains, and business partners.
- *Devices.* A device is any object made or adopted for a particular purpose. Typically, devices are mechanical or electronic equipment.
- *Service accounts.* A service account is an account created to provide security context for services running on an operating system. It is *not* used for logging into a system; rather, it is a nonhuman account to isolate an application.
- *Administrative/root accounts.* An administrative account, sometimes known as a *root account*, is the first account created when an operating system is installed. This account is used specifically by a system administrator.

TECH TIP

Most operating systems including Windows and Linux have the ability to create a service account that can be restricted from logging in as a normal user. A good practice is to create a lengthy and complex password and prevent it from being changed.

Risk

An important component of governance is addressing organizational risks. *Risk* is a situation that could cause harm, create a hazard, or otherwise cause problems for an organization. Risk affects **assets**, which are items, ideas, and people needed to operate an organization.

For example, *people assets* are people who bring talent to an organization. *Physical assets* are items such as equipment and the building in which the company operates. *Information assets* are data such as customer information, intellectual material, and financial documents. *IT assets* are information systems including hardware and software.

All assets are important to a company, and all are at risk. However, some are more essential to the daily operation of the organization than others; therefore, critical assets must be identified. **Critical assets** are those that are necessary to sustain business operations. For example, if a network goes down, it would be difficult to continue operations, so the network is a critical asset. However, if a printer stops working, accommodations can be made so the business does not stop.

Asset Life Cycle

The **asset life cycle** is the steps involved in managing an asset from its purchase until it is discarded. The steps of the life cycle include planning, requesting, purchasing, deploying, maintaining, and retiring an item of value, as shown in Figure 16-1.

1. *Planning* is the process of establishing and confirming asset requirements based on an evaluation of existing assets and their ability to meet anticipated needs.
2. *Requesting* occurs after a decision is made as to what asset is needed and how long it will last. Appropriate paperwork is completed after a budget is approved for the purchase.
3. *Purchasing* is the process in which bids are requested, if needed. Bids are reviewed and compared to determine the most cost-effective option. Once a bid is selected, a purchase order is completed, and the asset is purchased.
4. After the asset has been received by the organization, it is *deployed*, which means put in use.
5. Continuous *maintenance* is made to the asset to ensure it is in good working condition and the organization maximizes its investment.

Figure 16-1 The asset life cycle is the steps involved in managing an asset from its purchase until it is discarded.

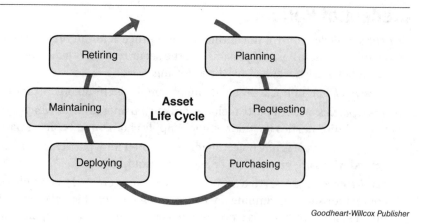

6. *Retiring* of an item occurs when the asset no longer works or becomes out of date.

5.3, 5.4

Asset Management

Organizational policies require that assets be managed effectively. **Asset management** requires all assets purchased be planned for effective use and tracked through the asset life cycle so sound financial decisions can be made. It involves tracking the location of each item, whether items are on-site and in the building or off-site at another facility. The *ISO 55001 Asset Management* standard provides a framework as a guide for organizations to create their own policies. ISO 55001 is one of the many regulations that help an organization maintain regulatory compliance and assess its **risk posture**, which is the overall cybersecurity program of an organization that provides protection from breaches and safeguards its data.

IT asset management (ITAM) is the tracking of all IT assets that reside in a business, including hardware and software systems. This is necessary for organizational security. Hardware and software must be maintained and updated when required and protected from damages and losses. In addition, equipment should be replaced when it is no longer valuable or efficient.

5.3

Change Management

Change management is a process or plan that describes the policies and practices of an organization to prepare, equip, and support individuals and staff to incorporate and adapt to changes made in IT systems. It includes managing configuration changes of desktop hardware as well as networks and other IT components that impact the security posture of an organization.

Organizational policies are necessary for change management to ensure that IT processes for modifications of current systems or purchase of new systems are followed.

- The person or department requesting a change is the *change requestor*. The request could be as simple as replacing a desktop computer or as complex as instituting a new inventory system.

- A higher authority in the organization must approve each request. The management team may have to sign off, or a *change review board* may be in place to review all IT change requests.

- After changes are approved, the *change manager* oversees and executes implementation. The manager could be the IT director or another appointed person within the organization.

Change Control

Change control is the approach to managing changes to ensure they are necessary, documented, and integrated as seamlessly as possible. Many organizations have a change management plan that outlines the roles, responsibilities, and policies for making IT changes. Standards are required to preserve the security of an organization.

An intricate component of change is clear communication. When overarching changes are made, a communication plan should be in place to notify employees of changes and training, if necessary, to ensure appropriate implementation and employee use.

Risk Management

Information assurance (IA) is the process of protecting an information system, including identifying vulnerabilities and risks for using, storing, and transmitting data. A key component of information assurance includes risk management. *Risk management* is the process of identifying and evaluating assets and their vulnerabilities while taking steps to avoid or minimize loss, should it occur. Risk management is a plan that enables professionals to identify and prioritize risks and create a risk-response plan to include preventive actions to reduce the possibility of risk.

Vulnerabilities and threats create risks for IT assets. A *vulnerability* is a flaw or potential for harm, while a *threat* is an event or action in which a vulnerability is exploited that endangers an enterprise environment. **Risk assessment** is a systematic process that involves identifying risks caused by threats and vulnerabilities associated with assets and ranking them with the most critical risks listed first. Risk assessment is the continuous process of reviewing information about assets. For the IT team, focus is on hardware, software, network, and all IT components that comprise the enterprise environment.

When conducting a risk assessment, specific questions help identify potential risks, such as the following:

- What are the assets in the organization?
- What vulnerabilities or threats exist that put assets at risk?
- What is the likelihood that threats exist?
- What is the impact of threats that actually happen?

Asset Identification

The first step when conducting a risk assessment is to identify organizational assets. Asset identification helps determine which assets are at risk and need protection. An *inventory* is a list of assets a business has on hand at any particular time. An inventory should include mission-critical systems, as well as everyday items needed by an organization to perform services and create products. Examples of IT assets are hardware, such as servers, printers, and copiers. These are *tangible assets* and can be seen and touched. The building in which you work is also a tangible asset. However, some assets are intangible. *Intangible assets* are items that are not physical. For example, a company's reputation is an intangible asset because it cannot be physically seen or touched.

Inventory reflects date of purchase, cost, and priority level for each asset. Date of purchase and cost are required to determine value for an asset when a replacement is necessary. A priority level establishes the importance of an asset in relation to other assets in the business. Examples of priority level are critical, high, medium, low, or very low, as shown in Figure 16-2.

✚ 5.3

TECH TIP

In addition to managing the typical assets of computers, servers, and printers, you should also manage networking infrastructure assets, such as switches, routers, firewalls, battery backup devices, mobile devices, cloud services, software, and volume licenses.

Figure 16-2 A priority level establishes the importance of an asset in relation to other assets in the business.

Category	Critical (C)	High (H)	Medium (M)	Low (L)	Very Low (VL)
Description	All staff are affected or unable to do their jobs.	A large number of staff are affected or unable to do their jobs.	A moderate number of staff are affected or unable to do their jobs properly.	A minimal number of staff are affected or are able to deliver an acceptable service, but doing so required extra time or effort.	A handful of staff is impacted but able to perform their jobs with little to no impact.
	All customers are affected or impacted, or customer data has been lost or stolen.	A large number of customers are affected or acutely disadvantaged in some way.	A moderate number of customers are affected or inconvenienced in some way.	A minimal number of customers are affected or inconvenienced, but not in a significant way.	Customers are not impacted or are marginally inconvenienced.
	The financial impact of the incident is, for example, likely to exceed $100,000.	The financial impact of the incident is, for example, likely to exceed $10,000 but will not exceed $100,000.	The financial impact of the incident is, for example, likely to exceed $1,000 but will not exceed $10,000.	The financial impact of the incident is, for example, likely to exceed $500 but will not exceed $1,000.	The financial impact of the incident is, for example, likely to exceed $100 but will not exceed $500.
	The damage to the business's reputation is potentially irreparable.	The damage to the business's reputation is likely to be significant.	The damage to the business's reputation is likely to be moderate.	The damage to the business's reputation is likely to be minimal.	There is no damage to the business's reputation.
	Someone has been injured.	Someone has been injured.	No injury has occurred.	No injury has occurred.	No injury has occurred.

Goodheart-Willcox Publisher

For example, if an employee notifies IT that a laptop is missing, you need to respond to that event. The *value* of replacing the laptop may be $1,000. However, if a company server is down, responding to the outage is a higher *priority level* because a server is required to maintain operations for the company as a whole. Replacement of an individual laptop could probably wait a few hours.

Vulnerability Assessment

A **vulnerability assessment** is the process of identifying and evaluating weaknesses in the networks and systems of an organization. It is a security-posture assessment that helps protect against threats that could put an organization at risk.

A vulnerability assessment assists in identifying potential risks and vulnerabilities of an organization. As stated previously, a *risk* is a situation that could cause harm, create a hazard, or otherwise cause problems for an organization. A *vulnerability* is a flaw or potential for harm.

Threat Assessment

A **threat assessment** is steps taken to identify or determine potential threats faced by an organization. A threat analysis helps track potential threats and identify the

- threat;
- consequences of the threat; and
- probability a threat will happen.

For example, an employee creates a weak password.

- The threat is a weak password.
- The consequence is a hacker can steal a weak password and harm a network.
- The probability of a password attack is generally high.

Threats are generally of an internal or external nature and can be environmental or man-made. *Internal threats* are those that exist within an organization, such as a disaster resulting from employees not following best practices or IT improperly configuring security software. Internal threats also include items such as legacy systems. *Legacy systems* are those that have been around for some time, are outdated, and can weaken security. Ultimately, these systems are replaced with current, efficient solutions.

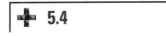 **5.4**

External threats are those that exist outside of an organization, such as hacking, inclement weather, and global pandemics. An example of an external threat is a supply chain attack. A *supply chain* is the businesses, people, and activities involved in turning raw materials into products and delivering them to end-users. A **supply chain attack** is a cyberattack in which a hacker infiltrates a system using a supply chain partner's access to an organization. Instead of attacking a company directly, a threat actor attacks through one of the members of the supply chain.

1.2, 5.4

Environmental disasters are events caused by humans that damage the environment, such as a forest fire as the result of a campfire that burns infrastructure and causes a business to close. Environmental disasters should not be confused with *natural disasters*, which are those caused by nature, such as floods, earthquakes, or other unexpected catastrophes. While severe weather, such as tornadoes or hurricanes, may not be common, if it does occur, it can be very destructive.

5.4

Man-made disasters are caused by humans and result in delays or business disruptions. Such disasters can be deliberate or accidental and typically are the result of intentional actions, errors, failures of safeguards, or negligence. For example, a fire broke out in a building and critical IT equipment was destroyed. Because of human error, backup tapes were not placed in a fireproof safe and all backup was lost. This is an internal man-made disaster that happened out of human carelessness, forcing the business to close because of loss of critical data.

5.4

Man-made risks can also be external. An external man-made disaster could be an automobile accident that cut the power to a building housing a server. The result, once again, is business disruption.

Risk Analysis

5.4

Risk analysis reviews the likelihood of a risk and the frequency with which it will occur. This information can help determine severity of the risk and its potential consequences. A heat map can assist with the task of conducting a risk analysis. A **heat map**, also known as a *risk matrix*, is a matrix that organizes risks into defined impact levels, as shown in Figure 16-3. Do not confuse this heat map with a wireless heat map, which is a type of site survey.

Risk awareness enables security practitioners to focus on the most common or intrusive threats faced by an organization. A basic question to answer is how much exposure can an organization tolerate? Better known as *risk appetite*, this assessment is about identifying how much risk an organization can tolerate before an action is pursued to take on the risk or do something about it.

5.4

A heat map takes into consideration risk controls used by the organization. *Risk controls* are frameworks used to safeguard assets and provide direction for handling risks for the good of the company. **Risk control self-assessment** is the process of

5.4

Figure 16-3 A heat map is a matrix that organizes risks into defined impact levels.

Impact Level	Description	Example
Catastrophic	Refers to events that stop or severely hinder an organization's functionality	Office is destroyed due to severe weather or fire
Major	Refers to events that have a major negative impact on an organization and its revenue	System is hacked and customer data is stolen
Significant	Refers to events that cause a loss of employee productivity or significant financial burden	Malware outbreak on a network
Minimal	Refers to events that create minor inconveniences for employees and may result in a change of process or procedure	Hardware failure such as a defective hard drive or fan
None	Refers to events that have no impact on an organization	Failure of a peripheral device, such as a wireless mouse or keyboard

Goodheart-Willcox Publisher

examining risks and the degree to which controls are effective. A review of the heat map can reveal if the company is using effective controls to handle risk.

Risk Impact

Risk impact is the estimated consequences or losses caused by a risk. The more extreme the risk, the more devastating the impact. Impact is a calculable value that can be determined by comparing estimated loss with costs associated with an asset. This provides an idea of how great a risk's impact could be to an organization.

Risk analyses use quantitative and qualitative assessments to prioritize risks. This provides information to identify risk exposure and prioritize the most critical risks.

Quantitative assessment is an analysis that uses numbers or monetary values. It is an objective method and not based on personal beliefs or opinions. Quantitative assessments require factual data, such as a specific value placed on an item. For example, suppose you know a replacement computer costs $400. The quantitative method determines monetary loss from the risk. Since the quantitative method assigns an objective value, such as monetary value, it is easy to compute loss.

A **qualitative assessment** is an analysis based on subjective opinion rather than data. For example, rating values of high, moderate, or low is one person's opinion; another person's view might differ. For example, the Chief Technology Officer of a company may think that a server is of higher value than the company website. The evaluation is purely subjective and not based on fact.

The higher the likelihood an event will occur, the greater the risk. **Annualized rate of occurrence (ARO)** is the expected number of times an incident will happen in one year. If over the course of a year a company expects four laptops to be lost or stolen, the ARO is 4. If a problem happens only once every two years, the ARO is 0.5. This is the *risk likelihood* of how probable a risk is to happen.

Risk Evaluation

A **risk register** is a tool used to list, categorize, and provide instructions for managing identified risks. It acts as a repository for all identified risks so each can be evaluated. A risk register includes important information, such as date of discovery, description of risk, likelihood, impact, severity, individual responsible for overseeing resolution, mitigation techniques, actions to take if mitigation fails (contingent

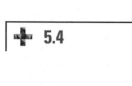

5.4

5.4

5.4

5.4

5.4

actions), notes, and status of risk, as shown in Figure 16-4. *Mitigating* means to make something less severe.

An important part of the analysis is determining value of assets at risk. *Asset valuation* is determining the market value of an asset. Regardless of how much an asset cost, its replacement value is important. In general, asset valuation can be either qualitative or quantitative, though quantitative measurements such as SLE and ALE typically enable better analysis and valuation.

Single loss expectancy (SLE) is the monetary value of a damaged asset. For example, if a company laptop was damaged beyond use, you would compute the cost for a replacement laptop including software and data restoration costs. The cost of the laptop is $1,500, replacement software is $200, and the data restoration fee is $300. Therefore, the total loss for one computer is $2,000.

Annualized loss expectancy (ALE) is the monetary value anticipated to be lost based on frequency of loss in one year. This amount is calculated by multiplying the SLE and the ARO (SLE × ARO = ALE). For example, you determine the SLE of a lost or stolen laptop is $2,000. You also project there will be four incidents related to this risk over the course of one year (ARO). In that scenario, the ALE is $8,000 ($2,000 × 4).

Response to Risk

An organization must decide on the types of responses or courses of action for identified risk. The generally accepted responses to risk are as follows:

- risk avoidance
- risk transfer
- risk mitigation
- risk acceptance

Risk Avoidance

Risk avoidance is the act of eliminating risk by avoiding agents that cause the risk. For example, a business choosing to be a cash-only establishment eliminates the risk of hacked credit card transactions and stolen credit card data. However, a trade-off for accepting only cash is that it may not be convenient for, or popular with, customers and business may be lost.

Risk Transfer

Risk transfer is a strategy that involves shifting risk to another party. *Risk transference* is assigning responsibility of risk-based loss to another party by means of a contract or insurance.

Purchasing insurance to cover the costs of recovering and restoring data is a way to transfer risk. Businesses often purchase cyber insurance to help mitigate exposure to Internet- or IT-based security breaches.

5.4

5.4

5.4

5.4

5.4

Figure 16-4 A risk register is a tool used to list, categorize, and provide instructions for managing identified risks.

ID	Date of Discovery	Description of Risk	Likelihood	Impact	Severity	Owner	Mitigation Action(s)	Contingent Action(s)	Notes	Status
0001	3/14/2020	Assets may not be updated in time to meet deadline	Low	High	Medium	J. McCoy	(1) Reallocate staff to assist (2) Hire temp worker to assist	(1) Push date of delivery from 2 weeks to 4 weeks	Update: Mitigation action 1 implemented 3/15/20	Open

Goodheart-Willcox Publisher

➕ 5.4

Risk Mitigation

Risk mitigation is the act of taking steps to reduce the effects of risks for an organization. Having backup or redundant hardware is an example of mitigating risk, because both can be used immediately in the event of a failure. An **inherent risk** is a risk that would happen if controls were not in place to mitigate it. Mitigation does not eliminate a risk; rather, it reduces the impact if the risk occurs. **Residual risk** refers to risk that remains after mitigation controls are implemented.

➕ 5.4

Risk Acceptance

Risk acceptance is making a decision to assume risk. This is an informed decision based on the likelihood and impact of the risk; it is not ignoring the issue. Risk acceptance usually happens after an attempt to minimize risk to an acceptable level. Assuming risk means making financial preparations for the possibility of future loss.

Data Governance

Data is information to which policies are applied. **Data governance** is the policies and procedures used by an organization to manage its data assets. It assists an organization in protecting the security of data and setting expectations for employees on how they handle company information. Data governance follows the CIA triad's underlying core security principles of data protection: confidentiality, integrity, and availability.

- *Confidentiality.* Data *confidentiality* assures data is respected and used as intended.
- *Integrity.* Data *integrity* is the assurance that information has not been modified.
- *Availability.* Data *availability* is making data available for access as needed.

➕ 5.5

Much of an organization's data is considered *sensitive*, which means it must be protected against unauthorized use. Examples of sensitive data include the following:

➕ 5.5

- **Personally identifiable information (PII)** is any data that can be used to pinpoint a specific person, such as Social Security or driver license numbers.
- *Health information* is data concerning a person's health such as blood type, x-ray results, and other health status indicators.
- *Financial information* is data pertaining to income, taxes, and other financial facts.

➕ 2.1

Data security is protection of data from intruders and the way in which a company secures its data from malicious events. To help protect sensitive data, Information Rights Management is sometimes used. **Information Rights Management (IRM)** is an IT security process that protects sensitive documents, such as health records, from unauthorized access. The process uses encryption, and information can generally be read but *cannot* be printed, edited, or manipulated in any way.

➕ 5.3

Compliance

To be in *compliance* means to follow organizational policies as well as regulatory policies. **Data compliance** is the practice of following organizational, industry, and governmental regulations to ensure data management and enable an organization to be accountable. Compliance regulations protect data such as customer information. Organizations *cannot* release information without permission of the owner. Data laws, such as HIPPA, protect citizens against the sharing of personal health information.

Privacy policies are internal guidelines for those who handle data. *Privacy notices* are statements to those outside an organization to define how company data is used and to whom information is released. There are generally three types of data.

- *Corporate data* is information owned by a corporation.
- *Governmental data* is information owned by the government.
- *Customer data* is any information collected from customers.

Terms of agreement state how personal data will be used. A data use agreement (DUA) is an agreement entered into before there is any use or disclosure of specified data.

A *Data Protection Impact Assessment (DPIA)* is an important part of an organization's accountability obligations as outlined in the General Data Protection Regulation (GDPR). A DPIA is a process used to analyze data to minimize risks of individuals when moving personal data. For example, consent must be given before an organization can collect data from a person. Companies must comply with this law.

Large organizations generally have a *privacy officer* who is responsible for setting data policies and procedures to keep data secure, as shown in Figure 16-5. In the absence of a privacy officer, a high-ranking manager, such as a CEO, assumes responsibility for data security. *Data policies* are the rules that dictate data management in an organization. Organizations create policies to ensure that only approved personnel have access to sensitive data and its management to avoid putting a business at risk.

Data Life Cycle

The **data life cycle** is the stages that data goes through from its initial creation to its eventual archival or deletion. This helps an organization manage the flow of data. The data life cycle follows six stages, as illustrated in Figure 16-6.

1. *Creation.* Sensitive data is created and generated in multiple formats, including e-mails, documents, spreadsheets, and websites, through data acquisition, entry, or capture.

2. *Role-based use.* Content is tagged according to security controls and classification levels. Tagging is reflective of an organization's security policies and compliance rules according to data roles and responsibility.

3. *Storage.* After its creation and tagging, data is stored and protected with proper access controls and encryption applied. A backup and recovery process for data storage is created.

Figure 16-5 In a large company, the responsibility of creating and managing data policies is divided among several different roles.

Data Roles and Responsibilities	
Data owner	Responsible for data compliance, policy management, and privilege usage
Data privacy officer (DPO)	Responsible for the overall data privacy by setting policies and procedures to ensure an organization's data remains secure
Data custodian/ steward	Defines and creates access rights to data as well as implements controls defined by the data steward
Data controller	Determines the purpose and means by which personal data is processed
Data processor	Processes personal data on behalf of the data controller, which is typically a third party

Goodheart-Willcox Publisher

✚	2.1
✚	5.5
✚	5.5
✚	5.5
✚	5.5

Figure 16-6 The data life cycle is the stages that data goes through from its initial creation to its eventual archival or deletion.

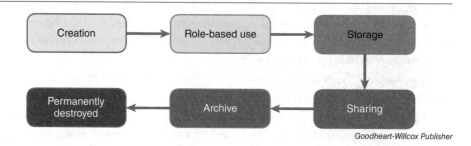

Goodheart-Willcox Publisher

4. *Sharing.* Data supports daily business activities and is shared with employees, customers, partners, and third-party members across different devices and platforms.

5. *Archive.* When data is no longer required, it is archived for future use.

6. *Permanently destroyed.* Obsolete data is deleted or removed from a system. Secure data destruction includes burning, shredding, pulping, or pulverizing.

Data sovereignty is a concept that states digital data is subject to the jurisdiction and laws of the country where the storage device is located. If data is stored in a country other than where a business is located, there may be legal ramifications. For example, some countries do not permit businesses to store or back up data to servers located in other countries, and data may be accessible to local governmental regulations that differ from the country of residence. When using a cloud vendor, it is important to identify this information and adjust contracts to reflect business preferences.

 2.1

 5.3

Data Clearance

Data clearance is an authorization that allows access to security data. Data is *classified* according to sensitivity. The government uses secret, top secret, sensitive, and unclassified as clearance levels. Businesses generally use clearance levels shown in Figure 16-7. The data classification depends on the type of organization.

 5.5

Figure 16-7 Data is classified according to sensitivity.

Data Classification	Description
Public	Freely accessible and available to the public without restrictions
Private	Medium level of restriction and contains personally identifiable, financial, or regulated information
Internal	Available only to those within a company, not the general public, low risk (customer information, employee handbooks)
Confidential	Personally identifiable, financial, or regulated information that could cause moderate risk to an organization (vendor contracts, employee reviews)
Proprietary	Information that belongs to an organization and is kept private
Sensitive	Data that must be protected from unauthorized access
Critical	Information that is important to the success of an organization
Restricted	Highly sensitive internal information requiring an NDA as unauthorized use could cause significant risk

Goodheart-Willcox Publisher

A business must respect data privacy and data security as required by law and ethical codes. A *data breach* occurs when private, confidential, or protected data is taken from an organization without permission. When a data breach occurs, it is the responsibility of the organization to notify the affected parties of the breach. *Security breach notification laws* require an entity to notify customers and parties about a breach and specific steps to be taken to remedy the situation based on state or federal laws. According to the law, notification must occur without delay and no later than 90 days after the incident.

When a breach occurs, an *escalation process* is necessary to notify all appropriate groups in an organization. An internal escalation plan notifies internal employees of a breach. An external escalation plan notifies external individuals and customers when appropriate.

A breach can be devastating to an organization. Examples of the consequences are as follows.

- *Reputation damage.* An organization's reputation is a significant, immeasurable asset. The way in which an organization is perceived influences customer attraction and retention. A data breach can cause a company to lose customers, revenue, and support from investors.

- *Identity theft.* Identity theft is the result of stolen personal private information used to assume the identity of an individual. Personal information can be employee or customer names, addresses, Social Security numbers, or other identification. Carelessly leaked personal information about employees or customers can cause legal issues for an organization.

- *Fines.* A data breach can be costly for an organization. When a data breach occurs, an organization is subject to regulatory fines. If a data breach exposes sensitive data, an organization may be subject to lawsuits, legal fees, and settlement fees.

- *Intellectual property (IP) theft.* **Intellectual property (IP)** is something that comes from a person's mind, such as an idea, invention, or process. IP theft involves stealing an organization's ideas, inventions, and processes. A breach of intellectual property can cost an organization trade secrets or other confidential information that could cause the company its livelihood.

TECH TIP

A number of online services can be used to determine whether confidential data has been exposed. For example, credit bureaus, such as Experian, often offer free dark web scans to determine if one's identity or e-mail address has been exposed. Typically, all users have to do is enter an e-mail address, and the website will determine if the address has been compromised and list any website associated with the e-mail account where data has been exposed.

Data Retention

A **data retention policy** identifies how long an organization must retain data. Data is required in forensic investigations or other situations in which evidence for an event is requested. Therefore, data must be retained and protected. Regulated data is retained according to specified laws. Unregulated data may be retained according to industry or the organization's data retention policies.

5.4

4.2, 5.3

Privacy-Enhancing Technology

A *privacy-enhancing technology (PET)* is a method of protecting data to help comply with data protection regulations and policies. Examples of protection techniques include the following.

Data Minimization

Data minimization is measures performed by an organization to limit the amount of personal data collected from individuals and process only information relevant to accomplishing specific tasks. Minimization also involves deleting data that is no longer required as well as setting time limits for the retention of data.

✚ 5.5 Data Masking

Data masking is a data security technique that involves copying a dataset but obfuscating any sensitive data. *Obfuscation* is the act of masking data so it is unclear or unintelligible but still usable. Data masking is a method of creating a structurally similar, but inauthentic, version of an organization's data used for different purposes, such as software testing and employee training. By using this technique, the original data is protected and remains intact while a functional substitute is used for occasions when the real data is not required.

✚ 2.1, 5.5 Tokenization

Tokenization is the method of protecting data by replacing it with tokens. A *token* is a random value, which represents original data, and the actual data is stored in a secured vault. Tokenization replaces sensitive data with unique identification symbols that retain all the essential information about the data without compromising its security. There is no mathematical relationship between the token and the actual data, and the process is irreversible. Tokenization prevents sensitive data from being stored on the business network.

✚ 4.1 Sanitization

Sanitization is the process of removing sensitive information, such as personally identifiable information, from documents, messages, and data sets. This allows people whom the data describe to remain anonymous to users. Sanitizing data or media is the best course of action to strengthen an organization's *security posture*, which is the actions, philosophies, and strategies for ensuring the security of an organization's software, hardware, network, and data.

Disk sanitization, sometimes referred to as *disk wiping* or *data sanitization*, is the irreversible and permanent removal of data from a storage device. Wiping a disk entails performing a low-level format where all data is overwritten with binary 0s and 1s. Most sanitization programs are developed to comply with the Department of Defense's acceptable wiping standard (DoD 5220.22-M), which requires all data to be overwritten with 0s, 1s, and random bit patterns.

The DoD 5220.22-M standard has become outdated by comparison to some of the newer technologies. As such, the National Institute for Standards and Technology (NIST) has created standards for disk sanitization. These standards are maintained in NIST's *800-88—Guidelines for Media Sanitization* document.

In scenarios where sanitization is not possible or desirable, physical destruction of media should be pursued. Physical destruction refers to rendering a storage device incapable of operation. This includes, but is not limited to, breaking, crushing, drilling, pulverizing, shredding, and burning. Many third-party vendors offer storage drive destruction as a service. If using a service provider, the destruction method should be confirmed, and security standards, such as chain of custody, should be followed. Once complete, the vendor should provide a certificate that confirms the media was destroyed.

✚ 5.5 Data Anonymization

Data anonymization is a form of sanitization with the intent of privacy protection through the removal of personally identifiable information (PII). Data anonymization can be reversed through a data mining strategy of de-anonymization. *De-anonymization* is the process of comparing anonymous data with public information with the goal of discovering the original owner of the data.

Pseudoanonymization

Pseudoanonymization is a de-identification procedure in which personally identifiable information fields within a data record are replaced with one or more artificial, or fake, identifiers. These false identifiers are known as *pseudonyms*. This is different from anonymization, which removes personally identifiable information. In pseudoanonymization, a pseudonym simply replaces a field or collection of fields in order to make the data record less identifiable while remaining usable for data processing and analysis.

Personnel Policies

Governance applies to how an organization addresses its employees. An employee of a business is often an organization's most important asset but can also be its greatest risk. As such, employees should be educated so they do not endanger the security of the organization and create unnecessary risk. Without proper education, employees can unknowingly become targets for malware and social engineering attacks. In addition, they can inadvertently cause problems due to improper system usage on their part as well as poor system configuration created by the business. Well-written policies outline rules for systems as well as employees.

Policy violations by employees are a common security risk. A **policy violation** occurs when an employee fails to follow a security policy effectively. This could be as simple as choosing weak passwords, leaving workstations unattended when not in use, or allowing people to enter through a door without swiping or checking their credentials.

Often, businesses underestimate the risks that existing employees can pose to data and systems. These threats may be from either malicious or inadvertent actions. Insider threats can go on for years without detection. Reasons why insider threats can go on without detection include the following.

- Differentiating between an employee conducting regular work and an employee committing harmful actions is difficult to identify.
- Employees find it easy to cover their actions.
- It is hard to prove guilt or malicious intent.

A comprehensive approach to user controls and organizational security policies is necessary in a business. Security policies provide guidance so employees understand behaviors expected of them. Defined expectations help to decrease potential employee threats. These policies should be reviewed periodically as technology and business processes change. In addition, polices should be reviewed on an annual basis to see if any changes should be implemented.

Background Checks

Before an employee is hired, a background check should be performed. A **background check** is a method of ensuring or authenticating an employee's job history, résumé, and credentials. A background check is completed before an employee is hired. Background checks should be commonplace for *all* potential employees, but are particularly important for anyone entrusted with sensitive data or access to network configurations and administration. A typical background check verifies a potential employee's education, past employment, and criminal history. Some also include credit checks. This information helps an employer decide if a potential employee has past issues that could possibly be a hiring risk for the organization.

Employment Contracts

Some organizations require a new employee to sign an employment contract. An **employment contract** defines the terms of employment between an employer and an employee. The contract describes how long the contract will last, how much the employee is paid, and the benefits provided by the business. An employment contract can also include information about trade secrets and termination of employment.

An employer might choose to require an employee to sign a nondisclosure agreement (NDA). Most NDAs specify that all data, notes, and records remain the property of the organization. *Intellectual property (IP)* is something that comes from a person's mind, such as an idea, invention, or process. Intellectual property laws protect a person's or a company's inventions, artistic works, and other intellectual property. IP theft committed by an employee who has access to intellectual property can be a risk for an organization. Requiring an NDA is an important step for IP theft risk avoidance.

Some employers may also require employees to sign a non-compete agreement. A *non-compete agreement* is a contract in which an employee agrees not to work for a competing business. This agreement may be in place while the employee is working for the company. However, it often extends for a period of time after the employee has left the company.

Acceptable Use Policy (AUP)

TECH TIP

The *Business Software Alliance (BSA)* is an international advocacy group and leading advocate that fights for proper licensing of software solutions. It was established by Microsoft Corp. and represents many of the world's largest software manufacturers. They promote education to companies about IP policies and security. BSA also can conduct software audits on behalf of their members.

All employees should be required to sign an acceptable use policy. An **acceptable use policy (AUP)** is a document that outlines information on proper usage of the network and related assets as defined by the owner of the network. The policy may include expectations for e-mail, computer, and personal device usage. Enforcing an AUP can help an organization reduce potential liabilities and risks by outlining appropriate use of and interaction with technology. An AUP

- sets rules defining what is and is not allowed when using network assets;
- identifies the amount of privacy a user or employee should expect when using the network;
- identifies procedures for incidents; and
- clearly defines consequences for individuals who do not comply with the terms in the policy, taking into account the severity and intent of the violation.

Users should be required to read, understand, and acknowledge understanding of the terms in the AUP by signing and dating a copy of the form. All who use an organization's network are bound by terms of an AUP, not just employees.

Of particular concern for an employer is a *software license compliance*, which can pose organizational risks. A *license* is the legal permission to use a software program. All software, and many websites, list rules called the *terms of use (TOU)*, sometimes known as *terms of service (TOS)*, that explain how and when software or downloaded files may be used. Employees who misuse a license put the organization at risk for a lawsuit.

Role-Based Awareness Training

Employees should receive role-based awareness training. **Role-based awareness training** assigns a role and provides training for individuals based on their positions within an organization. While every organization has its own unique environment, the following roles should be specifically addressed.

- The **data owner** is the role responsible for data compliance, policy management, and privilege usage.

- **User** is a role given to anyone who operates an application on a network. This role assumes responsibility for protecting information, even if access to data is limited.
- A **privileged user** is an elevated user role that has increased access to data and resources. As such, privileged users have greater responsibility for protecting data as well as being an increased risk to a system.
- The **system administrator** is the role responsible for managing applications that access data, even if the person does not use data directly. The person in this role should be aware of any security issues arising through management of software and security configurations.
- The **system owner** is the role that focuses on data protection, including redundancy, backups, and related policies and implementations.
- The **executive user** is the person who is responsible for the overall usage of a given application, evaluation of an application's operation, and making decisions about data usage.

Sender Policy Framework (SPF)

Another method of ensuring organizational security is to incorporate a sender policy framework. A **sender policy framework (SPF)** is an e-mail protocol used to validate the legitimacy of a sender's e-mail address. Organizations receive many e-mails during the course of a business day, some wanted and others unwanted. Most spammers, and those sending phishing e-mails, often spoof a legitimate e-mail address in use. To help control unwanted incoming e-mail, companies create sender policy frameworks.

To create SPFs, a network administrator generates special records for authorized senders and their accompanying IP addresses. These SPF records are included in the Domain Name System (DNS) using a TXT record. Inclusion in the network's DNS declares the validity of the e-mail associated to that IP address. When an e-mail arrives at the company, the e-mail provider software verifies the existence of an SPF record from the DNS. If the address is present, the e-mail is sent to the recipient. If the address is not there, the e-mail is refused entry to the system.

Mandatory Vacation

 5.3

Mandatory vacation is requiring an employee to take a vacation as designated by company policy. It is a way of managing employee attendance or presence within the organization for security reasons. Mandatory vacations force employees to take vacations so they are not on the premises or using company systems during a specified time. A user who is not following security policies or is committing data theft would be reluctant to leave for vacation in the fear previous actions are discovered in their absence. By enforcing this control, a person's access to a network and its resources is removed. During a user's vacation, it is easier to audit what the person has been working on, test passwords and other access levels, and compare network traffic levels to those when the user was present. For example, if traffic loads drop, this may indicate the user has been uploading or downloading a great deal of data. Traffic load drop may indicate a theft of data or data vandalism.

Job Rotation

5.3

Job rotation is a system of employment in which personnel cycle through different roles in an organization to gain new experiences and variety in a job. When mandatory vacation policies are implemented, users trained through job rotation step in to complete the assignments of the person on vacation. Some benefits to job rotation are shown in Figure 16-8.

Most importantly, with job rotation, multiple individuals can perform job duties. From a security perspective, job rotation helps to prevent or expose dangerous short-cuts or fraudulent activity. When a user rotates into a different position, settings can be checked and verified, as well as data and other aspects of the position.

Employee User Training

Organizations are responsible for all aspects of protecting the confidentiality, integrity, and availability of its data, but this responsibility does not rest solely with the security staff and upper management. *All* users in an organization need to understand their responsibilities in security protection and the security aspects related to their job functions. Employee user training provides this knowledge.

User training begins with the application of diversity of training techniques. *Diversity training* in the workplace includes recognizing, respecting, accepting, and valuing people from different backgrounds, cultures, or demographics. It includes age, race, nationality, gender, mental ability, physical ability, and other qualities that make an individual unique.

Diverse individuals require varied learning tools to comprehend new information. Security training with employees is more effective when games, simulations, and other interactive activities are applied rather than using traditional lectures and handouts as teaching tools.

- *Gamification* is the application of gaming designs and concepts to training scenarios to make learning more engaging and interactive for employees. Through interaction in a game scenario, employees can participate in imaginary cybersecurity incidents and apply team-building strategies to solve an incident.
- *Capture the flag (CTF)* is a security computer competition in which employees learn about cybersecurity as a member of a team. There are two formats typically used: jeopardy-style and attack-defend. In jeopardy, teams answer questions and the higher-scoring team wins the flag. In attack-defend, one team attacks the opposing team using hacking tools. The hacking team offensively attempts to break into the other team's network and steal its flag. The defending team must prevent its flag from capture by the offensive team. Then they switch roles and play again. In the simulation, the flag can be a file, folder, image, or similar important security items.
- *Computer-based training (CBT)* is training that uses computers to deliver instruction. Also known as *e-learning*, instruction is delivered over the Internet.
- *Phishing simulations* are a training technique for teaching and assessing employee awareness about fraudulent e-mails that often lead to other attacks. In

+ 5.3

+ 5.3

Figure 16-8 There are multiple benefits of an organization implementing job rotations.

Benefits of Job Rotation
▪ Encourages employees to continuously develop skills and knowledge
▪ Eliminates employee boredom with same routine
▪ Gives employees a break from strenuous job duties
▪ Helps identify where employees work best in an organization
▪ Installs a backup plan in the event an employee leaves the organization

this exercise, e-mails are written and disguised as legitimate e-mails to test the employee's understanding and recognition of phishing threats.

Additionally, user training should include various items. Some items include clean-desk policy, social media analysis, and e-mail policies. Additional items to include in user training are separation of duties, onboarding, and offboarding.

Clean-Desk Policy

A **clean-desk policy** is a human resource policy that outlines how an employee should leave a desk when not physically present. Such policies help deter insider threats to the organization. Typically included in the policy are directives for

- removing sensitive documents and placing in a secure location, such as a locked cabinet;
- disposing of paper documents properly; and
- protecting a computer against unauthorized access by shutting down or locking the computer when not using it.

Clean-desk policies help avoid accidental exposure of personally identifiable information (PII). *Personally identifiable information (PII)* is any data that can be used to pinpoint a specific person. A person's name, gender, address, telephone number, and e-mail address are all examples of PII. Unintentional exposure of private information can occur through an employee falling victim to social engineering attacks or even by something as simple as leaving the information open on a computer screen or on a desk.

PII is one of the most common insider threats. The information obtained through accidental exposure of PII can be used for blackmail, stalking, or identity theft, among other crimes. Additionally, it damages the integrity of an organization's information system and reputation. While there is no US federal law that mandates the handling of PII for businesses, some laws, such as HIPAA, specify that PII is protected under their coverage.

In the United States, NIST created a special publication, *NIST 800-122—Guide to Protecting the Confidentiality of Personally Identifiable Information (PII)*, to define personally identifiable information. This guide can assist an organization in developing security plans that protect the confidentiality of personal information.

Social Media Analysis

Social media analysis is the collecting of data from social media outlets so that an organization can evaluate policies needed for organizational security. *Social media security* is a process used to analyze social media data so an organization can protect itself against security threats. For example, social media postings can inadvertently expose confidential company information that can be used to launch social engineering attacks, or even breach physical security barriers.

E-Mail Policies

Employee use of personal e-mail is also a serious concern. Since employees' personal e-mail accounts are not created by IT staff, those accounts can be used to bypass protections that have been configured on corporate e-mail systems. These protections include malware protection, encryption, and configurations that search for potential data exposure in the body of the e-mails. Therefore, most organizations restrict the use of personal e-mail while using a company's network.

5.3

5.3

Separation of Duties

A key security practice related to personnel is **separation of duties**, which refers to having multiple people required to complete a job or task. With separation of duties, responsibilities are divided so no single individual has complete control of a task or assignment. This acts as a barrier to prevent fraud or other security issues and keeps any one person from compromising a job. For example, IT personnel may not have complete access to the entire network. A single person may have administrative access to routers but not to the Active Directory or the servers. This is common in businesses with large- or medium-sized IT departments.

Separating duties within an organization limits the scope of actions a user can perform, which strengthens the organization's security. A user cannot access or use what cannot be seen on the screen. Figure 16-9 shows the default user groups on a Windows 10 computer. These groups allow an administrator to set up privileges for users and limit the scope of what they can do. For example, to prevent a user from using the Remote Desktop program to access another computer on the network, simply do not add the user's account to that group. Custom security groups can be created to match the needs of an organization.

Onboarding

Onboarding is new-employee training used to instruct a user on rights and responsibilities expected when using the organization's network. During the onboarding process, it is important that new employees be trained on security awareness. Additionally, key policies, such as the AUP, should be explained and a copy given to the employee to read and sign to acknowledge receipt and acceptance of the policy.

Annual follow-up training for current employees is also important. Frequent repetition and exposure to information helps employees understand and retain the information. It also keeps employees informed of any policy changes or revisions.

Offboarding

Offboarding is an employment process that ensures users identify digital content they were working on and return all login credentials when they leave a business.

Figure 16-9 Separating duties in an organization limits the scope of actions a user can perform.

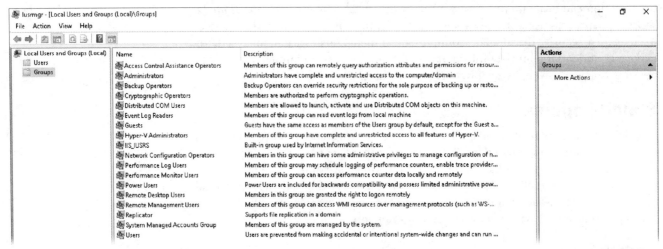

Offboarding is a critical aspect of organizational security. The process includes these following activities pertaining to the departing employee:

- The IT department disables user's account and deletes them as outlined in company policies.
- Company equipment, such as laptops or smartphones, are returned to the IT department. All data on the employee's work computer is removed, archived, or destroyed.
- The employee's name is removed from organizational charts and the e-mail system.

The final step in the offboarding process is an exit interview. The interview is typically conducted by a human resources representative at which time the person's login credentials, such as CAC cards, ID badges, and tokens, are returned as well as a debrief of digital content that person possesses. An exit interview is often used to determine why an employee is leaving the company as well as to review their experience of working for the company. The interview should also be used to promote data security measures, such as reminding employees of obligations of data confidentiality, and to determine if the employee has retained any data (physical or digital).

Third-Party Risk Management (TPRM)

⊹ 5.4

Policies for organizational security include third-party risk management. **Third-party risk management (TPRM)** is the process of identifying and controlling risks that occur when transacting business with third parties. Third-party risk, also referred to as *multi-party risk*, includes the following:

⊹ 5.3

- *Supply chain.* A supply chain is businesses, people, and activities involved in turning raw materials into products and delivering them to end-users. It is a business process that consists of companies, users, and resources working together to help produce and distribute a product from a supplier, to a manufacturer, and then to a customer.
- *Vendors.* Vendors, also known as *suppliers*, are companies that sell products or services to other businesses.
- *Business partners.* A business partner is a person(s) who shares ownership of a business. Each partner contributes to the business with money, property, labor, or expertise.

Engaging in business with others can put the security of your company at risk. For that reason, a framework should be in place that outlines policies for working with third parties.

Working with a third party requires contracts or agreements. Examples of common third-party agreements include the following:

⊹ 5.3

- *Service Level Agreement (SLA).* An SLA is a service contract between two parties, typically a vendor and a client, which explains services provided, responsibilities of each party, and guarantees of service.
- *Memorandum of Understanding (MOU).* An MOU is an agreement that businesses have in respect to what each party provides. An MOU is not legally enforceable. It is, however, a more formal agreement than an unwritten spoken agreement.
- *Measurement Systems Analysis (MSA).* An MSA is a detailed assessment of an organization's measurement system. An MSA evaluates the test method, measuring equipment, and an organization's entire process of obtaining measurements to ensure the integrity of data used for analysis. It is a process to ensure data between parties is intact and not corrupted.
- *Business Partnership Agreement (BPA).* A BPA is a written contract between two or more business partners to establish a partnership. The agreement outlines

the responsibilities of each partner, profit and loss distribution among the partners, and other general rules of the partnership.

- *End of Life (EOL).* An EOL is an announcement to customers indicating that a product is in the ends of its usefulness and will no longer be available. An EOL is also used to notify vendors to discontinue marketing, selling, or sustaining more of the product.
- *End of Service (EOS).* An EOS, also known as an *end of support,* is an agreement of when an organization will no longer provide services to a discontinued or unavailable product. This includes repairs, technical support, and availability of replacement parts.
- *Nondisclosure Agreement (NDA).* An NDA is a legal contract between two parties that restricts the signing party from distributing or sharing confidential information to anyone outside of the agreement.

SUMMARY

Governance

- Governance is the process of operating an organization. It is how an organization is operated and controlled through documented policies and procedures applied in the operation of business to establish organizational security.
- Organizational security includes safeguards used to protect an organization. It focuses on people, policies, and procedures.
- Governance guides an organization to be strategic through appropriate controls. Security controls are safeguards to minimize risks to assets of an organization
- Credential policies control the authentication process for an organization. Without these policies, unauthorized persons put the security of an organization at risk.

Risk

- Risk is a situation that could cause harm, create a hazard, or otherwise cause problems for an organization. It affects assets, which are items, ideas, and people needed to operate an organization. Examples include people, physical, information, IT, and critical assets.
- The asset life cycle is the steps involved in managing an asset. The steps include planning, requesting, purchasing, deploying, maintaining, and retiring an item of value.
- Asset management requires asset purchases be planned for effective use and tracked through their life cycles so that sound financial decisions can be made. Change management and change control are two key elements to managing changes to assets.
- IT asset management (ITAM) is the tracking of all IT assets that reside in a business, including hardware and software systems. This is necessary for organizational security.

Risk Management

- A key component of information assurance includes risk management. It is the process of identifying and evaluating assets and their vulnerabilities while taking steps to avoid or minimize loss, should it occur.
- Risk management is a plan that enables professionals to identify and prioritize risks and create a risk-response plan to include preventive actions to reduce the possibility of risk.
- Risk assessment is a systematic process that involves identifying risks caused by threats and vulnerabilities associated with assets and ranking them with the most critical risks listed first. It is the continuous process of reviewing information about assets.
- Risk assessment includes identifying assets at risk as well as potential vulnerabilities and threats that may occur.

Risk Analysis

- Risk analysis reviews the likelihood of a risk and the frequency with which it will occur. This helps determine severity of a risk and its potential consequences.
- A heat map assists with a risk analysis. It is a matrix that organizes risks into defined impact levels. The heat map takes into consideration risk controls used by the organization.
- Risk impact is the estimated consequences or losses caused by a risk to see how the risk could impact an organization. It is a calculable value that can be determined by comparing estimated loss with costs associated with an asset.
- A risk register is a tool used to list, categorize, and provide instructions for managing identified risks. It acts as a repository for all identified risks so each can be evaluated.
- An important part of the analysis is determining value of assets at risk. This is accomplished through asset valuation. SLE and ALE help determine the asset value.

Response to Risk

- An organization must decide on the types of responses or courses of action for identified vulnerabilities and threats.
- Risk avoidance is the act of eliminating risk by avoiding agents that cause the risk.
- Risk transfer is a strategy that involves shifting risk to another party. Risk transference is assigning responsibility of loss for risk to another party through a contract or insurance.
- Risk mitigation is the act of taking steps to reduce the effects of risks for an organization. It does not eliminate a risk; rather, mitigation reduces the impact if the risk occurs.
- Risk acceptance is making a decision to assume risk. This means making financial preparations for the possibility of future loss.

Data Governance

- Data governance is the policies and procedures used by an organization to manage its data assets. It assists in protecting the security of data and setting expectations for employees on how they handle company information.

- Data governance follows the CIA triad's underlying core security principles of data protection: confidentiality, integrity, and availability.
- Sensitive data must be protected against unauthorized use. Examples of sensitive data include PII, health information, and financial information.
- Data security is protection of data from intruders and the way in which a company secures its data from malicious events. To help protect sensitive data, Information Rights Management is sometimes used.
- Data governance includes following compliances, understanding the data life cycle, identifying proper data clearance levels, establishing data retention polices, and utilizing privacy-enhancing technology.

Personnel Policies

- Employees should be educated so they do not endanger the security of the organization and create unnecessary risk, especially from malware and social engineering attacks.
- Policy violations by employees are a common security risk. A policy violation occurs when an employee fails to follow a security policy effectively.
- Security policies provide guidance so employees understand behaviors that are expected of them. Defined expectations help to decrease potential employee threats.
- Types of personnel polices an organization can use to decrease risk include background checks, employment contracts, acceptable use policies (AUPs), role-based awareness training, sender policy framework (SPF), mandatory vacation, and job rotation.

Employee User Training

- Employee user training provides employees with the knowledge of their responsibilities in security protection and the security aspects related to their job functions.
- User training begins with the application of diversity of training techniques. Techniques include recognizing, respecting, accepting, and valuing people from different backgrounds, cultures, or demographics.
- Diverse individuals require varied learning tools to comprehend new information. Therefore, various tools should be used, such as gamification, capture the flag (CTF), computer-based training (CBT), and phishing simulations.
- User training should include various items, such as clean-desk and e-mail policies as well as social media analysis. Additional items to include are separation of duties, onboarding, and offboarding.

Third-Party Risk Management (TPRM)

- TPRM is the process of identifying and controlling risks that occur when transacting business with third parties, such as supply chains, vendors, and business partners.
- Engaging in business with others can put the security of a company at risk. Therefore, a framework should be in place that outlines policies for working with third parties.
- Working with a third party requires contracts or agreements. Common agreements include Service Level Agreement (SLA), Memorandum of Understanding (MOU), Measurement Systems Analysis (MSA), Business Partnership Agreement (BPA), End of Life (EOL), End of Service (EOS), and Nondisclosure Agreement (NDA).

REVIEW QUESTIONS

1. Discuss governance and its role in organizational security.

2. Explain the three categories of security controls.

3. Identify and explain each of the components of credential policies.

4. Identify assets at risk for an organization.

5. Briefly explain asset management and IT asset management (ITAM).

6. Summarize risk management.

7. Briefly explain internal, external, environmental, and man-made threats.

8. Discuss the role of risk analysis.

9. What is risk impact?

10. Briefly explain a risk register.

11. Explain four generally accepted responses to risk.

12. Summarize data governance and its role in asset security.

13. Identify and explain four potential consequences of a data breach for an organization.

14. Which data protection technique involves replacing personally identifiable information fields with one or more artificial identifiers?

15. Identify personnel policies implemented by organizations to decrease risks.

16. Define a *policy violation* and give an example.

17. List types of employee user training methods used by organizations.

18. What directives are typically included in a clean-desk policy?

19. Define *separation of duties* and how it acts as a barrier to prevent fraud and other security issues.

20. Summarize third-party risk management (TPRM).

✚ SAMPLE SECURITY+ EXAM QUESTIONS

1. Which of the following practices refers to following organizational and government regulations to ensure accountability of data usage?

   A. Data sovereignty

   B. Data clearance

   C. Data compliance

   D. Data minimization

2. Juan is a server engineer for a welding company. Which of the following would *best* help him harden a web server?

   A. Platform-based technical guides

   B. Data classification

   C. Security domains

   D. CIA triad

3. An organization is forced to comply with a request for information as part of a Freedom of Information Act (FOIA) request. Before they provide the requested information, they must remove private and personal data. Which of the following *best* describes the removal of such information?

A. Data obfuscation

B. Data sanitization

C. Data tokenization

D. Data masking

4. Alma works as a network engineer and is concerned about potential data risks occurring when a server must be logged in for a required service to run. Which of the following policy settings can she use to *best* protect data while the server is logged in?

A. Only use a service account to launch the required services.

B. Create a secondary administrator account that is only used for this service.

C. Prohibit non-IT access to the server.

D. Require all affected users to sign an NDA.

5. Which of the following *best* apply to data that has been requested in regard to a lawsuit over a data leak? (Choose 2)

A. Acceptable usage

B. Regulatory compliance rules

C. Data tokenization

D. Corporate retention policies

6. Akira works as a data security officer and recommends classifying data in a way so as to include labels such as Confidential, Private, Public, and Proprietary. Which is the *best* reason to follow this approach?

A. These labels make it easier to create data retention policies.

B. These labels make it easier to establish data access policies.

C. These labels make it easier to back up the data.

D. These labels make it easier to encrypt data.

7. Over the course of five years, an organization anticipates having to replace seven laptops. What is the ARO of laptop replacement in this organization?

A. 0.7

B. 5

C. 1.4

D. 7

8. A local library has reported it experiences a failure of a $600 laser printer every other year. What is the ALE for this printer?

A. $300

B. $600

C. $900

D. $1,200

9. Talia works as a security administrator for an agricultural business. Of the following issues that need to be resolved by Talia, which is *most likely* impacting a critical asset?

    A. There is a DNS server outage.

    B. The first floor MFP is offline.

    C. The server supporting the company intranet is down.

    D. Half of the offices on the second floor are suffering from intermittent VoIP connectivity.

10. The likelihood of an event, such as a hard drive failure in a critical asset, is measured in which yearly metric?

    A. ARO

    B. SLE

    C. ALE

    D. AV

LAB EXERCISES

Lab Activity 16-1: Security Policy Types

Security controls are based on the company's security policy. It makes more sense to create security policies specific to the topic at hand. The SANS Institute has created a detailed list of security policy templates that are free.

1. If directed by your instructor, you can form teams or work on this individually.

2. Launch a web browser and navigate to the SANS Institute website (www.sans.org).

3. Locate the free security resources, and then select the security policy samples or templates.

4. Choose a policy. Each team/individual should select a different policy, so check with the other teams. If there are more teams than policies, it is okay to repeat policies.

5. Download the policy template your team selected, and review its purpose.

6. Prepare a class presentation on the purpose and overview of the policy. Include information on how to check for compliance with the policy.

7. As a class, discuss the policies covered by each team. Should any be used in your classroom?

Lab Activity 16-2: Exploring State Data Security Laws

You must be familiar with the laws of all states in which your company does business. This includes interstate commerce in which the company engages. As a security professional, it is your responsibility to ensure compliance.

1. Launch a web browser, and navigate to the National Conference of State Legislatures website (www.ncsl.org). This site provides information related to state legislatures, including security laws for each state.

2. Use the site's search function, and conduct a search using the phrase security breach notification laws. In the results, select the link for the article of the same name.

3. Find your state on the list. Does your state have more than one law?

4. Click the link to the laws in your state. Read the text or description of the laws.

5. Open the laws for another state. How do they compare to the laws in your state?

6. Summarize some of the laws and penalties you see on these pages.

Lab Activity 16-3: Assets at Risk

An important task for the IT staff is to identify assets. After identifying assets, a value and level of importance need to be assigned to each.

1. Form teams of two to three students as directed by your instructor.

2. Select one person to record your observations in a spreadsheet.

3. Launch a spreadsheet program, and create the following columns.

Asset	Tangible or Intangible	Value	Priority Impact

Goodheart-Willcox Publisher

4. Look around your classroom for IT assets. This includes services and resources. If you have 20 classroom computers, for example, count those as one asset since they are all used by students.

5. List each asset in the first column.

6. Identify each asset as tangible or intangible in the second column.

7. Assign an estimated value for each asset in the third column. You may choose to use descriptive terms instead of a value.

8. Discuss with your team what you believe the priority impact would be if there is a loss of the asset. Use the examples in Figure 16-2. Enter the impact in the fourth column.

9. Share your team's findings with the class. Each team should then create one master list from the class findings.

10. Save the file. Your team will use it again later.

Lab Activity 16-4: Risk Factors

Knowing the causes of risks is important to identifying a risk. It is not enough just to identify a risk. You must also determine how likely the risk is to occur. For this activity, work in the same group as the last activity.

1. Open your group's vulnerability spreadsheet.

2. Add columns for vulnerability and likelihood.

Asset	Tangible or Intangible	Value	Priority Impact	Vulnerability	Likelihood

Goodheart-Willcox Publisher

3. For each asset, identify one vulnerability that could occur and its likelihood of occurring. Use these ratings for likelihood: seldom, occasionally, or frequently.

4. Share the results with your classmates.

5. Make any changes based on the work of other teams, and save your work.

Lab Activity 16-5: SLE, ARO, and ALE

The quantitative method relies on factual data. Using objective information, the SLE, ARO, and ALE can be set. For this activity, work in the same group as the last activity.

1. Open your group's vulnerability spreadsheet. It should include a classroom computer, either desktop, laptop, or tablet.

2. Research by the type of device you have and software installed. Determine what it would cost to replace this computer. This is the SLE for the loss of one of these devices.

3. Add a column to the spreadsheet for SLE, and enter your data.

4. Assume the device will fail twice each year.

5. What is the ALE for one of these devices?

Lab Activity 16-6: Risk Response

There are four basic ways to respond to risk. Each risk is different. A risk-response method may or may not be better than the others for a given risk. For this activity, work in the same group as the last activity.

1. Open your group's vulnerability spreadsheet.

2. Select two items from the list.

3. In a blank area in the spreadsheet under the list of assets, add the following information.

Risk Response			
Asset	Risk-Response Strategy	Rationale	Comments

Goodheart-Willcox Publisher

4. For each asset, discuss with your group which risk-response method you would choose. Then, enter the method in the Risk-Response Strategy column. At least one of the assets should use the mitigation method.

5. In the Rationale column, describe why your group selected the method.

6. For the mitigation method, identify all factors you could perform to mitigate the risk. Enter these in the Comments column.

7. If you select risk avoidance, identify some of the issues that will result from this choice. Enter these in the Comments column.

8. If you select risk transfer, identify where you will transfer this risk. Enter this in the Comments column.

9. If you select risk acceptance, list the possible losses. Enter these in the Comments column.

10. As directed, your team's spreadsheet information should be submitted, including data for Labs 15-1 through 15-4.

Lab Activity 16-7: Risk Assessment

In a risk-management strategy, there must be a complete understanding of the types of risks faced. A risk assessment involves identifying risks and ranking them with the most critical risks listed first. This activity uses Software Update Monitor software. Ensure the proper software is downloaded and installed before beginning the lab.

1. Open a web browser and navigate to the website www.kcsoftwares.com. Click on the **Downloads** page.

2. Each product includes an **Info** button that describes its purpose and functionality. What is the purpose of both SUMo and DUMo?

3. Using the respective **Download** buttons, download and install both SUMo and DUMo. Open SUMo. When it is first run, a wizard launches. Click on **Open SUMo Settings**, as shown in the following screen capture.

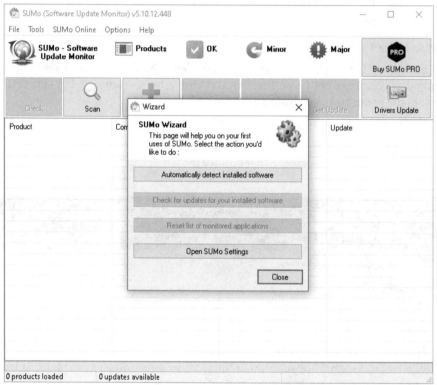

Goodheart-Willcox Publisher

4. Click the **Scan** button in the menu to begin scanning for installed software. This should take a few minutes. When the scan is finished, create a screen capture of the legend at the top of the screen detailing the products and their update status.

6. Sort the columns by clicking on the **File Path** column. Sometimes malicious or unknown software is installed in folders other than program files. Did you find programs installed outside the program files folders? If so, how many looked unusual or suspicious?

7. Another useful feature is the ability to export a list of programs to a spreadsheet program for documentation purposes. Select **Tools**>**Export**>**Spreadsheet File**. Create a screen capture of your result. How can creating this file help by creating a baseline of installed programs?

8. Close SUMo and install and run DUMo. Scan for drivers and updates. How many drivers were found, how many needed updates? Close DUMo when finished.

9. Summarize how including two programs can help you develop a risk-management plan.

CASE STUDY

Data Privacy Risks

In the summer of 2020, the US government announced it was considering banning two social media apps created in China: TikTok and WeChat. According to the White House proposal, this ban was intended to safeguard the privacy of US citizens, shield data about US citizens, and prevent governmental officials from tracking users or exploiting information that could lead to blackmail or social engineering threats. Earlier in the year, several US agencies as well as branches of the armed forces similarly banned the use of TikTok on governmental devices citing it as a cyber threat.

Security researchers compared TikTok's practices to those of other social media platforms. The results of that research included the following:

- TikTok scans and analyzes all the information entered in the composition and transmission of all messages, including those not sent. Facebook does the same thing in its Messenger app.
- TikTok acknowledges keystroke dynamics are tracked but does not specify how that data is used. This is interesting because most companies will not acknowledge if they participate in this practice.
- TikTok collects data about your device, including model, mobile carrier, time zone, resolution, apps, and operating system. This is standard across most apps.
- TikTok collects contacts from users' devices or social media platforms. This is common practice with most social media apps.
- TikTok's homepage includes a feed sent to users about interests, but no ability to use or modify this notification.

1. Other social media companies not based in China have had their data hacked and exposed, but those have not been banned or disallowed in any official capacity. To what extent do you think TikTok's location in China factors into its attention as a potential risk? Elaborate on your response.

2. TikTok and WeChat have massive user basis. Major US multinational companies raised concerns that banning WeChat could undermine their competitiveness in the Chinese markets. Do you think financial concerns should outweigh user privacy or potential national security concerns in this situation? Could this action have a retaliatory effect where other countries ban US apps in their countries? Expand on your opinions.

3. TikTok responded to the measures by agreeing to store data only on US soil with backups sent to Singapore, and the company hired an American CEO and operations team to run operations. These and other measures were not deemed enough protection, and the sale of TikTok is expected. Explain whether you think TikTok's response to the call for banning it were sufficient.

4. Most apps, including TikTok, have their privacy practices and notices in publicly accessible locations. To what extent does the responsibility of protecting sensitive data fall on the app user to accept or deny privacy implications?

5. What types of risk are associated with using TikTok? Explain how a TikTok user can evaluate, respond to, or mitigate those risks.

Incident Response and Digital Forensics

LEARNING OUTCOMES

- Define *incident response*.
- List and explain the steps in the incident response process.
- Summarize an incident response plan (IRP).
- Identify mitigation techniques used to secure an environment.
- Recognize common cybersecurity frameworks.
- Discuss digital forensics.
- Identify types of evidence to collect when securing an area.
- Explain the forensic procedure.
- Discuss data acquisition.
- Summarize a forensic report.
- Contrast cloud forensics with on-premises forensics.

KEY TERMS

artifact	digital forensics	preservation of evidence
chain of custody	eradication	quarantine
cloud forensics	incident response (IR)	screenshot
containment	incident response plan (IRP)	segmentation
counterintelligence	incident response process	stakeholder management
cybersecurity resilience	legal hold	strategic intelligence
data acquisition	memory dump	time offset
data dump (dd)	mirror image backup	time stamp
data evidence management	order of volatility	work-hour

SECURITY+ CERTIFICATION EXAM OBJECTIVES

The following Security+ Certification Exam Objectives are covered in this chapter.

- + 2.1: Response and recovery controls
- + 4.1: Forensics
- + 4.2: Incident response plans
- + 4.2: Incident response process
- + 4.2: Exercises
- + 4.2: Attack frameworks

- + 4.2: Stakeholder management
- + 4.2: Communication plan
- + 4.2: Incident response team
- + 4.2: Retention policies
- + 4.3: Retention
- + 4.3: Metadata

- + 4.4: Given an incident, apply mitigation techniques or controls to secure an environment.
- + 4.5: Explain the key aspects of digital forensics.

OVERVIEW

In the event of a security incident, there must be a plan of how to respond. An incident response plan prepares an organization to take appropriate steps when a cybersecurity attack happens. There is a structured method of incident response that enables organizations to identify, contain, and remove the threat. In addition, an incident response helps an organization recover from the incident and apply knowledge gained to improve future events.

Following a security event, there is the possibility that a criminal or civil prosecution may be necessary and a forensic investigation is required. This important undertaking involves the collection of digital evidence and ensuring the integrity of the process. Collection of evidence is called digital forensics, and understanding of the process of identifying types of evidence, collection procedures, and methods to acquire information about the cyber event is necessary.

SECURITY+ NOTE

No company is immune to cyberattacks, and the potential survivability for an organization may depend on the response to an incident. Digital devices and environments are vulnerable to cyberattacks, making the role of digital forensics increasing in importance. These are important topics that you will be tested on in the CompTIA Security+ Exam to measure your understanding of critical responsibilities.

Incident Response (IR)

 2.1

Incident response (IR) is acting against and recovering from a cybersecurity incident. A *cybersecurity incident* is an event, such as a data breach, that compromises systems or data of an organization and disrupts operations. Known as *response and recovery*, an incident response plan *responds* to an incident and protects data while minimizing *recovery* time.

An incident compromises confidentiality, integrity, or availability of data and systems. Some incidents are minor, whereas others are serious and require a formal investigation. **Cybersecurity resilience** is the ability of an organization to prepare for, respond to, and recover from a cyberattack. If an organization can defend itself against an attack, it is resilient. *Risk posture* is the overall cybersecurity program of an organization that provides protection from breaches and safeguards its data. Included is the overall management of protecting software and hardware, networks, services, and information of the enterprise.

Managerial controls are written and implemented to protect an organization and mitigate cybersecurity risks. *Security controls* are safeguards to minimize risks to assets of an organization. Incident response processes identify the attack, provide containment for the damages, and eradicate the cause. It involves planning and attention to detail for potential incidents, and a structured plan and organized approach will help resolve a situation. The **incident response process** outlines the steps taken when an incident occurs and becomes the main element of an IRP. An **incident response plan (IRP)** is a written document that provides instructions to follow when an incident occurs.

There are standard frameworks to assist in creating incident response process. National Institute of Standards and Technology (NIST) and SysAdmin, Audit, Network, and Security (SANS) Institute are reliable references.

Incident Response Process

The SANS Institute identifies six key phases of an incident response, as shown in Figure 17-1. An incident response plan should cover all six of these phases.

Preparation

Nobody wants to be caught off guard by an incident with no idea where to begin or what to investigate. Planning is a basic, yet critical, management function for all aspects of an organization and is necessary for incident response as well.

The first step of preparation is to conduct a risk assessment as outlined in Chapter 16. A *risk assessment* is a systematic process that involves identifying risks caused by threats and vulnerabilities associated with assets and ranking them with the most critical risks listed first. IT assets include networks, endpoints, servers, and any computing or mobile device used by an employee within the company.

A *communication plan* is a critical part of the preparation phase. Communication plans should include all stakeholders needing notification of an event when it occurs. *Stakeholders* include various levels of management as well as contacts outside the organization, such as selected vendors and customers directly impacted by a security attack on the company. **Stakeholder management** is the process of notifying those who need to be updated, anticipating questions, and managing their needs.

Identification

Identification is the stage in which a cybersecurity breach is determined and evidence is gathered and analyzed. The root cause of an incident is discovered, entry point of the threat is identified, and level of seriousness is summarized. For example, the root cause of a worm attack could be an e-mail attachment, malicious download, or via portable drive. Discovering how an incident occurred provides insight for preventing similar incidents in the future. During this stage, who, what, where, why, and how questions are answered about the security incident.

Containment

Containment is an action that limits further damage from an incident and ensures evidence is protected and not destroyed. Containment is a *mitigation* technique, which is the act of taking steps to reduce the effects of risks for an organization. Affected assets are segmented and endpoints are disconnected from the network. **Segmentation** is the act of dividing the components of the affected asset, such as the network and software, from other components for security purposes. Each segment should be isolated until the event is resolved.

Figure 17-1 The SANS Institute identifies six phases in the incident response process.

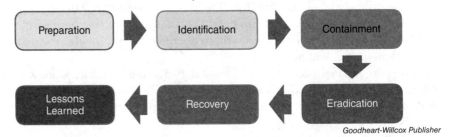

Goodheart-Willcox Publisher

Eradication

After the threat is contained, eradication can begin. **Eradication** is the process of evaluating damages, removing the root cause, and repairing the systems. In this phase, the primary goal is to restore the affected systems to their previous state while attempting to minimize potential losses of data.

Recovery

After an incident is eradicated, the situation recovers to normal operation. *Recovery* may involve reconnecting devices that were isolated. For example, after a computer is cleaned of a virus, it is reconnected to the network. All computer systems should be functioning normally at the completion of the recovery phase. The cost and damages of the security breach is also determined.

Lessons Learned

The final step is the post-incident responses. These are the lessons learned from resolving the incident. It is important to document how the incident occurred and identify steps needed to resolve it. Post-incident responses enable an IT staff to learn from an incident so safeguards can be implemented to prevent similar incidents. This final step can have a critical impact on preventing and resolving future incidents.

An *incident report* is a formal document that summarizes all details of an incident. An organization is required to retain all incident reports. Length of time to keep reports on file are dependent on the industry, type of incident, severity, and state or federal laws that might apply.

Cyber incidents that result in significant damage are reported to federal authorities. The federal agency that receives the initial report coordinates with other relevant federal stakeholders in responding to the incident. The federal government focuses their efforts on threat and asset responses. *Threat response* is the criminal aspect of countering malicious activity. *Asset response* includes protecting assets and mitigating vulnerabilities. This also allows the federal government to link related incidents and share information that protects other organizations.

Part of the post-incident response is to evaluate the risk assessment plan and its associated policies. It involves asking questions such as the following:

- Were there policies in place that may have prevented the incident?
- If so, why were they not followed?
- Should the risk assessment plan or policies be modified?

It is critical to analyze procedures and protocols that were not followed. This enables the organization to adjust policies, procedures, or even personnel. The lessons learned could help identify other areas where policies are not being followed. They may even help identify risks in areas that have not been considered or prioritized.

Incident Response Plan (IRP)

The way in which an organization responds to a computer-security incident should be in an incident response plan (IRP). A well-defined IRP enables an organization to

- identify a cyberattack incident;
- minimize damage caused by an incident; and
- find and fix the cause to prevent future incidents.

A comprehensive IRP prepares employees to handle events such as loss of data or a cybercrime. The goal is to return the organization to a safe, operational state after an incident has occurred. There are many templates available on the Internet to guide an organization when creating a formal plan.

The incident response process as defined by the organization should be included in the IRP. At a minimum, the following elements should be a part of an incident response plan:

- *Computer response team.* The computer incident response team (CIRT) consists of the *first responders* who react to incidents. A document is created that lists each team member contact information, assigned responsibilities, and degree of decision-making each possesses.
- *Reporting procedures.* Incident reporting procedures provide guidelines for reporting an incident, including to whom an incident is reported, how it is reported (via phone or e-mail), and other pertinent information such as urgency levels.
- *Glossary.* A glossary of current cyber incidents, each with a complete description or definition baseline for determining security threats, enables the observer to determine if the threat is truly a security incident.
- *Escalation guidelines.* Escalation statements explain how to determine when a threat is communicated to management and information to classify it as high, medium, and low. Some threats require escalation while others do not.
- *System information and tools.* Information, diagrams, etc. for systems in the organization subject to cyber threats must be available. Tools, such as vulnerability scanners, must be available.

An incident response plan should be tested before it is used to ensure it will work when needed. Therefore, most organizations conduct one or more of the following exercises:

- A *tabletop exercise* is a discussion-based exercise in which a scenario is presented to the team and conversations are conducted as to how it is solved.
- A *walk-through* is a functional exercise that tasks employees with validating plans and readiness by performing their duties in an environment similar to a real situation.
- A *war game* is a simulation in which an actual mock attack is staged. It is a full-scale exercise as close to the real thing as possible. It is a lengthy exercise and takes place on location using equipment and personnel called upon in a real event. Full-scale exercises are conducted by an organization or public agencies can be contracted.

There are agencies that provide guidance for conducting incident response exercises. For example, the Department of Homeland Security (DHS) offers resources for these exercises.

Mitigation Techniques

Mitigation is the act of reducing the severity of something. There are different mitigation techniques that can be used to secure an environment. These techniques include

- SOAR;
- configuration changes; and
- endpoint security solutions.

SOAR

4.4

SOAR, *Security Orchestration, Automation, and Response*, is a security solution that uses an array of software tools and solutions, allows for a collection of data from multiple sources, and generates an automatic response. For example, for a failed login, a response can be generated to a user and confirm if a user made the error. If it is true, a password reset is initiated. However, if the user did *not* perform these attempts, SOAR can quickly disable the account and begin an investigative response such as identifying the IP and MAC addresses of the attempts.

SOAR is a technique that enables an organization to simplify security operations for incident response through use of *playbooks* to provide a checklist needed to resolve an incident and *runbooks* that provide automation to accelerate the process.

Configuration Changes

4.4

Configuration changes can mitigate cybersecurity incidents. The following are suggested precautions:

- *Firewall rules* are essential and determine what is blocked to prevent unauthorized people from accessing data.
- *Mobile device management (MDM)* is a set of software tools that provides a single management platform to control, modify, and secure devices remotely. MDM enables correct configuration to avoid cybersecurity incidents.
- *Data loss prevention (DLP)* is a security strategy that detects potential data breaches or exfiltration transmissions to ensure that sensitive, confidential, or critical data does not leave the organization. Appropriate DLP software configuration detects and identifies sensitive or confidential data before it leaves an endpoint.
- *Content filters and URL filters* help control access to content on the Internet. They block customers and users from seeing information that the company does want made public.
- *Certificates* should be updated or revoked when a security concern exists.

Endpoint Security Solutions

Endpoint security is the practice of securing user endpoint devices on networks to prevent them from malicious activity and attacks. Endpoint-protection tools include the following:

4.4

- *Application whitelisting* is the process of specifying a list of approved applications or executable software permitted to run on a device or network. Software not on an application whitelist is denied permission to run. The automatic denial of applications is called *implicit deny*, or *deny-by-default*.
- *Application blacklisting* is the process of specifying a list of unapproved applications or executable software not permitted to run on a device or network.
- **Quarantine** is an action taken on a file infected with malware or virus. A quarantined file is moved to a portion on the storage disk where it cannot be accessed.
- *Isolation* of an endpoint removes it from the network. This keeps reinfection from occurring.

Cybersecurity Frameworks

An incident response plan is an important component of computer security, and frameworks provide best practices for creating organizational policies. *Cybersecurity frameworks* are policies and procedures written by cybersecurity experts to enhance security strategies in an enterprise environment. Frameworks assist in compliance with regulatory requirements to help improve security as well as overall objectives. Some noted frameworks are as follows:

- The *MITRE ATT&CK™ framework* is a comprehensive matrix of tactics and techniques used by threat hunters, red teamers, and defenders to better classify attacks and assess an organization's risk. MITRE ATT&CK™ is a globally accessible knowledge base of adversary tactics and techniques that was compiled by real-world observations. Figure 17-2 shows 11 tactics that cover the attack cycle to guide organizations in creating their own policies. Each tactic offers sub-techniques that provide detailed information about known attack mechanisms and actions including malware and script commands that form the basis of the attack.

- The *Diamond Model of Intrusion Analysis* is an approach to conducting intelligence on network intrusion threats. It got its name from the four interconnected elements that are the basis of any event as shown in Figure 17-3. Analysis of an event involves collecting and correlating information from each of these four elements to understand the full context of the threat.

- *Cyber Kill Chain* is a series of steps that follow a cyberattack from early stages to data exfiltration as shown in Figure 17-4. Lockheed Martin derived the kill chain framework from a military model originally established to identify, prepare to attack, engage, and destroy a target. The use of the kill chain can be used as a management tool to help continuously improve network defenses.

Digital Forensics

Digital forensics is the recovery, analysis, and protection of digital evidence from a crime scene to present in court. It is a branch of forensics that focuses on collecting

4.2

TECH TIP

The MITRE ATT&CK™ knowledge basis originally focused on attacks on Windows platforms and now contains adversary tactics and procedures that can impact Linux and macOS operating systems. It has also been expanded to cover behavior in mobile, cloud, and industrial control systems.

Figure 17-2 The MITRE ATT&CK™ framework identifies 11 tactics that cover the attack cycle to guide organization in creating their own policies.

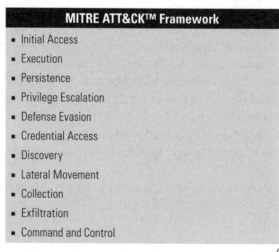

MITRE ATT&CK™ Framework

- Initial Access
- Execution
- Persistence
- Privilege Escalation
- Defense Evasion
- Credential Access
- Discovery
- Lateral Movement
- Collection
- Exfiltration
- Command and Control

Goodheart-Willcox Publisher

Figure 17-3 The Diamond Model of Intrusion Analysis is an approach to conducting intelligence on network intrusion threats.

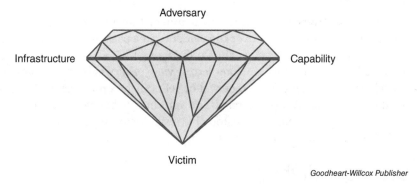

Diamond Model of Intrusion Analysis
Adversary
Infrastructure
Capability
Victim

Goodheart-Willcox Publisher

Figure 17-4 Cyber Kill Chain follows a series of eight steps that follow a cyberattack from early stages to data exfiltration.

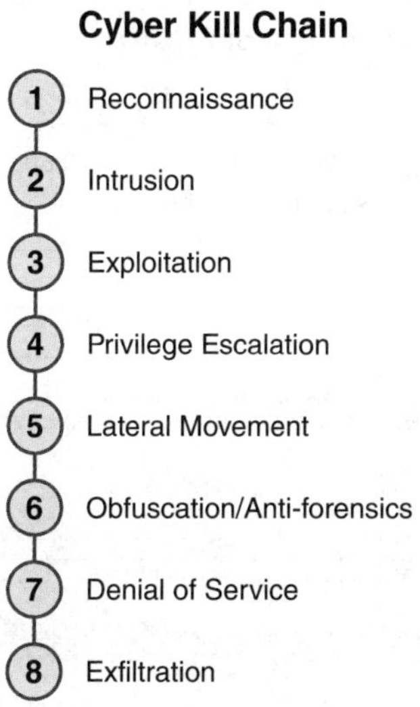

Cyber Kill Chain
1 Reconnaissance
2 Intrusion
3 Exploitation
4 Privilege Escalation
5 Lateral Movement
6 Obfuscation/Anti-forensics
7 Denial of Service
8 Exfiltration

Goodheart-Willcox Publisher

and investigating evidence related to a cybercrime. There are four main categories of digital forensics.

- *Computer forensics* applies to evidence found in computers and digital storage media. This includes laptops, desktops, operating systems, hard drives, and logs.
- *Mobile forensics* is the recovery of digital evidence or data from mobile devices. Cameras and USB drives are in this category.
- *Network forensics* involves the monitoring, collecting, and analyzing evidence related to a computer network.
- *Database forensics* is the recovery of digital information from a database, such as Oracle and Microsoft SQL.

When a cyberattack occurs, an incident response process is followed. Evidence is collected, analyzed, and reported by investigators to solve the incident. The evidence can also be used in court cases, if needed. *Admissible* means information relevant to decisions in a judicial proceeding. Requirements for admissible evidence are the evidence has not been corrupted and the chain of custody has been followed.

4.5

Chain of Custody

A **chain of custody** is a witnessed document that identifies those who maintain unbroken and total control over the evidence in a case. All evidence is logged on an *evidence-tracking document*, as shown in Figure 17-5, and used to record evidence, names of those who collected, handled, or were otherwise in possession of evidence, as well as when each person received or relinquished possession. A *custodial chain* must be intact, meaning there can be no gaps in who had possession of evidence and when. Any gaps in a chain of custody have significant legal ramifications, up to and including a mistrial or dismissal of charges.

4.5

Order of Volatility

An **order of volatility** defines the order or sequence in which digital evidence is collected. Data sources have varying degrees of preservation. *Volatile data* is data that would normally be lost if a computer were to shut down, such as data residing in the memory or cache. Evidence should be collected by starting with the most volatile and moving toward the least volatile of data.

Figure 17-5 An evidence-tracking document is used to record and track evidence as well as when a person received or relinquished possession of the evidence.

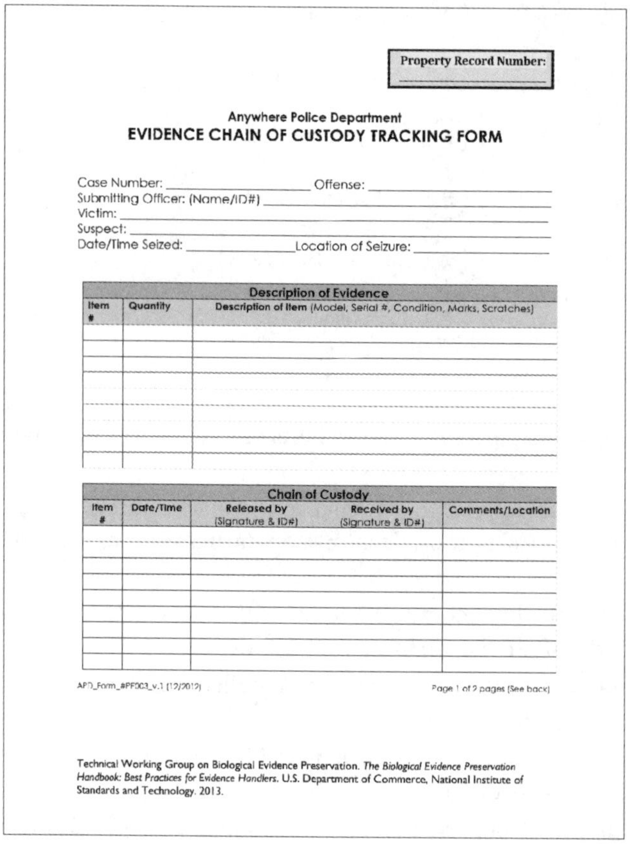

Property Record Number:

Anywhere Police Department

EVIDENCE CHAIN OF CUSTODY TRACKING FORM

Case Number: ____________ Offense: ____________
Submitting Officer: (Name/ID#) ____________
Victim: ____________
Suspect: ____________
Date/Time Seized: ____________ Location of Seizure: ____________

Description of Evidence		
Item #	Quantity	Description of Item (Model, Serial #, Condition, Marks, Scratches)

Chain of Custody				
Item #	Date/Time	Released by (Signature & ID#)	Received by (Signature & ID#)	Comments/Location

APD_Form_#PF003_v.1 (12/2012)

Page 1 of 2 pages (See back)

Technical Working Group on Biological Evidence Preservation. *The Biological Evidence Preservation Handbook: Best Practices for Evidence Handlers*. U.S. Department of Commerce, National Institute of Standards and Technology. 2013.

NIST

1. *CPU registers and cache.* The central processing unit (CPU) cache stores data that is currently being worked on by the CPU. Unlike regular random access memory (RAM), a system has less cache and is more likely to be overwritten sooner than data in the RAM. CPU cache is the most volatile of data and therefore should be collected first, if possible.

2. *Routing tables, ARP cache, process tables, and kernel statistics.* Kernel statistics move back and forth between cache and main memory.

3. *Live network connections.* This includes physical connection ports and wireless connections.

4. *Random-access memory (RAM).* The random-access memory (RAM) indicates what a system is performing. This includes user data in work, system and network processes, and application remnants. This evidence is lost when a device is turned off, so it is important to leave devices on when suspected to be involved in a security incident.

5. *Swap/pagefiles.* Swap files, also known as pagefiles, are temporary files used by operating systems to move unused data from RAM for temporary storage. Virtual memory is also known as a swap file. These files are on the system disk drive and able to extend the amount of RAM available to a computer. Since data is stored on the disk drive, it is less volatile than RAM and will not be lost if a computer is powered down. A swap file is rebuilt when the computer is powered back on. In other words, if you reboot the computer, you lose the virtual memory.

6. *Hard disk drives.* Data stored on a hard disk drive (HDD) remains on the drive after a computer or system is turned off. Data stored on an HDD includes any files, including low-level data such as the master boot record on a disk.

7. *OS.* Operating system (OS) includes temporary operating system files or variable configurations and information, including firmware and a copy of the registry. *Firmware* is the first program that runs on the CPU when it is turned on.

8. *Remote data and logins.* Remote data is external data to the computer of interest. Remote data can include items such as network cache and remote logs.

9. *Devices.* Data stored on devices includes any attached devices, such as USB storage devices, memory cards, and optical discs (CD/DVDs).

Secure the Area

Immediately following a cybercrime, the area should be secured. Securing the area prevents potential evidence from destruction, and failure could result in data being unusable in criminal or civil court proceedings. Securing the area includes dismissing any individual who is not part of the forensic team as well as ensuring devices are untouched and remain powered on to avoid the loss of digital evidence.

Securing the area is a way to preserve the evidence. Evidence must be preserved before it is collected to assure that it has not been tampered with. **Preservation of evidence** is the process of protecting evidence from change, corruption, alteration, or damage throughout its lifecycle. A **legal hold** prohibits employees from destroying documentation and other evidence or deleting data, documents, or items that may be relevant to an investigation. A legal hold is implemented to ensure evidence is preserved in an unaltered state before it is collected. **Data evidence management** is the policies and procedures used by an organization to manage data used as

+ 4.5

evidence in incident response cases. However, more data is not necessarily better. Only pertinent, quality data should be collected, analyzed, and retained.

Metadata

➕ 4.3, 4.5

Investigators search an entire system image for documentation and evidence, including files, folders, cache, cookies, e-mail, and mobile data. *Metadata* is data that gives information about other data, such as the author or creation time of a file. Metadata is data about data. Much time is spent searching through metadata to determine and record the time offset from when a file was created, accessed, or deleted. **Time offset** is the difference in hours and minutes added or subtracted from the *Coordinated Universal Time (UTC)* to get the current time whether it is standard time of daylight saving time. The UTC is the primary standard by which the world regulates clocks and time.

➕ 4.5

The *time-stamped history* of network access, e-mails, Internet searches, and all digital activities play a role in investigating a cybercrime. A **time stamp** is a digital record of when a specific event occurred in a specific time zone. The time-stamped history involves pulling data from the history of file changes, records of actions performed on a computer, and reported details from users. Once this information is gathered, the pieces of information are built into a chronological timeline of events. The timeline assists the investigation team in analyzing the process of events.

➕ 4.5

Event logs are documentation of evidence that provide an audit trail that records user and system events. Some of the information useful to an investigation includes documenting the date, time, and location of logons. In many cases, logs record if a login was local or remote. Other examples of useful forensic information are found in log entries that document when portable devices, such as cameras, mobile phones, and storage media, are connected to the computer. Connections to wireless networks record the time and date of the connection along with the SSID of the WLAN.

Capture the System Image

One of the first tasks that must happen is to capture the system image to preserve integrity and capture the data. To *capture the system image* is to create a snapshot of the current state of all settings and data on a computer.

➕ 4.5

It is important that forensic investigators can demonstrate the actions they conduct are on systems that have been unaltered. *Digital integrity* refers to digital data that has not been altered since its creation, transmission, or storage by an authorized source. If this assurance cannot be provided, the evidence may be viewed as tainted and not admissible in court proceedings.

Hash

➕ 4.5

When data is collected, a copy is made to preserve its current state. A copy uses hashes for integrity checks that prove a copy is original and not manipulated. *Hashing* is an algorithm performed on data to produce a number known as a hash. A *hash* is a collection of data used to compare the mirror image backup to verify that nothing has been modified, tampered, or corrupted. Normally, hard drives are not analyzed on the device in which it is installed; rather, it is copied to a working image. To ensure you are working on the exact same image, you must hash the original drive to achieve its hash value. Before beginning forensic analysis, compute the hash on the backup image. They should be identical.

Before beginning an analysis, forensics team members take a hash of the drive or the files on it. The hash is a computed value based on the contents of the drive as presented. For example, a hash of a hard drive is taken before beginning an examination and duplicated to another device. The original device is then safely stored. On the copied drive, before doing any analysis, the examiner computes a hash of the copied drive. The new computed value is compared with the hash file of the original drive or files. An example of comparing hash files is shown in Figure 17-6. If the values are the same, the data integrity is intact. If the values are *not* the same, the data has been manipulated or corrupted, and the contents cannot be used for analysis.

The two most prominent tools used for hashing are hardware- and software-based write blockers. *Write blocking* is a procedure that ensures changes have not been made to an original system image or a source disk. In essence, it turns a hard drive into a read-only device. A hardware-based write blocker is a physical device that attaches to the source disk and prevents any write activity to that drive. A software-based write blocker turns on write-blocking flags to ensure changes cannot be made. A software-based write blocker is typically used when a drive is mounted or accessible via the forensic workstation. Both write blockers preserve original content and maintain digital evidence integrity.

Checksum

A *checksum* is a value derived from data to ensure no errors occurred during transmission of the information. Checksums provide data integrity but do not verify data authenticity. As with hashes, checksums are computed prior to transmission of a file. On the receiving end, the checksum value is computed and must match the original value to ensure data integrity.

Digital Provenance

Digital provenance refers to the establishment of chain of custody. It ensures integrity has been maintained. Chain of custody remains intact and evidence collection was performed in an accountable and responsible manner.

Network Traffic and Logs

Network traffic and logs contain information recorded about a user's activity on a network. Data is collected from traffic from multiple locations including servers, switches, routers, firewalls, VPN appliances, and any location to which data travels. Network event logs can also contain critical information for identifying events related to the investigation as well as providing information for a timeline based on logins and other artifacts.

Figure 17-6 It is important to compare hashes between the original information and the copy to ensure the integrity of the data.

Goodheart-Willcox Publisher

Capture Video

Recording a video provides digital proof as evidence of an attack in an undisturbed state as well as time stamps the event. *Record time offset* is the difference between the time stamp on the video and the real time the event happened. A time stamp can be wrong, and investigators must establish the real time by using a legitimate time server. The video time stamp is compared to real time of the video to check for discrepancies.

All evidence must be preserved and unaltered. Video provides proof that evidence was obtained using acceptable standards and practices. This reduces the potential claims of alleged poor practices and evidence tampering. In addition to videotaping the crime scene, photographs are taken of papers, messages on a monitor, and even trash in a garbage or recycling can.

Interviews

The purpose of interviews is to gather data about the incident and document details about the event. It is imperative to call any witnesses to assist the investigation process and participate in an interview. A *witness* is a person who saw an event when it took place. The witness could be the user of the computer or device in question or the system administrator.

A witness can testify about how the event occurred, where and when it occurred, and other information related to the event in question. A witness can later testify in court as a voluntary participant.

Forensic Procedure

Procedures are necessary for an investigation of a cyberattack. A typical digital forensics procedure consists of the steps shown in Figure 17-7.

Strategic intelligence is the evaluation, analysis, and dissemination of evidence or data required for creating organizational policy that drives investigations. Rather than provide technical detail, this information is for management to make high-level decisions about investigations for the organization. Strategic intelligence plays a role in helping understand past forensic digital security events so current events can be remedied and future defenses put in place.

Counterintelligence is the gathering of information about the methods and extent of a cybercriminal's ability to obtain data from a system. Counterintelligence helps an organization be proactive and eliminate future attacks.

Logs are used to record evidence collected and relevant to investigative, criminal, or civil proceedings. Logs should be treated as critical evidence. In addition, log retention polices are established as a part of data evidence management.

To preserve data is to make sure the chain of custody is followed and evidence remains undisturbed. Once this is accomplished, evidence is collected and the data is analyzed and documented. Then a report is made to present the findings.

Throughout the forensic procedure, it is important to track work-hours and expenses of an investigation. A **work-hour** is the amount of work performed by an

Figure 17-7 The digital forensics procedure typically consists of five steps.

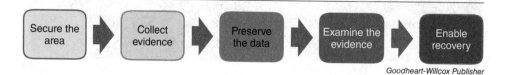

average employee in one hour. Recording work-hours demonstrates which individuals completed what tasks. It also tracks when individuals performed tasks and how long each task took to complete. After an investigation is completed, work-hours are used to determine the costs of the investigation. The hours can also be used as a baseline for future budgets.

Data Acquisition

Acquisition is the process of collecting evidence from the identified media that represents the evidence. **Data acquisition** is the capturing or collecting of volatile and non-volatile data. *Volatile data* is evidence stored in memory that will disappear when the device no longer has a power source. *Non-volatile data* is information that is stored and preserved, such as data saved to a hard drive. Examples of data acquisition tasks are as follows:

- *Create a snapshot.* A snapshot is a forensic image, which is a duplicate of media, such as a hard-disk drive.

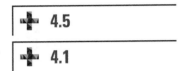

- *Create a data dump (dd) file.* A **data dump (dd)** is a disk image file that is a replica of a hard drive.
- *Create a memdump.* A **memory dump**, also known as a *memdump*, is a process that "dumps" the content of a computer's memory, including RAM, and stores it. The data is then analyzed.
- *Take screenshots.* A **screenshot**, also known as a *screen capture*, is a digital image of the current image displayed on a device's screen.
- *Create a mirror image backup.* A **mirror image backup** is a backup that replicates a hard drive, including any files and hidden data sectors stored on the drive.

Digital forensics applies forensic *data recovery*, which is the process of retrieving corrupted or damaged files from hard disks or removable media. *E-discovery* is the process of collecting easily accessible digital items, such as e-mails and calendars.

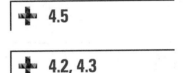

Digital data from a forensic investigation, such as e-mails and other documents, must be retained. *Retention policies* are guidelines for retaining and storing evidence as stipulated by laws or organizational policies. For electronic devices, this includes protection against static electricity. The use of special equipment, such as Faraday bags, can help protect static-sensitive devices—such as a hard drive, RAM, or video card—from damage. Other evidence should be packaged and secured with tamper-evident tape. Digital data from a forensic investigation, such as e-mail and other documents, must also be preserved and retained. Most organizations use electronic backups to retain data. All evidence should be stored in secure, fireproof areas.

Software is used as a tool to help the acquisition of evidence process. FTK® Imager is computer forensic software that provides a data preview tool used to assess electronic evidence to determine if further analysis is needed. Another example is WinHex, which is a universal hex editor used for forensic evidence gathering. By using WinHex, an investigator can view and edit any kind of file, perform data recovery, access physical RAM and other processors' virtual memory, and erase (wipe) confidential files securely.

Autopsy® is an open-source digital forensics platform capable of analyzing various types of digital media and mobile devices. It identifies, sorts, and catalogues various pieces of forensic data. Autopsy® has a plug-in architecture that enables extensibility from either custom-built or community-developed modules. Autopsy® is commonly used by law enforcement, military, and corporate examiners to investigate activities on a computer.

Forensic objects that contain evidence are **artifacts**. This may include computers, hard drives, flash drives, phones, e-mail, and documents. All evidence collected should be marked with evidence stickers, or *tags*, which help in the storage and processing of the evidence during the investigation. Each item is tagged with information on when and where it was collected and other pertinent information. Examples of useful artifacts include the following:

- Computer systems, including laptops
- Hard drives, including external drives and solid-state drives
- USB devices
- Removable media, including memory cards
- Mobile devices, including tablets, smartphones, and e-readers
- Peripheral devices, including mouse, keyboard, web and digital cameras, and scanners
- Digital and video cameras
- Surveillance equipment
- GPS equipment, video game consoles, and MP3 players
- Reference materials, including books

Forensic Report

The forensic report becomes part of the incident response report. Similar to other reports, it documents and gives detail about each step of the forensic process. Because the report can be used in a court hearing, it is subject to *nonrepudiation*, which is the assurance that an individual or group of people cannot deny the validity of something. This means a forensic report's conclusions are accurate and cannot be repudiated as the report was provided by a professional with appropriate training who used scientific methods for the investigation.

Cloud Forensics

Cloud forensics is applying digital forensics to the cloud environment rather than on the physical premises of an organization. A major difference in cloud vs. on-premises forensics is that cloud service providers operate in locations separate from the business using the cloud service. In a traditional digital forensic investigation, digital artifacts are obtained at the location or potential crime scene. In a cloud digital forensic investigation, artifacts are collected from cloud service provider (CSP) locations, which could be around the world. Evidence is generally presented in the location where it is discovered. This could mean that the business contracting the CSP may not have control over where the evidence or trial is held. *Data sovereignty* states digital data is subject to the jurisdiction and laws of the country where the evidence is located, and an investigation *must* abide by the requirements at the location. A trial could be held in another country and make it difficult for the business to monitor the proceedings.

A *data breach* is an incident where information is stolen or taken from a system without the permission, knowledge, or authorization of the system's owner. In the United States, all 50 states have data breach notification laws that require private and public entities to notify any individual of a data breach that involves personally identifiable information (PII). In an on-premises model, organizations must abide by US law. Cloud service providers, however, are subject to data breach laws enacted in the country in which the data is located. The organization that hires the CSP has no control over how the provider handles breach of data. This can put the organization in a tenuous position if data is breached and they cannot control how it is handled.

Maintaining a clear chain of custody of evidence in a cloud investigation can be difficult. In an on-premises model, investigators have access and complete control of the evidence and the chain of custody. In cloud forensics, the CSP is in control of the investigation and hires the team that collects evidence. The CSP is responsible for preservation and collection of data. If the team hired by the CSP is not properly trained, the integrity of the evidence could be considered tainted and inadmissible in court. The organization contracting the CSP normally has no input in the process.

Security precautions should be in place when using the cloud. When negotiating the contract, specifics should be discussed. Some of the topics that should be included in a contract about forensic investigations include the following:

- Amount of time in which the organization is notified after a breach of data
- Access to the CSP servers so the organization can collect its own data if an investigation is needed
- Geographical location of the data and legal requirements in that location

While the business is the owner of the data stored in the cloud, it is located on another vendor's system. Owners must trust that the cloud vendor is performing the safety and security measures as provided. However, trust alone does not provide for strong security. One method of ensuring the cloud service providers are using appropriate controls and remaining compliant is to conduct audits. In the contract between the business and cloud vendor should be a section entitled *Right to Audit*. The Right to Audit section should contain an *audit clause*, which is an agreement to provide relevant documentation. This clause should specify what the business is permitted to audit and when audits are permissible.

 4.5

SUMMARY

Incident Response (IR)

- Incident response (IR) is acting against and recovering from a cybersecurity incident.
- A cybersecurity incident is an event that compromises systems or data of an organization and disrupts operations. Some incidents are minor, whereas others are serious and require a formal investigation.
- The incident response process outlines the steps taken when an incident occurs. The process becomes the main elements of an IRP. An incident response plan (IRP) is a written document that provides instructions to follow when an incident occurs.

Incident Response Process

- The SANS Institute identifies six key phases of an incident response: preparation, identification, containment, eradication, recovery, and lessons learned.
- Preparation is necessary for incident response. Preparation involves conducting a risk assessment, creating a communication plan, and stakeholder management.

- Identification is determining where a cybersecurity breach is determined. The root cause of an incident is discovered, entry point of the threat is identified, and level of seriousness is summarized.
- Containment is an action that limits further damage from an incident and ensures no evidence is destroyed in the process. It is a mitigation technique.
- Eradication can begin after the threat is contained. It involves removing the cause of the incident by evaluating damages, removing the root cause, and repairing all systems.
- After eradication, the situation recovers to normal operation. All computer systems should be functioning normally at the completion of the recovery phase. The cost and damages of the security breach is also determined.
- The lessons learned are recorded in a post-incident response. From the response, IT staff can learn from the incident so safeguards can be put into place to prevent similar incidents.

Incident Response Plan (IRP)

- An incident response plan enables an organization to identify a cyberattack incident, minimize the damage, and find and fix the cause to prevent future incidents. The goal is to return the organization to a safe and operational state after an incident has occurred.
- An incident response plan should include a computer response team, reporting procedures, glossary, escalation guidelines, and system information and tools.
- An incident response plan should be tested before put to use to make sure it will work when needed. Therefore, an organization can use one of the following exercises: tabletop exercise, walk-through, and war game.

Mitigation Techniques

- Mitigation techniques include SOAR, configuration changes, and endpoint security solutions.
- SOAR uses an array of software tools and solutions that allows for a collection of data from multiple sources and generates an automatic response. It enables an organization to simplify security operations for incident response through playbooks and runbooks.
- Configuration changes can mitigate cybersecurity incidents. Suggested precautions include firewall rules, mobile device management (MDM), data loss prevention (DLP), content and URL filters, and certificates.
- Endpoint security is the practice of securing user endpoint devices on networks to prevent them from malicious activity and attacks. Common tools used include application whitelisting and blacklisting, quarantine, and isolation of an endpoint.

Cybersecurity Frameworks

- Frameworks provide best practices for creating organizational polices.
- Cybersecurity frameworks are policies and procedures written by cybersecurity experts to enhance cybersecurity strategies within an enterprise environment.
- Common frameworks include MITRE ATT&CK™, Diamond Model of Intrusion Analysis, and Cyber Kill Chain.

Digital Forensics

- Digital forensics is the recovery, analysis, and protection of digital evidence from a crime scene to present in court. It focuses on collecting and investigating evidence related to a cybercrime.

- When a cyberattack occurs, an incident response process is followed. Evidence is collected, analyzed, and reported by investigators to solve the incident. The evidence can also be used in court cases, if needed.
- Requirements for admissible evidence are the evidence has not been corrupted and the chain of custody has been followed. In addition, evidence is gathered following the order of volatility.

Secure the Area

- Immediately following a cybercrime, secure the area by dismissing any individual who is not part of the forensic team as well as ensuring devices are untouched and remain powered on. This prevents potential evidence from being destroyed.
- Securing the area is a way to preserve the evidence, which is the process of protecting evidence from change, corruption, alteration, or damage throughout its lifecycle.
- A legal hold prohibits employees from destroying or deleting data, documents, or other items that may be relevant to an investigation. It is implemented to ensure evidence is preserved in an unaltered state before it is collected.
- Types of evidence to collect include metadata, capturing the system image, network traffic and logs, and videos. It also includes conducting interviews with witnesses.

Forensic Procedure

- A typical digital forensic procedure consists of investigating, preserving data, analyzing data, documenting data, and presenting the data findings.
- Strategic intelligence is the evaluation, analysis, and dissemination of evidence or data required for creating organizational policy that drives investigations. It plays a role in helping understand past forensic digital security events so current events can be remedied and future defenses be put in place.
- Counterintelligence is the gathering of information about the methods and extent of a cybercriminal's ability to obtain data from a system. It helps an organization be proactive and eliminate future attacks.
- Throughout the forensic procedure, it is important to track work-hours and expenses of an investigation. Recording work-hours demonstrates which individuals completed what tasks. It also tracks when individuals did the tasks and how long it took to complete.

Data Acquisition

- Data acquisition is the capturing or collecting of volatile data and non-volatile data. Examples of acquisition tasks include create a snapshot, data dump file, memdump, and a mirror image backup. It also includes taking screenshots.
- Digital forensics applies forensic data recovery, which is the process of retrieving corrupted or damaged files from hard disks or removable media. E-discovery is the process of collecting easily accessible digital items.
- Digital data from a forensic investigation must be retained. Retention policies are guidelines for retaining and storing evidence as stipulated by laws or organizational policies.
- Software is used as a tool to help the acquisition of evidence process. Examples include FTK® Imager, WinHex, and Autopsy®.

- Forensic objects that contain evidence are artifacts. All evidence collected should be tagged with information on when and where it was collected and other pertinent information.

Forensic Report

- The forensic report becomes part of the incident response report. It documents and gives detail about each step of the forensic process.
- A forensic report can be used in court hearings. Therefore, it is subject to nonrepudiation. This means a forensic report's conclusions are accurate and cannot be repudiated.

Cloud Forensics

- Cloud forensics is applying digital forensics to the cloud environment rather than on the physical premises of an organization.
- A major difference in cloud vs. on-premises forensics is that cloud service providers operate in locations that are separate from the business using the cloud service. Artifacts are collected from cloud service provider locations, which could be around the world.
- In the on-premises model, organizations must abide by US law when data breaches occur. Cloud service providers are subject to data breach laws enacted in the country in which the data is located.
- Maintaining a clear chain of custody of evidence in a cloud investigation can be difficult compared to on-premises. In an on-premises model, investigators have access and complete control of the evidence and the chain of custody. In the cloud forensics, the CSP is in control of the investigation and hires the team that collects evidence.

REVIEW QUESTIONS

1. Define *incident response*.
2. Briefly explain cybersecurity resilience.
3. Explain the steps in the incident response process.
4. Differentiate between containment and segmentation.
5. Summarize an incident response plan (IRP).
6. Identify types of mitigation techniques used to secure an environment.
7. Define the roles of playbooks and runbooks.
8. Identify and explain four endpoint solutions used to mitigate cybersecurity incidents.
9. Explain three common cybersecurity frameworks.
10. Summarize digital forensics.
11. List the order that evidence should be collected according to the order of volatility.
12. Identify types of evidence to collect when securing an area.
13. What is the term for a digital record of when a specific event occurred in a specific time zone?
14. Identify and explain three elements of capturing the system image.

15. Explain the forensic procedure.

16. List three common software tools used to help the acquisition of evidence process.

17. Briefly explain data acquisition.

18. Identify and explain five data acquisition tasks.

19. Summarize a forensic report.

20. Contrast cloud forensics to on-premises forensics.

✚ SAMPLE SECURITY+ EXAM QUESTIONS

1. Which is a written document that provides instructions to be followed when an incident occurs?

    A. File signature

    B. Incident response plan (IRP)

    C. Jump bag

    D. CART

2. Which of the following describes those who should be notified as part of a communication plan?

    A. Stakeholders

    B. First responders

    C. Cloud service provider

    D. Law enforcement

3. Which of the following incidents would *most likely* be given the highest priority?

    A. A flash drive containing unencrypted spreadsheets of last month's sales projections has gone missing.

    B. A report containing public information is left in a printer.

    C. The guest account is not disabled on a computer.

    D. A server has been left unpatched.

4. Which of the following lists the correct order for addressing a security incident in which a user is found to have local admin rights on a secure computer?

    A. Remove the admin rights, and create a policy that details who should have admin rights.

    B. Document why this occurred, and remove the admin rights.

    C. Determine if this is a security incident, and remove the admin rights.

    D. Remove the admin rights, and contain any potential issues that may have occurred.

5. Of the following, which is *not* considered metadata?

    A. Creator of a file

    B. Time stamp of a file

    C. Date of last modification

    D. File name

6. What is the correct order of a digital forensic procedure?

    A. Investigate, document data, analyze data, preserve data, present data

    B. Preserve data, analyze data, investigate, document data, present data

    C. Investigate, preserve data, analyze data, document data, present data

    D. Document data, preserve data, analyze data, present data, investigate

7. A(n) _____ prohibits employees from destroying or deleting data, documents, or other items that may be relevant to an investigation.

    A. NDA

    B. write-blocker

    C. legal hold

    D. Faraday shielding bag

8. Which framework is a comprehensive matrix of tactics and techniques used by threat hunters to better classify attacks and assess an organization's risk?

    A. The MITRE ATT&CK™ framework

    B. The Diamond Model of Intrusion Analysis

    C. The Cyber Kill Chain

    D. Network forensic analysis

9. What is the difference between volatile and non-volatile data?

    A. Volatile data is data infected with malware; non-volatile data is clean data.

    B. Volatile data disappears when a computer is shut down; non-volatile data is stored until it is deleted.

    C. Volatile data is data currently in a state of quarantine; non-volatile data is data that has had malware removed.

    D. Volatile data is data that remains on a drive after a computer is shut down; non-volatile data is data that has been backed up to the cloud.

10. Which of the following examples of data collections is *most* volatile?

    A. Routing tables

    B. Pagefiles

    C. Hard drives

    D. OS

LAB EXERCISES

Lab 17-1: Incident Scoring

The United States Computer Emergency Readiness Team (US-CERT) has created a demonstration page to illustrate the National Cybersecurity and Communications Integration Center (NCCIC) cyber incident scoring system. Incidents are scored between 0 and 100. Once the score is assessed, a priority level is assigned. This website will give you an idea of how a score is assigned.

1. Launch a web browser, and navigate to the US-CERT website (www.us-cert.gov).

2. Use the site's search function, and search for nciss demo. In the search results, select the link for **NCISS Incident Scoring Demo.**

3. Scroll through the page, and notice the areas that are assessed and scored.

4. Consider this scenario: an employee lost a laptop that held unencrypted employee information, but nothing classified.

5. Make an appropriate selection in each area. Notice how the score is built as you make a selection in each area.

Lab 17-2: CSIRT Team

A CSIRT, or computer emergency response team, is responsible for the incident response plan. It must address all six phases of an incident. For this exercise, you will act as a member of a CSIRT.

1. Create a team with two or three classmates, as directed by your instructor.

2. Prepare a summary of how you would respond to the discovery of a keylogger on the system.

3. Record information on how you might approach the six phases. Be detailed, especially for the last three phases.

4. Discuss and share your team's approach with the class.

Lab 17-3: Computer Forensics Certification

The Certified Forensics Computer Examiner (CFCE) is one of the popular industry certifications in the forensics field. This exercise explores CFCE certification.

1. Launch a web browser, and navigate to the International Association of Computer Investigative Specialists website (www.iacis.com).

2. Click the Certification menu, and then click **CFCE** in the menu. The overview page is displayed.

3. What are the two phases that must be completed to obtain this certification? How does this differ from other certifications you are familiar with obtaining?

4. In the Certification menu, click **Certification FAQ**. Review the frequently asked questions.

5. In addition to a background check, what is the cost to enroll in the CFCE program?

6. Using the options in the **Training** menu, review some of the available classes. Which ones interest you?

Lab 17-4: Exif Data

Many digital documents, including images, may contain hidden information. Metadata can provide forensic investigators with important information.

1. Obtain the image file from your instructor, and open it in an image editor or by double-clicking the file. Look at the photograph. It could have been taken at any seaside location.

2. Close the image file.

3. In file explorer, right-click on the image file, and click **Properties** in the shortcut menu. The **Properties** dialog box is displayed.

4. Click the **Details** tab in the **Properties** dialog box, as shown. Review the Exif data. From this data, it is easy to determine what device took the photograph and when it was taken. The GPS data can be used to find the exact location where the photograph was taken.

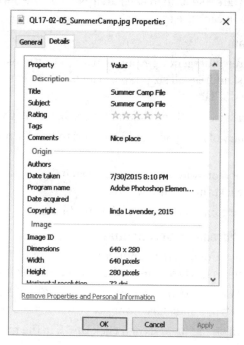

5. Latitude and longitude can be used to locate any place on Earth. Both are specified in degrees, minutes, and seconds. The latitude data for this image is 35 degrees, 12 minutes, 30.1699999999... seconds. The seconds value can be rounded to 30. These values can be entered into a geolocator website or converted to a decimal degree value and entered directly into the Google search engine.

6. To convert the latitude to a decimal degree value, take the seconds (30) and divide by 60. There are 60 seconds in one minute. The result is .5.

7. Add .5 to the minutes (12) and divide the result by 60. There are 60 minutes in one degree. The result is .2.

8. Add .2 to the degrees. The final decimal degree equivalent for the latitude of this image is 30.2 degrees.

9. Applying what you have learned, convert the longitude value for the photograph to a decimal degree value. What is the decimal degree value?

10. Launch a web browser, and navigate to Google Maps (maps.google.com). Enter the latitude decimal value, a space, a dash, and the longitude decimal value. The dash indicates the western hemisphere. Where was the photograph taken?

CASE STUDY

Confidential Information

It has been widely recognized that members of CSIRT teams often face ethical dilemmas as they respond to incidents. To help guide these members, the GIAC published a code of ethics to encourage high ethical and appropriate conduct. This can be found on the SANS website. Search for GIAC code of ethics to locate the document. Consider a situation in which a CSIRT member responds to a call about the company's payroll report left unattended on a printer. The print job is tracked to the payroll clerk, who is a close friend of the responder. The responder chooses to give the print job back to the payroll clerk with a verbal warning and no further action.

1. Was this an appropriate and ethical response? Why or why not?

2. If you feel a different response was needed, explain what you would have done differently.

Business Continuity and Disaster Recovery

LEARNING OUTCOMES

- Define *business continuity*.
- Identify elements included in a business-impact analysis.
- Explain a disaster recovery plan and the steps involved.

KEY TERMS

archive bit	generator	RAID 1
business continuity	hot site	RAID 1+0
business continuity plan (BCP)	incremental backup	RAID 5
business-impact analysis (BIA)	IT contingency plan (ITCP)	recovery point objective (RPO)
cold site	mean time between failures (MTBF)	recovery site
copy backup	mean time to failure (MTTF)	recovery time objective (RTO)
data backup	mean time to repair (MTTR)	redundancy
differential backup	mission-critical functions and systems	resilience
disaster recovery plan (DRP)	multipathing	restoration order
failover	network-attached storage (NAS)	single point of failure (SPOF)
failover cluster	power distribution unit (PDU)	storage area network (SAN)
fault tolerance	power surge	uninterruptible power supply (UPS)
full backup	RAID 0	warm site

SECURITY+ CERTIFICATION EXAM OBJECTIVES

The following Security+ Certification Exam Objectives are covered in this chapter.

- **+** 2.1: Site resiliency
- **+** 2.5: Redundancy
- **+** 2.5: Geographic dispersal
- **+** 2.5: Disk
- **+** 2.5: Power

- **+** 2.5: Replication
- **+** 2.5: Backup types
- **+** 2.5: High availability
- **+** 2.5: Restoration order
- **+** 4.2: Disaster recovery plan

- **+** 4.2: Business continuity plan
- **+** 4.2: Continuity of operation planning (COOP)
- **+** 5.4: Business impact analysis

OVERVIEW

According to statistics, global economic losses due to natural disasters total approximately $232 billion, ranking natural disasters among the most negatively impactful events on business. However, business operations are affected by man-made disasters or events as well, including hacking, terrorism, sabotage, and general human errors. The ability of a business to continue operating despite catastrophes and adverse actions is vital to its longevity, reputation, and financial health.

To best prepare for the worst-case scenario of operational shutdown, a business should create a business-impact analysis (BIA) to identify how a failure or outage threatens a company's ability to restore operations in a manner that aligns with recovery objectives. The BIA provides the basis for organizations to develop disaster recovery plans (DRPs) to define how operations and computer systems will recover in the event of a natural or man-made disaster. The development of these plans can help mitigate the impact of a negative event before it occurs. In this chapter, you will learn about business continuity; business-impact analyses (BIAs), including resilience and redundancy; and disaster recovery plans (DRPs), including data backups, restoration, and recovery.

SECURITY+ NOTE

Information security specialists, because of their technical knowledge, are typically included in the creation of strategies and plans to promote business continuity. The CompTIA Security+ Certification Exam will test your knowledge of redundant and fault-tolerant solutions, as well as the planning and recovery of data to ensure business continuity. Therefore, it is important for you to understand the impact of a disaster on not only an organization's network but also the business as a whole.

Business Continuity

Business continuity is the ability of a business to remain operational before, during, and after a catastrophic event has occurred. The inability to open or provide services is extremely costly for a business and results in the reduction of revenue and profit. Employees may not be able to work, which could translate to lost wages and a negative impact on the economy. An organization must be prepared and focused on the continuation of its business and the protection of critical assets and services.

A **business continuity plan (BCP)** is a comprehensive and proactive plan that provides the steps needed to keep a business operational before, during, and after a disaster. It is a strategy to address how to sustain critical functions within 12 hours of a disaster and up to 30 days before returning to normal operation, while relocating personnel to another facility. According to NIST, a *continuity of operations plan (COOP)* is another term for a business continuity plan.

 4.2

A business must be able to defend itself and guarantee that the business will continue operation. The plan takes into consideration the CIA triad of confidentiality, integrity, and access and how each component of the business will recover from the disruption.

There are multiple components of business continuity planning, as shown in Figure 18-1. Similar to an incident response plan, crisis communication is of major importance. A *crisis communication plan* is a plan that outlines what a business should do during a crisis as well as throughout the hours and days that follow a disaster. A business must be prepared to address stakeholders to provide details of the disaster and outline the way in which the business will approach communication.

Figure 18-1 Business continuity planning comprises multiple steps and components.

Business Continuity Planning Checklist	
1	Management team reviews policies created for governance, risk, and organizational compliance
2	Develop business continuity plan
3	Develop disaster recovery plan
4	Review both plans and implement changes if needed
5	Test both plans to identify weaknesses or shortcomings
6	Maintain plans and update if needed

Goodheart-Willcox Publisher

Business-Impact Analysis (BIA)

One of the first steps in establishing a business continuity plan is to perform a business-impact analysis. A **business-impact analysis (BIA)** is a detailed process that determines the potential consequences of business disruptions and uses data to develop recovery strategies. It includes financial and nonfinancial assessments that an emergency or crisis has on a business, as well as the following:

- *Impact on life* is how business interruptions affect the well-being of an organization's employees and customers as well as other stakeholders.
- *Impact on property* is the effect business interruptions have on physical, tangible assets.
- *Impact on safety* is the effect of business interruptions on the physical protections of its employees.
- *Impact on reputation* is the result of business interruptions on the perceived status of an organization to its customers.
- *Impact on finance* is the after-effect of funding of an organization.

Most BIAs include an impact on privacy assessment. This assessment identifies data at risk, such as personally identifiable information (PII), which must be protected at all times. The privacy officer is responsible for setting data policies and procedures to keep data secure to ensure business continuity.

A BIA identifies **mission-critical functions and systems**, which are the essential functions and systems necessary to keep a business operational. These are the most essential services that must function continuously in order for a company to be successful. The negative consequences could be financial loss or damage to a business's reputation. Mission-critical applications and services are unique to each business or organization.

Continuity planning requires that a *site risk assessment* be performed to determine mission-critical system vulnerabilities associated with the site at which the company is located. When a disaster strikes, management must be aware of factors that comprise the facility and assets prone to damage from a disaster. In a site risk assessment, vulnerabilities such as building construction materials, security systems, and sprinkler systems are assessed and determination is made as to how each would survive a disaster. Of specific importance to IT professionals, a record of where each IT item is located is necessary so removal of critical assets can occur as soon as possible immediately following an event.

High Availability

BIA identifies downtime maximums before damage occurs. *High availability (HA)* is the ability of a system to remain available with no interruption. Systems with high availability minimize downtime and maximize uptime. High availability provides **failover**, which is the action of switching from primary equipment to secondary equipment with no human intervention and with little or no interruption. Failover seamlessly switches to a reliable standby source and can be achieved by incorporating a **failover cluster**, which is a group of servers that coordinate to maintain availability of resources. If one node fails, another node in the cluster takes over.

Despite best efforts, companies must plan for the possibility that there will be unexpected downtime and potential loss of data. Senior management must plan for this possibility and determine objectives for restoration of data and systems. The two primary objectives are recovery point objective (RPO) and recovery time objective (RTO).

- The **recovery point objective (RPO)** is the maximum amount of data that an organization can afford to lose after operations cease. A backup strategy must take this time into account.

- The **recovery time objective (RTO)** is the target time by which applications and systems must be restored to avoid unacceptable consequences after a disaster. A rating system can be used to define *maximum* amount of time that can be lost. Figure 18-2 shows an example of a rating system.

➕ 5.4

Resilience

A BIA reviews systems for resilience. **Resilience** is the ability of a system to recover from a disruption in an acceptable amount of time. By improving its resilience, a business can be proactive in preventing disasters.

Resilience can be improved by forecasting potential hardware faults. Hardware experiences wear and tear that can cause mechanical elements to fail. It is impossible to prevent all failures from occurring; however, by analyzing failure rates, it is possible to predict when hardware might fail, which can help avoid disasters. Measurements to assist with this analysis include the following:

- MTBF
- MTTF
- MTTR

MTBF

➕ 5.4

Mean time between failures (MTBF) is a measure of the average time that passes before a fault occurs. *Mean* is an average. The manufacturer computes MTBF during the quality control process. An example of MTBF information that may appear in a user manual for hard drives appears in Figure 18-3.

Rating	Description
Extremely Critical (1 to 3 days)	These are essential services needed to fulfill operational, legal, or safety issues.
Critical (4 to 14 days)	These services are critical to the organization's ability to operate. Failure to restore them within 14 days could cause significant issues.
Important (15 to 30 days)	These services or resources support the critical applications. If they are not functioning, there will be minimal impact on the organization's operation.
Noncritical (Over 30 days)	If these applications or resources are not restored, they will have little to no impact on normal business operations.

Goodheart-Willcox Publisher

Figure 18-2 A rating system should be used to define the maximum amount of time that can be lost.

4.2 Reliability

4.2.1 Mean Time Between Failures (MTBF) and Annualized Failure Rate (AFR)

This disk drive will experience a mean time between failures (MTBF) rate of 1,000,000 hours or an annualized failure rate (AFR) of 0.73% over a service life of seven (7) years under these conditions:

- 8,760 hours of power-on condition per year
- Drive-reported temperature not exceeding 90°F (32°C)
- Ambient temperature not exceeding 75°F (25°C)
- Workload that is not excessive
- Dust contamination levels at the drive per ISO 14644-1 Class 8 standards

MTBF and AFR are for the population of a production run and do not apply to individual units.

Goodheart-Willcox Publisher

Instead of MTBF, some manufacturers use *annualized failure rate (AFR)*, which calculates the *probable* percentage of drive failures in one year due to supplier issue. Comparatively, MTBF provides the average number of service hours before a failure *may* occur. Some manufacturers may use the terms MTBF and AFR interchangeably. However, the two figures are technically different.

MTTF

Mean time to failure (MTTF) is the average amount of time an irreparable asset operates before it fails. MTTF is displayed as a number that represents functional hours before failure occurs. For example, if a manufacturer lists the MTTF as 1,000,000 hours, this implies the drive should last *on average* over 100 years. Another way to represent this value is with *power-on hours (POH)*.

MTTF is sometimes represented as a bathtub curve as shown in Figure 18-4. In a bathtub curve, failures typically occur early and late in the life of a hard drive. Failures during the middle part of the drive's life are not common.

Figure 18-4 A bathtub curb shows the hard drive failures occur at the beginning and the end of the drive's life while there are few failures in the middle.

Goodheart-Willcox Publisher

MTTR

Mean time to repair (MTTR) is a calculation for the average time it takes to repair or replace a failed component. This applies to *all* equipment, not just hard drives. This calculation includes repair time, delivery time of the new component, and testing of the replacements. A typical hard drive can be replaced almost immediately. However, not all IT hardware is readily available. Some systems may require special-order parts or consultation with a specialized contractor.

Redundancy

Redundancy is a way to support resilience and business continuity. **Redundancy** is duplication of systems to increase dependability. For example, if one server shuts down, a backup server should be in place so operations do not shut down. **Fault tolerance** is the ability of a system to operate without interruption when one or more components fail. Fault tolerance depends on redundancy.

RAID

RAID is an acronym that stands for *redundant array of independent disks* or *redundant array of inexpensive disks*. RAID arrangements provide *disk redundancy* by writing to two or more disks simultaneously. By writing to multiple disks, data can be recovered in the event of one disk failing. Commonly used RAID solutions include the following.

RAID 0

RAID 0, also known as *disk striping*, is a RAID configuration in which multiple hard drives work in synchronization with each other when saving or retrieving data. There must be a minimum of two hard disks to implement RAID 0, which supports a maximum of 32 disks. RAID 0 does not provide fault tolerance but does provide increased performance.

Although there are multiple drives, they logically work together as one drive. Each drive's read-write arm is located in the same spot on each drive, as shown in Figure 18-5. If each drive is 1 TB in size, this RAID array will operate as one logical

Drives operate in unison

Disk 1   Disk 2

Goodheart-Willcox Publisher; (hard drives) HomeArt/Shutterstock.com

Figure 18-5 In a RAID 0 configuration, multiple hard drives work together as if they were one drive.

drive with 2 TB total of disk space. Therefore, only one instruction is needed for both drives. For example, the instruction may be "retrieve data from platter 1, location C." This speeds up the reading and writing of data.

Data is written, or *striped*, across the array in passes, as illustrated in Figure 18-6. In pass 1, part of the data is written on Drive 1 (A1). The next part is written in the same location on Drive 2 (A2). In the second pass, data is written in the next location on Drive 1 (B1). This is followed by data written in the same location on Drive 2 (B2).

RAID 1

RAID 1 is a RAID system that uses two hard drives, each a mirror or copy of the other drive. When data is written to one drive, it is automatically written to the second drive as shown in Figure 18-7. This solution is called *disk mirroring.* Unlike RAID 0, the main reason to choose this solution is to increase fault tolerance. Should one of the hard drives in a RAID 1 array fail, the other drive will continue to provide access to data. However, a RAID 1 array with one failed drive is *not* considered a fault-tolerant situation until the bad drive is replaced.

Keep in mind, with RAID 1, half of the total disk space is used for mirroring. If Drive 1 is 1 TB and Drive 2 is 1 TB, there is *not* a total of 2 TB. The total amount of disk space available for data is 1 TB.

RAID 5

RAID 5 is a RAID setup that combines the performance of RAID 0 with fault tolerance. Data is written across at least three drives similar to a striping array (RAID 0). RAID 5 is known as *disk striping with parity.* It requires a minimum of three drives but can host up to 32 drives. On the third drive, a value called parity is created and written. *Parity* is an additional digit of information that helps recover data in the event one of the drives fails. In each pass of writing data, the parity bit is switched to a different drive, as shown in Figure 18-8. The parity information can be used to recreate the missing data. Assume the third drive in Figure 18-8 fails. On the first pass, no data loss has occurred. A1 and A2 are still available. On the second pass, the data at B2 is lost. The parity written on Drive 2 will recreate the missing data.

Figure 18-6 In RAID 0, data is written, or striped, across the array in passes.

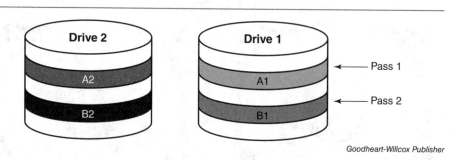

Goodheart-Willcox Publisher

Figure 18-7 In RAID 1, data is written to one drive and is automatically written the same way to the second drive.

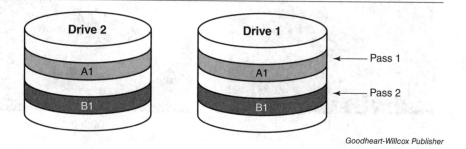

Goodheart-Willcox Publisher

Figure 18-8 Data is written across at least three drives similar to RAID 0, but it includes a parity bit to help recover data.

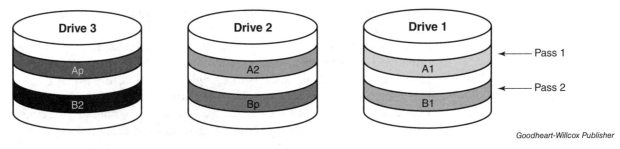

Goodheart-Willcox Publisher

A RAID 5 array can only suffer the loss of a single drive in the array. If more than one drive fails, the array is no longer considered fault tolerant and data will be inaccessible. Parity can only be used to recreate the missing data on a single physical disk.

Total disk space depends on the number of drives in the array. Assume each drive in a RAID 5 array of three drives is 1 TB of storage for a total of 3 TB. Only two of the drives can store data because a parity bit must always be written. Therefore, $1/n$ is the amount of space used for parity, where n is the number of drives in the array. In this example, 1/3, or 1 TB, is the amount of space dedicated to parity. The remaining space is dedicated to data, which in this example is 2 TB.

RAID 1+0

RAID 1+0 is a RAID array that combines RAID 1 and RAID 0. It is not called "RAID ten," but it is often written without the plus symbol (+). RAID 1+0 is sometimes called a *stripe of mirrors, nested RAID*, or *hybrid RAID*. This version of RAID requires at least four physical disks. Since a mirror requires exactly two drives, RAID 1+0 has pairings of mirrored drives, as shown in Figure 18-9. The drives are then striped for performance. This provides for fault tolerance with high availability.

Figure 18-9 In RAID 1+0, two drives are mirrored to form a group, and there are at least two groups across which data is striped.

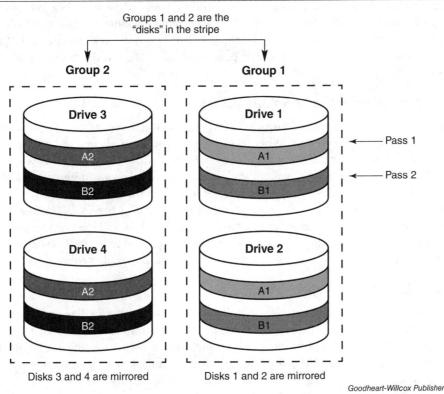

Goodheart-Willcox Publisher

Multipathing

Multipathing, also called *SAN multipathing* or *I/O multipathing (MPIO)*, is the creation of alternative routes between a server and storage device. At times, the route data takes between a server and storage device fails due to a broken cable or an unplugged device. When only one path exists and fails, a user has no recourse to obtain the needed data. This creates a **single point of failure (SPOF)**, which is a risk that occurs when a system part fails and causes the entire system to stop working. Providing multiple possible paths for data to traverse eliminates the single point of failure by allowing data to continue traveling on another route.

Power

When creating a BIA, availability of redundant power is examined. Servers and essential hosts rely on electrical power, and any fluctuation in electricity can cause surges, spikes, or outages. A **power surge** is a fluctuation in the supplied voltage. Power surges are often called *power spikes*. A fluctuation lasting longer than three nanoseconds is a surge; fewer than three nanoseconds is a spike. Power surges result in an unstable flow of electricity to a device. In the United States, standard voltage for a wall outlet is 120 volts. If power rises above this voltage, a computer system may not be able to handle it. This could lead to damage, even if a fluctuation only lasts a few nanoseconds.

Generator

Fault tolerance is the ability of a system to operate without interruption when a component fails. Fault-tolerant systems use backups, such as generators, to ensure continuation of service. A **generator** is a device that creates electricity. Hospitals, emergency centers, and similar organizations must have critical equipment running at all times.

A standby generator is typically located outside a building and fueled by natural gas or diesel fuel. These generators start automatically when there is a loss of electricity from the public electrical grid. A transfer switch isolates the building from the electrical grid to prevent generated electricity from feeding back into the grid. When electricity is restored to the grid, the generator shuts off, and the transfer switch is reset.

Uninterruptible Power Supply (UPS)

An **uninterruptible power supply (UPS)** is a device that acts as a power source when the main power fails. When the main power shuts downs, a UPS provides almost instant protection from interruption. Since it runs on a battery that will eventually deplete and power down, a UPS is not as powerful as a generator, but it does provide temporary power to perform necessary preventive measures, such as backing up data, saving works in progress, etc. The amount of time a UPS can provide power depends on the capacity of its battery and the electrical load connected to it. It may be able to provide power for several minutes or several hours. Even a few minutes is enough time to save your work and safely shut down the system.

Dual Supply

A *dual power supply* is created by installing multiple power supplies on a device so that each power supply provides half the power needed to run the device. However, each has the capability of running the computer on its own, meaning one supply will continue functioning if the other goes down. A dual power supply provides the advantage of not having to take the device offline. Instead, the defective power

TECH TIP

A *smart UPS*, also called an *intelligent UPS*, is one that not only provides emergency power but also manages, monitors, and can automatically shut down equipment attached to it. Most of these UPS devices include an additional slot in which an interface card can be inserted to control such services as network connectivity and temperature or humidity monitoring.

supply connection is removed and replaced while the second supply continues providing uninterrupted power. The process of replacing defective hardware without powering down a machine is called *hot-swapping*. An example of hot-swappable dual supply is shown in Figure 18-10.

+ 2.5

Power Distribution Units (PDUs)

+ 2.5

A **power distribution unit (PDU)** is a device that distributes electrical power. PDUs are used in data centers to support power required to run networked servers. There are a number of different PDU types, as referenced in Figure 18-11.

The use of rack-installed PDUs (rPDUs) provides an extra layer of protection from power outages by switching from one power supply to another in the event of failure. While a PDU enables a certain degree of fault tolerance, installing only one PDU creates a single point of failure. Therefore, it is suggested to use multiple PDUs to add additional layers of tolerance to power.

Figure 18-10 A dual power supply is created by installing multiple power supplies on a device so that each power supply provides half the power needed to run the device.

SasaStock/Shutterstock.com

Figure 18-11 A power distribution unit (PDU) is a device that distributes electrical power.

PDU Type	Function
Basic	Provides power to any connection device
Intelligent	Also called *networked PDU*; provides power to devices and enables remote management
Metered	Monitors locally connected devices in real time using built-in meters to prevent overloads
Monitored	Monitors real-time load levels of remotely connected devices and warns administrators of overloads
Switched	Monitors load levels of locally connected devices, avoids potential overloads using built-in meter, and controls individual outlets remotely
Automatic transfer switch	Provides redundant power sources for devices that do not have their own power supplies and automatically switches to secondary power source if primary source fails
Hot-swap	Enables hot-swap of online UPS systems
Dual circuit	Provides independent power to devices with redundant power supplies

Goodheart-Willcox Publisher

Disaster Recovery Plan (DRP)

A *disaster recovery plan (DRP)* is a part of the continuity of business plan. A **disaster recovery plan (DRP)** is a customized, structured plan to resume infrastructure and IT services that shut down due to a disaster and ensure continuity of business operations. It is a *functional recovery plan* that includes procedures and strategies aimed at restoring hardware, applications, and data to meet the needs of the recovery of a business. A DRP is the plan for addressing critical data and applications in a hardware or software failure or destruction of facilities. Where a business continuity plan is typically concerned with the overall business, a DRP is a detailed response for regaining functionality of computer and network systems.

A DRP looks at how an organization can *continue operations* during and after a disruptive or catastrophic event. The DRP is an essential component of the business continuity plan that provides the step-by-step structure to resume mission-critical functions quickly.

Disaster recovery plans should be scalable. *Scalability* is the ability to accommodate additional resources or changes as needed. In the content of recovery, scalability refers to the ability to adapt the plans, outcomes, or goals as needed through recovery or continuity efforts and a contingency plan should be created. An **IT contingency plan (ITCP)** is a supplemental plan enacted in the event the DRP is not successful or feasible. A contingency plan can provide interim measures to continue operations or restore services. For example, the plan could address moving operations to another physical location or using alternative equipment.

Data Backup

The first step in a DRP is ensuring that an organization's data has a backup. Critical data is determined by an organization and includes items such as legal documents, financial data, and information needed on a daily basis to operate the business.

A **data backup**, sometimes called *archiving*, is the process of copying data from one location to another medium. Backup involved making copies of original data and storing off-site. Backup enables data restoration if something happens to the original copy of the data. There are three general types of backup, as shown in Figure 18-12.

- A **full backup** is a copy of all files. This is the easiest type of backup from which to restore because all the data is included in the backup.

TECH TIP

The US government has resources for Information Technology Disaster Recovery planning on its disaster-planning website, www.ready.gov. Also included on the site are links to templates, tools, and other options to prepare for possible disasters and appropriate recovery measures.

Figure 18-12 A data backup, sometimes called *archiving*, is the process of copying data from one location to another medium. There are three general types of backup: full, incremental, and differential.

Type	Description	Archive Bit	Restore Information
Full	All files are backed up.	The archive bit is cleared on each file after the file is backed up.	Easiest type to restore; all data are included in the backup.
Incremental	Only files that were changed or created since the last backup will be backed up. A full backup first must be created before the incremental backup cycles can start.	The archive bit is cleared on each file after the file is backed up.	The full backup must be restored first, then the incremental backups are restored in the order they were created.
Differential	Only files that were changed or created since the full backup will be backed up. A full backup first must be created before the differential backup cycles can start.	The archive bit is *not* cleared after backup.	The full backup must be restored first, then the last differential backup is restored.

Goodheart-Willcox Publisher

- An **incremental backup** is a series of sequential backups in which the first day begins with a full backup, and each remaining day in the cycle creates copies of files that have changed or been created since the last backup. The system knows which files to back up because the files are flagged with an attribute called an archive bit. An **archive bit** is a single bit within a file indicating if a file has been backed up or not. When a bit is *on*, it indicates the file is new or changed and needs a backup. Bits are placed on data when it is first created, moved to a new location, or altered. In an incremental backup, after a file is backed up, the archive bit is cleared.

- A **differential backup** is a series of sequential backups that starts with a full backup, and the subsequent backups include copies of only the files that have changed or been created since the last full backup. Unlike incremental backups, differential backups do *not* clear archive bits after files are backed up.

An *online backup* is accessible from any device with an Internet connection. Online backups offer the convenience of accessing data from virtually anywhere, but an organization is at the mercy of the vendor hosting the online storage. One popular example of an online backup is SAN.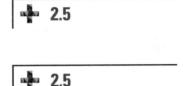

A **storage area network (SAN)**, also called a *storage network*, is a computer network that provides access to consolidated storage devices. A SAN accesses storage devices such as RAIDs, tape drives, and storage servers. In a SAN environment, a networked storage device appears as if it is connected directly to the computer from which a user is accessing it. SAN backups offer an increased level of security because SANs are typically inaccessible through the organization's local network. This means that if a LAN is breached, backups are inaccessible to a hacker.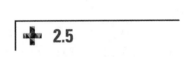

A replication varies slightly from a backup. A backup refers to data stored off-site, where as a *replication* is a copy of data that is stored on-site. Examples of replication include the following:

- A network-attached storage backup is one that archives data to a NAS device. **Network-attached storage (NAS)** is a data storage method in which a storage server or device is connected to a network and enables storage and retrieval from one centralized source. NAS systems offer flexibility and scalability, meaning that an organization can always add additional storage space as needed. In a sense, NAS backups enable organizations to function as though cloud infrastructure exists on-site since data is stored in a separate, but easily accessible, networked location.

- A *cloud backup*, also called *remote backup*, is a strategy of backing up data to an off-site, virtual, or cloud-based server as opposed to a local server. Cloud backups are popular off-site backup methods.

- *Virtual machine (VM) replication* is a process used to create exact backups of virtual machines.

- *Offline backups* are traditional backup methods in which data is copied to a device and stored off-site. Examples of offline backups include tape, disk, and copied backups. While offline backups do not offer the same accessibility as online backups, they are faster and provide physical access to data.

- An *image backup*, also referred to as a *snapshot*, is a data backup method in which software captures an image of a hard drive and its contents. A *disk image* is a file that stores the contents and structure of a hard disk. Image backups protect everything on a disk, including boot information, the OS, data, and user settings. They also enable administrators to restore or recover only needed data.

- *Magnetic tape* has large capacities, low cost, ease with which additional drives can be added, long lifespan, efficiency, portability, and off-line security. However, they are susceptible to failure and slow restoration of data.

- *Disk backup*, also called *backup-to-disk*, is a backup method in which data is stored on a hard disk. Disk backups have large storage capabilities and offer a much faster recovery time than tape backups.
- A **copy backup**, also called a *backup file*, copies designated files but does not clear the files' archive bits. This type of backup serves as a duplicate of data and is used to restore original files in the event of deletion or corruption.

Data backup can be stored on- or off-site. While storing backups on-site may be convenient, it is hardly the safest option. Putting distance between the business location and backup media is highly recommended. *Geographic dispersal* is the process of distributing redundancy across geographic areas. The best practice is to store backups off-site at a restricted location, such as a bank vault or other secure location. However, storing backups in an employee's home is not a recommended strategy since an organization has no control over the backup and cannot ensure its integrity or availability.

✚ 2.5

Restoration Order

When your organization moves into recovery mode, you must determine the order in which you will restore operations. A **restoration order** is the priority order of restoration of services or applications. A *priority list* is determined based on which services or applications are most essential and then planning accordingly. This is generally a management decision carried out by IT staff. For example, the highest priority might be getting your sales teams back online so they can begin taking and processing orders, while having access to the company intranet may not be a critical or essential service. This may be a dynamic list, meaning this list can change by company direction or time of year. It is important the list is reviewed often by management and senior IT staff and updated in the business-continuity planning document.

✚ 2.1

Recovery Sites

A data recovery strategy is created that includes data replication and backup that can be used until a business is operational. Data recovery follows the CIA triad of data confidentiality, integrity, and availability.

As part of the DRP, recovery sites are necessary to protect assets. A **recovery site** is a place in which a business can operate temporarily until the business site is up and running again. There are three types of recovery sites, as illustrated in Figure 18-13. Each one varies in time of recovery and cost of the implementation.

A **cold site** is a location that provides necessary office space needed to move operations, but it contains no operational equipment. Instead, a customer must provide and install necessary equipment and restore data backups required to resume business operations. Cold sites are the least costly of all recovery site solutions, but it also takes the longest to restore operations.

A **warm site** is a facility with minimal equipment in place to resume business operations. Warm sites may include hardware such as servers to provide network connections, but an organization is responsible for installing additional equipment and transferring data to the new location. Additionally, some systems may require OS configuration to ensure full operability.

A **hot site** is a duplication of a current, fully functional site. It has all the equipment needed to move operations in a short amount of time. Hot sites often include servers, cooling systems, and other necessary production equipment. This type of recovery site provides a near-immediate restoration of operations but can be extremely costly to maintain.

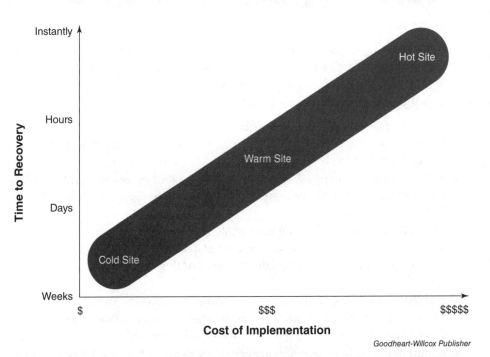

Figure 18-13 A recovery site is a place in which a business can operate temporarily until the business site is up and running again. Each type of site varies in time and cost.

Goodheart-Willcox Publisher

SUMMARY

Business Continuity

- Business continuity is the ability of a business to remain operational before, during, and after a catastrophic event has occurred. An organization must be prepared and focused on the continuation of its business and the protection of critical assets and services.

- A business continuity plan (BCP), or COOP, is a comprehensive and proactive plan that provides the steps needed to keep a business operational before, during, and after a disaster.

- A BCP must be able to defend itself and guarantee that the business will continue operation. The plan must also take the CIA triad into consideration as well as how each component of the business will recover.

Business-Impact Analysis (BIA)

- A business-impact analysis (BIA) is one of the first steps in establishing a BCP. A BIA is a detailed process that determines the potential consequences of business disruptions and uses data to develop recovery strategies.

- A BIA categorizes financial and nonfinancial impacts that an emergency or crisis has on a business. It also includes an impact on privacy assessment by identifying data at risk.

- The analysis also identifies mission-critical (essential) functions and critical systems, which are the essential functions and systems necessary to keep a business operational. A site risk assessment is performed to identify mission-critical vulnerabilities.

- A BIA identifies downtime maximums before damage occurs by identifying the high availability, reviewing systems for resilience, and utilizing redundancies to support resilience and business continuity.

Disaster Recovery Plan (DRP)

- A disaster recovery plan (DRP) is a customized, structured plan to resume infrastructure and IT services that shut down due to a disaster and ensure continuity of business operations.
- A DRP is a functional recovery plan that includes procedures and strategies aimed at restoring hardware, applications, and data to meet the needs of the recovery of a business.
- Disaster recovery plans should be scalable. In the content of recovery, scalability refers to the ability to adapt the plans, outcomes, or goals as needed through recovery or continuity efforts, and a contingency plan should be created.
- The first step in a DRP is ensuring that an organization's information has a backup. Once backups are determined, an organization can move forward with determining the order in which operations will be restored.
- As part of the DRP, backup sites are necessary to protect assets. A recovery site is a place in which a business can operate temporarily until the business site is up and running again. Examples include cold, warm, and hot sites.

REVIEW QUESTIONS

1. Define *business continuity*.
2. Explain a business continuity plan.
3. What is a crisis communication plan?
4. Identify elements included in a business-impact analysis.
5. Briefly explain five financial and nonfinancial impacts that an emergency or crisis can have on a business.
6. Define *mission-critical functions and systems*.
7. State the difference between a recovery point objective (RPO) and a recovery time objective (RTO).
8. Explain MTBF, MTTF, and MTTR.
9. What does RAID stand for?
10. What is the main reason an individual would choose RAID 1?
11. Explain RAID 5.
12. Briefly explain multipathing.
13. Identify and explain four methods that can protect an organization's systems during a power surge.
14. Explain a disaster recovery plan and the steps involved.
15. What is an IT contingency plan (ITCP)?
16. Identify and explain three general types of backup.
17. List examples of replication methods.
18. Explain *geographic dispersal*.

19. Summarize a restoration order.

20. Explain the three types of recovery sites.

➕ SAMPLE SECURITY+ EXAM QUESTIONS

1. Which should be done *first* when creating a BCP?

    A. Designate an order of succession.

    B. Create the steps for a DRP.

    C. Decide on an RPO.

    D. Perform a BIA on critical operations.

2. Which indicator is used to help a business make decisions about how fast it needs to be operational?

    A. RPO

    B. SPF

    C. RTO

    D. BIA

3. Which of the following provides detailed steps for restoring services after a disaster?

    A. BIA

    B. DRP

    C. BCP

    D. RPO

4. Which of the following *best* describes a fault-tolerant solution?

    A. Multiple network cards installed in a busy server

    B. A surge protector attached to a printer

    C. The use of a RAID 5 array in a file server

    D. Performing a daily backup

5. A company has determined it must be very quick in moving to another location following a catastrophic event. It estimates it must be operational within four hours in order to prevent significant operational disruption. Which choice should this company select?

    A. Cold site

    B. Warm site

    C. Hot site

    D. Alternate location

6. Which version of RAID provides increased performance, but does *not* provide any fault tolerance?

    A. RAID 1

    B. RAID 5

    C. RAID 0

    D. RAID 1+0

7. Your company chooses to configure six 1-TB drives for a RAID 5 array. What percentage of the drives will be used for parity?

   A. 17 percent

   B. 20 percent

   C. 83 percent

   D. 100 percent

8. Which is the *best* choice for a company that is trying to minimize overall backup time during the week?

   A. Full backup every day

   B. Full backup on Monday and incremental backups each of the remaining weekdays

   C. Full backup on Monday and differential backups each of the remaining days of the week

   D. Full backup on Monday and switch between incremental and differential backups each of the remaining weekdays

9. Your organization's recovery plan requires that power remain available to devices for up to 10 days following an outage. Which of the following would most likely provide power for that duration?

   A. UPS

   B. Standby generator

   C. PDU

   D. Dual supply

10. Which is the *most* effective method of backing up data on a virtual machine?

    A. Snapshot

    B. Cloud Backup

    C. Full + Incremental

    D. Full + Differential

LAB EXERCISES

Lab Activity 18-1: Governmental Resources

The Federal Emergency Management Agency (FEMA) has created many resources for businesses to use to plan for emergency preparedness. These are available for free on its website.

1. Launch a web browser, and navigate to the FEMA website (www.fema.gov).

2. Using the site's search function, enter the search phrase every business should have a plan.pdf. In the search results, locate the 12-page booklet of the same name, and click the link to go to that page.

3. On the next page, open the PDF file.

4. Scroll through the document. In the section Continuity Planning, what are the four items a company needs to identify to stay operational?

5. The Continuity Planning section talks about succession of management. Why is this important?

6. Review additional tips in the document, including identifying business suppliers, calling trees, and planning for employees with disabilities. Describe why it is important to practice the plan with employees.

7. The document also mentions the www.ready.gov website. Navigate to this site.

8. Click the **Business Continuity Planning** link, and consider the following scenario:

> You have been hired as a consultant to a regional real-estate company with four physical locations in one city and another two locations in a nearby town. The company employs 45 individuals from sales agents, web design and graphic arts, and administrative employees and maintains an active web page with links for each house they sell. You want to begin by providing an overview on why they need a business continuity plan. Using a presentation program such as PowerPoint or Prezi, create a presentation focusing on the need for a continuity plan. Describe the four stages in the process diagram by using relevant examples. Keep the language of the presentation simple and on the appropriate level of technical understanding.

9. Submit as instructed.

Lab Activity 18-2: Windows Archive Settings

In Microsoft Windows, the A bit can be set or removed using the Command Prompt. You can also use the Command Prompt to view the current setting for files in a folder.

1. Applying what you have learned, open the Windows Command Prompt.

2. Change to your working folder for this class.

3. Enter the **attrib** command. This displays all files and their current attributes. If a file is flagged for backup, the A bit will be listed, as shown. If the A bit is not listed, the file will not be backed up. Hint: If you have too many, enter attrib | more.

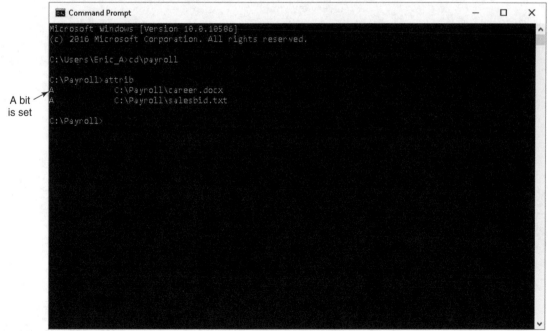

Goodheart-Willcox Publisher

4. Enter the **dir** command and the /aa switch. This is another way to view the files that have the A bit set in the current folder. The /aa switch stands for attribute, archive.

5. Enter attrib -a. This removes the A bit from all files in the current folder.

6. Enter copy con newfile.txt, then enter test as the textual content in the file, and finally press the [Ctrl][Z] key combination and press [Enter] to exit editing mode and save the file.

7. Enter attrib newfile.txt. Notice the A bit is set because the file is new.

8. Enter attrib +a. This adds the A bit to all files in the current folder.

Lab Activity 18-3: Windows Backup Program

One of the changes made in Windows 10 was the location of the backup system. While a backup created in an older system such as Windows 7 can be used in Windows 10, the system for creating backup is in a new location.

1. Click the Windows **Start** button, and then click **Settings**.

2. In the **Settings** window, click **Update & Security**.

3. In the **Update & Security** window, click **Backup** on the left-hand side. You must first add a drive.

4. Click the **Add a drive** button (+). Windows will look for any usable external drives. Once it finds a usable drive, select it.

5. After a drive is selected, click the **More options** link to display the **Backup Options** window, as shown. Scroll through this window to review the options. Several folders will likely be specified for backup. Also notice the settings for how often to create backups and how long to keep backups.

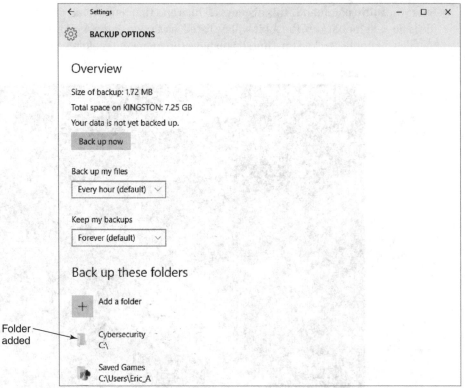

Goodheart-Willcox Publisher

6. Click the **Add a folder** button (+). Then, navigate to your working folder on the local hard drive, and select it. The folder is now listed at the bottom of the **Backup Options** window and will be included in the backup.

7. Click the **Back up my files** drop-down arrow, and click **Daily** in the drop-down list. The backup will be created once each day. This is the longest interval allowed in the Windows 10 backup system.

8. Click the back button at the top of the window to return to the **Update & Security** window. Note: your instructor may tell you to disable the backup at this point.

Lab Activity 18-4: Evaluating Site Choices

Identify which type of alternate site you feel is best for each of the following scenarios and why. Choose from cold, warm, or hot sites. Consider some of the environmental factors that could influence your choices. After you choose the alternate site, where would you suggest it be located? Be detailed in your responses.

1. An executive jet service with its only headquarters located in Southern California

2. The data center for a private university located in upstate New York

3. A hospital network in Baton Rouge, LA, that maintains patient health records and other pertinent medical information in electronic format

CASE STUDY

Continuity of Operations

In 2017, Avalution Consulting, a business continuity and IT disaster-recovery consultation firm, suffered flooding as the result of cold temperatures causing a water pipe to burst in their offices. In response, Avalution activated the company's crisis management team (CMT) to assess the situation and review corresponding business continuity plans.

The business-continuity coordinator issued an emergency notification to employees instructing them to switch to remote work strategies and kept them informed as to when additional communication should be expected. The notice included a requirement for employees to acknowledge receipt of the information and confirm the ability to work remotely.

Fortunately, prior to this event, Avalution identified single points of failure and incorporated as much redundancy as possible. Due to a high level of resiliency and quick response and activation of business continuity plans, employees were back in the office within a month and delivery of services was not impacted.

1. How does this example demonstrate the importance of business continuity planning?

2. What steps can an organization take to be proactive in mitigating downtime after a disaster?

3. To what extent does Avalution's response demonstrate an effective business continuity plan?

4. In your opinion, is it more important for a business to plan for specific events, such as a burst water pipe or fire, or for loss of specific assets, such as a building or equipment? Explain your position.

LEARNING OUTCOMES

- Identify three important documents used for getting a job.
- Compare and contrast applying online versus in person for the application process.
- Summarize preparing for an interview.
- Explain two tasks to be completed after an interview.
- Discuss the hiring process.
- Cite examples of soft skills important for professionals to apply in the workplace.
- Explain three techniques that can help with time management.
- Summarize working with a team.
- Explain job acquisition and advancement.
- Discuss professional success.

KEY TERMS

active listening	employment verification	office politics
attitude	ethics	portfolio
behavioral question	hypothetical question	problem-solving
collaboration skills	integrity	professionalism
confidence	job-acquisition skills	reference
conflict resolution	leadership	resilience
cover message	lifelong learning	résumé
critical-thinking skills	mock interview	teamwork
decision-making	morals	time management
diversity awareness	networking	work ethic
empathy		

OVERVIEW

Obtaining a certification is the first step in finding gainful, long-lasting employment. In today's workforce, employers desire not only those with the necessary job-specific skills but also the ability to interact with a diverse employee population as well as customers. The Security+ Certification confirms your knowledge and abilities in security information, but it will not prove communication or employability skills. It is up to you to develop, confirm, and convey those areas. This chapter discusses information needed for finding and applying for jobs; interviewing; the hiring process; and skills desired by most employers.

Getting a Job

When seeking employment, it will be necessary to create a résumé and cover letter. Some job applications may also require a career portfolio. Each document should be professionally written and formatted.

Résumé

A **résumé** is a document that profiles a person's career goals, education, and work history. Its purpose is to prove to a potential employer that a person's experiences and skills match the qualifications of the job. Think of a résumé as a snapshot that tells the employer who you are and why you would be an asset as an employee.

The first impression most employers will have of you is your résumé. It is a reflection of your professional image, so it should be well written, error free, and fit on one page, as shown in Figure 19-1. A simple format should be used with top and bottom margins approximately one inch. Side margins should also be one inch but can be adjusted as needed to fit the résumé on one page. Font selection should be conservative and professional, such as Calibri 11 pt. or Times New Roman 12 pt. Decorative fonts are distracting and should never be used on a résumé. A typical résumé is organized into the following sections:

- contact information
- objective
- education
- work experience
- memberships and professional affiliations
- community service experience
- honors, awards, and publications

A section should only be included if you have relevant information to list. For example, if you do not belong to a professional organization, do not use this heading.

The job description for which you are applying may note specific hard skills, as well as soft skills, that the employer is requesting. The *education* section is a good place to list relevant skills that highlight your qualifications for the job.

When saving a résumé, use your name and the word *résumé* in the filename. For example, if your name were Latisha Turgess, your filename would be LatishaTurgessResume. This helps the employer identify to whom the résumé belongs.

Cover Message

A **cover message** is a letter or e-mail sent with a résumé to introduce and summarize the reasons the applicant is applying for a job. It is a sales message written to persuade the reader to grant an interview. A cover message provides an opportunity to focus a potential employer's attention on the individual's background, important soft skills and hard skills required for the position, and work experience that matches the job the person is seeking.

Writing a cover message is an important part of applying for a job. It sets the tone for the résumé that follows. A cover message should focus on your qualifications without being boastful, while expressing why you are a good fit for the company. It should not repeat details found in the résumé. Rather, it should highlight your key qualifications that are specific to the job for which you are applying. The message should also explain how you heard about the position.

A cover message, like all professional communication, must be completely error free. Whether it is a printed letter or an e-mail message, standard letter formatting should be followed. Figure 19-2 shows an example of a cover message that will be printed and mailed. Figure 19-3 shows an example of a cover message that will be sent by e-mail.

Figure 19-1 A résumé is a document that profiles a person's career goals, education, and work history.

Latisha Turgess

518 Burnett Road, Randallstown, MD 21123
(555) 555-1234
lturgess@e-mail.com
www.linkedin.com/in/latishaturgess

Objective: To use my computer security certification and skills to obtain a position as a security specialist.

Education: Bachelor degree. June, 20--, University of Maryland, College Park, MD
Major: Computer Science, Data and System Security Specialization

Relevant Courses: Programming Language Technologies and Paradigms
Design and Analysis of Computer Algorithms
Network Design and Infrastructure   Operating Systems
Cryptology   Computer and Network Security

Relevant Skills: System Architecture Design   Information Assurance
System Troubleshooting   Risk Management
Vulnerability Evaluation   Linux, Windows, and Mac Administration

Clearance and Certifications: TS/SCI Clearance, May 20--
CompTIA Security+ Certification, May 20--

Work Experience: August, 20-- to present
Network Technician, McHenry Manufacturing, Baltimore, MD
Assist in installation of workstations, network cable, devices; perform troubleshooting, maintenance, and repair of systems and network; create and install system images; conduct regular vulnerability and threat assessment evaluations; schedule and coordinate third-part pen testing

January, 20-- to August 20--
University of Maryland IT Help Desk
Provide student and faculty help desk support

Honors: Dean's list four years

Figure 19-2 A cover message is a letter or e-mail sent with a résumé to introduce and summarize the reasons the applicant is applying for a job.

39 Lucas Lane
Jasper, TN 37347
June 5, 20--

Ms. Cheryl Lynn Sebastian
Director of Administration
Jefferson City Convention & Visitors Buerau, Inc.
100 E. High Street
Jefferson City, MO 65101

Dear Ms. Sebastian:

The position you advertised in the *Network Journal* on March 14 for a systems security trainee is exactly the kind of job I am seeking. According to your ad, this position requires good systems administration skills. As you can see by my résumé, my education and work experience in Linux and Windows administration prepared me well for this position.

For the past two years, I worked as a part-time network assistant in a position with the Jasper Community College. I gained experience administering systems in Linux and Windows environments, as well as coordinating with external vendors for services as needed. I also had the opportunity to shadow full-time staff as they sought to upgrade network infrastructure and attend departmental meetings, where I learned the importance of ensuring confidentiality, integrity, and availability of system data.

As the enclosed résumé shows, I will graduate from the University of Missouri in early June. While in college, I took several security courses, which helped me develop my skills in data security. Those classes prepared me to sit for and obtain a CompTIA Security+ Certification. Through the university, I was also able to receive governmental clearances.

I would like very much to meet you and hope that you will contact me by phone or e-mail to schedule an interview for the position. If I do not hear from you within the next few weeks, I hope you will not mind if I follow up with a phone call.

Sincerely yours,

Pat Accura

Pat Accura

Enclosure

Figure 19-3 When applying online, a cover message can be sent in an e-mail. Note that the applicant attached their résumé to the e-mail.

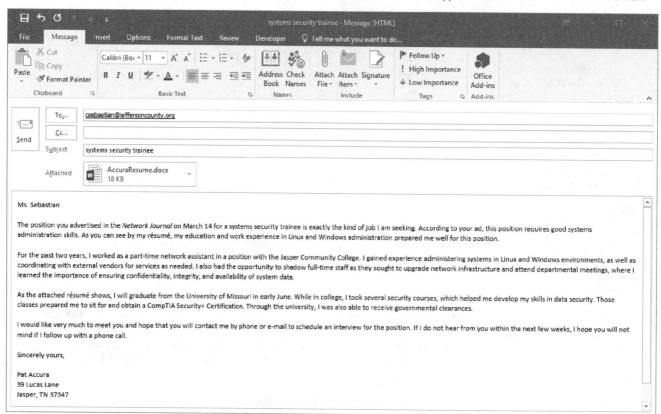

Ms. Sebastian

The position you advertised in the *Network Journal* on March 14 for a systems security trainee is exactly the kind of job I am seeking. According to your ad, this position requires good systems administration skills. As you can see by my résumé, my education and work experience in Linux and Windows administration prepared me well for this position.

For the past two years, I worked as a part-time network assistant in a position with the Jasper Community College. I gained experience administering systems in Linux and Windows environments, as well as coordinating with external vendors for services as needed. I also had the opportunity to shadow full-time staff as they sought to upgrade network infrastructure and attend departmental meetings, where I learned the importance of ensuring confidentiality, integrity, and availability of system data.

As the attached résumé shows, I will graduate from the University of Missouri in early June. While in college, I took several security courses, which helped me develop my skills in data security. Those classes prepared me to sit for and obtain a CompTIA Security+ Certification. Through the university, I was also able to receive governmental clearances.

I would like very much to meet you and hope that you will contact me by phone or e-mail to schedule an interview for the position. If I do not hear from you within the next few weeks, I hope you will not mind if I follow up with a phone call.

Sincerely yours,

Pat Accura
39 Lucas Lane
Jasper, TN 37347

Goodheart-Willcox Publisher

Portfolio

When applying for a job, it will be necessary to tell the employer why you are qualified for the position. To support your qualifications, you may need to create a portfolio. A **portfolio** is a selection of related materials that are collected and organized to show the qualifications, skills, and talents that support an individual's career or personal goals.

There are some common elements generally included in a portfolio such as photocopies of certifications, diplomas, and professional licenses. Samples of work, letters of recommendation, and any documents that show a talent or skill appropriate for the position should also be a part of a portfolio. Examples of additional items are shown in Figure 19-4.

Résumés, generally, do not include references but may be included as a separate document in a portfolio. A **reference** is a person who knows an applicant's skills,

Figure 19-4 A portfolio is a selection of related materials that are collected and organized to show the qualifications, skills, and talents that support an individual's career or personal goals.

Examples of Portfolio Elements	
• Diploma	• References
• Professional license(s)	• Résumé
• Letter of introduction	• Transcripts
• Letter(s) of recommendation	• Video(s) (presentations or other talents)
• Military record and award(s)	

Goodheart-Willcox Publisher

talents, or personal traits and is willing to recommend the individual. These individuals can be someone for whom you have worked or with whom you provided community service. However, you should not list relatives as references.

Consider which references can best recommend you for the position for which you are applying. Always get permission from the person before using the individual's name as a reference, and notify the person the companies and positions for which you are applying.

There are multiple ways to prepare a portfolio for presentation. The method you choose should allow the viewer to easily navigate and find items. The simplest approach is to print and organize your portfolio material in a binder. Alternatively, you could create an electronic presentation with slides that have links to documents, videos, graphics, or sound files. Another option is to place the files on a CD or USB flash drive.

Websites are another method for presenting a digital portfolio. A personal website can be created to host the files with a main page and links to various sections. Each section page could have links to pages with documents, videos, graphics, or sound files. Alternatively, LinkedIn can be a good place to house portfolio documents. If you place your material on a site owned by a company, read the user agreement for rules of use.

A portfolio is a living document and should be updated regularly. Before going to an interview, it is a good idea to review the material in your portfolio and make sure it is up-to-date. In addition, it may need customizing for the specific job interview.

Application Process

The process of applying for employment typically involves completing a job application form along with submitting a résumé and cover message. Some job employment opportunities may also require the submission of a portfolio.

In today's market, the job application process is typically completed online. However, some employers utilize the traditional process of an applicant physically visiting the human resources department and applying in person.

Before applying for a position, confirm the application process described in the job advertisement. A call to the company's human resources department can also help clarify what is expected by the employer.

Applying Online

The first step in applying online may be to complete an online job application. A *job application* is an employment form that requests contact information, education, and work experience. Even though much of this information may be repeated on your résumé, many companies require an official job application to be completed.

Next, you may be required to upload a résumé, copy and paste information into a form on the site, or send it as an e-mail attachment. Be aware that copying and pasting text into a form usually strips out formatting such as tabs, indentations, and bold type. Avoid pasting text that is formatted in any way. Even if the formatting is retained, it can make the information difficult to read when the employer accesses the application. You may need to adjust the layout of your résumé after uploading it or pasting it into an online application form.

Carefully review each document before clicking the **Submit** button. Applying online does not mean you can ignore proper spelling, grammar, and usage. Your application materials will be the employer's first impression of you. Submitting an application with misspellings or other errors may persuade an employer to eliminate you as a serious candidate.

There may be an opportunity to include a cover letter and portfolio with the application. Follow the directions on the website for attaching additional employment materials.

Applying in Person

The traditional way of applying for employment is to visit the human resources office of the company to which you are applying. When you arrive, be prepared to complete a job application. Write neatly and use only blue or black ink. Carefully review the form before submitting it. Like a résumé or cover message, a job application needs to be free of spelling, grammar, and usage errors.

Bring with you a copy of your résumé, cover message, and portfolio. All documents should be on the same high-quality, white or off-white paper and printed using a laser printer. Do not fold or staple the documents. Instead, use a large envelope, file folder, or paperclip to keep the pages together. If using an envelope or folder, print your name on the outside and list the components included.

Preparing for an Interview

If your résumé and cover letter have passed the employer's screening process, you may be invited to interview. A first interview may be conducted either over the phone or in person.

To prepare for a job interview, learn as much as you can about the position as well as the company. People in your professional network may be able to help you find information about the position or company.

Much information can be obtained from the company's website, which will likely have an *About Us* section. This section of the website may include press releases, annual reports, and information on the company's products or services. You may also consider calling the human resources department for additional information. The human resources department often has materials specifically developed for potential employees. When you call the company, use your best telephone etiquette while speaking with the person who answers the phone. Introduce yourself, state your purpose for calling, and be prepared with a list of questions to ask. Be polite and say "please" and "thank you" when speaking with each person so that you make a positive impression.

Interview Questions

Interview questions are intended to assess an applicant's skills and abilities and to explore an individual's personality. Answers to these questions will help determine whether a candidate will fit in with the company team and the manager's leadership style. Interviewers also want to assess an individual's critical-thinking skills by asking the interviewee to cite specific examples of completed projects or problems the individual solved. During the interview, the applicant's communication skills will also be observed.

Common Questions

Before the interview, try to anticipate questions the interviewer is likely to ask you. The following are some common interview questions:

- What are your strengths?
- What are your weaknesses?

- What about this position interests you?
- What do you plan to be doing five years from now?
- Why do you want to work for this organization?

Write down your answers to these questions. Practice answering the questions while in front of a mirror. An important part of the communication process is nonverbal communication—body language is especially important. Practicing in front of a mirror allows you to see your nonverbal communication.

Another way to prepare for an interview is to conduct a mock interview with a friend or instructor. A **mock interview** is a practice interview conducted with another person. Practice until you can respond with your planned responses naturally and without reading them. The more prepared you are, the more relaxed, organized, competent, and professional you will appear to the interviewer.

Hypothetical Questions

Interviewers may also ask hypothetical questions. **Hypothetical questions** require a candidate to imagine a situation and describe how they would act. Frequent topics of hypothetical questions relate to working with and getting along with coworkers. For example, "How would you handle a disagreement with a coworker?" You cannot prepare specific answers to these questions, so you need to rely on your ability to think on your feet.

For these types of questions, the interviewer is aware that you are being put on the spot. In addition to what you say, you should consider other aspects of your answer as well. Body language is first and foremost. Avoid fidgeting and looking at the ceiling while thinking of your answer. Instead, look at the interviewer and calmly take a moment to compose your thoughts. Keep your answer brief. If your answer runs on too long, you risk losing your train of thought. Try to relate the question to something that is familiar to you and answer honestly.

Do not try to figure out what the interviewer wants you to say. Showing that you can remain poised and project confidence carries a lot of weight, even if your answer is not ideal. In many cases, the interviewer is not as interested in *what* your response is as much as *how* you responded. Was your response quick and thoughtful? Did you ramble? Did you stare blankly at the interviewer before responding?

Behavioral Questions

Interviewers may ask behavioral questions. **Behavioral questions** are questions that draw on an individual's previous experiences and decisions. Your answers to these types of questions indicate past behavior, which may be used to predict future behavior and success in a position. The following are some examples of behavioral questions:

- Tell me about a time when you needed to assume a leadership position in a group. What were the challenges, and how did you help the group meet its goals?
- Describe a situation where you needed to be creative in order to help a client with a problem.
- Describe a situation when you made a mistake. How did you correct the mistake and what measures did you put in place to ensure it did not happen a second time?

Again, you cannot prepare specific answers to these questions. Remain poised, answer honestly, and keep your answers focused on the question. Making direct eye contact with the interviewer can project a positive impression.

Questions an Employer Should Not Ask

State and federal laws prohibit employers from asking questions on certain topics. It is important to know these topics so you can be prepared if such a question comes up during an interview. It is illegal for employers to ask questions about a job candidate's religion, national origin, gender, or disability. Questions about age can only be asked if a minimum age is required by law for a job. The following are some examples of questions an employer is not permitted to ask a candidate:

- What is your religion?
- Are you married?
- What is your nationality?
- Are you disabled?
- Do you have children?
- How much do you weigh?

If you are presented with similar questions during the interview, remain professional. You are not obligated to provide an answer. You could respond, "Please explain how that relates to the job." Alternatively, you could completely avoid the question by saying, "I would rather not answer personal questions."

Questions to Ask the Employer

Keep in mind that the questions you ask, and how you ask them, reveal details about your personality. In the early stages of the interview process, your questions should demonstrate that you would be a valuable employee and are interested in learning about the company. The following are some questions you may want to ask:

- What are the specific duties of this position?
- What is company policy or criteria for employee promotions?
- Do you have a policy for providing on-the-job training?
- When do you expect to make your hiring decision?
- What is the anticipated start date?

Some questions are not appropriate until after you have been offered the job. Questions related to pay and benefits, such as vacation time, should not be asked in the interview unless the employer brings them up. Sometimes, however, an interviewer may ask for your salary expectations. If you prefer not to answer at the time of the interview, you can simply tell the interviewer that the salary is negotiable.

Dress for an Interview

A face-to-face interview is typically the first time a potential employee is seen by a company representative. First impressions are important, so professional dress is critical. When dressing for an interview, consider what you wish your professional image to portray. Figure 19-5 identifies typical attire worn for a job interview.

The easiest rule to follow is to dress in a way that shows you understand the work environment and know the appropriate attire. Interviewing apparel should be somewhat more formal than is called for in the work environment. For example, if the work environment were business-casual dress, a business-professional outfit with a jacket would be appropriate at the interview. If the work environment requires a uniform, business-casual dress might be appropriate for the interview.

It is better to dress conservatively than in trendy clothing. Employers expect interviewees to present their best image in appearance, as well as skills and qualifications. Dressing more conservatively than needed is not likely to be viewed as a disadvantage. However, dressing too casually, too trendy, or wearing inappropriate

Appropriate Attire for a Job Interview	
Women	**Men**
Wear a suit or dress with a conservative length.	Wear a conservative suit of a solid color.
Choose solid colors over prints or flowers.	Wear a long-sleeved shirt, either white or a light color.
Wear pumps with a moderate heel or flats.	Tie should be a solid color or a conservative print.
Keep any jewelry small.	Wear loafers or lace-up shoes with dark socks.
Have a well-groomed hairstyle.	Avoid wearing jewelry.
Use little makeup.	Have a well-groomed haircut.
Avoid perfume or apply it very lightly.	Avoid cologne.
Nails should be manicured and of moderate length without decals.	Nails should be neatly trimmed.
Cover all tattoos.	Cover all tattoos.

Goodheart-Willcox Publisher

Figure 19-5 Appropriate dress for an interview can display one's professionalism.

clothing is likely to cost you the job. Additionally, personal expressions, such as visible tattoos or piercings, may be seen as inappropriate for the workplace by the employer.

After the Interview

Saying thank you and leaving the building does not mark the end of the job-interview process. After the interview has ended, it is important to send a thank-you message to the person, or persons, with whom you met and evaluate the experience. Performing these actions will ensure that you not only stay on the radar of the company, but improve your skills before your next interview as well.

Thank-You Message

Immediately after an interview, and no later than 24 to 48 hours, a *thank-you message* should be written to the interviewer. It may be in the form of a printed letter sent through the mail or an e-mail. Remind the person, or persons, of your name and reiterate your enthusiasm, but do not be pushy. Extend your appreciation for the interviewer's time. An example of a thank-you message is shown in Figure 19-6.

Figure 19-6 A thank-you message should be sent immediately after an interview.

Dear Ms. Cary:

Thank you for the opportunity to discuss the position of associate fashion designer.

I am very excited about the possibility of working for Clothing Design Specialists. The job is exactly the sort of challenging opportunity I had hoped to find. I believe my educational background and internship experience will enable me to make a contribution, while also learning and growing on the job.

Please contact me if you need any additional information. I look forward to hearing from you.

Sincerely,

Goodheart-Willcox Publisher

Interview Evaluation

Evaluate your performance as soon as you can after the interview. Asking yourself the following questions can help in evaluating your performance:

- Was I adequately prepared with knowledge about the company and the position?
- Did I remember to bring copies of my résumé, list of references, portfolio, and any other requested documents to the interview?
- Was I on time for the interview?
- Did I talk too much or too little?
- Did I honestly and completely answer the interviewer's questions?
- Did I dress appropriately?
- Did I display nervous behavior, such as fidgeting, or forget things I wanted to say?
- Did I come across as composed and confident?
- Which questions could I have handled better?

Every job interview is an opportunity to practice. If you discover that you are not interested in the job, do not feel as though your time was wasted. Make a list of the things you feel you did correctly and things you would do differently next time.

Hiring Process

A successful interviewing process may lead to a job offer with the company for which an applicant has applied to work. Most companies make a job offer contingent on employment verification, reference checks, background checks, and credit checks. In addition, the applicant may be required to submit to drug testing. If the applicant passes the screenings, the job offer is generally made official, employment forms are completed, and the new employee starts the job.

Employee Checks

Employment verification is a process through which the information provided on an applicant's résumé is checked to verify that it is correct. Former employers typically verify only the dates of employment, position title, and other objective data of employees who are no longer at the company. Most employers will not provide opinions about employees, such as whether or not the employee was considered a good worker. Reference checks are also made at this time.

Another important part of the employment process is a background check. A *background check* is an investigation into personal data about a job applicant. This information is available from governmental records and other sources. The employer should inform you that a background check will be conducted. The company must ask for written permission before obtaining the background check report. A person is not legally obligated to give permission, but an employer can reject a candidate based on insufficient or unverified background information.

When granted permission by a job applicant, an employer may perform a credit check on that person. A credit report reflects a person's credit history, which some employers use as an indicator of a person's level of responsibility. There is no solid evidence that credit history will indicate an applicant's performance, but it is a common screening device. Many states have regulations on how credit reports can be used and employers may not be able to run this check.

In states where permitted, companies may require drug and alcohol screenings of job applicants. These screenings are commonly performed at a sterile, off-site location, such as a lab, and may be a blood, urine, saliva, or other medical test. A failed drug or alcohol test can result in not being offered a job.

In addition to governmental sources, many employers use Internet search engines, such as Google, to search for information on candidates. Employers may also check social networking websites, such as Facebook and Twitter. Be aware of this before posting any personal information or photos. These checks might work to your advantage or against you, depending on what the employer finds. It is up to you to ensure that the image you project on social networking sites is not embarrassing or, worse, preventing you from achieving your career goals.

Employment Forms

After the job applicant is successful in the hiring process and is offered the job, a considerable amount of time will be spent in the human resources department completing necessary forms for employment. Common employment forms include Form I-9, Form W-4, and benefit forms. Come prepared with the personal information required to complete a multitude of forms. You will need your Social Security number, contact information for emergencies, and other personal information.

Form I-9

A *Form I-9 Employment Eligibility Verification* is used to verify an employee's identity and that the individual is authorized to work in the United States. This form is from the US Citizen and Immigration Services, a governmental agency within the US Department of Homeland Security. Both citizens and noncitizens are required to complete this form. An example of a Form I-9 is shown in Figure 19-7.

The Form I-9 must be signed in the presence of an authorized representative of the human resources department. Documentation of identity must be presented at the time the form is signed. Acceptable documentation commonly used includes a valid driver's license, a state-issued photo ID, or a passport.

Figure 19-7 A *Form I-9 Employment Eligibility Verification* is used to verify an employee's identity and that the individual is authorized to work in the United States.

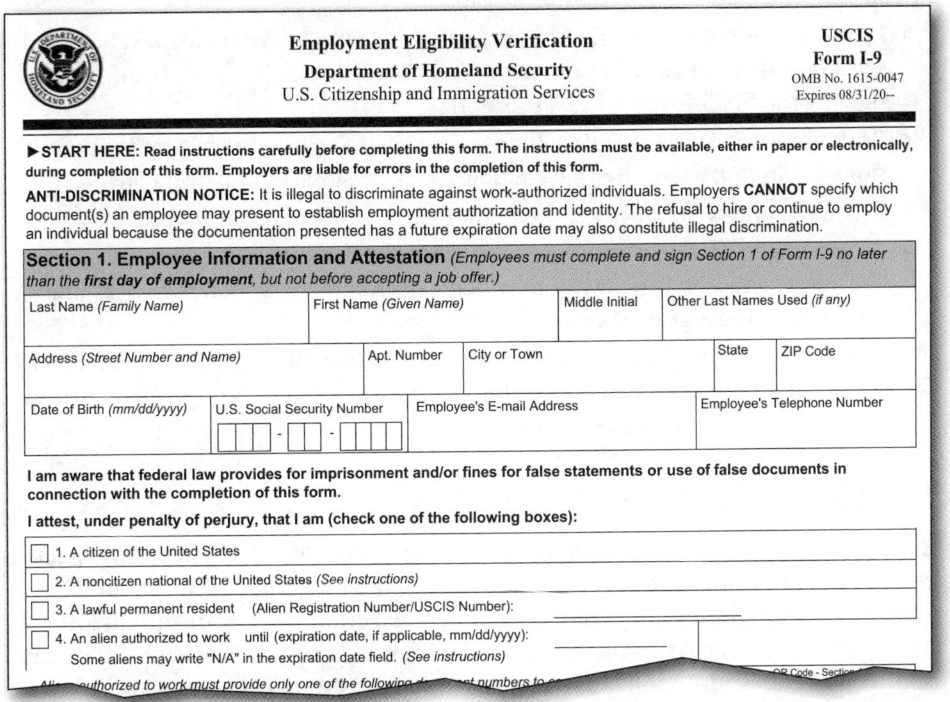

Employment Eligibility Verification
Department of Homeland Security
U.S. Citizenship and Immigration Services

USCIS
Form I-9
OMB No. 1615-0047
Expires 08/31/20--

▶ **START HERE: Read instructions carefully before completing this form. The instructions must be available, either in paper or electronically, during completion of this form. Employers are liable for errors in the completion of this form.**

ANTI-DISCRIMINATION NOTICE: It is illegal to discriminate against work-authorized individuals. Employers **CANNOT** specify which document(s) an employee may present to establish employment authorization and identity. The refusal to hire or continue to employ an individual because the documentation presented has a future expiration date may also constitute illegal discrimination.

Section 1. Employee Information and Attestation *(Employees must complete and sign Section 1 of Form I-9 no later than the **first day of employment**, but not before accepting a job offer.)*

Last Name *(Family Name)*	First Name *(Given Name)*	Middle Initial	Other Last Names Used *(if any)*

Address *(Street Number and Name)*	Apt. Number	City or Town	State	ZIP Code

Date of Birth *(mm/dd/yyyy)*	U.S. Social Security Number	Employee's E-mail Address	Employee's Telephone Number

I am aware that federal law provides for imprisonment and/or fines for false statements or use of false documents in connection with the completion of this form.

I attest, under penalty of perjury, that I am (check one of the following boxes):

☐ 1. A citizen of the United States
☐ 2. A noncitizen national of the United States *(See instructions)*
☐ 3. A lawful permanent resident (Alien Registration Number/USCIS Number): ____________
☐ 4. An alien authorized to work until (expiration date, if applicable, mm/dd/yyyy): ____________
Some aliens may write "N/A" in the expiration date field. *(See instructions)*

Source: US Department of Homeland Security

Form W-4

A *Form W-4 Employee's Withholding Allowance Certificate* is used by the employer to determine the appropriate amount of taxes to withhold from an employee's paycheck. Deductions are based on marital status and the number of dependents claimed, including the employee. The amounts withheld are forwarded to the appropriate governmental agency.

At the end of the year, the employer sends the employee a *Form W-2 Wage and Tax Statement* to use when filing income tax returns. This form summarizes all wages and deductions for the year for an individual employee.

Benefits Forms

The human resources department will provide a variety of forms that are specific to the compensation package offered by the employer. These forms may include health insurance, life insurance, corporate membership, or profit-sharing enrollment forms. Be prepared to complete multiple forms on your first day.

Soft Skills

To be successful in a new job, you will need soft skills. *Soft skills* are skills used to help an individual find a job, perform in the workplace, and gain success in a job or career. They are also known as *interpersonal skills*, *human relations skills*, and *employability skills*. These skills enable a person to interact with others in a positive manner.

Like all other employees, IT professionals must conduct themselves with professionalism in the workplace. **Professionalism** is the act of exhibiting appropriate character, judgment, and behavior by a person trained to perform a job. It is an acquired soft skill of knowing how to interact with others in a manner that is conducive for everyone to be successful in their responsibilities. Professionals have the skills and abilities to perform specific job tasks and work well with others. The following attributes are exhibited by professionals:

- Professionals show *initiative* and make the first step to take charge. When they see a task that needs attention or a decision to be made, they are comfortable making the first move to find a solution.
- Professionals are *responsible*, which means they are accountable for their actions, accepting when they have made good decisions or bad decisions.
- Professionals are *confident* in their abilities to lead and motivate others.
- Professionals *dress* in a manner appropriate for the job and workplace. Self-representation is behavior in which a person reflects their own personal image. It includes good grooming and hygiene.

In all situations, professionals apply soft skills. Examples of soft skills important for professionals to exhibit include ethics, respecting diversity, a positive attitude, confidence, and professional etiquette.

Ethics

Students and employees are expected to make good decisions. They are also expected to act ethically. **Ethics** are rules of behavior based on a group's ideas about what is right and wrong. These groups can be society, social groups, or organizations. **Morals** are an individual's ideas of what is right and wrong. Ethical actions result when a person, a business, or an organization applies ethics and moral behavior.

Integrity is the honesty of a person's actions. People show their integrity through their senses of ethics and morals. You can show integrity by following laws and policies. Another way is to respect the property of your employer and coworkers. People with integrity can identify the far-reaching effects of their actions. In addition, they are reliable.

Work ethic is the belief that honest work is a reward on its own. It is a soft skill that can help a person be successful. Coming to school on time and respecting your instructors and classmates are ways to demonstrate a good work ethic. Other ways include taking direction willingly and exhibiting motivation to accomplish a task.

Diversity

Another soft skill needed for the workplace is diversity awareness. *Diversity* means having people from different backgrounds, demographics, or cultures come together in a group. Diversity can include age, race, nationality, gender, mental ability, physical ability, and other qualities that make individuals unique from one another. **Diversity awareness** is the ability to embrace the unique traits of others. You can show this by working in a friendly way with all people. It is vital to respect cultural differences found in the workplace.

A diverse workforce has many benefits. Diverse employees can help a company create products and services that might be new in the marketplace. New ways of thinking are a benefit of hiring people with varied backgrounds. Diversity also increases the pool of potential candidates. This can result in a more effective workforce.

Diversity does not come without challenges. Special training might be required for workers to learn how to communicate in a diverse workplace. Employees may have to adjust their ways of thinking to work with a diverse population.

Positive Attitude

Professionals exhibit a positive attitude in their job performance and workplace interactions. **Attitude** is how personal thoughts or feelings affect a person's outward behavior. It is a combination of how you feel, what you think, and what you do. Attitude is how an individual sees oneself, as well as how others perceive the individual. A person with a *positive attitude* is optimistic and looks at the upside of a situation rather than the downside.

Attitude influences the way an IT professional performs in a job situation. Positive people are enthusiastic and show interest in their jobs and activities in which they participate. They are eager to learn new tasks and make an effort to have productive relationships with those around them.

People who have positive attitudes are generally more resilient. **Resilience** is a person's ability to cope with and recover from change or adversity. IT professionals face many challenges in the workplace. Having resilience helps them aptly handle challenges in one aspect of their lives while not letting it affect other aspects. They can bounce back even when they feel as though they have been knocked down.

Confidence

An important element to the professional image of an IT professional is confidence. **Confidence** is being certain and secure about one's own abilities and judgment. Effective IT professionals have confidence and know what they are good at doing and how to best use their abilities to achieve goals of the organization. Successful IT professionals are confident, humble, and take charge of situations. An important role of the position is to be in control and responsible.

Professional Etiquette

IT professionals are expected to have good manners in their dealings with internal customers as well as those outside the organization. *Etiquette* is the art of using good manners in any situation. *Professional etiquette* is using good manners in a professional or business setting. It means to be courteous as well as acting and speaking appropriately in all situations. Examples of professional etiquette expected from IT professionals are shown in Figure 19-8.

IT professionals spend a lot of time on the phone solving computer issues with others. *Telephone etiquette* is using good manners when speaking on the telephone. It involves being courteous to the person on the other end of the phone no matter how upset the person may be on the receiving end. Volume and tone of voice are also important when talking on the phone.

Listening is an intellectual process that combines hearing with evaluating. It is a critical soft skill for IT professionals. A person who is listening makes an effort to pay attention and process what is heard. **Active listening** is fully processing what a person says and interacting with the person who is speaking.

An important component of listening is to demonstrate empathy. **Empathy** is having the ability to share someone else's emotions and showing understanding of how the other person is feeling.

Time Management

Time management is the practice of organizing time and work assignments to increase personal efficiency. It is a *self-management skill*, which is a skill that enables an individual to control and make the best of their time and abilities. Time-management skills help IT professionals work efficiently, meet deadlines, and keep appointments. Without time-management skills, it would be nearly impossible for an IT professional to accomplish what is necessary to keep a team or company operating efficiently.

Prioritize

To *prioritize* tasks means to determine the order of importance in which tasks are to be completed. Tasks are prioritized by determining which ones should be completed before others. For example, you *have* to attend to a patch management task in a timely manner. You *do not have* to check personal social media sites while you are at work. Therefore, checking social media should not be on your list of tasks for the day.

Figure 19-8 Professional etiquette is using good manners in a professional or business setting.

Ways to Exhibit Etiquette
• Compose a thank-you letter after somebody does something extraordinary for you.
• Show thoughtfulness and politeness to each individual with whom you come in contact.
• Praise those around you when they contribute in a constructive way.
• Wait to speak until it is your turn.
• Arrive on time to each conference and appointment.
• Address each individual with whom you speak by his or her name.
• Turn off your digital devices when in a conference or discussion.
• Shake hands when meeting somebody for the first time.
• Show you are listening when involved in a dialogue.
• Respect the workspaces of your colleagues.
• Do not let your movements or discussions become a disruption.

Goodheart-Willcox Publisher

Use a Calendar

All appointments and meetings should be recorded on a calendar, preferably in the calendar that is part of an e-mail program. Personal vacations or appointments should also be noted on the same calendar. Entering all commitments on the same calendar helps avoid missed meetings and scheduling conflicts.

Create a To-Do List

Creating a list of tasks to do each day is one simple way to manage time and an easy way to track tasks. As each task is finished, a line should be drawn through it. Any listings that are not deleted should be forwarded to the next day.

Working with a Team

Demonstrating teamwork skills is vital in the workplace. **Teamwork** is the cooperative efforts of team members to reach a goal. A *team* consists of two or more people working together to reach a common goal. Effective team members are people who contribute ideas and effort. They contribute to the success of the team by doing things such as brainstorming answers, volunteering, and acting in accordance with their assigned roles. They are cooperative and work well with others on and outside of the team.

People who are positive contributors show leadership qualities, even when they are not in leadership roles. **Leadership** is the ability to influence others to reach a goal. Effective team members also have collaboration skills. **Collaboration skills** are behaviors for working with others. Effective team members help others. They support other team members and their leaders. These people take initiative when appropriate. Another way to demonstrate teamwork skills is to request help when needed.

When people work together, there is likely to be some conflict. A *conflict* is a strong disagreement between two or more people or a difference that prevents agreement. Conflict can be positive when people learn from the disagreements. Positive solutions can result when conflict is handled in a proper manner. **Conflict resolution** is the process of resolving disputes. Following a conflict-resolution model can help a team solve differences, as shown in Figure 19-9. Conflict resolution requires each party to show *emotional control*. This means each person directs their reactions toward a desirable result. You can show conflict-resolution skills by discussing solutions to conflicts in the workplace.

Formal methods of conflict resolution might be required in some cases. *Negotiation* is people coming together in an attempt to reach an agreement. Sometimes, mediation is needed in negotiation. *Mediation* is the inclusion of a neutral person to help the parties resolve their dispute. This person is called a *mediator*.

Problem-solving is the process used to evaluate a situation and find a solution. Closely related to problem-solving is decision-making. **Decision-making** is the process of taking a course of action after weighing the benefits and costs of alternate actions. In this process, the outcome can be an action or opinion. Decision-making is a logical process that always ends up with a choice. There are five general steps to the decision-making process, as shown in Figure 19-10.

A clear idea of the problem first must be formulated in order to find the best approach. Then, potential solutions to the challenge should be listed and analyzed. After considering all potential solutions, the one that best fits the situation can be selected. The solution can be a single alternative or some blend of alternatives. Once a decision is made, it should be executed. After time has passed, the solution can be analyzed to determine if it was the correct course of action.

Figure 19-9 Conflict resolution is the process of resolving disputes.

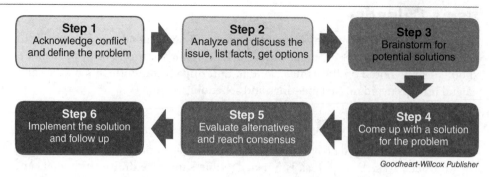

Goodheart-Willcox Publisher

Figure 19-10 Decision-making is the process of taking a course of action after weighing the benefits and costs of alternate actions.

Decision-Making Process

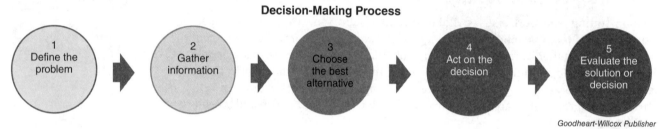

Goodheart-Willcox Publisher

Both decision-making and problem-solving involve critical-thinking skills. **Critical-thinking skills** provide the ability to make sound judgments. Critical-thinking skills involve being unbiased about the possibilities. Applying critical-thinking skills is an important part of problem-solving. You can also show critical-thinking and problem-solving skills by identifying resources that might help solve a problem.

Job Acquisition and Advancement

Job-acquisition skills are those skills used to obtain employment, such as writing a résumé and properly filling out an application. These are vital as you move into the workplace. You will need to prepare to apply for a job. It will be necessary to create a résumé. Write and format this document so it appears professional. It will be the first impression you make on an employer.

An employer will screen all résumés it receives. If your résumé passes the screening process, you may be asked to interview. To prepare for a job interview, learn as much as you can about the position. Also, learn about the company. People in your network might be able to help you find this information.

Networking means talking with people you know and making new relationships that can lead to potential career or job opportunities. The more contacts you make, the greater your opportunities for finding career ideas. Talking with people you know can help you evaluate career opportunities. It also may lead to potential jobs. Many people use LinkedIn to create a professional network and look for career opportunities. As with all social media sites, take care in what you post.

In order to be successful in getting a job, it is vital to have the skills required to cooperate. It is also vital to have the technical skills necessary to complete the tasks. Obtaining certifications is one way to prove you have the requisite technical skills.

Getting a job is only the first step in building a career. As you gain experience, strive to advance in your career. *Promotion* is advancing to the next level in a company's hierarchy. Promotions must be earned. They are not automatically given. Identify what is needed to seek promotion. These steps include taking advantage of professional development opportunities, offering to take on extra assignments, and learning new skills. Show you can follow company rules. Prove you have the skills needed for the higher position. Demonstrate the soft skills required to work with coworkers.

A good attitude about learning includes a sense of responsibility for your own education. Strive to be a lifelong learner. **Lifelong learning** is the voluntary attainment of knowledge throughout life. A lifelong learner looks for chances to acquire information throughout life. This may be for personal or professional use. Some of your learning will come from formal schooling. Other learning will come from life experiences and a desire to improve your mind. You can always improve your professional skills to stay current in your field and promote personal progress.

Professional Success

Professional success means different things to different people. A personal sense of accomplishment and satisfaction gained from working in a chosen profession is a sign of success for many people. Others seek professional advancement as an indicator of success. Advancement can be measured by a promotion, new job title, or other forms of recognition that help an individual attain a desired career status. The measure of job success is unique to each individual.

To attain advancement, it is important to exhibit confidence in personal performance and the ability to interact in the workplace. It also requires taking control of your career and learning how to manage up and appropriately deal with office politics within the organization.

Manage Up

"Manage up" is a common term in the workplace. *Managing up* is the efforts of an employee to establish a working relationship with a supervisor so the employer's professional needs are met as well as the employee's own needs. It is the act of demonstrating professional behavior and working toward the goals of a supervisor and the company.

To manage up is to show basic respect toward your supervisor. It is the act of maintaining a good attitude, volunteering your services when needed, and learning how to make a supervisor look good. Successful employees determine what the manager wants and how to show support. This includes being proactive in situations that demand attention. Knowing how to help a manger can make an employee an asset to the team and to the company. It can also position an individual for promotions when they arise.

Some people confuse "managing up" with "playing up." *Playing up* is going through the motions of building a relationship with a supervisor and displaying professional behavior, but the motivation behind the actions is not genuine. Someone who plays up to a superior is only looking to gain influence and does not have the best interests of the company in mind. This is often demonstrated through flattery, insincere praise, and eager attentiveness toward a supervisor. Playing up is often called *brown-nosing*.

Office Politics

Office politics are inevitable in most organizations. **Office politics** are the behaviors that individuals practice to gain advantages over others in the workplace. It is a struggle for power. Engaging in office politics is considered inappropriate at best and is often unethical. Some individuals believe the more they know about company business, the more power they will have. Others want to secure a friendship with upper IT professionals or with those who can help them climb the ladder for promotions.

Gossipers may say unkind things about coworkers to try to make them look worse. Some workers withhold information from a coworker to maintain an advantage over the individual. Many times office politics result in a coworker being the target of someone's negative behavior. Unfortunately, while an employee can avoid participating in office politics, the employee cannot prevent others from engaging in them.

SUMMARY

Getting a Job

- It is necessary to create a résumé and cover letter when seeking employment. Some applications may also require a portfolio. All three should be professionally written and formatted.
- A résumé is a document that profiles a person's career goals, education, and work history. It is a snapshot of who you are and why you would be an asset as an employee.
- A cover message is a letter or e-mail sent with a résumé to introduce and summarize the reasons the applicant is applying for a job. It is a sales message written to persuade the reader to grant an interview.
- A portfolio is a selection of related materials that are collected and organized to show the qualifications, skills, and talents that support an individual's career or personal goals. A portfolio can help support your qualifications for a position.

Application Process

- The process of applying for employment typically involves completing a job application form along with submitting a résumé and cover message.
- Today, the job application process is typically completed online. The first step is to complete an online job application. Next, you may be required to upload a résumé, copy and paste information into a form on the site, or send it as an e-mail attachment.
- When applying online, carefully review each document before clicking the **Submit** button. Applying online does not mean you can ignore proper spelling, grammar, and usage.
- Some employers still utilize the traditional process of applying in person by visiting the human resource department and completing an application. It is important to write neatly, use only blue or black ink, and have no errors.
- When applying in person, make sure to bring a copy of your résumé, cover message, and portfolio.

Preparing for an Interview

- To prepare for a job interview, learn as much as you can about the position as well as the company. Information can be obtained from the company's website or the human resources department.
- Interview questions are intended to assess an applicant's skills and abilities and to explore an individual's personality.

- Before the interview, try to anticipate questions the interviewer is likely to ask you. Write down answers to potential questions and practice answering questions in a mock interview. In addition, prepare questions you wish to ask the interviewer during the interview.
- Professional dress is critical in interviews. Consider what you wish your professional image to portray. The easiest rule to follow is to dress in a way that shows you understand the work environment and know the appropriate attire.

After the Interview

- Immediately after an interview, a thank-you message should be written to the interviewer. Remind the person, or persons, of your name and reiterate your enthusiasm as well as extend your appreciation for their time.
- Evaluate your performance as soon as you can after the interview by asking yourself various reflection questions. Make a list of the things you feel you did correctly and things you would do differently next time.

Hiring Process

- A successful interviewing process may lead to a job offer with the company for which an applicant has applied to work.
- Before an employee is hired, employment checks are completed. These checks can include an employment verification, background check, and credit check. In some states, a drug and alcohol screening may also be completed.
- Employers utilize government sources as well as Internet search engines to search for information on candidates. Employers may also check social networking websites.
- Once the hiring process is completed, the new employee will be required to complete several necessary forms for employment. Common forms include Form I-9, Form W-4, and benefit forms.

Soft Skills

- Soft skills are skills used to help an individual find a job, perform in the workplace, and gain success in a job or career. These skills enable a person to interact with others in a positive manner.
- Professionalism is the act of exhibiting appropriate character, judgment, and behavior by a person trained to perform a job. It is an acquired soft skill of knowing how to interact with others in a manner that is conducive for everyone to be successful in their responsibilities.
- In all situations, professionals apply soft skills. Examples of soft skills important for professionals to exhibit include ethics, respecting diversity, a positive attitude, confidence, and professional etiquette.

Time Management

- Time management is the practice of organizing time and work assignments to increase personal efficiency. It is a self-management skill that enables an individual to control and make the best of their time and abilities.
- Three techniques that can help an individual with time management include prioritizing tasks, using a calendar, and creating a to-do list.

Working with a Team

- Teamwork is the cooperative efforts of team members to reach a goal. Effective team members are people who contribute ideas, effort, and success of the team.

- Effective team members are positive contributors and show leadership qualities, even when not in leadership roles. They also have collaboration skills. Effective team members help and support others and their leaders as well as ask for help when needed.
- When people work together, there is likely to be some conflict. Positive solutions can result when conflict is handled in a proper manner. This can be accomplished through conflict resolution.
- Sometimes, formal methods of conflict resolution might be required. Negotiation is people coming together in an attempt to reach an agreement. Mediation is sometimes needed in negotiation.
- Two additional skills for team members to have are problem-solving and decision-making skills. These involve critical-thinking skills, which provide the ability to make sound judgments and being unbiased about the possibilities.

Job Acquisition and Advancement

- Job-acquisition skills are those skills used to obtain employment. One example is networking. This can increase your opportunities for finding career ideas as well as leading to potential jobs.
- To be successful in acquiring a job, it is vital to have the skills required to cooperate as well as to have the technical skills necessary to complete the tasks. Obtaining certifications is one way to prove you have the requisite technical skills.
- As you gain experience, strive to advance in your career through promotions, which is advancing to the next level in a company's hierarchy. Remember promotions are not automatically given; they are earned.
- A good attitude about learning includes a sense of responsibility for your own education. Strive to be a lifelong learner. A lifelong learner looks for chances to acquire information throughout life.

Professional Success

- Professional success means different things to different people. It can be a personal sense of accomplishment from working a chosen profession or acquiring professional advancement.
- To attain advancement, it is important to exhibit confidence in personal performance and the ability to interact in the workplace.
- Success also requires taking control of your career and learning how to manage up and appropriately deal with office politics within the organization.

REVIEW QUESTIONS

1. Identify three important documents used for getting a job.
2. Briefly explain a cover message.
3. Define *reference* and give examples of who can be one.
4. Compare and contrast applying online versus in person for the application process.
5. Summarize preparing for an interview.
6. Which type of interview question is the following example: How would you handle a disagreement with a coworker?

7. List four examples of questions an interviewer is *not* allowed to ask.

8. Explain two tasks to be completed after an interview.

9. State five examples of questions to ask yourself to help evaluate your interview performance.

10. Summarize the hiring process.

11. What information is typically obtained in employment verification?

12. Which employment form is used by the employer to determine the appropriate amount of taxes to withhold from an employee's paycheck?

13. Identify and explain five examples of soft skills important for professionals to apply in the workplace.

14. Briefly explain four attributes that are exhibited by professionals.

15. Explain three techniques that can help with time management.

16. Summarize working with a team.

17. Explain job acquisition and advancement.

18. What is lifelong learning?

19. Discuss professional success.

20. What is the difference between managing up and playing up?

CASE STUDY

Résumé Fraud

Mina Chang served as Deputy Assistant Secretary of the Bureau of Conflict and Stabilization Operations for the State Department under the administration of President Donald Trump. Her position began in April 2019 until she resigned in November of the same year. Her tenure in the office was cut short after NBC News reported inconsistencies in her résumé and background.

It was reported that Chang's résumé stated she was an alumna of Harvard Business School and had graduated from multiple prestigious schools, including the Army War College. Among other inconsistencies, she claimed that she was part of a United Nations panel and that she addressed both the Democratic and Republican national conventions in 2016. In reality, Chang only attended a seven-week course at Harvard and spoke in the cities where the conventions were held, not at the party conventions.

Chang was forced to resign from her position in the State Department in November 2019 and continues to face allegations of misrepresentation. It is likely these lies will follow Mina Chang for the remainder of her career.

1. What impact does the act of committing résumé fraud have on a person's integrity?

2. Why do you think people falsify their résumés?

3. To what extent does résumé fraud affect a person's professional image?

4. Can a person recover professionally after their résumé has been publicly exposed as being false? Explain your answer.

Appendix A

CompTIA Security+ SY0-601 Exam Correlation Chart

The following chart lists the objectives for CompTIA Security+ SY0-601 Exam and their point(s) of coverage within the *Security Essentials* textbook.

1.0 Threats, Attacks, and Vulnerabilities

1.1 Compare and contrast different types of social engineering techniques.

Objective	Chapter(s)	Heading(s)
Phishing	2	Phishing
Smishing		Smishing
Vishing		Vishing
Spam		Spam
Spam over Internet Messaging (SPIM)		Spam over Internet Messaging (SPIM)
Spear phishing		Spear Phishing
Dumpster diving		Dumpster Diving
Shoulder surfing		Shoulder Surfing
Pharming		Pharming
Tailgating	5	Mantraps
Eliciting information	2	Eliciting Information
Whaling		Whale Phishing
Prepending		Prepending
Identity fraud		Identity Fraud
Invoice scams		Invoice Scams
Credential harvesting		Credential Harvesting
Reconnaissance	2	Shoulder Surfing
	3	Reconnaissance
Hoax	2	Hoax
Impersonation		Impersonation
Watering hole attack		Watering Hole
Typo squatting	7	Typo Squatting
Influence campaigns	2	Influence Campaigns
Hybrid warfare		Hybrid Warfare
Social media		Social Media

Continued

Objective	Chapter(s)	Heading(s)
Principles (reasons for effectiveness)	2	Social Engineering
Authority		
Intimidation		
Consensus		
Scarcity		
Familiarity		
Trust		
Urgency		

1.2: Given a scenario, analyze potential indicators to determine the type of attack.

Objective	Chapter(s)	Heading(s)
Malware	2	Malware Attacks
Ransomware		Ransomware
Trojans		Trojan
Worms		Worm
Potentially unwanted programs (PUPs)		Potentially Unwanted Program (PUP)
Fileless virus		Fileless Virus
Command and control		Malware Attacks
Bots		
Cypto malware		Ransomware
Logic bombs		Logic Bomb
Spyware		Keylogger
Keyloggers		
Remote access Trojan (RAT)		Trojan
Rootkit		Rootkit
Backdoor		Backdoor
Password attacks		
Spraying	9	Password Spraying
Dictionary		Dictionary Attack
Brute Force		Brute Force
Offline		Password Attacks
Online		
Rainbow tables		Rainbow Table
Plaintext/unencrypted		Plaintext/Unencrypted
Physical attacks	2	Physical Attacks
Malicious universal serial bus (USB) cable		Malicious USB Cables
Malicious flash drive		Malicious Flash Drives
Card cloning		Card Cloning and Skimming
Skimming		

Continued

Objective	Chapter(s)	Heading(s)
Adversarial artificial intelligence (AI)	2	Adversarial Artificial Intelligence (AI) Attack
Tainted training data for machine learning (ML)		
Security or machine learning algorithms		
Supply-chain attacks	16	Threat Assessment
Cloud-based vs. on-premises attacks	15	Cloud Vulnerabilities
Cryptographic attacks		
Birthday	9	Birthday Attack
Collision		Collision Attack
Downgrade		Downgrade Attack

1.3: Given a scenario, analyze potential indicators associated with application attacks.

Objective	Chapter(s)	Heading(s)
Privilege escalation	7	Privilege Escalation
Cross-site scripting		Cross-Site Scripting
Injections		
Structured query language (SQL)	7	SQL Injection
Dynamic link library (DLL)		DLL Injection
Lightweight directory access protocol (LDAP)		LDAP Injections
Extensible markup language (XML)		XML Injections
Pointer/object dereference		Pointer Dereference
Directory traversal		Directory Traversal
Buffer overflow		Buffer Overflow
Race conditions		Race Conditions
Time of check/time of use		
Error handling		Error Handling
Improper input handling		
Replay attack	14	Replay Attacks
Session replays		
Integer overflow	7	Integer Overflow
Request forgeries		Request Forgeries
Server-side		
Client-side		
Cross-site		
Application programming interface (API) attacks		Application Programming Interface (API) Attacks
Resource exhaustion		Application Vulnerabilities
Memory leak		Memory Leak
Secure sockets layer (SSL) stripping		SSL Stripping

Continued

Objective	Chapter(s)	Heading(s)
Driver manipulation	7	Driver Manipulation
Shimming		
Refactoring		
Pass the hash	9	Pass the Hash

1.4: Given a scenario, analyze potential indicators associated with network attacks.

Objective	Chapter(s)	Heading(s)
Wireless		
Evil twin	14	Evil Twins
Rogue access point		
Bluesnarfing		Bluejacking and Bluesnarfing
Bluejacking		
Disassociation		Disassociation
Jamming		Jamming
Radio frequency identifier (RFID)		RFID Attacks
Near field communication (NFC)		NFC Attacks
Initialization vector (IV)		Initialization Vectors (IVs)
Man in the middle	9	Downgrade Attack
Man in the browser	7	SSL Stripping
Layer 2 attacks		
Address resolution protocol (ARP) poisoning	1	LAN
	13	ARP Poisoning
Media access control (MAC) flooding	12	Flood Guards
MAC cloning	13	MAC Cloning
Domain name system (DNS)		
Domain hijacking	13	Domain Hijacking
DNS poisoning		DNS Poisoning
Universal resource locator (URL) redirection		URL Redirection
Domain reputation		Domain Reputation
Distributed denial of service (DDoS)		Denial of Service Attacks
Network application		
Operational technology (OT)		
Malicious code or script execution		Malicious Code and Script Execution
PowerShell		
Python		
Bash		
Macros		
Visual Basic for Application (VBA)		

1.5: Explain different threat actors, vectors, and intelligence sources.

Objective	Chapter(s)	Heading(s)
Actors and threats	2	Threat Actors
Advanced persistent threat (APT)		State Actor
Insider threats		Insiders
State actors		State Actor
Hacktivists		Hacktivist
Script kiddies		Script Kiddie
Criminal syndicates		Criminal Syndicate
Hackers		Hackers
White hat		
Black hat		
Gray hat		
Shadow IT		Insiders
Competitors		Competitors
Attributes of actors		Attributes of Threat Actors
Internal/external		
Level of sophistication/capability		
Resources/funding		
Intent/motivation		
Vectors		Vectors
Direct access		
Wireless		
E-mail		
Supply chain		
Social media		
Removable media		
Cloud		
Threat intelligence sources		Threat Intelligence Sources
Open source intelligence (OSINT)		Open-Source Intelligence (OSINT)
Closed/proprietary		Closed/Proprietary Sources
Vulnerability databases		Open-Source Intelligence (OSINT)
Public/private information sharing centers		Information Sharing Centers
Dark web		Dark Web
Indicators of compromise		Threat Intelligence Sources
Automated indicator sharing (AIS)		Automated Indicator Sharing
Structured threat information exchange (STIX)/Trusted automated exchange of indicator information (TAXII)		Structured Threat Information eXpression (STIX)
		Trusted Automated Exchange of Indicator Information (TAXII)
Predictive analysis	7	Software Diversity
Threat maps	2	Closed/Proprietary Sources

Continued

Objective	Chapter(s)	Heading(s)
Threat intelligence sources (continued)		
File/code repositories	7	DevOps
Research sources		
Vendor websites	2	Open-Source Intelligence (OSINT)
Vulnerability feeds		
Conferences		
Academic journals		
Request for comments (RFC)		
Local industry groups		
Social media		Social Media
Threat feeds		Open-Source Intelligence (OSINT)
Adversary tactics, techniques. and procedures (TTP)		

1.6: Explain the security concerns associated with various types of vulnerabilities.

Objective	Chapter(s)	Heading(s)
Cloud-based vs. on-premises	15	Cloud Vulnerabilities
Zero-day	2	Zero-Day Vulnerability
Weak configurations		Weak Configurations
Open permissions		Open Permissions
Unsecured root accounts		Unsecured Root Accounts
Errors		Errors
Weak encryption		Weak Encryption
Unsecure protocols		Unsecure Protocols
Default settings		Default Settings
Open ports and services		Open Ports and Services
Third-party risks		Third-Party Risks
Vendor management		Vendor Management
System integration		
Lack of vendor support		
Supply chain		Supply Chain
Outsourced code development		Outsourced Code Development
Data storage		Data Storage
Improper or weak patch management	6	Patch Management
Firmware		
Operating system (OS)		
Applications		

Continued

Objective	Chapter(s)	Heading(s)
Legacy platforms	2	Legacy Platforms
Impacts		Vulnerabilities
Data loss		
Data breaches		
Data exfiltration		
Identity theft		
Financial		
Reputation		
Availability loss		

1.7: Summarize the techniques used in security assessment.

Objective	Chapter(s)	Heading(s)
Threat hunting	3	Threat Hunting
Intelligence fusion		
Threat feeds		Threat Intelligence Feeds
Advisories and bulletins		Advisories and Bulletins
Maneuver		Maneuvers
Vulnerability scans		Vulnerability Scan
False positives		Scanner Output
False negatives		
Log reviews		
Credentialed vs. non-credentialed		Vulnerability Scan
Intrusive vs. non-intrusive		Vulnerability Scanners
Application		Vulnerability Scanning Techniques
Web application		
Network		
Common Vulnerabilities and Exposures (CVE)/Common Vulnerability Scoring System (CVSS)		Common Vulnerabilities and Exposure Resource
Configuration review		Scanner Output
Syslog/Security information and event management (SIEM)		Syslog
		Security Information and Event Management (SIEM)
Review reports		Syslog
Packet capture		Security Information and Event Management (SIEM)
Data inputs		
User behavior analysis		
Sentiment analysis		
Security monitoring		

Continued

Objective	Chapter(s)	Heading(s)
Syslog/Security information and event management (SIEM) (continued)	3	
Log aggregation		Security Information and Event Management (SIEM)
Log collectors		
Security orchestration, automation, response (SORAR)		SOAR

1.8: Explain the techniques used in penetration testing.

Objective	Chapter(s)	Heading(s)
Penetration testing	3	Penetration Testing
White box		Types of Pen Tests
Black box		
Gray box		
Rules of engagement		Rules of Engagement
Lateral movement		Lateral Movement
Privilege escalation		Escalation of Privilege
Persistence		Persistence
Cleanup		Penetration Testing Cleanup
Bug bounty		Penetration Testing
Pivoting		Pivot
Passive and active reconnaissance		Reconnaissance
Drones/unmanned aerial vehicle (UAV)		Passive Reconnaissance
Way flying		
War driving		
Footprinting		
OSINT		
Exercise types		Exercise Types
Red team		
Blue team		
White team		
Purple team		

2.0 Architecture and Design

2.1: Explain the importance of security concepts in an enterprise environment.

Objective	Chapter(s)	Heading(s)
Configuration management		
Diagrams	12	Configuration Management
Baseline configuration	3	Establishing Baselines
	12	Configuration Management
Standard naming conventions	4	Standard Naming Convention
	12	Configuration Management
Internet protocol (IP) schema		
Data sovereignty	15	Storage
	16	Data Life Cycle
Data protection		
Data loss prevention (DLP)	6	Data Loss Prevention (DLP)
Masking	9	Obfuscation
Encryption		Encryption
At rest		Cryptography
In transit/motion		
In processing		
Tokenization	6	Database Hardening
	16	Tokenization
Rights management		Data Governance
Hardware security module (HSM)	8	MicroSD Hardware Security Module
Geographical considerations	12	Geographical Considerations
Cloud access security broker (CASB)	15	Secure Cloud Access
Response and recovery controls	17	Incident Response (IR)
Secure Sockets Layer (SSL)/Transport Layer Security (TLS) Inspection	12	Other Security Devices
Hashing	9	Hashing
API considerations	15	Applications
		Cloud Native Controls vs. Third-Party Solutions
Site resiliency	18	Recovery Sites
Hot site		
Cold site		
Warm site		

Continued

Objective	Chapter(s)	Heading(s)
Deception and disruption		
Honeypots	12	Honeypot
Honeyfiles		Honeyfile
Honeynets		Honeypot
Fake telemetry		Fake Telemetry
DNS sinkhole		DNS Sinkhole

2.2: Summarize virtualization and cloud-computing concepts.

Objective	Chapter(s)	Heading(s)
Cloud models		
Infrastructure as a service (IaaS)	15	Infrastructure as a Service (IaaS)
Platform as a service (PaaS)		Platform as a Service (PaaS)
Software as a service (SaaS)		Software as a Service (SaaS)
Anything as a service (XaaS)		Anything as a Service (XaaS)
Public		Public Cloud
Community		Community Cloud
Private		Private Cloud
Hybrid		Hybrid Cloud
Cloud service providers		Cloud Service Providers (CSPs)
Managed service provider (MSP)/Managed security service provider (MSSP)		
On-premises vs. off-premises		Cloud Computing
Fog computing		Non-Cloud Services
Edge computing		
Thin client		
Containers		Container Security
Micro-services/API		Applications
Infrastructure as code		
Software-defined networking (SDN)		
Software-defined visibility (SDV)		
Serverless architecture		Serverless Architecture
Services integration		Cloud Services
Resources policies		Resource Policies
Transit gateway		Hardware
Virtualization		Virtualization
Virtual machine (VM) sprawl avoidance		VM Sprawl Avoidance
VM escape protection		VM Escape Protection

2.3: Summarize secure application development, deployment, and automation concepts.

Objective	Chapter(s)	Heading(s)
Environment		
Development	7	Application Development
		Secure Application Development
Test		Test Environment
Staging		Staging Environment
Production		Production Environment
Quality assurance (QA)		Test Environment
Provisioning and deprovisioning		Development Resources
Integrity measurement		Integrity Measurement
Secure coding techniques		
Normalization	7	Normalization
Stored procedures		Stored Procedures
Obfuscation/camouflage		Obfuscation
Code reuse/dead code		Code Reuse
Server-side vs. client-side execution and validation		Proper Input Validation
Memory management		Memory Management
Use of third-party libraries and software development kits (SDKs)		Code Reuse
Data exposure		Data Exposure
Open Web Application Security Project (OWASP)		Secure Coding Techniques
Software diversity		Software Diversity
Complier		
Binary		
Automation/scripting		DevOps
Automated courses of action		
Continuous monitoring		
Continuous validation		
Continuous integration		
Continuous delivery		
Continuous deployment		
Elasticity		Elasticity
Scalability		Scalability
Version control		Version Control

2.4: Summarize authentication and authorization design concepts.

Objective	Chapter(s)	Heading(s)
Authentication methods		
Directory services	4	Directory Services
Federation		Federated Identity Management (FIM)
Attestation		Authentication and Access Control
Technologies		
Time-based on-time password (TOTP)	5	Tokens
HMAC-based one-time password (HOTP)		
Short message service (SMS)	4	Authentication and Access Control
Token key		Token
	5	Tokens
Static codes	8	Multifunction Printers
Authentication applications	4	Tokens
Push notifications	8	Authentication
Phone call		
Smart card authentication	5	Smart Card
Biometrics	4	Standard Biometrics
Fingerprint		
Retina		
Iris		
Facial		
Voice		
Vein		
Gait analysis		
Efficacy rates		
False acceptance		
False rejection		
Crossover error rate		
Multifactor authentication (MFA) factors and attributes	4	Multifactor Authentication
Factors		
Something you know		
Something you have		
Something you are		
Attributes		
Somewhere you are		
Something you can do		
Something you exhibit		
Someone you know		
Authentication, authorization, and accounting (AAA)	4	Authentication and Access Control
Cloud vs. on-premises requirements	15	Authentication

2.5: Given a scenario, implement cybersecurity resilience.

Objective	Chapter(s)	Heading(s)
Redundancy	18	Redundancy
Geographic dispersal		Data Backup
Disk		
Redundant array of inexpensive (RAID) levels	18	RAID
Multipath		Multipathing
Network		
Load balancers	7	Scalability
	12	Load Balancer
Network interface card (NIC) teaming		
Power		
Uninterruptible power supply (UPS)	18	Uninterruptible Power Supply (UPS)
Generator		Generator
Dual supply		Multiple Power Supplies
Managed power distributed units (PDUs)		Power Distribution Units (PDUs)
Replication		
Storage area network (SAN)	18	Data Backup
VM		
On-premises vs. cloud	15	Cloud Security Controls
Backup types		
Full	18	Data Backup
Incremental		
Snapshot		
Differential		
Tape		
Disk		
Copy		
Network attached storage (NAS)		
SAN		
Cloud	15	Cloud Backup and Recovery
	18	Data Backup
Image	18	Data Backup
Online vs. offline		
Offsite storage		
Distance considerations		
Non-persistence	12	Non-Persistence
Revert to known state		
Last known good configuration		
Live boot media		

Continued

Objective	Chapter(s)	Heading(s)
High availability	18	High Availability
Scalability	7	Scalability
	18	Disaster Recovery Plan
Restoration order		Restoration Order
Diversity		
Technologies	1	Security Domains
Vendors	1	Security Domains
Crypto	9	Cryptography
Controls	1	Security Domains

2.5: Explain the security implications of embedded and specialized systems.

Objective	Chapter(s)	Heading(s)
Embedded systems	8	Embedded Systems
Raspberry Pi		Raspberry Pi
Field-programmable gate array (FPGA)		Field-Programmable Gate Array (FPGA)
Arduino		Arduino
System control and data acquisition (SCADA)/Industrial control system (ICS)		Industrial Control Systems (ICS)
Facilities		
Industrial		
Manufacturing		
Energy		
Logistics		
Internet of Things (IoT)		Internet of Things (IoT)
Sensors		Internet of Things (IoT)
Smart devices		Smart Devices
Wearables		Wearable Technology
Facility automation		Industrial Control Systems (ICS)
Weak defaults		Internet of Things (IoT)
Specialized		
Medical systems	8	Wearable Technology
		Medical Systems
Vehicles		Vehicles
Aircraft		Aircraft
Smart meters		Smart Meters

Continued

Objective	Chapter(s)	Heading(s)
Voice over IP (VoIP)	8	VoIP
Heating, ventilation, air conditioning (HVAC)		Industrial-Control Systems (ICS)
Drones/AVs		Drones
Multifunction printer (MFP)		Multifunction Printers
Real-time operating system (RTOS)		Real-Time Operating System (RTOS)
Surveillance systems		Surveillance Systems
System on a chip (SoC)		System on a Chip (SoC)
Communication considerations		
5G	14	Cellular Generations
Narrowband		Narrowband
Baseband radio		Baseband
Subscriber identity module (SIM) cards		SIM Cards
Zigbee		Zigbee
Constraints	8	Constraints of Embedded Systems
Power		
Computer		
Network		
Crypto		
Inability to patch		
Authentication		
Range		
Cost		
Implied trust		

2.7: Explain the importance of physical security controls.

Objective	Chapter(s)	Heading(s)
Bollards/barricades	5	Barricades
Mantraps		Mantraps
Badges		Identification Badges
Alarms		Alarms
Signage		Signage
Cameras		Closed-Circuit Television (CCTV)
Motion recognition		
Object detection		
Closed-circuit television (CCTV)		
Industrial camouflage		Industrial Camouflage
Personnel		Personnel
Guards		
Robot sentries		

Continued

Objective	Chapter(s)	Heading(s)
Personnel (continued)	5	Personnel
Reception		
Two-person integrity/control		
Locks		Lock Access and Cable Locks
Biometrics		
Electronic		
Physical		
Cable locks		
USB data blocker	2	USB Data Blocker
Lighting	5	Lighting
Fencing		Fencing
Fire suppression		Fire Control
Sensors		Hot and Cold Aisles
Motion detection		Lighting
		Alarms
Noise detection		Alarms
Proximity reader		Gated Entrance
		Lock Access and Cable Locks
Moisture detection		Water Control
Cards		Gated Entrance
		Lock Access and Cable Locks
Temperature		Temperature Control
Drones/UAV	8	Drones
Visitor logs	5	Logs
Faraday cages		Data Signal Protection
Air gap	5	Air-Gap Network
Demilitarized zone (DMZ)	12	Demilitarized Zone (DMZ)
Protected cable distribution	5	Protected Distribution and Cabling
Secure areas		
Air gap	5	Mantraps
Vault		Safes and Vaults
Safe		Safes and Vaults
Hot aisle		Hot and Cold Aisles
Cold aisle		Hot and Cold Aisles
Secure data destruction		Data Destruction
Burning		Destroying Paper-Based Data
Shredding		
Pulping		

Continued

Objective	Chapter(s)	Heading(s)
Secure data destruction (continued)	5	
Pulverizing		Physical Destruction
Degaussing		Destroying Data on Digital Media
Third-party solutions		Physical Destruction Tech Tip

2.8: Summarize the basics of cryptographic concepts.

Objective	Chapter(s)	Heading(s)
Digital signatures	10	Public Key Infrastructure
Key length	9	Encryption
Key stretching		Key Stretching
Salting		
Hashing		Hashing
Key exchange		Symmetric Encryption
Elliptical-curve cryptography		Elliptical-Curve Cryptography
Perfect forward secrecy		Symmetric Encryption
Quantum		Quantum Cryptography
Communications		
Computing		
Post-quantum		Quantum Cryptography
Ephemeral		Encryption
Modes of operation		
Authenticated		
Unauthenticated		
Counter		
Blockchain	10	Blockchains
Public ledgers		
Cipher suites	9	Symmetric Algorithm Types
Stream		
Block		
Symmetric vs. asymmetric		Symmetric Encryption
		Asymmetric Encryption
Lightweight cryptography		Low-Power Devices
Steganography		Steganography
Audio		
Video		
Image		
Homomorphic encryption	9	Low Latency

Continued

Objective	Chapter(s)	Heading(s)
Common use cases		
Low power devices	9	Low-Power Devices
Low latency		Low Latency
High resiliency		High Resiliency
Supporting confidentiality		Confidentiality
Supporting integrity		Integrity
Supporting obfuscation		Obfuscation
Supporting authentication		Authentication
Supporting nonrepudiation		Nonrepudiation
Resource vs. security constraints		Low-Power Devices
Limitations		
Speed	9	Cryptography Limitation
Size		Encryption
Weak keys		Cryptography Limitations
Time		
Longevity		Encryption
Predictability		
Reuse		Cryptography Limitations
Entropy		Encryption
Computational overheads		Low-Power Devices
Resource vs. security constraints		

3.0 Implementation

3.1: Given a scenario, implement secure protocols.

Objective	Chapter(s)	Heading(s)
Protocols		
Domain Name System Security Extension (DNSSEC)	13	DNS Poisoning Attack
SSH	10	SSH
	13	Secure Shell (SSH)
Secure/multipurpose Internet mail exchanger (S/MIME)	10	S/MIME
	13	Figure 13-1
Secure real-time protocol (SRTP)	10	SRTP
	13	Figure 13-1
LDAPS	13	Lightweight Directory Access Protocol, Secure (LDAPS)
File transfer protocol, secure (FTPS)		File Transfer Protocol (FTP)
Secured file transfer protocol (SFTP)		

Continued

Objective	Chapter(s)	Heading(s)
Protocols (continued)		
Simple Network Management Protocol, version 3 (SNMPv3)	5	Hot and Cold Aisles
	13	Figure 13-1
Hypertext transfer protocol over SSL/TLS (HTTPS)	10	HTTPS
	13	Figure 13-1
IPSec	10	IP Security
	13	Figure 13-1
Authentication header (AH)/Encapsulated security payload (ESP)	10	IP Security
Tunnel/Transport		
Secure post office protocol (POP)/Internet message access protocol (IMAP)	13	E-Mail Protocols
Use cases		
Voice and audio	13	Secure Protocols
Time synchronization		Figure 13-1
E-mail and web		
File transfer		
Directory Services	4	Directory Services
	13	Secure Protocols
		Figure 13-1
Remote access	13	Secure Protocols
Domain name resolution		Figure 13-1
Routing and switching		
Network address allocation		
Subscription services		

3.2: Given a scenario, implement host or application security solutions.

Objective	Chapter(s)	Heading(s)
Endpoint protection	6	Endpoint Protection
Antivirus		Antivirus and Antimalware
Antimalware		
Endpoint detection and response (EDR)		Endpoint Detection and Response
DLP		Data Loss Prevention (DLP)
Next-generation firewall		Firewall
Host intrusion-prevention system (HIPS)		Host Intrusion Systems
Host intrusion-detection system (HIDS)		
Host-based firewall		Firewall

Continued

Objective	Chapter(s)	Heading(s)
Boot integrity	6	Boot Integrity
Boot security/Unified Extensible Firmware Interface (UEFI)		UEFI
Measured boot		Measured Boot
Boot attestation		Boot Attestation
Database		Database Hardening
Tokenization		
Salting		
Hashing		
Application security		
Input validation	7	Input Validation
Secure cookies		Secure Cookies
Hypertext Transfer Protocol (HTTP) headers		Secure HTTP Headers
Code signing		Code Reuse
Whitelisting		Application Hardening
Blacklisting		
Secure coding practices		Normalization
		Stored Procedures
		Obfuscation
		Code Reuse
		Proper Input Validation
		Memory Management
		Data Exposure
Static code analysis		Black-Box Testing
Manual code review		
Dynamic code analysis		
Fuzzing		
Hardening		
Open ports and services	6	Services
		Ports
Registry		Securing the Windows Registry
Disk encryption		Disk Encryption
OS		Operating System Hardening
Patch management		Patch Management
Third-party updates		
Auto-update		
Self-encrypting drive (SED)/full disk encryption (FDE)		Disk Encryption
Opal		

Continued

Objective	Chapter(s)	Heading(s)
Hardware root of trust	6	Measured Boot
Trusted Platform Module (TPM)		
Sandboxing	7	Code Testing

3.3: Given a scenario, implement secure network designs.

Objective	Chapter(s)	Heading(s)
Load balancing	12	Load Balancer
Active/active		
Active/passive		
Scheduling		
Virtual IP		
Persistence		
Network segmentation		
Virtual local area network (VLAN)	12	Virtual Local Area Network (VLAN)
DMZ		Demilitarized Zone (DMZ)
East-west traffic		Microsegmentation
Extranet		Intranets and Extranets
Intranet		
Zero trust		Incorporating Zero Trust
Virtual private network (VPN)		
Always on	12	Virtual Private Network (VPN)
Split tunnel vs. full tunnel		
Remote access vs. site-to-site		
IPSec		VPN Protocols
SSL/TLS	10	SSL/TLS
HTML5	12	VPN Protocols
Layer 2 tunneling protocol (L2TP)		
DNS	13	DNS
Network access control (NAC)		Network Access Control (NAC)
Agent and agentless		
Out-of-band management		Out-of-Band Management
Port security		
Broadcast storm prevention	12	Loop Prevention
Bridge Protocol Data Unit (BPDU) guard		
Loop prevention		
Dynamic Host Configuration Protocol (DHCP) snooping		DHCP Snooping
Media access control (MAC) filtering		Port Security
	14	MAC Address Filtering

Continued

Objective	Chapter(s)	Heading(s)
Network appliances		
Jump servers	12	Jump Server
Proxy servers		Proxy Server
Forward		
Reverse		
Network-based intrusion-detection system (NIDS)/ network-based intrusion-prevention system (NIPS)		Intrusion-Detection System Intrusion-Prevention System
Signature based		Signature-Based Monitoring
Heuristic/behavior		Heuristic-Based Monitoring
Anomaly		Anomaly-Based Monitoring
Inline vs. passive		Intrusion-Detection System Intrusion-Prevention System
HSM	8	MicroSD Hardware Security Module
	12	Other Security Devices
Sensors		Intrusion-Detection Systems
Collectors		
Aggregators		Switch
Firewalls		
Web application firewall (WAF)	12	Web Application Firewall
Next-generation firewall	6	Firewall
Stateful	12	Stateful-Inspection Firewall
Stateless		Stateless-Inspection Firewall
Unified threat management (UTM)		Unified Threat Management
Network address translation (NAT) gateway		Network Address Translation
Content/URL filter		Content Filter
Open-source vs. proprietary		Firewalls
Hardware vs. software		
Appliance vs. host-based vs. virtual		
Access control list (ACL)		Access Control Lists (ACLs)
Route security		Route Security
Quality of service (QoS)		Secure Network Design
Implications of IPv6		Internet Protocol (IP) Schema
Port spanning/port mirroring		Intrusion-Detection System
Port taps		
Monitoring services	13	Monitoring Services
File integrity monitors		File Integrity Monitoring

3.4: Given a scenario, install and configure wireless security settings.

Objective	Chapter(s)	Heading(s)
Cryptographic protocols		
Wi-Fi protected access II (WPA2)	14	Wi-Fi Protected Access II (WPA2)
Wi-Fi protected access III (WPA3)		Wi-Fi Protected Access III (WPA3)
Counter-mode/CBC-MAC protocol (CCMP)		Wi-Fi Protected Access 2 (WPA2)
Simultaneous Authentication of Equals (SAE)		Wi-Fi Protected Access III (WPA3)
Authentication protocols		
Extensible Authentication Protocol (EAP)	14	Wi-Fi Protected Access (WPA)
Protected Extensible Application Protocol (PEAP)		PEAP
EAP-FAST		EAP-FAST
EAP-TLS		EAP-TLS
EAP-TTLS		EAP-TTLS
IEEE 802.1X	5	Smart Card
	14	802.1X
Remote Authentication Dial-In User Sever (RADIUS) Federation	4	Remote Access Authentication
	14	802.1X
Methods		
Pre-shared key (PSK) vs. Enterprise Vs. Open	14	Wireless Security Methods
		Wi-Fi Protected Access (WPA)
		802.1X
Wi-Fi Protected Setup (WPS)		Wi-Fi Protected Setup (WPS)
Captive Portals		Captive Portal
Installation considerations		
Site surveys	14	Site Survey
Heat maps		Predictive Site Survey
Wi-Fi analyzers		Wi-Fi Survey
Channel overlays		Site Survey
Wireless access point (WAP) placement		Antennae Types and Placement
Controller and access point security		Wireless Access Point

3.5: Given a scenario, implement secure mobile solutions.

Objective	Chapter(s)	Heading(s)
Connection methods and receivers		
Cellular	8	Cellular
	14	Cellular
Wi-Fi	8	Wi-Fi
	14	WLAN

Continued

Objective	Chapter(s)	Heading(s)
Connection methods and receivers (continued)		
Bluetooth	8	Bluetooth
	14	Bluetooth
NFC		NFC
Infrared		Infrared
USB	8	USB
Point to point	14	Antennae Types and Placement
Point to multipoint		
Global Positioning System (GPS)	8	Physical Security
	14	GPS
RFID		Radio Frequency Identification (RFID)
Mobile device management (MDM)		
Application management	8	Management Tools
Content management		
Remote wipe		Physical Security
Geofencing		
Geolocation		
Screen locks		Authentication
Push notifications		Authentication
		Push Notification
Passwords and pins		Management Tools
Biometrics		Authentication
Context-aware authentication		Context-Aware Authentication
Containerization		Storage Segmentation
Storage segmentation		
Full device encryption		Mobile Devices
Mobile devices		
MicroSD HSM	8	MicroSD Hardware Security Module
MDM/Unified endpoint management (UEM)		Management Tools
Mobile application management (MAM)		
SEAndorid		SEAndorid
Enforcement and monitoring of:		
Third-party app stores	8	Third-Party App Stores
Rooting/jailbreaking		Bypassing Device Restrictions
Sideloading		Third-Party App Stores
Custom firmware		Custom and Unauthorized Firmware
Carrier unlocking		Bypassing Device Restrictions
Firmware over-the-air (OTA) updates		Custom and Unauthorized Firmware
Camera use		Cameras and Microphones

Continued

Objective	Chapter(s)	Heading(s)
SMS/Multimedia message service (MMS)/Rich communication services (RCS)	8	Text-Message Threats
External media		External Media
USB on the go (OTG)		USB
Recording microphone		Cameras and Microphones
GPS tagging		Physical Security
Wi-Fi direct/ad hoc		Wi-Fi
Tethering		Bluetooth
Hotspot		Wi-Fi
Payment methods		Mobile Payments
Deployment models		Mobile Devices
Bring your own device (BYOD)		
Corporate-owned personally enabled (COPE)		
Choose your own device (CYOD)		
Corporate-owned		
Virtual desktop infrastructure (VDI)		

3.6: Given a scenario, apply cybersecurity solutions to the cloud.

Objective	Chapter(s)	Heading(s)
Cloud security controls		
High availability across zones	15	High Availability across Zones
Resource policies		Resource Policies
Secrets management		Secrets Management
Integration and auditing		Integration and Auditing
Storage		Storage
Permissions		
Encryptions		
Replication		
High availability		
Network		
Virtual networks	15	Virtual Networks
Public and private subnets		
Segmentation		Segmentation
API inspection and integration		Cloud Native Controls vs. Third-Party Solutions
Compute		
Security groups	15	Security Groups
Dynamic resource allocation		Integration and Auditing
Instance awareness		Servers

Continued

Objective	Chapter(s)	Heading(s)
Compute (continued)		
Virtual private cloud (VPS) endpoint	15	Virtual Networks
Container security		Containers
Solutions		
CASB	15	Secure Cloud Access
Application security		Containers
Next-generation secure web gateway (SWG)		Next-Generation Secure Web Gateway (SWG)
Firewall considerations in a cloud environment		
Cost	15	Firewalls
Need for segmentation		Segmentation
Open Systems Interconnection (OSI) layers		Firewalls
		Segmentation
Cloud native controls vs. third-party solutions		Cloud Native Controls vs. Third-Party Solutions

3.7: Given a scenario, implement identity and account management controls.

Objective	Chapter(s)	Heading(s)
Identity		
Identity provider (IdP)	4	Security Assertion Markup Language (SAML)
Attributes		Security Assertion Markup Language (SAML)
		Attributes
Certificates	10	Digital Certificate
Tokens	4	Tokens
	5	Token
SSH Keys	10	SSH
Smart cards	5	Smart Cards
Account types	4	Account Types
User account		
Shared and generic accounts/credentials		
Guest accounts		
Service accounts		
Account policies		
Password complexity	4	Password Policy
Password history		
Password reuse		
Time of day		Group-Based Access Control
Network location		
Geofencing		Somewhere You Are
Geotagging		
Geolocation		

Continued

Objective	Chapter(s)	Heading(s)
Account policies (continued)		
Time-based logins	8	Context-Aware Authentication
Access policies	4	Account Policy Enforcement
Account permissions		Auditing
Account audits		Account Auditing
Impossible travel time/risky login	8	Authentication
		Context-Aware Authentication
Lockout	4	Account Policy Enforcement
	8	Lockout
Disablement	4	Account Policy Enforcement

3.8: Given a scenario, implement authentication and authorization solutions.

Objective	Chapter(s)	Heading(s)
Authentication management		
Password keys	4	Weak Passwords Tech Tip
Password vaults	8	Management Tools
TPM	6	Measured Boot
HSM	8	MicroSD Hardware Security Module
Knowledge-based authentication	4	What You Know
Authentication		
EAP	12	Extensible Authentication Protocol (EAP)
	14	Wi-Fi Protected Access (WPA)
Challenge Handshake Authentication Protocol (CHAP)	12	Challenge Handshake Authentication Protocol (CHAP)
Password Authentication Protocol (PAP)		Password Authentication Protocol (PAP)
802.1X	5	Smart Card
	14	802.1X
RADIUS	4	Remote Access Authentication
	14	802.1X
Single sign-on (SSO)	4	Single Sign-On (SSO)
Security Assertions Markup Language (SAML)		Security Assertion Markup Language (SAML)
Terminal Access Controller Access Control System Plus (TACACS+)		Remote Access Authentication
OAuth		OAuth
OpenID		OpenID Connect
Kerberos		Directory Authentication

Continued

Objective	Chapter(s)	Heading(s)
Access control schemes		
Attribute-based access control (ABAC)	4	Attribute-Based Access Control (ABAC)
Role-based access control		Discretionary Access Control (DAC)
Rule-based access control		Discretionary Access Control (DAC)
MAC		Mandatory Access Control (MAC)
Discretionary access control (DAC)		Discretionary Access Control (DAC)
Conditional access	8	Securing Mobile Devices
Privilege access management	4	Account Management Practices
		Account Types
		File System Permissions
File system permissions		File System Permissions

3.9: Given a scenario, implement public key infrastructure.

Objective	Chapter(s)	Heading(s)
Public key infrastructure (PKI)		
Key management	10	Public Key Infrastructure
Certificate authority (CA)		Certificate Authority
Intermediate CA		Certificate Signing Request (CSR)
Registration authority (RA)		
Certificate revocation list (CRL)		Certificate Revocation List (CRL)
Certificate attributes		Certificate Attributes
Online Certificate Status Protocol (OCSP)		Online Certificate Status Protocol (OCSP)
Certificate signing request (CSR)		Certificate Signing Request (CSR)
CN		Certificate Attributes
SAN		Subject Alternative Name (SAN) Certificate
Expiration		PKI Management
Types of certificates		
Wildcard	10	Wildcard Certificate
SAN		Subject Alternative Name (SAN) Certificate
Code signing		Code Signing
Self-signed		Self-Signed Digital Certificates
Machine/computer		Machine
E-mail		E-Mail
User		User
Root		Root Digital Certificates
Domain validation		Domain Validation (DV) Certificate
Extended validation		Extended Validation (EV) Certificate

Continued

Objective	Chapter(s)	Heading(s)
Certificate formats	10	Certificate Formats
Distinguished encoding rules (DER)		
Privacy enhanced mail (PEM)		
Personal information exchange (PFX)		
.cer		
P12		
P7B		
Concepts		
Online vs. offline CA	10	Certificate Signing Request (CSR)
Stapling		Online Certificate Status Protocol (OCSP)
Pinning		Pinning
Trust model		Trust Model
Key escrow		PKI Management
Certificate chaining		Certificate Chaining

4.0 Operations and Incident Response

4.1: Given a scenario, use the appropriate tool to assess organizational security.

Objective	Chapter(s)	Heading(s)
Network reconnaissance and discovery		
tracert/traceroute	11	Tracert
nslookup/dig		NSlookup and dig
ipconfig/ifconfig		IPConfig
nmap	13	Nmap
ping/pathping	11	Ping
		Pathping
hping	13	hping
netstat		Netstat
netcat		Netcat
IP scanners		IP Scanners
arp	11	ARP
route		Route
curl	13	Curl
theHarvester		Harvester
sn1per		Sn1per
scanless		Scanless
dnsenum		DNSenum
Nessus		Nessus
Cuckoo		Cuckoo

Continued

Objective	Chapter(s)	Heading(s)
File manipulation		
head	11	Piping
tail		Piping
cat		Cat
grep		Grep
chmod		Chmod
logger		Logger
Shell and script environments		
SSH	13	Secure Shell (SSH)
PowerShell	11	Windows PowerShell
Python		Python
OpenSSL		OpenSSL
Packet capture and replay	13	Packet Capture and Replay
Tcpreplay		
Tcpdump		
Wireshark		
Forensics	17	Data Acquisition
dd		
Memdump		
WinHex		
FTK imager		
Autopsy		
Exploitation frameworks	13	Exploitation Frameworks
Password crackers	9	Password Cracking
Data sanitization	5	Disk Sanitization
	16	Sanitization

4.2: Summarize the importance of policies, processes, and procedures for incident response.

Objective	Chapter(s)	Heading(s)
Incident response plans	17	Incident Response Plan (IRP)
Incident response process		
Preparation	17	Preparation
Identification		Identification
Containment		Containment
Eradication		Eradication
Recovery		Recovery
Lessons learned		Lessons Learned

Continued

Objective	Chapter(s)	Heading(s)
Exercises	17	Incident Response Plan (IRP)
Tabletop		
Walkthroughs		
Simulations		
Attack frameworks		Cybersecurity Frameworks
MITRE ATT&CK		
The Diamond Model of Intrusion Analysis		
Cyber Kill Chain		
Stakeholder management		Preparation
Communication plan		Preparation
Disaster recovery plan	18	Disaster Recovery Plan (DRP)
Business continuity plan		Business Continuity
Continuity of operation planning (COOP)		Business Continuity
Incident response team	17	Incident Response Plan (IRP)
Retention policies	16	Data Retention
	17	Data Acquisition

4.3: Given an incident, utilize appropriate data sources to support an investigation.

Objective	Chapter(s)	Heading(s)
Vulnerability scan output	3	Scanner Output
SIEM dashboards	3	Security Information and Event Management (SIEM)
Sensor		
Sensitivity		
Trends		
Alerts		
Correlation		
Log files	3	Log Files
Network	13	Log Files
System		
Application		
Security		
Web		
DNS		
Authentication		
Dump files		
VoIP and call managers		
Session Initiation Protocol (SIP) traffic		
syslog/rsyslog/syslog-ng	3	Syslog
	13	Syslog

Continued

Objective	Chapter(s)	Heading(s)
journalctl	3	Syslog
	13	Syslog
nxlog	3	Syslog
	13	Syslog
Retention	17	Data Acquisition
Bandwidth monitors	13	Bandwidth Monitors
Metadata	17	Metadata
E-mail		
Mobile		
Web		
File		
Netflow/sflow	13	Netflow
		sFlow
Echo		ICMP Monitoring
IPfix		IPfix
Protocol analyzer output		Packet Capture and Replay

4.4: Given an incident, apply mitigation techniques or controls to secure an environment.

Objective	Chapter(s)	Heading(s)
Reconfigure endpoint security solutions		
Application whitelisting	6	Application Hardening
	17	Endpoint Security Solutions
Application blacklisting	6	Application Hardening
	17	Endpoint Security Solutions
Quarantine	17	Endpoint Security Solutions
Configuration changes		
Firewall rules	17	Configuration Changes
MDM	8	Management Tools
		Physical Security
		Authentication
		Push Notification
		Context-Aware Authentication
		Storage Segmentation
		Mobile Devices
	17	Configuration Changes
DLP	6	Data Loss Prevention (DLP)
	17	Configuration Changes
Content filter/URL filter	17	Configuration Changes
Update or revoke certificates		Configuration Changes

Continued

Objective	Chapter(s)	Heading(s)
Isolation	17	Endpoint Security Solutions
Containment		Containment
Segmentation		Containment
Secure Orchestration, Automation, and Response (SOAR)		SOAR
Runbooks		
Playbooks		

4.5: Explain the key aspects of digital forensics.

Objective	Chapter(s)	Heading(s)
Documentation/evidence		
Legal hold	17	Secure the Area
Video		Capture Video
Admissibility		Preserve the Data
Chain of custody		Chain of Custody
Timeliness of sequence of events		Metadata
Time stamps		
Time offset		
Tags		Data Acquisition
Reports		Forensics Report
Event logs		Metadata
Interviews		Interviews
Acquisition		
Order of volatility	17	Order of Volatility
Disk		
Random-access memory (RAM)		
Swap/pagefile		
OS		
Device		
Firmware		
Snapshot		Data Acquisition
Cache		Order of Volatility
Network		Order of Volatility
Artifacts		Data Acquisition
On-premises vs. cloud		Cloud Forensics
Right to audit clauses		
Regulatory/jurisdiction		
Data breach notification laws		

Continued

Objective	Chapter(s)	Heading(s)
Integrity	17	Capture the System Image
Hashing		Hash
Checksums		Checksum
Provenance		Digital Provenance
Preservation		Secure the Area
E-discovery		Data Acquisition
Data recovery		
Nonrepudiation		Forensics Report
Strategic intelligence/counterintelligence		Forensics Procedure

5.0 Governance, Risk, and Compliance

5.1: Compare and contrast various types of controls.

Objective	Chapter(s)	Heading(s)
Category	16	Strategies
Managerial		
Operational		
Technical		
Control type	5	Security Controls
Preventive	16	Control Types
Detective		
Corrective		
Deterrent		
Compensating		
Physical		

5.2: Explain the importance of applicable regulations, standards, or frameworks that impact organizational security posture.

Objective	Chapter(s)	Heading(s)
Regulations, standards, and legislation	1	Regulatory Compliance
General Data Protection Regulation (GDPR)		
National, territory, or state laws		
Payment Card Industry Data Security Standard (PCI DSS)		Payment Card Industry Data Security Standard (PCI DSS)
Key frameworks		
Center for Internet Security (CIS)	1	CIS Critical Security Controls
National Institute of Standards and Technology (NIST) RMF/CSF		NIST Framework for Improving Critical Infrastructure Cybersecurity
International Organization for Standardization ISO) 27001/27002/27701/31000		ISO Standards

Continued

Objective	Chapter(s)	Heading(s)
Key frameworks (continued)		
SSAE SOC2 Type II/III	1	SSAE SOC2
Cloud Security alliance	15	Cloud Security Controls
Cloud control matrix		
Reference architecture		
Benchmarks/secure configuration guides	1	Information Security Plan
Platform/vendor-specific guides		System
Web server		
OS		
Application server		
Network infrastructure devices		

5.3: Explain the importance of policies to organizational security.

Objective	Chapter(s)	Heading(s)
Personnel		
Acceptable use policy	16	Acceptable Use Policy
Job rotation		Job Rotation
Mandatory vacation		Mandatory Vacation
Separation of duties		Separation of Duties
Least privilege		Least Privilege
Clean desk space		Clean-Desk Policy
Background checks		Background Checks
Nondisclosure agreement (NDA)		Employment Contracts
Social media analysis		Social Media Analysis
Onboarding	4	Employee Onboarding and Offboarding
	16	Onboarding
Offboarding	4	Employee Onboarding and Offboarding
	16	Offboarding
User training		Employee User Training
Gamification		
Capture the flag		
Phishing campaigns		
Phishing simulations		Employee User Training
Computer-based training (CBT)		Employee User Training
Role-based training		Role-Based Awareness Training
Diversity of training techniques		Employee User Training

Continued

Objective	Chapter(s)	Heading(s)
Third-party risk management	16	Third-Party Risk Management
Vendors		
Supply chain		
Business partners		
Service level agreement (SLA)		
Memorandum of understanding (MOU)		
Measurement systems analysis (MSA)		
Business partnership agreement (BPA)		
End of life (EOL)		
End of service (EOS)		
NDA		
Data		
Classification	16	Data Clearance
Governance		Governance
Retention		Data Retention
Credential policies		Credential Policies
Personnel		
Third party		
Devices		
Service accounts		
Administrator/root accounts		
Organizational policies		
Change management	16	Change Management
Change control		
Asset management		Asset Management

5.4: Summarize risk management processes and concepts.

Objective	Chapter(s)	Heading(s)
Risk types		
External	16	Threat Assessment
Internal		
Legacy systems		
Multiparty		Third-Party Risk Management (TPRM)
IP theft		Data Clearance
Software compliance/licensing		Acceptable Use Policy
Risk management strategies		
Acceptance	16	Risk Acceptance
Avoidance		

Continued

Objective	Chapter(s)	Heading(s)
Risk management strategies (continued)		
Transference	16	Risk Transfer
Cybersecurity insurance		
Mitigation		Risk Mitigation
Risk analysis		
Risk register	16	Risk Evaluation
Risk matrix/heat map		Risk Analysis
Risk control assessment		
Risk control self-assessment		
Risk awareness		Risk Management
Inherent risk		Risk Mitigation
Residual risk		
Control risk		Risk Analysis
Risk appetite		
Regulations that affect risk posture		Asset Management
Risk assessment types		Risk Impact
Qualitative		
Quantitative		
Likelihood of occurrence		
Impact		
Asset value		Risk Evaluation
Single loss expectancy (SLE)		
Annualized loss expectancy (ALE)		
Annualized rate of occurrence (ARO)		Risk Impact
Disasters		Threat Assessment
Environmental		
Man-made		
Internal vs. external		
Business impact analysis		
Recovery time objective (RTO)	18	High Availability
Recovery point objective (RPO)		High Availability
Mean time to repair (MTTR)		MTTR
Mean time between failures (MTBF)		MTBF
Functional recovery plans		Disaster Recovery Plan (DRP)
Single point of failure		Multipathing
Disaster recovery plan (DRP)		Disaster Recovery Plan (DRP)
Mission essential functions		Business Impact Analysis
Identification of critical systems		
Site risk assessment		Business Continuity

5.5: Explain privacy and sensitive data concepts in relation to security.

Objective	Chapter(s)	Heading(s)
Organizational consequences of privacy breaches	16	Data Clearance
Reputation damage		
Identity theft		
Fines		
IP theft		
Notifications of breaches		
Escalation		
Public notifications and disclosures		
Data types		
Classifications	16	Data Clearance
Public		Figure 16-3
Private		
Sensitive		
Confidential		
Critical		
Proprietary		
Personally identifiable information (PII)		Governance
Health information		
Financial information		
Government data		
Customer data		
Privacy enhancing technologies		
Data minimization	16	Data Minimization
Data masking		Data Masking
Tokenization		Tokenization
Anonymization		Data Anonymization
Pseudoanonymization		Pseudoanonymization
Roles and responsibilities		Governance
Data owners		Figure 16-1
Data controller		
Data processor		
Data custodian/steward		
Data privacy officer (DPO)		
Information life cycle		Data Life Cycle
Impact assessment	.	Governance
Terms of agreement		Governance
Privacy notice		Governance

Appendix B

ASCII Characters

This table shows the ASCII characters along with the binary and hex equivalents. Characters listed as UP are unprintable.

ASCII Character	Binary	Hex
UP	00000000	00
UP	00000001	01
UP	00000010	02
UP	00000011	03
UP	00000100	04
UP	00000101	05
UP	00000110	06
UP	00000111	07
UP	00001000	08
UP	00001001	09
UP	00001010	0A
UP	00001011	0B
UP	00001100	0C
UP	00001101	0D
UP	00001110	0E
UP	00001111	0F
UP	00010000	10
UP	00010001	11
UP	00010010	12
UP	00010011	13
UP	00010100	14
UP	00010101	15
UP	00010110	16
UP	00010111	17
UP	00011000	18
UP	00011001	19
UP	00011010	1A
UP	00011011	1B
UP	00011100	1C

ASCII Character	Binary	Hex
UP	00011101	1D
UP	00011110	1E
UP	00011111	1F
(space)	00100000	20
!	00100001	21
"	00100010	22
#	00100011	23
$	00100100	24
%	00100101	25
&	00100110	26
'	00100111	27
(	00101000	28
)	00101001	29
*	00101010	2A
+	00101011	2B
,	00101100	2C
-	00101101	2D
.	00101110	2E
/	00101111	2F
0	00110000	30
1	00110001	31
2	00110010	32
3	00110011	33
4	00110100	34
5	00110101	35
6	00110110	36
7	00110111	37
8	00111000	38
9	00111001	39

Continued

ASCII Character	Binary	Hex
:	00111010	3A
;	00111011	3B
<	00111100	3C
=	00111101	3D
>	00111110	3E
?	00111111	3F
@	01000000	40
A	01000001	41
B	01000010	42
C	01000011	43
D	01000100	44
E	01000101	45
F	01000110	46
G	01000111	47
H	01001000	48
I	01001001	49
J	01001010	4A
K	01001011	4B
L	01001100	4C
M	01001101	4D
N	01001110	4E
O	01001111	4F
P	01010000	50
Q	01010001	51
R	01010010	52
S	01010011	53
T	01010100	54
U	01010101	55
V	01010110	56
W	01010111	57
X	01011000	58
Y	01011001	59
Z	01011010	5A
[	01011011	5B
\	01011100	5C
]	01011101	5D

ASCII Character	Binary	Hex
^	01011110	5E
_	01011111	5F
`	01100000	60
a	01100001	61
b	01100010	62
c	01100011	63
d	01100100	64
e	01100101	65
f	01100110	66
g	01100111	67
h	01101000	68
i	01101001	69
j	01101010	6A
k	01101011	6B
l	01101100	6C
m	01101101	6D
n	01101110	6E
o	01101111	6F
p	01110000	70
q	01110001	71
r	01110010	72
s	01110011	73
t	01110100	74
u	01110101	75
v	01110110	76
w	01110111	77
x	01111000	78
y	01111001	79
z	01111010	7A
{	01111011	7B
		01111100	7C
}	01111101	7D
~	01111110	7E
UP	01111111	7F
€	10000000	80
UP	10000001	81

Continued

ASCII Character	Binary	Hex
‚	10000010	82
ƒ	10000011	83
„	10000100	84
…	10000101	85
†	10000110	86
‡	10000111	87
ˆ	10001000	88
‰	10001001	89
Š	10001010	8A
‹	10001011	8B
Œ	10001100	8C
UP	10001101	8D
Ž	10001110	8E
UP	10001111	8F
UP	10010000	90
'	10010001	91
'	10010010	92
"	10010011	93
"	10010100	94
•	10010101	95
–	10010110	96
—	10010111	97
˜	10011000	98
™	10011001	99
š	10011010	9A
›	10011011	9B
œ	10011100	9C
UP	10011101	9D
ž	10011110	9E
Ÿ	10011111	9F
UP	10100000	A0
¡	10100001	A1
¢	10100010	A2
£	10100011	A3
¤	10100100	A4
¥	10100101	A5

ASCII Character	Binary	Hex
¦	10100110	A6
§	10100111	A7
¨	10101000	A8
©	10101001	A9
ª	10101010	AA
«	10101011	AB
¬	10101100	AC
-	10101101	AD
®	10101110	AE
¯	10101111	AF
°	10110000	B0
±	10110001	B1
²	10110010	B2
³	10110011	B3
´	10110100	B4
µ	10110101	B5
¶	10110110	B6
·	10110111	B7
¸	10111000	B8
¹	10111001	B9
º	10111010	BA
»	10111011	BB
¼	10111100	BC
½	10111101	BD
¾	10111110	BE
¿	10111111	BF
À	11000000	C0
Á	11000001	C1
Â	11000010	C2
Ã	11000011	C3
Ä	11000100	C4
Å	11000101	C5
Æ	11000110	C6
Ç	11000111	C7
È	11001000	C8
É	11001001	C9

Continued

ASCII Character	Binary	Hex
Ê	11001010	CA
Ë	11001011	CB
Ì	11001100	CC
Í	11001101	CD
Î	11001110	CE
Ï	11001111	CF
Đ	11010000	D0
Ñ	11010001	D1
Ò	11010010	D2
Ó	11010011	D3
Ô	11010100	D4
Õ	11010101	D5
Ö	11010110	D6
×	11010111	D7
Ø	11011000	D8
Ù	11011001	D9
Ú	11011010	DA
Û	11011011	DB
Ü	11011100	DC
Ý	11011101	DD
Þ	11011110	DE
ß	11011111	DF
à	11100000	E0
á	11100001	E1
â	11100010	E2
ã	11100011	E3
ä	11100100	E4
å	11100101	E5

ASCII Character	Binary	Hex
æ	11100110	E6
ç	11100111	E7
è	11101000	E8
é	11101001	E9
ê	11101010	EA
ë	11101011	EB
ì	11101100	EC
í	11101101	ED
î	11101110	EE
ï	11101111	EF
ð	11110000	F0
ñ	11110001	F1
ò	11110010	F2
ó	11110011	F3
ô	11110100	F4
õ	11110101	F5
ö	11110110	F6
÷	11110111	F7
ø	11111000	F8
ù	11111001	F9
ú	11111010	FA
û	11111011	FB
ü	11111100	FC
ý	11111101	FD
þ	11111110	FE
ÿ	11111111	FF

Appendix C

CompTIA Security+ (SY0-601) Acronym List

Acronym	Definition
3DES	Triple Digital Encryption Standard
AAA	Authentication, Authorization, and Accounting
ABAC	Attribute-based Access Control
ACL	Access Control List
AES	Advanced Encryption Standard
AES256	Advanced Encryption Standards 256 bit
AH	Authentication Header
AI	Artificial Intelligence
AIS	Automated Indicator Sharing
ALE	Annualized Loss Expectancy
AP	Access Point
API	Application Programming Interface
APT	Advanced Persistent Threat
ARO	Annualized Rate of Occurrence
ARP	Address Resolution Protocol
ASLR	Address Space Layout Randomization
ARP	Active Server Page
ATT&CK	Adversarial Tactics, Techniques, and Common Knowledge
AUP	Acceptable Use Policy
AV	Antivirus
BASH	Bourne Again Shell
BCP	Business Continuity Planning
BGP	Border Gateway Protocol
BIA	Business Impact Analysis
BIOS	Basic Input/Output System
BPA	Business Partnership Agreement
BPDU	Bridge Protocol Data Unit
BYOD	Bring Your Own Device
CA	Certificate Authority
CAC	Common Access Card
CAPTCHA	Completely Automated Public Turing Test to Tell Computers and Humans Apart
CAR	Corrective Action Report

Continued

Acronym	Definition
CASB	Cloud Access Security Broker
CBC	Cipher Block Chaining
CBT	Computer-Based Training
CCMP	Counter-Mode/CBC-Mac Protocol
CCTV	Closed-Circuit Television
CERT	Computer Emergency Response Team
CFB	Cipher Feedback
CHAP	Challenge Handshake Authentication Protocol
CIO	Chief Information Officer
CIRT	Computer Incident Response Team
CIS	Center for Internet Security
CMS	Content Management System
COOP	Continuity of Operation Planning
COPE	Corporate Owned Personal Enabled
CP	Contingency Planning
CRC	Cyclical Redundancy Check
CRL	Certificate Revocation List
CSO	Chief Security Officer
CSP	Cloud Service Provider
CSR	Certificate Signing Request
CSRF	Cross-Site Request Forgery
CSU	Channel Service Unit
CTM	Counter-Mode
CTO	Chief Technology Officer
CVE	Common Vulnerabilities and Exposures
CVSS	Common Vulnerability Scoring System
CYOD	Choose Your Own Device
DAC	Discretionary Access Control
DBA	Database Administrator
DDoS	Distributed Denial of Service
DEP	Data Execution Prevention
DER	Distinguished Encoding Rules
DES	Digital Encryption Standard
DHCP	Dynamic Host Configuration Protocol
DHE	Diffie-Hellman Ephemeral
DKIM	Domain Keys Identified Mail
DLL	Dynamic Link Library
DLP	Data Loss Prevention

Continued

Acronym	Definition
DMARC	Domain Message Authentication Reporting and Conformance
DMZ	Demilitarized Zone
DNAT	Destination Network Address Transaction
DNS	Domain Name Service (Server)
DNSSEC	Domain Name System Security Extensions
DoS	Denial of Service
DPO	Data Privacy Officer
DRP	Disaster Recovery Plan
DSA	Digital Signature Algorithm
DSL	Digital Subscriber Line
EAP	Extensible Authentication Protocol
ECB	Electronic Code Book
ECC	Elliptic Curve Cryptography
ECCDHE	Elliptic Curve Diffie-Hellman Ephemeral
ECDSA	Elliptic Curve Digital Signature Algorithm
EDR	Endpoint Detection and Response
EFS	Encrypted File System
EOL	End of Life
EOS	End of Service
ERP	Enterprise Resource Planning
ESN	Electronic Serial Number
ESP	Encapsulated Security Payload
FACL	File System Access Control List
FDE	Full Disk Encryption
FPGA	Field Programmable Gate Array
FRR	False Rejection Rate
FTP	File Transfer Protocol
FTPS	Secured File Transfer Protocol
GCM	Galois Counter Mode
GDPR	General Data Protection Regulation
GPG	Gnu Privacy Guard
GPO	Group Policy Object
GPS	Global Positioning System
GPU	Graphics Processing Unit
GRE	Generic Routing Encapsulation
HA	High Availability
HDD	Hard Disk Drive
HIDS	Host-based Intrusion-Detection System

Continued

Acronym	Definition
HIPS	Host-based Intrusion-Prevention System
HMAC	Hashed Message Authentication Code
HOTP	HMAC-based One Time Password
HSM	Hardware Security Module
HTML	HyperText Markup Language
HTTP	Hypertext Transfer Protocol
HTTPS	Hypertext Transfer Protocol over SSL/TLS
HVAC	Heating, Ventilation, Air Conditioning
IaaS	Infrastructure as a Service
ICMP	Internet Control Message Protocol
ICS	Industrial Control Systems
IDEA	International Data Encryption Algorithm
IDF	Intermediate Distribution Frame
IdP	Identity Provider
IDS	Intrusion-Detection System
IEEE	Institute of Electrical and Electronics Engineers
IKE	Internet Key Exchange
IM	Instant Messaging
IMAP4	Internet Message Access Protocol v4
IoC	Indicators of Compromise
IoT	Internet of Things
IP	Internet Protocol
IPSec	Internet Protocol Security
IR	Incident Response
IRC	Internet Relay Chat
IRP	Incident Response Plan
ISO	International Organization for Standardization
ISP	Internet Service Provider
ISSO	Information Systems Security Officer
ITCP	IT Contingency Plan
IV	Initialization Vector
KDC	Key Distribution Center
KEK	Key Encryption Key
L2TP	Layer 2 Tunneling Protocol
LAN	Local Area Network
LDAP	Lightweight Directory Access Protocol
LEAP	Lightweight Extensible Authentication Protocol
MaaS	Monitoring as a Service

Continued

Acronym	Definition
MAC	Mandatory Access Control
MAC	Media Access Control
MAC	Message Authentication Code
MAM	Mobile Application Management
MAN	Metropolitan Area Network
MBR	Master Boot Record
MD5	Message Digest 5
MDF	Main Distribution Frame
MDM	Mobile Device Management
MFA	Multifactor Authentication
MFD	Multi-Function Device
MFP	Multi-Function Printer
MITM	Man in the Middle
ML	Machine Learning
MMS	Multimedia Message Service
MOA	Memorandum of Agreement
MOU	Memorandum of Understanding
MPLS	Multi-Protocol Label Switching
MSA	Measurement Systems Analysis
MSCHAP	Microsoft Challenge Handshake Authentication Protocol
MSP	Managed Service Provider
MSSP	Managed Security Service Provider
MTBF	Mean Time Between Failures
MTTF	Mean Time to Failure
MTTR	Mean Time to Recover
MTU	Maximum Transmission Unit
NAC	Network Access Control
NAS	Network Attached Storage
NAT	Network Address Translation
NDA	Non-Disclosure Agreement
NFC	Near Field Communication
NFV	Network Functions Virtualization
NIC	Network Interface Card
NIDS	Network-based Intrusion-Detection System
NIPS	Network-based Intrusion-Prevention System
NIST	National Institute of Standards & Technology
NTFS	New Technology File System
NTLM	New Technology LAN Manager

Continued

Acronym	Definition
NTP	Network Time Protocol
OAUTH	Open Authorization
OCSP	Online Certificate Status Protocol
OID	Object Identifier
OS	Operating System
OSI	Open Systems Interconnection
OSINT	Open Source Intelligence
OSPF	Open Shortest Path First
OT	Operational Technology
OTA	Over The Air
OTG	On The Go
OVAL	Open Vulnerability Assessment Language
OWASP	Open Web Application Security Project
P12	PKCS #12
P2P	Peer to Peer
PaaS	Platform as a Service
PAC	Proxy Auto Configuration
PAM	Privileged Access Management
PAM	Pluggable Authentication Modules
PAP	Password Authentication Protocol
PAT	Port Address Translation
PBKDF2	Password Based Key Derivation Function 2
PBX	Private Branch Exchange
PCAP	Packet Capture
PCI DSS	Payment Card Industry Data Security Standard
PDU	Power Distribution Unit
PEAP	Protected Extensible Authentication Protocol
PED	Personal Electronic Device
PEM	Privacy Enhanced Mail
PFS	Perfect Forward Secrecy
PFX	Personal Information Exchange
PGP	Pretty Good Privacy
PHI	Personal Health Information
PII	Personally Identifiable Information
PIC	Personal Identity Verification
PKCS	Public Key Cryptography Standards
PKI	Public Key Infrastructure
POP	Post Office Protocol

Continued

Acronym	Definition
POTS	Plain Old Telephone Service
PPP	Point-to-Point Protocol
PPTP	Point-to-Point Tunneling Protocol
PSK	Pre-Shared Key
PTZ	Pan-Tilt-Zoom
PUP	Potentially Unwanted Program
QA	Quality Assurance
QoS	Quality of Service
RA	Recovery Agent
RA	Registration Authority
RACE	Research and Development in Advanced Communications Technologies in Europe
RAD	Rapid Application Development
RADIUS	Remote Authentication Dial-in User Server
RAID	Redundant Array of Inexpensive Disks
RAM	Random Access Memory
RAS	Remote Access Server
RAT	Remote Access Trojan
RC4	Rivest Cipher version 4
RCS	Rich Communication Services
RFC	Request for Comments
RFID	Radio Frequency Identifier
RIPEMD	RACE Integrity Primitives Evaluation Message Digest
ROI	Return on Investment
RPO	Recovery Point Objective
RSA	Rivest, Shamir, & Adleman
RTBH	Remote Triggered Black Hole
RTO	Recovery Time Objective
RTOS	Real-Time Operating System
RTP	Real-Time Transport Protocol
S/MIME	Secure/Multipurpose Internet Mail Extensions
SaaS	Software as a Service
SAE	Simultaneous Authentication of Equals
SAML	Security Assertions Markup Language
SAN	Storage Area Network
SAN	Subject Alternative Name
SCADA	System Control and Data Acquisition
SCAP	Security Content Automation Protocol
SCEP	Simple Certificate Enrollment Protocol

Continued

Acronym	Definition
SDK	Software Development Kit
SDLC	Software Development Life Cycle
SDLM	Software Development Life-cycle Methodology
SDN	Software Defined Networking
SDV	Software Defined Visibility
SED	Self-Encrypting Drives
SHE	Structured Exception Handler
SFTP	Secured File Transfer Protocol
SHA	Secure Hashing Algorithm
SHTTP	Secure Hypertext Transfer Protocol
SIEM	Security Information and Event Management
SIM	Subscriber Identity Module
SIP	Session Initiation Protocol
SLA	Service Level Agreement
SLE	Single Loss Expectancy
SMS	Short Message Service
SMTP	Simple Mail Transfer Protocol
SMTPS	Simple Mail Transfer Protocol Secure
SNMP	Simple Network Management Protocol
SOAP	Simple Object Access Protocol
SOAR	Security Orchestration, Automation, Response
SoC	System on Chip
SOC	Security Operations Center
SPF	Sender Policy Framework
SPIM	Spam over Internet Messaging
SQL	Structured Query Language
SQLi	SQL Injection
SRTP	Secure Real-Time Protocol
SSD	Solid State Drive
SSH	Secure Shell
SSL	Secure Sockets Layer
SSO	Single Sign On
STIX	Structured Threat Information eXchange
STP	Shielded Twisted Pair
SWA	Secure Web Gateway
TACAS+	Terminal Access Controller Access Control System
TAXII	Trusted Automated eXchange of Indicator Information
TCP/IP	Transmission Control Protocol/Internet Protocol

Continued

Acronym	Definition
TGT	Ticket Granting Ticket
TKIP	Temporal Key Integrity Protocol
TLS	Transport Layer Security
TOTP	Time-based One Time Password
TPM	Trusted Platform Module
TSIG	Transaction Signature
TTP	Tactics, Techniques, and Procedures
UAT	User Acceptance Testing
UAV	Unmanned Aerial Vehicle
UDP	User Datagram Protocol
UEFI	Unified Extensible Firmware Interface
UEM	Unified Endpoint Management
UPS	Uninterruptable Power Supply
URI	Uniform Resource Identifier
URL	Universal Resource Locator
USB	Universal Serial Bus
USB OTG	USB On The Go
UTM	Unified Threat Management
UTP	Unshielded Twisted Pair
VBA	Visual Basic
VDE	Virtual Desktop Environment
VDI	Virtual Desktop Infrastructure
VLAN	Virtual Local Area Network
VLSM	Variable Length Subnet Masking
VM	Virtual Machine
VoIP	Voice over IP
VPC	Virtual Private Cloud
VPN	Virtual Private Network
VTC	Video Teleconferencing
WAF	Web Application Firewall
WAP	Wireless Access Point
WEP	Wired Equivalent Privacy
WIDS	Wireless Intrusion Detection System
WIPS	Wireless Intrusion Prevention System
WORM	Write Once Read Many
WPA	WiFi Protected Access
WPS	WiFi Protected Setup
WTLS	Wireless TLS

Continued

Acronym	Definition
XaaS	Anything as a Service
XML	Extensible Markup Language
XOR	Exclusive Or
XSRF	Cross-Site Request Forgery
XSS	Cross-Site Scripting

Appendix D

Number Conversion Table

Decimal	Binary	Octal	Hexadecimal
0	000000	0	0
1	000001	1	1
2	000010	2	2
3	000011	3	3
4	000100	4	4
5	000101	5	5
6	000110	6	6
7	000111	7	7
8	001000	10	8
9	001001	11	9
10	001010	12	A
11	001011	13	B
12	001100	14	C
13	001101	15	D
14	001110	16	E
15	001111	17	F
16	010000	20	10
17	010001	21	11
18	010010	22	12
19	010011	23	13
20	010100	24	14
21	010101	25	15
22	010110	26	16
23	010111	27	17
24	011000	30	18
25	011001	31	19
26	011010	32	1A
27	011011	33	1B
28	011100	34	1C
29	011101	35	1D
30	011110	36	1E
31	011111	37	1F

Decimal	Binary	Octal	Hexadecimal
32	100000	40	20
33	100001	41	21
34	100010	42	22
35	100011	43	23
36	100100	44	24
37	100101	45	25
38	100110	46	26
39	100111	47	27
40	101000	50	28
41	101001	51	29
42	101010	52	2A
43	101011	53	2B
44	101100	54	2C
45	101101	55	2D
46	101110	56	2E
47	101111	57	2F
48	110000	60	30
49	110001	61	31
50	110010	62	32
51	110011	63	33
52	110100	64	34
53	110101	65	35
54	110110	66	36
55	110111	67	37
56	111000	70	38
57	111001	71	39
58	111010	72	3A
59	111011	73	3B
60	111100	74	3C
61	111101	75	3D
62	111110	76	3E
63	111111	77	3F

Continued

Glossary

A

acceptable use policy (AUP). Document that outlines information on proper usage of the network and related assets as defined by the owner of the network.

access control list (ACL). List of permissions associated with network objects that control which device is allowed on a given subnet. (12)

account audit. Examination, assessment, or evaluation of an account. (4)

account expiration. Process that will automatically disable an account after the expiration date is met. (4)

account maintenance. Routine review of accounts, including permissions and usage patterns, compared against an organization's operational and security needs. (4)

active-active configuration. Operational modality in which all load balancers are actively operating. (12)

Active Directory (AD). Directory service developed by Microsoft for Windows networks that authenticates users in a Windows network. (4)

active listening. Fully processing what a person says and interacting with the person who is speaking. (19)

active-passive configuration. Operational modality in which one load balancer is responsible for distributing network traffic while a second balancer operates passively unless the first balancer fails. (12)

active reconnaissance. Active discovery and gathering of data by using tools to interact with a system. (3)

administrative control. Type of control that develops and enforces policies, procedures, and processes in an effort to regulate human interaction with a device or network. (5)

Advanced Encryption Standard (AES). Symmetric block cipher that requires 128-, 192-, or 256-bit keys; also known as *Rijndael encryption*. (9)

advanced persistent threat (APT). Stealth network attack, typically state-sponsored, that gains unauthorized access to a computer system or network and intentionally remains undetected for extended periods of time. (2)

adversarial AI attack. Malicious development and use of sophisticated AI systems to behave in a manner that benefits an attacker. (2)

adware. Software installed on a computer that collects data about the user, such as websites the person visits, and then redirects advertising sites to the web browser based on browsing habits. (2)

affinity scheduling. Scheduling protocol that distributes loads based on which device is best capable of handling a given load. (12)

aggregation switch. Networking device used to combine multiple network connections in a single switch. (12)

aggregator. Device or service provider used to consolidate and serve multiple other devices or users with either its own functionalities or by forwarding transmissions in a compressed or more efficient way. (12)

agile model. Software development life cycle model in which solutions evolve through team member collaboration and follow core values. (7)

air gap. Area is designed to be completely isolated from secure areas of a building or room. (5)

air-gap network. Computer network designed to be completely isolated from other networks, including connections to the Internet. (5)

algorithm. Set of procedures resulting from a mathematical formula; also called a *cipher*. (9)

alias. Alternate name for designating a file or fields in PowerShell. (11)

annualized loss expectancy (ALE). Monetary value anticipated to be lost based on frequency of loss in one year. (16)

annualized rate of occurrence (ARO). Expected number of times an incident will happen in one year. (16)

anomaly. Deviation from expected network activity. (12)

anomaly monitoring. Method that detects anomalies in a network's traffic statistics. (12)

ANT. Wireless communication standard that facilitates transmissions using electromagnetic radio fields between devices of a very close proximity. (14)

antispoofing. Technique that identifies and protects against IP spoofing by blocking inbound traffic originating from a suspect network address. (12)

Anything as a Service (XaaS). Collective term that refers to the delivery of any service through the Internet. (15)

API attack. Use of malicious code or exploitation of vulnerable code within an application programming interface (API). (7)

append. To add data to an existing data set. (11)

application development. Collective process of designing, programming, testing, and quality controlling a computer program to meet specific needs of a business. (7)

Note: The number in parentheses following each definition indicates the chapter in which the term can be found.

application management. Download, distribution, and control of apps through centralized tools and services. (8)

application programming interface (API). Set of tools and programs that enables interactions between applications and components and provides communication between a client and server. (7)

application scanning. Scanning software applications to identify weak configurations, out-of-date software patches, and other vulnerabilities. (3)

application security (AppSec). Process of developing software that is free from vulnerabilities before it goes into production. (7)

archive bit. Single bit within a file indicating if a file has been backed up or not. (18)

Arduino. Open-source platform used for creating electronics projects. (8)

armored virus. Computer virus designed to prevent security analysts from reading source code by attempting to disassemble or prevent access to the code. (2)

arp command. Windows command-line tool used to view and modify entries in the Address Resolution Protocol (ARP) cache. (11)

ARP poisoning. Attack in which a spoofed Address Resolution Protocol (ARP) message is sent onto a LAN and causes network traffic to be sent to the attacker; also called *ARP spoofing*. (1)

artifact. Forensic object that contains evidence. (17)

artificial intelligence (AI). Branch of computer science aimed at simulating intelligence in machines. (2)

asset. Items, ideas, and people needed to operate an organization. (16)

asset life cycle. Steps involved in managing an asset from its purchase until it is discarded. (16)

asset management. Process that requires all assets purchased be planned for effective use and tracked through the asset life cycle

so sound financial decisions can be made. (16)

asymmetric encryption. Encryption method that uses two mathematically related keys, a public key and a private key, to encrypt and decrypt data. (9)

attack surface. All the locations where an attacker can enter and cause a security risk. (1)

attitude. How personal thoughts or feelings affect a person's outward behavior. (19)

attribute. Characteristic a person possesses. (2)

attribute-based access control (ABAC). Access control system that uses attributes or characteristics assigned to a user and compares them to attributes or characteristics that are assigned to the data. (4)

authentication. Process of validating or verifying a user's identity. (1)

authentication header (AH). Security feature used to authenticate the sender and determine if there are any changes to the data during transmission. (12)

automated alert and trigger. Rules that generate and inform administrators about specific events or incidents to streamline the process of reviewing data. (3)

automated patch management service. Program that automatically scans, downloads, and installs patches when available from the vendor; also known as *auto-update*. (6)

automation. Use of technology to perform processes without human intervention. (7)

availability. Data can be accessed when needed. (1)

B

backdoor. Type of malware that creates a secret or unknown access point into a system. (2)

background check. Method of ensuring or authenticating an employee's job history, résumé, and credentials. (16)

bandwidth monitor. Network tool that allows an administrator to monitor

and analyze inbound and outbound network traffic and usage. (13)

banner grabbing. Act of requesting information about computer systems or services on a remote system. (3)

baseband. Refers to a frequency's original range before it is converted through modulation. (14)

baseline. Starting point from which data comparisons are made. (3)

batch file. Single file in which a command, series of commands, or set of instructions to be processed in sequence is listed. (11)

bcrypt. Cipher based on the Blowfish block cipher with a nonce added to the password. (9)

behavioral biometrics. Study that identifies measurable patterns in human activities. (4)

behavioral question. Interview question that draws on an individual's previous experiences and decisions. (19)

binary. File in which content must be interpreted by a program or hardware processor that knows in advance how the file is formatted. (7)

biometric authentication. Identity and access management concept and physical security control in which a user must provide a physical characteristic in addition to a username and password. (4)

birthday attack. Cryptographic attack that attempts to exploit the birthday paradox. (9)

black box test. Penetration test in which the tester has no knowledge of the system. (3)

black-hat hacker. Hacker who usually operates outside the law. (2)

blacklisting. Process of specifying a list of unapproved applications or executable software that is not permitted to run on a device or network. (6)

blockchain. List of records—called *blocks*—that are linked together using cryptography. (10)

block cipher. Cipher that encrypts blocks of data in a fixed size at one time. (9)

blocked port. Communication port that has been shut down so data cannot be transmitted through the port. (6)

Blowfish cryptography. Free symmetric cryptographic encryption originally designed to replace the DES cipher. (9)

bluejacking. Bluetooth-based concern in which somebody sends an unsolicited message, such as an advertisement, via Bluetooth. (14)

bluesnarfing. Bluetooth-based attack in which a hacker exploits a Bluetooth connection to steal data from a Bluetooth-enabled device. (14)

Bluetooth. Wireless connection that enables mobile devices to share data via short-range, ad-hoc communication sessions. (8)

bollard. Vertical cylinders permanently installed to prevent vehicles from passing. (5)

boot attestation. Mechanism that allows software to prove its identity. (6)

boot integrity. Assurance that a computer is booting from a secure drive and running only authorized programs. (6)

BPDU guard. Switch feature that uses STP/RSTP to prevent Bridge Protocol Data Units (BPDUs) from being accepted on a given port. (12)

bring your own device (BYOD). Strategy that allows employees, partners, and other personnel to use their personal devices to conduct business and connect to an organization's networks. (8)

broadcast storm. Accumulation of a high volume of traffic on a network in a short period of time; sometimes called *broadcast radiation*. (12)

brute-force attack. Intensive attack that tries every possible combination of letters, numbers, and special characters to determine the key. (9)

buffer overflow. Occurs when there is more data in the buffer than it can handle. (7)

buffer-overflow attack. Cyberattack in which a hacker exploits a buffer overflow, resulting in extra data written to memory outside of the buffer. (7)

bug-bounty program. Initiative that offers rewards to those who identify flaws and vulnerabilities found in their program. (2)

business continuity. Ability of a business to remain operational before, during, and after a catastrophic event has occurred. (18)

business continuity plan (BCP). Comprehensive and proactive plan that provides the steps needed to keep a business operational before, during, and after a disaster. (18)

business-impact analysis (BIA). Detailed process that determines the potential consequences of business disruptions and uses data to develop recovery strategies. (18)

C

CAC reader. Device that senses the microchip in the CAC and determines if it contains the correct information to allow access. (4)

camouflaged code. Code written in a way that makes it difficult for someone to read or interpret. (7)

Canonical Encoding Rules Certificate (CER). Certificate format that can have its data encoded by DER or using Base64. (10)

captive portal. Web page a user must view when connecting to a wireless network before broad access to the network is granted. (14)

card cloning. Act of stealing a credit card by copying card numbers and data and attaching them to a bogus card; also called *skimming*. (2)

carrier unlocking. Legal process of disconnecting a phone from a wireless provider's network. (8)

cat command. Linux-based utility used to view and create files, display contents of multiple files simultaneously, or redirect the contents of multiple files into a single file; short for concatenate. (11)

cell. Coverage provided by the base station of a cellular network is contained within a specified geographic area. (14)

cellular. Network technology that enables communication through mobile devices by using a system of stations and transceivers that make up a cellular network. (8)

cellular network. Type of wireless network in which transmissions are distributed over groups of geographic areas called *cells*. (8)

centralized patch management. Method of patch deployment that enables administrators to push updates to devices from a central point within a network. (6)

certificate authority (CA). Trusted third-party source that issues and validates digital certificates. (10)

certificate chaining. Act of linking one certificate to another to establish trust between them. (10)

certificate management. Processes, procedures, and steps taken to ensure digital certificates are current and stored properly. (10)

certificate revocation list (CRL). List of all canceled digital certificates. (10)

certificate-signing request (CSR). Request for a digital certificate that contains an applicant's public key, additional identification information, and integrity protection. (10)

chain of custody. Witnessed document that identifies those who maintain unbroken and total control over the evidence in a case. (17)

Challenge Handshake Authentication Protocol (CHAP). Protocol in which an authenticating server sends a challenge to a client after the client establishes a connection to the server. (12)

change control. Approach to managing changes to ensure they are necessary, documented, and integrated as seamlessly as possible. (16)

change management. Process or plan that describes the policies and practices of an organization to prepare, equip, and support individuals and staff to incorporate and adapt to changes made in IT systems. (16)

channel overlay. Overlapping channel that enables resiliency in a wireless network. (14)

chmod command. Linux-based command that enables a user to change file and folder permissions. (11)

choose your own device (CYOD). Strategy in which a company selects the type of devices approved for connection to their network, but the employee chooses and owns the device. (8)

CIA triad. Consists of the three underlying core security principles of data protection: confidentiality, integrity, and availability. (1)

Cipher Block Chaining (CBC). Encryption mode in which randomization is performed on a key. (10)

cipher suite. Combination of message authentication code, encryption, and authentication algorithms used with Transport Layer Security (TLS) and Secure Sockets Layer (SSL) for connections between a browser and server. (9)

ciphertext. Disguised or encoded format of information. (9)

Clarifying Lawful Overseas Use of Data (CLOUD) Act. Federal law that provides oversight into data storage on cloud providers. (15)

clean-desk policy. Human resource policy that outlines how an employee should leave a desk when not physically present. (16)

clickjacking. Malicious attack that occurs when a user is tricked into clicking a concealed link. (7)

client. Device that requests and accesses services or resources from a server. (6)

client-side request forgery. Attack that exploits vulnerabilities on a client's device; also known as *universal cross-site scripting (UXSS).* (7)

client-side validation. Input validation for which user input is confirmed by a client web browser; also called *client-side execution.* (7)

closed-circuit television (CCTV). System in which video cameras transmit signals to a centralized monitoring location. (5)

closed port. Communication port that does not have a process actively listening to it. (6)

closed threat intelligence source. Commercial product that requires an account and payment to access its resources to extract information; also known as a *proprietary intelligence source.* (2)

cloud access security broker (CASB). Set of services or software tools that enable an organization's enterprise security policies to extend to its data stored in the cloud. (15)

cloud application security. Policies and procedures that govern information exchanges that occur in cloud environments, such as Microsoft Office 365. (15)

cloud audit. Independent examination of cloud service controls in terms of items such as privacy impact and performance. (15)

cloud backup. Strategy of backing up data to an off-site, virtual, or cloud-based server as opposed to a local server; also called an *online backup* or *remote backup.* (15)

cloud computing. Using remote servers on the Internet to host, access, and store data rather than using a personal computer or local server using a pay-per-use service model. (15)

cloud forensics. Applying digital forensics to the cloud environment rather than on the physical premises of an organization. (17)

cloud governance. Policies and procedures used by an organization to manage its processes associated with the cloud. (15)

cloud infrastructure. Infrastructure that consists of computing hardware, software, and other components necessary to provide the required infrastructure for delivering business operations from a remote location. (15)

cloud instance. Virtualized server installation within a cloud-computing environment. (15)

cloud model. Way in which cloud infrastructure is provisioned for use. (15)

cloud security. Protection of data transmitted and stored in the cloud as well as methods used to protect against vulnerabilities and reduce attacks. (15)

cloud security control. Process that enables a cloud architecture to protect against vulnerabilities and mitigate malicious attacks. (15)

cloud service provider (CSP). Vendor that provides IT services over the Internet. (15)

cloud storage. Digital storage that involves using remote servers hosted on the Internet to *store* data rather than *process* data. (15)

cmdlet. Program in PowerShell; pronounced *command-let.* (11)

code reuse. Practice of using existing code in a new application. (7)

code signature. Digital signature placed on code to verify its authenticity and integrity. (7)

code signing. Adding a code signature to an application. (7)

cold site. Location that provides necessary office space needed to move operations, but it contains no operational equipment. (18)

collaboration skills. Behaviors for working with others. (19)

collision. Error in which two different inputs produce the same message digest. (9)

command and control (C&C) attack. Malware attack that programs the infected machine to signal the attacker's server for instruction. (2)

command-line interface (CLI). Text-based user interface that executes actions within the computer by entering textual commands instead of employing a mouse or touch screen. (11)

command prompt. Command-line interface for entering commands manually. (11)

common access card (CAC). Smart card that contains security information about the user stored on a microchip similar to microchipped credit cards. (4)

common name (CN). Fully qualified domain name (FQDN) of the web server that is to receive a certificate. (10)

Common Vulnerabilities and Exposure (CVE). List of known security threats identified by the US Department of Homeland Security. (3)

Common Vulnerability Scoring System (CVSS). Open industry standard used to assess system vulnerabilities and their severity. (3)

community cloud. Cloud-computing resource shared by everyone in an affiliated organization and not available to anyone outside of the organization. (15)

company-owned, personally enabled (COPE). Strategy in which a company owns and provides a device for an employee's work. (8)

compensating control. Type of control that provides an alternative action in the event a typical control cannot be used. (5)

compiler. Program that converts code from a programming language into machine language. (7)

compliance. Adhering to laws, regulations, and standards as set forth by a governing body. (1)

conditional access. Configuration and control of devices to determine if access is granted to services or locations. (8)

confidence. Being certain and secure about one's own abilities and judgment. (19)

confidentiality. Condition of being private or secret. (1)

configuration management (CM). Process of maintaining computers, servers, and applications in a preferred, consistent state to ensure a system's performance remains as efficient as possible despite changes made over time. (12)

configuration review. Act of monitoring and assessing settings and policies set forth for a system. (3)

configuration-compliance scanner. Security configuration assessment that determines if a target's configuration settings comply with an organization's configuration guidelines. (3)

conflict resolution. Process of resolving disputes. (19)

container. Executable software that contains applications and utilizes the host operating system; also called an *application cell*. (15)

containerization. Separation of various data types into separate storage pools, called *containers* or *lockers*, so storage can be managed separately. (8)

container security. Processes, policies, and procedures implemented to ensure containers run as designed. (15)

containment. Action that limits further damage from an incident and ensures evidence is protected and not destroyed. (17)

content filter. Software- or hardware-based technology often incorporated in a firewall to monitor Internet traffic and prevent access to blacklisted websites, files, and services; also called a *URL filter*. (12)

context-aware authentication. Configuration setting that uses situational information—such as location, identity, and time of day—to verify a user. (8)

controller-based access point (controller-based AP). Access point that receives and transmits wireless traffic and is managed by a wireless LAN controller (WLC). (14)

copy backup. Data storage method that copies designated files but does not clear the files' archive bits; also called a *backup file*. (18)

corrective control. Type of control that isolates and limits damage caused by an incident. (5)

correlation engine. Software application that has been programmed to understand relationships. (12)

counterintelligence. Gathering of information about the methods and extent of a cyber criminal's ability to obtain data from a system. (17)

Counter Mode (CTR). Block cipher mode of operation that mandates both the sender and receiver of a message access a counter, which generates a new value every time a cipher block is exchanged. (10)

Counter Mode with Cipher Block Chaining Message Authentication Code Protocol (CCMP). Wireless encryption standard designed to be used with wireless LANs. (14)

cover message. Letter or e-mail sent with a résumé to introduce and summarize the reasons the applicant is applying for a job. (19)

credential harvesting. Technique designed to obtain a user's login name and password for systems. (2)

credential management. Actions taken to manage a user's login credentials and other factors associated with a user's account. (4)

credentialed scan. Scan that requires credentials of an account registered to a device being scanned. (3)

criminal syndicate. Group of criminals in local, national, or international enterprises who engage in illegal activity for profit. (3)

critical asset. Asset that is necessary to sustain business operation. (16)

critical-thinking skills. Skills that provide the ability to make sound judgments. (19)

crossover error rate (CER). Point where the false acceptance rates and false rejection rates are equal. (4)

cross-site request forgery (CSRF). Attack that tricks a web browser into executing an unwanted or undesired action by manipulating an application to which a user is logged in; also referred to as *XSRF*. (7)

cross-site scripting (XSS) attack. Widespread attack method in which hackers inject client-side scripts into pages of a trusted website. (7)

cryptographic attack. Attacks attempting to break the secrecy of encrypted data or discovering the value of the private encryption key used to mask the data. (9)

cryptographic modules. Combinations of hardware, firmware, and software that perform cryptographic functions. (10)

cryptographic service provider (CSP). Hardware- or software-based library that implements coding or decoding functions so that an encryption algorithm is executed; also called a *crypto service*. (10)

cryptomalware. Ransomware, or any other malware, that requires the use of cryptocurrency for return of access to data. (2)

cryptoperiod. Span of time for which a key is authorized for use. (9)

Cuckoo. Open-source automated malware analysis system; also known as *Cuckoo Sandbox*. (13)

curl. Network reconnaissance and discovery command used to transfer data to and from a server using various protocols to request information and analyze the resulting information; short for *client URL*. (13)

current directory. Directory in which a user is working. (11)

custom firmware. Firmware modified by a third party to provide new features or access previously locked-down functionalities; also known as *after-market firmware*. (8)

cyberattack. Attempt to steal, damage, or destroy data or a computer system. (2)

cybercrime. Umbrella term that describes any criminal activity committed using a computer or the Internet. (2)

cybersecurity. Process of protecting an enterprise environment against unintended or malicious changes or use that involves access from individuals and systems on the Internet. (2)

cybersecurity resilience. Ability of an organization to prepare for, respond to, and recover from a cyberattack. (17)

D

dark web. Part of the Internet that is not easily accessible to the average user; also called the *darknet*. (2)

data acquisition. Capturing or collecting of volatile and non-volatile data. (17)

data anonymization. Form of sanitization with the intent of privacy protection through the removal of personally identifiable information (PII). (16)

data-at-rest. Data that is being stored on a computer network. (9)

data backup. Process of copying data from one location to another medium; sometimes called *archiving*. (18)

database. Structured, organized collection of data. (6)

data canary. Known value placed at the end of the assigned buffer space. (7)

data center. Facility specifically designed to store and manage vast quantities of data. (5)

data clearance. Authorization that allows access to security data. (16)

data compliance. Practice of following organizational, industry, and governmental regulations to ensure data management and enable an organization be accountable. (16)

data dump (dd). Disk image file that is a replica of a hard drive. (17)

Data Encryption Standard (DES). Symmetric-key algorithm that requires keys to be 56 bits in length. (9)

data evidence management. Policies and procedures used by an organization to manage data used as evidence in incident response cases. (17)

data exposure. Occurs when sensitive, personal, or confidential data is accidentally exposed to users. (7)

data governance. Policies and procedures used by an organization to manage its data assets. (16)

data input. Methods used in syslog to collect and record data within logs. (3)

data-in-transit. Data transmitted across a network during a session; also called *data-in-motion*. (9)

data-in-use. Data actively being used by computer or system memory; also called *data-in-processing*. (9)

data life cycle. Stages that data goes through from its initial creation to its eventual archival or deletion. (16)

data loss prevention (DLP). Security strategy that detects potential data breaches or exfiltration transmissions to ensure that sensitive, confidential, or critical data is transferred outside the organization. (6)

data masking. Data security technique that involves copying a dataset but obfuscating any sensitive data. (16)

data minimization. Measures performed by an organization to limit the amount of personal data collected from individuals and process only information relevant to accomplishing specific tasks. (16)

data owner. Role responsible for data compliance, policy management, and privilege usage. (16)

data purging. Removal of existing data from the drive. (5)

data retention policy. Policy that identifies how long an organization must retain data. (16)

dead code. Source code that is no longer used. (7)

deception technology. Security tools and techniques designed to prevent a threat actor who has already breached a network from doing any damage. (12)

decision-making. Process of taking a course of action after weighing the benefits and costs of alternate actions. (19)

defense in depth. Having multiple, redundant levels of protection in the event that one level fails; also known as *layered security*. (1)

deference attack. Deference error that is intentionally triggered. (7)

degaussing. Rearranges magnetic fields by randomizing the patterns of magnetization. (5)

demilitarized zone (DMZ). Segment of a network that allows some public access and borders a private network where the public access is blocked; also called a *screened subnet* or a *perimeter network*. (12)

denial of service (DoS) attack. Cyberattack that prevents rightful users from accessing systems. (2)

deprovisioning. Removal of resource access from team members when those resources are no longer required. (7)

detective control. Type of control that identifies incidents that are in progress or have recently occurred and categorizes them according to specific characteristics. (5)

deterrent control. Type of control that attempts to dissuade attacks or violations from occurring. (5)

device driver. Software program that instructs a piece of hardware how to operate. (11)

DevOps. Philosophy that incorporates security concepts in the collaboration among developers, managers, and other IT and operational staff from development through production and support; short for *developer operations*. (7)

dictionary attack. Software-based password-cracking method that uses a list of words and their precomputed hash values to determine a user's password. (9)

differential backup. Series of sequential backups that starts with a full backup, and the subsequent backups include copies of only the files that have changed or been created since the last full backup. (18)

dig command. Linux command-line equivalent to the Windows-based **nslookup** command; stands for *digital information grouper*. (11)

digital certificate. Electronic file digitally signed and used to verify that a public key belongs specifically to that person or entity. (10)

digital forensics. Recovery, analysis, and protection of digital evidence from a crime scene to present in court. (17)

digital signature. Computed value used to validate the sender of a digital file, such as an e-mail or document. (10)

directory. Location or hierarchical folder structure for storing files on a computer. (4)

directory traversal. Attack in which hackers get beyond the web server's root directory and execute commands. (7)

disabled service. Locked service not permitted to run on a computer. (6)

disablement. Act of leaving an account intact but unable to be used for authentication. (4)

disassociation attack. Form of a denial of service attack in which the hacker disconnects a user from their wireless network by sending a disassociation signal to the user. (14)

disaster recovery plan (DRP). Customized, structured plan to resume infrastructure and IT services that shut down due to a disaster and ensure continuity of business operations. (18)

discretionary access control (DAC). Access control method in which a user can be granted additional rights to data beyond what is allowed by the individual's assigned access level. (4)

disk encryption. Process of converting all data on a hard disk into unreadable characters by applying a security key. (6)

disk sanitization. Irreversible and permanent removal of data from a storage device; also known as *disk wiping*. (5)

Distinguished Encoding Rules (DER). Certificate that encodes the public key in binary code. (10)

distributed denial of service (DDoS) attack. DoS attack in which many hosts are contributing in attacking the victim. (2)

distributed-trust model. Trust model in which the workload of signing a certificate is distributed among several intermediate CAs. (10)

distro. Unique operating system based off a Linux kernel and package management system; also called *distribution*. (11)

diversity awareness. Ability to embrace the unique traits of others. (19)

DLL injection. Technique used to insert code into a running program, forcing the program to load a Dynamic Link Library. (7)

DNS attack. Cyberattack in which vulnerabilities within the Domain Name System are exploited. (13)

dnsenum command. Network reconnaissance command that displays DNS information and retrieves DNS servers and entries within an organization. (13)

DNS poisoning. Attack that occurs when an entry is embedded in the victim's local DNS cache that redirects a legitimate URL to an incorrect IP address. (13)

DNS Security Extensions (DNSSEC). Suite of specifications that requires all responses from a DNS server be digitally signed to ensure they come from an authorized source. (13)

DNS sinkhole. DNS server used to prevent the resolution of host names of specific URLs. (12)

domain hijacking. Attempt to transfer the ownership or registration and control of the domain from the rightful owner. (7)

Domain Name System (DNS). Hierarchical, decentralized protocol that maps a domain name to a corresponding IP address. (13)

downgrade attack. Attack in which a hacker forces a system to switch to a lower or less-secure cryptographic standard. (9)

doxing. Theft and release of personal, private, or identifying information. (2)

drive-by download. Attack that occurs when a user visits an infected web page from which ransomware is automatically downloaded to a computer without a user's knowledge. (2)

driver manipulation. Type of attack in which a threat actor accesses and modifies device drivers within an operating system in an effort to bypass security measures or take control of a device. (7)

driver shim. Library of compiled code that translates commands so a program can run on multiple platforms. (7)

drone. Unmanned, remote-controlled robot that can fly autonomously using an RTOS or controlled remotely by an operator; often called an *unmanned aerial vehicle (UAV)* or *unscrewed aerial vehicle*. (8)

dumpster diving. Act of digging through trash for useful or valuable information. (2)

Dynamic Host Configuration Protocol (DHCP). Network management protocol used to assign an IP address automatically when a client connects to a network. (13)

Dynamic Host Configuration Protocol (DHCP) snooping. Layer-2 security technology built into a switch that prevents unauthorized DHCP servers from assigning IP addresses to clients. (12)

E

EAP-Flexible Authentication via Secure Tunneling (FAST). Authentication protocol created by Cisco to replace a previously unsecure version of EAP called Lightweight EAP (LEAP). (14)

EAP over Transport Layer Security (EAP-TLS). Protocol that provides certificate-based authentication. (14)

EAP Tunnel Transport Layer Security (EAP-TTLS). Extension of EAP-TLS that allows communication to be sent through a protected tunnel. (14)

east-west traffic. Traffic that flows from one server to another within an organization's data center. (12)

edge computing. Non-cloud service model that collects information and processes it on devices that are close in proximity. (15)

efficacy rate. Frequency in which an intended result is achieved. (4)

elasticity. Application's ability to change resources dynamically as needs change. (7)

electromagnetic radiation (EMR). Signals emitted from printers, computers, monitors, microwaves, transmission lines, and other devices. (5)

Electronic Codebook (ECB). Cryptographic mode in which a message is divided into blocks with each block separately encrypted using the same key. (10)

elliptical-curve cryptography (ECC). Encryption method based on numbers located on an elliptical curve rather than using prime numbers. (9)

embedded system. Combination of hardware and software contained within a larger device used to complete a specific task. (8)

EMI shielding. Barrier placed around wires to block EMI from interfering with the electrical signals in the wires. (5)

empathy. Having the ability to share someone else's emotions and showing understanding of how the other person is feeling. (19)

employment contract. Document that defines the terms of employment between an employer and an employee. (16)

employment verification. Process through which the information provided on an applicant's résumé is checked to verify that it is correct. (19)

encapsulating security payload (ESP). Alternative to authentication header (AH) that authenticates the header as well as encrypts the data.

encryption. Process of converting data into unreadable characters by applying a security key. (2)

encryption key. Random string of alphanumeric characters used to encrypt or decrypt a message. (9)

endpoint. Device that functions as a physical endpoint on a network. (6)

endpoint detection and response (EDR). Tools and technology used to monitor devices continuously to identify malicious attacks on endpoint devices. (6)

endpoint protection. Practice of securing user endpoint devices on networks to prevent them from malicious activity and attacks; also known as *endpoint security*. (6)

enterprise environment. Devices, architecture, and design of a professional organization's computer network system. (2)

enterprise mobility management (EMM). Enterprise organization's processes and policies for operations of mobile devices used in the business. (8)

entropy. Degree of randomness with which a key is generated. (9)

environmental disaster. Event caused by humans that damages the environment, such as a forest fire as the result of a campfire that burns infrastructure and causes a business to close. (16)

eradication. Process of evaluating damages, removing the root cause, and repairing the systems. (17)

escalation of privilege. Test that attempts to move from a normal user to achieve root or admin privileges while accessing a system. (3)

ethical hacking. Umbrella term that refers to all hacking methods performed and sanctioned by an organization to identify potential vulnerabilities or attack vectors within a system. (3)

ethics. Rules of behavior based on a group's ideas about what is right and wrong. (19)

event deduplication. Process that merges identical events into a single event. (3)

evil twin router. Illegitimate router that carries the same service set identifier (SSID) as the desired access point (AP). (14)

executive user. Person who is responsible for the overall usage of a given application, evaluation of an application's operation, and making decisions about data usage. (16)

explicit permissions. Permissions given to a user to access a specific folder, file, or network drive. (4)

exploitation framework. Software package that contains apps and tools used to analyze and replicate attacks during vulnerability assessments. (13)

Extensible Authentication Protocol (EAP). Authentication protocol framework that outlines secure transport and usage of information. (12)

extranet. Type of intranet that can be partially accessed by authorized users outside an organization. (12)

F

facial recognition. Uses software that scans a person's facial features to confirm identity. (4)

facility automation. Digital transformation to automatic or electronic control for monitoring of systems crucial to facility operation, such as lighting; surveillance; energy management; heating, ventilation, and air-conditioning (HVAC) systems; and temperature control. (8)

failover. Action of switching from primary equipment to secondary equipment with no human intervention and with little or no interruption. (18)

failover cluster. Group of servers that coordinate to maintain availability of resources. (18)

fake telemetry. False data recorded through simulations; also called *deception telemetry*. (12)

false acceptance rate (FAR). Measurement of how likely a biometric feature incorrectly grants access to an unauthorized person. (4)

false negative. Occurs when a scanner is unable to find vulnerabilities when there really are vulnerabilities present. (3)

false positive. Occurs when a scanner registers a vulnerability when none is present. (3)

false rejection rate (FRR). Measurement of how likely a biometric feature will incorrectly deny an authorized person access to the system. (4)

Faraday cage. Blocks electromagnetic signals and distributes them around the exterior of the cage, preventing the signals from reaching the protected equipment. (5)

fat access point. Network device that exists independently from other network devices and can manage authentication, encryption, and other wireless functions; sometimes called an *autonomous AP*. (14)

fault tolerance. Ability of a system to operate without interruption when one or more components fail. (18)

federated identity management (FIM). Agreement between a group of organizations to allow subscribers to use one set of credentials to access all networks belonging to the organizations in the group. (4)

field-programmable gate array (FPGA). Programmable hardware circuit used to carry out logical operations. (8)

file integrity monitor (FIM). Security control or process that monitors changes made to files stored on a computer and validates the integrity of software, including the operating system; also called a *file integrity check (FIC)*. (13)

fileless virus. Virus that uses a computer system's software, files, and applications to launch malware, often through PowerShell scripts. (2)

File Transfer Protocol (FTP). Protocol that enables the transmission of files between devices connected over the Internet. (13)

File Transfer Protocol/SSL (FTPS). Extension to File Transfer Protocol (FTP) that has SSH functionality with an added second channel for secure transmissions. (13)

fingerprint scanner. Device that reads the unique skin layers of a person's fingerprint to confirm that person's identity. (4)

firewall. Network security tool that acts as a barrier or protection against unwanted data transfer at entry points by monitoring incoming and outgoing network traffic, (6)

Firewall as a Service (FWaaS). Method of delivering a firewall and other advanced security tools to the cloud environment. (15)

firmware. Read-only software program on a hardware device that provides instructions for the device to communicate with other hardware. (6)

firmware OTA update. Patch or system update for a mobile device distributed through a wireless provider as an over-the-air (OTA) update. (8)

flood guard. Firewall-type feature that limits the amount of memory a switch can use to store data for each port. (12)

fog computing. Decentralized model in which computing activities take place on devices that are not physically close but connected by a LAN. (15)

footprinting. Gathering information about a system; also called *pre-attack technique*. (3)

forked. Term for a program that has been modified to create an entirely new development branch that is a separate program. (11)

forward proxy server. Internet-facing proxy server used to intercept and forward requests from a local network to the Internet, typically through a firewall, on behalf of the user; also called a *forward proxy*. (12)

framework. Document that defines policies and processes that outline the way in which information is managed in an organization. (1)

full backup. Copy of all files. (18)

full-device encryption (FDE). Technology that renders data stored on a hard drive unreadable without an encryption key to unlock it; also known as *drive encryption*. (6)

fuzzing. Automated testing technique in which a program attempts to find coding errors or bugs in implantation of code, such as invalid, unexpected, or misconfigured data; also called *fuzz testing*. (7)

G

gait analysis. Identity confirmation based on analysis of the way a person walks. (4)

Galois/Counter Mode (GCM). Process that encrypts and processes message authentication codes (MACs). (10)

generator. Device that creates electricity. (18)

geofencing. Process of using GPS or RFID to create a virtual boundary, allowing management to establish a geographic area and disable or allow devices or features based on the user's proximity to that area. (4)

geolocation. Act of identifying the geographical coordinates of a device. (4)

governance. Process of operating an organization. (16)

GPS tagging. Act of including GPS information to media, such as photos taken from a mobile device; also known as *geotagging*. (4)

gray box test. Penetration test in which the tester has some knowledge of the system. (3)

gray-hat hacker. Hacker who does not necessarily harm others but does not ask permission before conducting attacks or accessing systems. (2)

grep command. Helpful Linux utility used to search for plain-text data. (11)

group-based access control. Procedure in which users are assigned into groups, sometimes known as roles, and each group is assigned permissions. (4)

guest network. Open network that is separate from a primary network and allows anyone to gain access without permission. (12)

guest operating system. Software installed and running on a virtual system; or *guest OS*. (15)

H

hacking attack. Attempt to break into a computer system to steal data. (2)

hacktivist. Hacker who is motivated to hack based on ideals or personal beliefs. (2)

hardening. Security method that relies on tools, techniques, and actions to reduce IT vulnerabilities in an enterprise environment. (6)

hard link. Link that points directly to the original data. (11)

hardware root of trust. Hardware that serves as a starting point in a chain of trust. (6)

hardware security module (HSM). Cryptographic device that stores or manages encryption keys and performs cryptographic functions. (8)

hash-based message authentication code (HMAC). Message-authentication code that employs a cryptographic key as well as a hash in order to authenticate the sender. (9)

hashing. Mathematical function that creates a value based on the data. (9)

hash table. Data set that contains cracked passwords with preconstructed hashes for every password entered into the table. (9)

heat map. Matrix that organizes risks into defined impact levels; also known as a *risk matrix*. (16)

heuristic-based monitoring. Method in which scanning is applied to normal processes to determine if a threat exists; also known as *behavioral-based monitoring*. (12)

heuristic methodology. Approach to finding previously undetected, unwanted programs or variants of known viruses. (2)

hexadecimal numbering system. Base-16 numbering system that uses 16 characters (0–9, A–F) to represent numbers. (11)

hierarchical-trust model. Trust model in which there is just one master CA, known as the *root CA*. (10)

high availability (HA). Ability of a system to remain available with no interruption. (15)

high resilience. Ability to recover from failure or lack of resources quickly. (9)

hoax. Falsehood that a person believes is genuine. (2)

home directory. Directory where a user stores personal files. (11)

homomorphic encryption. Encryption method in which data is converted into ciphertext that can be analyzed, searched, and modified without the need to decrypt the information. (9)

honeyfile. Fake file located on a network folder share. (12)

honeynet. Network intentionally established and configured to be vulnerable to attract attackers and study their methods. (12)

honeypot. Computer or server loaded with files or applications that appear to be authentic and placed in a network zone with limited security. (12)

host. Device that is accessible over a network. (6)

host intrusion-detection system (HIDS). Security tool that passively examines and analyzes activity to and from an endpoint device and provides notifications of security threats. (6)

host intrusion-prevention system (HIPS). Security-monitoring program that monitors and analyzes incoming and outgoing traffic flow and immediately halts traffic if malicious activity is suspected. (6)

host operating system. Software installed on a device that interacts with that device's hardware; or *host OS*. (15)

host security. Methods used to secure an operating system, file structure, and applications used on a host from unauthorized activity or access. (6)

hosted service. Resource deployment method in which data servers, storage devices, and networking resources are utilized using a remote connection for which services are contracted. (15)

hot and cold aisles. Layout design in which server racks are arranged in rows with cold air entering the room on one side and hot air exiting the room on the other side (5)

hot site. Duplication of a current, fully functional site. (18)

hotspot. Publicly accessible, often unsecured, Internet access point. (8)

hping command. Network reconnaissance command that is used to scan and analyze ports, conduct network security audits, and test firewalls; also called *hping3 command*. (13)

HTTP header. Block of data composed of fields that contain information used in an HTTP transmission. (7)

hybrid cloud. Cloud model that combines public, private, or community clouds. (15)

hybrid cryptography. Form of encryption that merges the functionality of symmetric and asymmetric cryptography. (9)

hybrid warfare. Military strategy that combines political, conventional, and cyberwarfare to disseminate false information. (2)

Hypertext Markup Language version 5 (HTML5). Fifth revision of the HTML standard that can be used as a secure remote access solution. (12)

Hypertext Transfer Protocol Secure (HTTPS). Extension of the Hypertext Transfer Protocol (HTTP) used for secure communication over the Internet; sometimes referred to as *Hypertext Transfer Protocol over SSL/TLS.* (10)

hypervisor. Software program that monitors and manages virtual operating systems. (15)

hypothetical question. Interview question that requires a candidate to imagine a situation and describe how they would act. (19)

I

ICMP echo request. Query message sent to a destination machine to establish connectivity. (13)

identity fraud. Social engineering attack in which a hacker uses stolen information to obtain additional data or access to a secure account of a victim. (2)

IEEE 802.1X. Wireless networking standard that provides more security than other standards by employing port-based security. (5)

ifconfig. Linux equivalent of the Windows **ipconfig** command; command that returns information about network adapters and related TCP/IP information. (11)

impersonation. Social engineering technique in which hackers pretend to be another person to obtain information. (2)

implicit permissions. Permissions a user receives through another object, such as a group. (4)

impossible travel time restriction. Safeguard that prevents access to a user if the system detects the user traveled between two locations faster than anticipated. (8)

in-band. Management method in which an intrusion-detection system (IDS) is connected to the network and manages devices using common protocols of the network. (12)

incident response (IR). Acting against and recovering from a cybersecurity incident. (17)

incident response plan (IRP). Written document that provides instructions to follow when an incident occurs. (17)

incident response process. Process that outlines the steps taken when an incident occurs and becomes the main element of an incident response plan (IRP). (17)

incremental backup. Series of sequential backups in which the first day begins with a full backup, and each remaining day in the cycle creates copies of files that have changed or been created since the last backup. (18)

indicators of compromise (IoC). Evidence that identifies a cyberattack. (2)

industrial camouflage. Concept in which a company designs a facility in a way that makes it unappealing or uninteresting to a potential attacker. (5)

industrial control system (ICS). Umbrella term that describes various types of systems, tools, and instrumentation used to operate or automate industrial processes. (8)

industry standard. Set of rules adopted by a particular industry. (1)

influence campaign. Wide-scale operation that focuses on the spread of false or misleading information in an effort to make a group of people think or behave a certain way. (2)

information assurance (IA). Process of protecting an information system, including identifying vulnerabilities and risks for using, storing, and transmitting data. (1)

Information Rights Management (IRM). IT security process that protects sensitive documents, such as health records, from unauthorized access. (16)

information security. Processes and procedures designed to prevent the loss of data integrity, detect ongoing vulnerabilities and threats, and mitigate and response to threats; also referred to as *infosec.* (1)

information security plan. Set of procedures that describes an organization's computer network and details how company data will be protected and kept confidential; also referred to as a *security plan.* (1)

information sharing center (ISC). Industry-specific consortium of business owners and IT personnel working together to collect, analyze, and distribute timely information to its members about cyber threats. (2)

infrared (IR). Wireless communication technology that conveys data through infrared radiation. (14)

Infrastructure as a Service (IaaS). Cloud-computing service in which a vendor provides the customer with virtualized infrastructure over the Internet. (15)

infrastructure as code (IaC). Management of hardware and software through machine-readable files as opposed to physical configuration. (7)

inherent risk. Risk that would happen if controls were not in place to mitigate it. (16)

inherited permissions. Permissions a user receives by default when a child of a parent object is created. (4)

initial exploitation. Act of a pen tester using the information gathered during reconnaissance in an attempt to gain entry to a network. (3)

injection attack. Attack in which a hacker is able to supply input that exploits a vulnerability in an application. (7)

input validation. Programming configuration in which an input field rejects any characters that do not match its function or could cause a malfunction; also called *form validation.* (7)

insider. Threat actor who has infiltrated an organization with the intent of committing cybercrime against the employer. (2)

integer overflow. Condition in which an arithmetic operation results in a number that is too large to be stored in the memory space allocated for the result. (7)

integer overflow attack. Attack that occurs when an attacker alters a variable's value to something outside the variable's intended range. (7)

integrity. Refers to an unchanged, unimpaired, or unaltered state. (1)

integrity. Honesty of a person's actions. (19)

integrity measurement. Measurement and identification of changes made to a system as compared to its baseline. (7)

intellectual property (IP). Something that comes from a person's mind, such as an idea, invention, or process. (16)

intelligence fusion. Combination of intelligence information from many sources to create a comprehensive threat profile. (3)

intermediate CA. Subordinate certificate authority that manages specific needs, such as confirming identities and processing requests. (10)

Internet Key Exchange Protocol version 2 (IKEv2). Tunneling protocol that uses the IPSec tunneling protocol over UDP on port 500 to establish a security association. (12)

Internet Mail Access Protocol (IMAP). More recent and advanced e-mail protocol that enables mail to be stored on and accessed from a server. (13)

Internet of Things (IoT). Connection of nontraditional computing devices to the Internet. (1)

intranet. Private Internet environment for an organization's internal use only. (12)

intrusive test. Test in which the scanner tries to exploit vulnerabilities. (3)

invoice scam. Social engineering attack in which fraudulent invoices are submitted to targeted organizations in an effort to obtain money. (2)

ipconfig command. Windows command-line tool that displays all devices connected to a network. (11)

IP Flow Information Export (IPFix). Network flow standard that provides for the export of the flow of information from routers, switches, firewalls, and other devices located in the network infrastructure. (13)

IP scanner. Tool that searches a network for IP addresses and other relevant information regarding network devices. (13)

IP Security (IPSec). Security protocol that can be used to encrypt and secure data traveling over computer networks using the TCP/IP protocol. (12)

IP spoofing. Creation of a fake IP address that matches a local IP address so malicious external traffic appears to be originating from inside the network. (12)

iris scanner. Confirms a person's identity by reading the characteristics of a person's iris. (4)

IT asset management (ITAM). Asset management process that involves tracking of all IT assets that reside in a business, including hardware and software systems. (16)

IT contingency plan (ITCP). Supplemental plan enacted in the event the DRP is not successful or feasible. (18)

J

jailbreaking. Process of allowing an iOS device to bypass device restrictions. (8)

jamming. Intentionally interfering with wireless signals to prevent a transmission from being usable. (14)

Jersey walls. Tee-shaped walls usually made of concrete to prevent vehicles from passing. (5)

job-acquisition skills. Skills used to obtain employment, such as writing a résumé and properly filling out an application. (19)

job rotation. System of employment in which personnel cycle through different roles in an organization to gain new experiences and variety in a job. (16)

jump server. Network appliance used to access and manage devices in a separate security zone; also known as a *pivot server* or *jump host.* (12)

K

Kerberos. Standard authentication protocol on all versions of Microsoft Server when using the Active Directory. (4)

key escrow. Process in which keys are managed by a trusted third party, such as a certificate authority. (10)

key exchange. Process in which the cryptographic key is exchanged, or shared, between a sender and a receiver. (9)

key length. Number of bits in a cryptographic algorithm's key; also called *key size.* (9)

keylogger. software or a hardware device that tracks a user's keystrokes on a keyboard. (2)

key pair. Public and private key used in combination for asymmetric encryption. (9)

key strength. Resiliency of the key used to resist attack. (9)

key stretching. Process of making passwords longer, more complex, and harder to crack. (9)

key-stretching algorithm. Algorithm that intentionally limits the ability of an attacker to decode passwords by requiring increased time to create a digest. (9)

L

lateral movement. Moving from one compromised host to another host within the network. (3)

Layer 2 Tunneling Protocol (L2TP). Tunneling protocol used by Internet service providers to enable operation of a VPN over the Internet. (12)

LDAP injection attack. Injection attack in which an attacker exploits web applications that use constructed Lightweight Directory Access Protocol (LDAP) statements. (7)

LDAPS. Secure form of LDAP, where LDAP is used with SSL to send directory communications encrypted. (4)

leadership. Ability to influence others to reach a goal. (19)

legacy platform. Operating system or embedded system that is no longer in widespread use; also called a *legacy operating system.* (2)

legal hold. Prohibits employees from destroying documentation and other evidence or deleting data, documents, or items that may be relevant to an investigation. (17)

library. Collection of programming code used in software development. (7)

lifelong learning. Voluntary attainment of knowledge throughout life. (19)

lightweight cryptography. Encryption method that uses a small footprint so that it can meet standards while accommodating low-power devices and/or low computational complexity. (9)

Lightweight Directory Access Protocol (LDAP). Protocol that provides standards and ensures that directories or directory services are constructed and used in the same manner. (4)

Linux. Open-source computer operating system derived from the UNIX operating system. (11)

LM hash. Old (pre-Windows NT) method of encrypting local passwords; also called *LAN Manager hash.* (9)

load balancer. Network device that sends requests to various servers on a network based on predefined factors. (7)

load balancing. Distribution of processing needs over multiple servers; often referred to as *scheduling.* (7)

location-based policy. Control used to grant or deny access based on a user's location. (4)

log aggregation. Automated gathering of log and event data from hosts and network devices throughout the network. (3)

log analysis. Process of setting policies regarding the collection, review, and analysis of log data. (3)

log collector. Service that assembles logs from various event sources through a network environment. (3)

logger command. Linux-based command that enables an administrator to make notes in the syslog log file located in the **/var/log** directory. (11)

logic bomb. Malicious software that deploys when conditions exist that the malware is seeking; the time and date are irrelevant. (2)

log file. Record of events that occur during a server or computer operation; also called an *event log.* (3)

log management. Process of generating, transmitting, analyzing, archiving, and disposing of log data. (3)

log review. Assessment and analysis of vulnerability scan logs. (3)

loop prevention. Incorporation of protocols that prevent a switch from creating a continuous loop of traffic that ultimately floods the switch with needless packets. (12)

low latency. Processing data with minimal delays. (9)

M

MAC cloning. Attack in which a threat actor configures a host using the MAC address of a different, validated host; also known as *MAC spoofing.* (13)

machine learning (ML). Ability for computer algorithms to improve automatically through experience. (2)

MAC filtering. Access control method by which a MAC address is used to determine access to a network. (12)

MAC flooding. Network attack in which multiple MAC addresses are assigned to one physical port on a switch. (12)

macro virus. Macro written in the same language as software applications and programmed to carry out a malicious intent. (2)

malicious USB cable. USB cable that, when plugged into a USB device, injects keystrokes onto a computer enabling an attacker to download malware. (2)

malware. Computer code intentionally written to cause some form of harm; also known as *malicious software.* (2)

malware attack. Action of a hacker installing malicious software on another person's device with the intent of accessing data for personal gain. (2)

managed security service provider (MSSP). Vendor that manages a customer's IT security environment. (15)

managed service provider (MSP). Vendor that manages a customer's IT operations environment. (15)

managerial control. Security control that uses management or administrative processes to implement and measure performance as well as intervene and take corrective actions when needed. (16)

mandatory access control (MAC). Security strategy that sets a strict level of access to resources based on criteria set by a network administrator. (4)

mandatory vacation. Requiring an employee to take a vacation as designated by company policy. (16)

man-in-the-browser (MITB) attack. Internet threat that infects a web browser and covertly modifies web pages, transaction content, or preferences. (7)

man-in-the-middle attack. Network attack in which legitimate communication is intercepted and a fictitious response is forged and sent to the sender. (9)

man-made disaster. Event caused by humans that results in delays or business disruptions. (16)

mantrap. Physical access control system used to trap a person between two sets of interlocking doors. (5)

manual code review. Process of reading source code, line-by-line, to locate and identify vulnerabilities. (7)

mean time between failures (MTBF). Measure of the average time that passes before a fault occurs. (18)

mean time to failure (MTTF). Average amount of time an irreparable asset operates before it fails. (18)

mean time to repair (MTTR). Calculation for the average time it takes to repair or replace a failed component. (18)

Measured Boot. Boot feature that provides protection from rootkits and other malware that launch during an operating system boot process. (6)

memory dump. Process that "dumps" the content of a computer's memory, including RAM, and stores it; also known as a *memdump*. (17)

memory leak. Vulnerability that occurs when memory allocated for a program is not freed when the program is completed. (7)

method. Set of instructions that specifies an action to be performed on an object. (11)

microSD HSM. Lightweight security solution that implements cryptographic key management in a microSD card. (8)

microsegmentation. Security technique that enables administrators to split a network's attack surface by logically dividing the network into segments based on individual workloads. (12)

microservice. Software application development method made up of reusable components used in a cloud-native application; also known as *microservice architecture*. (15)

Microsoft Challenge Handshake Authentication Protocol (MS-CHAP). Microsoft's version of the Challenge Handshake Authentication Protocol. (12)

mirror image backup. Backup that replicates a hard drive, including any files and hidden data sectors stored on the drive. (17)

mission-critical functions and systems. Essential functions and systems necessary to keep a business operational. (18)

mobile application management (MAM). Solution that provides specific functionality by enabling administrators to lock or disable apps and the data stored within them. (8)

mobile content management (MCM). Solution that enables a company to have control over mobile devices, device content, and how devices access data located on company systems. (8)

mobile device management (MDM). Set of software tools that provides a single management platform to control, modify, and secure devices remotely. (8)

mock interview. Practice interview conducted with another person. (19)

monitoring service. Software-based utilities that continually observe an individual device or network as a whole for hardware errors or interruptions or performance anomalies and notify an administrator in the event an error or outage is detected. (13)

morals. Individual's ideas of what is right and wrong. (19)

multifactor authentication. Using multiple independent credentials, rather than just one, to verify user identification. (4)

multifunction printer (MFP). Output device that uses embedded systems to perform printing, faxing, copying, scanning, and e-mail functions; often called a *multifunction device (MFD)*. (8)

multimedia messaging service (MMS). Messaging service that allows for photo, video, or audio to be included in a message. (8)

multipathing. Creation of alternative routes between a server and storage device; also called *SAN multipathing* or *I/O multipathing (MPIO)*. (18)

N

narrowband (NB). Radio communication method that utilizes a narrow set, or *band*, of frequencies within a given communication channel. (14)

NAT gateway. Managed service that bridges the connection between a local network and the Internet by translating IP addresses from private to public or vice versa. (12)

near-field communication (NFC). Wireless communication standard that facilitates transmissions using electromagnetic radio fields between devices of a very close proximity. (14)

netcat command. Versatile utility that can read and write data using the TCP/IP protocol. (13)

NetFlow. Network protocol created by Cisco that collects IP traffic as it flows in and out of a network interface card and allows for monitoring of the network in real time. (13)

netstat command. Network reconnaissance and discovery command-line utility that allows a user to view TCP and UDP connections, routing tables, and other network interface and protocol statistics. (13)

network access control (NAC). Network solution that unifies endpoint security by verifying that a host meets minimum standards before it is allowed to connect to a network; also known as a *host health check*. (13)

network address translation (NAT). Method of remapping an IP address so a device with a private address can be used on a public network such as the Internet. (12)

network administration. Operational tasks that provide ongoing support, management, and maintenance to enable a network to run efficiently. (13)

network-attached storage (NAS). Data storage method in which a storage server or device is connected to a network and enables storage and retrieval from one centralized source. (18)

networking. Talking with people you know and making new relationships that can lead to potential career or job opportunities. (19)

network interface card (NIC) teaming. Act of combining network interface cards (NICs) to function as one logical NIC called a *bond*. (12)

network security assessment. Audit or review of security measures in place on a computer network conducted to identify or locate previously unknown vulnerabilities. (13)

network segmentation. Act of dividing a network into smaller sections, called *network segments* or *subnetworks*, to separate data to reduce its exposure. (12)

network TAP. Networking device installed inside a network to monitor traffic; also called a *port TAP*. (12)

network vulnerability scanner. Vulnerability scanners that focus on potentially vulnerable network activities. (3)

New Technology File System (NTFS) permissions. Permissions used to manage access to folders, files, or resources stored on an NTFS-based system. (4)

next-generation firewall. Firewall that can run at all levels of the OSI model to monitor and filter traffic based data inside packet headers or the packet's payload on header or application data; also known as a *next-gen firewall*. (6)

next-generation secure web gateway (SWG). Cloud-based solution that can prevent malware, protect data, filter content, manage applications, and detect threats. (15)

nmap. Text-based protocol analyzer that scans networks; discovers hosts, services, and port information; analyzes the results to identify open ports; and creates educated guesses on the operating systems in use. (13)

nonce. Arbitrarily chosen, unique number used only once in communication; comes from the phrase *number used once*. (9)

noncredentialed scan. Scan that does not require credentials to access the system; also called a *nonauthenticated scan*. (3)

nondisclosure agreement (NDA). Legal contract between two parties that restricts the signing party from distributing or sharing confidential information to anyone outside of the agreement. (2)

non-intrusive test. Test in which a system is scanned without causing harm to its target. (3)

non-persistence. Actions taken and configurations implemented to ensure unwanted data is not retained when new devices are added and instead, a clean disk image is used. (12)

nonrepudiation. Assurance that an individual or group of people cannot deny the validity of something. (1)

nonrepudiation process. Systematic process in which the origins and alterations to a data set are tracked according to the user account that made them. (1)

normalization. Process of organizing data in a database to reduce redundancies and improve performance. (7)

north-south traffic. Flow of traffic from an organization's data center to an outside location. (12)

nslookup command. Windows command-line tool used to locate information related to the domain name system (DNS). (11)

NTLM hash. Microsoft's most recent password-encryption method; also called *New Technology LAN Manager hash*. (9)

null pointer exception. Type of error that occurs when a value of NULL is stored in a valid memory area. (7)

NXlog. Multiplatform log management tool that includes support for Android and Windows platforms. (3)

O

obfuscation. Act of masking something to make it unclear. (7)

object. Self-contained resource that stores information about itself in properties and provides program code used to interact with it. (11)

object detection. Type of artificial intelligence technology that is able to identify preprogrammed objects. (5)

object identifier (OID). Numeric value that identifies the application or service for which the certificate is used. (10)

offboarding. Interview with an exiting employee to gather all login credentials. (4)

office politics. Behaviors that individuals practice to gain advantages over others in the workplace. (19)

off-premises model. Organization accesses and stores data in an off-site facility. (15)

onboarding. New-employee training to acquaint the individual with the organization as well as explain rights and responsibilities expected when using the organization's network. (4)

Online Certificate Status Protocol (OCSP). Internet protocol for obtaining the status of a certificate. (10)

on-premises model. Organization purchases hardware and software needed for business operations and uses them on-site. (15)

open port. Communication port that actively accepts TCP or UDP connections. (2)

open security. Wireless connection that requires no authentication and offers no encryption; also called an *open connection*. (14)

open service. Service permitted to run on a computer. (2)

open-source intelligence (OSINT). Data collected from public sources as well as government sites. (2)

open-source software. Software that has unlocked source code that can be modified by anyone. (11)

OpenSSL. Open-source command-line tool used by network administrators for cryptographic management. (11)

Open Systems Interconnect (OSI) model. Conceptual framework that outlines how hardware and software function together to form a communications network. (6)

Open Web Application Security Project (OWASP). Nonprofit organization that provides unbiased information about application security. (7)

operational control. Security control implemented by people who carry out day-to-day operations of a business. (16)

orchestration. Integration of different technologies, including security and non-security tools to work together. (3)

order of volatility. Order or sequence in which digital evidence is collected. (17)

out-of-band. Management method in which the intrusion-detection system (IDS) has an access server connected to a management port on each device. (12)

out-of-band management (OOBM). Method of remotely managing and controlling infrastructure using an interface separate from the primary connection. (12)

P

packet capture. Act of intercepting a data packet as it crosses a specific network point. (3)

packet-filtering firewall. Firewall that examines all data packets and either forwards or drops them based on predefined rules that designate where a packet can go. (12)

packet replay. Review of previously captured data packets; also known as *traffic replay*. (13)

packet sniffer. Tool that uses a network interface card (NIC) to capture raw data traveling on network media and replay it for analysis. (13)

passive reconnaissance. Discovery and gathering of data without the target being aware it is happening. (3)

pass-the-hash attack. Attack in which a hacker intercepts or steals a message digest, sends it to a remote system, and is authenticated as an acceptable user. (9)

Password Authentication Protocol (PAP). Unencrypted password-based authentication protocol that used Point-to-Point Protocol (PPP) to validate users. (12)

Password-Based Key Derivation Function 2 (PBKDF2). Key-stretching technique in which a pseudorandom function, such as a hashing operation, and a salt is added to an input password. (9)

password complexity. Level of difficulty associated with a password. (4)

password cracker. Device or application that recovers a password stored on a system or compares potential passwords against hashes. (9)

password lockout. Policy that prevents access to an account after an established number of failed login attempts is met. (4)

password management. Controlling the methods in which users create passwords to gain access to a company network. (8)

password recovery. Process for providing an existing or new password to a user as a replacement for a lost password. (4)

password spraying. Cryptographic attack that attempts to access a large number of user account names with just a few commonly used passwords. (9)

password vault. Repository for passwords protected by a master password. (8)

patch. Update provided by a vendor to correct errors or bugs in software or improve its operation. (6)

patch management. Process of deploying patches to networked devices to keep all devices up to date. (6)

path validation. Process of verifying a digital certificate is safe and not revoked. (10)

pathping command. TCP/IP utility that provides information about network latency and identifies the hops between the source address and the destination address. (11)

payload. Actions of malicious code. (2)

pen register. Device that captures *outgoing* phone numbers, e-mail data, or Internet addresses of communications between parties. (1)

penetration exercise. Test that examines the security defenses of an organization. (3)

penetration testing. Process in which white-hat hackers are given permission to access a system in an attempt to penetrate defenses to locate vulnerabilities; also called *pen testing*. (3)

penetration testing authorization. Permission given by a company or organization to another party to access or hack a system in an effort to determine how susceptible the system is to unauthorized access or penetration. (3)

perfect forward secrecy (PFS). Cryptographic security feature in which a key is changed from one encrypted conversation to another conversation or is changed after a message is sent. (9)

permission. Authorization assigned to a user that allows the individual to access a given resource within a computer network. (4)

permission audit and review. Process of re-evaluating the permission set established for an account to determine if the same permission set can be renewed, or if more or fewer restrictions are necessary. (4)

persistence. Act of a pen tester attempting to maintain a connection after a successful exploit. (3)

personal cloud. Cloud-computing resource that allows a user to manage their own cloud service to store files or offer services within a household; often referred to as a *home cloud*. (15)

personal identity verification (PIV). US governmental standard for smart cards. (5)

Personal Information Exchange (PFX). Certificate type used to create certificates for authentication. (10)

personally identifiable information (PII). Any data that can be used to pinpoint a specific person, such as Social Security or driver license numbers. (16)

pharming. Process of setting up a website that looks legitimate and credible but used to steal personal information entered by users. (2)

phishing. Social engineering attack in which an attacker attempts to obtain a user's personal information, through fake e-mails that appear to be real. (2)

physical control. Tangible control used to protect the physical assets of an organization. (5)

physical network segregation. Act of isolating or segmenting a network so it is not accessible to unauthorized personnel. (5)

ping command. Windows command-line tool used to test the connection between two networked devices. (11)

pinning. Process of associating a host or client application with an *expected* certificate or public key. (10)

piping. Act of directing the results of one command into the input syntax of another command. (11)

pivot. Point of a penetration test in which the tester refocuses attention from the initial point of entry to begin looking for targets and other resources on a network. (3)

PKCS#7. Standard used to sign or encrypt messages under a PKI and is often used for single sign-on (SSO). (10)

PKCS#12. Standard that defines a file format used to store private keys along with their corresponding public key certificate. (10)

PKI management. Managing certificates, authorizing keys, storing keys, and other tasks to safeguard keys. (10)

plaintext. Original form of information. (9)

Platform as a Service (PaaS). Cloud service that allows a customer to develop, run, and manage their applications in the cloud. (15)

pointer dereference error. Vulnerability that occurs when a value has not been obtained from the correct area; also called an *object deference.* (7)

Point-to-Point Tunneling Protocol (PPTP). Networking protocol for connecting to VPNs. PPTP is the most outdated of the tunneling protocols. (12)

policy. Set of rules that can automatically control access to resources. (4)

policy violation. Occurs when an employee fails to follow a security policy effectively. (16)

polymorphic virus. Virus that changes its characteristics in an attempt to avoid detection from antivirus programs. (2)

portfolio. Selection of related materials that are collected and organized to show the qualifications, skills, and talents that support an individual's career or personal goals. (19)

port mirroring. Method of traffic monitoring in which data packets are copied from one switch port to another; also known as *Switched Port Analyzer (SPAN)* or *port spanning.* (12)

port scanner. Application designed to probe a server or host for open ports. (3)

port scanning. Method that determines the status of communication ports on a system. (3)

port security. Traffic-control feature that prevents unknown or unauthorized devices from forwarding packets. (12)

Post Office Protocol (POP). Legacy e-mail protocol that enables users to retrieve incoming e-mail messages. (13)

post-quantum cryptography. Cryptographic measures that are intended to be secure against attacks generated from a quantum computer; sometimes referred to as *quantum-proof cryptography, quantum-safe cryptography,* or *quantum-resistant cryptography.* (9)

potentially unwanted program (PUP). Program that has been approved for download, but may not be wanted, by a user. (2)

power distribution unit (PDU). Device that distributes electrical power. (18)

power surge. Fluctuation in the supplied voltage; often called *power spikes.* (18)

PowerShell. Powerful command-line interface shell integrated in Windows.NET technologies. (3)

predictive analysis. Examination of data, statistical modeling, and machine learning techniques to quantify the likelihood of a future cyber threat. (3)

predictive site survey. Visual representation of wireless signal strength, often depicted as a map, within a network; also called a *wireless heat map.* (14)

prepending. Technique in which characters are added to the beginning of a text, phrase, word, etc. with the goal of influencing how a user receives or interprets the message. (2)

preservation of evidence. Process of protecting evidence from change, corruption, alteration, or damage throughout its lifecycle. (17)

pre-shared key (PSK). Authentication method used in WLAN security that requires a key value before granting access to an access point or wireless devices. (14)

pre-shared symmetric key (PSK). Secret value previously shared between two parties; also called a *secret algorithm.* (9)

pretexting. Using a lie or scam to obtain private information. (1)

preventive control. Type of control that prevents an incident from occurring. (5)

Privacy Enhanced Mail (PEM). Certificate type that provides integrity and confidentiality to e-mail messages. (10)

private cloud. Cloud-computing resource owned and managed by a single private organization. (15)

private key. Encryption key that does not need protection. (9)

privileged user. Elevated user role that has increased access to data and resources. (16)

privilege escalation. Act of exploiting a coding error, design flaw, or oversight to gain elevated access to data that would normally be restricted. (7)

problem-solving. Process used to evaluate a situation and find a solution. (19)

process. Actively running computer program. (11)

professionalism. Act of exhibiting appropriate character, judgment, and behavior by a person trained to perform a job. (19)

property. Data embedded into an object. (11)

Protected EAP (PEAP). Open-standard authentication protocol created jointly by Cisco, Microsoft, and RSA to protect EAP communications. (14)

protective distribution system (PDS). Set of safeguards implemented to protect data sent over electromagnetic media against EMR hijacking. (5)

protocol. Industry-accepted standardized format that allows communication between devices. (12)

provider. Program that organizes data in specialized groups to be easily viewed and managed. (11)

provisioning. Practice of providing access and resources to network services needed for employees to complete their jobs. (7)

proxy firewall. Network security device that protects a network by filtering a packet's data as well as its header. (12)

proxy server. Server that functions as a gateway between a local network and the Internet. (12)

pseudoanonymization. De-identification procedure in which personally identifiable information fields within a data record are replaced with one or more artificial, or fake, identifiers. (16)

pseudo-random number generator (PRNG). Number-generation algorithm that creates a sequence of numbers that appear to be randomly generated but is actually based on the same starting number. (9)

public cloud. Cloud-computing resource that provides services to anyone. (15)

public key. Key that does not need to be protected. (9)

Public Key Cryptography Standards (PKCS). Set of standards devised and published by RSA Security. (10)

public key infrastructure (PKI). Set of policies, hardware, and procedures necessary for creating, distributing, managing, storing, or revoking public keys used in digital certificates. (10)

public ledger. Record-keeping system that details the representation of blocks in a chain while preventing its contents from being edited without authorization. (10)

pulping. Process of putting paper in a tank of water and chemically removing the ink from the paper fibers. (5)

push notification. Message or alert that appears on a mobile device without user interaction. (8)

push notification service. System in place to send notifications to devices. (8)

Python. Versatile programming language often used for web, mobile app, and desktop app development. (11)

Q

qualitative assessment. Analysis based on subjective opinion rather than data. (16)

Quality of Service (QoS). Set of technologies that enable a network to run priority applications and deliver as expected despite limited capacity or connectivity. (12)

quantitative assessment. Analysis that uses numbers or monetary values. (16)

quantum communication. Digital communication that uses photons, or tiny particles of light, to transfer data along fiber-optic lines. (9)

quantum computing. New area of computer science that uses quantum theory to enable computing bits to exist in more than one state. (9)

quantum cryptography. Cryptographic science in which quantum mechanics is used to encrypt data. (9)

quarantine. Action taken on a file infected with malware or virus by moving the infected file to a portion on the storage disk where it cannot be accessed. (17)

R

race condition. Software vulnerability in which two simultaneous lines of executable code, called *threads*, attempt to access a shared resource. (7)

radio-frequency identification (RFID). Wireless technology that uses electromagnetic fields to automatically identify objects and track tags or smart labels that are attached to the objects. (14)

RADIUS Federation. Method where users can connect and authenticate to one network while using credentials from another network. (14)

RAID 0. RAID configuration in which multiple hard drives work in synchronization with each other when saving or retrieving data; also known as *disk striping*. (18)

RAID 1. RAID system that uses two hard drives, each a mirror or copy of the other drive; also known as *disk mirroring*. (18)

RAID 1+0. RAID array that combines RAID 1 and RAID 0; sometimes called a *stripe of mirrors, nested RAID,* or *hybrid RAID*. (18)

RAID 5. RAID setup that combines the performance of RAID 0 with fault tolerance; also known as *disk striping with parity*. (18)

rainbow table. Precomputed table of calculations used to speed up the password cracking process by using a hashing function and reduction function. (9)

ransomware. Malware that encrypts data so the user cannot access it unless a fee, or ransom, is paid to the hacker. (2)

Raspberry Pi. Low-cost, single-board computer the size of a credit card and powered by a system on a chip (SoC). (8)

real-time operating system (RTOS). Operating system designed specifically for the SoC in an embedded system. (8)

recertification. Process of renewing a user account, including permissions, access control, and group membership. (4)

reconnaissance. Act of eliciting information from or about a target. (2)

recovery point objective (RPO). Maximum amount of data that an organization can afford to lose after operations cease. (18)

recovery site. Place in which a business can operate temporarily until the business site is up and running again. (18)

recovery time objective (RTO). Target time by which applications and systems must be restored to avoid unacceptable consequences after a disaster. (18)

redundancy. Duplication of systems to increase dependability. (18)

refactoring. Process of modifying or restructuring existing code without changing any external behavior. (7)

reference. Person who knows an applicant's skills, talents, or personal traits and is willing to recommend the individual. (19)

reference architecture. Document, or a set of documents, that provides recommendations of structures and integration of IT products and solutions. (15)

registration authority (RA). Authority that verifies a certificate-signing request and informs a certificate authority to issue the digital certificate. (10)

remote access Trojan (RAT). Form of malware that allows a hacker to use an embedded backdoor to gain administrative control of a victim's computer. (2)

Remote Authentication Dial-In User Service (RADIUS). Connectionless protocol that uses the User Datagram Protocol (UDP) as its transport protocol. (4)

Remote Authentication Dial-In User Service (RADIUS) server. Identity and access authentication server that functions on both wired and wireless networks. (14)

remote wipe. Remote-erase feature that, when activated, returns a device to its original factory settings. (8)

replay attack. Wireless attack in which a hacker captures login credentials during an initial attack, stores them, and retransmits them at another time. (14)

residual risk. Risk that remains after mitigation controls are implemented. (16)

resilience. Ability of a system to recover from a disruption in an acceptable amount of time. (7)

resilience. Person's ability to cope with and recover from change or adversity. (19)

resource exhaustion. Occurs when computer resources required to execute actions are depleted, preventing action from occurring. (7)

resource policy. Policy that specifies permissions for who can access and act on resources. (15)

resource vs. security constraint. Limitation in providing cryptography based on the demands of the algorithm compared to available power. (9)

restoration order. Priority order of restoration of services or applications. (18)

résumé. Document that profiles a person's career goals, education, and work history. (19)

retinal scanner. Device that scans a person's retina to confirm their identity. (4)

reverse proxy server. Internal-facing proxy server that sits behind a firewall, processes incoming requests from the Internet, and routes them to the correct internal server. (12)

rich communication services (RCS). Mobile device communication protocol with more features and options than SMS. (8)

right. Ability to perform a type of action on the computer; also known as a *privilege*. (4)

risk. Situation that could cause harm, create a hazard, or otherwise cause problems for an organization. (1)

risk acceptance. Making a decision to assume risk. (16)

risk analysis. Reviews the likelihood of a risk and the frequency with which it will occur. (16)

risk assessment. Systematic process that involves identifying risks caused by threats and vulnerabilities associated with assets and ranking them with the most critical risks listed first. (16)

risk avoidance. Act of eliminating risk by avoiding agents that cause the risk. (16)

risk awareness. Enables security practitioners to focus on the most common or intrusive threats faced by an organization. (16)

risk control self-assessment. Process of examining risks and the degree to which controls are effective. (16)

risk impact. Estimated consequences or losses caused by a risk. (16)

risk management. Process of identifying and evaluating assets and their vulnerabilities while taking steps to avoid or minimize loss, should it occur. (1)

risk mitigation. Act of taking steps to reduce the effects of risks for an organization. (16)

risk posture. Overall cybersecurity program of an organization that provides protection from breaches and safeguards its data. (16)

risk register. Tool used to list, categorize, and provide instructions for managing identified risks. (16)

risk transfer. Strategy that involves shifting risk to another party. (16)

Rivest Cipher 4 (RC4) cryptography. Stream cipher characterized by a variable-size cipher and a random algorithm based on permutation. (9)

rogue access point (rogue AP). Unauthorized access point that enables a hacker to circumvent network security. (14)

role-based access control (RBAC). Access control method in which rights are assigned to a role instead of manually to each individual user. (4)

role-based awareness training. Assigns a role and provides training for individuals based on their positions within an organization. (16)

root certificate. Certificate that reflects the highest point in the chain of trust for certificate authorities. (10)

rooting. Process of bypassing device restrictions on an Android device to access administrator-level privileges. (8)

rootkit. Type of malware that infects a computer before the operating system loads, making it difficult to remove. (2)

round-robin scheduling. Scheduling protocol rotation in which the amount of time permitted for a process to run is applied to each process in equal amounts and in circular order without priority; also known as *cyclic executive scheduling*. (12)

route command. Window command-line tool that enables a user to view the local routing table and make changes if necessary. (11)

rsyslog. Open-source software utility used with Unix and Linux systems to forward messages; variation of *syslog*. (3)

rule-based access control. Control strategy in which user access is determined by a set of rules established by an administrator. (4)

rules of engagement (RoE). Document that specifies in detail the manner in which penetration testing will be conducted. (3)

S

salting. Process that adds additional insignificant data to the end of data to create a different hash value. (6)

sandboxing. Act of running software in an isolated environment, called a *sandbox*, that is separate from other programs so if errors occur, they will not spread to other programs. (7)

scalability. Ability of a program to cope with increased loads, such as customers and new features, and continue functioning as needed. (7)

scanless. Python-based command line utility that performs port scanning on websites using a variety of online scanning tools. (13)

screen filter. Attaches to a computer monitor and prevents visibility of onscreen information from any person who is not sitting directly in front of the screen; also known as a *privacy filter*. (5)

screen lock. Security setting that requires authentication to access a device's home screen. (8)

screenshot. Digital image of the current image displayed on a device's screen; also known as a *screen capture*. (17)

script. Custom file containing commands and functions to be processed in order. (7)

script kiddie. Slang term used to describe an individual who uses premade tools to perform an attack. (2)

secondary logon. Provides a way for entering a secondary set of credentials. (4)

secrets management. Practice of using specific tools, policies, and procedures for ensuring the confidentiality and availability of information through digital authentication. (15)

Secure Boot. Feature of UEFI that ensures a computer uses only software trusted by a manufacturer for booting purposes. Secure Boot enables UEFI to check digital signatures. (6)

secure-configuration guide. Guide that provides assistance to security personnel for the secure configuration of hardware devices in an effort to prevent unauthorized access or attacks. (1)

Secure File Transfer Protocol (SFTP). Secure alternative to FTP that uses a single channel to transmit and receive data; also known as *SSH File Transfer Protocol*. (13)

Secure Multipurpose Internet Mail Extension (S/MIME). E-mail signing protocol used to increase the security of e-mail transactions. (10)

Secure Real-Time Protocol (SRTP). Secure extension to the Real-Time Transport Protocol (RTP) for protecting Voice over IP (VoIP) communications. (10)

secure shell (SSH). Secured protocol used to provide remote administrative management of servers, routers, switches, and other devices. (10)

Secure Socket Tunneling Protocol (SSTP). VPN tunneling protocol that provides support for traffic over an SSL/TLS encrypted connection. (12)

Secure Sockets Layer (SSL) protocol. Protocol that provides authentication and encryption between two computers. (10)

Secure Sockets Layer (SSL) stripping. Attack in which a threat actor removes encryption protection of an HTTPS transmission without user knowledge. (7)

secure token. Device that stores information to authenticate a person's identity. (5)

Security Account Manager (SAM). Local database of users and groups on a Windows system. (9)

Security as a Service (SECaaS). Business model that integrates security services into the infrastructure of an organization. (15)

Security Assertion Markup Language (SAML). Open standard that allows the exchange of authentication and authorization information to provide SSO options over the Internet with federated systems. (4)

security assessment. Periodic exercise that evaluates a company's security preparedness. (3)

security automation. Automatic handling and processing of security-related tasks to identify vulnerabilities without human intervention. (3)

security configuration management (SCM). Management and control of configurations for an information system with the goal of enabling security and managing risk. (12)

security control. Tool or process used to reduce risk to assets by slowing, minimizing, or stopping a threat. (5)

security domain. List of people, devices, and systems that must comply with a security policy. (1)

Security Enhancements for Android (SEAndroid). Android-specific security tool that prevents apps or processes from accessing data and resources they are not allowed to access. (8)

security group. Virtual firewall solution that filters traffic entering and exiting a cloud environment. (15)

security information and event management (SIEM) system. Software product that supports organizational security by real-time collecting and compiling log data generated in a network and producing analyzed results and reports. (3)

security posture. Actions, philosophies, and strategies for ensuring the security of an organization's software, hardware, network, and data. (1)

security through obscurity. Flawed concept that a system is secure as long as only authorized people understand how the security functions. (9)

security zone. Segmented section of a network and contains systems that have limited access to the internal network. (12)

segmentation. Act of dividing the components of the affected asset, such as the network and software, from other components for security purposes. (17)

self-encrypting drive (SED). Storage drive that automatically encrypts stored data. (6)

sender policy framework (SPF). E-mail protocol used to validate the legitimacy of a sender's e-mail address. (16)

sentiment analysis. Security feature that assesses social attitudes and opinions to make predictions about likely outcomes. (3)

separation of duties. Security practice of having multiple people required to complete a job or task. (16)

serverless architecture. Cloud service that provides on-demand software and hosting on an as-used basis; also known as *serverless computing* or *function as a service (FaaS)*. (15)

server-side request forgery (SSRF). Attack in which an attacker is able to access a server, which is used to generate HTTP requests to a desired or targeted website. (7)

server-side validation. Input validation for which user input is confirmed by a server; also called *server-side execution*. (7)

service. Program that runs in the background of an operating system to provide specific features and functionality. (11)

services integration. System of cloud tools and technologies that connect systems, applications, data, and IT environments to provide real-time exchange of information. (15)

session hijacking. Attack that occurs when an attacker exploits a computer session and gains access to a system or its data. (7)

session key. Symmetric key that verifies its integrity and used for the duration of a session between a sender and receiver. (9)

session replay attack. Type of replay attack in which an attacker steals a session ID and reuses it to impersonate an authorized user; also known as a *playback attack*. (14)

sFlow. Proprietary packet sampling protocol that enables the capture of packet metadata, such as statistics, infrastructure, and routing information; short for *sampled flow*. (13)

shadow IT. Use of information systems, devices, hardware, applications, or services without explicit approval of a central IT staff. (2)

share permissions. Permissions that determine the level of access to a given file or folder for other network users. (4)

shell. Software that provides a direct method of running commands to the kernel. (11)

Shibboleth. Open-source project that provides single sign-on and allows websites to make authorization decisions on an individual level. (4)

shimming. Practice of using a driver shim to force a program to run on a program for which it was not intended. (7)

short messaging service (SMS). Text-messaging service that limits messages to 160 characters. (8)

shoulder surfing. Observing a person keying their information on a keyboard. (2)

sideloading. Process of installing applications from one device to another instead of using an official app-distribution method. (8)

SIEM correlation. SIEM feature that searches through aggregated data and reports common characteristics. (3)

SIEM dashboard. Tool that summarizes data and transforms it into useful information to provide simple security monitoring. (3)

SIEM log. Records of events that are reviewed or analyzed. (3)

signature-based monitoring. Method that examines network traffic or searches for patterns to compare against a predefined signature database. (12)

Simultaneous Authentication of Equals (SAE). Password-based security authentication method that replaced the PSK method used by WPA2. (14)

single loss expectancy (SLE). Monetary value of a damaged asset. (16)

single point of failure (SPOF). Risk that occurs when a system part fails and causes the entire system to stop working. (18)

single sign-on (SSO). Authentication service that allows a user to use one login and password combination to access a set of services. (4)

skimmer. Hardware device that attaches to a Point of Sale (PoS) device, reads credit card data simultaneously with the PoS device, and then copies the information from the card's magnetic strip into memory. (2)

smart card. Card that contains an embedded circuit or chip that stores information used to authorize or authenticate a person's identity and access to resources or physical locations. (5)

smart card authentication. Employs the use of digital certificates to authenticate a person's identity, encrypt data transfer, and allow for digital signatures. (5)

smart device. Electronic device capable of performing important processes such as autonomous computing operations and context-aware functions. (8)

smart meter. Digital electricity meter that records information such as electrical or water consumption by a residence or organization in predefined intervals. (8)

smart sensor. Device that receives, interprets, and computes data from its physical surroundings to perform predefined functions or actions based on specific input. (8)

smishing. Variation of a phishing attack in which a user is tricked into downloading malware or providing confidential information via text message; often styled as *SMiShing*. (2)

SMTP querying. Act of using the Simple Mail Transfer Protocol (SMTP) system to obtain e-mail account information. (3)

sn1per. Automated network reconnaissance tool that collects data during vulnerability assessments and penetration tests. (13)

SNMPv3. Most recent version of SNMP and enables authentication as well as encryption. (5)

SOAR. Security solution that uses an array of software tools and solutions that allows for a collection of data from multiple sources and generates an automatic response; stands for *Security Orchestration, Automation, and Response*. (3).

social media analysis. Collecting of data from social media outlets so that an organization can evaluate policies needed for organizational security. (16)

Software as a Service (SaaS). Complete software distribution solution from the cloud that eliminates the need to install resources locally. (15)

software-defined networking (SDN). Approach to management of a network using the application of code. (15)

software-defined visibility (SDV). Process that allows automation between software programs through a set of open, RESTful APIs, which allow them to interact directly. (15)

software development kit (SDK). Collection of software development tools in one installable package. (7)

software development life cycle (SDLC). Conceptual process used to create, deploy, and maintain a software application; also called a *software* or *application development process*. (7)

software diversity. Practice of transforming software into different forms before deployment. (7)

spam. Unsolicited bulk messages. (2)

spam over Internet messaging (SPIM). Specific form of unwanted messages that arrive as Internet messages, instant messages, or notifications. (2)

spear phishing. Variation of a phishing attack in which a recipient is deliberately chosen as a target of an attack. (2)

spyware. Type of software that unobtrusively spies on a user's activities. (2)

SQL injection attack. Code-injection technique in which a hacker inputs SQL-formatted commands in a user-input field. (7)

SSH key. Pair of access credential keys used by the SSH protocol to confirm a person's identity. (10)

SSL decryptor. Device dedicated to the decryption of SSL traffic. (10)

SSL/TLS accelerator. Dedicated device or installed SCSI or PCI card that is connected to the web server. (10)

SSL/TLS handshake process. Encryption process that includes verification of digital certificates based on asymmetric encryption. (10)

stakeholder management. Process of notifying those who need to be updated, anticipating questions, and managing their needs. (17)

stand-alone access point (stand-alone AP). Access point that requires individual configuration but has appropriate functionality to accept data and forward it to the appropriate device. (14)

standard biometrics. Unique physical characteristics of a person used for authentication. (4)

standard naming convention. Set of rules that dictates how account names are created or established. (4)

state actor. Hacker who is financially supported by a sovereign political entity. (2)

stateful firewall. Firewall that monitors packets over an established period of time and accepts only packets that were previously tracked. (12)

stateless firewall. Firewall designed to protect networks based on static information, such as source and destination addresses or ports. (12)

state-sponsored hacking. Work of a governmental body to disrupt or impair an organization, individual, or other governments. (2)

static code. Authentication and access password or PIN that is unique to the individual and does not change automatically. (8)

static code analyzer. Tool that analyzes code for known vulnerabilities and errors, such as using unsafe libraries and input validation, buffer overflow, or injection errors. (7)

steganography. Practice of hiding a file, text, image, or video inside another file. (9)

storage area network (SAN). Computer network that provides access to consolidated storage devices; also called a *storage network*. (18)

storage segmentation. Separation of company or organization data from personal data on a mobile device. (8)

stored procedure. Prepared SQL code that can be saved and reused when accessing databases and executing tasks. (7)

strategic intelligence. Evaluation, analysis, and dissemination of evidence or data required for creating organizational policy that drives investigations. (17)

stream cipher. Algorithm that encrypts each bit of data at one time by repeatedly taking one character and replacing it with another. (9)

Structured Query Language (SQL). Programming language used for managing a database that contains multiple linked tables; pronounced like *sequel*. (7)

Structured Threat Information eXpression (STIX). Standardized language developed by the MITRE Corporation and the OASIS Cyber Threat Intelligence (CTI) technical committee to discuss cyber threat information. (2)

subscriber identity module (SIM) card. Integrated circuit that stores a cellular device's international mobile subscriber identity (IMSI) number and related key. (14)

substitution cipher. Cryptographic algorithm in which each letter or character of a word is replaced by a different letter or character. (9)

supply chain. Businesses, people, and activities involved in turning raw materials into products and delivering them to end-users. (2)

supply chain attack. Cyberattack in which a hacker infiltrates a system using a supply-chain partner's access to an organization. (16)

supply chain vulnerability. Potential malicious events that can occur in the supply chain. (2)

switch. Modifier added to a command to enforce specific parameters and help limit or narrow the possible results. (11)

symbolic link. One made to another *link*, not directly to the original data. (11)

symmetric encryption. Encryption method that uses a single key to encrypt and decrypt data. (9)

system administrator. Role responsible for managing applications that access data, even if the person does not use data directly. (16)

system control and data acquisition (SCADA) system. Embedded system used to monitor an interface with controls for machines and equipment in an industrial process; also known as a *supervisory control and data acquisition system*. (8)

System Health Agent (SHA). Program that performs a self-check on the client. (13)

system integration. Process of linking various IT systems, services, and software to enable a unified functional system between companies. (2)

system logging protocol (syslog). Standard event logging protocol used to send system and event log information to a specific server, called the *syslog server*. (3)

system on a chip (SoC). Integrated circuit that includes all fundamental computing components including a central processing unit (CPU), memory, storage, and input/output ports all on a single chip. (8)

system owner. Role that focuses on data protection, including redundancy, backups, and related policies and implementations. (16)

T

tailgating. Occurs when an unauthorized person walks into a facility with, or right behind, authorized people to appear as if with them. (5)

tcpdump command. Linux command that is a text-based solution that functions as a packet sniffer and allows users to capture and analyze packets to view data as it is collected, as well as its protocol and direction of datagram. (13)

teamwork. Cooperative efforts of team members to reach a goal. (19)

technical control. Type of control that uses technology that automates device management for access and application of confidential data. (5)

TEMPEST. National Security Agency (NSA) specification and North Atlantic Treaty Organization (NATO) certification that attempts to counter the act of spying on information systems through leaking electromagnetic emanations. (5)

Terminal Access Controller Access-Control System (TACACS). Cisco proprietary protocol and authentication service that forwards user credentials to a central server. (4)

tethering. Use of an Internet-enabled device to share an online connection with a connected device through Bluetooth or Wi-Fi. (8)

theHarvester. Network reconnaissance command-line utility that gathers information such as e-mails, subdomains, employee names, IP address, and open ports from public sources, among other data. (13)

thin access point. Access point that does not contain all the management and configuration functions found in a fat access point. (14)

thin client. Computing devices that do not contain internal storage. (15)

third-party risk management (TPRM). Process of identifying and controlling risks that occur when transacting business with third parties. (16)

threat. Event or action in which a vulnerability is exploited endangering an enterprise environment. (2)

threat actor. Individual, nation state, or organization responsible for a security incident, attack, or other type of event that affect's an organization's security; also called a *threat agent* or *malicious actor*. (2)

threat assessment. Steps taken to identify or determine potential threats faced by an organization. (16)

threat hunting. Practice of proactively searching for cyber threats and vulnerabilities not already detected or identified in a network. (3)

threat intelligence. Information regarding threats, threat actors, and other potentially harmful actions that could occur in an enterprise environment. (2)

threat intelligence feed. Real-time streams of data that provide information on potential cyber threats and risks. (3)

threat map. Visual representations of a cyber threat occurring at any given time across the world; also known as a *cyberattack map*. (2)

time-based login. Procedure that enables authentication of a user by either detecting the user's presence at a pre-established time or accounting for an interval of time for the user to travel to another location. (8)

time bomb. Malicious software that does not launch immediately when a system is infected, but relies on some type of trigger. (2)

time management. Practice of organizing time and work assignments to increase personal efficiency. (19)

time-of-day restriction. Control that is used to limit when a user or group of users can access an account. (4)

time offset. Difference in hours and minutes added or subtracted from the *Coordinated Universal Time (UTC)* to get the current time whether it is standard time of daylight saving time. (17)

time stamp. Digital record of when a specific event occurred in a specific time zone. (17)

time synchronization. Process that ensures all devices agree on the correct time. (3)

token. Device used to gain access to a resource. (4)

tokenization. Method of protecting data by replacing it with tokens. (6)

tracert command. Windows command-line utility that displays the path a data packet takes across a network. (11)

transit gateway. Transit hub used to interconnect a company's virtual private cloud (VPC) and on-premises network. (15)

Transport Layer Security (TLS). Cryptographic protocol designed to provide security between networked computers. (10)

transport mode. IPSec mode that encrypts only the data and ESP information, not the original packet. (12)

transposition cipher. Cryptographic algorithm in which letters are rearranged within each word in the text. (9)

Triple DES (3DES) cryptography. Symmetric-key block cipher that employs DES encryption but uses two or three keys for a much stronger algorithm. (9)

Trojan. Malware hidden inside software that appears to be harmless. (2)

Trusted Automated Exchange of Indicator Information (TAXII). AIS standard that defines the method of information exchanges, including data formatted with STIX standards between partners. (2)

Trusted Platform Module (TPM). Chip located in a computer's hardware that runs authentication checks on hardware, software, and firmware. (6)

trust model. Relationship between parties. (10)

tunneling. Process of using a VPN to encrypt data before transmitting it across a remote connection. (12)

tunnel mode. IPSec mode that encrypts the IP header of the original packet. (12)

turnstile. Device with bars or other obstruction to alternately block an entryway and allow only one person to enter at a time. (5)

Twofish cryptography. Block cipher that encrypts data in 128-bit blocks and key sizes up to 256 bits and is the successor to Blowfish. (9)

typo squatting. Social engineering attack in which a hacker registers a web domain name that is similar to a trusted website to take advantage of users making a typographical mistake when entering a web address; also called *URL hijacking*. (7)

U

unified endpoint management (UEM). Class of software tools that provides management for various types of endpoints, including mobile devices, PCs, and Internet-enabled devices. (8)

Unified Extensible Firmware Interface (UEFI). Firmware interface that adds enhanced security measures to a boot process. (6)

unified threat management (UTM) device. All-in-one security device that enables a network to be managed using one appliance. (12)

uninterruptible power supply (UPS). Device that acts as a power source when the main power fails. (18)

universal resource locator (URL) redirection. Technique used to reroute one domain to another; also called *URL forwarding*. (13)

uptime. Measurement expressed as a percentage of time that the cloud storage system is working and available. (15)

URL redirection attack. Network attack that redirects a user from a valid web page to a malicious copy, often for phishing campaigns. (13)

usage audit and review. Process of evaluating the types, frequency, and purpose of applications used by a given account. (4)

USB data blocker. Device that prevents unauthorized transfer of information as well as the installation of malware to a device. (2)

USB On-the Go (USB OTG). USB connection that enables multiple mobile devices to be connected without using a computer. (8)

user. Role given to anyone who operates an application on a network. (16)

user account control (UAC). Microsoft technology used to govern security by limiting what a standard user is able to do on a system. (4)

user behavior analysis (UBA). Security assessment that monitors user behavior and compares it to established baseline information. (3)

V

vein scanner. Device that identifies characteristics of a person's blood vessels using infrared light. (4)

vendor management. Process of procuring and managing the services of a third party. (2)

vendor-specific guide. Guide written by a vendor for specific models of hardware. (1)

vendor support. Act of a vendor providing training, help desk responses, and other follow-up services for a contract. (2)

version control. Method of tracking changes to a file; also called *source control*. (7)

virtual IP (VIP) address. IP address that does not correspond to physical network devices. (12)

virtualization. Means of managing or presenting computer resources virtually as opposed to physically. (8)

virtual local area network (VLAN). Technology that enables remote users to be grouped logically even when connected to different switches. (12)

virtual machine (VM) escape. Security concern that occurs when a program breaks out of the virtual environment and interacts directly with a host. (15)

virtual machine (VM) sprawl. Security concern that occurs when deployment of virtual machines is abundant and improperly managed. (15)

virtual private network (VPN). Virtual network connection that provides a way to encrypt data traveling through unsecured public networks, such as the Internet. (12)

virus. Malicious software code that is unleashed and attempts to perform destructive content on computer systems or data. (2)

vishing. Attack like phishing, but involves an attack conducted by phone. (2)

VLAN access control list (VACL). Permission set that provides access control for packets traveling into or out of a virtual local area network (VLAN). (12)

Voice over IP (VoIP). Networking protocol used to deliver voice traffic over standard network connections. (8)

voice recognition. Uses software that authenticates a person's unique vocal characteristics. (4)

VPN concentrator. Device that collects virtual private network (VPN) connections and delivers traffic to the appropriate VPN node. (12)

vulnerability. Flaw or potential for harm. (2)

vulnerability assessment. Process of identifying and evaluating weaknesses in the networks and systems of an organization. (16)

vulnerability scan. Security assessment that searches a computer or network for potential vulnerabilities or weak security configurations. (3)

vulnerability scanner. Software that automates the process of scanning computer systems for potential security weaknesses in software, configurations, and other settings. (3)

vulnerable business process. Set of activities by a business that can be easily exploited by a threat actor. (8)

W

war driving. Act of moving around, usually in a vehicle, and searching for wireless networks. (3)

war flying. Act of detecting wireless networks using airplanes or drones/unmanned aerial vehicles to search for open access points. (3)

warm site. Facility with minimal equipment in place to resume business operations. (18)

waterfall model. Development life cycle model that follows a sequential process in which each step is completed before moving to the next step. (7)

watering hole attack. Social engineering attack that occurs when an attacker targets an individual in a specific group, organization, or IP address range. (2)

weak configuration. Inadequate security controls in a device or system. (2)

wearable technology. Type of IoT device worn by a consumer that houses a minicomputer for performing specific functions; also called *wearables*. (8)

web application. Application that runs dynamically through a web browser as script without requiring software to be installed; also called *web apps*. (7)

web application firewall (WAF). Specific firewall used to protect web applications by filtering and monitoring HTTP traffic between applications and the Internet. (7)

web application scanner. Tools that scan web applications for web-based vulnerabilities, such as scripting attacks, dangerous files, out-of-date versions, and unsecure configurations. (3)

whale phishing. Phishing attack targeting individuals who have a high net worth or a high business status; also known as *whaling*. (2)

white box test. Penetration test for which the tester is given complete information and full knowledge of the system. (3)

white-hat hacker. Generally ethical and law-abiding individuals who often break into networks with permission to study or reveal vulnerabilities. (2)

whitelisting. Process of specifying a list of approved applications or executable software permitted to run on a device or network. (6)

Wi-Fi. Wireless networking technology that uses radio waves instead of copper-core or fiber-optic cable. (1)

Wi-Fi ad-hoc network. Wireless network in which two or more devices connect to one another directly instead of communicating through a wireless router or access point. (8)

Wi-Fi analyzer. Device used to locate wireless signals and signal strength in a physical location. (14)

Wi-Fi Direct. Wireless connection that allows device-to-device communication without the use of a centralized network. (8)

Wi-Fi Protected Access (WPA). Wireless security standard that replaced WEP and offers more security in terms of keys and user authentication. (14)

Wi-Fi Protected Access II (WPA2). Second generation of WPA that provides stronger security protections and better control of network access. (14)

Wi-Fi Protected Access III (WPA3). Newest generation of Wi-Fi security and provides advanced security protocols to the communication of wireless transmissions. (14)

Wi-Fi Protected Setup (WPS). Network security setting and standard for wireless networks. (14)

Wi-Fi survey. Service that combines a predictive survey with analysis by a network engineer to determine what is needed to deploy a wireless network at a given location. (14)

wildcard character. Character used to represent one or more unknown characters in a string of text. (11)

Windows Management Instrumentation (WMI). Infrastructure in Windows for managing data and operations. (11)

Windows Registry. Hierarchical configuration database containing information, settings, options, and values for a given installation of the Windows operation system. (6)

wireless access point (WAP). Networking device that provides access to a connection between a wireless network and a physical cable-based network; also known as an *access point (AP)*. (14)

wireless cracker. Tool designed to break the encryption protections of a wireless local area network (WLAN). (14)

wireless LAN controller (WLC). Device that manages multiple access points in a network. (14)

wireless local area network (WLAN). Wireless networking technology that uses radio waves rather than a copper-core or fiber-optic cable; also called *Wi-Fi*. (14)

wireless network security. Process of enabling security on a wireless local area network. (14)

wireless router. Device that has the same capabilities of an access point but also adds functionality to wireless connections to LANs or WANs. (14)

wireless site survey. Process of planning, designing, and documenting a wireless network environment. (14)

work ethic. Belief that honest work is a reward on its own. It is a soft skill that can help a person be successful. (19)

work-hour. Amount of work performed by an average employee in one hour. (17)

worm. Form of malware that infects a system with its payload and moves or spreads from one infected computer to another through open network connections. (2)

WORM device. Storage device that allows data to be saved but not changed. (3)

X

X.509. Format used for public certificates to ensure consistent formatting. (10)

XML injection. Attack method in which a hacker inserts script with the goal of compromising logic of an XML application. (7)

Z

zero-day vulnerability. Serious flaw that exists in software and remains unknown until exploited by hackers. (2)

zero-level formatting. Process in which new data is written over existing data to destroy the existing data. (8)

zero trust. Security model in which no one from inside or outside the network is trusted by default and all users attempting to access network resources are required to verify their identities. (12)

Zigbee. Telecommunication network standard based on IEEE's 802.15.4 personal area network standard. (14)

Index

A

acceptable use policy (AUP), 520
access control lists (ACLs), 373
access management controls, 117–119
account audit, 133
account expiration, 128
account maintenance, 133
account management practices, 127–131
    account types, 127–128
    policy enforcement, 128–131
active-active configuration, 373
Active Directory (AD), 120
active listening, 594
active-passive configuration, 373
active reconnaissance, 78
Address Resolution Protocol (ARP)
    poisoning, 426
administrative control, 153
Advanced Encryption Standard (AES),
    277
advanced persistent threat (APT), 29
adversarial AI attack, 41
adversarial artificial intelligence (AI)
    attack, 41–42
adware, 36
affinity scheduling, 373
aggregation switch, 370
aggregator, 375
agile model, 212
air gap, 161
air-gap network, 162
algorithm, 273
alias, 339
annualized loss expectance (ALE), 513
annualized rate of occurrence (ARO), 512
anomaly, 380
anomaly monitoring, 380
ANT, 458
antennae types and placement, 455–456
antispoofing, 373
antivirus and antimalware, 183
Anything as a Service (XaaS), 483
API attack, 224
append, 336
application attacks, 224–229
application development and security,
    208–237

application development, defined, 209
application development environment
    (ADE), 210
application hardening, 194–195
application management, 243
application process, 585–586
    in person, 586
    online, 585
application programming interface
    (API), 224
application scanning, 74
application security (AppSec), 215
application vulnerabilities, 221–223
archive bit, 571
Arduino, 260
armored virus, 40
arp command, 330
ARP poisoning, 14
artifacts, 550
artificial intelligence (AI), 41
assessing network security, 416–419
asset identification, 509
asset life cycle, 507
asset management, 508
assets, 507
asymmetric encryption, 278–280
    Diffie-Hellman, 278–279
    Digital Signature Algorithm (DSA),
        280
    elliptical-curve cryptography, 279
    Rivest-Shamir-Adleman (RSA), 279
attack surface, 11
attack vectors, 31
attitude, 593
attribute, 30
attribute-based access control (ABAC),
    118–119
attributes, 116–117
authentication, 5, 109–110, 272, 486
authentication and access control,
    109–110
authentication header (AH), 393
automated alert and trigger, 86
automated indicator sharing (AIS),
    33–34
automated patch management service,
    189
automation, 213

availability, 5
availability zones, 487

B

backdoor, 40
background check, 519
band selection, 454–455
bandwidth monitors, 432
banner grabbing, 78
barricades, 156
baseband, 460
baseline, 80
baseline configuration, 385
baselines and performance, 80–82
    establishing, 80–81
    monitoring, 82
Basic Input/Output System (BIOS), 191
batch file, 335
Bcrypt, 283
behavioral biometrics, 117
behavioral questions, 587
binary, 216
biometric authentication, 115
birthday attack, 286
black box test, 76
black-hat hacker, 30
blacklisting, 195
block cipher, 276
block cipher operation modes, 315–317
blockchain, 316
blocked port, 187
blowfish cryptography, 278
bluejacking, 463
bluesnarfing, 463
Bluetooth, 241, 458
bollard, 156
boot attestation, 193
boot integrity, 192
BPDU guard, 371
bridge, 370
bring your own device (BYOD), 240
broadcast storm, 371
brute-force attack, 277
buffer overflow, 222
buffer-overflow attack, 222
bug-bounty program, 52
business continuity and data recovery,
    560–579

Q

qualitative assessment, 512
Quality of Service (QoS), 368
quantitative assessment, 512
quantum communication, 287
quantum computing, 287
quantum cryptography, 287–288
quarantine, 541

R

race condition, 223
radio-frequency identification (RFID), 459
RADIUS Federation, 450
RAID 0, 565
RAID 1, 566
RAID 1+0, 567
RAID 5, 566
rainbow table, 284
ransomware, 39
Raspberry Pi, 256, 259–260
real-time operating system (RTOS), 249
recertification, 133
reconnaissance, 42, 78–79
    active, 78–79
    passive, 78
recovery point objective (RPO), 563
recovery site, 572
redundancy, 565
refactoring, 229
reference, 584
reference architecture, 488
registration authority (RA), 302
regulatory compliance, 15–20
remote access domain, 14–15
remote access Trojan (RAT), 38
Remote Authentication Dial-In User
    Service (RADIUS), 127
Remote Authentication Dial-In User
    Service (RADIUS) server, 449
remote wipe, 244
replay attack, 462
request forgery, 226
residual risk, 514
resilience, 216. 563, 593
resource exhaustion, 221
resource policies, 488
resource vs. security constraint, 275
restoration order, 572
résumé, 582
retinal scanner, 115
reverse proxy server, 374
revocation, 304–306
RFID attacks, 464

rich communication services (RCS), 248
right, 127
risk, 4, 507–509
    acceptance, 514
    analysis, 511–513
    assessment, 509
    avoidance, 513
    awareness, 511
    impact, 512
    management, 4, 509–513
    mitigation, 514
    posture, 508
    register, 512
    response, 513–514
    transfer, 513
risk control self-assessment, 511
Rivest Cipher 4 (RC4) cryptography, 278
rogue access point (rogue AP), 462
role-based access control (RBAC), 118
role-based awareness training, 520
root accounts, 53
root certificate, 307
rooting, 248
rootkit, 40
round-robin scheduling, 373
route command, 330
routers, 372–373
rsyslog, 84
rule-based access control, 118
rules of engagement (RoE), 76
    scope, 76
running program, 350

S

salting, 195
sandboxing, 210
sanitization, 518
Sarbanes-Oxley Act (SOX), 19
scalability, 216
scanless, 423
scanner output, 74–75
screen filter, 157
screen lock, 245
screenshot, 549
script, 214
script kiddie, 28
secondary logon, 124
secrets management, 489
secure application development, 215–217
secure area of incident, 545–548
Secure Boot, 193
secure code review, 221
secure coding techniques, 217–221
secure-configuration guide, 7

secure cookies, 220
Secure File Transfer Protocol (SFTP), 411
Secure Multipurpose Internet Mail
    Extension (S/MIME), 313
secure network administration, 408–445
secure network design, 366–407
secure protocols, 409–410
Secure Real-Time Protocol (SRTP), 313
secure shell (SHH), 313, 411
Secure Sockets Layer (SSL) protocol, 311
Secure Sockets Layer (SSL) stripping, 229
Secure Socket Tunneling Protocol (STP),
    392
secure token, 158
security
    assessment, 71
    automation, 87
    controls, 153–154
    data destruction, 167–169
    devices, 375–381
        placement, 386–388
    domains, 11–15, 21
    evaluation, 70–107
        advisories and bulletins, 73
        evaluating, 71
        penetration testing, 75–77
        threat hunting, 71–73
        vulnerability scan, 73–74
    facility physical controls, 154–166
    group, 486
    insider threats, 166–167
    IT physical controls, 161–166
    personnel, 156–159
    physical, 152–179
    posture, 7
    protected distribution and cabling,
        159
    zone, 375, 381–382
Security Account Manager (SAM), 285
Security as a Service (SECaaS), 484
Security Assertion Markup Language
    (SAML), 125
security configuration management
    (SCM), 385
Security Enhancements for Android
    (SEAndroid), 246
security information and event
    management (SIEM), 85–87
security orchestration, automation, and
    response (SOAR), 87, 541
security through obscurity, 272
segmentation, 488, 538
self-encrypting drive (SED), 194
self-signed digital certificate, 309
sender policy framework (SPF), 521
sentiment analysis, 86